CLASSICS OF ORGANIZATION THEORY

Second Edition

Jay M. Shafritz
University of Pittsburgh

J. Steven Ott
University of Maine

The Dorsey Press
Chicago, Illinois 60604

ISBN 0-256-05526-2

Library of Congress Catalog Card No. 86–50819

Printed in the United States of America

3 4 5 6 7 8 9 0 K 4 3 2 1 0 9 8

Preface

Few things are as satisfying to writers as the opportunity to do a second edition. It gives the chance not only to correct mistakes, but also to take full advantage of all the advice that comes from those who read the first edition. This second version has had the benefits of our maturing judgment and several years of additional pondering on the subject of organization theory—not to mention the advice of our friendly critics.

The second edition has been completely restructured and rewritten to reflect both the changes in the field of organization theory and our developing thoughts. Sections have been added on "power and politics" and "organizational culture," two newer schools or perspectives of organization theory that literally did not exist when the first edition was published. Also, about one half of the selections are new—either additions or replacements. The Introduction has been expanded substantially and now represents a fairly extensive overview of organization theory. We have highlighted the ebbs and flows in the development of organization theory over the last century and have added a chronology of organization theory that should help place works in historical perspective.

As with the first edition, we encourage communications from the scholarly and practitioner communities. Given sufficient encouragement, we will continue revising this book until we get it right.

One of the authors of the first edition is missing from the second. Our colleague and valued friend, Philip H. Whitbeck, formerly the Director of Administration of the Johnson Space Center, National Aeronautics and Space Administration, died suddenly in 1983. We will always be in his debt for his insightful contributions to our understanding of organization theory, for his work on the first edition of this book, and for allowing us to know an executive of such character, ability, and integrity, as is usually only found in fiction.

Many others contributed to this book by providing valuable insights. A mere listing of their names is entirely inadequate thanks. However, we simply cannot let the opportunity pass the thank Albert C. Hyde of San Francisco State University; Marshall Kaplan, E. Samuel Overman, and Mark Emmert, our colleagues at the University of Colorado at Denver; and Howard E. McCurdy of The American University.

v

Only a very few people truly influence the way we look at and think about important things. As J. Steven Ott's teacher, adviser, master's thesis committee chair, and co-author at the Sloan School of Management at M.I.T. in the early 1960s, Edgar H. Schein became a significant influence at an important time in his life. According to Ott, "I was repeatedly astounded by his ability to ask the right question—the question that would require me to pull my thinking up out of a state of nonclarity—to separate confusion from complexity. Thus, more than twenty years later, as my interest in organization theory was rekindled, it was no surprise to discover that Ed once again was having a most significant influence on my thinking. This time, his influence was by way of his insightful writings on organizational culture, including for example his conceptually sound formal definition of organizational culture, his emphasis on the developmental view of people in organizations and the importance of learning theory, and his methodological concepts for identifying organizational culture." Thus, a particular acknowledgment to Edgar H. Schein.

And, we collectively thank the authors and publishers of these classics for their permissions to reproduce their work.

Jay M. Shafritz
J. Steven Ott

Contents

Chapter III "MODERN" STRUCTURAL ORGANIZATION THEORY 166

Introduction *166*

Chapter IV SYSTEMS AND CONTINGENCY THEORIES OF ORGANIZATION 234

Introduction *234*

List of Figures and Tables

Introduction

This book is about organization theory. By *organization* we mean a social unit with some particular purposes. By *theory* we mean a proposition or set of propositions that seeks to explain or predict something. The something in this case is how groups and individuals behave in varying organizational structures and circumstances. This is obviously important information for any manager or leader to have. It is hardly an exaggeration to say that the world is ruled by the underlying premises of organization theory, and that it has been ever since humankind first organized itself for hunting, war, and even family life. Indeed, the newest thing about organization theory is the study of it.

Only in the twentieth century has intellectual substance and tradition been given to a field that was the instinctual domain of adventuresome entrepreneurs and cunning politicos. Organization theory lay largely dormant over the centuries until society found a practical use for it—to help manage the ever-burgeoning national (as opposed to local) industries and institutions that increasingly run the twentieth century. When the problems of managing an organization grew to be more than one head could cope with, the search for guidance on how to manage and arrange large-scale organizations became as noble a quest as the secular world of business could offer. If a commercial society ever had prophets, they were those pioneers of the scientific management movement who claimed that the path to ever-greater prosperity was to be found in the relentless search for the "one best way." They were offering society a theory—abstract guidance for those who knew where they wanted to go but didn't quite know how to get there. They already knew what Kurt Lewin would assert years later: "there is nothing so practical as a good theory." (Morrow, 1969)

Peter Drucker (1954) once observed that the thrust toward scientific management "may well be the most powerful as well as the most lasting contribution America has made to Western thought since the Federalist Papers." Of course, the scientific management movement was just the beginning of a continuous search for the most effective means by which people can be organized into social units in order to achieve the goals of their companies, their governments, or themselves. What was once said of the first atomic bomb is now said of the first U.S. voyage to the moon: It was as much an achievement of organization as it was of engineering and science.

Have our more recent theories of organization kept pace with our industrial and technical achievements? Maybe. But certainly yes when they are compared with the "primitive" notions of the scientific management movement. Yet many of the basics remain the same—remain as givens. The laws of physics and gravity do not change with intellectual fashions or technological advances; nor do the basic social and physical characteristics of people change. Just as those who would build space ships have to start by studying Newton, those who would design and manage organizations must start with Taylor and Fayol. The future will always build upon what is enduring from the past. That is the rationale for this book—to provide those who seek to understand and/or to advance organization theory with a convenient place to find the essentials, indeed the classics, of organization theory's past. However old some of these articles may be, they are not dated. A classic *is* a classic because it continues to be of value to each new generation of students and practitioners who study organizations.

The basic elements of organizations have remained relatively constant through history: Organizations have purposes (which may be explicit or implicit), attract participants, acquire and allocate resources to accomplish goals, use some form of structure to divide and coordinate activities, and rely on certain members to lead or manage others. Although the elements of organizations have remained relatively constant, their purposes, structures, ways of doing things, and methods for coor-·dinating activities have always varied widely. The variations largely (but not exclusively) reflect an organization's adaptation to its environment. Organizations are "open systems" that are influenced by and have an impact on the world around them. The world around organizations includes, for example, their sources of inputs (like raw materials, capital, and labor), markets, technology, politics, and the surrounding society's culture and subcultures. Inherently, organizations are part of the society and the culture in which they exist and function. Human behavior and thus organizational behavior is heavily influenced by culturally rooted beliefs, values, assumptions, and behavioral norms affecting all aspects of organizational life.

Theories about organizations do not develop in a vacuum. They reflect what is going on in the world—including the existing culture. Thus, contributions to organization theory vary over time and across cultures and subcultures. The advent of the factory system, World War II, the "flower child"/anti-establishment/self-development era of the 1960s, and the computer/information society of the 1970s all substantially influenced the evolution of organization theory. In order to truly understand organization theory as it exists today, one must appreciate the historical contexts through which it developed and the cultural milieus during and in which important contributions were made to its body of knowledge. In order to help readers place writings in their historical contexts, *A Chronology of Organization Theory*, a review of the major events and publications in the field, follows this introduction.

CRITERIA FOR SELECTION

The editors are neither so vain nor so foolish as to assert that these are *the* classics of organization theory. The academic study of organization theory rests upon a foundation of primary and secondary sciences: It draws significantly from such disciplines as sociology, psychology, social psychology, cultural anthropology, political science, economics, business administration, and public administration. It draws with less force, but still importantly, from mathematics, statistics, systems theory, industrial engineering, philosophy and ethics, history, and the computer sciences. The field is so diverse that there can be no single definitive list of *the classics*. The editors readily admit that some important contributors and contributions to the field have not found their way into this collection. Omitting some was very painful. However, considerations of space and balance necessarily prevailed.

We used several criteria for making our selections. First, we asked ourselves: "Should the serious student of organization theory be expected to be able to identify this author and his or her basic themes?" If the answer was yes, then it was so because such a contribution has long been, or is increasingly being recognized as, an important theme by a significant writer. While we expect to be criticized for excluding other articles and writers, it will be much more difficult to honestly criticize us for our inclusions; the writers and pieces chosen are among the most widely quoted and reprinted theorists in the field of organization theory. The possible exceptions are those writers chosen to represent the newer "schools" or "frameworks" of organization theory—particularly "power and politics" and "organizational culture." Most of the significant writing in these two schools has been done since 1980, and some of the most impressive works are as recent as 1985. Obviously, the very new articles have not been quoted as extensively as those written ten, twenty, or thirty years earlier. Thus, the editors had to make more subjective judgments about inclusions and exclusions in these chapters. For example, we selected pieces for the chapter on organizational culture by Burton Clark, Meryl Louis, Thomas Peters, Edgar Schein, and Caren Siehl and Joanne Martin over more widely distributed works such as Peters and Waterman's *In Search of Excellence*, Deal and Kennedy's *Corporate Cultures*, Stanley Davis' *Managing Corporate Culture*, and Ralph Kilmann's *Beyond the Quick Fix*. In our judgment, the inclusions will fare better against the test of time.

The second criterion is related to the first: Each article or portion of a book had to make a basic statement that has been consistently echoed or attacked over the years. In other words, the selection had to be important—significant—in the sense that it must have been (or will be) an integral part of the foundation for the subsequent building of the field of organization theory.

The third criterion was that articles had to be readable. Those readers who have already had reason to peruse the literature of organization theory will appreciate the importance of this criterion.

The inclusion of articles from the more recent schools raises questions about the editors' choices of chapters for grouping selections. For example, why did we include "power and politics" and "organizational culture" but not "symbolic management"? Why is there no chapter on "the human relations school" or, as it is often known, "organizational behavior"? What is the basis for our distinction between the "modern structuralists" and the "systemists"? Where are the human behavior-oriented, early "classical philosophers" like Mary Parker Follett, Chester Barnard, Fritz Roethlisberger, and Elton Mayo? The answers to questions such as these reflect the editors' conceptual and historical construction of organization theory—tempered by the need to limit the size of this volume. As such, it is crucially important for the reader to understand "where we are coming from." Thus we provide rather extensive historical and conceptual overviews to our six chapters. Each chapter presents a school or perspective of organization theory. Since there is no universally accepted set of schools, a few words of explanation are in order.

A FRAMEWORK: THE "SCHOOLS" OF ORGANIZATION THEORY

There is no such thing as *the* theory of organizations. Rather, there are many theories that attempt to explain and predict how organizations and the people in them will behave in varying organizational structures, cultures, and circumstances. Some theories of organization are compatible with and build upon others—in what they explain or predict, the aspects of organizations they consider to be important, their assumptions about organizations and the world at large from which they are created, and the methods for studying organizations that work well. They use the same language or jargon. These groupings of compatible theories and theorists usually are called alternately schools, perspectives, traditions, frameworks, models, paradigms or, occasionally, eras of organization theory.

Organization theorists from one school will quote and cite each others' works regularly. However, they usually ignore theorists and theories from other schools—or acknowledge them only negatively. In 1961, Harold Koontz described management theory as a "semantics jungle." In 1963, Arthur Kuriloff examined the various schools of organization theory and found that "each is at odds with others, each defends its own position, each claims that the others have major deficiencies." But that was way back in 1963, and we have come a long way since then. Haven't we? Twenty years after Kuriloff's statement, Graham Astley and Andrew Van de Ven (1983) observed: "The problem is that different schools of [organizational] thought tend to focus only on single sides of issues and use such different logics and vocabularies that they do not speak to each other directly." A year later, Lee Bolman and Terrence Deal (1984) remarked: "Within the social sciences, major schools of thought have evolved, each with its own view of organizations, its own well-defined concepts and assumptions, and its own ideas about how managers can best bring social collectives under control."

It is reasonable to conclude that not only is there no consensus on what constitutes knowledge in organization theory, but there is not likely to be any such consensus in the foreseeable future. Anyone who studies this subject is free to join the school of organization theory of his or her choice and is free to accept the philosophic boundaries of one group of serious thinkers over another. But before casting your lot with one school and excluding others, consider the options. Examine each school's strengths and weaknesses. See if its philosophy is in harmony with your already established beliefs, assumptions, and predispositions. You may find that no single school deserves your loyalty, that they each contain important information and insights that are useful in differing circumstances. Remember these are schools with no tuition, no classes, and no grades. They exist only as intellectual constructs and as mutual support networks of organization theorists. They have one primary purpose: to organize and extend knowledge about organizations and how to study them.

Just as there is disagreement among the various schools about what makes organizations tick, there also are different views about the best way to group organization theories into schools. A few examples of different views on the schools of organization theory are summarized in Figure 1.

Each of the major schools of organization theory is associated with a period in time. For example, the Classical School was at its prime in the 1920s and 1930s, and the Neoclassical School in the 1940s and 1950s. Each school had its beginnings while another was dominant, gradually gained acceptance, and eventually replaced its predecessor as the dominant school. Some years later, another school came along to challenge and eventually take its position. Once-dominant schools of organization theory may lose the center stage, but they do not die. Their thinking influences subsequent schools—even those that reject their basic assumptions and tenets. Important works from these earlier schools become the timeless classics.

This cycling of schools through struggling ascendancy, dominance, challenge by other schools, and reluctant decline is not unique to organization theory. Thomas Kuhn (1970) postulated that this dialectic process is common in all sciences—including physics, mathematics, and psychiatry. It is quite common for schools that are close to each other chronologically to have widely divergent basic assumptions about the object of their theories.

Despite their differences, most of the better-known approaches to grouping organization theories into schools (including those summarized in Figure 1) have commonalities. First, they group theories by their perspectives on organizations—in other words, by basic assumptions about humans and organizations, and by those aspects of organizations that they see as most important for understanding organizational behavior. Second, they usually group the theories by the period of time during which the most important contributions were written. However, there are other organization theorists who use different approaches for labeling the schools. For example, Harold Koontz in "The Management Jungle Revisited" (1980) has expanded his list from six to eleven approaches to the study of management and organizational theory. We find Koontz's more current categorization system, with its Interpersonal Behavior Approach, Cooperative Social System Approach, and Sociotechnical Systems Approach, to be far too detailed to be useful.

Graham Astley and Andrew Van de Ven (1983) have used a very different logic to classify schools of organization "thought" into four basic views based on two analytical dimensions: the level of organizational analysis (micro or macro) and the emphasis placed on deterministic versus voluntaristic assumptions about

FIGURE 1 • A FEW EXAMPLES OF HOW SCHOLARS HAVE GROUPED SCHOOLS OF ORGANIZATION THEORY

Author	Schools
Scott, W. G. (1961). Organization theory: An overview and an appraisal. *Academy of Management Journal.*	The Classical Doctrine Neoclassical Theory Modern Theory
Koontz, H. (1961). The management theory jungle. *Academy of Management Journal.*	Management Process School Empirical Approach (or Case Approach) Human Behavior School Social System School Decision Theory School Mathematics School
Hutchinson, J. G. (1967). *Organizations: Theory and classical concepts.* New York: Holt, Rinehart & Winston.	Scientific Management Environmental and Human Relations School Man as a Decision Maker Current Theories of Management 1. Operational School 2. Empirical School 3. Human Behavior School 4. Social Systems School 5. Decision Theory School 6. Mathematical School
Scott, W. G. & Mitchell, T. R. (1972). *Organization theory* (rev. ed.). Homewood, IL: Dorsey Press.	The Scientific Management Movement The Human Relations and Industrial Humanism Movements Classical Theory Neoclassical Critique The Systems Concept (Unlabeled, but including) Personality Dynamics and Motivation, Attitudes, and Group Dynamics Organization Processes (Communication Processes, Decision Processes, Balance and Conflict Processes, Status and Role Processes, Influence Processes, Leadership Processes, and Technological Processes) Organization Change
George, C. S. Jr., (1972). *The history of management thought.* Englewood Cliffs, NJ: Prentice-Hall.	Traditional School: Scientific Management Behavioral School Management Process School Quantitative School
Perrow, C. (1973, Summer). The short and glorious history of organizational theory. *Organizational Dynamics.*	Scientific Management Human Relations Bureaucracy ("A Comeback") Power, Conflict and Decisions The Technological Qualification Goals, Environments and Systems
Pfeffer, J. (1981). *Power in organizations.* Marshfield, MA: Pitman Publishing.	Rational Choice Models Bureaucratic Models of Decision Making Decision Process Models Political Models
Bolman, L. & Deal, T. (1984). *Modern approaches to understanding and managing organizations.* San Francisco: Jossey-Bass.	Structural/Systems Frame Human Resources Frame Power Frame Symbolic Frame

human nature. Thus Astley and Van de Ven conclude that organization theories can be grouped into the cells of a two-by-two matrix. (See Figure 2.) Their voluntaristic-to-deterministic dimension (the horizontal continuum in Figure 2) classifies theories by their assumptions about individual organization members' autonomy and self-direction versus the assumption that behavior in organizations is determined by structural constraints. The macro-to-micro continuum (the vertical continuum in Figure 2) groups organization theories by their focus on communities of organizations or single organizations.

THE ORGANIZATION OF THIS BOOK

Although different approaches such as Astley and Van de Ven's (1983) and Koontz's (1980) are insightful and thought provoking, they are not well suited to a historical development of organization theory. And, it is our contention that the historical approach offers some clear advantages for the student. Organization theory tends to be cumulative—theorists and schools of theorists learn from and build upon each other's works. Sometimes the cumulative building of organization theory has been accomplished through the adoption of prior theorists' assumptions, logic, and empirical research methods and findings. In other instances, the building process has advanced by *rejecting* prior assumptions and theories (Kuhn, 1970). Thus, the

FIGURE 2 • ASTLEY AND VAN DE VEN'S FOUR VIEWS OF ORGANIZATION

Macro Level		
	Natural Selection View	Collective Action View
	System-Structural View	Strategic Choice View
Micro Level	Deterministic Orientation	Voluntaristic Orientation

Examples of Some Representative Organization Theorists for Each of the Four Views

System-Structural View: Gulick and Urwick (1937), Fayol (1949), Merton (1940), Blau and Scott (1962), Lawrence and Lorsch (1967), James D. Thompson (1967)

Strategic Choice View: Blau (1964), Feldman and March (1981), Strauss et al. (1963), Weick (1979), Bittner (1965)

Natural Selection View: Aldrich (1979), Hannan and Freeman (1977), Porter (1981), Pfeffer and Salancik (1978)

Collective Action View: Emery and Trist (1973), Hawley (1950, 1968), Schon (1971)

Adapted from Astley, W. G., & Van de Ven, A. H. (1983). Central perspectives and debates in organization theory. *Administrative Science Quarterly, 28.*

editors have used a more traditional, historically oriented approach that allows the reader to follow the ebbs and flows within and between the schools. The reader can gain a quick overview of the historical development of organization theory by referring to the *Chronology of Organization Theory* that follows this introduction. Our "schools" and their corresponding chapters are listed below:

1. The Classical School
2. The Neoclassical School
3. The "Modern" Structural School
4. The Systems and Contingency School
5. The Power and Politics School
6. The Organizational Culture School

Each school is discussed in detail in the first pages of each of the respective chapters.

Although we have attempted to include only selections that fit into one school, many works (which are not reprinted here) span the boundaries of schools—no matter how tightly those boundaries are defined and drawn. For example, Rosabeth Moss Kanter's writings (1977 and 1983) blend power and politics, human relations, and organizational culture perspectives. Cohen and March's (1974) concept of "organized anarchy" bridges the power politics and the organizational culture schools. Argyris and Schön's (1978) notion of "theories for action" incorporates theory and research from the human relations and the organizational culture schools. Thus the reader should remember that the schools—as well as the chapters—reflect a period in time as well as a perspective on organizations. Within each chapter, most of the selections are presented in chronological order so that the reader may gain a sense of the evolution of thought in the field.

In selecting the chapters to frame the contributions, the editors were faced with one particularly difficult decision: whether or not to include the human relations school or, as it is often labeled, the field of organizational behavior. Unquestionably, the human relations school is one of the most important perspectives of organization theory. It incorporates a wealth of behavioral science theories that address such variables as motivation, leadership, group and intergroup dynamics, interactions between people and structure, and the application of applied behavioral sciences to organizational change processes (organization development or OD). The human relations school incorporates the works of such luminaries as Argyris, Beckhard, Bennis, French and Bell, Fiedler, Gouldner, Hersey and Blanchard, Herzberg, Lewin, Likert, Maslow, McGregor, Schein, Tannenbaum, and Vroom—to name only a few. How could we possibly omit such an extensive and vital part of organization theory? The answer lies in the question. The field of organizational behavior is too vast and contains too many important works. It is a field of study unto itself. It requires a volume of its own, and scores of excellent texts and readers on organizational behavior are already on the market. The decision to omit the human relations school was painful but necessary. Clint Eastwood as Dirty Harry was fond of saying, "a man has to know his limitations." The same holds true for a textbook. Thus, we made a calculated decision to focus not or the microperspective of organizational behavior—*the way individuals behave in organizations*—but rather to focus on the macroperspective of organization theory—*how and why organizations behave as they do.*

BIBLIOGRAPHIC REFERENCES

Aldrich, H. (1979). *Organizations and environments.* Englewood Cliffs, NJ: Prentice-Hall.

Argyris, C., & Schön, D. A. (1978). *Organizational learning: A theory of action perspective.* Reading, MA: Addison-Wesley Publishing.

Astley, W. G., & Van de Ven, A. H. (1983, June). Central perspectives and debates in organization theory. *Administrative Science Quarterly, 28,* 245–270.

Bittner, E. (1965). The concept of organization. *Social Research, 32*(3), 239–255.

Blau, P. M. (1964). *Exchange and power in social life.* New York: John Wiley & Sons.

Blau, P. M., & Scott, R. G. (1962). *Formal organizations.* San Francisco: Chandler Publishing.

Bolman, L. G., & Deal, T. E. (1984). *Modern approaches to understanding and managing organizations.* San Francisco: Jossey-Bass.

Cohen, M. D., & March, J. G. (1974). *Leadership and ambiguity: The American college president.* New York: McGraw-Hill.

Drucker, P. F. (1954). *The practice of management.* New York: Harper & Row.

Emery, F. E., and Trist, E. L. (1973). *Towards a social ecology: Contextual appreciations of the future in the present.* New York: Plenum Press.

Fayol, H. (1949). *General and industrial management.* London: Pitman Publishing. (Original work published 1916)

Feldman, M. S., & March, J. G. (1981). Information in organizations as signal and symbol. *Administrative Science Quarterly, 26,* 171–186.

George, C. S., Jr. (1972). *The history of management thought.* Englewood Cliffs, NJ: Prentice-Hall.

Gulick, L., & Urwick, L. (Eds.). (1937). *Papers on the science of administration.* New York: Institute of Public Administration.

Hannan, M., & Freeman, J. (1977). The population ecology of organizations. *American Journal of Sociology, 82,* 929–964.

Hawley, A. (1950). *Human ecology: A theory of community structure.* New York: Ronald Press.

Hawley, A. (1968). Human ecology. In D. L. Sills (Ed.). *The international encyclopedia of the social sciences* (Vol. 4, pp. 328–337). New York: Crowell-Collier & Macmillan.

Hutchinson, J. G. (1967). *Organizations: Theory and classical concepts.* New York: Holt, Rinehart, & Winston.

Kanter, R. M. (1977). *Men and women of the corporation.* New York: Basic Books.

Kanter, R. M. (1983). *The changemasters.* New York: Simon & Schuster.

Koontz, H. (1961). The management theory jungle. *Academy of Management Journal, 4* 174–188.

Koontz, H. (1980). The management theory jungle revisited. *Academy of Management Review, 5,* 175–187.

Kuhn, T. S. (1970). *The structure of scientific revolutions* (2nd ed., enlarged). Chicago: University of Chicago Press.

Lawrence. P. R., & Lorsch, J. W. (1967). *Organization and environment.* Cambridge, MA: Harvard University Press.

Marrow, A. J. (1969). *The practical theorist: The life and works of Kurt Lewin.* New York: Basic Books.

Merton, R. K. (1940). Bureaucratic structure and personality. *Social Forces, 18,* 560–568.

Perrow, C. (1973, Summer). The short and glorious history of organizational theory. *Organizational Dynamics*.

Pfeffer, J. (1981). *Power in organizations*. Marshfield, MA: Pitman Publishing.

Pfeffer, J., & Salancik, G. R. (1978). *The external control of organizations: A resource dependence perspective*. New York: Harper & Row.

Porter, M. E. (1981). The contributions of industrial organization to strategic management. *Academy of Management Review, 6,* 609–620.

Schön, D. A. (1971). *Beyond the stable state*. New York: Basic Books.

Scott, W. G. (1961, April). Organization theory: An overview and an appraisal. *Academy of Management Journal, 7–26.*

Scott, W. G., & Mitchell, T. R. (1972). *Organization theory* (rev. ed.). Chicago: Dorsey Press.

Strauss, A., Schatzman, L., Erlich, D., Bucher, R., & Sabshin, M. (1963). The hospital and its negotiated order. In E. Friedson (Ed.), *The hospital in modern society* (pp. 147–169). New York: Free Press.

Thompson, J. D. (1967). *Organizations in action*. New York: McGraw-Hill.

Weick, K. E. (1979). *The social psychology of organizing* (2nd ed.). Reading, MA: Addison-Wesley Publishing.

Wren, D. A. (1972). *The evolution of management thought*. New York: Ronald Press.

A CHRONOLOGY OF ORGANIZATION THEORY

1491 B.C.   During the exodus from Egypt, Jethro, the father-in-law of Moses, urges Moses to delegate authority over the tribes of Israel along hierarchical lines.

500 B.C.   Sun Tzu's *The Art of War* recognizes the need for hierarchical organization, interorganizational communications, and staff planning.

400 B.C.   Socrates argues for the universality of management as an art unto itself.

360 B.C.   Aristotle in *The Politics* asserts that the specific nature of executive powers and functions cannot be the same for all states (organizations), but must reflect their specific cultural environment.

370 B.C.   Xenophon records the first known description of the advantages of the division of labor when he describes an ancient Greek shoe factory.

1513   Machiavelli in *The Discourses* urges the principle of unity of command: "It is better to confide any expedition to a single man of ordinary ability, rather than to two, even though they are men of the highest merit, and both having equal ability."

1532   Machiavelli's book of advice to all would-be leaders, *The Prince*, is published five years after its author's death; it will become the progenitor of all "how to succeed" books that advocate practical rather than moral actions.

1776   Adam Smith's *The Wealth of Nations* discusses the optimal organization of a pin factory; this becomes the most famous and influential statement of the economic rationale of the factory system and the division of labor.

1813   Robert Owen in his "Address to the Superintendents of Manufactories" puts forth the revolutionary idea that managers should pay as much attention to their "vital machines" (employees) as to their "inanimate machines."

1832   Charles Babbage's On the Economy of Machinery and Manufactures anticipates many of the notions of the scientific management movement, including "basic principles of management" such as the division of labor.

1855   Daniel C. McCallum in his annual report as superintendent of the New York and Erie Railroad Company states his six basic principles of administration; the first was to use internally generated data for managerial purposes.

1885   Captain Henry Metcalfe, the manager of an army arsenal, published The Cost of Manufactures and the Administration of Workshops, Public and Private, which asserts that there is a "science of administration" that is based upon principles discoverable by diligent observation.

1886   Henry R. Towne's paper "The Engineer as an Economist," read to the American Society of Mechanical Engineers, encourages the scientific management movement.

1902   Vilfredo Pareto becomes the "father" of the concept of "social systems"; his societal notions would later by applied by Elton Mayo and the human relationists in an organizational context.

1903   Frederick W. Taylor publishes Shop Management.

1904   Frank B. and Lillian M. Gilbreth marry; they then proceed to produce many of the pioneering works on time and motion study, scientific management, applied psychology, and twelve children.

1910   Louis D. Brandeis, an associate of Frederick W. Taylor (and later Supreme Court Justice) coins and popularizes the term scientific management in his Eastern Rate Case testimony before the Interstate Commerce Commission by arguing that railroad rate increases should be denied because the railroads could save "a million dollars a day" by applying scientific management methods.

1911   Frederick W. Taylor publishes The Principles of Scientific Management.

1912   Harrington Emerson publishes The Twelve Principles of Efficiency, which put forth an interdependent but coordinated management system.

1913   Hugo Munsterberg's Psychology and Industrial Efficiency calls for the application of psychology to industry.

1914   Robert Michels in his analysis of the workings of political parties and labor unions, Political Parties, formulates his iron law of oligarchy: "who says organization, says oligarchy."

1916   In France, Henri Fayol publishes his *General and Industrial Management,* the first complete theory of management.

1922   Max Weber's structural definition of bureaucracy is published posthumously; it uses an "ideal-type" approach to extrapolate from the real world the central core of features that characterizes the most fully developed form of bureaucratic organization.

1924   Hawthorne studies begin at the Hawthorne Works of the Western Electric Company in Chicago; they last until 1932 and lead to new thinking about the relationships among work environment, human motivation, and productivity.

1926   Mary Parker Follett in calling for "power with" as opposed to "power over" anticipates the movement toward more participatory management styles.

1931   Mooney and Reiley in *Onward Industry* (republished in 1939 as *The Principles of Organization*) show how the newly discovered "principles of organization" have really been known since ancient times.

1933   Elton Mayo's *The Human Problems of an Industrial Civilization* is the first major report on the Hawthorne studies, the first significant call for a human relations movement.

1937   Luther Gulick's "Notes on the Theory of Organization" draws attention to the functional elements of the work of an executive with his mnemonic device POSDCORB.

1938   Chester I. Barnard's *The Functions of the Executive,* his sociological analysis of organizations, encourages and foreshadows the postwar revolution in thinking about organizational behavior.

1939   Roethlisberger and Dickson publish *Management and the Worker,* the definitive account of the Hawthorne studies.

1940   Robert K. Merton's article "Bureaucratic Structure and Personality" proclaims that Max Weber's "ideal-type" bureaucracy has inhibiting dysfunctions leading to inefficiency and worse.

1941   James Burnham in *The Managerial Revolution* asserts that as the control of large organizations passes from the hands of the owners into the hands of professional administrators, the society's new governing class will be the possessors not of wealth but of technical expertise.

1943   Abraham Maslow's "needs hierarchy" first appears in his *Psychological Review* article, "A Theory of Human Motivation."

1946   Herbert A. Simon's "The Proverbs of Administration" attacks the principles approach to management for being inconsistent and often inapplicable.

1947 National Training Laboratories for Group Development (now called the NTL Institute for Applied Behavioral Science) is established to do research on group dynamics and later sensitivity training.

Herbert A. Simon's *Administrative Behavior* urges that a true scientific method be used in the study of administrative phenomena, that the perspective of logical positivism should be used in dealing with questions of policy-making, and that decision making is the true heart of administration.

1948 Dwight Waldo publishes *The Administrative State*, which attacks the "gospel of efficiency" that dominated administrative thinking prior to World War II.

Norbert Wiener coins the term *cybernetics* in his book with the same title, which becomes a critical foundation concept for the systems school of organizational theory.

1949 Philip Selznick in *TVA and the Grass Roots* discovers "cooptation" when he examines how the Tennessee Valley Authority subsumed new external elements into its policy-making process in order to prevent those elements from becoming a threat to the organization.

In his *Public Administration Review* article, "Power and Administration," Norton E. Long finds that power is the lifeblood of administration, and that managers had to more than just apply the scientific method to problems— they had to attain, maintain, and increase their power or risk failing in their mission.

Rufus E. Miles, Jr., of the Bureau of the Budget first states Miles' Law: "Where you stand depends on where you sit."

Air Force Captain Edsel Murphy first states Murphy's Law: "If anything can go wrong, it will."

1950 George C. Homans publishes *The Human Group*, the first major application of "systems" to organizational analysis.

1951 Kurt Lewin proposes a general model of change consisting of three phases, "unfreezing, change, refreezing," in his *Field Theory in Social Science;* this model becomes the conceptual frame for organization development.

Ludwig von Bertalanffy's article "General Systems Theory: A New Approach to the Unity of Science" is published in *Human Biology;* his concepts will become *the* intellectual basis for the systems approach to organizational thinking.

1954 Peter Drucker's book, *The Practice of Management*, popularizes the concept of management by objectives.

Alvin Gouldner's *Patterns of Industrial Bureaucracy* describes three possible responses to a formal bureaucratic structure: "mock," where the formal rules are ignored by both management and labor; "punishment-centered," where management seeks to enforce rules that workers resist; and "representative," where rules are both enforced and obeyed.

1956   William H. Whyte, Jr., first profiles *The Organization Man*, an individual within an organization who accepts its values and finds harmony in conforming to its policies.

In the premier issue of *Administrative Science Quarterly*, Talcott Parsons' article "Suggestions for a Sociological Approach to the Theory of Organizations" defines an organization as a social system that focuses on the attainment of specific goals and contributes, in turn, to the accomplishment of goals of the larger organization or society itself.

Kenneth Boulding's *Management Science* article, "General Systems Theory—The Skeleton of Science" integrates Wiener's concept of cybernetics with von Bertalanffy's general systems theory; this will become the most quoted introduction to the systems concept of organization.

1957   C. Northcote Parkinson discovers his law that "work expands so as to fill the time available for its completion."

Chris Argyris asserts in his first major book, *Personality and Organization*, that there is an inherent conflict between the personality of a mature adult and the needs of modern organizations.

Douglas M. McGregor's article, "The Human Side of Enterprise," distills the contending traditional (authoritarian) and humanistic managerial philosophies into Theory X and Theory Y; applies the concept of "self-fulfilling prophesies" to organizational behavior.

Philip Selznick in *Leadership in Administration* anticipates many of the 1980s' notions of "transformational leadership" when he asserts that the function of an institutional leader is to help shape the environment in which the institution operates and to define new institutional directions through recruitment, training, and bargaining.

Alvin W. Gouldner in "Cosmopolitans and Locals" identifies two latent social roles that tend to manifest themselves in organizations: cosmopolitans," who have small loyalty to the employing organization, high commitment to specialized skills, and an outer-reference group orientation; and "locals," who have high loyalty to the employing organization, a low commitment to specialized skills, and an inner-reference group orientation.

1958   March and Simon in *Organizations* seek to inventory and classify all that is worth knowing about the behavioral revolution in organization theory.

1959 Charles A. Lindblom's "The Science of 'Muddling Through' " rejects the rational model of decision making in favor of incrementalism.

Herzberg, Mausner, and Snyderman's *The Motivation to Work* puts forth the motivation-hygiene theory of worker motivation.

Cyert and March postulate that power and politics impact on the formation of organizational goals; their "A Behavioral Theory of Organizational Objectives" is an early precursor of the power and politics school.

1960 Richard Neustadt's *Presidential Power* asserts that the president's (or any executive's) essential power is that of persuasion.

Herbert Kaufman's *The Forest Ranger* shows how organizational and professional socialization can develop the will and capacity to conform in employees.

1961 Victor A. Thompson's *Modern Organization* finds that there is "an imbalance between ability and authority" causing bureaucratic dysfunctions all over the place.

Harold Koontz's "Management Theory Jungle" describes thinking about management as a "semantics jungle."

Burns and Stalker's *The Management of Innovation* articulates the need for different types of management systems (organic or mechanistic) under differing circumstances.

Rensis Likert's *New Patterns of Management* offers an empirically based defense of participatory management and organization development techniques.

Amatai Etzioni in *A Comparative Analysis of Complex Organizations* argues that organizational effectiveness is affected by the match between an organization's goal structure and its compliance structure.

1962 Robert Presthus' *The Organizational Society* presents his threefold classification of patterns of organizational accommodation: "upward-mobiles," who identify and accept the values of the organization; "indifferents," who reject such values and find personal satisfaction off the job; and "ambivalents," who want the rewards of organizational life but can't cope with the demands.

Blau and Scott in their *Formal Organizations: A Comparative Approach* assert that all organizations include both a formal and informal element, and that it is impossible to know and understand the true structure of a formal organization without a similar understanding of its parallel informal organization.

David Mechanic's *Administrative Science Quarterly* article, "Sources of Power of Lower Participants in Complex Organizations," anticipates the power and politics perspective of organization theory.

1963 Cyert and March in *A Behavioral Theory of the Firm* demonstrate that corporations tend to "satisfice" rather than engage in economically rational profit-maximizing behavior.

1964 Blake and Mouton's *The Managerial Grid* uses a graphic gridiron to explain management styles and their potential impacts on an organization development program.

Michel Crozier in *The Bureaucratic Phenomenon* defines a bureaucracy as "an organization which cannot correct its behavior by learning from its errors."

Bertram M. Gross publishes his two-volume *The Managing of Organizations*, an historical analysis of thinking about organizations from ancient times to the present.

1965 Don K. Price publishes *The Scientific Estate* in which he posits that decisional authority flows inexorably from the executive suite to the technical office.

Robert L. Kahn's *Organizational Stress* is the first major study of the mental health consequences of organizational role conflict and ambiguity.

James G. March edits the huge *Handbook of Organizations*, which sought to summarize all existing knowledge on organization theory and behavior.

1966 Katz and Kahn in *The Social Psychology of Organizations* seek to unify the findings of behavioral science on organizational behavior through open systems theory.

Warren Bennis in *Changing Organizations* sounds the death knell for bureaucratic institutions because they are inadequate for a future that will demand rapid organizational change, participatory management, and the growth of a more professionalized work force.

1967 James D. Thompson's *Organizations in Action* seeks to close the gap between open and closed systems theory by suggesting that organizations deal with the uncertainty of their environments by creating specific elements designed to cope with the outside world while other elements are able to focus on the rational nature of technical operations.

Anthony Downs' *Inside Bureaucracy* seeks to develop laws and propositions that would aid in predicting the behavior of bureaus and bureaucrats.

John Kenneth Galbraith's *The New Industrial State* asserts that the control of modern corporations has passed to the technostructure and that this technostructure is more concerned with stability than profits.

Antony Jay in *Management and Machiavelli* applies Machiavelli's political principles (from *The Prince*) to modern organizational management.

1968 Harold Wilensky's *Organizational Intelligence* presents the pioneering study of the flow and perception of information in organizations.

Walker and Lorsch grapple with the perennial structural issue of whether to design organizations by product or function in their *Harvard Business Review* article, "Organizational Choice: Product vs. Function."

1969 Laurence J. Peter promulgates his principle that "in a hierarchy every employee tends to rise to his level of incompetence."

Lawrence and Lorsch in *Organization and Environment* call for a contingency theory that can deal with the appropriateness of different theories under differing circumstances; they state that organizations must solve the problem of simultaneous differentiation and integration.

1970 Burton Clark's *The Distinctive College* identifies ways that three colleges created and maintained their distinctiveness through the management of symbols.

1971 Graham T. Allison's *Essence of Decision* demonstrates the inadequacies of the view that the decisions of a government are made by a "single calculating decisionmaker" who has control over the organizations and officials within his government.

1972 Wildcat strike at General Motors Lordstown, Ohio, automobile assembly plant calls national attention to the dysfunctions of dehumanized and monotonous work.

Harlan Cleveland in *The Future Executive* asserts that decision making in the future will call for "continuous improvisation on a general sense of direction."

Charles Perrow's *Complex Organizations* is a major defense of bureaucratic forms of organization and an attack on those writers who think that bureaucracy can be easily, fairly, or inexpensively replaced.

Kast and Rosenzweig in their *Academy of Management Journal* article, "General Systems Theory: Applications for Organization and Management," assess the level of successful application of general systems theory in organizations and advocate a contingency theory as a less abstract and more applicable theoretical approach.

1973 Jay Galbraith in *Designing Complex Organizations* articulates the systems/contingency view that the amount of information an organization needs is a function of the levels of its uncertainty, interdependence of units and functions, and adaptation mechanisms.

1976 Michael Maccoby psychoanalytically interviews 250 corporate managers and discovers *The Gamesman*, a manager whose main interest lies in "competitive activity where he can prove himself a winner."

1977   In *Matrix*, Davis and Lawrence caution against using a matrix form of organization unless there exist specific organizational conditions that are conducive to its success.

Rosabeth Moss Kanter in *Men and Women of the Corporation* describes the unique problems women encounter with power and politics in organizations.

1978   Thomas J. Peters' *Organizational Dynamics* article, "Symbols, Patterns, and Settings: An Optimistic Case for Getting Things Done," is the first major analysis of symbolic management in organizations to gain significant attention in the "mainstream" literature of organization theory.

1979   Rosabeth Moss Kanter's *Harvard Business Review* article, "Power Failure in Management Circuits," identifies organizational positions that tend to have power problems; then argues that powerlessness is often more of a problem than power for organizations.

Structuring Organizations is published, the first book in Henry Mintzberg's integrative series on "The Theory of Management Policy."

1981   Jeffrey Pfeffer's *Power in Organizations* integrates the tenets and applications of the power and politics school of organization theory.

Thomas Ouchi's *Theory Z* and Pascale and Athos' *The Art of Japanese Management* popularize the Japanese management "movement."

1982   Organizational culture becomes "hot" in the general business literature with such books as Peters and Waterman's *In Search of Excellence*, Deal and Kennedy's *Corporate Culture*, and *Business Week's* cover story on "Corporate Culture."

1983   Henry Mintzberg's *Power in and Around Organizations* molds the power and politics school of organizational theory into an integrative theory of management policy.

Meryl R. Louis' article, "Organizations as Cultural-Bearing Milieux," becomes the first readable, integrative statement of the organizational cultural school's assumptions and positions.

1984   Segiovanni and Corbally edit the first notable collection of papers on the organizational culture perspective, *Leadership and Organizational Culture*.

Siehl and Martin report the findings of the first major quantitative and qualitative empirical study of organizational culture in their "The Role of Symbolic Management: How Can Managers Effectively Transmit Organizational Culture?"

1985   Edgar Schein writes the most comprehensive and integrative statement of the organizational culture school in his *Organizational Culture and Leadership*.

CHAPTER I

Classical Organization Theory

No single date can be pinpointed as the beginning of serious thinking about how organizations work and how they should be structured and managed. One can trace writings about management and organizations as far back as the known origins of commerce. Much can be learned from the early organizations of the Egyptians, Hebrews, Greeks, and Romans. If we were to take the time, we could make the case that much of what we know about organization theory has its origins in ancient and medieval times. After all, it was Aristotle who first wrote of the importance of culture to management systems, and Machiavelli who gave the world the definitive analysis of the use of power.

In order to give the reader a sense of organization theory's deep roots in earlier eras, we offer two examples of ancient wisdom on organization management. The first of our ancient examples is from the Book of Exodus, Chapter 18 (see box), in which Jethro, Moses' father-in-law, chastises Moses for failing to establish an organization through which he could delegate his responsibility for the administration of justice. In Verse 25, Moses accepts Jethro's advice and "chose able men out of all Israel, and made them heads over the people, rulers of thousands, rulers of hundreds, rulers of fifties, and rulers of tens." Moses continued to judge the "hard cases," but his rulers judged "every small matter" themselves. This concept of "management by exception" would later be developed for modern audiences by Frederick Winslow Taylor.

In the second ancient example (see chapter selection 1), Socrates anticipates the arguments for "generic management" and "principles of management" as he explains to Nicomachides that a leader who "knows what he needs, and is able to provide it, [can] be a good president, whether he have the direction of a chorus, a family, a city, or an army." (Xenophon, 1869). Socrates lists and discusses the duties of all good presidents—of public and private institutions—and emphasizes the similarities. This is the first known statement that organizations as entities are basically alike; that a manager who could cope well with one would be equally adept at coping with others—even though their purposes and functions might be widely disparate.

While it is always great fun to delve into the wisdom of the ancients, most analysts of the origins of organization theory view the beginnings of the factory

EXODUS
Chapter 18

13 And it came to pass on the morrow, that Moses sat to judge the people: and the people stood by Moses from the morning unto the evening.

14 And when Moses' father-in-law saw all that he did to the people, he said, "What *is* this thing that thou doest to the people? why sittest thou thyself alone, and all the people stand by thee from morning unto even?"

15 And Moses said unto his father-in-law, "Because the people come unto me to inquire of God:

16 When they have a matter, they come unto me; and I judge between one and another, and I do make *them* know the statutes of God, and his laws."

17 And Moses' father-in-law said unto him, "The thing that thou doest is not good.

18 Thou wilt surely wear away, both thou, and this people that *is* with thee: for this thing *is* too heavy for thee: thou art not able to perform it thyself alone.

19 Hearken now unto my voice, I will give thee counsel, and God shall be with thee: Be thou for the people to God-ward, that thou mayest bring the causes unto God:

20 And thou shalt teach them ordinances and laws, and shalt shew them the way wherein they must walk, and the work that they must do.

21 Moreover thou shalt provide out of all the people able men, such as fear God, men of truth, hating covetousness; and place *such* over them, *to be* rulers of thousands, *and* rulers of hundreds, rulers of fifties, and rulers of tens:

22 And let them judge the people at all seasons: and it shall be, *that* every great matter they shall bring unto thee, but every small matter they shall judge: so shall it be easier for thyself, and they shall bear *the burden* with thee.

23 If thou shalt do this thing, and God command thee *so*, then thou shalt be able to endure, and all this people shall also go to their place in peace."

24 So Moses hearkened to the voice of his father-in-law, and did all that he had said.

25 And Moses chose able men out of all Israel, and made them heads over the people, rulers of thousands, rulers of hundreds, rulers of fifties, and rulers of tens.

26 And they judged the people at all seasons: the hard causes they brought unto Moses, but every small matter they judged themselves.

27 And Moses let his father-in-law depart; and he went his way into his own land.

system in Great Britain in the eighteenth century as the birthpoint of complex economic organizations and, consequently, of the field of organization theory.

Classical organization theory, as its name implies, was the first theory of its kind, is considered traditional, and continues to be the base upon which other schools of organization theory have built. Thus, an understanding of classical organization theory is essential not only because of its historical interest but also, more importantly, because subsequent analyses and theories presume a knowledge of it.

The classical school dominated organization theory into the 1930s and remains highly influential today (Merkle, 1980). Over the years, classical organization theory expanded and matured. Its basic tenets and assumptions, however, which were rooted in the industrial revolution of the 1700s and the professions of mechanical engineering, industrial engineering, and economics, have never changed. They were only expanded upon, refined, and made more sophisticated. These fundamental tenets are that:

1. Organizations exist to accomplish production-related and economic goals.
2. There is one best way to organize for production, and that way can be found through systematic, scientific inquiry.
3. Production is maximized through specialization and division of labor.
4. People and organizations act in accordance with rational economic principles.

The evolution of any theory must be viewed in context. The beliefs of early management theorists about how organizations worked or should work were a direct reflection of the societal values of their times. And the times were harsh. It was well into the twentieth century before the industrial workers of the United States and Europe began to enjoy even limited "rights" as organizational citizens. Workers were not viewed as individuals but as the interchangeable parts in an industrial machine whose parts were made of flesh only when it was impractical to make them of steel.

The advent of power-driven machinery and hence the modern factory system spawned our current concepts of economic organizations and organization for production. Power-driven equipment was expensive. Production workers could not purchase and use their own equipment as they had their own tools. Remember the phrase for being fired—"get the sack." It comes from the earliest days of the industrial revolution when a dismissed worker literally was given a sack in which to gather up his tools. Increasingly, workers without their own tools and often without any special skills had to gather for work where the equipment was—in factories. Expensive equipment had to produce enough output to justify their acquisition and maintenance costs.

The advent of the factory system presented managers of organizations with an unprecedented array of new problems. Managers had to arrange for heavy infusions of capital, plan and organize for reliable large-scale production, coordinate and control activities of large numbers of people and functions, contain costs (this was hardly a concern under "cottage industry" production), and maintain a trained and motivated work force.

Under the factory system, organizational success resulted from well-organized production systems that kept machines busy and costs under control. Industrial and mechanical engineers—and their machines—were the keys to production. Organizational structures and production systems were needed to take best advantage of the machines. Organizations, it was thought, should work like machines, using people, capital, and machines as their parts. Just as industrial engineers sought to design "the best" machines to keep factories productive, industrial and mechanical engineering-type thinking dominated theories about "the best way" to organize for production. Thus, the first theories of organizations were concerned primarily with the anatomy—or structure—of formal organizations. This was the milieu, or the environment, the mode of thinking, that shaped and influenced the tenets of classical organization theory.

Centralization of equipment and labor in factories, division of specialized labor, management of specialization, and economic paybacks on factory equipment all were concerns of the Scottish economist Adam Smith's work, *An Inquiry into the Nature and Causes of the Wealth of Nations* (1776). The historian Arnold Toynbee (1956) identified Adam Smith (1723–1790) and James Watt (1736–1819) as the two people who were most responsible for pushing the world into industrialization. Watt, of course, invented the steam engine.

Smith, who is considered the "father" of the academic discipline of economics, provided the intellectual foundation for laissez-faire capitalism. *The Wealth of Nations* (1776) devotes its first chapter, "Of the Division of Labour," to a discussion of the optimum organization of a pin factory. Why? Because specialization of labor was one of the pillars of Smith's "invisible hand" market mechanism in which the greatest rewards would go to those who were the most efficient in the competitive marketplace. Traditional pin makers could produce only a few dozen pins a day. When organized in a factory with each worker performing a limited operation, they could produce tens of thousands a day. Smith's "Of the Division of Labour" is reprinted here because, coming as it did at the dawn of the Industrial Revolution, it is the most famous and influential statement on the economic rationale of the factory system. Smith revolutionized thinking about economics and organizations. Thus we have operationally defined 1776, the year in which *Wealth of Nations* was published, as the beginning point of organization theory as an applied science and academic discipline. Besides, 1776 was a good year for other events as well.

Charles Babbage (1792–1871), the British scientist and mathematician who is considered the intellectual "father" of the modern computer, was studying different manufacturing methods to produce one of his many inventions. His studies led him to conclude that there were basic principles of management (including the division of labor), that those principles could be learned through experience, and that they could be applied broadly. He alluded to these conclusions in *On the Economy of Machinery and Manufactures* (1832). His chapter, "On the Division of Labour," which is included here, clearly benefited from the earlier writing of Adam

Smith, but Babbage carried the concept considerably farther—as is obvious from the conclusions about pervasive principles of management. Sixty years later, Babbage's conclusions would influence the thinking and writing of Frederick Winslow Taylor and his followers and, therefore, of the scientific management movement.

About twenty years after Babbage proposed general principles of management, Daniel C. McCallum (1815–1878), the visionary general superintendent of the New York and Erie Railroad, elucidated general principles of organization that "may be regarded as settled and necessary" (1856). His principles included division of responsibilities, power commensurate with responsibilities, and a reporting system that allowed managers to know promptly if responsibilities were "faithfully executed" and to identify errors and "delinquent" subordinates. McCallum, who is also credited with creating the first modern organization chart, had an enormous influence on the managerial development of the American railroad industry.

In systematizing America's first big business before the Civil War, McCallum provided the model principles and procedures of management for the big businesses that would follow after the war. He became so much *the* authority on running railroads that as a major general during the Civil War, he was chosen to run the Union's military rail system. While McCallum was highly influential as a practitioner, he was no scholar, and the only coherent statement of his general principles comes from an annual report he wrote for the New York and Erie Railroad. Excerpts from his "Superintendent's Report" of March 25, 1856, are reprinted here.

During the 1880s, two practicing managers in the United States independently discovered that generally applicable principles of administration could be determined through systematic, scientific investigation—about thirty years before Taylor's *The Principles of Scientific Management* or Fayol's *General and Industrial Management*. The first, Captain Henry Metcalfe (1847–1917) of the United States Army's Frankford Arsenal in Philadelphia, urged managers to record production events and experiences systematically so that they could use the information to improve production processes. He published his propositions in *The Cost of Manufactures and the Administration of Workshops, Public and Private* (1885), which also pioneered in applying "pre-scientific management" methods to the problems of managerial control and asserted that there is a "science of administration" based upon principles discoverable by diligent observation. Although Metcalfe's work is important historically, it is so similar to that of Taylor's and others that it is not included here as a selection.

The second prescientific management advocate of the 1880s was Henry R. Towne (1844–1924), co-founder and president of the Yale & Towne Manufacturing Company. In 1886, Towne proposed that shop management was of equal importance to engineering management and that the American Society of Mechanical Engineers (ASME) should take a leadership role in establishing a multicompany, engineering/management "database" on shop practices or "the management of works." The information could then be shared among established and new enterprises. Several years later, his proposal was adopted by ASME. His paper presented to the society, entitled "The Engineer as an Economist," was published in *Transactions of the American Society of Mechanical Engineers* (1886) and is reprinted here. Historians have often considered Towne's paper the first "call" for scientific management.

Interestingly, Towne had several significant associations with Frederick Winslow Taylor. The two of them were fellow draftsmen at the Midvale Steel works during the 1880s. Towne gave Taylor one of his first true opportunities to succeed at applying scientific management principles at Yale & Towne in 1904. Towne also nominated Taylor for the presidency of ASME in 1906, and thus provided him with an international forum for advocating scientific management. (Upon election, Taylor promptly reorganized the ASME according to scientific management principles.)

While the ideas of Adam Smith, Charles Babbage, Frederick Winslow Taylor, and others are still dominant influences on the design and management of organizations, it was Henri Fayol (1841–1925), a French executive engineer, who developed the first comprehensive theory of management. While Taylor was tinkering with the technology employed by the individual worker, Fayol was theorizing about all of the elements necessary to organize and manage a major corporation. Fayol's major work, *Administration Industrielle et Generale* (published in France in 1916), was almost ignored in the United States until Constance Storr's English translation, *General and Industrial Management*, appeared in 1949. Since that time, Fayol's theoretical contributions have been widely recognized and his work is considered fully as significant as that of Taylor.

Fayol believed that his concept of management was universally applicable to every type of organization. While he had six principles: technical (production of goods), commercial (buying, selling, and exchange activities), financial (raising and using capital), security (protection of property and people), accounting, and managerial (coordination, control, organization, planning, and command of people); Fayol's primary interest and emphasis was on his final principle—managerial. His managerial principle addressed such variables as division of work, authority and responsibility, discipline, unity of command, unity of direction, subordination of individual interest to general interest, remuneration of personnel, centralization, scalar chains, order, equity, stability of personnel tenure, initiative, and esprit de corps. Reprinted here is Fayol's "General Principles of Management," a chapter from his *General and Industrial Management*.

About one hundred years after Adam Smith declared the factory to be the most appropriate means of mass production, Frederick Winslow Taylor and a group of his followers were "spreading the gospel" that factory workers could be much more productive if their work was designed scientifically. Taylor, the acknowledged father of the scientific management movement, pioneered the development of time-and-motion studies, originally under the name "Taylorism" or the "Taylor system." "Taylorism" or its successor scientific management was not a single invention but rather a series of methods and organizational arrangements designed by Taylor and his associates to increase the efficiency and speed of machine-shop production. Premised upon the notion that there was "one best way" of accomplishing any given task, Taylor's scientific management sought to increase output by discovering the fastest, most efficient, and least fatiguing production methods.

The job of the scientific manager, once the "one best way" was found, was to impose this procedure upon his or her organization. Classical organization theory derives from a corollary of this proposition. If there was one best way to accomplish any given production task, then correspondingly, there must also be one best way to accomplish any task of social organization—including organizing firms. Such principles of social organization were assumed to exist and to be waiting to be discovered by diligent scientific observation and analysis.

Scientific management, as espoused by Taylor, also contained a powerful, puritanical, social message. Taylor (1911) offered scientific management as the way for firms to increase profits, get rid of unions, "increase the thrift and virtue of the working classes," and raise productivity so that the broader society could enter a new era of harmony based on higher consumption of mass-produced goods by members of the laboring classes.

Scientific management emerged as a national movement during a series of events in 1910. The railroad companies in the eastern states filed for increased freight rates with the Interstate Commerce Commission. The railroads had been receiving poor press, being blamed for many things including a cost-price squeeze that was bankrupting farmers. Thus the rate hearings received extensive media coverage. Louis D. Brandeis, a self-styled populist lawyer who would later be a Supreme Court justice, took the case against the railroads without pay. Brandeis called in Harrington Emerson, a consultant who had "systematized" the Santa Fe Railroad, to testify that the railroads did not need increased rates: they could "save a million dollars a day" by using what Brandeis initially called "scientific management" methods (Urwick, 1956). At first, Taylor was reluctant to use the phrase because it sounded too academic. But, the ICC hearings meant that the national scientific management boom was underway, and Taylor was its leader.

Taylor had a profound—almost revolutionary—effect on the fields of business and public administration. Taylor gained credence for the notion that organizational operations could be planned and controlled systematically by experts using scientific principles. Many of Taylor's concepts and precepts are still in use today. The legacy of scientific management is substantial. Taylor's best known work is his 1911 book, *The Principles of Scientific Management*, but he also wrote numerous accounts on the subject. Reprinted here is an article, also entitled "The Principles of Scientific Management," which was the summary of an address given by him on March 3, 1915, two weeks prior to his death.

Several of Taylor's associates subsequently gained wide recognition including, for example, Frank (1868–1924) and Lillian (1878–1972) Gilbreth of *Cheaper by the Dozen* (1948) and "therblig" (Spriegel & Myers, 1953) fame, Henry Laurence Gantt (1861–1919) who invented the Gantt chart for planning work output (Alford, 1932), and Carl G. Barth (1860–1939) who, among his other accomplishments, in 1908 convinced the dean of the new Harvard Business School to adopt "Taylorism" as the "foundation concept" of modern management (Urwick, 1956).

In contrast with the fervent advocates of scientific management, Max Weber (1864–1920) was a brilliant analytical sociologist who happened to study bureaucratic organizations. Bureaucracy has emerged as a dominant feature of the contemporary world. Virtually everywhere one looks in both developed and developing nations, economic, social, and political life are influenced extensively by bureaucratic organizations. Typically *bureaucracy* is used to refer to a specific set of structural arrangements. It is also used to refer to specific patterns of behavior—patterns that are not restricted to formal bureaucracies. It is widely assumed that the structural characteristics of organizations properly defined as "bureaucratic" influence the behavior of individuals—whether clients or bureaucrats—who interact with them. Contemporary thinking along these lines began with the work of Max Weber. His analysis of bureaucracy, first published in 1922, remains the single most influential statement and the point of departure for all further analyses on the subject (including those of the "modern structuralists" in Chapter III).

Drawing upon studies of ancient bureaucracies in Egypt, Rome, China, and the Byzantine Empire, as well as on the more modern ones emerging in Europe during the nineteenth and early part of the twentieth centuries, Weber used an "ideal-type" approach to extrapolate from the real world the central core of features characteristic of the most fully developed bureaucratic form of organization. Weber's "Characteristics of Bureaucracy," which is included here, is neither a description of reality nor a statement of normative preference. In fact, Weber feared the potential implications of bureaucracies. Rather, his "ideal-type" bureaucracy is merely an identification of the major variables or features that characterize this type of social institution.

Luther Gulick's (1892–) "Notes on the Theory of Organization," which clearly was influenced by the work of Henri Fayol, is one of the major statements of the "principles" approach to managing the functions of organizations. It appeared in *Papers on the Science of Administration*, a collection that he and Lyndall Urwick edited in 1937. It was here that Gulick introduced his famous mnemonic, POSDCORB, which stood for the seven major functions of executive management—planning, organizing, staffing, directing, coordinating, reporting, and budgeting. Gulick's principles of administration also included unity of command and span of control. Overall, the *Papers* was a statement of the "state of the art" of organization theory. The study of organizations through analysis of management functions continues within the field of organization theory.

Daniel A. Wren (1972) once observed that "the development of a body of knowledge about how to manage has . . . evolved within a framework of the economic, social, and political facets of various cultures. Management thought is both a process in and a product of its cultural environment." The selections we have chosen to represent the classical school of organization theory vividly demonstrate Wren's thesis. Looking through 1986 "lenses," it is tempting to denigrate the contributions of the classicalists—to view them as narrow and simplistic. In the context of their times, however, they were brilliant pioneers. Their thinking provided invaluable foundations for the field of organization theory, and their influence upon organization theory and theorists continues today.

BIBLIOGRAPHIC REFERENCES

Alford, L. P. (1932). *Henry Laurence Gantt: Leader in industry.* New York: Harper & Row.

Babbage, C. (1832). *On the economy of machinery and manufactures.* Philadelphia, PA: Carey & Lea.

Fayol, H. (1949). *General and industrial management* (C. Storrs, Trans.) London: Pitman Publishing Co. (Original work published 1916)

George, C. S., Jr. (1972). *The history of management thought.* (2nd ed.). Englewood Cliffs, NJ: Prentice-Hall.

Gilbreth, F. B., Jr., & Carey, E. G. (1948). *Cheaper by the dozen.* New York: Grosset & Dunlap.

Gulick, L. (1937). Notes on the theory of organization. In L. Gulick & L. Urwick (Eds.), *Papers on the science of administration* (pp. 3–13). New York: Institute of Public Administration.

McCallum, D. C. (1856). Superintendent's report, March 25, 1856. In *Annual report of the New York and Erie Railroad Company for 1855.* In A. D. Chandler, Jr. (Ed.), *The railroads* (pp. 101–108). New York: Harcourt Brace & Jovanovich.

Merkle, J. A. (1980). *Management and ideology: The legacy of the international scientific management movement.* Berkeley, CA: University of California Press.

Metcalfe, H. (1885). *The cost of manufactures and the administration of workshops, public and private.* New York: John Wiley & Sons.

Smith, A. (1776). Of the division of labour. In A. Smith, *The wealth of nations* (chap. 1).

Spriegel, W. R., & Myers, C. E. (Eds.). (1953). *The writings of the Gilbreths.* Homewood, IL: Richard D. Irwin.

Taylor, F. W. (1911). *The principles of scientific management.* New York: W. W. Norton.

Taylor, F. W. (1916, December). The principles of scientific management. *Bulletin of the Taylor Society.* An abstract of an address given by the late Dr. Taylor before the Cleveland Advertising Club, March 3, 1915.

Towne, H. R. (1886, May). The engineer as an economist. *Transactions of the American Society of Mechanical Engineers, 7,* 428–432. Paper presented at a meeting of the Society, Chicago, IL.

Toynbee, A. (1956). *The industrial revolution.* Boston: Beacon Press. (Original publication 1884)

Urwick, L. (1956). *The golden book of management.* London: Newman, Neame.

Weber, M. (1922). Bureaucracy. In H. Gerth & C. W. Mills (Eds.), *Max Weber: Essays in sociology.* Oxford, UK: Oxford University Press.

Wren, D. A. (1972). *The evolution of management thought.* New York· Ronald Press.

Xenophon. (1869). *The memorabilia of Socrates,* (Rev. J. S. Watson, Trans.) New York: Harper & Row.

1
Socrates Discovers Generic Management

Seeing Nicomachides, one day, coming from the assembly for the election of magistrates, he asked him, "Who have been chosen generals, Nicomachides?"

"Are not the Athenians the same as ever, Socrates?" he replied; "for they have not chosen me, who am worn out with serving on the list, both as captain and centurion, and with having received so many wounds from the enemy (he then drew aside his robe, and showed the scars of the wounds), but have elected Antisthenes, who has never served in the heavy-armed infantry, nor done any thing remarkable in the cavalry, and who indeed knows nothing, but how to get money."

"Is it not good, however, to know this," said Socrates, "since he will then be able to get necessaries for the troops?"

"But merchants," replied Nicomachides, "are able to collect money; and yet would not on that account, be capable of leading an army."

"Antisthenes, however," continued Socrates, "is given to emulation, a quality necessary in a general. Do you not know that whenever he has been chorus-manager he has gained the superiority in all his choruses?"

"But, by Jupiter," rejoined Nicomachides, "there is nothing similar in managing a chorus and an army."

"Yet Antisthenes," said Socrates, "though neither skilled in music nor in teaching a chorus, was able to find out the best masters in these departments."

"In the army, accordingly," exclaimed Nicomachides, "he will find others to range his troops for him, and others to fight for him!"

"Well, then," rejoined Socrates, "if he finds out and selects the best men in military affairs, as he has done in the conduct of his choruses, he will probably attain superiority in this respect also; and it is likely that he will be more willing to spend money for a victory in war on behalf of the whole state, than for a victory with a chorus in behalf of his single tribe."

"Do you say, then, Socrates," said he, "that it is in the power of the same man to manage a chorus well, and to manage an army well?"

"I say," said Socrates, "that over whatever a man may preside, he will, if he knows what he needs, and is able to provide it, be a good president, whether he have the direction of a chorus, a family, a city, or an army."

"By Jupiter, Socrates," cried Nicomachides, "I should never have expected to hear from you that good managers of a family would also be good generals."

"Come, then," proceeded Socrates, "let us consider what are the duties of each of them, that we may understand whether they are the same, or are in any respect different."

Source: Xenophon, *The Anabasis or Expedition of Cyrus and the Memorabilia of Socrates*, trans. J. S. Watson (N.Y.: Harper & Row, 1869), 430–433.

"By all means."

"Is it not, then, the duty of both," asked Socrates, "to render those under their command obedient and submissive to them?"

"Unquestionably."

"Is it not also the duty of both to intrust various employments to such as are fitted to execute them?"

"That is also unquestionable."

"To punish the bad, and to honor the good, too, belongs, I think, to each of them."

"Undoubtedly."

"And is it not honorable in both to render those under them well-disposed toward them?"

"That also is certain."

"And do you think it for the interest of both to gain for themselves allies and auxiliaries or not?"

"It assuredly is for their interest."

"Is it not proper for both also to be careful of their resources?"

"Assuredly."

"And is it not proper for both, therefore, to be attentive and industrious in their respective duties?"

"All these particulars," said Nicomachides, "are common alike to both; but it is not common to both to fight."

"Yet both have doubtless enemies," rejoined Socrates.

"That is probably the case," said the other.

"Is it not for the interest of both to gain the superiority over those enemies?"

"Certainly; but to say something on that point, what, I ask, will skill in managing a household avail, if it be necessary to fight?"

"It will doubtless in that case, be of the greatest avail," said Socrates; "for a good manager of a house, knowing that nothing is so advantageous or profitable as to get the better of your enemies when you contend with them, nothing so unprofitable and prejudicial as to be defeated, will zealously seek and provide every thing that may conduce to victory, will carefully watch and guard against whatever tends to defeat, will vigorously engage if he sees that his force is likely to conquer, and, what is not the least important point, will cautiously avoid engaging if he finds himself insufficiently prepared. Do not, therefore, Nicomachides," he added, "despise men skillful in managing a household; for the conduct of private affairs differs from that of public concerns only in magnitude; in other respects they are similar; but what is most to be observed, is, that neither of them are managed without men, and that private matters are not managed by one species of men, and public matters by another; for those who conduct public business make use of men not at all differing in nature from those whom the managers of private affairs employ; and those who know how to employ them conduct either public or private affairs judiciously, while those who do not know will err in the management of both."

2
Of the Division of Labour
Adam Smith

The greatest improvement in the productive powers of labour, and the greater
part of the skill, dexterity, and judgment
with which it is any where directed, or
applied, seem to have been the effects
of the division of labour.

The effects of the division of labour,
in the general business of society, will
be more easily understood, by considering in what manner it operates in some
particular manufactures. It is commonly
supposed to be carried furthest in some
very trifling ones; not perhaps that it
really is carried further in them than in
others of more importance: but in those
trifling manufactures which are destined
to supply the small wants of but a small
number of people, the whole number of
workmen must necessarily be small; and
those employed in every different branch
of the work can often be collected into
the same workhouse, and placed at once
under the view of the spectator. In those
great manufactures, on the contrary,
which are destined to supply the great
wants of the great body of the people,
every different branch of the work employs so great a number of workmen,
that it is impossible to collect them all
into the same workhouse. We can seldom see more, at one time, than those
employed in one single branch. Though
in such manufactures, therefore, the
work may really be divided into a much
greater number of parts, than in those
of a more trifling nature, the division is

not near so obvious, and has accordingly
been much less observed.

To take an example, therefore, from
a very trifling manufacture; but one in
which the division of labour has been
very often taken notice of, the trade of
the pin-maker; a workman not educated
to this business (which the division of
labour has rendered a distinct trade),
nor acquainted with the use of the machinery employed in it (to the invention
of which the same division of labour has
probably given occasion), could scarce,
perhaps, with his utmost industry, make
one pin in a day, and certainly could not
make twenty. But in the way in which
this business is now carried on, not only
the whole work is a peculiar trade, but
it is divided into a number of branches,
of which the greater part are likewise
peculiar trades. One man draws out the
wire, another straights it, a third cuts it,
a fourth points it, a fifth grinds it at the
top for receiving the head; to make the
head requires two or three distinct operations; to put it on, is a peculiar business, to whiten the pins is another; it is
even a trade by itself to put them into
the paper; and the important business of
making a pin is, in this manner, divided
into about eighteen distinct operations,
which, in some manufactories, are all
performed by distinct hands, though in
others the same man will sometimes perform two or three of them. I have seen
a small manufactory of this kind where

Source: Adam Smith, *The Wealth of Nations* (1776), Chapter 1. Footnotes omitted.

ten men only were employed, and where some of them consequently performed two or three distinct operations. But though they were very poor, and therefore but indifferently accommodated with the necessary machine, they could, when they exerted themselves, make among them about twelve pounds of pins in a day. There are in a pound upwards of four thousand pins of a middling size. Those ten persons, therefore, could make among them upwards of forty-eight thousand pins in a day. Each person, therefore, making a tenth part of forty-eight thousand pins, might be considered as making four thousand eight hundred pins in a day. But if they had all wrought separately and independently, and without any of them having been educated to this peculiar business, they certainly could not each of them have made twenty, perhaps not one pin in a day; that is, certainly, not the two hundred and fortieth, perhaps not the four thousand eight hundredth part of what they are at present capable of performing, in consequence of a proper division and combination of their different operations.

In every other art and manufacture, the effects of the division of labour are similar to what they are in this very trifling one; though, in many of them, the labour can neither be so much subdivided, nor reduced to so great a simplicity of operation. The division of labour, however, so far as it can be introduced, occasions, in every art, a proportionable increase of the productive powers of labour. The separation of different trades and employments from one another, seems to have taken place, in consequence of this advantage. This separation too is generally carried furthest in those countries which enjoy the highest degree of industry and improvement; what is the work of one man in a rude state of society, being generally that of several in an improved one. In every improved society, the farmer is generally nothing but a farmer; the manufacturer, nothing but a manufacturer. The labour too which is necessary to produce any one complete manufacture, is almost always divided among a great number of hands. How many different trades are employed in each branch of the linen and woollen manufactures, from the growers of the flax and the wool, to the bleachers and smoothers of the linen, or to the dyers and dressers of the cloth! The nature of agriculture, indeed, does not admit of so many subdivisions of labour, nor of so complete a separation of one business from another, as manufactures. It is impossible to separate so entirely, the business of the grazier from that of the corn-farmer, as the trade of the carpenter is commonly separated from that of the smith. The spinner is almost always a distinct person from the weaver; but the ploughman, the harrower, the sower of the seed, and the reaper of the corn, are often the same. The occasions for those different sorts of labour returning with the different seasons of the year, it is impossible that one man should be constantly employed in any one of them. This impossibility of making so complete and entire a separation of all the different branches of labour employed in agriculture, is perhaps the reason why the improvement of the productive powers of labour in this art, does not always keep pace with their improvement in manufactures. The most opulent nations, indeed, generally excel all their neighbours in agriculture as well as in manufactures; but they are commonly more distinguished by their superiority in the latter than in the former. Their lands are in general better cultivated, and having more labour and expence bestowed upon them, produce more in proportion to the extent and natural fertility of the ground. But this superiority of produce is seldom much more than in proportion to the superiority of labour and expence. In agriculture, the labour of the rich country is not always much more productive than that of the poor; or, at least, it is never so much more productive, as it commonly is in manufactures. The corn of the rich country, therefore, will not always, in the same degree of goodness, come cheaper to market than that of the poor. The corn of Poland, in the same degree of goodness, is as cheap as that of France, notwithstanding the superior opulence and improvement of the latter country. The corn of France is, in the corn provinces, fully as good, and in most years nearly about the same price with the corn of England, though, in opulence and improvement, France is perhaps inferior to England. The corn lands of England, however, are better cultivated than those of France, and the corn lands of France are said to be much better cultivated than those of Poland. But though the poor country, notwithstanding the inferiority of its cultivation, can, in some measure, rival the rich in the cheapness and goodness of its corn, it can pretend to no such competition in its manufactures; at least if those manufactures suit the soil, climate, and situation of the rich country. The silks of France are better and cheaper than those of England, because the silk manufacture, at least under the present high duties upon the importation of raw silk, does not so well suit the climate of England as that of France. But the hardware and the coarse woollens of England are beyond all comparison superior to those of France, and much cheaper too in the same degree of goodness. In Poland there are said to be scarce any manufactures of any kind, a

few of those coarser household manufactures excepted, without which no country can well subsist.

This great increase of the quantity of work, which, in consequence of the division of labour, the same number of people are capable of performing, is owing to three different circumstances; first, to the increase of dexterity in every particular workman; secondly, to the saving of the time which is commonly lost in passing from one species of work to another; and lastly, to the invention of a great number of machines which facilitate and abridge labour, and enable one man to do the work of many.

First, the improvement of the dexterity of the workman necessarily increases the quantity of the work he can perform; and the division of labour, by reducing every man's business to some one simple operation, and by making this operation the sole employment of his life, necessarily increases very much the dexterity of the workman. A common smith, who, though accustomed to handle the hammer, has never been used to make nails, if upon some particular occasion he is obliged to attempt it, will scarce, I am assured, be able to make above two or three hundred nails in a day, and those too very bad ones. A smith who has been accustomed to make nails, but whose sole or principal business has not been that of a nailer, can seldom with his utmost diligence make more than eight hundred or a thousand nails in a day. I have seen several boys under twenty years of age who had never exercised any other trade but that of making nails, and who, when they exerted themselves, could make, each of them, upwards of two thousand three hundred nails in a day. The making of a nail, however, is by no means one of the simplest operations. The same person blows the bellows, stirs or mends the fire as there is occasion, heats the iron, and forges every part of the nail: In forging the head too he is obliged to change his tools. The different operations into which the making of a pin, or of a metal button, is subdivided, are all of them much more simple, and the dexterity of the person, of whose life it has been the sole business to perform them, is usually much greater. The rapidity with which some of the operations of those manufactures are performed, exceeds what the human hand could, by those who had never seen them, be supposed capable of acquiring.

Secondly, the advantage which is gained by saving the time commonly lost in passing from one sort of work to another, is much greater than we should at first view be apt to imagine it. It is impossible to pass very quickly from one kind of work to another, that is carried on in a different place, and with quite different tools. A country weaver, who cultivates a small farm, must lose a good deal of time in passing from his loom to his field, and from the field to his loom. When the two trades can be carried on in the same workhouse, the loss of time is no doubt much less. It is even in this case, however, very considerable. A man commonly saunters a little in turning his hand from one sort of employment to another. When he first begins the new work he is seldom very keen and hearty; his mind, as they say, does not go to it, and for some time he rather trifles than applies to good purpose. The habit of sauntering and of indolent careless application, which is naturally, or rather necessarily acquired by every country workman who is obliged to change his work and his tools every half hour, and to apply his hand in twenty different ways almost every day of his life; renders him almost always slothful and lazy, and incapable of any vigorous application even on the most pressing occasions. Independent, therefore, of his deficiency

in point of dexterity, this cause alone must always reduce considerably the quantity of work which he is capable of performing.

Thirdly, and lastly, every body must be sensible how much labour is facilitated and abridged by the application of proper machinery. It is unnecessary to give any example. I shall only observe, therefore, that the invention of all those machines by which labour is so much facilitated and abridged, seems to have been originally owing to the division of labour. Men are much more likely to discover easier and readier methods of attaining any object, when the whole attention of their minds is directed towards that single object, than when it is dissipated among a great variety of things. But in consequence of the division of labour, the whole of every man's attention comes naturally to be directed towards some one very simple object. It is naturally to be expected, therefore, that some one or other of those who are employed in each particular branch of labour should soon find out easier and readier methods of performing their own particular work, wherever the nature of it admits of such improvement. A great part of the machines made use of in those manufactures in which labour is most subdivided, were originally the inventions of common workmen, who, being each of them employed in some very simple operation, naturally turned their thoughts towards finding out easier and readier methods of performing it. Whoever has been much accustomed to visit such manufactures, must frequently have been shewn very pretty machines, which were the inventions of such workmen, in order to facilitate and quicken their own particular part of the work. In the first fire-engines, a boy was constantly employed to open and shut alternately the communication between the boiler and the cylinder, according as the piston either ascended or descended. One of those boys, who loved to play with his companions, observed that, by tying a string from the handle of the valve which opened this communication to another part of the machine, the valve would open and shut without his assistance, and leave him at liberty to divert himself with his playfellows. One of the greatest improvements that has been made upon this machine, since it was first invented, was in this manner the discovery of a boy who wanted to save his own labour.

All the improvements in machinery, however, have by no means been the inventions of those who had occasion to use the machines. Many improvements have been made by the ingenuity of the makers of the machines, when to make them become the business of a peculiar trade; and some by that of those who are called philosophers or men of speculation, whose trade it is not to do any thing, but to observe every thing; and who, upon that account, are often capable of combining together the powers of the most distant and dissimilar objects. In the progress of society, philosophy or speculation becomes, like every other employment, the principal or sole trade and occupation of a particular class of citizens. Like every other employment too, it is subdivided into a great number of different branches, each of which affords occupation to a peculiar tribe or class of philosophers; and this subdivision of employment in philosophy, as well as in every other business, improves dexterity, and saves time. Each individual becomes more expert in his own peculiar branch, more work is done upon the whole, and the quantity of science is considerably increased by it.

It is the great multiplication of the productions of all the different arts, in consequence of the division of labour,

which occasions, in a well-governed society, that universal opulence which extends itself to the lowest ranks of the people. Every workman has a great quantity of his own work to dispose of beyond what he himself has occasion for; and every other workman being exactly in the same situation, he is enabled to exchange a great quantity of his own goods for a great quantity, or, what comes to the same thing, for the price of a great quantity of theirs. He supplies them abundantly with what they have occasion for, and they accommodate him as amply with what he has occasion for, and a general plenty diffuses itself through all the different ranks of the society.

Observe the accommodation of the most common artificer or day-labourer in a civilized and thriving country, and you will perceive that the number of people of whose industry a part, though but a small part, has been employed in procuring him this accommodation, exceeds all computation. The woollen coat, for example, which covers the day-labourer, as coarse and rough as it may appear, is the produce of the joint labour of a great multitude of workmen. The shepherd, the sorter of the wool, the wool-comber or carder, the dyer, the scribbler, the spinner, the weaver, the fuller, the dresser, with many others, must all join their different arts in order to complete even this homely production. How many merchants and carriers, besides, must have been employed in transporting the materials from some of those workmen to others who often live in a very distant part of the country! How much commerce and navigation in particular, how many ship-builders, sailors, sail-makers, rope-makers, must have been employed in order to bring together the different drugs made use of by the dyer, which often come from the remotest corners of the world! What a variety of labour too is necessary in order to produce the tools of the meanest of those workmen! To say nothing of such complicated machines as the ship of the sailor, the mill of the fuller, or even the loom of the weaver, let us consider only what a variety of labour is requisite in order to form that very simple machine, the shears with which the shepherd clips the wool. The miner, the builder of the furnace for smelting the ore, the feller of the timber, the burner of the charcoal to be made use of in the smelting-house, the brick-maker, the brick-layer, the work-men who attend the furnace, the millwright, the forger, the smith, must all of them join their different arts in order to produce them. Were we to examine, in the same manner, all the different parts of his dress and household furniture, the coarse linen shirt which he wears next his skin, the shoes which cover his feet, the bed which he lies on, and all the different parts which compose it, the kitchen grate at which he prepares his victuals, the coals which he makes use of for that purpose, dug from the bowels of the earth, and brought to him perhaps by a long sea and a long land carriage, all the other utensils of his kitchen, all the furniture of his table, the knives and forks, the earthen or pewter plates upon which he serves up

and divides his victuals, the different hands employed in preparing his bread and his beer, the glass window which lets in the heat and the light, and keeps out the wind and the rain, with all the knowledge and art requisite for preparing that beautiful and happy invention, without which these northern parts of the world could scarce have afforded a very comfortable habitation, together with the tools of all the different work-men employed in producing those different conveniences; if we examine, I say, all these things, and consider what a variety of labour is employed about each of them, we shall be sensible that without the assistance and cooperation of many thousands, the very meanest person in a civilized country could not be provided, even according to, what we very falsely imagine, the easy and simple manner in which he is commonly accommodated. Compared, indeed, with the more extravagant luxury of the great, his accommodation must no doubt appear extremely simple and easy; and yet it may be true, perhaps, that the accommodation of an European prince does not always so much exceed that of an industrious and frugal peasant, as the accommodation of the latter exceeds that of many an African king. . . .

3
On the Division of Labour
Charles Babbage

Perhaps the most important principle on which the economy of a manufacture depends, is the *division of labour* amongst the persons who perform the work. The first application of this principle must have been made in a very early stage of society; for it must soon have been apparent, that more comforts and conveniences could be acquired by one man restricting his occupation to the art of making bows, another to that of building houses, a third boats, and so on. This division of labour into trades was not, however, the result of an opinion that the general riches of the community would be increased by such an arrangement: but it must have arisen from the circumstance, of each individual so employed discovering that he himself could thus make a greater profit of his labour than by pursuing more varied occupations. Society must have made considerable advances before this principle could have been carried into the workshop; for it is only in countries which have attained a high degree of civilization, and in articles in which there is a great competition amongst the producers, that the most perfect system of the division of labour is to be observed. The principles on which the advantages of this system depend, have been much the subject of discussion amongst writers on Political Economy; but the relative importance of their influence does not appear, in all cases, to have been estimated with sufficient precision. It is my intention, in the first instance, to state shortly those principles, and then to point out what appears to me to have been omitted by those who have previously treated the subject.

1. *Of the time required for learning.* It will readily be admitted, that the portion of time occupied in the acquisition of any art will depend on the difficulty of its execution; and that the greater the number of distinct processes, the longer will be the time which the apprentice must employ in acquiring it. Five or seven years have been adopted, in a great many trades, as the time considered requisite for a lad to acquire a sufficient knowledge of his art, and to repay by his labour, during the latter portion of his time, the expense incurred by his master at its commencement. If, however, instead of learning all the different processes for making a needle, for instance, his attention be confined to one operation, a very small portion of his time will be consumed unprofitably at the commencement, and the whole of the rest of it will be beneficial to his master: and if there be any competition amongst the masters, the apprentice will be able to make better terms, and diminish the period of his servitude. Again; the facility of acquiring skill in a single process, and the early period of life at which it can be made a source of profit, will induce a greater number of parents to bring up

Source: Charles Babbage, *On the Economy of Machinery and Manufactures* (Philadelphia: Carey & Lea, 1832), 121–140.

their children to it; and from this circumstance also, the number of workmen being increased, the wages will soon fall.

A certain quantity of material will be consumed unprofitably, or spoiled by every person who learns an art; and, as he applies himself to each new process, he will waste a certain quantity of the raw material, or of the partly manufactured commodity. But whether one man commits this waste in acquiring successively each process, or many persons separately learn the several processes, the quantity of waste will remain the same: in this view of the subject, therefore, the division of labour will neither increase nor diminish the price of production.

2. Another source of the advantage resulting from the division of labour is, that *time is always lost from changing from one occupation to another*. When the human hand, or the human head, has been for some time occupied in any kind of work, it cannot instantly change its employment with full effect. The muscles of the limbs employed have acquired a flexibility during their exertion, and those to be put in action a stiffness during rest, which renders every change slow and unequal in the commencement. A similar result seems to take place in any change of mental exertion; the attention bestowed on the new subject is not so perfect at the first commencement as it becomes after some exercise. Long habit also produces in the muscles exercised a capacity for enduring fatigue to a much greater degree than they could support under other circumstances.

Another cause of the loss of time in changing from one operation to another, arises from the employment of different tools in the two processes. If these tools are simple in their nature, and the change is not frequently repeated, the loss of time is not considerable; but in many processes of the arts the tools are of great

delicacy, requiring accurate adjustment whenever they are used. In many cases the time employed in adjusting, bears a large proportion to that employed in using the tool. The sliding-rest, the dividing and the drilling-engine, are of this kind; and hence in manufactories of sufficient extent, it is found to be good economy to keep one machine constantly employed in one kind of work: one lathe, for example, having a screw motion to its sliding-rest along the whole length of its bed, is kept constantly making cylinders; another, having a motion for rendering uniform the velocity of the work at the point at which it passes the tool, is kept for facing surfaces; whilst a third is constantly employed in cutting wheels.

3. *Skill acquired by frequent repetition of the same processes.* The constant repetition of the same process necessarily produces in the workman a degree of excellence and rapidity in his particular department, which is never possessed by one person who is obliged to execute many different processes. This rapidity is still farther increased from the circumstance that most of the operations in factories, where the division of labour is carried to a considerable extent, are paid for as piece work. It is difficult to estimate in numbers the effect of this cause upon production. In nail-making, Adam Smith has stated, that it is almost three to one; for, he observes, that a smith accustomed to make nails, but whose whole business has not been that of a nailer, can make only from eight hundred to a thousand per day; whilst a lad who had never exercised any other trade, can make upwards of two thousand three hundred a day.

Upon an occasion when a large issue of bank-notes was required, a clerk at the Bank of England signed his name, consisting of seven letters, including the

initial of his Christian name, five thousand three hundred times during eleven
working hours; and he also arranged the
notes he had signed in parcels of fifty
each. In different trades the economy of
production arising from this cause, will
necessarily be different. The case of nail-
making is perhaps, rather an extreme
one. It must, however, be observed that,
in one sense, this is not a permanent
source of advantage; for, although it acts
at the commencement of an establishment, yet every month adds to the skill
of the workmen; and at the end of three
or four years they will not be very far
behind those who have practised only
the particular branch of their art.

4. *The division of labour suggests the
contrivance of tools and machinery to execute its processes.* When each process,
by which any article is produced, is the
sole occupation of one individual, his
whole attention being devoted to a very
limited and simple operation, any improvement in the form of his tools, or
in the mode of using them, is much more
likely to occur to his mind than if it were
distracted by a greater variety of circumstances. Such an improvement in the
tool is generally the first step towards a
machine. If a piece of metal is to be cut
in a lathe, for example, there is one
angle at which the cutting- tool must be
held to ensure the cleanest cut; and it
is quite natural that the idea of fixing
the tool at that angle should present itself to an intelligent workman. The necessity of moving the tool slowly, and
in a direction parallel to itself, would
suggest the use of a screw, and thus arises
the sliding-rest. It was probably the idea
of mounting a chisel in a frame, to prevent its cutting too deeply, which gave
rise to the common carpenter's plane.
In cases where a blow from a hammer is
employed, experience teaches the proper
force required. The transition from the
hammer held in the hand to one

mounted upon an axis, and lifted regularly to a certain height by some mechanical contrivance, requires perhaps
a greater degree of invention. Yet it is
not difficult to perceive, that, if the
hammer always falls from the same
height, its effect must be always the same.

When each process has been reduced
to the use of some simple tool, the union
of all these tools, actuated by one moving power, constitutes a machine. In
contriving tools and simplifying processes, the operative workmen are, perhaps, most successful; but it requires far
other habits to combine into one machine these scattered arts. A previous
education as a workman in the peculiar
trade, is undoubtedly a valuable prelim-
inary; but in order to make such combinations with any reasonable expectation of success, an extensive knowledge
of machinery, and the power of making
mechanical drawings, are essentially
requisite. These accomplishments are
now much more common than they were
formerly; and their absence was, perhaps, one of the causes of the multitude
of failures in the early history of many
of our manufactures.

Such are the principles usually assigned as the causes of the advantage
resulting from the division of labour. As
in the view I have taken of the question,
the most important and influential cause
has been altogether unnoticed, I shall
re-state those principles in the words of
Adam Smith: "The great increase in the
quantity of work, which, in consequence of the division of labour, the same
number of people are capable of performing, is owing to three different circumstances: first, to the increase of dexterity in every particular workman;
secondly, to the saving of time, which
is commonly lost in passing from one
species of work to another; and, lastly,
to the invention of a great number of
machines which facilitate and abridge

labour, and enable one man to do the work of many." Now, although all these are important causes, and each has its influence on the result; yet it appears to me, that any explanation of the cheapness of manufactured articles, as consequent upon the division of labour, would be incomplete if the following principle were omitted to be stated.

That the master manufacturer, by dividing the work to be executed into different processes, each requiring different degrees of skill and force, can purchase exactly that precise quantity of both which is necessary for each process; whereas, if the whole work were executed by one workman, that person must possess sufficient skill to perform the most difficult, and sufficient strength to execute the most laborious, of the operations into which the art is divided.[1]

As the clear apprehension of this principle, upon which so much of the economy arising from the division of labour depends, is of considerable importance, it may be desirable to illustrate it, by pointing out its precise and numerical application in some specific manufacture. The art of making needles is, perhaps, that which I should have selected as comprehending a very large number of processes remarkably different in their nature; but the less difficult art of pin-making, has some claim to attention, from its having been used by Adam Smith, in his illustration of the subject; and I am confirmed in the choice, by the circumstance of our possessing a very accurate and minute description of that art, as practised in France above half a century ago.

Pin-making. In the manufacture of pins in England the following processes are employed:—

1. *Wire-drawing.* The brass wire used for making pins is purchased by the manufacturer in coils of about twenty-two inches in diameter, each weighing about thirty-six pounds. The coils are wound off into smaller ones of about six inches' diameter, and between one and two pounds' weight. The diameter of this wire is now reduced by drawing it repeatedly through holes in steel plates, until it becomes of the size required for the sort of pins intended to be made. During the process of drawing the wire through these holes it becomes hardened, and it is necessary to anneal it in order to prevent its breaking; and, to enable it to be still farther reduced, it is annealed two or three times, according to the diminution of diameter required. The coils are then soaked in sulphuric acid, largely diluted with water, in order to clean them, and are then beaten on stone for the purpose of removing any oxidated coating which may adhere to them. This process is usually performed by men, who draw and clean from thirty to thirty-six pounds of wire a day. They are paid at the rate of five farthings per pound, and generally earn about 3s. 6d. per day.

M. Perronet made some experiments on the extension the wire undergoes by this process at each hole: he took a piece of thick Swedish brass wire, and found

	Feet	Inch
Its length to be before drawing	3	8
After passing the first hole	5	5
———— second hole	7	2
———— third hole	7	8

It was now, annealed, and the length became

	Feet	Inch
After passing the fourth hole	10	8
——————— fifth hole	13	1
——————— sixth hole	16	8
And finally, after passing through six other holes	144	0

The holes through which the wire was drawn were not, in this experiment, of regularly decreasing diameter; and it is extremely difficult to make such holes, and still more to preserve them in their original dimensions.

2. *Straightening the Wire.* The coil of wire now passes into the hands of a woman, assisted by a boy or girl. A few nails, or iron pins, not quite in a line, are fixed into one end of a wooden table about twenty feet in length; the end of the wire is passed alternately between these nails, and is then pulled to the other end of the table. The object of this process is to straighten the wire, which had acquired a uniform curvature in the small coils into which it had been wound. The length thus straightened is cut off, and the remainder of the coil is drawn into similar lengths. About seven nails or pins are employed in straightening the wire, and their adjustment is a matter of some nicety. It seems, that by passing the wire between the first three nails or pins, a bend is produced in an opposite direction to that which the wire had in the coil; this bend, by passing the next two nails, is reduced to another of larger curvature in the first direction, and so on till the curvature is at last so large that it may be confounded with a straight line.

3. *Pointing.* A man next takes about three hundred of these straightened pieces in a parcel, and putting them into a gauge, cuts off from one end, by means of a pair of shears, moved by his foot, a portion equal in length to rather more than six pins. He continues this operation until the entire parcel is reduced into similar pieces. The next step is to sharpen the ends: for this purpose the operator sits before a steel mill, which is kept rapidly revolving; and taking up a parcel between the finger and the thumb of each hand, he passes the ends before the mill, taking care with his fingers and thumbs to make each wire slowly revolve upon its axis. The mill consists of a cylinder about six inches in diameter, and two and a half inches broad, faced with steel, which is cut in the manner of a file. Another cylinder is fixed on the same axis at a few inches distant; the file on the edge of which is of a finer kind, and is used for finishing off the points. Having thus pointed all the pieces at one end, he reverses them, and performs the same process on the other. This process requires considerable skill, but it is not unhealthy whilst the similar process in needle-making is remarkably destructive of health. The pieces, now pointed at both ends, are next placed in gauges, and the pointed ends are cut off, by means of shears, to the proper length of which the pins are to be made. The remaining portions of the wire are now equal to about four pins in length, and are again pointed at each end, and their ends again cut off. This process is repeated a third time, and the small portion of wire left in the middle is thrown amongst the waste, to be

melted along with the dust arising from the sharpening. It is usual for a man, his wife, and a child, to join in performing these processes; and they are paid at the rate of five farthings per pound. They can point from thirty-four to thirty-six and a half pounds per day, and gain from 6s. 6d. to 7s., which may be apportioned thus: 5s. 6d. to the man, 1s. to the woman, 6d. to the boy or girl.

4. *Twisting and Cutting the Heads.* The next process is making the heads. For this purpose a boy takes a piece of wire, of the same diameter as the pin to be headed, which he fixes on an axis that can be made to revolve rapidly by means of a wheel and strap connected with it. This wire is called the mould. He then takes a smaller wire, which having passed through an eye in a small tool held in his left hand, he fixes close to the bottom of the mould. The mould is now made to revolve rapidly by means of the right hand, and the smaller wire coils round it until it has covered the whole length of the mould. The boy now cuts the end of the spiral connected with the foot of the mould, and draws it off. When a sufficient quantity of heading is thus made, a man takes from thirteen to twenty of these spirals in his left hand, between his thumb and three outer fingers; these he places in such a manner that two turns of the spiral shall be beyond the upper edge of a pair of shears, and with the forefinger of the same hand he feels these two projecting turns. With his right hand he closes the shears; and the two turns of the spiral being cut off, drop into a basin. The position of the forefinger prevents the heads from flying about when cut off. The workmen who cut the heads are usually paid at the rate of 2½d. to 3d. per pound for large, but a higher price is given for the smaller heading. Out of this they pay the boy who spins the spiral; he re-

ceives from 4d. to 6d. per day. A good workman can cut from six to about thirty pounds of heading per day, according to its size.

5. *Heading.* The process of fixing the head on the body of the pin is usually executed by women and children. Each operator sits before a small steel stake, having a cavity, into which one half of the intended head will fit; immediately above is a steel die, having a corresponding cavity for the other half of the head: this latter die can be raised by a pedal moved by the foot. The cavities in the centre of these dies are connected with the edge by a small groove, to admit of the body of the pin, which is thus prevented from being flattened by the blow of the die. The operator with his left hand dips the pointed end of the body of a pin into a tray of heads; having passed the point through one of them, he carries it along to the other end with the forefinger. He now takes the pin in the right hand, and places the head in the cavity of the stake, and, lifting the die with his foot, allows it to fall on the head. This blow tightens the head on the shank, which is then turned round, and the head receives three or four blows on different parts of its circumference. The women and children who fix the heads are paid at the rate of 1s. 6d. for every twenty thousand. A skilful operator can with great exertion do twenty thousand per day; but from ten to fifteen thousand is the usual quantity: children head a much smaller number; varying, of course, with the degree of their skill. The weight of the hammer is from seven to ten pounds, and it falls through a very small space, perhaps from one to two inches. About one percent are spoiled in the process; these are picked out afterwards by women, and are reserved with the waste from other processes for the melting-pot. The form of the dies

in which the heads are struck is varied according to the fashion of the time; but the repeated blows to which it is subject renders it necessary that it should be repaired after it has been used for about thirty pounds of pins.

6. *Tinning.* The pins are now fit to be tinned, a process which is usually executed, by a man, assisted by his wife, or by a lad. The quantity of pins operated upon at this stage is usually fifty-six pounds. They are first placed in a pickle, in order to remove any grease or dirt from their surface, and also to render that surface rough, which facilitates the adherence of the tin with which they are to be covered. They are then placed in a boiler full of a solution of tartar in water, in which they are mixed with a quantity of tin in small grains. They are generally kept boiling for about two hours and a half, and are then removed into a tub of water into which some bran has been thrown; this is for the purpose of washing them. They are then taken out, and, being placed in wooden trays, are well shaken in dry bran: this removes any water adhering to them; and by giving the wooden tray a peculiar kind of motion, the pins are thrown up, and the bran gradually flies off, and leaves them behind in the tray. The man who pickles and tins the pins usually gets one penny per pound for the work, and employs himself, during the boiling of one batch of pins, with drying those previously tinned. He can earn about 9s. per day; but out of this he pays about 3s. for his assistant.

7. *Papering.* The arranging of pins side by side in paper is generally performed by women. The pins come from the last process in wooden bowls, with the points projecting in all directions. A woman takes up some, and places them on the teeth of a comb, whilst, by a few shakes, some of the pins fall back into the bowl, and the rest, being caught by

their heads, are detained between the teeth of the comb. Having thus arranged them in a parallel direction, she fixes the requisite number between two pieces of iron, having twenty-five small grooves, at equal distances; and having previously doubled the paper, she presses it against the points of the pins until they have passed through the two folds which are to retain them. The pins are then relieved from the grasp of the tool, and the process repeated with others. A woman gains about 1s. 6d. per day by papering; but children are sometimes employed, who earn from 6d. per day, and upwards.

Having thus described the various processes of pin-making, without entering into the minuter details, and having stated the usual cost of each, it will be convenient to present a tabular view [Table 1] of the time occupied by each process, and its cost, as well as of the sums which can be earned by the persons who confine themselves solely to each process. As the rate of wages is itself fluctuating, and as the prices paid and quantities executed have been given between certain limits, it is not to be expected that this table can represent with the minutest accuracy the cost of each part of the work, nor even that it shall accord perfectly with the prices above given: but it has been drawn up with some care, and will be quite sufficient for that general view, and for those reasonings, which it is meant to illustrate. A table nearly similar will be subjoined [Table 2], which has been deduced from a statement of M. Perronet, respecting the art of pin-making in France, about seventy years ago.

English Manufacture. Pins, "Elevens," 5,546 weigh one pound; "*one dozen*" = 6,932 pins weigh twenty ounces, and require six ounces of paper.

French Manufacture. Cost of 12,000 pins, N. 6, each being eight-tenths of

TABLE 1

Name of the Process	Work-men	Time of Making 1 lb. of Pins (hours)	Cost of Making 1 lb. of Pins (pence)	Work-man Earns per Day (s) (d)		Price of Making Each Part of a Single Pin, in Millionths of a Penny
1. Drawing Wire	Man	.3636	1.2500	3	3	225
2. Straightening the Wire {	Woman	.3000	.2840	1	0	51
	Girl	.3000	.1420	0	6	26
3. Pointing	Man	.3000	1.7750	5	3	319
4. Twisting and { Cutting the Heads	Boy	.0400	.0147	0	4½	3
	Man	.0400	.2103	5	4½	38
5. Heading	Woman	4.0000	5.0000	1	3	901
6. Tinning, or { Whitening	Man	.1071	.6666	6	0	121
	Woman	.1071	.3333	3	0	60
7. Papering	Woman	2.1314	3.1973	1	6	576
		7.6892	12.8732			2,320

TABLE 2

Name of the Process	Time of Making Twelve Thousand Pins (hours)	Cost of Making Twelve Thousand Pins (pence)	Workman Usually Earns per Day (pence)	Expense of Tools and Material (pence)
1. Wire	—	—	—	24.75
2. Straightening and Cutting {	1.2	.5	4.5	—
Coarse Pointing	1.2	.625	10.0	—
Turning Wheel*	1.2	.875	7.0	—
3. Fine Pointing	.8	.5	9.375	—
Turning Wheel	1.2	.5	4.75	—
Cutting off Pointed Ends	.6	.375	7.5	—
Turning Spiral	.5	.152	3.0	—
4. Cutting off Heads {	.8	.375	5.625	—
Fuel to Anneal Ditto	—	—	—	.125
5. Heading	12.0	.333	4.25	—
6. Tartar for Cleaning {	—	—	—	.5
Tartar for Whitening	—	—	—	.5
7. Papering	4.8	.5	2.0	—
Paper	—	—	—	1.0
Wear of Tools	—	—	—	2.0
	24.3	4.708		

*The expense of turning the wheel appears to have arisen from the person so occupied being unemployed during half his time, whilst the pointer went to another manufactory.

an English inch in length; with the cost of each operation:—deduced from the observations and statement of M. Perronet:—as they were manufactured in France about 1760.

It appears from the analysis we have given of the art of pin-making, that it occupies rather more than seven hours and a half of time, for ten different individuals working in succession on the same material, to convert it into a pound of pins; and that the total expense of their labour, each being paid in the joint ratio of his skill and of the time he is employed, amounts very nearly to 1s. 1d. But from an examination of the first of these tables, it appears that the wages earned by the persons employed vary from 4½d. per day up to 6s., and consequently the skill which is required for their respective employments may be measured by those sums. Now it is evident, that if one person be required to make the whole pound of pins, he must have skill enough to earn about 5s. 3d. per day whilst he is pointing the wires or cutting off the heads from the spiral coil,—and 6s. when he is whitening the pins; which three operations together would occupy little more than the seventeenth part of his time. It is also apparent, that during more than one half of his time he must be earning only 1s. 3d. per day in putting on the heads, although his skill, if properly employed, would, in the same time, produce nearly five times as much. If therefore we were to employ, for each of the processes, the man who whitens the pins, and who earns 6s. per day, even supposing that he could make the pounds of pins in an equally short time, yet we must pay him for his time 46.14 pence or about 3s. 10d. *The pins would therefore cost in making, three times and three quarters as much as they now do by the application of the division of labour.* The higher the skill required of the workman in any one process of a manufacture, and the smaller

the time during which it is employed, so much the greater will be the advantage of separating that process from the rest, and devoting one person's attention entirely to it. Had we selected the art of needle-making as our illustration, the economy arising from the division of labour would have been still larger; for the process of tempering the needles requires great skill, attention, and experience; and although from three to four thousand are tempered at once, the workman is paid a very high rate of wages. In another process of the same art, dry-pointing, which is also executed with great rapidity, the wages earned by the workman reach from 7s. to 12s., 15s., and even, in some instances, to 20s. per day; whilst other processes in the same art are carried on by children paid at the rate of 6d. per day.

Some farther reflections are suggested by the preceding analysis; but it may be convenient, previously, to place before the reader a brief description of a machine for making pins, invented by an American. It is highly ingenious in point of contrivance, and, in respect to its economical principles, will furnish a strong and interesting contrast with the manufacture of pins by the human hand. In this machine a coil of brass wire is placed on an axis; one end of this wire is drawn by a pair of rollers through a small hole in a plate of steel, and is held there by a forceps. As soon as the machine is put in action—

1. The forceps draws the wire on to a distance equal in length to one pin: a cutting edge of steel then descends close to the hole through which the wire entered, and severs a piece equal in length to one pin.

2. The forceps holding this wire moves on until it brings the wire into the centre of the *chuck* of a small lathe, which opens to receive it. Whilst the forceps returns to fetch another piece of wire, the lathe revolves rapidly, and

grinds the projecting end of the wire upon a steel mill, which advances towards it.

3. After this first or coarse pointing, the lathe stops, and another forceps takes hold of the half-pointed pin, (which is instantly released by the opening of the *chuck*,) and conveys it to a similar *chuck* of another lathe, which receives it, and finishes the pointing on a finer steel mill.

4. This mill again stops, and another forceps removes the pointed pin into a pair of strong steel clams, having a small groove in them by which they hold the pin very firmly. A part of this groove, which terminates at that edge of the steel clams which is intended to form the head of the pin, is made conical. A small round steel punch is now driven forcibly against the end of the wire thus clamped, and the head of a pin is partially formed by compressing the wire into the conical cavity.

5. Another pair of forceps now removes the pin to another pair of clams, and the head of the pin is completed by a blow from a second punch, the end of which is slightly concave. Each pair of forceps returns as soon as it has delivered its burden; and thus there are always five pieces of wire at the same moment in different stages of advance towards a finished pin. The pins so formed are received in a tray, and whitened and papered in the usual manner. About sixty pins can thus be made by this machine in one minute; but each process occupies exactly the same time in performing.

In order to judge of the value of such a machine, compared with hand labour, it would be necessary to inquire:—1. To what defects pins so made are liable? 2. What advantages they possess over those made in the usual way? 3. What is the prime cost of a machine for making them? 4. What is the expense of keeping it in repair? 5. What is the expense of moving it and attending to it?

1. Pins made by the machine are more likely to bend, because as the head is punched up out of the solid wire, it ought to be in a soft state to admit of this process. 2. Pins made by the machine are better than common ones, because they are not subject to losing their heads. 3. With respect to the prime cost of a machine, it would be very much reduced if numbers should be required. 4. With regard to its wear and tear, experience only can decide the question: but it may be remarked, that the steel clams or dies in which the heads are punched up, will wear quickly unless the wire has been softened by annealing; and that if it has been softened, the bodies of the pins will bend too readily. Such an inconvenience might be remedied, either by making the machine spin the heads and fix them on, or by annealing only that end of the wire which is to become the head of the pin: but this would cause a delay between the operations, since the brass is too brittle while heated to bear a blow without crumbling. 5. On comparing the time occupied by the machine with that stated in the analysis, we find, except in the process of heading, if time alone is considered, that the human hand is more rapid. Three thousand six hundred pins are pointed by the machine in one hour, whilst a man can point fifteen thousand six hundred in the same time. But in the process of heading, the rapidity of the machine is two and a half times that of the human hand. It must, however, be observed, that the process of grinding does not require the application of force to the machine equal to that of one man; for all the processes we have described are executed at once by the machine, and one labourer can easily work it.

NOTE

1. I have already stated, that this principle presented itself to me after a personal examination of a number of manufactories and workshops devoted to different purposes; but I have since

found that it has been distinctly stated, in the work of Gioja, *Nuovo Prospetto delle Scienze*

Economiche, 6 tom. 4to. Milano, 1815, tom. i. capo iv.

4
Superintendent's Report

OFFICE GENERAL SUP'T N.Y. &
ERIE R. R.
New York, March 25, 1856

HOMER RAMSDELL, ESQ.
PRESIDENT OF THE NEW YORK AND
ERIE RAILROAD COMPANY:

SIR:
The magnitude of the business of this road, its numerous and important connections, and the large number of employés engaged in operating it, have led many, whose opinions are entitled to respect, to the conclusion, that a proper regard to details, which enter so largely into the elements of success in the management of all railroads, cannot possibly be attained by any plan that contemplates its organization as a whole; and in proof of this position, the experience of shorter roads is referred to, the business operations of which have been conducted much more economically.

Theoretically, other things being equal, a long road should be operated for a less cost per mile than a short one. This position is so clearly evident and so generally admitted, that its truth may be assumed without offering any arguments in support of it; and, notwithstanding the reverse, so far as *practical* results are considered, has generally been the case, we must look to other causes than the mere difference in length of roads for a solution of the difficulty.

A Superintendent of a road fifty miles in length can give its business his personal attention, and may be almost constantly upon the line engaged in the direction of its details; each employé is familiarly known to him, and all questions in relation to its business are at once presented and acted upon; and any system, however imperfect, may under such circumstances prove comparatively successful.

In the government of a road five hundred miles in length a very different state of things exists. Any system which might be applicable to the business and extent of a short road, would be found entirely inadequate to the wants of a long one; and I am fully convinced, that in the want of a system perfect in its details, properly adapted and vigilantly enforced, lies the true secret of their failure; and that this disparity of cost per mile in operating long and short roads, is not produced by *a difference in length,* but is in proportion to the perfection of the system adopted.

Entertaining these views, I had the honor, more than a year since, to submit for your consideration and approval a plan for the more effective organization of this department. The system then proposed has to some extent been introduced, and experience, so far, affords the strongest assurances that when fully

---

Source: Daniel C. McCallum, "Superintendent's Report," March 25, 1856, in *Annual Report of the New York and Erie Railroad Company for 1855* (New York, 1856).

carried out, the most satisfactory results will be obtained.

In my opinion a system of operations, to be efficient and successful, should be such as to give to the principal and responsible head of the running department a complete daily history of details in all their minutiae. Without such supervision, the procurement of a satisfactory annual statement must be regarded as extremely problematical. The fact that dividends are earned without such control does not disprove the position, as in many cases the extraordinarily remunerative nature of an enterprise may ensure satisfactory returns under the most loose and inefficient management.

It may be proper here to remark that in consequence of that want of adaptation before alluded to, we cannot avail ourselves to any great extent of the plan of organization of shorter lines in framing one for this, nor have we any precedent or experience upon which we can fully rely in doing so. Under these circumstances, it will scarcely be expected that we can at once adopt any plan of operations which will not require amendment and a reasonable time to prove its worth. A few general principles, however, may be regarded as settled and necessary in its formation, amongst which are:

1. A proper division of responsibilities.
2. Sufficient power conferred to enable the same to be fully carried out, that such responsibilities may be real in their character.
3. The means of knowing whether such responsibilities are faithfully executed.
4. Great promptness in the report of all derelictions of duty, that evils may be at once corrected.
5. Such information, to be obtained through a system of daily reports and checks that will not embarrass principal officers, nor lessen their influence with their subordinates.
6. The adoption of a system, as a whole, which will not only enable the General Superintendent to detect errors immediately, but will also point out the delinquent.

5

The Engineer as an Economist

Henry R. Towne

The monogram of our national initials, which is the symbol of our monetary unit, the dollar, is almost as frequently conjoined to the figures of an engineer's calculations as are the symbols indicating feet, minutes, pounds, or gallons. The final issue of his work, in probably a majority of cases, resolves itself into a question of dollars and cents, of relative or absolute values. This statement, while true in regard to the work of all engineers, applies particularly to that of the mechanical engineer, for the reason that his functions, more frequently than in the case of others, include the executive duties of organizing and superintending the operations of industrial establishments, and of directing the labor of the

Source: Transactions of The American Society of Mechanical Engineers, Vol. 7 (Paper presented at May 1886 meeting of the Society, Chicago), 428–432.

artisans whose organized efforts yield the fruition of his work.

To insure the best results, the organization of productive labor must be directed and controlled by persons having not only good executive ability, and possessing the practical familiarity of a mechanic or engineer with the goods produced and the processes employed, but having also, and equally, a practical knowledge of how to observe, record, analyze and compare essential facts in relation to wages, supplies, expense accounts, and all else that enters into or affects the economy of production and the cost of the product. There are many good mechanical engineers;—there are also many good "business men";—but the two are rarely combined in one person. But this combination of qualities, together with at least some skill as an accountant, either in one person or more, is essential to the successful management of industrial works, and has its highest effectiveness if united in one person, who is thus qualified to supervise, either personally or through assistants, the operations of all departments of a business, and to subordinate each to the harmonious development of the whole.

Engineering has long been conceded a place as one of the modern arts, and has become a well-defined science, with a large and growing literature of its own, and of late years has subdivided itself into numerous and distinct divisions, one of which is that of mechanical engineering. It will probably not be disputed that the matter of shop management is of equal importance with that of engineering, as affecting the successful conduct of most, if not all, of our great industrial establishments, and that the *management of works* has become a matter of such great and far-reaching importance as perhaps to justify its classification also as one of the modern arts.

The one is a well-defined science, with a distinct literature, with numerous journals and with many associations for the interchange of experience; the other is unorganized, is almost without literature, has no organ or medium for the interchange of experience, and is without association or organization of any kind. A vast amount of accumulated experience in the art of workshop management already exists, but there is no record of it available to the world in general, and each old enterprise is managed more or less in its own way, receiving little benefit from the parallel experience of other similar enterprises, and imparting as little of its own to them; while each new enterprise, starting *de novo* and with much labor, and usually at much cost for experience, gradually develops a more or less perfect system of its own, according to the ability of its managers, receiving little benefit or aid from all that may have been done previously by others in precisely the same field of work.

Surely this condition of things is wrong and should be remedied. But the remedy must not be looked for from those who are "business men" or clerks and accountants only; it should come from those whose training and experience has given them an understanding of both sides (viz.: the mechanical and the clerical) of the important questions involved. It should originate, therefore, from those who are also engineers, and, for the reasons above indicated, particularly from mechanical engineers. Granting this, why should it not originate from, and be promoted by The American Society of Mechanical Engineers?

To consider this proposition more definitely, let us state the work which requires to be done. The questions to be considered, and which need recording and publication as conducing to discussion and the dissemination of useful knowledge in this specialty, group themselves under two principal heads, namely: Shop Management, and Shop Accounting. A third head may be named which is subordinate to, and partly included in each of these, namely: Shop Forms and Blanks. Under the head of Shop Management fall the questions of organization, responsibility, reports, systems of contract and piece work, and all that relates to the executive management of works, mills and factories. Under the head of Shop Accounting fall the questions of time and wages systems, determination of costs, whether by piece or day-work, the distribution of the various expense accounts, the ascertainment of profits, methods of book-keeping, and all that enters into the system of accounts which relates to the manufacturing departments of a business, and to the determination and record of its results.

There already exists an enormous fund of information relating to such matters, based upon actual and most extensive experience. What is now needed is a medium for the interchange of this experience among those whom it interests and concerns. Probably no better way for this exists than that obtaining in other instances, namely, by the publication of papers and reports, and by meetings for the discussion of papers and interchange of opinions.

The subject thus outlined, however distinct and apart from the primary functions of this society, is, nevertheless, germane to the interests of most, if not all, of its members. Conceding this, why should not the functions of the society be so enlarged as to embrace this new field of usefulness? This work, if undertaken, may be kept separate and distinct from the present work of the society by organizing a new "section" (which might be designated the "Economic Section"), the scope of which would embrace all papers and discussions relating to the topics herein referred to. The meetings of this section could be held either separately from, or immediately following the regular meetings of the society, and its papers could appear as a supplement to the regular transactions. In this way all interference would be avoided with the primary and chief business of the society, and the attendance at the meetings of the new section would naturally resolve itself into such portion of the membership as is interested in the objects for which it would be organized.

As a single illustration of the class of subjects to be covered by the discussions and papers of the proposed new section, and of the benefit to be derived therefrom, there may be cited the case of a manufacturing establishment in which there are now in use, in connection with the manufacturing accounts and exclusive of the ordinary commercial accounts, some twenty various forms of special record and account books, and more than one hundred printed forms and blanks. The primary object to which all of these contribute is the systematic recording of the operations of the different departments of the works, and the computation therefrom of such statistical information as is essential to the efficient management of the business, and especially to increased economy of production. All of these special books and forms have been the outgrowth of experience extending over many years, and represent a large amount of thoughtful planning and intelligent effort at constant development and improvement. The methods thus arrived at would undoubtedly be of great value to others engaged in similar operations, and particularly to persons engaged in

FIGURE 1

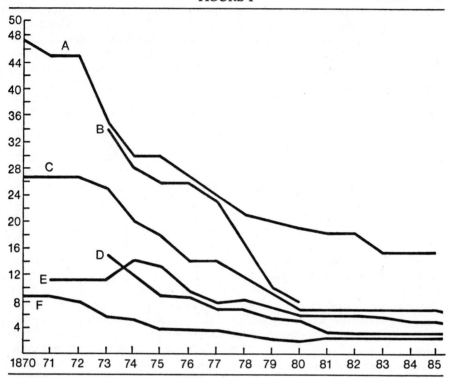

organizing and starting new enterprises. It is probable that much, if not all, of the information and experience referred to would be willingly made public through such a channel as is herein suggested, particularly if such action on the part of one firm or corporation would be responded to in like manner by others, so that each member could reasonably expect to receive some equivalent for his contributions by the benefit which he would derive from the experience of others.

In the case of the establishment above referred to, a special system of contract and piece-work has been in operation for some fifteen years, the results from which, in reducing the labor cost on certain products without encroaching upon the earnings of the men engaged, have been quite striking. A few of these results selected at random, are indicated by the accompanying diagram (Figure 1), the diagonal lines on which represent the fluctuations in the labor cost of certain special products during the time covered by the table, the vertical scale representing values.

Undoubtedly a portion of the reductions thus indicated resulted from improved appliances, larger product, and increased experience, but after making due allowance for all of these, there remains a large portion of the reduction which, to the writer's knowledge, is fairly attributable to the operation of the peculiar piece-work system adopted. The details and operations of this system would probably be placed before the society, in due time, through the channel of the proposed new section, should the latter take definite form.

Other, and probably much more valuable, information and experience relating to systems of contract and piecework would doubtless be contributed by other members, and in the aggregate a great amount of information of a most valuable character would thus be made available to the whole membership of the society.

In conclusion, it is suggested that if the plan herein proposed commends itself favorably to the members present at the meeting at which it is presented, the subject had best be referred to a special committee, by whom it can be carefully considered, and by whom, if it seems expedient to proceed further, the whole matter can be matured and formulated in an orderly manner, and thus be so presented at a future meeting as to enable the society then intelligently to act upon the question, and to decide whether or not to adopt the recommendations made by such committee.

6
General Principles of Management
Henri Fayol

The managerial function finds its only outlet through the members of the organization (body corporate). Whilst the other functions bring into play material and machines the managerial function operates only on the personnel. the soundness and good working order of the body corporate depend on a certain number of conditions termed indiscriminately principles, laws, rules. For preference I shall adopt the term principles whilst dissociating it from any suggestion of rigidity, for there is nothing rigid or absolute in management affairs, it is all a question of proportion. Seldom do we have to apply the same principle twice in identical conditions; allowance must be made for different changing circumstances, for men just as different and changing and for many other variable elements.

Therefore principles are flexible and capable of adaptation to every need; it is a matter of knowing how to make use of them, which is a difficult art requiring intelligence, experience, decision and proportion. Compounded of tact and experience, proportion is one of the foremost attributes of the manager. There is no limit to the number of principles of mangement, every rule or managerial procedure which strengthens the body corporate or facilitates its functioning has a place among the principles so long, at least, as experience confirms its worthiness. A change in the state of affairs can be responsible for change of rules which had been engendered by that state.

I am going to review some of the principles of management which I have most frequently had to apply; viz.—

1. Division of work.
2. Authority.
3. Discipline.
4. Unity of command.
5. Unity of direction.

Source: Henri Fayol, *General and Industrial Management,* trans. Constance Storrs (London: Pitman Publishing, Ltd., 1949), 19–42. (Original work published 1916.) Reprinted by permission.

6. Subordination of individual interests to the general interest.
7. Remuneration.
8. Centralization.
9. Scalar chain (line of authority).
10. Order.
11. Equity.
12. Stability of tenure of personnel.
13. Initiative.
14. Esprit de corps.

1. DIVISION OF WORK

Specialization belongs to the natural order; it is observable in the animal world, where the more highly developed the creature the more highly differentiated its organs; it is observable in human societies where the more important the body corporate[1] the closer is the relationship between structure and function. As society grows, so new organs develop destined to replace the single one performing all functions in the primitive state.

The object of division of work is to produce more and better work with the same effort. The worker always on the same part, the manager concerned always with the same matters, acquire an ability, sureness, and accuracy which increase their output. Each change of work brings in its train an adaptation which reduces output. Division of work permits of reduction in the number of objects to which attention and effort must be directed and has been recognized as the best means of making use of individuals and of groups of people. It is not merely applicable to technical work, but without exception to all work involving a more or less considerable number of people and demanding abilities of various types, and it results in specialization of functions and separation of powers. Although its advantages are universally recognized and although possibility of progress is inconceivable without the specialized work of learned men and artists, yet division of work has its limits which experience and a sense of proportion teach us may not be exceeded.

2. AUTHORITY AND RESPONSIBILITY

Authority is the right to give orders and the power to exact obedience. Distinction must be made between a manager's official authority deriving from office and personal authority, compounded of intelligence, experience, moral worth, ability to lead, past services, etc. In the make up of a good head personal authority is the indispensable complement of official authority. Authority is not to be conceived of apart from responsibility, that is apart from sanction—reward or penalty—which goes with the exercise of power. Responsibility is a corollary of authority, it is its natural consequence and essential counterpart, and wheresoever authority is exercised responsibility arises.

The need for sanction, which has its origin in a sense of justice, is strengthened and increased by this consideration, that in the general interest useful actions have to be encouraged and their opposite discouraged. Application of sanction to acts of authority forms part of the conditions essential for good management, but it is generally difficult to effect, especially in large concerns. First, the degree of responsibility must be established and then the weight of the sanction. Now, it is relatively easy to establish a workman's responsibility for his acts and a scale of corresponding sanctions; in the case of a foreman it is somewhat difficult, and proportionately as one goes up the scalar chain of businesses, as work grows more complex, as the number of workers involved increases, as the final result is more remote, it is increasingly difficult to isolate the share of the initial act of authority in the ultimate result and to establish the degree of responsibility of the manager. The measurement of this responsibility and its equivalent in material terms elude all calculation.

Sanction, then, is a question of kind, custom, convention, and judging it one must take into account the action itself, the attendant circumstances and potential repercussions. Judgment demands high moral character, impartiality and firmness. If all these conditions are not fulfilled there is a danger that the sense of responsibility may disappear from the concern.

Responsibility valiantly undertaken and borne merits some consideration; it is a kind of courage everywhere much appreciated. Tangible proof of this exists in the salary level of some industrial leaders, which is much higher than that of civil servants of comparable rank but carrying no responsibility. Nevertheless, generally speaking, responsibility is feared as much as authority is sought after, and fear of responsibility paralyses much initiative and destroys many good qualities. A good leader should possess and infuse into those around him courage to accept responsibility.

The best safeguard against abuse of authority and against weakness on the part of a higher manager is personal integrity and particularly high moral character of such a manager, and this integrity, it is well known, is conferred neither by election nor ownership.

3. DISCIPLINE

Discipline is in essence obedience, application, energy, behaviour, and outward marks of respect observed in accordance with the standing agreements between the firm and its employees, whether these agreements have been freely debated or accepted without prior discussion, whether they be written or implicit, whether they derive from the wish of the parties to them or from rules and customs, it it these agreements which determine the formalities of discipline.

Discipline, being the outcome of different varying agreements, natually appears under the most diverse forms; obligations of obedience, application, energy, behaviour, vary, in effect, from one firm to another, from one group of employees to another, from one time to another. Nevertheless, general opinion is deeply convinced that discipline is absolutely essential for the smooth running of business and that without discipline no enterprise could prosper.

This sentiment is very forcibly expressed in military hand-books, where it runs that "Discipline constitutes the chief strength of armies." I would approve unreservedly of this aphorism were it followed by this other, "Discipline is what leaders make it." The first one inspires respect for discipline, which is a good thing, but it tends to eclipse from view the responsibility of leaders, which is undesirable, for the state of discipline of any group of people depends essentially on the worthiness of its leaders.

When a defect in discipline is apparent or when relations between superiors and subordinates leave much to be desired, responsibility for this must not be cast heedlessly, and without going further afield, on the poor state of the team, because the ill mostly results from the ineptitude of the leaders. That, at all events, is what I have noted in various parts of France, for I have always found French workmen obedient and loyal provided they are ably led.

In the matter of influence upon discipline, agreements must set side by side with command. It is important that they be clear and, as far as is possible, afford satisfaction to both sides. This is not easy. Proof of that exists in the great strikes of miners, railwaymen, and civil servants which, in these latter years, have jeopardized national life at home and elsewhere and which arose out of agreements in dispute or inadequate legislation.

For half a century a considerable change has been effected in the mode of agreements between a concern and its employees. The agreements of former days fixed by the employer alone are being replaced, in ever increasing measure, by understandings arrived at by discussion between an owner or group of owners and workers' associations. Thus each individual owner's responsibility has been reduced and is further diminished by increasingly frequent state intervention in labour problems. Nevertheless, the setting up of agreements binding a firm and its employees from which disciplinary formalities emanate, should remain one of the chief preoccupations of industrial heads.

The well-being of the concern does not permit, in cases of offence against discipline, of the neglect of certain sanctions capable of preventing or minimizing their recurrence. Experience and tact on the part of a manager are put to the proof in the choice and degree of sanctions to be used, such as remonstrances, warning, fines, suspensions, demotion, dismissal. Individual people and attendant circumstances must be taken into account. In fine, discipline is respect for agreements which are directed at achieving obedience, application, energy, and the outward marks of respect. It is incumbent upon managers at high levels as much as upon humble employees, and the best means of establishing and maintaining it are—

1. Good superiors at all levels.
2. Agreements as clear and fair as possible.
3. Sanctions (penalties) judiciously applied.

4. UNITY OF COMMAND

For any action whatsoever, an employee should receive orders from one superior only. Such is the rule of unity of command, arising from general and ever-present necessity and wielding an influence on the conduct of affairs, which to my way of thinking, is at least equal to any other principle whatsoever. Should it be violated, authority is undermined, discipline is in jeopardy, order disturbed and stability threatened. This rule seems fundamental to me and so I have given it the rank of principle. As soon as two superiors wield their authority over the same person or department, uneasiness makes itself felt and should the cause persist, the disorder increases, the malady takes on the appearance of an animal organism troubled by a foreign body, and the following consequences are to be observed: either the dual command ends in disappearance or elimination of one of the superiors and organic well-being is restored, or else the organism continues to wither away. In no case is there adaptation of the social organism to dual command.

Now dual command is extremely common and wreaks havoc in all concerns, large or small, in home and in state. The evil is all the more to be feared in that it worms its way into the social organism on the most plausible pretexts. For instance—

(a) In the hope of being better understood or gaining time or to put a stop forthwith to an undesirable practice, a superior S^2 may give orders directly to an employee E without going via the superior S^1. If this mistake is repeated there is dual command with its consequences, viz., hesitation on the part of the subordinate, irritation and dissatisfaction on the part of the superior set aside, and disorder in the work. It will be seen later that it is possible to bypass the scalar chain when necessary, whilst avoiding the drawbacks of dual command.

(b) The desire to get away from the immediate necessity of dividing up authority as between two colleagues, two friends, two members of one family, results at times in dual command reigning at the top of a concern right from the outset. Exercising the same powers and having the same authority over the same men, the two colleagues end up inevitably with dual command and its consequences. Despite harsh lessons, instances of this sort are still numerous. New colleagues count on their mutual regard, common interest, and good sense to save them from every conflict, every serious disagreement and, save for rare exceptions, the illusion is short-lived. First an awkwardness makes itself felt, then a certain irritation and, in time, if dual command exists, even hatred. Men cannot bear dual command. A judicious assignment of duties would have reduced the danger without entirely banishing it, for between two superiors on the same footing there must always be some question ill-defined. But it is riding for a fall to set up a business organization with two superiors on equal footing without assigning duties and demarcating authority.

(c) Imperfect demarcation of departments also leads to dual command: two superiors issuing orders in a sphere which each thinks his own, constitutes dual command.

(d) Constant linking up as between different departments, natural intermeshing of functions, duties often badly defined, create an ever-present danger of dual command. If a knowledgeable superior does not put it in order, footholds are established which later upset and compromise the conduct of affairs.

In all human associations, in industry, commerce, army, home, state, dual command is a perpetual source of conflicts, very grave sometimes, which have special claim on the attention of superiors of all ranks.

5. UNITY OF DIRECTION

This principle is expressed as: one head and one plan for a group of activities having the same objective. It is the condition essential to unity of action, coordination of strength and focusing of effort. A body with two heads is in the social as in the animal sphere a monster, and has difficulty in surviving. Unity of direction (one head one plan) must not be confused with unity of command (one employee to have orders from one superior only). Unity of direction is provided for by sound organization of the body corporate, unity of command turns on the functioning of the personnel. Unity of command cannot exist without unity of direction, but does not flow from it.

6. SUBORDINATION OF INDIVIDUAL INTEREST TO GENERAL INTEREST

This principle calls to mind the fact that in a business the interest of one employee or group of employees should not prevail over that of the concern, that the interest of the home should come before that of its members and that the interest of the state should have pride of place over that of one citizen or group of citizens.

It seems that such an admonition should not need calling to mind. But ignorance, ambition, selfishness, laziness, weakness, and all human passions tend to cause the general interest to be lost sight of in favour of individual interest and a perpetual struggle has to be waged against them. Two interests of a different order, but claiming equal respect, confront each other and means must be found to reconcile them. That represents one of the great difficulties of management. Means of effecting it are—

1. Firmness and good example on the part of superiors.
2. Agreements as fair as is possible.
3. Constant supervision.

7. REMUNERATION OF PERSONNEL

Remuneration of personnel is the price of services rendered. It should be fair and, as far as is possible, afford satisfaction both to personnel and firm (employee and employer). The rate of remuneration depends, firstly, on circumstances independent of the employer's will and employee's worth, viz. cost of living, abundance or shortage of personnel, general business conditions, the economic position of the business, and after that it depends on the value of the employee and mode of payment adopted. Appreciation of the factors dependent on the employer's will and on the value of employees, demands a fairly good knowledge of business, judgement, and impartiality. Later on in connection with selecting personnel we shall deal with assessing the value of employees; here only the mode of payment is under consideration as a factor operation on remuneration. The method of payment can exercise considerable influence on business progress, so the choice of this method is an important problem. It is also a thorny problem which in practice has been solved in widely different ways, of which so far none has proved satisfactory. What is generally looked for in the method of payment is that—

1. It shall assure fair remuneration.
2. It shall encourage keenness by rewarding well-directed effort.

3. It shall not lead to overpayment going beyond reasonable limits.

I am going to examine briefly the modes of payment in use for workers, junior managers, and higher managers.

Workers

The various modes of payment in use for workers are—

1. Time rates.
2. Job rates.
3. Piece rates.

These three modes of payment may be combined and give rise to important variations by the introduction of bonuses, profit-sharing schemes, payment in kind, and nonfinancial incentives.

1. Time Rates. Under this system the workman sells the employer, in return for a predetermined sum, a day's work under definite conditions. This system has the disadvantage of conducing to negligence and of demanding constant supervision. It is inevitable where the work done is not susceptible to measurement and in effect it is very common.

2. Job Rates. Here payment made turns upon the execution of a definite job set in advance and may be independent of the length of the job. When payment is due only on condition that the job be completed during the normal work spell, this method merges into time rate. Payment by daily job does not require as close a supervision as payment by the day, but it has the drawback of levelling the output of good workers down to that of mediocre ones. The good ones are not satisfied, because they feel that they could earn more; the mediocre ones find the task set too heavy.

3. Piece Rates. Here payment is related to work done and there is no limit. This system is often used in workshops where a large number of similar articles have to be made, and is found where the product can be measured by weight, length, or cubic capacity, and in general is used wherever possible. It is criticized on the grounds of emphasizing quantity at the expense of quality and of provoking disagreements when rates have to be revised in the light of manufacturing improvements. Piece-work becomes contract work when applied to an important unit of work. To reduce the contractor's risk, sometimes there is added to the contract price a payment for each day's work done.

Generally, piece rates give rise to increased earnings which act for some time as a stimulus, then finally a system prevails in which this mode of payment gradually approximates to time rates for a pre-arranged sum.

The above three modes of payment are found in all large concerns; sometimes time rates prevail, sometimes one of the other two. In a workshop the same workman may be seen working now on piece rates, not on time rates. Each one of these methods had its advantages and drawbacks, and their effectiveness depends on circumstances and the ability of superiors. Neither method nor rate of payment absolves management from competence and tact, and keenness of workers and peaceful atmosphere of the workshop depend largely upon it.

Bonuses

To arouse the worker's interest in the smooth running of the business, sometimes an increment in the nature of a bonus is added to the time-, job- or piece-rate: for good time keeping, hard work, freedom from machine breakdown, output, cleanliness, etc. The relative importance, nature and qualifying conditions of these bonuses are very varied. There are to be found the small daily supplement, the monthly sum, the annual award, shares or portions of shares distributed to the most meritorious, and also even profit-sharing schemes such as,

for example, certain monetary allocations distributed annually among workers in some large firms. Several French collieries started some years back the granting of a bonus proportional to profits distributed or to extra profits. No contract is required from the workers save that the earning of the bonus is subject to certain conditions, for instance, that there shall have no strike during the year, or that absenteeism shall not have exceeded a given number of days. This type of bonus introduced an element of profit-sharing into miners' wages without any prior discussion as between workers and employer. The workman did not refuse a gift, largely gratuitous, on the part of the employer, that is, the contract was a unilateral one. Thanks to a successful trading period the yearly wages have been appreciably increased by the operation of the bonus. But what is to happen in lean times? This interesting procedure is as yet too new to be judged, but obviously it is no general solution of the problem.

In the mining industry there is another type of bonus, dependent upon the selling price of coal. The sliding scale of wages depending on a basic rate plus a bonus proportionate to the local selling price, which had long flourished in Wales, but was discontinued when minimum wages legislation came into force, is to-day the principle regulating the payment of miners in the Nord and Pas de Calais *départements*, and has also been adopted in the Loire region. This system established a certain fixed relationship between the prosperity of the colliery and the miner's wage. It is criticized on the grounds that it conduces to limitation of production in order to raise selling price. So we see that it is necessary to have recourse to a variety of methods in order to settle wages questions. The problem is far from being settled to everyone's satisfaction and all solutions are hazardous.

Profit-Sharing

1. Workers. The idea of making workers share in profits is a very attractive one and it would seem that it is from there that harmony as between Capital and Labour should come. But the practical formula for such sharing has not yet been found. Workers' profit-sharing has hitherto come up against insurmountable difficulties of application in the case of large concerns. Firstly, let us note that it cannot exist in enterprises having no monetary objective (State services, religion, philanthropic, scientific societies) and also that it is not possible in the case of businesses running at a loss. Thus profit-sharing is excluded from a great number of concerns. There remain the prosperous business concerns and of these latter the desire to reconcile and harmonize workers' and employers' interests is nowhere so great as in French mining and metallurgical industries. Now, in these industries I know of no clear application of workers' profit-sharing, whence it may be concluded forthwith that the matter is difficult, if not impossible. It is very difficult indeed. Whether a business is making a profit or not the worker must have an immediate wage assured him, and a system which would make workers' payment depend entirely on eventual future profit is unworkable. But perhaps a part of wages might come from business profits. Let us see. Viewing all contingent factors, the workers' greater or lesser share of activity or ability in the final outcome of a large concern is impossible to assess and is, moreover, quite insignificant. The portion accruing to him of distributed dividend would at the most be a few centimes on a wage of five francs for instance, that is to say the smallest extra effort, the stroke of a pick or of a file

operating directly on his wage, would prove of greater advantage to him. Hence the worker has no interest in being rewarded by a share in profits proportionate to the effect he has upon profits. It is worthy of note that, in most large concerns, wages increases, operative now for some twenty years, represent a total sum greater than the amount of capital shared out. In effect, unmodified real profit-sharing by workers of large concerns has not yet entered the sphere of practical business politics.

2. Junior Managers. Profit-sharing for foremen, superintendents, engineers, is scarcely more advanced than for workers. Nevertheless, the influence of these employees on the results of a business is quite considerable, and if they are not consistently interested in profits the only reason is that the basis for participation is difficult to establish. Doubtless managers have no need of monetary incentive to carry out their duties, but they are not indifferent to material satisfactions and it must be acknowledged that the hope of extra profit is capable of arousing their enthusiasm. So employees at middle levels should, where possible, be induced to have an interest in profits. It is relatively easy in businesses which are starting out or on trial, where exceptional effort can yield outstanding results. Sharing may then be applied to overall business profits or merely to the running of the particular department of the employee in question. When the business is of long standing and well run the zeal of a junior manager is scarcely apparent in the general outcome, and it is very hard to establish a useful basis on which he may participate. In fact, profit-sharing among junior managers in France is very rare in large concerns. Production or workshop output bonuses—not to be confused with profit-sharing—are much more common.

3. Higher Managers. It is necessary to go right up to top management to find a class of employee with frequent interest in the profits of large-scale French concerns. The head of the business, in view of his knowledge, ideas, and actions, exerts considerable influence on general results, so it is quite natural to try and provide him with an interest in them. Sometimes it is possible to establish a close connection between his personal activity and its effects. Nevertheless, generally speaking, there exist other influences quite independent of the personal capability of the manager which can influence results to a greater extent than can his personal activity. If the manager's salary were exclusively dependent upon profits, it might at times be reduced to nothing. There are besides, businesses being built up, wound up, or merely passing through temporary crisis, wherein management depends no less on talent than in the case of prosperous ones, and wherein profit-sharing cannot be a basis for remuneration for the manager. In fine, senior civil servants cannot be paid on a profit-sharing basis. Profit-sharing, then, for either higher managers or workers is not a general rule of remuneration. To sum up, then: profit-sharing is a mode of payment capable of giving excellent results in certain cases, but is not a general rule. It does not seem to me possible, at least for the present, to count on this mode of payment for appeasing conflict between Capital and Labour. Fortunately, there are other means which hitherto have been sufficient to maintain relative social quiet. Such methods have not lost their power and it is up to managers to study them, apply them, and make them work well.

Payment in Kind, Welfare Work, Non-Financial Incentives

Whether wages are made up of money only or whether they include various additions such as heating, light, housing, food, is of little consequence provided that the employee be satisfied.

From another point of view, there is no doubt that a business will be better served in proportion as its employees are more energetic, better educated, more conscientious and more permanent. The employer should have regard, if merely in the interests of the business, for the health, strength, education, morale, and stability of his personnel. These elements of smooth running are not acquired in the workshop alone, they are formed and developed as well, and particularly, outside it, in the home and school, in civil and religious life. Therefore, the employer comes to be concerned with his employees outside the works and here the question of proportion comes up again. Opinion is greatly divided on this point. Certain unfortunate experiments have resulted in some employers stopping short their interest, at the works gate and at the regulation of wages. The majority consider that the employer's activity may be used to good purpose outside the factory confines provided that there be discretion and prudence, that it be sought after rather than imposed, be in keeping with the general level of education and taste of those concerned and that it have absolute respect for their liberty. It must be benevolent collaboration, not tyrannical stewardship, and therein lies an indispensable condition of success.

The employer's welfare activities may be of various kinds. In the works they bear on matters of hygiene and comfort: ventilation, lighting, cleanliness, canteen facilities. Outside the works they bear on housing accommodation, feeding, education, and training. Provident schemes come under this head.

Non-financial incentives only come in in the case of large scale concerns and may be said to be almost exclusively in the realm of government work. Every mode of payment likely to make the personnel more valuable and improve its lot in life, and also to inspire keenness on the part of employees at all levels, should be a matter for managers' constant attention.

8. CENTRALIZATION

Like division of work, centralization belongs to the natural order; this turns on the fact that in every organism, animal or social, sensations converge towards the brain or directive part, and from the brain or directive part orders are sent out which set all parts of the organism in movement. Centralization is not a system of management good or bad of itself, capable of being adopted or discarded at the whim of managers or of circumstances; it is always present to a greater or less extent. The question of centralization or decentralization, is a simple question of proportion, it is a matter of finding the optimum degree for the particular concern. In small firms, where the manager's orders go directly to subordinates there is absolute centralization; in large concerns, where a long scalar chain is interposed between manager and lower grades, orders and counter-information too, have to go through a series of intermediaries. Each employee, intentionally or unintentionally, puts something of himself into the transmission and execution of orders and of information received too. He does not operate merely as a cog in a machine. What appropriate share of initiative may be left to intermediaries depends on the personal character of the manager, on his moral worth, on the reliability of his subordinates, and also on the condition of the business. The degree of centralization must vary according to different cases. The objective to pursue is the optimum utilization of all faculties of the personnel.

If the moral worth of the manager, his strength, intelligence, experience, and swiftness of thought allow him to have a wide span of activities he will be able to carry centralization quite far and reduce his seconds in command to mere executive agents. If, conversely, he prefers to have greater recourse to the experience, opinions, and counsel of his colleagues whilst reserving to himself the privilege of giving general directives, he can effect considerable decentralization.

Seeing that both absolute and relative value of manager and employees are constantly changing, it is understandable that the degree of centralization or decentralization may itself vary constantly. It is a problem to be solved according to circumstances, to the best satisfaction of the interests involved. It arises, not only in the case of higher authority, but for superiors at all levels and not one but can extend or confine, to some extent, his subordinates' initiative.

The finding of the measure which shall give the best overall yield: that is the problem of centralization or decentralization. Everything which goes to increase the importance of the subordinate's rôle is decentralization, everything which goes to reduce it is centralization.

9. SCALAR CHAIN

The scalar chain is the chain of superiors ranging from the ultimate authority to the lowest ranks. The line of authority is the route followed—via every link in the chain—by all communications which start from or go to the ultimate authority. This path is dictated both by the need for some transmission and by the principle of unity of command, but it is not always the swiftest. It is even at times disastrously lengthy in large concerns, notably in governmental ones. Now, there are many activities whose success turns on speedy execution, hence respect for the line of authority must be reconciled with the need for swift action.

Let us imagine that section F has to be put into contact with section P in a business whose scalar chain is represented by the double ladder G—A—Q thus—

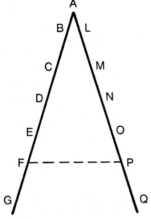

By following the line of authority the ladder must be climbed from F to A and then descended from A to P, stopping at each rung, then ascended again from P to A, and descended once more from A to F, in order to get back to the starting point. Evidently it is much simpler and quicker to go directly from F to P by making use of FP as a "gang plank" and that is what is most often done. The scalar principle will be safeguarded if managers E and O have authorized their respective subordinates F and P to treat directly, and the position will be fully regularized if F and P inform their respective superiors forthwith of what they have agreed upon. So long as F and P remain in agreement, and so long as their actions are approved by their immediate superiors, direct contact may be maintained, but from the instant that agreement ceases or there is no approval from the superiors direct contact comes to an end, and the scalar chain is straightway resumed. Such is the actual procedure

to be observed in the great majority of businesses. It provides for the usual exercise of some measure of initiative at all levels of authority. In the small concern, the general interest, viz. that of the concern proper, is easy to grasp, and the employer is present to recall this interest to those tempted to lose sight of it. In government enterprise the general interest is such a complex, vast, remote thing, that it is not easy to get a clear idea of it, and for the majority of civil servants the employer is somewhat mythical and unless the sentiment of general interest be constantly revived by higher authority, it becomes blurred and weakened and each section tends to regard itself as its own aim and end and forgets that it is only a cog in a big machine, all of whose parts must work in concert. It becomes isolated, cloistered, aware only of the line of authority.

The use of the "gang plank" is simple, swift, sure. It allows the two employees F and P to deal at one sitting, and in a few hours, with some question or other which via the scalar chain would pass through twenty transmissions, inconvenience many people, involve masses of paper, lose weeks or months to get to a conclusion less satisfactory generally than the one which could have been obtained via direct contact as between F and P.

It is possible that such practices, as ridiculous as they are devasting, could be in current use? Unfortunately there can be little doubt of it in government department affairs. It is usually acknowledged that the chief cause is fear of responsibility. I am rather of the opinion that it is insufficient executive capacity on the part of those in charge. If supreme authority A insisted that his assistants B and L made use of the "gang plank" themselves and made its use incumbent upon their subordinates C and M, the habit and courage of taking responsibility would be established and at the same time the custom of using the shortest path.

It is an error to depart needlessly from the line of authority, but it is an even greater one to keep to it when detriment to the business ensues. The latter may attain extreme gravity in certain conditions. When an employee is obliged to choose between the two practices, and it is impossible for him to take advice from his superior, he should be courageous enough and feel free enough to adopt the line dictated by the general interest. But for him to be in this frame of mind there must have been previous precedent, and his superiors must have set him the example—for example must always come from above.

10. ORDER

The formula is known in the case of material things "A place for everything and everything in its place." The formula is the same for human order. "A place for everyone and everyone in his place."

Material Order

In accordance with the preceding definition, so that material order shall prevail, there must be a place appointed for each thing and each thing must be in its appointed place. Is that enough? Is it not also necessary that the place shall have been well chosen? The object of order must be avoidance of loss of material, and for this object to be completely realized not only must things be in their place suitably arranged but also the place must have been chosen so as to facilitate all activities as much as possible. If this last condition be unfulfilled, there is merely the appearance of order. Appearance of order may cover over real disorder. I have seen a works yard used as a store for steel ingots in which the

material was well stacked, evenly arranged and clean and which gave a pleasing impression of orderliness. On close inspection it could be noted that the same heap included five or six types of steel intended for different manufacture all mixed up together. Whence useless handling, lost time, risk of mistakes because each thing was not in its place. It happens, on the other hand, that the appearance of disorder may actually be true order. Such is the case with papers scattered about at a master's whim which a well-meaning but incompetent servant re-arranges and sticks in neat piles. The master can no longer find his way about them. Perfect order presupposes a judiciously chosen place and the appearance of order is merely a false or imperfect image of real order. Cleanliness is a corollary of orderliness, there is no appointed place for dirt. A diagram representing the entire premises divided up into as many sections as there are employees responsible facilitates considerably the establishing and control of order.

Social Order

For social order to prevail in a concern there must, in accordance with the definition, be an appointed place for every employee and every employee be in his appointed place. Perfect order requires, further, that the place be suitable for the employee and the employee for the place—in English idiom, "The right man in the right place."

Thus understood, social order presupposes the successful execution of the two most difficult managerial activities: good organization and good selection. Once the posts essential to the smooth running of the business have been decided upon and those to fill such posts have been selected, each employee occupies that post wherein he can render most service. Such is perfect social order "A place for each one and each one in his place." That appears simple, and naturally we are so anxious for it to be so that when we hear for the twentieth time a government departmental head assert this principle, we conjure up straightway a concept of perfect administration. This is a mirage.

Social order demands precise knowledge of the human requirements and resources of the concern and a constant balance between these requirements and resources. Now this balance is most difficult to establish and maintain and all the more difficult the bigger the business, and when it has been upset and individual interests resulted in neglect or sacrifice of the general interest, when ambition, nepotism, favouritism, or merely ignorance, has multiplied positions without good reason or filled them with incompetent employees, much talent and strength of will and more persistence than current instability of ministerial appointments presupposes, are required in order to sweep away abuses and restore order.

As applied to government enterprise the principle of order "a place for each one and each one in his place," takes on an astounding breadth. It means national responsibility towards each and all, everyone's destiny mapped out, national solidarity, the whole problem of society. I will stay no longer over this disturbing extension of the principle of order. In private businesses and especially in those of restricted scope it is easier to maintain proportion as between selection and requirements. As in the case of orderly material arrangement, a chart or plan makes the establishment and control of human arrangement much more easy. This represents the personnel in entirety, and all selections of the concern together with the people occupying them. This chart will come up again in the chapter on Organization.

11. EQUITY

Why equity and not justice? Justice is putting into execution established conventions, but conventions cannot foresee everything, they need to be interpreted or their inadequacy supplemented. For the personnel to be encouraged to carry out its duties with all the devotion and loyalty of which it is capable it must be treated with kindliness, and equity results from the combination of kindliness and justice. Equity excludes neither forcefulness nor sternness and the application of it requires much good sense, experience, and good nature.

Desire for equity and equality of treatment are aspirations to be taken into account in dealing with employees. In order to satisfy these requirements as much as possible without neglecting any principle or losing sight of the general interest, the head of the business must frequently summon up his highest faculties. He should strive to instil a sense of equity throughout all levels of the scalar chain.

12. STABILITY OF TENURE OF PERSONNEL

Time is required for an employee to get used to new work and succeed in doing it well, always assuming that he possesses the requisite abilities. If when he has got used to it, or before then, he is removed, he will not have had time to render worthwhile service. If this be repeated indefinitely the work will never be properly done. The undesirable consequences of such insecurity of tenure are especially to be feared in large concerns, where the settling in of managers is generally a lengthy matter. Much time is needed indeed to get to know men and things in a large concern in order to be in a position to decide on a plan of action, to gain confidence in oneself, and inspire it in others. Hence it has often been recorded that a mediocre manager who stays is infinitely preferable to outstanding managers who merely come and go.

Generally the managerial personnel of prosperous concerns is stable, that of unsuccessful ones is unstable. Instability of tenure is at one and the same time cause and effect of bad running. The apprenticeship of a higher manager is generally a costly matter. Nevertheless, changes of personnel are inevitable; age, illness, retirement, death, disturb the human make-up of the firm, certain employees are no longer capable of carrying out their duties, whilst others become fit to assume greater responsibilities. In common with all the other principles, therefore, stability of tenure and personnel is also a question of proportion.

13. INITIATIVE

Thinking out a plan and ensuring its success is one of the keenest satisfactions for an intelligent man to experience. It is also one of the most powerful stimulants of human endeavour. This power of thinking out and executing is what is called initiative, and freedom to propose and to execute belongs too, each in its way, to initiative. At all levels of the organizational ladder zeal and energy on the part of employees are augmented by initiative. The initiative of all, added to that of the manager, and supplementing it if need be, represents a great source of strength for businesses. This is particularly apparent at difficult times; hence it is essential to encourage and develop this capacity to the full.

Much tact and some integrity are required to inspire and maintain everyone's initiative, within the limits imposed, by respect for authority and for discipline. The manager must be able to sacrifice some personal vanity in order to grant this sort of satisfaction to subordinates. Other things being equal, moreover, a manager able to permit the exercise of initiative on the part of subordinates is infinitely superior to one who cannot do so.

14. ESPRIT DE CORPS

"Union is strength." Business heads would do well to ponder on this proverb. Harmony, union among the personnel of a concern, is great strength in that concern. Effort, then, should be made to establish it. Among the countless methods in use I will single out specially one principle to be observed and two pitfalls to be avoided. The principle to be observed is unity of command; the dangers to be avoided are (a) a misguided interpretation of the motto "divide and rule," (b) the abuse of written communications.

(a) *Personnel must not be split up.* Dividing enemy forces to weaken them is clever, but dividing one's own team is a grave sin against the business. Whether this error results from inadequate managerial capacity or imperfect grasp of things, or from egoism which sacrifices general interest to personal interest, it is always reprehensible because harmful to the business. There is no merit in sowing dissension among subordinates; any beginner can do it. On the contrary, real talent is needed to co-ordinate effort, encourage keenness, use each man's abilities, and reward each one's merit without arousing possible jealousies and disturbing harmonious relations.

(b) *Abuse of written communications.* In dealing with a business matter or giving an order which requires explanation to complete it, usually it is simpler and quicker to do so verbally than in writing. Besides, it is well known that differences and misunderstandings which a conversation could clear up, grow more bitter in writing. Thence it follows that, wherever possible, contacts should be verbal; there is a gain in speed, clarity and harmony. Nevertheless, it happens in some firms that employees of neighbouring departments with numerous points of contact, or even employees within a department, who could quite easily meet, only communicate with each other in writing. Hence arise increased work and complications and delays harmful to the business. At the same time, there is to be observed a certain animosity prevailing between different departments or different employees within a department. The system of written communications usually brings this result. There is a way of putting an end to this deplorable system and that is to forbid all communications in writing which could easily and advantageously be replaced by verbal ones. There again, we come up against a question of proportion.

It is not merely by the satisfactory results of harmony obtaining as between employees of the same department that the power of unity is shown: commercial agreements, unions, associations of every kind, play an important part in business management.

The part played by association has increased remarkably in half a century. I remember, in 1860, workers of primary industries without cohesion, without common bond, a veritable cloud of individual dust particles; and out of that the union has produced collective associations, meeting employers on equal terms. At that same time, bitter rivalry prevailed between large firms, closely similar, which has given place gradually to friendly relations, permitting of the settlement of most common interests by joint agreement. It is the beginning of a new era which already has profoundly modified both habits and ideas, and industrial heads should take this development into account. . . .

There I bring to an end this review of principles, not because the list is exhausted—this list has no precise limits—but because to me it seems at the moment especially useful to endow management theory with a dozen or so well-established principles, on which it is appropriate to concentrate general discussion. The foregoing principles are those to which I have most often had recourse. I have simply expressed my personal opinion in connection with them. Are they to have a place in the management code which is to be built up? General discussion will show.

This code is indispensable. Be it a case of commerce, industry, politics, religion, war, or philanthropy, in every concern there is a management function to be performed, and for its performance there must be principles, that is to say acknowledged truths regarded as proven on which to rely. And it is the code which represents the sum total of these truths at any given moment.

Surprise might be expressed at the outset that the eternal moral principles, the laws of the Decalogue and Commandments of the Church are not sufficient guide for the manager, and that a special code is needed. The explanation is this: the higher laws of religious or moral order envisage the individual only, or else interests which are not of this world, whereas management principles aim at the success of associations of individuals and at the satisfying of economic interests. Given that the aim is different, it is not surprising that the means are not the same. There is no identity, so there is no contradiction. Without principles one is in darkness and chaos; interest, experience, and proportion are still very handicapped, even with the best principles. The principle is the lighthouse fixing the bearings, but it can only serve those who already know the way into port.

NOTE

1. *"Body corporate."* Fayol's term "corps social," meaning all those engaged in a given corporate activity in any sphere, is best rendered by this somewhat unusual term because (a) it retains his implied biological metaphor; (b) it represents the structure as distinct from the process of organization. The term will be retained in all contexts where these two requirements have to be met. (Translator's note.)

7
The Principles of Scientific Management
Frederick Winslow Taylor

By far the most important fact which faces the industries of our country, the industries, in fact, of the civilized world, is that not only the average worker, but nineteen out of twenty workmen throughout the civilized world firmly believe that it is for their best interests to go slow instead of to go fast. They firmly believe that it is for their interest to give as little work in return for the money that they get as is practical. The reasons for this belief are twofold, and I do not believe that the workingmen are to blame for holding these fallacious views.

If you will take any set of workmen in your own town and suggest to those men that it would be a good thing for them in their trade if they were to double their output in the coming year, each man turn out twice as much work and become twice as efficient, they would say, "I do not know anything about other people's trades; what you are saying about increasing efficiency being a good thing may be good for other trades, but I know that the only result if you come to our trade would be that half of us would be out of a job before the year was out." That to the average workingman is an axiom; it is not a matter subject to debate at all. And even among the average business men of this country that opinion is almost universal. They firmly believe that that would be the result of a great increase in efficiency, and yet directly the opposite is true.

THE EFFECT OF LABOR-SAVING DEVICES

Whenever any labor-saving device of any kind has been introduced into any trade—go back into the history of any trade and see it—even though that labor-saving device may turn out ten, twenty, thirty times that output that was originally turned out by men in that trade, the result has universally been to

Source: Bulletin of the Taylor Society (December 1916). An abstract of an address given by the late Dr. Taylor before the Cleveland Advertising Club, March 3, 1915, two weeks prior to his death. It was repeated the following day at Youngstown, Ohio, and this presentation was Dr. Taylor's last public appearance.

make work for more men in that trade, not work for less men.

Let me give you one illustration. Let us take one of the staple businesses, the cotton industry. About 1840 the power loom succeeded the old hand loom in the cotton industry. It was invented many years before, somewhere about 1780 or 1790, but it came in very slowly. About 1840 the weavers of Manchester, England, saw that the power loom was coming, and they knew it would turn out three times the yardage of cloth in a day that the hand loom turned out. And what did they do, these five thousand weavers of Manchester, England, who saw starvation staring them in the face? They broke into the establishments into which those machines were being introduced, they smashed them, they did everything possible to stop the introduction of the power loom. And the same result followed that follows every attempt to interfere with the introduction of any labor-saving device, if it is really a labor-saving device. Instead of stopping the introduction of the power loom, their opposition apparently accelerated it, just as opposition to scientific management all over the country, bitter labor opposition today, is accelerating the introduction of it instead of retarding it. History repeats itself in that respect. The power loom came right straight along.

And let us see the result in Manchester. Just what follows in every industry when any labor-saving device is introduced. Less than a century has gone by since 1840. The population of England in that time has not more than doubled. Each man in the cotton industry in Manchester, England, now turns out, at a restricted estimate ten yards of cloth for every yard of cloth that was turned out in 1840. In 1840 there were 5,000 weavers in Manchester. Now there are 265,000. Has that thrown men out of work? Has the introduction of labor-saving machinery, which has multiplied the output per man by tenfold, thrown men out of work?

What is the real meaning of this? All that you have to do is to bring wealth into this world and the world uses it. That is the real meaning. The meaning is that where in 1840 cotton goods were a luxury to be worn only by rich people when they were hardly ever seen on the street, now every man, woman, and child all over the world wears cotton goods as a daily necessity.

Nineteen-twentieths of the real wealth of this world is used by the poor people, and not the rich, so that the working-man who sets out as a steady principle to restrict output is merely robbing his own kind. That group of manufacturers which adopts as a permanent principle restriction of output, in order to hold up prices, is robbing the world. The one great thing that marks the improvement of this world is measured by the enormous increase in output of the individuals in this world. There is fully twenty times the output per man now that there was three hundred years ago. That marks the increase in the real wealth of the world; that marks the increase of the happiness of the world, that gives us the opportunity for shorter hours, for better education, for amusement, for art, for music, for everything that is worthwhile in this world—goes right straight back to this increase in the output of the individual. The workingmen of today live better than the king did three hundred years ago. From what does the progress the world has made come? Simply from the increase in the output of the individual all over the world.

THE DEVELOPMENT OF SOLDIERING

The second reason why the workmen of this country and of Europe deliberately restrict output is a very simple one. They, for this reason, are even less to blame than they are for the other. If, for example, you are manufacturing a pen, let us assume for simplicity that a pen can be made by a single man. Let us say that the workman is turning out ten pens per day, and that he is receiving $2.50 a day for his wages. He has a progressive foreman who is up to date, and that foreman goes to the workman and suggests, "Here, John, you are getting $2.50 a day, and you are turning out ten pens. I would suggest that I pay you 25 cents for making that pen." The man takes the job, and through the help of his foreman, through his own ingenuity, through his increased work, through his interest in his business, through the help of his friends, at the end of the year he finds himself turning out twenty pens instead of ten. He is happy, he is making $5, instead of $2.50 a day. His foreman is happy because, with the same room, with the same men he had before, he has doubled the output of his department, and the manufacturer himself is sometimes happy, but not often. Then someone on the board of directors asks to see the payroll, and he finds that we are paying $5 a day where other similar mechanics are only getting $2.50, and in no uncertain terms he announces that we must stop ruining the labor market. We cannot pay $5 a day when the standard rate of wages is $2.50; how can we hope to compete with surrounding towns? What is the result? Mr. Foreman is sent for, and he is told that he has got to stop ruining the labor market of Cleveland. And the foreman goes back to his workman in sadness, in depression, and tells his workman, "I am sorry, John, but I have got to cut the price down for that pen; I cannot let you earn $5 a day; the board of directors has got on to it, and it is ruining the labor market; you ought to be willing to have the price reduced. You cannot earn more than $3 or $2.75 a day, and I will have to cut your wages so that you will only get $3 a day." John, of necessity accepts the cut, but he sees to it that he never makes enough pens to get another cut.

CHARACTERISTICS OF THE UNION WORKMAN

There seem to be two divergent opinions about the workmen of this country. One is that a lot of the trade unions' workmen, particularly in this country, have become brutal, have become dominating, careless of any interests but their own, and are a pretty poor lot. And the other opinion which those same trade unionists hold of themselves is that they are pretty close to little gods. Whichever view you may hold of the workingmen of this country, and my personal view of them is that they are a pretty fine lot of fellows, they are just about the same as you and I. But whether you hold the bad opinion or the good opinion, it makes no difference. Whatever the workingmen of this country are or whatever they are not, they are not fools. And all that is necessary is for a workingman to have but one object lesson, like that I have told you, and he soldiers for the rest of his life.

There are a few exceptional employers who treat their workmen differently, but I am talking about the rule of the country. Soldiering is the absolute rule with all workmen who know their business. I am not saying it is for their interest to soldier. You cannot blame them for it. You cannot expect them to be large enough minded men to look at the proper view of the matter. Nor is the man who cuts the wages necessarily to blame. It is simply a misfortune in industry.

THE DEVELOPMENT OF SCIENTIFIC MANAGEMENT

There has been, until comparatively recently, no scheme promulgated by which the evils of rate cutting could be properly avoided, so soldiering has been the rule.

Now the first step that was taken toward the development of those methods, of those principles, which rightly or wrongly have come to be known under the name of scientific management—the first step that was taken in an earnest endeavor to remedy the evils of soldiering; an earnest endeavor to make it unnecessary for workmen to be hypocritical in this way, to deceive themselves, to deceive their employers, to live day in and day out a life of deceit, forced upon them by conditions—the very first step that was taken toward the development was to overcome that evil. I want to emphasize that, because I wish to emphasize the one great fact relating to scientific management, the greatest factor: namely, that scientific management is no new set of theories that has been tried on by any one at every step. Scientific management at every step has been an evolution, not a theory. In all cases the practice has preceded the theory, not succeeded it. In every case one measure after another has been tried out, until the proper remedy has been found. That series of proper eliminations, that evolution, is what is called scientific management. Every element of it has had to fight its way against the elements that preceded it, and prove itself better or it would not be there tomorrow.

All the men that I know of who are in any way connected with scientific management are ready to abandon any scheme, any theory in favor of anything else that could be found that is better. There is nothing in scientific management that is fixed. There is no one man, or group of men, who have invented scientific management.

What I want to emphasize is that all of the elements of scientific management are an evolution, not an invention. Scientific management is in use in an immense range and variety of industries. Almost every type of industry in this country has scientific management working successfully. I think I can safely say that on the average in those establishments in which scientific management has been introduced, the average workman is turning out double the output he was before. I think that is a conservative statement.

THE WORKMEN THE CHIEF BENEFICIARIES

Three or four years ago I could have said there were about fifty thousand men working under scientific management, but now I know there are many more. Company after company is coming under it, many of which I know nothing about. Almost universally they are working successfully. This increasing of the output per individual in the trade, results, of course, in cheapening the product; it results, therefore, in larger profit usually to the owners of the business; it results also, in many cases, in a lowering of the selling price, although that has not come to the extent it will later. In the end the public gets the good. Without any question, the large good which so far has come from scientific management has come to the worker. To the workmen has come, practically right off as soon as scientific management is introduced, an increase in wages amounting from 33 to 100 percent, and yet that is not the greatest good that comes to the workmen from scientific management. The great good comes from the fact that, under scientific management, they look upon their employers as the best friends they have in the world;

the suspicious watchfulness which characterizes the old type of management, the semi-antagonism, or the complete antagonism between workmen and employers is entirely superseded, and in its place comes genuine friendship between both sides. That is the greatest good that has come under scientific management. As a proof of this in the many businesses in which scientific management has been introduced, I know of not one single strike of workmen working under it after it had been introduced, and only two or three while it was in process of introduction. In this connection I must speak of the fakers, those who have said they can introduce scientific management into a business in six months or a year. That is pure nonsense. There have been many strikes stirred up by that type of man. Not one strike has ever come, and I do not believe ever will come, under scientific management.

WHAT SCIENTIFIC MANAGEMENT IS

What is scientific management? It is no efficiency device, nor is it any group of efficiency devices. Scientific management is no new scheme for paying men, it is no bonus system, no piecework system, no premium system of payment; it is no new method of figuring costs. It is no one of the various elements by which it is commonly known, by which people refer to it. It is not time study nor man study. It is not the printing of a ton or two of blanks and unloading them on a company and saying, "There is your system, go ahead and use it." Scientific management does not exist and cannot exist until there has been a complete mental revolution on the part of the workmen working under it, as to their duties toward themselves and toward their employers, and a complete mental

revolution in the outlook for the employers, toward their duties, toward themselves, and toward their workmen. And until this great mental change takes place, scientific management does not exist. Do you think you can make a great mental revolution in a large group of workmen in a year, or do you think you can make it in a large group of foremen and superintendents in a year? If you do, you are very much mistaken. All of us hold mighty close to our ideas and principles in life, and we change very slowly toward the new, and very properly too.

Let me give you an idea of what I mean by this change in mental outlook. If you are manufacturing a hammer or a mallet, into the cost of that mallet goes a certain amount of raw materials, a certain amount of wood and metal. If you will take the cost of the raw materials and then add to it that cost which is frequently called by various names—overhead expenses, general expense, indirect expense; that is, the proper share of taxes, insurance, light, heat, salaries of officers and advertising—and you have a sum of money. Subtract that sum from the selling price, and what is left over is called the surplus. It is over this surplus that all of the labor disputes in the past have occurred. The workman naturally wants all he can get. His wages come out of that surplus. The manufacturer wants all he can get in the shape of profits, and it is from the division of this surplus that all the labor disputes have come in the past—the equitable division.

The new outlook that comes under scientific management is this: The workmen, after many object lessons, come to see and the management come to see that this surplus can be made so great, providing both sides will stop their pulling apart, will stop their fighting and will push as hard as they can to get as cheap an output as possible, that there is no occasion to quarrel. Each side can get more than ever before. The acknowledgment of this fact represents a complete mental revolution.

INTELLIGENT OLD-STYLE MANAGEMENT

There is one more illustration of the new and great change which comes under scientific management. I can make it clearer, perhaps, by contrasting it with what I look upon as the best of the older types of management. If you have a company employing five hundred or a thousand men, you will have in that company perhaps fifteen different trades. The workmen in those trades have learned absolutely all that they know, not from books, not by being taught, but they have learned it traditionally. It has been handed down to them, not even by word of mouth in many cases, but by seeing what other men do. One man stands alongside of another man and imitates him. That is the way the trades are handed down, and my impression is that trades are now picked up just as they were in the Middle Ages.

The manufacturer, the manager, or the foreman who knows his business realizes that his chief function as a manager—I am talking now of the old-fashioned manager—ought to be to get the true initiative of his workman. He wants the initiative of the workman, their hard work, their good will, their ingenuity, their determination to do all they can for the benefit of his firm. If he knows anything about human nature, if he has thought over the problems, he must realize that in order to get the initiative of his workmen, in order to modify their soldiering, he must do something more for his men than other employers are doing for their men under similar circumstances. The wise manager, under the old type of management, deliberately sets out to do something better for his workmen than his competitors are doing, better than he himself has ever done before. It takes a good while for the workmen to stop looking for that "nigger in the woodpile," but if the manager keeps at them long enough he will get the confidence of the men, and when he does workmen of all kinds will respond by giving a great increase in output. When he sets out to do better for his men than other people do for theirs, the workmen respond liberally when that time comes. I refer to this case as being the highest type of management, the case in which the managers deliberately set out to do something better for their workmen than other people are doing, and to give them a special incentive of some kind, to which the workmen respond by giving a share at least of their initiative.

WHAT SCIENTIFIC MANAGEMENT WILL DO

I am going to try to prove to you that the old style of management has not a ghost of a chance in competition with the principles of scientific management. Why? In the first place, under scientific management, the initiative of the workmen, their hard work, their goodwill, their best endeavors are obtained with absolute regularity. There are cases all the time where men will soldier, but they become the exception, as a rule, and they give their true initiative under scientific management. That is the least of the two sources of gain. The greatest source of gain under scientific management comes from the new and almost unheard-of duties and burdens which are voluntarily assumed, not by the workmen, but by the men on the management side. These are the things which make scientific management a success.

These new duties, these new burdens undertaken by the management have rightly or wrongly been divided into four groups, and have been called the principles of scientific management.

The first of the great principles of scientific management, the first of the new burdens which are voluntarily undertaken by those on the management side is the deliberate gathering together of the great mass of traditional knowledge which, in the past, has been in the heads of the workmen, recording it, tabulating it, reducing it in most cases to rules, laws, and in many cases to mathematical fomulae, which, with these new laws, are applied to the cooperation of the management to the work of the workmen. This results in an immense increase in the output, we may say, of the two. The gathering in of this great mass of traditional knowledge, which is done by the means of motion study, time study, can be truly called the science.

Let me make a prediction. I have before me the first book, so far as I know, that has been published on motion study and on time study. That is, the motion study and time study of the cement and concrete trades. It contains everything relating to concrete work. It is of about seven hundred pages and embodies the motions of men, the time and the best way of doing that sort of work. It is the first case in which a trade has been reduced to the same condition that engineering data of all kinds have been reduced, and it is this sort of data that is bound to sweep the world.

I have before me something which has been gathering for about fourteen years, the time or motion study of the machine shop. It will take probably four or five years more before the first book will be ready to publish on that subject. There is a collection of sixty or seventy thousand elements affecting machine-shop work. After a few years, say three, four or five years more, some one will be ready to publish the first book giving the laws of the movements of men in the machine shop—all the laws, not only a few of them. Let me predict, just as sure as the sun shines, that is going to come in every trade. Why? Because it pays, for no other reason. That results in doubling the output in any shop. Any device which results in an increased output is bound to come in spite of all opposition, whether we want it or not. It comes automatically.

THE SELECTION OF THE WORKMAN

The next of the four principles of scientific management is the scientific selection of the workman, and then his progressive development. It becomes the duty under scientific management of not one, but of a group of men on the management side, to deliberately study the workmen who are under them; study them in the most careful, thorough and painstaking way; and not just leave it to the poor, overworked foreman to go out and say, "Come on, what do you want? If you are cheap enough I will give you a trial."

That is the old way. The new way is to take a great deal of trouble in selecting the workmen. The selection proceeds year after year. And it becomes the duty of those engaged in scientific management to know something about the workmen under them. It becomes their duty to set out deliberately to train the workmen in their employ to be able to do a better and still better class of work than ever before, and to then pay them higher wages than ever before. This deliberate selection of the workmen is the second of the great duties that devolve on the management under scientific management.

BRINGING TOGETHER THE SCIENCE AND THE MAN

The third principle is the bringing together of this science of which I have spoken and the trained workmen. I say bringing because they don't come together unless someone brings them. Select and train your workmen all you may, but unless there is some one who will make the men and the science come together, they will stay apart. The "make" involves a great many elements. They are not all disagreeable elements. The most important and largest way of "making" is to do something nice for the man whom you wish to make come together with the science. Offer him a plum, something that is worthwhile. There are many plums offered to those who come under scientific management—better treatment, more kindly treatment, more consideration for their wishes, and an opportunity for them to express their wants freely. That is one side of the "make." An equally important side is, whenever a man will not do what he ought, to either make him do it or stop it. If he will not do it, let him get out. I am not talking of any mollycoddle. Let me disabuse your minds of any opinion that scientific management is a mollycoddle scheme.

I have a great many union friends. I find they look with especial bitterness on this word "make." They have been used to doing the "making" in the past. That is the attitude of the trade unions, and it softens matters greatly when you can tell them the facts, namely, that in our making the science and the men come together, nine-tenths of our trouble comes with the men on the management side in making them do their new duties. I am speaking of those who have been trying to change from the old system to the new. Nine-tenths of our troubles come in trying to make the men on the management side do what they ought to do, to make them do the new duties, and take on these new burdens, and give up their old duties. That softens this word "make."

THE PRINCIPLE OF THE DIVISION OF WORK

The fourth principle is the plainest of all. It involves a complete re-division of the work of the establishment. Under the old scheme of management, almost all of the work was done by the workmen. Under the new, the work of the establishment is divided into two large parts. All of that work which formerly was done by the workmen alone is divided into two large sections, and one of those sections is handed over to the management. They do a whole division of the work formerly done by the workmen. It is this real cooperation, this genuine division of the work between the two sides, more than any other element which accounts for the fact that there never will be strikes under scientific management. When the workman realizes that there is hardly a thing he does that does not have to be preceded by some act of preparation on the part of management, and when that workman realizes when the management falls down and does not do its part, that he is not only entitled to a kick, but that he can register that kick in the most forcible possible way, he cannot quarrel with the men over him. It is teamwork. There are more complaints made every day on the part of the workmen that the men on the management side fail to do their duties than are made by the management that the men fail. Every one of the complaints of the men have to be heeded, just as much as the complaints from the management that the workmen do not do their share. That is characteristic of scientific management. It represents a democracy, co-operation, a genuine division of work which never existed before in this world.

THE PROOF OF THE THEORY

I am through now with the theory. I will try to convince you of the value of these four principles by giving you some practical illustrations. I hope that you will look for these four elements in the illustrations. I shall begin by trying to show the power of these four elements when applied to the greatest kind of work I know of that is done by man. The reason I have heretofore chosen pig-iron for an illustration is that it is the lowest form of work that is known.

A pig of iron weighs about ninety-two pounds on an average. A man stoops down and, with no other implement than his hands, picks up a pig of iron, walks a few yards with it, and drops it on a pile. A large part of the community has the impression that scientific management is chiefly handling pig-iron. The reason I first chose pig-iron for an illustration is that, if you can prove to any one the strength, the effect, of those four principles when applied to such rudimentary work as handling pig-iron, the presumption is that it can be applied to something better. The only way to prove it is to start at the bottom and show those four principles all along the line. I am sorry I cannot, because of lack of time, give you the illustration of handling pig-iron. Many of you doubt whether there is much of any science in it. I am going to try to prove later with a high class mechanic that the workman who is fit to work at any type of work is almost universally incapable of understanding the principles without the help of some one else. I will use shoveling because it is a shorter illustration, and I will try to show what I mean by the science of shoveling, and the power

which comes to the man who knows the science of shoveling. It is a high art compared with pig-iron handling.

THE SCIENCE OF SHOVELING

When I went to the Bethlehem Steel Works, the first thing I saw was a gang of men unloading rice coal. They were a splendid set of fellows, and they shoveled fast. There was no loafing at all. They shoveled as hard as you could ask any man to work. I looked with the greatest of interest for a long time, and finally they moved off rapidly down into the yard to another part of the yard and went right at handling iron ore. One of the main facts connected with that shoveling was that the work those men were doing was that, in handling the rice coal, they had on their shovels a load of 3¾ pounds, and when the same men went to handling ore with the same shovel, they had over 38 pounds on their shovels. Is it asking too much of anyone to inquire whether 3¾ pounds is the right load for a shovel, or whether 38 pounds is the right load for a shovel? Surely if one is right the other must be wrong. I think that is a self-evident fact, and yet I am willing to bet that that is what workmen are doing right now in Cleveland.

That is the old way. Suppose we notice that fact. Most of us do not notice it because it is left to the foreman. At the Midvale works, we had to find out these facts. What is the old way of finding them out? The old way was to sit down and write one's friends and ask them the questions. They got answers from contractors about what they thought it ought to be, and then they averaged them up, or took the most reliable man, and said, "That is all right; now we have a shovel load of so much." The more common way is to say, "I want a good shovel foreman." They will send for the foreman of the shovelers and put the job up to him to find what is the proper load to put on a shovel. He will tell you right off the bat. I want to show you the difference under scientific management.

Under scientific management you ask no one. Every little trifle,—there is nothing too small,—becomes the subject of experiment. The experiments develop into a law; they save money; they increase the output of the individual and make the thing worthwhile. How is this done? What we did in shoveling experiments was to deliberately select two first class shovelers, the best we knew how to get. We brought them into the office and said, "Jim and Mike, you two fellows are both good shovelers. I have a proposition to make to you. I am going to pay you double wages if you fellows will go out and do what I want you to do. There will be a young chap go along with you with a pencil and a piece of paper, and he will tell you to do a lot of fool things, and you will do them, and he will write down a lot of fool things, and you will think it is a joke, but it is nothing of the kind. Let me tell you one thing: if you fellows think that you can fool that chap you are very much mistaken, you cannot fool him at all. Don't get it through your heads you can fool him. If you take this double wages, you will be straight and do what you are told." They both promised and did exactly what they were told. What we told them was this: "We want you to start in and do whatever shoveling you are told to do, and work at just the pace, all day long, that when it comes night you are going to be good and tired, but not tired out. I do not want you exhausted or anything like that, but properly tired. You know what a good day's work is. In other words, I do not want any loafing business or any overwork business. If you find yourself overworked and getting too tired, slow

down." Those men did that and did it in the most splendid kind of way day in and day out. We proved their cooperation because they were in different parts of the yard, and they both got near enough the same results. Our results were duplicated.

I have found that there are a lot of schemes among my working friends, but no more among them than among us. They are good, straight fellows if you only treat them right, and put the matter up squarely to them. We started in at a pile of material, with a very large shovel. We kept innumerable accurate records of all kinds, some of them useless. Thirty or forty different items were carefully observed about the work of those two men. We counted the number of shovelfuls thrown in a day. We found with a weight of between thirty-eight and thirty-nine pounds on the shovel, the man made a pile of material of a certain height. We then cut off the shovel, and he shoveled again and with a thirty-four pound load his pile went up and he shoveled more in a day. We again cut off the shovel to thirty pounds, and the pile went up again. With twenty-six pounds on the shovel, the pile again went up, and at twenty-one and one-half pounds the men could do their best. At twenty pounds the pile went down, at eighteen it went down, and at fourteen it went down, so that they were at the peak of twenty-one and one-half pounds. There is a scientific fact. A first class shoveler ought to take twenty-one and one-half pounds on his shovel in order to work to the best possible advantage. You are not giving that man a chance unless you give him a shovel which will hold twenty-one pounds.

The men in the yard were run by the old fashioned foreman. He simply walked about with them. We at once took their shovels away from them. We built a large labor tool room which held ten to fifteen different kinds of shoveling implements so that for each kind of material that was handled in that yard, all the way from rice coal, ashes, coke, all the way up to ore, we would have a shovel that would just hold twenty-one pounds, or average twenty-one. One time it would hold eighteen, the next twenty-four, but it will average twenty-one.

When you have six hundred men laboring in the yard, as we had there, it becomes a matter of quite considerable difficulty to get, each day, for each one of those six hundred men, engaged in a line one and one-half to two miles long and a half mile wide, just the right shovel for shoveling material. That requires organization to lay out and plan for those men in advance. We had to lay out the work each day. We had to have large maps on which the movements of the men were plotted out a day in advance. When each workman came in the morning, he took out two pieces of paper. One of the blanks gave them a statement of the implements which they had to use, and the part of the yard in which they had to work. That required organization planning in advance.

One of the first principles we adopted was that no man in that labor gang could work on the new way unless he earned sixty percent higher wages than under the old plan. It is only just to the workman that he shall know right off whether he is doing his work right or not. He must not be told a week or month after, that he fell down. He must know it the next morning. So the next slip that came out of the pigeon hole was either a white or yellow slip. We used the two colors because some of the men could not read. The yellow slip meant that he had not earned his sixty per cent higher wages. He knew that he could not stay in that gang and keep on getting yellow slips.

TEACHING THE MEN

I want to show you again the totally different outlook there is under scientific management by illustrating what happened when that man got his yellow slips. Under the old scheme, the foreman could say to him, "You are no good, get out of this; no time for you, you cannot earn sixty percent higher wages; get out of this! Go!" It was not done politely, but the foreman had no time to palaver. Under the new scheme what happened? A teacher of shoveling went down to see that man. A teacher of shoveling is a man who is handy with a shovel, who has made his mark in life with a shovel, and yet who is a kindly fellow and knows how to show the other fellow what he ought to do. When that teacher went there he said, "See here, Jim, you have a lot of those yellow slips, what is the matter with you? What is up? Have you been drunk? Are you tired? Are you sick? Anything wrong with you? Because if you are tired or sick we will give you a show somewhere else." "Well, no, I am all right." "Then if you are not sick, or there is nothing wrong with you, you have forgotten how to shovel. I showed you how to shovel. You have forgotten something, now go ahead and shovel and I will show you what is the matter with you." Shoveling is a pretty big science, it is not a little thing.

If you are going to use the shovel right you should always shovel off an iron bottom; if not an iron bottom, a wooden bottom; and if not a wooden bottom a hard dirt bottom. Time and again the conditions are such that you have to go right into the pile. When that is the case, with nine out of ten materials it takes more trouble and more time and more effort to get the shovel into the pile than to do all the rest of the shoveling. That is where the effort comes.

Those of you again who have taught the art of shoveling will have taught your workmen to do this. There is only one way to do it right. Put your forearm down onto the upper part of your leg, and when you push into the pile, throw your weight against it. That relieves your arm of work. You then have an automatic push, we will say, about eighty pounds, the weight of your body thrown on to it. Time and again we would find men whom we had taught to shovel right were going at it in the old way, and of course they could not do a day's work. The teacher would simply stand over that fellow and say, "There is what is the matter with you, Jim, you have forgotten to shovel into the pile."

You are not interested in shoveling, you are not interested in whether one way or the other is right, but I do hope to interest you in the difference of the mental attitude of the men who are teaching under the new system. Under the new system, if a man falls down, the presumption is that it is our fault at first, that we probably have not taught the man right, have not given him a fair show, have not spent time enough in showing him how to do his work.

Let me tell you another thing that is characteristic of scientific management. In my day, we were smart enough to know when the boss was coming, and when he came up we were apparently really working. Under scientific management, there is none of that pretense. I cannot say that in the old days we were delighted to see the boss coming around. We always expected some kind of roast if he came too close. Under the new, the teacher is welcomed; he is not an enemy, but a friend. He comes there to try to help the man get bigger wages, to show him how to do something. It is the great mental change, the change in the

outlook that comes, rather than the details of it.

DOES SCIENTIFIC MANAGEMENT PAY?

It took the time of a number of men for about three years to study the art of shoveling in that yard at the Bethlehem Steel Works alone. They were carefully trained college men, and they were busy all the time. That costs money, the tool room costs money, the clerks we had to keep there all night figuring up how much the men did the day before cost money, the office in which the men laid out and planned the work cost money. The very fair and proper question, the only question to ask is "Does it pay?" because if scientific management does not pay, there is nothing in it; if it does not pay in dollars and cents, it is the rankest kind of nonsense. There is nothing philanthropic about it. It has got to pay, because business which cannot be done on a profitable basis ought not to be done on a philanthropic basis, for it will not last. At the end of three and one-half years we had a very good chance to know whether or not it paid.

Fortunately in the Bethlehem Steel Works they had records of how much it cost to handle the materials under the old system, where the single foreman led a group of men around the works. It costs them between seven and eight cents a ton to handle materials, on an average throughout the year. After paying for all this extra work I have told you about, it cost between three and four cents a ton to handle materials, and there was a profit of between seventy-five and eighty thousand dollars a year in that yard by handling those materials in the new way. What the men got out of it was this: Under the old system there were between four and six hundred men handling the material in that yard, and when we got through there were about one hundred and forty. Each one was earning a great deal more money. We made careful investigation and found they were almost all saving money, living better, happier; they are the most contented set of laborers to be seen anywhere. It is only by this kind of justification, justification of a profit for both sides, an advantage to both sides, that scientific management can exist.

I would like to give you one more illustration. I want to try to prove to you that even the highest class mechanic cannot possibly understand the philosophy of his work, cannot possibly understand the laws under which he has to operate. There is a man who has had a high school education, an ingenious fellow who courts variety in life, to whom it is pleasant to change from one kind of work to another. He is not a cheap man, he is rather a high grade man among the machinists of this country. The case of which I am going to tell you is one in which my friend Barth went to introduce scientific management in the works of an owner, who, at between 65 and 70 years of age, had built up his business from nothing to almost five thousand men. They had a squabble, and after they got through, Mr. Barth made the proposition, "I will take any machine that you use in your shop, and I will show you that I can double the output of that machine." A very fair machine was selected. It was a lathe on which the workman had been working about twelve years. The product of that shop is a patented machine with a good many parts, 350 men working making those parts year in and year out. Each man had ten or a dozen parts a year.

The first thing that was done was in the presence of the foreman, the superintendent and the owner of the establishment. Mr. Barth laid down the way

in which all of the parts were to be machined on that machine by the workman. Then Mr. Barth, with one of his small slide rules, proceeded to analyze the machine. With the aid of this analysis, which embodies the laws of cutting metals, Mr. Barth was able to take his turn at the machine; his gain was from two and one-half times to three times the amount of work turned out by the other man. This is what can be done by science as against the old rule of thumb knowledge. That is not exaggeration; the gain is as great as that in many cases.

Let me tell you something. The machines of this country, almost universally in the machine shops of our country, are speeded two or three hundred percent wrong. I made that assertion before the tool builders in Atlantic City. I said, "Gentlemen, in your own shops, many of your machines are two and three hundred percent wrong in speeds. Why? Because you have guessed at it." I am trying to show you what are the losses under the old opinions, the difference between knowledge on the one hand and guesswork on the other.

In 1882, at the end of a long fight with the machinists of the Midvale Steel Works, I went there as a laborer, and finally became a machinist after serving my apprenticeship outside. I finally got into the shop, and worked up to the place of a clerk who had something wrong with him. I then did a little bit more work than the others were doing, not too much. They came to me and said, "See here, Fred, you are not going to be a piecework hog." I said, "You fellows mean that you think I am not going to try to get any more work off these machines? I certainly am. Now I am on the other side, and I am going to be straight with you, and I will tell you so in advance." They said, "All right then, we will give you fair notice you will be outside the fence inside of six weeks." Let me tell you gentlemen, if any of you have been through a fight like that, trying to get workmen to do what they do not want to do, you will know the meanness of it, and you will never want to go into another one. I never would have gone into it if I had known what was ahead of me. After the meanest kind of a bitter fight, at the end of three years, we fairly won out and got a big increase in output. I had no illusion at the end of that time as to my great ability or anything else. I knew that those workmen knew about ten times as much as I did about doing the work. I set out deliberately to get on our side some of that knowledge that those workmen had.

Mr. William Sellers was the president, and he was a man away beyond his generation in progress. I went to him and said, "I want to spend quite a good deal of money trying to educate ourselves on the management side of our works. I do not know much of anything, and I am just about in the same condition as all the rest of the foremen around here." Very reluctantly, I may say, he allowed us to start to spend money. That started the study of the art of cutting metals. At the end of six months, from the standpoint of how to cut the metal off faster, the study did not amount to anything, but we unearthed a gold mine of information. Mr. Sellers laughed at me, but when I was able to show him the possibilities that lay ahead of us, the number of things we could find out, he said, "Go ahead." So until 1889, that experiment went straight ahead day in and day out. That was done because it paid in dollars and cents.

After I left the Midvale Steel Works, we had no means of figuring those experiments except the information which we had already gotten. Ten different machines were built to develop the art of cutting metals, so that almost continuously from 1882 for twenty-six years, all sorts of experiments went on to determine the twelve great elements that go to make up the art of cutting metals. I am trying to show you just what is going to take place in every industry throughout this world. You must know those facts if you are going to manufacture cheaply, and the only way to know them is to pay for them.

THE DISCOVERY OF HIGH SPEED STEEL

Twelve elements do not sound very many, but they are difficult elements. One of the twelve elements was the discovery of high speed steel, that is, it resulted from a careful series of experiments to determine the proper chemical composition, plus the proper heat treatment of tool steel in order to get the highest cutting speed out of it. It was a series of most carefully tried scientific experiments lasting through three years, which led gradually up to the discovery of high speed steel. Most people think it was an accident. Not at all. It was at the expense of about $50,000 in work, in wages, and in the manufacture of steels. That is one of the twelve elements. There are eleven others. Among the others is this one, simplest of all. We found very early that if we threw a heavy stream of cold water on the tip of the tool, the cooling effect was such that we could run forty percent faster. Mr. Sellers was skeptical, and it was pretty hard to make him believe the truth. He tore down the old shop and built an entirely new shop in order to get that forty percent increase. He had his overhead supply of water brought down to each machine so that it could be adjusted quickly, and by means of that it gave us that forty percent increase.

Gentlemen, think of it, only one machine shop in twenty years followed that. It was explained to the manufacturers, and the average man said, "Oh, hell, what's the use." There is the answer.

I also want to try to show you why the high class mechanic cannot possibly compete with this science. The working out of those twelve elements resulted in the development of twelve large mathematical formulas, and in order to figure out the two great things that every mechanic has to know when he sets a tool in a lathe and goes to cutting metals,— what speed and what feed shall be used,—requires the solution of a mathematical problem containing twelve unknown quantities. If any one tries to solve those twelve unknown quantities with a pencil and paper, it takes about six hours. For eighteen years we had mathematicians all the time employed trying to solve that problem, and it paid because we got nearer and nearer to the solution. At the end of eighteen years, instead of taking six hours to solve the problem, it can be solved in twenty seconds by all of the workmen. That brings this problem right down to the level of every day practical common sense.

THE EFFECT ON THE WORKMAN

Almost every one says, "Why, yes, that may be a good thing for the manufacturer, but how about the workmen? You are taking all the initiative away from that workman, you are making a machine out of him; what are you doing for him? He becomes merely a part of the machine." That is the almost universal impression. Again let me try to sweep aside the fallacy of that view by an illustration. The modern surgeon without a doubt is the finest mechanic in the world. He combines the greatest manual dexterity with the greatest knowledge of implements and the greatest knowledge of materials on which he is working. He is a true scientist, and he is a very highly skilled mechanic.

How does the surgeon teach his trade to the young men who come to the medical school? Does he say to them, "Now, young men, we belong to an older generation than you do, but the new generation is going to far outstrip anything that has been done in our generation; therefore, what we want of you is your initiative. We must have your brains, your thought, with your initiative. Of course, you know we old fellows have certain prejudices. For example, if we were going to amputate a leg, when we come down to the bone we are accustomed to take a saw, and we use it in that way and saw the bone off. But, gentlemen, do not let that fact one minute interfere with your originality, with your initiative, if you prefer an axe or a hatchet." Does the surgeon say this? He does not. He says, "You young men are going to outstrip us, but we will show you how. You shall not use a single implement in a single way until you know just which one to use, and we will tell you which one to use, and until you know how to use it, we will tell you how to use that implement, and after you have learned to use that implement our way, if you then see any defects in the implements, any defects in the method, then invent; but, invent so that you can invent upwards. Do not go inventing things which we discarded years ago."

That is just what we say to our young men in the shops. Scientific Management makes no pretense that there is any finality in it. We merely say that the collective work of thirty or forty men in this trade through eight or ten years has gathered together a large amount of data. Every man in the establishment must start that way, must start our way, then if he can show us any better way, I do not care what it is, we will make an experiment to see if it is better. It will be named after him, and he will get a prize for having improved on one of our standards. There is the way we make progress under scientific management.

There is your justification for all this. It does not dwarf initiative, it makes true initiative. Most of our progress comes through our workmen, but comes in a legitimate way.

8
Bureaucracy
Max Weber

1. CHARACTERISTICS OF BUREAUCRACY

Modern officialdom functions in the following specific manner:

I. *There is the principle of fixed and official jurisdictional areas, which are generally ordered by rules, that is, by laws or administrative regulations.* [Italics added]

1. The regular activities required for the purposes of the bureaucratically governed structure are distributed in a fixed way as official duties.

2. The authority to give the commands required for the discharge of these duties is distributed in a stable way and is strictly delimited by rules concerning the coercive means, physical, sacerdotal, or otherwise, which may be placed at the disposal of officials.

3. Methodical provision is made for the regular and continuous fulfillment of these duties and for the execution of the corresponding rights; only persons who have the generally regulated qualifications to serve are employed.

In public and lawful government these three elements constitute "bureaucratic authority." In private eco-

nomic domination, they constitute bureaucratic "management." Bureaucracy, thus understood, is fully developed in political and ecclesiastical communities only in the modern state, and, in the private economy, only in the most advanced institutions of capitalism. Permanent and public office authority, with fixed jurisdiction, is not the historical rule but rather the exception. This is so even in large political structures such as those of the ancient Orient, the Germanic and Mongolian empires of conquest, or of many feudal structures of state. In all these cases, the ruler executes the most important measures through personal trustees, table-companions, or court-servants. Their commissions and authority are not precisely delimited and are temporarily called into being for each case.

II. *The principles of office hierarchy and of levels of graded authority mean a firmly ordered system of super- and subordination in which there is a supervision of the lower offices by the higher ones.* Such a system offers the governed the possibility of appealing the decision of a lower office to its higher authority, in a definitely

Source: From *From Max Weber: Essays in Sociology* edited and translated by H. H. Gerth and C. Wright Mills. Copyright 1946 by Oxford University Press, Inc.; renewed 1973 by Hans H. Gerth. Reprinted by permission of the publisher. Footnotes omitted.

regulated manner. With the full development of the bureaucratic type, the office hierarchy is monocratically organized. The principle of hierarchical office authority is found in all bureaucratic structures: in state and ecclesiastical structures as well as in large party organizations and private enterprises. It does not matter for the character of bureaucracy whether its authority is called "private" or "public."

When the principle of jurisdictional "competency" is fully carried through, hierarchical subordination—at least in public office—does not mean that the "higher" authority is simply authorized to take over the business of the "lower." Indeed, the opposite is the rule. Once established and having fulfilled its task, an office tends to continue in existence and be held by another incumbent.

III. The management of the modern office is based upon written documents ("the files"), which are preserved in their original or draught form. There is, therefore, a staff or subaltern officials and scribes of all sorts. The body of officials actively engaged in a "public" office, along with the respective apparatus of material implements and the files, make up a "bureau." In private enterprise, "the bureau" is often called "the office."

In principle, the modern organization of the civil service separates the bureau from the private domicile of the official, and, in general, bureaucracy segregates official activity as something distinct from the sphere of private life. Public monies and equipment are divorced from the private property of the official. This condition is everywhere the product of a long development. Nowadays, it is found in public as well as in private enterprises; in the latter, the principle extends even to the leading entrepreneur. In principle, the executive office is separated from the household, business from

private correspondence, and business assets from private fortunes. The more consistently the modern type of business management has been carried through the more are these separations the case. The beginnings of this process are to be found as early as the Middle Ages.

It is the peculiarity of the modern entrepreneur that he conducts himself as the "first official" of his enterprise, in the very same way in which the ruler of a specifically modern bureaucratic state spoke of himself as "the first servant" of the state. The idea that the bureau activities of the state are intrinsically different in character from the management of private economic offices is a continental European notion and, by way of contrast, is totally foreign to the American way.

IV. Office management, at least all specialized office management—and such management is distinctly modern—usually presupposes thorough and expert training. This increasingly holds for the modern executive and employee of private enterprises, in the same manner as it holds for the state official.

V. When the office is fully developed, official activity demands the full working capacity of the official, irrespective of the fact that his obligatory time in the bureau may be firmly delimited. In the normal case, this is only the product of a long development, in the public as well as in the private office. Formerly, in all cases, the normal state of affairs was reversed: official business was discharged as a secondary activity.

VI. The management of the office follows general rules, which are more or less stable, more or less exhaustive, and which can be learned. Knowledge of these rules represents a special technical learning which the officials possess. It involves jurisprudence, or administrative or business management.

The reduction of modern office management to rules is deeply embedded in its very nature. The theory of modern public administration, for instance, assumes that the authority to order certain matters by decree—which has been legally granted to public authorities—does not entitle the bureau to regulate the matter by commands given for each case, but only to regulate the matter abstractly. This stands in extreme contrast to the regulation of all relationships through individual privileges and bestowals of favor, which is absolutely dominant in patrimonialism, at least in so far as such relationships are not fixed by sacred tradition.

2. THE POSITION OF THE OFFICIAL

All this results in the following for the internal and external position of the official:

I. Office holding is a "vocation." This is shown, first, in the requirement of a firmly prescribed course of training, which demands the entire capacity for work for a long period of time, and in the generally prescribed and special examinations which are prerequisites of employment. Furthermore, the position of the official is in the nature of a duty. This determines the internal structure of his relations, in the following manner: Legally and actually, office holding is not considered a source to be exploited for rents or emoluments, as was normally the case during the Middle Ages and frequently up to the threshold of recent times. Nor is office holding considered a usual exchange of services for equivalents, as is the case with free labor contracts. Entrance into an office, including one in the private economy, is considered an acceptance of a specific obligation of faithful management in return for a secure existence. It is decisive for the specific nature of modern loyalty to an office that, in the pure type, it does not establish a relationship to a *person*, like the vassal's or disciple's faith in feudal or in patrimonial relations of authority. Modern loyalty is devoted to impersonal and functional purposes. Behind the functional purposes, of course, "ideas of culture-values" usually stand. These are *ersatz* for the earthly or supra-mundane personal master: ideas such as "state," "church," "community," "party," or "enterprise" are thought of as being realized in a community; they provide an ideological halo for the master.

The political official—at least in the fully developed modern state—is not considered the personal servant of a ruler. Today, the bishop, the priest, and the preacher are in fact no longer, as in early Christian times, holders of purely personal charisma. The supramundane and sacred values which they offer are given to everybody who seems to be worthy of them and who asks for them. In former times, such leaders acted upon the personal command of their master; in principle, they were responsible only to him. Nowadays, in spite of the partial survival of the old theory, such religious leaders are officials in the service of a functional purpose, which in the present-day "church" has become routinized and, in turn, ideologically hallowed.

II. The personal position of the official is patterned in the following way:

1. Whether he is in a private office or a public bureau, the modern official always strives and usually enjoys a distinct *social esteem* as compared with the governed. His social position is guaranteed by the prescriptive rules of rank order and, for the political official, by special definitions of the criminal code against "insults of officials" and "contempt" of state and church authorities.

The actual social position of the official is normally highest where, as in old civilized countries, the following conditions prevail: a strong demand for administration by trained experts; a strong and stable social differentiation, where the official predominantly derives from socially and economically privileged strata because of the social distribution of power; or where the costliness of the required training and status conventions are binding upon him. The possession of educational certificates—to be discussed elsewhere—are usually linked with qualification for office. Naturally, such certificates or patents enhance the "status element" in the social position of the official. For the rest this status factor in individual cases is explicitly and impassively acknowledged; for example, in the prescription that the acceptance or rejection of an aspirant to an official career depends upon the consent ("election") of the members of the official body. This is the case in the German army with the officer corps. Similar phenomena, which promote this guild-like closure of officialdom, are typically found in patrimonial and, particularly, in prebendal officialdoms of the past. The desire to resurrect such phenomena in changed forms is by no means infrequent among modern bureaucrats. For instance, they have played a role among the demands of the quite proletarian and expert officials (the *tretyj* element) during the Russian revolution.

Usually the social esteem of the officials as such is especially low where the demand for expert administration and the dominance of status conventions are weak. This is especially the case in the United States; it is often the case in new settlements by virtue of their wide fields for profitmaking and the great instability of their social stratification.

2. The pure type of bureaucratic official is *appointed* by a superior authority.

An official elected by the governed is not a purely bureaucratic figure. Of course, the formal existence of an election does not by itself mean that no appointment hides behind the election—in the state, especially, appointment by party chiefs. Whether or not this is the case does not depend upon legal statutes but upon the way in which the party mechanism functions. Once firmly organized, the parties can turn a formally free election into the mere acclamation of a candidate designated by the party chief. As a rule, however, a formally free election is turned into a fight, conducted according to definite rules, for votes in favor of one of two designated candidates.

In all circumstances, the designation of officials by means of an election among the governed modifies the strictness of hierarchical subordination. In principle, an official who is so elected has an autonomous position opposite the superordinate official. The elected official does not derive his position "from above" but "from below," or at least not from a superior authority of the official hierarchy but from powerful party men ("bosses"), who also determine his further career. The career of the elected official is not, or at least not primarily, dependent upon his chief in the administration. The official who is not elected but appointed by a chief normally functions more exactly, from a technical point of view, because, all other circumstances being equal, it is more likely that purely functional points of consideration and qualities will determine his selection and career. As laymen, the governed can become acquainted with the extent to which a candidate is expertly qualified for office only in terms of experience, and hence only after his service. Moreover, in every sort of selection of officials by election, parties quite naturally give decisive weight not to expert considerations but to the services a follower renders to the party boss. This holds for all kinds of procurement of officials by elections, for the designation of formally free, elected officials by party bosses when they determine the slate of candidates, or the free appointment by a chief who has himself been elected. The contrast, however, is relative: substantially similar conditions hold where legitimate monarchs and their subordinates appoint officials, except that the influence of the followings are then less controllable.

Where the demand for administration by trained experts is considerable, and the party followings have to recognize an intellectually developed, educated, and freely moving "public opinion," the use of unqualified officials falls back upon the party in power at the next election. Naturally, this is more likely to happen when the officials are appointed by the chief. The demand for a trained administration now exists in the United States, but in the large cities, where immigrant votes are "corralled," there is, of course, no educated public opinion. Therefore, popular elections of the administrative chief and also of his subordinate officials usually endanger the expert qualification of the official as well as the precise functioning of the bureaucratic mechanism. It also weakens the dependence of the officials upon the hierarchy. This holds at least for the large administrative bodies that are difficult to supervise. The superior qualification and integrity of federal judges, appointed by the President, as over against elected judges in the United States is well known, although both types of officials have been selected primarily in terms of party considerations. The great changes in American metropolitan administrations demanded by reformers have proceeded essentially from elected mayors working with an apparatus of officials who were appointed by them. These reforms have thus come about in a "Caesarist" fashion. Viewed technically, as an organized form of authority, the efficiency of "Caesarism," which often grows out of democracy, rests in general upon the position of the "Caesar" as a free trustee of the masses (of the army or of the citizenry), who is unfettered by tradition. The "Caesar" is thus the unrestrained master of a body of highly qualified military officers and officials whom he selects freely and personally without regard to tradition or to any other considerations. This "rule of the personal genius," however, stands in contradiction to the formally "democratic" principle of a universally elected officialdom.

3. Normally, the position of the official is held for life, at least in public bureaucracies; and this is increasingly the case for all similar structures. As a factual rule, *tenure for life* is presupposed, even where the giving of notice or periodic reappointment occurs. In contrast to the worker in a private enterprise, the official normally holds tenure. Legal or actual life-tenure, however, is not recognized as the official's right to the possession of office, as was the case with many structures of authority in the past. Where legal guarantees against arbitrary dismissal or transfer are developed, they merely serve to guarantee a strictly objective discharge of specific office duties free from all personal considerations. In Germany, this is the case for all juridical and, increasingly, for all administrative officials.

Within the bureaucracy, therefore, the measure of "independence," legally guaranteed by tenure, is not always a source of increased status for the official whose position is thus secured. Indeed, often the reverse holds, especially in old cultures and communities that are highly differentiated. In such communities, the stricter the subordination under the arbitrary rule of the master, the more it guarantees the maintenance of the conventional seigneurial style of living for the official. Because of the very absence of these legal guarantees of tenure, the conventional esteem for the official may rise in the same way as, during the Middle Ages, the esteem of the nobility of office rose at the expense of esteem for the freemen, and as the king's judge surpassed that of the people's judge. In Germany, the military officer or the administrative official can be removed from office at any time, or at least far more readily than the "independent judge," who never pays with loss of his office for even the grossest offense against the "code of honor" or against social conventions of the salon. For this very reason, if other things are equal, in the eyes of the master stratum the judge is considered less qualified for social intercourse than are officers and administrative officials, whose greater dependence on the master is a greater guarantee of their conformity with status conventions. Of course, the average official strives for a civil-service law, which would materially secure his old age and provide increased guarantees against his arbitrary removal from office. This striving, however, has its limits. A very strong development of the "right to the office" naturally makes it more difficult to staff them with regard to technical efficiency, for such a development decreases the career opportunities of ambitious candidates for office. This makes for the fact that officials, on the whole, do not feel their dependency upon those at the top. This lack of a feeling of dependency, however, rests primarily upon the inclination to depend upon one's equals rather than upon the socially inferior and governed strata. The present conservative movement among the Badenia clergy, occasioned by the anxiety of a presumably threatening separation of church and state, has been expressly determined by the desire not to be turned "from a master into a servant of the parish."

4. The official receives the regular *pecuniary* compensation of a normally fixed *salary* and the old age security provided by a pension. The salary is not measured like a wage in terms of work done, but according to "status," that is, according to the kind of function (the "rank") and, in addition, possibly, according to the length of service. The relatively great security of the official's income, as well as the rewards of social esteem, make the office a sought-after position, especially in countries which no longer provide opportunities for colonial profits. In such countries, this situation permits relatively low salaries for officials.

5. The official is set for a "*career*" within the hierarchical order of the public service. He moves from the lower, less important, and lower paid to the higher positions. The average official naturally desires a mechanical fixing of the conditions of promotion: if not of the offices, at least of the salary levels. He wants these conditions fixed in terms of "seniority," or possibly according to grades achieved in a developed system of expert examinations. Here and there, such examinations actually form a character *indelebilis* of the official and have lifelong effects on his career. To this is joined the desire to qualify the right to office and the increasing tendency toward status group closure and economic security. All of this makes for a tendency to consider the offices as "prebends" of those who are qualified by educational certificates. The necessity of taking general personal and intellectual qualifications into consideration, irrespective of the often subaltern character of the educational certificate, has led to a condition in which the

highest political offices, especially the positions of "ministers," are principally filled without reference to such certificates.

9
Notes on the Theory of Organization
Luther Gulick

Every large-scale or complicated enterprise requires many men to carry it forward. Wherever many men are thus working together the best results are secured when there is a division of work among these men. The theory of organization, therefore, has to do with the structure of co-ordination imposed upon the work-division units of an enterprise. Hence it is not possible to determine how an activity is to be organized without, at the same time, considering how the work in question is to be divided. Work division is the foundation of organization; indeed, the reason for organization.

1. THE DIVISION OF WORK

It is appropriate at the outset of this discussion to consider the reasons for and the effect of the division of work. It is sufficient for our purpose to note the following factors.

Why Divide Work?
Because men differ in nature, capacity and skill, and gain greatly in dexterity by specialization; Because the same man cannot be at two places at the same time; Because the range of knowledge and skill is so great that a man cannot within his life-span know more than a small fraction of it. In other words, it is a question of human nature, time, and space.

In a shoe factory it would be possible to have 1,000 men each assigned to making complete pairs of shoes. Each man would cut his leather, stamp in the eyelets, sew up the tops, sew on the bottoms, nail on the heels, put in the laces, and pack each pair in a box. It might take two days to do the job. One thousand men would make 500 pairs of shoes a day. It would also be possible to divide the work among these same men, using the identical hand methods, in an entirely different way. One group of men would be assigned to cut the leather, another to putting in the eyelets, another to stitching up the tops, another to sewing on the soles, another to nailing on the heels, another to inserting the laces and packing the pairs of shoes. We know from common sense and experience that there are two great gains in this latter process: first, it makes possible the better utilization of the varying skills and aptitudes of the different workmen, and encourages the development of specialization; and second, it eliminates the time that is lost when a workman turns from a knife, to a punch, to a needle and awl, to a hammer, and moves from table to bench, to anvil, to

Source: Luther Gulick and Lyndall Urwick, eds., *Papers on the Science of Administration* (New York: Institute of Public Administration, 1937), 3–13.

stool. Without any pressure on the workers, they could probably turn out twice as many shoes in a single day. There would be additional economies, because inserting laces and packing could be assigned to unskilled and low-paid workers. Moreover, in the cutting of the leather there would be less spoilage because the less skillful pattern cutters would all be eliminated and assigned to other work. It would also be possible to cut a dozen shoe tops at the same time from the same pattern with little additional effort. All of these advances would follow, without the introduction of new labor saving machinery.

The introduction of machinery accentuates the division of work. Even such a simple thing as a saw, a typewriter, or a transit requires increased specialization, and serves to divide workers into those who can and those who cannot use the particular instrument effectively. Division of work on the basis of the tools and machines used in work rests no doubt in part on aptitude, but primarily upon the development and maintenance of skill through continued manipulation.

Specialized skills are developed not alone in connection with machines and tools. They evolve naturally from the materials handled, like wood, or cattle, or paint, or cement. They arise similarly in activities which center in a complicated series of interrelated concepts, principles, and techniques. These are most clearly recognized in the professions, particularly those based on the application of scientific knowledge, as in engineering, medicine, and chemistry. They are none the less equally present in law, ministry, teaching, accountancy, navigation, aviation, and other fields.

The nature of these subdivisions is essentially pragmatic, in spite of the fact that there is an element of logic underlying them. They are therefore subject to a gradual evolution with the advance of science, the invention of new machines, the progress of technology and the change of the social system. In the last analysis, however, they appear to be based upon differences in individual human beings. But it is not to be concluded that the apparent stability of "human nature," whatever that may be, limits the probable development of specialization. The situation is quite the reverse. As each field of knowledge and work is advanced, constituting a continually larger and more complicated nexus of related principles, practices and skills, any individual will be less and less able to encompass it and maintain intimate knowledge and facility over the entire area, and there will thus arise a more minute specialization because knowledge and skill advance while man stands still. Division of work and integrated organization are the bootstraps by which mankind lifts itself in the process of civilization.

The Limits of Division

There are three clear limitations beyond which the division of work cannot to advantage go. The first is practical and arises from the volume of work involved in man-hours. Nothing is gained by subdividing work if that further subdivision results in setting up a task which requires less than the full time of one man. This is too obvious to need demonstration. The only exception arises where space interferes, and in such cases the part-time expert must fill in his spare time at other tasks, so that as a matter of fact a new combination is introduced.

The second limitation arises from technology and custom at a given time and place. In some areas nothing would be gained by separating undertaking from the custody and cleaning of churches, because by custom the sexton is the undertaker; in building construction it is extraordinarily difficult to redivide certain aspects of electrical and plumbing work and to combine them in a more effective way, because of the jurisdictional conflicts of craft unions; and it is clearly impracticable to establish a division of cost accounting in a field in which no technique of costing has yet been developed.

This second limitation is obviously elastic. It may be changed by invention and by education. If this were not the fact, we should face a static division of labor. It should be noted, however, that a marked change has two dangers. It greatly restricts the labor market from which workers may be drawn and greatly lessens the opportunities open to those who are trained for the particular specialization.

The third limitation is that the subdivision of work must not pass beyond physical division into organic division. It might seem far more efficient to have the front half of the cow in the pasture grazing and the rear half in the barn being milked all of the time, but this organic division would fail. Similarly there is no gain from splitting a single movement or gesture like licking an envelope, or tearing apart a series of intimately and intricately related activities.

It may be said that there is in this an element of reasoning in a circle; that the test here applied as to whether an activity is organic or not is whether it is divisible or not—which is what we set out to define. This charge is true. It must be a pragmatic test. Does the division work out? Is something vital destroyed and lost? Does it bleed?

The Whole and the Parts

It is axiomatic that the whole is equal to the sum of its parts. But in dividing up any "whole," one must be certain that every part, including unseen elements and relationships, is accounted for. The marble sand to which the Venus de Milo may be reduced by a vandal does not equal the statue, though every last grain be preserved; nor is a thrush just so much feathers, bones, flesh and blood; nor a typewriter merely so much steel, glass, paint, and rubber. Similarly a piece of work to be done cannot be subdivided into the obvious component parts without great danger that the central design, the operating relationships, the imprisoned idea, will be lost.

A simple illustration will make this clear. One man can build a house. He can lay the foundation, cut the beams and boards, make the window frames and doors, lay the floors, raise the roof, plaster the walls, fit in the heating and water systems, install the electric wiring, hang the paper, and paint the structure. But if he did, most of the work would be done by hands unskilled in the work; much material would be spoiled, and the work would require many months of his time. On the other hand, the whole job of building the house might be divided among a group of men. One man could do the foundation, build the chimney, and plaster the walls; another could erect the frame, cut the timbers and the boards, raise the roof, and do all the carpentry; another all the plumbing; another all the paper hanging and painting; another all the electric wiring. But this would not make a house unless someone—an architect—made a plan for the house, so that each skilled worker could know what to do and when to do it.

When one man builds a house alone he plans as he works; he decides what to do first and what next, that is, he "co-ordinates the work." When many men work together to build a house this part of the work, the co-ordinating, must not be lost sight of.

In the "division of the work" among the various skilled specialists, a specialist in planning and coordination must be sought as well. Otherwise, a great deal of time may be lost, workers may get in each other's way, material may not be on hand when needed, things may be done in the wrong order, and there may even be a difference of opinion as to where the various doors and windows are to go. It is self-evident that the more the work is subdivided, the greater is the danger of confusion, and the greater is the need of overall supervision and coordination. Co-ordination is not something that develops by accident. It must be won by intelligent, vigorous, persistent, and organized effort.

2. THE CO-ORDINATION OF WORK

If subdivision of work is inescapable, co-ordination becomes mandatory. There is, however, no one way to co-ordination. Experience shows that it may be achieved in two primary ways. These are:

1. By organization, that is, by interrelating the subdivisions of work by allotting them to men who are placed in a structure of authority, so that the work may be co-ordinated by orders of superiors to subordinates, reaching from the top to the bottom of the entire enterprise.
2. By the dominance of an idea, that is, the development of intelligent singleness of purpose in the minds and wills of those who are working together as a group, so that each worker will of his own accord fit his task into the whole with skill and enthusiasm.

These two principles of co-ordination are not mutually exclusive, in fact, no enterprise is really effective without the extensive utilization of both.

Size and time are the great limiting factors in the development of co-ordination. In a small project, the problem is not difficult; the structure of authority is simple, and the central purpose is real to every worker. In a large complicated enterprise, the organization becomes involved, the lines of authority tangled, and there is danger that the workers will forget that there is any central purpose, and so devote their best energies only to their own individual advancement and advantage.

The interrelated elements of time and habit are extraordinarily important in coordination. Man is a creature of habit. When an enterprise is built up gradually from small beginnings the staff can be "broken in" step by step. And when difficulties develop, they can be ironed out, and the new method followed from that point on as a matter of habit, with the knowledge that that particular difficulty will not develop again. Routines may even be mastered by drill as they are in the army. When, however, a large new enterprise must be set up or altered overnight, then the real difficulties of co-ordination make their appearance. The factor of habit, which is thus an important foundation of co-ordination when time is available, becomes a serious handicap when time is not available, that is, when rules change. The question of co-ordination therefore must be approached with different emphasis in small and in large enterprises; in simple and in complex situations; in stable and in new or changing organizations.

Co-ordination through Organization

Organization as a way of co-ordination requires the establishment of a system of authority whereby the central purpose or objective of an enterprise is translated into reality through the combined efforts of many specialists, each working in his own field at a particular time and place.

It is clear from long experience in human affairs that such a structure of authority requires not only many men at work in many places at selected times, but also a single directing executive authority.[1] The problem of organization thus becomes the problem of building up between the executive at the center and the subdivisions of work on the periphery of an effective network of communication and control.

The following outline may serve further to define the problem:

I. First Step: Define the job to be done, such as the furnishing of pure water to all of the people and industries within a given area at the lowest possible cost;

II. Second Step: Provide a director to see that the objective is realized;

III. Third Step: Determine the nature and number of individualized and specialized work units into which the job will have to be divided. As has been seen above, this subdivision depends partly upon the size of the job (no ultimate subdivision can generally be so small as to require less than the full time of one worker) and upon the status of technological and social development at a given time;

IV. Fourth Step: Establish and perfect the structure of authority between the director and the ultimate work subdivisions.

It is this fourth step which is the central concern of the theory of organization. It is the function of this organization (IV) to enable the director (II) to co-ordinate and energize all of the subdivisions of work (III) so that the major objective (I) may be achieved efficiently.

The Span of Control

In this undertaking we are confronted at the start by the inexorable limits of human nature. Just as the hand of man can span only a limited number of notes on the piano, so the mind and will of man can span but a limited number of immediate managerial contacts. The problem has been discussed brilliantly by Graicunas in his paper included in this collection. The limit of control is partly a matter of the limits of knowledge, but even more is it a matter of the limits of time and of energy. As a result the executive of any enterprise can personally direct only a few persons. He must depend upon these to direct others, and upon them in turn to direct still others, until the last man in the organization is reached.

This condition placed upon all human organization by the limits of the span of control obviously differs in different kinds of work and in organizations of different sizes. Where the work is of a routine, repetitive, measurable and homogeneous character, one man can perhaps direct several score workers. This is particularly true when the workers are all in a single room. Where the work is diversified, qualitative, and particularly when the workers are scattered, one man can supervise only a few. This diversification, dispersion, and non-measurability is of course most evident at the very top of any organization. It follows that the limitations imposed by the span of control are most evident at the top of an organization, directly under the executive himself.

But when we seek to determine how many immediate subordinates the director of an enterprise can effectively supervise, we enter a realm of experience which has not been brought under sufficient scientific study to furnish a final answer. Sir Ian Hamilton says, "The nearer we approach the supreme head of the whole organization, the more we ought to work towards groups of three; the closer we get to the foot of the whole organization (the Infantry of the Line), the more we work towards groups of six."[2]

The British Machinery of Government Committee of 1918 arrived at the conclusion that "The Cabinet should be small in number—perferably ten or, at most, twelve."[3]

Henri Fayol said "[In France] a minister has twenty assistants, where the Administrative Theory says that a manager at the head of a big undertaking should not have more than five or six."[4]

Graham Wallas expressed the opinion that the cabinet should not be increased "beyond the number of ten or twelve at which organized oral discussion is most efficient."[5]

Léon Blum recommended for France a prime minister with a technical cabinet modelled after the British War Cabinet, which was composed of five members.[6]

It is not difficult to understand why there is this divergence of statement among authorities who are agreed on the fundamentals. It arises in part from the differences in the capacities and work habits of individual executives observed, and in part from the noncomparable character of the work covered. It would seem that insufficient attention has been devoted to three factors, first, the element of diversification of function; second, the element of time; and third, the element of space. A chief of public works can deal effectively with more direct subordinates than can the general of the army, because all of his immediate subordinates in the department of public works will be in the general field of engineering, while in the army there will be many different elements, such as communications, chemistry, aviation, ordnance, motorized service, engineering, supply, transportation, etc., each with its own technology. The element of time is also of great significance as has been indicated above. In a stable organization the chief executive can deal with more immediate subordinates than in a new or changing organization. Similarly, space influences the span of control. An organization located in one building can be supervised through more immediate subordinates than can the same organization if scattered in several cities. When scattered there is not only need for more supervision, and therefore more supervisory personnel, but also for a fewer number of contacts with the chief executive because of the increased difficulty faced by the chief executive in learning sufficient details about a far-flung organization to do an intelligent job. The failure to attach sufficient importance to these variables has served to limit the scientific validity of the statements which have been made that one man can supervise but three, or five, or eight, or twelve immediate subordinates.

These considerations do not, however, dispose of the problem. They indicate rather the need for further research. But without further research we may conclude that the chief executive of an organization can deal with only a few immediate subordinates; that this number is determined not only by the nature of the work, but also by the nature of the executive; and that the number of immediate subordinates in a large, diversified and dispersed organization must be even less than in a homogeneous and unified organization to achieve the same measure of coordination.

One Master

From the earliest times it has been recognized that nothing but confusion arises under multiple command. "A man cannot serve two masters" was adduced as a theological argument because it was already accepted as a principle of human relation in everyday life. In administration this is known as the principle of "unity of command."[7] The principle may be stated as follows: A workman subject to orders from several superiors will be confused, inefficient, and irresponsible; a workman subject to orders from but one superior may be methodical, efficient, and responsible. Unity of command thus refers to those who are commanded, not to those who issue the commands.[8]

The significance of this principle in the process of co-ordination and organization must not be lost sight of. In building a structure of co-ordination, it is often tempting to set up more than one boss for a man who is doing work which has more than one relationship. Even as great a philosopher of management as Taylor fell into this error in setting up separate foremen to deal with machinery, with materials, with speed, etc., each with the power of giving orders directly to the individual workman.[9] The rigid adherence to the principle of unity of command may have its absurdities; these are, however, unimportant in comparison with the certainty of confusion, inefficiency and irresponsibility which arise from the violation of the principle.

Technical Efficiency

There are many aspects of the problem of securing technical efficiency. Most of these do not concern us here directly. They have been treated extensively by such authorities as Taylor, Dennison, and Kimball, and their implications for general organization by Fayol, Urwick, Mooney, and Reiley. There is, however, one efficiency concept which concerns us deeply in approaching the theory of organization. It is the principle of homogeneity.

It has been observed by authorities in many fields that the efficiency of a group working together is directly related to the homogeneity of the work they are performing, of the processes they are utilizing, and of the purposes which actuate them. From top to bottom, the group must be unified. It must work together.

It follows from this (1) that any organizational structure which brings together in a single unit work divisions which are non-homogeneous in work, in technology, or in purpose will encounter the danger of friction and inefficiency; and (2) that a unit based on a given specialization cannot be given technical direction by a layman.

In the realm of government it is not difficult to find many illustrations of the unsatisfactory results of non-homogeneous administrative combinations. It is generally agreed that agricultural development and education cannot be administered by the same men who enforce pest and disease control, because the success of the former rests upon friendly co-operation and trust of the farmers, while the latter engenders resentment and suspicion. Similarly, activities like drug control established in protection of the consumer do not find appropriate homes in departments dominated by the interests of the producer. In the larger cities and in states it has been found that hospitals cannot be so well administered by the health department directly as they can be when set up independently in a separate department, or at least in a bureau with extensive autonomy, and it is generally agreed that public welfare administration and police administration require separation, as do public health administration and welfare administration, though both of these combinations may be found in successful operation under special conditions. No one would think of combining water supply and public education, or tax administration and public recreation. In every one of these cases, it will be seen that there is some element either of work to be done, or of the technology used, or of the end sought which is non-homogeneous.

Another phase of the combination of incompatible functions in the same office may be found in the common American practice of appointing unqualified laymen and politicians to technical positions or to give technical direction to highly specialized services. As Dr. Frank J. Goodnow pointed out a generation ago, we are faced here by two heterogeneous functions, "politics" and "administration," the combination of which cannot be undertaken within the structure of the administration without producing inefficiency.

Caveamus Expertum

At this point a word of caution is necessary. The application of the principle of homogeneity has its pitfalls. Every highly trained technician, particularly in the learned professions, has a profound sense of omniscience and a great desire for complete independence in the service of society. When employed by government he knows exactly what the people need better than they do themselves, and he knows how to render this service. He tends to be utterly oblivious of all other needs, because, after all, is not his particular technology the road to salvation? Any restraint applied to him is "limitation of freedom," and any criticism "springs from ignorance and jealousy." Every budget increase he secures is "in the public interest," while every increase secured elsewhere is "a sheer waste." His efforts and maneuvers to expand are "public education" and "civic organization," while similar efforts by others are "propaganda" and "politics."

Another trait of the expert is his tendency to assume knowledge and authority in fields in which he has no competence. In this particular, educators, lawyers, priests, admirals, doctors, scientists, engineers, accountants, merchants and bankers are all the same— having achieved technical competence or "success" in one field, they come to think this competence is a general quality detachable from the field and inherent in themselves. They step without embarrassment into other areas. They do not remember that the robes of authority of one kingdom confer no sovereignty in another; but that there they are merely a masquerade.

The expert knows his "stuff." Society needs him, and must have him more and more as man's technical knowledge becomes more and more extensive. But history shows us that the common man is a better judge of his own needs in the long run than any cult of experts. Kings and ruling classes, priests and prophets, soldiers and lawyers, when permitted to rule rather than serve mankind, have in the end done more to check the advance of human welfare than they have to advance it. The true place of the expert is, as A. E. said so well, "on tap, not on top." The essential validity of democracy rests upon this philosophy, for democracy is a way of government in which the common man is the final judge of what is good for him.

Efficiency is one of the things that is good for him because it makes life richer and safer. That efficiency is to be secured more and more through the use of technical specialists. These specialists have no right to ask for, and must not be given freedom from supervisory control, but in establishing that control, a government which ignores the conditions of efficiency cannot expect to achieve efficiency.

3. ORGANIZATIONAL PATTERNS

Organization Up or Down?

One of the great sources of confusion in the discussion of the theory of organization is that some authorities work and think primarily from the top down, while others work and think from the bottom up. This is perfectly natural because some authorities are interested primarily in the executive and in the problems of central management, while others are interested primarily in individual services and activities. Those who work from the top down regard the organization as a system of subdividing the enterprise under the chief executive, while those who work from the bottom up, look upon organization as a system of combining the individual units of work into aggregates which are in turn subordinated to the chief executive. It may be argued that either approach leads to a consideration of the entire problem, so that it is of no great significance which way the organization is viewed. Certainly it makes this very important practical difference: those who work from the top down must guard themselves from the danger of sacrificing the effectiveness of the individual services in their zeal to achieve a model structure at the top, while those who start from the bottom, must guard themselves from the danger of thwarting co-ordination in their eagerness to develop effective individual services.

In any practical situation the problem of organization must be approached from both top and bottom. This is particularly true in the reorganization of a going concern. May it not be that this practical necessity is likewise the sound process theoretically? In that case one would develop the plan of an organization or reorganization both from the top downward and from the bottom upward, and would reconcile the two at the center. In planning the first subdivisions under the chief executive, the principle of the limitation of the span of control must apply; in building up the first aggregates of specialized functions, the principle of homogeneity must apply. If any enterprise has such an array of functions that the first subdivisions from the top down

do not readily meet the first aggregations from the bottom up, then additional divisions and additional aggregates must be introduced, but at each further step there must be a less and less rigorous adherence to the two conflicting principles until their juncture is effected.

An interesting illustration of this problem was encountered in the plans for the reorganization of the City of New York. The Charter Commission of 1934 approached the problem with the determination to cut down the number of departments and separate activities from some 60 to a manageable number. It was equally convinced after conferences with officials from the various city departments that the number could not be brought below 25 without bringing together as "departments" activities which had nothing in common or were in actual conflict. This was still too many for effective supervision by the chief executive. As a solution it was suggested by the author that the charter provide for the subdividing of the executive by the appointment of three or four assistant mayors to whom the mayor might assign parts of his task of broad supervision and co-ordination. Under the plan the assistant mayors would bring all novel and important matters to the mayor for decision, and through continual intimate relationship know the temper of his mind on all matters, and thus be able to relieve him of great masses of detail without in any way injecting themselves into the determination of policy. Under such a plan one assistant mayor might be assigned to give general direction to agencies as diverse as police, parks, hospitals, and docks without violating the principle of homogeneity any more than is the case by bringing these activities under the mayor himself, which is after all a paramount necessity under a democratically controlled government. This is not a violation of the principle of ho-mogeneity *provided* the assistant mayors keep out of the technology of the ser-vices and devote themselves to the broad aspects of administration and co-ordi-nation, as would the mayor himself. The assistants were conceived of as parts of the mayoralty, not as parts of the service departments. That is, they represented not the apex of a structure built from the bottom up, but rather the base of a structure extended from the top down, the object of which was to multiply by four the points of effective contact be-tween the executive and the service de-partments.[10]

Organizing the Executive

The effect of the suggestion presented above is to organize and institutionalize the executive function as such so that it may be more adequate in a compli-cated situation. This is in reality not a new idea. We do not, for example, ex-pect the chief executive to write his own letters. We give him a private secretary, who is part of his office and assists him to do this part of his job. This secretary is not a part of any department, he is a subdivision of the executive himself. In just this way, though on a different plane, other phases of the job of the chief ex-ecutive may be organized.

Before doing this, however, it is nec-essary to have a clear picture of the job itself. This brings us directly to the ques-tion, "What is the work of the chief executive? What does he do?"

The answer is POSDCORB.

POSDCORB is, of course, a made-up word designed to call attention to the various functional elements of the work of a chief executive because "adminis-tration" and "management" have lost all specific content.[11] POSDCORB is made up of the initials and stands for the fol-lowing activities:

Planning, that is working out in broad outline the things that need to be done and the methods for doing them to ac-complish the purpose set for the en-terprise;

Organizing, that is the establishment of the formal structure of authority through which work subdivisions are arranged, defined and co-ordinated for the de-fined objective;

Staffing, that is the whole personnel func-tion of bringing in and training the staff and maintaining favorable conditions of work;

Directing, that is the continuous task of making decisions and embodying them in specific and general orders and in-structions and serving as the leader of the enterprise;

Co-ordinating, that is the all important duty of interrelating the various parts of the work;

Reporting, that is keeping those to whom the executive is responsible informed as to what is going on, which thus in-cludes keeping himself and his subor-dinates informed through records, re-search, and inspection;

Budgeting, with all that goes with bud-geting in the form of fiscal planning, accounting, and control.

This statement of the work of a chief executive is adapted from the functional analysis elaborated by Henri Fayol in his "Industrial and General Administra-tion." It is believed that those who know administration intimately will find in this analysis a valid and helpful pattern, into which can be fitted each of the major activities and duties of any chief exec-utive.

If these seven elements may be ac-cepted as the major duties of the chief executive, it follows that they *may* be separately organized as subdivisions of the executive. The need for such sub-division depends entirely on the size and complexity of the enterprise. In the larg-est enterprises, particularly where the chief executive is as a matter of fact unable to do the work that is thrown upon him, it may be presumed that one or more parts of POSDCORB should be suborganized.

NOTES

1. I.e., when *organization is the basis of coordination.* Wherever the central executive authority is composed of several who exercise their functions jointly by majority vote, as on a board, this is from the standpoint of organization still a "single authority"; where the central executive is in reality composed of several men acting freely and independently, then organization cannot be said to be the basis of co-ordination; it is rather the dominance of an idea and falls under the second principle stated above.

2. Sir Ian Hamilton, "The Soul and Body of an Army." Arnold, London, 1921, p. 230.

3. Great Britain. Ministry of Reconstruction. Report of the Machinery of Government Committee. H. M. Stationery Office, London, 1918, p. 5.

4. Henri Fayol, "The Administrative Theory in the State." Address before the Second International Congress of Administrative Science at Brussels, September 13, 1923. Paper IV in this collection.

5. Graham Wallas, "The Great Society." Macmillan, London and New York, 1919, p. 264.

6. Léon Blum, "La Réforme Gouvernementale." Grasset, Paris, 1918. Reprinted in 1936, p. 59.

7. Henri Fayol, "Industrial and General Administration." English translation by J. A. Coubrough. International Management Association, Geneva, 1930.

8. Fayol terms the latter "unity of direction."

9. Frederick Winslow Taylor, "Shop Management." Harper and Brothers, New York and London, 1911, p. 99.

10. This recommendation was also presented to the Thatcher Charter Commission of 1935, to which the author was a consultant. A first step in this direction was taken in Sec. 9, Chap. 1 of the new charter which provides for a deputy mayor, and for such other assistance as may be provided by ordinance.

11. See Minutes of the Princeton Conference on Training for the Public Service, 1935, p. 35. See also criticism of this analysis in Lewis Meriam, "Public Service and Special Training," University of Chicago Press, 1936, pp. 1, 2, 10 and 15, where this functional analysis is misinterpreted as a statement of qualifications for appointment.

CHAPTER II

Neoclassical Organization Theory

There is no precise definition of *neoclassical* in the context of organization theory. The general connotation is that of a theoretical perspective that revises and/or is critical of classical organization theory—particularly for minimizing issues related to the humanness of organizational members, coordination needs among administrative units, internal-external organizational relations, and organizational decision processes. The major writers of the classical school did their most significant work before World War II. The Neoclassical writers gained their reputations as organization theorists by attacking the classical writers from the end of the war through the 1950s. Because classical theories were, to a large measure, derived intellectually rather than empirically, their artificial assumptions left them vulnerable to attack. Theorists of the classical period thought that organizations should be based on universally applicable, scientific principles.

In spite of their frequent and vigorous attacks upon the classicalists, the neoclassicalists did not develop a body of theory that could adequately replace the classical school. The neoclassical school modified, added to, and somewhat extended classical theory. It attempted to blend assumptions of classical theory with concepts that subsequently were used by later organization theorists from all subsequent schools. The neoclassical school attempted to save classical theory by introducing modifications based upon research findings in the behavioral sciences. It did not have a bona fide theory of its own. To a great extent, it was an "anti-school."

Despite its limitations, the neoclassical school was very important in the historical development of organization theory. But, like a rebellious teenager, neoclassical theory could not permanently stand on its own. It was a transitional, somewhat reactionary school. Why then was the neoclassical school so important? First, because it initiated the theoretical movement away from the oversimplistic mechanistic views of the classical school. The neoclassicalists challenged some of the basic tenets of the classical school *head on*. And, remember, the classical school was the *only* school at that time. Organization theory and classical organization theory were virtually synomomous.

Secondly, in the process of challenging the classical school, the neoclassicalists raised issues and initiated theories that became central to the foundations of most of the schools that have followed. The neoclassical school was a critically important forerunner. Most serious post-1960 articles from *any* school of organization theory cite neoclassical theorists. All of the neoclassical selections that we have chosen to include in this chapter are important precursors of the human relations, "modern" structural, systems, power and politics, and organizational culture schools of organization theory.

Herbert A. Simon certainly was the most influential of the neoclassical organization theorists. He was the first to seriously challenge the tenets of classical organization theory. In his widely quoted 1946 *Public Administration Review* article, "The Proverbs of Administration" (the first selection in this chapter), Simon is devastating in his criticism of the classical approach to "general principles of management," such as those proposed by Fayol, Gulick, and others, as being inconsistent, conflicting, and inapplicable to many of the administrative situations facing managers. He suggests that such "principles" as "span of control" and "unity of command" can, with equal logic, be applied in diametrically opposed ways to the same set of circumstances. Simon concludes that the so-called principles of administration are instead proverbs of administration. The basic themes of the article later were incorporated in his landmark book, *Administrative Behavior* (1947).

One of the major themes of the neoclassical organization theorists was that organizations did not and could not exist as self-contained islands isolated from their environments. As might be expected, the first significant efforts to "open up" organizations (theoretically speaking) came from analysts whose professional identities required them to take a broad view of things—sociologists.

One such sociologist, Philip Selznick, in his 1948 *American Sociological Review* article, "Foundations of the Theory of Organization," (which is reprinted here) asserts that while it is possible to describe and design organizations in a purely rational manner, such efforts can never hope to cope with the nonrational aspects of organizational behavior. In contrast with the classical theorists, Selznick maintains that organizations consist of individuals whose goals and aspirations might not necessarily coincide with the formal goals of the organization, rather than simply a number of positions for management to control. Selznick is perhaps best known for his concept of "cooptation," which describes the process of an organization bringing and subsuming new elements into its policy-making process in order to prevent such elements from becoming a threat to the organization or its mission. The fullest account of Selznick's "cooptation" is found in *TVA and the Grass Roots*, his 1949 case study of how the Tennessee Valley Authority first gained local support for its programs.

Recently, Selznick's approach to studying organizations and his intellectual separation between the concepts of "organization" and "institution" have been lauded as models of organizational theory insightfulness and usefulness by several members of the organizational culture school. One such article, "The Role of Symbolic Management: How Can Managers Effectively Transmit Organizational Culture?" by Caren Siehl and Joanne Martin, is in our Chapter VI. Two other important examples of Selznick's continuing influence are Alan Wilkins' 1983 article "Organizational Stories as Symbols Which Control the Organization," and Joanne Martin and Melanie Powers' 1983 article "Truth or Corporate Propaganda: The Value of a Good War Story."

One of the most renowned American sociologists, Talcott Parsons, presents an approach to the analysis of formal organizations using the general theory of social systems. In his 1956 *Administrative Science Quarterly* article, "Suggestions for a Sociological Approach to the Theory of Organizations," which is reprinted here, Parsons defines an organization as a social system that focuses on the attainment of specific goals and contributes, in turn, to the accomplishment of goals of a more comprehensive system, such as the larger organization or society itself. Parsons has been widely cited by theorists from the "modern" structural school. For example, Eisenstadt (1958), Etzioni (1961), and Gordon and Babchuk (1959) use Parsons' system for classifying organizations by purposes, as the basis for their analytical typologies.

We have mentioned Philip Selznick and Talcott Parsons, and selections by each are reprinted here. Many other sociologists made major contributions to the neoclassical school and to the general development of the field of organization theory, but space prohibits including their works. For example, Melville Dalton (1950 and 1959) focused on structural frictions between line and staff units and between the central office of an organization and geographically dispersed facilities. His work drew attention to some of the universal ingredients of conflict within organizations and to problems of educating and socializing managers. William F. Whyte (1948) studied *Human Relations in the Restaurant Business* in order to understand and describe stresses resulting from interrelations and status differences in the workplace.

Perhaps the most comprehensive of the neoclassical critiques came in 1957, when James G. March and Herbert A. Simon published *Organizations*, a summary of the knowledge about organization theory/behavior that had been generated primarily by the behavioral science movement. Reprinted here is their well-known section concerning the dysfunctions of bureaucracies, "Theories of Bureaucracy." The piece begins by reviewing the models of bureaucratic behavior developed by three contemporary sociologists—Robert K. Merton (1940), Philip Selznick (1949), and Alvin W. Gouldner (1954). In each case, the sociologists found that efforts to achieve bureaucratic objectives resulted in unforeseen and dysfunctional consequences because individuals responded in personal ways to organizational stimuli. These studies helped to reveal the dynamic—as opposed to static—nature of organizations and provided a framework for further exploration of the impacts of systems on individuals and, more importantly, the impacts of individuals on systems.

As we mentioned earlier, Herbert Simon and his associates at the Carnegie Institute of Technology (now, Carnegie-Mellon University) also were major developers of theories of organizational decision making. Simon was a firm believer that decision making should be the focus of a new "administrative science." For example, Simon (1947) asserted that organizational theory is, in fact, the theory of the bounded rationality of human beings who "satisfice" because they do not have the intellectual capacity to maximize. He (1960) also drew a distinction between "programmed" and "unprogrammed" organizational decisions and highlighted the importance of the distinction for management information systems. His work on administrative science and decision making went in two major directions: first, he was a pioneer in developing the "science" of improved organizational decision making through quantitative methods such as operations research and computer technology. Secondly, and perhaps even more important, was his leadership in studying the processes by which administrative organizations make decisions. Herbert Simon's extensive contributions continue to influence the field of organization theory in the 1980s.

Two of Simon's colleagues at Carnegie Tech during the early 1960s, R. M. Cyert and James G. March, analyze the impacts of power and politics on the establishment of organizational goals in "A Behavioral Theory of Organizational Objectives" (reprinted here). This was a perspective that did not receive serious attention from organizational theorists until the mid-1970s. Cyert and March discuss the formation and activation of coalitions, and negotiations to impose coalitions' demands on the organization. The article subsequently was merged into their widely cited 1963 book, *A Behavioral Theory of the Firm*, which postulated that corporations tended to "satisfice" rather than engage in economically rational profit-maximizing behavior.

The neoclassical school played a very important role in the evolution of organization theory. Its writers provided the intellectual and empirical impetus to break the classicalists' simplistic, mechanically oriented, monopolistic dominance of the field. Neoclassicalists also paved the way—opened the door—for the soon-to-follow explosions of thinking from the human relations, "modern" structural, systems, power and politics, and organizational culture perspectives of organizations.

BIBLIOGRAPHIC REFERENCES

Cyert, R. M., & March, J. G. (1959). Behavioral theory of organizational objectives. In M. Haire (Ed.), *Modern organization theory* (pp. 76–90). New York: John Wiley & Sons.

Cyert, R. M., & March, J. G. (1963). *A behavioral theory of the firm.* Englewood Cliffs, NJ: Prentice-Hall.

Dalton, M. (1950, June). Conflicts between staff and line managerial officers. *American Sociological Review*, 342–351.

Dalton, M. (1959). *Men who manage.* New York: John Wiley & Sons.

Durkheim, E. (1947). *The division of labor in society.* George Simpson (Trans). New York: Free Press. (Original work published 1893)

Etzioni, A. (1961). *A comparative analysis of complex organizations.* New York: Free Press.

Gordon, C. W., & Babchuk, N. (1959). A typology of voluntary associations. *American Sociological Review, 24*, 22–29.

Gouldner, A. W. (1954). *Patterns of industrial democracy.* Glencoe, IL: Free Press.

March, J. G., & Simon, H. A. (1958). *Organizations.* New York: John Wiley & Sons.

Martin, J., & Powers, M. E. (1983). Truth or corporate propaganda: The value of a good war story. In L. R. Pondy, P. J. Frost, G. Morgan, & T. C. Dandridge (Eds.), *Organizational symbolism* (pp. 93–107). Greenwich, CT: JAI Press.

Merton, R. K. (1940). Bureaucratic structure and personality. *Social Forces, 18*, 560–568.

Parsons, T. (1956, June). Suggestions for a sociological approach to the theory of organizations. *Administrative Science Quarterly, 1*, 63–85.

Selznick, P. (1948). Foundations of the theory of organization. *American Sociological Review, 13*, 25–35.

Selznick, P. (1949). *TVA and the grass roots.* Berkeley, CA: University of California Press.

Siehl, C., & Martin, J. (1984). The role of symbolic management: How can managers effectively transmit organizational culture? In J. G. Hunt, D. M. Hosking, C. A. Schriesheim, & R. Stewart (Eds.), *Leaders and managers* (pp. 227–269). New York: Pergamon Press.

Simon, H. A. (1946, Winter). The proverbs of administration. *Public Administration Review, 6*, 53–67.

Simon, H. A. (1947). *Administrative behavior.* New York: Macmillan.

Simon, H. A. (1957). *Administrative behavior* (2nd ed.). New York: Macmillan.

Simon, H. A. (1960). *The new science of management decisions.* New York: Harper & Row.

Whyte, W. F. (1948). *Human relations in the restaurant business.* New York: McGraw-Hill.

Wilkins, A. A. (1983). Organizational stories as symbols which control the organization. In L. R. Pondy, P. J. Frost, G. Morgan, & T. C. Dandridge (Eds.), *Organizational symbolism* (pp. 93–107). Greenwich, CT: JAI Press.

10
The Proverbs of Administration
Herbert A. Simon

A fact about proverbs that greatly enhances their quotability is that they almost always occur in mutually contradictory pairs. "Look before you leap!"—but "He who hesitates is lost."

This is both a great convenience and a serious defect—depending on the use to which one wishes to put the proverbs in question. If it is a matter of rationalizing behavior that has already taken place or justifying action that has already been decided upon, proverbs are ideal. Since one is never at a loss to find one that will prove his point—or the precisely contradictory point, for that matter—they are a great help in persuasion, political debate, and all forms of rhetoric.

But when one seeks to use proverbs as the basis of a scientific theory, the situation is less happy. It is not that the propositions expressed by the proverbs are insufficient; it is rather that they prove too much. A scientific theory should tell what is true but also what is false. If Newton had announced to the world that particles of matter exert either an attraction or a repulsion

Source: Reprinted from *Public Administration Review* 6 (Winter 1946): 53–67. © 1946 by The American Society for Public Administration, 1225 Connecticut Avenue, N. W., Washington, D.C. All rights reserved. Footnotes renumbered.

on each other, he would not have added much to scientific knowledge. His contribution consisted in showing that an attraction was exercised and in announcing the precise law governing its operation.

Most of the propositions that make up the body of administrative theory today share, unfortunately, this defect of proverbs. For almost every principle one can find an equally plausible and acceptable contradictory principle. Although the two principles of the pair will lead to exactly opposite organizational recommendations, there is nothing in the theory to indicate which is the proper one to apply.[1]

It is the purpose of this paper to substantiate this sweeping criticism of administrative theory, and to present some suggestions—perhaps less concrete than they should be—as to how the existing dilemma can be solved.

SOME ACCEPTED ADMINISTRATIVE PRINCIPLES

Among the more common "principles" that occur in the literature of administration are these:

1. Administrative efficiency is increased by a specialization of the task among the group.
2. Administrative efficiency is increased by arranging the members of the group in a determinate hierarchy of authority.
3. Administrative efficiency is increased by limiting the span of control at any point in the hierarchy to a small number.
4. Administrative efficiency is increased by grouping the workers, for purposes of control, according to (a) purpose, (b) process, (c) clientele, or (d) place. (This is really an elaboration of the first principle but deserves separate discussion.)

Since these principles appear relatively simple and clear, it would seem that their application to concrete problems of administrative organization would be unambiguous and that their validity would be easily submitted to empirical test. Such, however, seems not to be the case. To show why it is not, each of the four principles just listed will be considered in turn.

Specialization. Administrative efficiency is supposed to increase with an increase in specialization. But is this intended to mean that *any* increase in specialization will increase efficiency? If so, which of the following alternatives is the correct application of the principle in a particular case?

1. A plan of nursing should be put into effect by which nurses will be assigned to districts and do all nursing within that district, including school examinations, visits to homes or school children, and tuberculosis nursing.
2. A functional plan of nursing should be put into effect by which different nurses will be assigned to school examinations, visits to homes of school children, and tuberculosis nursing. The present method of generalized nursing by districts impedes the development of specialized skills in the three very diverse programs.

Both of these administrative arrangements satisfy the requirement of specialization—the first provides specialization by place; the second, specialization by function. The principle of specialization is of no help at all in choosing between the two alternatives.

It appears that the simplicity of the principle of specialization is a deceptive simplicity—a simplicity which conceals fundamental ambiguities. For "specialization" is not a condition of efficient administration; it is an inevitable characteristic of all group effort, however efficient or inefficient that effort may be.

Specialization merely means that different persons are doing different things—and since it is physically impossible for two persons to be doing the same thing in the same place at the same time, two persons are always doing different things.

The real problem of administration, then, is not to "specialize," but to specialize in that particular manner and along those particular lines which will lead to administrative efficiency. But, in thus rephrasing this "principle" of administration, there has been brought clearly into the open its fundamental ambiguity: "Administrative efficiency is increased by a specialization of the task among the group in the direction which will lead to greater efficiency."

Further discussion of the choice between competing bases of specialization will be undertaken after two other principles of administration have been examined.

Unity of Command. Administrative efficiency is supposed to be enhanced by arranging the members of the organization in a determinate hierarchy of authority in order to preserve "unity of command."

Analysis of this "principle" requires a clear understanding of what is meant by the term "authority." A subordinate may be said to accept authority whenever he permits his behavior to be guided by a decision reached by another, irrespective of his own judgment as to the merits of that decision.

In one sense the principle of unity of command, like the principle of specialization, cannot be violated; for it is physically impossible for a man to obey two contradictory commands—that is what is meant by "contradictory commands." Presumably, if unity of command is a principle of administration, it must assert something more than this physical impossibility. Perhaps it asserts this: that it is undesirable to place a member of

an organization in a position where he receives orders from more than one superior. This is evidently the meaning that Gulick attaches to the principle when he says,

> The significance of this principle in the process of co-ordination and organization must not be lost sight of. In building a structure of co-ordination, it is often tempting to set up more than one boss for a man who is doing work which has more than one relationship. Even as great a philosopher of management as Taylor fell into this error in setting up separate foremen to deal with machinery, with materials, with speed, etc., each with the power of giving orders directly to the individual workman. The rigid adherence to the principle of unity of command may have its absurdities; these are, however, unimportant in comparison with the certainty of confusion, inefficiency and irresponsibility which arise from the violation of the principle.[2]

Certainly the principle of unity of command, thus interpreted, cannot be criticized for any lack of clarity or any ambiguity. The definition of authority given above should provide a clear test whether, in any concrete situation, the principle is observed. The real fault that must be found with this principle is that it is incompatible with the principle of specialization. One of the most important uses to which authority is put in organization is to bring about specialization in the work of making decisions, so that each decision is made at a point in the organization where it can be made most expertly. As a result, the use of authority permits a greater degree of expertness to be achieved in decision making than would be possible if each operative employee had himself to make all the decisions upon which his activity is predicated. The individual fireman does not decide whether to use a two-inch hose or a fire extinguisher; that is decided for him by his officers, and the decision is communicated to him in the form of a command.

However, if unity of command, in Gulick's sense, is observed, the decisions of a person at any point in the administrative hierarchy are subject to influence through only one channel of authority; and if his decisions are of a kind that require expertise in more than one field of knowledge, then advisory and informational services must be relied upon to supply those premises which lie in a field not recognized by the mode of specialization in the organization. For example, if an accountant in a school department is subordinate to an educator, and if unity of command is observed, then the finance department cannot issue direct orders to him regarding the technical, accounting aspects of his work. Similarly, the director of motor vehicles in the public works department will be unable to issue direct orders on care of motor equipment to the fire-truck driver.[3]

Gulick, in the statement quoted above, clearly indicates the difficulties to be faced if unity of command is not observed. A certain amount of irresponsibility and confusion are almost certain to ensue. But perhaps this is not too great a price to pay for the increased expertise that can be applied to decisions. What is needed to decide the issue is a principle of administration that would enable one to weigh the relative advantages of the two courses of action. But neither the principle of unity of command nor the principle of specialization is helpful in adjudicating the controversy. They merely contradict each other without indicating any procedure for resolving the contradiction.

If this were merely an academic controversy—if it were generally agreed and had been generally demonstrated that unity of command must be preserved in all cases, even with a loss in expertise—

one could assert that in case of conflict between the two principles, unity of command should prevail. But the issue is far from clear, and experts can be arranged on both sides of the controversy. On the side of unity of command there may be cited the dictums of Gulick and others.[4] On the side of specialization there are Taylor's theory of functional supervision, Macmahon and Millett's idea of "dual supervision," and the practice of technical supervision in military organization.[5]

It may be, as Gulick asserts, that the notion of Taylor and these others is an "error." If so, the evidence that it is an error has never been marshalled or published—apart from loose heuristic arguments like that quoted above. One is left with a choice between equally eminent theorists of administration and without any evidential basis for making that choice.

What evidence there is of actual administrative practice would seem to indicate that the need for specialization is to a very large degree given priority over the need for unity of command. As a matter of fact, it does not go too far to say that unity of command, in Gulick's sense, never has existed in any administrative organization. If a line officer accepts the regulations of an accounting department with regard to the procedure for making requisitions, can it be said that, in this sphere, he is not subject to the authority of the accounting department? In any actual administrative situation authority is zoned, and to maintain that this zoning does not contradict the principle of unity of command requires a very different definition of authority from that used here. This subjection of the line officer to the accounting department is no different, in principle, from Taylor's recommendation that in the matter of work programming a workman be subject to one foreman, in the matter of machine operation to another.

The principle of unity of command is perhaps more defensible if narrowed down to the following: In case two authoritative commands conflict, there should be a single determinate person whom the subordinate is expected to obey; and the sanctions of authority should be applied against the subordinate only to enforce his obedience to that one person.

If the principle of unity of command is more defensible when stated in this limited form, it also solves fewer problems. In the first place, it no longer requires, except for settling conflicts of authority, a single hierarchy of authority. Consequently, it leaves unsettled the very important question of how authority should be zoned in a particular organization (i.e., the modes of specialization) and through what channels it should be exercised. Finally, even this narrower concept of unity of command conflicts with the principle of specialization, for whenever disagreement does occur and the organization members revert to the formal lines of authority, then only those types of specialization which are represented in the hierarchy of authority can impress themselves on decisions. If the training officer of a city exercises only functional supervision over the police training officer, then in case of disagreement with the police chief, specialized knowledge of police problems will determine the outcome while specialized knowledge of training problems will be subordinated or ignored. That this actually occurs is shown by the frustration so commonly expressed by functional supervisors at their lack of authority to apply sanctions.

Span of Control. Administrative efficiency is supposed to be enhanced by limiting the number of subordinates who report directly to any one administrator to a small number—say six. This notion that the "span of control" should be narrow is confidently asserted as a third incontrovertible principle of administration. The usual common-sense arguments for restricting the span of control are familiar and need not be repeated here. What is not so generally recognized is that a contradictory proverb of administration can be stated which, though it is not so familiar as the principle of span of control, can be supported by arguments of equal plausibility. The proverb in question is the following: Administrative efficiency is enhanced by keeping at a minimum the number of organizational levels through which a matter must pass before it is acted upon.

This latter proverb is one of the fundamental criteria that guide administrative analysis in procedures simplification work. Yet in many situations the results to which this principle leads are in direct contradiction to the requirements of the principle of span of control, the principle of unity of command, and the principle of specialization. The present discussion is concerned with the first of these conflicts. To illustrate the difficulty, two alternative proposals for the organization of a small health department will be presented—one based on the restriction of span of control, the other on the limitation of number of organization levels:

1. The present organization of the department places an administrative overload on the health officer by reason of the fact that all eleven employees of the department report directly to him and the further fact that some of the staff lack adequate technical training. Consequently, venereal disease clinic treatments and other details require an undue amount of the health officer's personal attention.

It has previously been recommended that the proposed medical officer be placed in charge of the venereal disease and chest clinics and all child hygiene work. It is further recommended that one of the inspectors be designated chief inspector and placed in charge of all the department's inspectional activities and that one of the nurses be designated as head nurse. This will relieve the health commissioner of considerable detail and will leave him greater freedom to plan and supervise the health program as a whole, to conduct health education, and to coordinate the work of the department with that of other community agencies. If the department were thus organized, the effectiveness of all employees could be substantially increased.

2. The present organization of the department leads to inefficiency and excessive red tape by reason of the fact that an unnecessary supervisory level intervenes between the health officer and the operative employees, and that those four of the twelve employees who are best trained technically are engaged largely in "overhead" administrative duties. Consequently, unnecessary delays occur in securing the approval of the health officer on matters requiring his attention, and too many matters require review and re-review.

The medical officer should be left in charge of the venereal disease and chest clinics and child hygiene work. It is recommended, however, that the position of chief inspector and head nurse be abolished and that the employees now filling these positions perform regular inspectional and nursing duties. The details of work scheduling now handled by these two employees can be taken care of more economically by the secretary to the health officer, and, since broader matters of policy have, in any event, always required the personal attention of the health officer, the abolition of these two positions will eliminate a wholly unnecessary step in review, will allow an expansion of inspectional and nursing services, and will permit at least a beginning to be made in the recommended program of health education. The number of persons reporting directly to the health officer will be increased to nine, but since there are few matters requiring the coordination of these employees, other than the work schedules and policy questions referred to above, this change will not materially increase his work load.

The dilemma is this: in a large organization with complex interrelations between members, a restricted span of control inevitably produces excessive red tape, for each contact between organization members must be carried upward until a common superior is found. If the organization is at all large, this will involve carrying all such matters upward through several levels of officials for decision and then downward again in the form of orders and instructions—a cumbersome and time-consuming process.

The alternative is to increase the number of persons who are under the command of each officer, so that the pyramid will come more rapidly to a peak, with fewer intervening levels. But this, too, leads to difficulty, for if an officer is required to supervise too many employees, his control over them is weakened.

If it is granted, then, that both the increase and the decrease in span of control has some undesirable consequences, what is the optimum point? Proponents of a restricted span of control have suggested three, five, even eleven, as suitable numbers, but nowhere have they explained the reasoning which led them to the particular number they selected. The principle as stated casts no light on this very crucial question. One is reminded of current arguments about the proper size of the national debt.

Organization by Purpose, Process, Clientele, Place. Administrative efficiency is supposed to be increased by grouping workers according to (a) purpose, (b) process, (c) clientele, or (d) place. But from the discussion of specialization it is clear that this principle is internally inconsistent; for purpose, process, clientele, and place are competing bases of organization, and at any given point of division the advantages of three must be sacrificed to secure the advantages of the fourth. If the major departments of a city, for example, are organized on the basis of major purpose, then it follows that all the physicians, all the lawyers, all the engineers, all the statisticians will not be located in a single department exclusively composed of members of their profession but will be distributed among the various city departments needing their services. The advantages of organization by process will thereby be partly lost.

Some of these advantages can be regained by organizing on the basis of process *within* the major departments. Thus there may be an engineering bureau within the public works department, or the board of education may have a school health service as a major division of its work. Similarly, within smaller units there may be division by area or by clientele: e.g., a fire department will have separate companies located throughout the city, while a welfare department may have intake and case work agencies in various locations. Again, however, these major types of specialization cannot be simultaneously achieved, for at any point in the organization it must be decided whether specialization at the next level will be accomplished by distinction of major purpose, major process, clientele, or area.

The conflict may be illustrated by showing how the principle of specialization according to purpose would lead to a different result from specialization according to clientele in the organization of a health department.

1. Public health administration consists of the following activities for the prevention of disease and the maintenance of healthful conditions: (1) vital statistics; (2) child hygiene—prenatal, maternity, postnatal, infant, preschool, and school health programs; (3) communicable disease control; (4) inspection of milk, foods, and drugs; (5) sanitary inspection; (6) laboratory service; (7) health education.

One of the handicaps under which the health department labors is the fact that the department has no control over school health, that being an activity of the county board of education, and there is little or no coordination between that highly important part of the community health program and the balance of the program which is conducted by the city-county health unit. It is recommended that the city and county open negotiations with the board of eduction for the transfer of all school health work and the appropriation therefor to the joint health unit. . . .

2. To the modern school department is entrusted the care of children during almost the entire period that they are absent from the parental home. It has three principal responsibilities toward them: (1) to provide for their education in useful skills and knowledge and in character; (2) to provide them with wholesome play activities outside school hours; (3) to care for their health and to assure the attainment of minimum standards of nutrition.

One of the handicaps under which the school board labors is the fact that, except for school lunches, the board has no control over child health and nutrition, and there is little or no coordination between that highly important part of the child development program and the balance of the program which is conducted by the board of education. It is recommended that the city and county open negotiations for the transfer of all health work for children of school age to the board of education.

Here again is posed the dilemma of choosing between alternative, equally plausible, administrative principles. But this is not the only difficulty in the present case, for a closer study of the situation shows there are fundamental ambiguities in the meanings of the key terms—"purpose," "process," "clientele," and "place."

"Purpose" may be roughly defined as the objective or end for which an activity is carried on; "process" as a means for accomplishing a purpose. Processes, then, are carried on in order to achieve purposes. But purposes themselves may generally be arranged in some sort of hierarchy. A typist moves her fingers in order to type; types in order to reproduce a letter, reproduces a letter in order that an inquiry may be answered. Writing a letter is then the purpose for which the typing is performed; while writing a letter is also the process whereby the purpose of replying to an inquiry is achieved. It follows that the same activity may be described as purpose or as process.

This ambiguity is easily illustrated for the case of an administrative organization. A health department conceived as a unit whose task it is to care for the health of the community is a purpose organization; the same department conceived as a unit which makes use of the medical arts to carry on its work is a process organization. In the same way, an education department may be viewed as a purpose (to educate) organization, or a clientele (children) organization; the forest service as a purpose (forest conservation), process (forest management), clientele (lumbermen and cattlemen utilizing public forests), or area (publicly owned forest lands) organization. When concrete illustrations of this sort are selected, the lines of demarcation between these categories become very hazy and unclear indeed.

"Organization by major purpose," says Gulick, " . . . serves to bring together in a single large department all of those who are at work endeavoring to render a particular service."[6] But what is a particular service? Is fire protection a single purpose, or is it merely a part of the purpose of public safety?—or is it a combination of purposes including fire prevention and fire fighting? It must be concluded that there is no such thing as a purpose, or a unifunctional (single-purpose) organization. What is to be considered a single function depends entirely on language and techniques.[7] If the English language has a comprehensive term which covers both of two subpurposes it is natural to think of the two together as a single purpose. If such a term is lacking, the two subpurposes become purposes in their own right. On the other hand, a single activity may contribute to several objectives, but since they are technically (procedurally) inseparable, the activity is considered a single function or purpose.

The fact, mentioned previously, that purposes form a hierarchy, each subpurpose contributing to some more final and comprehensive end, helps to make clear the relation between purpose and process. "Organization by major process," says Gulick, ". . . tends to bring together in a single department all of those who are at work making use of a given special skill or technology, or are members of a given profession."[8] Consider a simple skill of this kind—typing. Typing is a skill which brings about a means-end coordination of muscular movements, but at a very low level in the means-end hierarchy. The content of the typewritten letter is indifferent to the skill that produces it. The skill consists merely in the ability to hit the letter "t" quickly whenever the letter "t" is required by the content and to hit the letter "a" whenever the letter "a" is required by the content.

There is, then, no essential difference between a "purpose" and a "process," but only a distinction of degree. A "process" is an activity whose immediate purpose is at a low level in the hierarchy of means and ends, while a "purpose" is a collection of activities whose orienting value or aim is at a high level in the means-end hierarchy.

Next consider "clientele" and "place" as bases of organization. These categories are really not separate from purpose, but a part of it. A complete statement of the purpose of a fire department would have to include the area served by it: "to reduce fires losses on property in the city of X." Objectives of an administrative organization are phrased in terms of a service to be provided and an area for which it is provided. Usually, the term "purpose" is meant to refer only to the first element, but the second is just as legitimately an aspect of purpose. Area of service, of course, may be a specified clientele quite as well as a geographical area. In the case of an agency which works on "shifts," time will be a third dimension of purpose—to provide a given service in a given area (or to a given clientele) during a given time period.

With this clarification of terminology, the next task is to reconsider the problem of specializing the work of an organization. It is no longer legitimate to speak of a "purpose" organization, a "process" organization, a "clientele" organization, or an "area" organization. The same unit might fall into any one of these four categories, depending on the nature of the larger organizational unit of which it was a part. A unit providing public health and medical services for school-age children in Multnomah County might be considered (1) an "area" organization if it were part of a unit providing the same service for the

state of Oregon; (2) a "clientele" organization if it were part of a unit providing similar services for children of all ages; (3) a "purpose" or a "process" organization (it would be impossible to say which) if it were part of an education department.

It is incorrect to say that Bureau A is a process bureau; the correct statement is that Bureau A is a process bureau *within* Department X.[9] This latter statement would mean that Bureau A incorporates all the processes of a certain kind in Department X, without reference to any special subpurposes, subareas, or subclientele of Department X. Now it is conceivable that a particular unit might incorporate all processes of a certain kind but that these processes might relate to only certain particular subpurposes of the department purpose. In this case, which corresponds to the health unit in an education department mentioned above, the unit would be specialized by both purpose and process. The health unit would be the only one in the education department using the medical art (process) and concerned with health (subpurpose).

Even when the problem is solved of proper usage for the terms "purpose," "process," "clientele," and "area," the principles of administration give no guide as to which of these four competing bases of specialization is applicable in any particular situation. The British Machinery of Government Committee had no doubts about the matter. It considered purpose and clientele as the two possible bases of organization and put its faith entirely in the former. Others have had equal assurance in choosing between purpose and process. The reasoning which leads to these unequivocal conclusions leaves something to be desired. The Machinery of Government Committee gives this sole argument for its choice:

Now the inevitable outcome of this method of organization [by clientele] is a tendency to Lilliputian administration. It is impossible that the specialized service which each Department has to render to the community can be of as high a standard when its work is at the same time limited to a particular class of persons and extended to every variety of provision for them, as when the Department concentrates itself on the provision of the particular service only by whomsoever required, and looks beyond the interest of comparatively small classes.[10]

The faults in this analysis are obvious. First, there is no attempt to determine how a service is to be recognized. Second, there is a bald assumption, absolutely without proof, that a child health unit, for example, in a department of child welfare could not offer services of "as high a standard" as the same unit if it were located in a department of health. Just how the shifting of the unit from one department to another would improve or damage the quality of its work is not explained. Third, no basis is set forth for adjudicating the competing claims of purpose and process—the two are merged in the ambiguous term "service." It is not necessary here to decide whether the committee was right or wrong in its recommendation; the important point is that the recommendation represented a choice, without any apparent logical or empirical grounds, between contradictory principles of administration.

Even more remarkable illustrations of illogic can be found in most discussions of purpose versus process. They would be too ridiculous to cite if they were not commonly used in serious political and administrative debate.

For instance, where should agricultural education come: in the Ministry of Education, or of Agriculture? That depends on whether we want to see the best farming taught, though possibly by old methods, or a possibly out-of-date style of farming, taught in the most modern and compelling manner. The question answers itself.[11]

But does the question really answer itself? Suppose a bureau of agricultural education were set up, headed, for example, by a man who had had extensive experience in agricultural research or as administrator of an agricultural school, and staffed by men of similarly appropriate background. What reason is there to believe that if attached to a Ministry of Education they would teach old-fashioned farming by new-fashioned methods, while if attached to a Ministry of Agriculture they would teach new-fashioned farming by old-fashioned methods? The administrative problem of such a bureau would be to teach new-fashioned farming by new-fashioned methods, and it is a little difficult to see how the departmental location of the unit would affect this result. "The question answers itself" only if one has a rather mystical faith in the potency of bureau-shuffling as a means for redirecting the activities of an agency.

These contradictions and competitions have received increasing attention from students of administration during the past few years. For example, Gulick, Wallace, and Benson have stated certain advantages and disadvantages of the several modes of specialization, and have considered the conditions under which one or the other mode might best be adopted.[12] All this analysis has been at a theoretical level—in the sense that data have not been employed to demonstrate the superior effectiveness claimed for the different modes. But though theoretical, the analysis has lacked a theory. Since no comprehensive framework has been constructed within which the discussion could take place, the analysis has tended either to the logical one-sidedness which characterizes the examples quoted above or to inconclusiveness.

The Impasse of Administrative Theory. The four "principles of administration" that were set forth at the beginning of this paper have now been subjected to critical analysis. None of the four survived in very good shape, for in each case there was found, instead of an unequivocal principle, a set of two or more mutually incompatible principles apparently equally applicable to the administrative situation.

Moreover, the reader will see that the very same objections can be urged against the customary discussions of "centralization" versus "decentralization," which usually conclude, in effect, that "on the one hand, centralization of decision-making functions is desirable; on the other hand, there are definite advantages in decentralization."

Can anything be salvaged which will be useful in the construction of an administrative theory? As a matter of fact, almost everything can be salvaged. The difficulty has arisen from treating as "principles of administration" what are really only criteria for describing and diagnosing administrative situations. Closet space is certainly an important item in the design of a successful house; yet a house designed entirely with a view to securing a maximum of closet space—all other considerations being forgotten—would be considered, to say the least, somewhat unbalanced. Similarly, unity of command, specialization by purpose, and decentralization are all items to be considered in the design of an efficient administrative organization. No single one of these items is of sufficient importance to suffice as a guiding principle for the administrative analyst. In the design of administrative organizations, as in their operation, overall efficiency must be the guiding criterion.

Mutually incompatible advantages must be balanced against each other, just as an architect weighs the advantages of additional closet space against the advantages of a larger living room.

This position, if it is a valid one, constitutes an indictment of much current writing about administrative matters. As the examples cited in this chapter amply demonstrate, much administrative analysis proceeds by selecting a single criterion and applying it to an administrative situation to reach a recommendation; while the fact that equally valid, but contradictory, criteria exist which could be applied with equal reason, but with a different result, is conveniently ignored. A valid approach to the study of administration requires that *all* the relevant diagnostic criteria be identified; that each administrative situation be analyzed in terms of the entire set of criteria; and that research be instituted to determine how weights can be assigned to the several criteria when they are, as they usually will be, mutually incompatible.

AN APPROACH TO ADMINISTRATIVE THEORY

This program needs to be considered step by step. First, what is included in the description of administrative situations for purposes of such an analysis? Second, how can weights be assigned to the various criteria to give them their proper place in the total picture?

The Description of Administrative Situations. Before a science can develop principles, it must possess concepts. Before a law of gravitation could be formulated, it was necessary to have the notions of "acceleration" and "weight." The first task of administrative theory is to develop a set of concepts that will permit the description in terms relevant to the theory of administrative situations. These concepts, to be scientifically useful, must be operational; that is, their meanings must correspond to empirically observable facts or situations. The definition of *authority* given earlier in this paper is an example of an operational definition.

What is a scientifically relevant description of an organization? It is a description that, so far as possible, designates for each person in the organization what decisions that person makes and the influences to which he is subject in making each of these decisions. Current descriptions of administrative organizations fall far short of this standard. For the most part, they confine themselves to the allocation of *functions* and the formal structure of *authority.* They give little attention to the other types of organizational influence or to the system of communications.[13]

What does it mean, for example to say: "The department is made up of three bureaus. The first has the function of _____, the second the function of _____, and the third the function of _____?" What can be learned from such a description about the workability of the organizational arrangement? Very little, indeed. For from the description there is obtained no idea of the degree to which decisions are centralized at the bureau level or at the departmental level. No notion is given as to the extent to which the (presumably unlimited) authority of the department over the bureau is actually exercised or by what mechanisms. There is no indication of the extent to which systems of communication assist the coordination of the three bureaus or, for that matter, to what extent coordination is required by the nature of their work. There is no description of the kinds of training the members of the bureau have undergone or of the extent to which this training permits decentralization at the bureau

level. In sum, a description of administrative organizations in terms almost exclusively of functions and lines of authority is completely inadequate for purposes of administrative analysis.

Consider the term "centralization." How is it determined whether the operations of a particular organization are "centralized" or "decentralized"? Does the fact that field offices exist prove anything about decentralization? Might not the same decentralization take place in the bureaus of a centrally located office? A realistic analysis of centralization must include a study of the allocation of decisions in the organization and the methods of influence that are employed by the higher levels to affect the decisions at the lower levels. Such an analysis would reveal a much more complex picture of the decision-making process than any enumeration of the geographical locations of organizational units at the different levels.

Administrative description suffers currently from superficiality, oversimplification, lack of realism. It has confined itself too closely to the mechanism of authority and has failed to bring within its orbit the other, equally important, modes of influence on organizational behavior. It has refused to undertake the tiresome task of studying the actual allocation of decision-making functions. It has been satisfied to speak of "authority," "centralization," "span of control," "function," without seeking operational definitions of these terms. Until administrative description reaches a higher level of sophistication, there is little reason to hope that rapid progress will be made toward the identification and verification of valid administrative principles.

Does this mean that a purely formal description of an administrative organization is impossible—that a relevant description must include an account of the content of the organization's decisions? This is a question that is almost impossible to answer in the present state of knowledge of administrative theory. One thing seems certain: content plays a greater role in the application of administrative principles than is allowed for in the formal administrative theory of the present time. This is a fact that is beginning to be recognized in the literature of administration. If one examines the chain of publications extending from Mooney and Reilley, through Gulick and the President's Committee controversy, to Schuyler Wallace and Benson, he sees a steady shift of emphasis from the "principles of administration" themselves to a study of the *conditions* under which competing principles are respectively applicable. Recent publications seldom say that "organization should be by purpose," but rather that "under such and such conditions purpose organization is desirable." It is to these conditions which underlie the application of the proverbs of administration that administrative theory and analysis must turn in their search for really valid principles to replace the proverbs.

The Diagnosis of Administrative Situations. Before any positive suggestions can be made, it is necessary to digress a bit and to consider more closely the exact nature of the propositions of administrative theory. The theory of administration is concerned with how an organization should be constructed and operated in order to accomplish its work efficiently. A fundamental principle of administration, which follows almost immediately from the rational character of "good" administration, is that among several alternatives involving the same expenditure that one should always be selected which leads to the greatest accomplishment of administrative objectives; and among several alternatives that lead to the same accomplishment that

one should be selected which involves the least expenditure. Since this "principle of efficiency" is characteristic of any activity that attempts rationally to maximize the attainment of certain ends with the use of scarce means, it is as characteristic of economic theory as it is of administrative theory. The "administrative man" takes his place alongside the classical "economic man."[14]

Actually, the "principle" of efficiency should be considered a definition rather than a principle: it is a definition of what is meant by "good" or "correct" administrative behavior. It does not tell *how* accomplishments are to be maximized, but merely states that this maximization is the aim of administrative activity, and that administrative theory must disclose under what conditions the maximization takes place.

Now what are the factors that determine the level of efficiency which is achieved by an administrative organization? It is not possible to make an exhaustive list of these but the principal categories can be enumerated. Perhaps the simplest method of approach is to consider the single member of the administrative organization and ask what the limits are to the quantity and quality of his output. These limits include (*a*) limits on his ability to perform and (*b*) limits on his ability to make correct decisions. To the extent that these limits are removed, the administrative organization approaches its goal of high efficiency. Two persons, given the same skills, the same objectives and values, the same knowledge and information, can rationally decide only upon the same course of action. Hence, administrative theory must be interested in the factors that will determine with what skills, values, and knowledge the organization member undertakes his work. These are the "limits" to rationality with which the principles of administration must deal.

On one side, the individual is limited by those skills, habits, and reflexes which are no longer in the realm of the conscious. His performance, for example, may be limited by his manual dexterity or his reaction time or his strength. His decision-making processes may be limited by the speed of his mental processes, his skill in elementary arithmetic, and so forth. In this area, the principles of administration must be concerned with the physiology of the human body and with the laws of skill-training and of habit. This is the field that has been most successfully cultivated by the followers of Taylor and in which has been developed time-and-motion study and the therblig.

On a second side, the individual is limited by his values and those conceptions of purpose which influence him in making his decisions. If his loyalty to the organization is high, his decisions may evidence sincere acceptance of the objectives set for the organization; if that loyalty is lacking, personal motives may interfere with his administrative efficiency. If his loyalties are attached to the bureau by which he is employed, he may sometimes make decisions that are inimical to the larger unit of which the bureau is a part. In this area the principles of administration must be concerned with the determinants of loyalty and morale, with leadership and initiative, and with the influences that determine where the individual's organizational loyalties will be attached.

On a third side, the individual is limited by the extent of his knowledge of things relevant to his job. This applies both to the basic knowledge required in decision-making—a bridge designer must know the fundamentals of mechanics—and to the information that is required to make his decisions appropriate to the given situation. In this area, administrative theory is concerned with such fundamental questions as these: What are the limits on the mass of knowledge that human minds can accumulate and apply? How rapidly can knowledge be assimilated? How is specialization in the administrative organization to be related to the specializations of knowledge that are prevalent in the community's occupational structure? How is the system of communication to channel knowledge and information to the appropriate decision-points? What types of knowledge can, and what types cannot, be easily transmitted? How is the need for intercommunication of information affected by the modes of specialization in the organization? This is perhaps the *terra incognita* of administrative theory, and undoubtedly its careful exploration will cast great light on the proper application of the proverbs of administration.

Perhaps this triangle of limits does not completely bound the area of rationality, and other sides need to be added to the figure. In any case, this enumeration will serve to indicate the kinds of considerations that must go into the construction of valid and noncontradictory principles of administration.

An important fact to be kept in mind is that the limits of rationality are variable limits. Most important of all, consciousness of the limits may in itself alter them. Suppose it were discovered in a particular organization, for example, that organizational loyalties attached to small units had frequently led to a harmful degree of intraorganizational competition. Then, a program which trained members of the organization to be conscious of their loyalties, and to subordinate loyalties to the smaller group to those of the large, might lead to a very considerable alteration of the limits in that organization.[15]

A related point is that the term "rational behavior" as employed here, refers to rationality when that behavior is evaluated in terms of the objectives of the larger organization; for, as just pointed out, the difference in direction of the individual's aims from those of the larger organization is just one of those elements of nonrationality with which the theory must deal.

A final observation is that, since administrative theory is concerned with the nonrational limits of the rational, it follows that the larger the area in which rationality has been achieved the less important is the exact form of the administrative organization. For example, the function of plan preparation, or design, if it results in a written plan that can be communicated interpersonally without difficulty, can be located almost anywhere in the organization without affecting results. All that is needed is a procedure whereby the plan can be given authoritative status, and this can be provided in a number of ways. A discussion, then, of the proper location for a planning or designing unit is apt to be highly inconclusive and is apt to hinge on the personalities in the organization and their relative enthusiasm, or lack of it, toward the planning function rather than upon any abstract principles of good administration.[16]

On the other hand, when factors of communication or faiths or loyalty are crucial to the making of a decision, the location of the decision in the organization is of great importance. The method of allocating decisions in the army, for instance, automatically provides (at least in the period prior to the actual battle) that each decision will be made where the knowledge is available for coordinating it with other decisions.

Assigning Weights to the Criteria. A first step, then, in the overhauling of the proverbs of administration is to develop a vocabulary, along the lines just suggested, for the description of administrative organization. A second step, which has also been outlined, is to study the limits of rationality in order to develop a complete and comprehensive enumeration of the criteria that must be weighed in evaluating an administrative organization. The current proverbs represent only a fragmentary and unsystematized portion of these criteria.

When these two tasks have been carried out, it remains to assign weights to the criteria. Since the criteria, or "proverbs," are often mutually competitive or contradictory, it is not sufficient merely to identify them. Merely to know, for example, that a specified change in organization will reduce the span of control is not enough to justify the change. This gain must be balanced against the possible resulting loss of contact between the higher and lower ranks of the hierarchy.

Hence, administrative theory must also be concerned with the question of the weights that are to be applied to these criteria—to the problems of their relative importance in any concrete situation. This question is not one that can be solved in a vacuum. Arm-chair philosophizing about administration—of which the present paper is an example—has gone about as far as it can profitably go in this particular direction. What is needed now is empirical research and experimentation to determine the relative desirability of alternative administrative arrangements.

The methodological framework for this research is already at hand in the principle of efficiency. If an administrative organization whose activities are susceptible to objective evaluation be subjected to study, then the actual change in accomplishment that results from modifying administrative arrangements in these organizations can be observed and analyzed.

There are two indispensable conditions to successful research along these lines. First, it is necessary that the objectives of the administrative organization under study be defined in concrete terms so that results, expressed in terms of these objectives, can be accurately measured. Second, it is necessary that sufficient experimental control be exercised to make possible the isolation of the particular effect under study from other disturbing factors that might be operating on the organization at the same time.

These two conditions have seldom been even partially fulfilled in so-called "administrative experiments." The mere fact that a legislature passes a law creating an administrative agency, that the agency operates for five years, that the agency is finally abolished, and that a historical study is then made of the agency's operations is not sufficient to make of that agency's history an "administrative experiment." Modern American legislation is full of such "experiments" which furnish orators in neighboring states with abundant ammunition when similar issues arise in their bailiwicks, but which provide the scientific investigator with little or nothing in the way of objective evidence, one way or the other.

In the literature of administration, there are only a handful of research studies that satisfy these fundamental conditions of methodology—and these are, for the most part, on the periphery of the problem of organization. There are, first of all, the studies of the Taylor group which sought to determine the technological conditions of efficiency. Perhaps none of these is a better example of the painstaking methods of science than Taylor's own studies of the cutting of metals.[17]

Studies dealing with the human and social aspects of administration are even rarer than the technological studies. Among the more important are the whole series of studies on fatigue, starting in Great Britain during World War I and culminating in the Westinghouse experiments.[18]

In the field of public administration, almost the sole example of such experimentation is the series of studies that have been conducted in the public welfare field to determine the proper case loads for social workers.[19]

Because, apart from these scattered examples, studies of administrative agencies have been carried out without benefit of control or of objective measurements of results, they have had to depend for their recommendations and conclusions upon *a priori* reasoning proceeding from "principles of administration." The reasons have already been stated why the "principles" derived in this way cannot be more than "proverbs."

Perhaps the program outlined here will appear an ambitious or even a quixotic one. There should certainly be no illusions, in undertaking it, as to the length and deviousness of the path. It is hard to see, however, what alternative remains open. Certainly neither the practitioner of administration nor the theoretician can be satisfied with the poor analytic tools that the proverbs provide him. Nor is there any reason to believe that a less drastic reconversion than that outlined here will rebuild those tools to usefulness.

It may be objected that administration cannot aspire to be a "science"; that by the nature of its subject it cannot be more than an "art." Whether true or false, this objection is irrelevant to the present discussion. The question of how "exact" the principles of administration can be made is one that only experience can answer. But as to whether they should be logical or illogical there can be no debate. Even an "art" cannot be founded on proverbs.

NOTES

1. Lest it be thought that this deficiency is peculiar to the science—or "art"—of administration, it should be pointed out that the same trouble is

shared by most Freudian psychological theories, as well as by some sociological theories.

2. Luther Gulick, "Notes on the Theory of Organization," in Luther Gulick and L. Urwick (eds.), *Papers on the Science of Administration* (Institute of Public Administration, Columbia University, 1937), p. 9.

3. This point is discussed in Herbert A. Simon, "Decision-Making and Administrative Organization," 4 *Public Administration Review* 20–21 (Winter, 1944).

4. Gulick, "Notes on the Theory of Organization," p. 9; L. D. White, *Introduction to the Study of Public Administration* (Macmillan Co., 1939), p. 45.

5. Frederick W. Taylor, *Shop Management* (Harper & Bros., 1911), p. 99; Macmahon, Millett, and Ogden, *The Administration of Federal Work Relief* (Public Administration Service, 1941), pp. 265–68; and L. Urwick, who describes British army practice in "Organization as a Technical Problem," Gulick and Urwick (eds.), *op. cit.*, pp. 67–69.

6. *Op. cit.*, p. 21.

7. If this is correct, then any attempt to prove that certain activities belong in a single department because they relate to a single purpose is doomed to fail. See, for example, John M. Gaus and Leon Wolcott, *Public Administration and the U.S. Department of Agriculture* (Public Administration Service, 1940).

8. *Op. cit.*, p. 23.

9. This distinction is implicit in most of Gulick's analysis of specialization. However, since he cites as examples single departments within a city, and since he usually speaks of "grouping activities" rather than "dividing work," the relative character of these categories is not always apparent in this discussion (*op. cit.*, pp. 15–30).

10. *Report of the Machinery of Government Committee* (H. M. Stationery Office, 1918).

11. Sir Charles Harris, "Decentralization," 3 *Journal of Public Administration* 117–33 (April, 1925).

12. Gulick, "Notes on the Theory of Organization," pp. 21–30; Schuyler Wallace, *Federal Departmentalization* (Columbia University Press, 1941); George C. S. Benson, "International Administrative Organization," 1 *Public Administration Review* 473–86 (Autumn, 1941).

13. The monograph by Macmahon, Millett, and Ogden, *op. cit.*, perhaps approaches nearer than any other published administrative study to the

sophistication required in administrative description. See, for example, the discussion on pp. 233–36 of headquarters-field relationships.

14. For an elaboration of the principle of efficiency and its place in administrative theory see Clarence E. Ridley and Herbert A. Simon, *Measuring Municipal Activities* (International City Managers' Association, 2nd ed., 1943), particularly Chapter 1 and the preface to the second edition.

15. For an example of the use of such training, see Herbert A. Simon and William Divine, "Controlling Human Factors in an Administrative Experiment," 1 *Public Administration Review* 487–92 (Autumn, 1941).

16. See, for instance, Robert A. Walker, *The Planning Function in Urban Government* (University of Chicago Press, 1941), pp. 166–75. Walker makes out a strong case for attaching the planning agency to the chief executive. But he rests his entire case on the rather slender reed that "as long as the planning agency is outside the governmental structure . . . planning will tend to encounter resistance from public officials as an invasion of their responsibility and jurisdiction." This "resistance" is precisely the type of nonrational loyalty which has been referred to previously, and which is certainly a variable.

17. F. W. Taylor, *On the Art of Cutting Metals* (American Society of Mechanical Engineers, 1907).

18. Great Britain, Ministry of Munitions, Health of Munitions Workers Committee, *Final Report* (H. M. Stationery Office, 1918); F. J. Roethlisberger and William J. Dickson, *Management and the Worker* (Harvard University Press, 1939).

19. Ellery F. Reed, *An Experiment in Reducing the Cost of Relief* (American Public Welfare Administration, 1937); Rebecca Staman, "What Is the Most Economical Case Load in Public Relief Administration?" 4 *Social Work Technique* 117–21 (May-June, 1938); Chicago Relief Administration, *Adequate Staff Brings Economy* (American Public Welfare Association, 1939); Constance Hastings and Saya S. Schwartz, *Size of Visitor's Caseload as a Factor in Efficient Administration of Public Assistance* (Philadelphia County Board of Assistance, 1939); Simon et al., *Determining Work Loads for Professional Staff in a Public Welfare Agency* (Bureau of Public Administration, University of California, 1941).

11
Foundations of the Theory of Organization
Philip Selznick

Trades unions, governments, business corporations, political parties, and the like are formal structures in the sense that they represent rationally ordered instruments for the achievement of stated goals. "Organization," we are told, "is the arrangement of personnel for facilitating the accomplishment of some agreed purpose through the allocation of functions and responsibilities."[1] Or, defined more generally, formal organization is "a system of consciously coordinated activities or forces of two or more persons."[2] Viewed in this light, formal organization is the structural expression of rational action. The mobilization of technical and managerial skills requires a pattern of coordination, a systematic ordering of positions and duties which defines a chain of command and makes possible the administrative integration of specialized functions. In this context *delegation* is the primordial organizational act, a precarious venture which requires the continuous elaboration of formal mechanisms of coordination and control. The security of all participants, and of the system as a whole, generates a persistent pressure for the institutionalization of relationships, which are thus removed from the uncertainties of individual fealty or sentiment. Moreover, it is necessary for the relations within the structure to be determined in such a way that individuals will be interchangeable and the organization will thus

be free of dependence upon personal qualities.[3] In this way, the formal structure becomes subject to calculable manipulation, an instrument of rational action.

But as we inspect these formal structures we begin to see that they never succeed in conquering the nonrational dimensions of organizational behavior. The latter remain at once indispensable to the continued existence of the system of coordination and at the same time the source of friction, dilemma, doubt, and ruin. This fundamental paradox arises from the fact that rational action systems are inescapably imbedded in an institutional matrix, in two significant senses: (1) the action system—or the formal structure of delegation and control which is its organizational expression—is itself only an aspect of a concrete social structure made up of individuals who may interact as *wholes*, not simply in terms of their formal roles within the system; (2) the formal system, and the social structure within which it finds concrete existence, are alike subject to the pressure of an institutional environment to which some overall adjustment must be made. The formal administrative design can never adequately or fully reflect the concrete organization to which it refers, for the obvious reason that no abstract plan or pattern can—or may, if it is to be useful—exhaustively describe an empirical

Source: From *American Sociological Review* 13 (1948): 25–35. Copyright © 1948 American Sociological Association. Reprinted by permission.

totality. At the same time, that which is not included in the abstract design (as reflected, for example, in a staff-and-line organization chart) is vitally relevant to the maintenance and development of the formal system itself.

Organization may be viewed from two standpoints which are analytically distinct but which are empirically united in a context of reciprocal consequences. On the one hand, any concrete organizational system is an economy; at the same time, it is an adaptive social structure. Considered as an economy, organization is a system of relationships which define the availability of scarce resources and which may be manipulated in terms of efficiency *and* effectiveness. It is the economic aspect of organization which commands the attention of management technicians and, for the most part, students of public as well as private administration.[4] Such problems as the span of executive control, the role of staff or auxiliary agencies, the relation of headquarters to field offices, and the relative merits of single or multiple executive boards are typical concerns of the science of administration. The coordinative scalar, and functional principles, as elements of the theory of organization, are products of the attempt to explicate the most general features of organization as a "technical problem" or, in our terms, as an economy.

Organization as an economy is, however, necessarily conditioned by the organic states of the concrete structure, outside of the systematics of delegation and control. This becomes especially evident as the attention of leadership is directed toward such problems as the legitimacy of authority and the dynamics of persuasion. It is recognized implicitly in action and explicitly in the work of a number of students that the possibility of manipulating the system of coordination depends on the extent to which

that system is operating within an environment of effective inducement to individual participants and of conditions in which the stability of authority is assured. This is in a sense the fundamental thesis of Barnard's remarkable study, *The Functions of the Executive*. It is also the underlying hypothesis which makes it possible for Urwick to suggest that "proper" or formal channels in fact function to "confirm and record" decisions arrived at by more personal means.[5] We meet it again in the concept of administration as a process of education, in which the winning of consent and support is conceived to be a basic function of leadership.[6] In short, it is recognized that control and consent cannot be divorced even within formally authoritarian structures.

The indivisibility of control and consent makes it necessary to view formal organizations as *cooperative* systems, widening the frame of reference of those concerned with the manipulation of organizational resources. At the point of action, of executive decision, the economic aspect of organization provides inadequate tools for control over the concrete structure. This idea may be readily grasped if attention is directed to the role of the individual within the organizational economy. From the standpoint of organization as a formal system, persons are viewed functionally, in respect to their *roles*, as participants in assigned segments of the cooperative system. But in fact individuals have a propensity to resist depersonalization, to spill over the boundaries of their segmentary roles, to participate as *wholes*. The formal systems (at an extreme, the disposition of "rifles" at a military perimeter) cannot take account of the deviations thus introduced, and consequently break down as instruments of control when relied upon alone. The whole individual raises new problems for the organization, partly because of the needs of his own personality, partly because he brings with him a set of established habits as well, perhaps, as commitments to special groups outside of the organization.

Unfortunately for the adequacy of formal systems of coordination, the needs of individuals do not permit a single-minded attention to the stated goals of the system within which they have been assigned. The hazard inherent in the act of delegation derives essentially from this fact. Delegation is an organizational act, having to do with formal assignments to functions and powers. Theoretically, these assignments are made to roles or official positions, not to individuals as such. In fact, however, delegation necessarily involves concrete individuals who have interests and goals which do not always coincide with the goals of the formal system. As a consequence, individual personalities may offer resistance to the demands made upon them by the official conditions of delegation. These resistances are not accounted for within the categories of coordination and delegation, so that when they occur they must be considered as unpredictable and accidental. Observations of this type of situation within formal structures are sufficiently commonplace. A familiar example is that of delegation to a subordinate who is also required to train his own replacement. The subordinate may resist this demand in order to maintain unique access to the "mysteries" of the job, and thus insure his indispensability to the organization.

In large organizations, deviations from the formal system tend to become institutionalized, so that "unwritten laws" and informal associations are established. Institutionalization removes such deviations from the realm of personality differences, transforming them into a persistent structural aspect of formal organizations.[7] These institutionalized rules and modes of informal cooperation are normally attempts by participants in the formal organization to control the group relations which form the environment of organizational decisions. The informal patterns (such as cliques) arise spontaneously, are based on personal relationships, and are usually directed to the control of some specific situation. They may be generated anywhere within a hierarchy, often with deleterious consequences for the formal goals of the organization, but they may also function to widen the available resources of executive control and thus contribute to rather than hinder the achievement of the stated objectives of the organization. The deviations tend to force a shift away from the purely formal system as the effective determinant of behavior to (1) a condition in which informal patterns buttress the formal, as through the manipulation of sentiment within the organization in favor of established authority; or (2) a condition wherein the informal controls effect a consistent modification of formal goals, as in the case of some bureaucratic patterns.[8] This trend will eventually result in the formalization of erstwhile informal activities, with the cycle of deviation and transformation beginning again on a new level.

The relevance of informal structures to organizational analysis underlines the significance of conceiving of formal organizations as cooperative systems. When the totality of interacting groups and individuals becomes the object of inquiry, the latter is not restricted by formal, legal, or procedural dimensions. The *state of the system* emerges as a significant point of analysis, as when an internal situation charged with conflict qualifies and informs actions ostensibly determined by formal relations and objectives. A proper understanding of the organizational process must make it possible to interpret changes in the formal system—new appointments or rules or reorganizations—in their relation to the informal and unavowed ties of friendship, class loyalty, power cliques, or external commitment. This is what it means "to know the score."

The fact that the involvement of individuals as whole personalities tends to limit the adequacy of formal systems of coordination does not mean that organizational characteristics are those of individuals. The organic, emergent character of the formal organization considered as a cooperative system must be recognized. This means that the *organization* reaches decisions, takes action, and makes adjustments. Such a view raises the question of the relation between organizations and persons. The significance of theoretical emphasis upon the cooperative *system* as such is derived from the insight that certain actions and consequences are enjoined independently of the personality of the individuals involved. Thus, if reference is made to the "organization-paradox"—the tension created by the inhibitory consequences of certain types of informal structures within organizations—this does not mean that individuals themselves are in quandaries. It is the nature of the interacting consequences of divergent interests within the organization which creates the condition, a result which may obtain independently of the consciousness or the qualities of the individual participants. Similarly, it seems useful to insist that there are qualities and needs of leadership, having to do with position and role, which are persistent despite variations in the character or personality of individual leaders themselves.

Rational action systems are characteristic of both individuals and organizations. The conscious attempt to mobilize available internal resources (*e.g.*, self-discipline) for the achievement of a stated goal—referred to here as an economy or a formal system—is one aspect of individual psychology. But the personality considered as a dynamic system of interacting wishes, compulsions, and restraints defines a system which is at once essential and yet potentially deleterious to what may be thought of as the "economy of learning" or to individual rational action. At the same time, the individual personality is an adaptive structure, and this, too, requires a broader frame of reference for analysis than the categories of rationality. On a different level, although analogously, we have pointed to the need to consider organizations as cooperative systems and adaptive structures in order to explain the context of and deviations from the formal systems of delegation and coordination.

To recognize the sociological relevance of formal structures is not, however, to have constructed a theory of organization. It is important to set the framework of analysis, and much is accomplished along this line when, for example, the nature of authority in formal organizations is reinterpreted to emphasize the factors of cohesion and persuasion as against legal or coercive sources.[9] This redefinition is logically the same as that which introduced the conception of the self as social. The latter helps make possible, but does not of itself fulfill, the requirements for a dynamic theory of personality. In the same way, the definition of authority as conditioned by sociological factors of sentiment and cohesion—or more generally the definition of formal organizations as cooperative systems—only sets the stage, as an initial requirement, for the formulation of a theory of organization.

STRUCTURAL-FUNCTIONAL ANALYSIS

Cooperative systems are constituted of individuals interacting as wholes in relation to a formal system of coordination. The concrete structure is therefore a resultant of the reciprocal influences of the formal and informal aspects of organization. Furthermore, this structure is itself a totality, an adaptive "organism" reacting to influences upon it from an external environment. These considerations help to define the objects of inquiry; but to progress to a system of predicates *about* these objects it is necessary to set forth an analytical method which seems to be fruitful and significant. The method must have a relevance to empirical materials, which is to say, it must be more specific in its reference than discussions of the logic or methodology of social science.

The organon which may be suggested as peculiarly helpful in the analysis of adaptive structures has been referred to as "structural-functional analysis."[10] This method may be characterized in a sentence: *Structural-functional analysis relates contemporary and variable behavior to a presumptively stable system of needs and mechanisms.* This means that a given empirical system is deemed to have basic needs, essentially related to self-maintenance; the system develops repetitive means of self-defense; and day-to-day activity is interpreted in terms of the function served by that activity for the maintenance and defense of the system. Put thus generally, the approach is applicable on any level in which the determinate "states" of empirically isolable systems undergo self-impelled and repetitive transformations when impinged upon by external conditions. This self-impulsion suggests the relevance of the term "dynamic," which is often used in referring to physiological, psychological, or social systems to which this type of analysis has been applied.[11]

It is a postulate of the structural-functional approach that the basic need of all empirical systems is the maintenance of the integrity and continuity of the system itself. Of course, such a postulate is primarily useful in directing attention to a set of "derived imperatives" or needs which are sufficiently concrete to characterize the system at hand.[12] It is perhaps rash to attempt a catalogue of these imperatives for formal organizations, but some suggestive formulation is needed in the interests of setting forth the type of analysis under discussion. In formal organizations, the "maintenance of the system" as a generic need may be specified in terms of the following imperatives:

(1) *The security of the organization as a whole in relation to social forces in its environment.* This imperative requires continuous attention to the possibilities of encroachment and to the forestalling of threatened aggressions or deleterious (though perhaps unintended) consequences from the actions of others.

(2) *The stability of the lines of authority and communication.* One of the persistent reference-points of administrative decision is the weighing of consequences for the continued capacity of leadership to control and to have access to the personnel or ranks.

(3) *The stability of informal relations within the organization.* Ties of sentiment and self-interest are evolved as unacknowledged but effective mechanisms of adjustment of individuals and subgroups to the conditions of life within the organization. These ties represent a cementing of relationships which sustains the formal authority in day-to-day operations and widens opportunities for effective communication.[13]

Consequently, attempts to "upset" the informal structure, either frontally or as an indirect consequence of formal reorganization, will normally be met with considerable resistance.

(4) *The continuity of policy and of the sources of its determination.* For each level within the organization, and for the organization as a whole, it is necessary that there be a sense that action taken in the light of a given policy will not be placed in continuous jeopardy. Arbitrary or unpredictable changes in policy undermine the significance of (and therefore the attention to) day-to-day action by injecting a note of capriciousness. At the same time, the organization will seek stable roots (or firm statutory authority or popular mandate) so that a sense of the permanency and legitimacy of its acts will be achieved.

(5) *A homogeneity of outlook with respect to the meaning and role of the organization.* The minimization of disaffection requires a unity derived from a common understanding of what the character of the organization is meant to be. When this homogeneity breaks down, as in situations of internal conflict over basic issues, the continued existence of the organization is endangered. On the other hand, one of the signs of "healthy" organization is the ability to effectively orient new members and readily slough off those who cannot be adapted to the established outlook.

This catalogue of needs cannot be thought of as final, but it approximates the stable system generally characteristic of formal organizations. These imperatives are derived, in the sense that they represent the conditions for survival or self-maintenance of cooperative systems of organized action. An inspection of these needs suggests that organizational survival is intimately connected with the struggle for relative prestige, both for the organization and for elements and individuals within it. It may therefore be useful to refer to a *prestige-survival motif* in organizational behavior as a shorthand way of relating behavior needs, especially when the exact nature of the

needs remains in doubt. However, it must be emphasized that prestige-survival in organizations does not derive simply from like motives in individuals. Loyalty and self-sacrifice may be individual expressions of organizational or group egotism and self-consciousness.

The concept of organizational need directs analysis to the *internal relevance* of organizational behavior. This is especially pertinent with respect to discretionary action undertaken by agents manifestly in pursuit of formal goals. The question then becomes one of relating the specific act of discretion to some presumptively stable organizational need. In other words, it is not simply action plainly oriented internally (such as in-service training) but also action presumably oriented externally which must be inspected for its relevance to internal conditions. This is of prime importance for the understanding of bureaucratic behavior, for it is of the essence of the latter that action formally undertaken for substantive goals be weighed and transformed in terms of its consequences for the position of the officialdom.

Formal organizations as cooperative systems on the one hand, and individual personalities on the other, involve structural-functional homologies, a point which may help to clarify the nature of this type of analysis. If we say that the individual has a stable set of needs, most generally the need for maintaining and defending the integrity of his personality or ego; that there are recognizable certain repetitive mechanisms which are utilized by the ego in its defense (rationalization, projection, regression, etc.); and that overt and variable behavior may be interpreted in terms of its relation to these needs and mechanisms—on the basis of this logic we may discern the typical pattern of structural-functional analysis as set forth above. In this sense, it is possible to speak of a

"Freudian model" for organizational analysis. This does not mean that the substantive insights of individual psychology may be applied to organizations, as in vulgar extrapolations from the individual ego to whole nations or (by a no less vulgar inversion) from strikes to frustrated workers. It is the *logic*, the *type* of analysis which is pertinent.

This homology is also instructive in relation to the applicability of generalizations to concrete cases. The dynamic theory of personality states a set of possible predicates about the ego and its mechanisms of defense, which inform us concerning the propensities of individual personalities under certain general circumstances. But these predicates provide only tools for the analysis of particular individuals, and each concrete case must be examined to tell which operate and in what degree. They are not primarily organs of prediction. In the same way, the predicates within the theory of organization will provide tools for the analysis of particular cases. Each organization, like each personality, represents a resultant of complex forces, an empirical entity which no single relation or no simple formula can explain. The problem of analysis becomes that of selecting among the possible predicates set forth in the theory of organization those which illuminate our understanding of the materials at hand.

The setting of structural-functional analysis as applied to organizations requires some qualification, however. Let us entertain the suggestion that the interesting problem in social science is not so much why men act the way they do as why men in certain circumstances *must* act the way they do. This emphasis upon constraint, if accepted, releases us from an ubiquitous attention to behavior in general, and especially from any undue fixation upon statistics. On the other

hand, it has what would seem to be salutary consequence of focusing inquiry upon certain necessary relationships of the type "if . . . then," for example: If the cultural level of the rank and file members of a formally democratic organization is below that necessary for participation in the formulation of policy, then there will be pressure upon the leaders to use the tools of demagogy.

Is such a statement universal in its applicability? Surely not in the sense that one can predict without remainder the nature of all or even most political groups in a democracy. Concrete behavior is a resultant, a complex vector, shaped by the operation of a number of such general constraints. But there is a test of general applicability: it is that of noting whether the relation made explicit must be *taken into account* in action. This criterion represents an empirical test of the significance of social generalizations. If a theory is significant it will state a relation which will either (1) be taken into account as an element of achieving control; or (2) be ignored only at the risk of losing control and will evidence itself in a ramification of objective or unintended consequences.[14] It is a corollary of this principle of significance that investigation must search out the underlying factors in organizational action, which requires a kind of intensive analysis of the same order as psychoanalytic probing.

A frame of reference which invites attention to the constraints upon behavior will tend to highlight tensions and dilemmas, the characteristic paradoxes generated in the course of action. The dilemma may be said to be the handmaiden of structural-functional analysis, for it introduces the concept of *commitment* or *involvement* as fundamental to organizational analysis. A dilemma in human behavior is represented by an inescapable commitment which cannot be reconciled with the needs of the organism or the social system. There are many spurious dilemmas which have to do with verbal contradictions, but inherent dilemmas to which we refer are of a more profound sort, for they reflect the basic nature of the empirical system in question. An economic order committed to profit as its sustaining incentive may, in Marxist terms, sow the seed of its own destruction. Again, the anguish of man, torn between finitude and pride, is not a matter of arbitrary and replaceable assumptions but is a reflection of the psychological needs of the human organism, and is concretized in his commitment to the institutions which command his life; he is in the world and of it, inescapably involved in its goals and demands; at the same time, the needs of the spirit are compelling, proposing modes of salvation which have continuously disquieting consequences for worldly involvements. In still another context, the need of the human organism for affection and response necessitates a commitment to elements of the culture which can provide them; but the rule of the super-ego is uncertain since it cannot be completely reconciled with the need for libidinal satisfaction.

Applying this principle to organizations we may note that there is a general source of tension observable in the split between "the motion and the act." Plans and programs reflect the freedom of technical or ideal choice, but organized action cannot escape involvement, a commitment to personnel or institutions or procedures which effectively qualifies the initial plan. *Der Mensch denkt, Gott lenkt.* In organized action, this ultimate wisdom finds a temporal meaning in the recalcitrance of the tools of action. We are inescapably committed to the mediation of human structures which are at once indispensable to our goals and at the same time stand between them

and ourselves. The selection of agents generates immediately a bifurcation of interest, expressed in new centers of need and power, placing effective constraints upon the arena of action, and resulting in tensions which are never completely resolved. This is part of what it means to say that there is a "logic" of action which impels us forward from one undesired position to another. Commitment to dynamic, self-activating tools is of the nature of organized action; at the same time, the need for continuity of authority, policy, and character are pressing, and require an unceasing effort to master the instruments generated in the course of action. This generic tension is specified within the terms of each cooperative system. But for all we find a persistent relationship between *need* and *commitment* in which the latter not only qualifies the former but unites with it to produce a continuous state of tension. In this way, the notion of constraint (as reflected in tension or paradox) at once widens and more closely specifies the frame of reference for organizational analysis.

For Malinowski, the core of functionalism was contained in the view that a cultural fact must be analyzed in its setting. Moreover, he apparently conceived of his method as pertinent to the analysis of all aspects of cultural systems. But there is a more specific problem, one involving a principle of selection which serves to guide inquiry along significant lines. Freud conceived of the human organism as an adaptive structure, but he was not concerned with all human needs, nor with all phases of adaptation. For his system, he selected those needs whose expression is blocked in some way, so that such terms as repression, inhibition, and frustration became crucial. All conduct may be thought of as derived from need, and all adjustment represents the reduction of need. But not all needs are relevant to the systematics of dynamic psychology; and it is not adjustment as such but reaction to frustration which generates the characteristic modes of defensive behavior.

Organizational analysis, too, must find its selective principle; otherwise the indiscriminate attempts to relate activity functionally to needs will produce little in the way of significant theory. Such a principle might read as follows: *Our frame of reference is to select out those needs which cannot be fulfilled within approved avenues of expression and thus must have recourse to such adaptive mechanisms as ideology and to the manipulation of formal processes and structures in terms of informal goals.* This formulation has many difficulties, and is not presented as conclusive, but it suggests the kind of principle which is likely to separate the quick and the dead, the meaningful and the trite, in the study of cooperative systems in organized action.[15]

The frame of reference outlined here for the theory of organization may now be identified as involving the following major ideas: (1) the concept of organizations as cooperative systems, adaptive social structures, made up of interacting individuals, subgroups, and informal plus formal relationships; (2) structural-functional analysis, which relates variable aspects of organization (such as goals) to stable needs and self-defensive mechanisms; (3) the concept of recalcitrance as a quality of the tools of social action, involving a break in the continuum of adjustment and defining an environment of constraint, commitment, and tension. This frame of reference is suggested as providing a specifiable *area of relations* within which predicates in the theory of organization will be sought, and at the same time setting forth principles of selection and relevance in our approach to the data of organization.

It will be noted that we have set forth this frame of reference within the overall context of social action. The significance of events may be defined by their place and operational role in a means-end scheme. If functional analysis searches out the elements important for the maintenance of a given structure, and that structure is one of the materials to be manipulated in action, then that which is functional in respect to the structure is also functional in respect to the action system. This provides a ground for the significance of functionally derived theories. At the same time, relevance to control in action is the empirical test of their applicability or truth.

COOPTATION AS A MECHANISM OF ADJUSTMENT

The frame of reference stated above is in fact an amalgam of definition, resolution, and substantive theory. There is an element of *definition* in conceiving of formal organizations as cooperative systems, though of course the interaction of informal and formal patterns is a question of fact; in a sense, we are *resolving* to employ structural-functional analysis on the assumption that it will be fruitful to do so, though here, too, the specification of needs or derived imperatives is a matter for empirical inquiry; and our predication of recalcitrance as a quality of the tools of action is itself a *substantive theory*, perhaps fundamental to a general understanding of the nature of social action.

A theory of organization requires more than a general frame of reference, though the latter is indispensable to inform the approach of inquiry to any given set of materials. What is necessary is the construction of generalizations concerning transformations within and among cooperative systems. These generalizations represent, from the standpoint of particular cases, possible predicates which are relevant to the materials as we know them in general, but which are not necessarily controlling in all circumstances. A theory of transformations in organization would specify those states of the system which resulted typically in predictable, or at least understandable, changes in such aspects of organization as goals, leadership, doctrine, efficiency, effectiveness, and size. These empirical generalizations would be systematized as they were related to the stable needs of the cooperative system.

Changes in the characteristics of organizations may occur as a result of many different conditions, not always or necessarily related to the processes of organization as such. But the theory of organization must be selective, so that explanations of transformations will be sought within its own assumptions or frame of reference. Consider the question of size. Organizations may expand for many reasons—the availability of markets, legislative delegations, the swing of opinion—which may be accidental from the point of view of the organizational process. To explore changes in size (as of, say, a trades union) as related to changes in nonorganizational conditions may be necessitated by the historical events to be described, but it will not of itself advance the frontiers of the theory of organization. However, if "the innate propensity of all organizations to expand" is asserted as a function of "the inherent instability of incentives"[16] then transformations have been stated within the terms of the theory of organization itself. It is likely that in many cases the generalization in question may represent only a minor aspect of the empirical changes, but these organizational relations must be made explicit if the theory is to receive development.

In a frame of reference which specifies needs and anticipates the formulation of a set of self-defensive responses or mechanisms, the latter appear to constitute one kind of empirical generalization or "possible predicate" within the general theory. The needs of organizations (whatever investigation may determine them to be) are posited as attributes of all organizations, but the responses to disequilibrium will be varied. The mechanisms used by the system in fulfillment of its needs will be repetitive and thus may be described as a specifiable set of assertions within the theory of organization, but any given organization may or may not have recourse to the characteristic modes of response. Certainly no given organization will employ all of the possible mechanisms which are theoretically available. When Barnard speaks of an "innate propensity of organization to expand," he is in fact formulating one of the general mechanisms, namely, expansion, which is a characteristic mode of response available to an organization under pressure from within. These responses necessarily involve a transformation (in this case, size) of some structural aspect of the organization.

Other examples of the self-defensive mechanisms available to organizations may derive primarily from the response of these organizations to the institutional environments in which they live. The tendency to construct ideologies, reflecting the need to come to terms with major social forces, is one such mechanism. Less well understood as a mechanism of organizational adjustment is what we may term *cooptation.* Some statement of the meaning of this concept may aid in clarifying the foregoing analysis.

Cooptation is the process of absorbing new elements into the leadership or policy-determining structure of an organization as a means of averting threats to its stability or existence. This is a defensive mechanism, formulated as one of a number of possible predicates available for the interpretation of organizational behavior. Cooptation tells us something about the process by which an institutional environment impinges itself upon an organization and effects changes in its leadership and policy. Formal authority may resort to cooptation under the following general conditions:

(1) When there exists a hiatus between consent and control, so that the legitimacy of the formal authority is called into question. The "indivisibility" of consent and control refers, of course, to an optimum situation. Where control lacks an adequate measure of consent, it may revert to coercive measures or attempt somehow to win the consent of the governed. One means of winning consent is to coopt elements into the leadership or organization, usually elements which in some way reflect the sentiment, or possess the confidence of the relevant public or mass. As a result, it is expected that the new elements will lend respectability or legitimacy to the organs of control and thus reestablish the stability of formal authority. This process is widely used, and in many different contexts. It is met in colonial countries, where the organs of alien control reaffirm their legitimacy by coopting native leaders into the colonial administration. We find it in the phenomenon of "crisis-patriotism" wherein normally disfranchised groups are temporarily given representation in the councils of government in order to win their solidarity in a time of national stress. Cooptation is presently being considered by the United States Army in its study of proposals to give enlisted personnel representation in the court-martial machinery—a clearly adaptive response to stresses made explicit during the war, the lack of confidence in the administration of army justice. The "unity" parties of totalitarian states are another form of cooptation; company unions or some employee representation

plans in industry are still another. In each of these cases, the response of formal authority (private or public, in a large organization or a small one) is an attempt to correct a state of imbalance by *formal* measures. It will be noted, moreover, that what is shared is the *responsibility* for power rather than power itself. These conditions define what we shall refer to as *formal cooptation.*

(2) Cooptation may be a response to the pressure of specific centers of power. This is not necessarily a matter of legitimacy or of a general and diffuse lack of confidence. These may be well established; and yet organized forces which are able to threaten the formal authority may effectively shape its structure and policy. The organization in respect to its institutional environment—or the leadership in respect to its ranks—must take these forces into account. As a consequence, the outside elements may be brought into the leadership or policy-determining structure, may be given a place as a recognition of and concession to the resources they can independently command. The representation of interests through administrative constituencies is a typical example of this process. Or, within an organization, individuals upon whom the group is dependent for funds or other resources may insist upon and receive a share in the determination of policy. This form of cooptation is typically expressed in informal terms, for the problem is not one of responding to a state of imbalance with respect to the "people as a whole" but rather one of meeting the pressure of specific individuals or interest-groups which are in a position to enforce demands. The latter are interested in the substance of power and not its forms. Moreover, an open acknowledgement of capitulation to specific interests may itself undermine the sense of legitimacy of the formal authority within the community. Consequently, there is a positive pressure to refrain from explicit recognition of the relationship established. This form of the cooptative mechanism, having to do with the sharing of power as a response to specific pressures, may be termed *informal cooptation.*

Cooptation reflects a state of tension between formal authority and social power. The former is embodied in a particular structure and leadership, but the latter has to do with subjective and objective factors which control the loyalties and potential manipulability of the community. Where the formal authority is an expression of social power, its stability is assured. On the other hand, when it becomes divorced from the sources of social power its continued existence is threatened. This threat may arise from the sheer alienation of sentiment or from the fact that other leaderships have control over the sources of social power. Where a formal authority has been accustomed to the assumption that its constituents respond to it as individuals, there may be a rude awakening when organization of those constituents on a non-governmental basis creates nuclei of power which are able effectively to demand a sharing of power.[17]

The significance of cooptation for organizational analysis is not simply that there is a change in or a broadening of leadership, and that this is an adaptive response, but also that *this change is consequential for the character and role of the organization.* Cooptation involves commitment, so that the groups to which adaptation has been made constrain the field of choice available to the organization or leadership in question. The character of the coopted elements will necessarily shape (inhibit or broaden) the modes of action available to the leadership which has won adaptation and security at the price of commitment. The concept of cooptation thus implicitly sets forth the major points of the frame of reference outlined above: it is an adaptive response of a cooperative system to a stable need, generating transformations which reflect constraints enforced by the recalcitrant tools of action.

NOTES

1. John M. Gaus, "A Theory of Organization in Public Administration," in *The Frontiers of Public Administration* (Chicago: University of Chicago Press, 1936), p. 66.

2. Chester I. Barnard, *The Functions of the Executive* (Cambridge: Harvard University Press, 1938), p. 73.

3. Cf. Talcott Parsons' generalization (after Max Weber) of the "law of the increasing rationality of action systems," in *The Structure of Social Action* (New York: McGraw-Hill, 1937), p. 752.

4. See Luther Gulick and Lydall Urwick (editors), *Papers on the Science of Administration* (New York: Institute of Public Administration, Columbia University, 1937); Lydall Urwick, *The Elements of Administration* (New York, Harper, 1943); James D. Mooney and Alan C. Reiley, *The Principles of Organization* (New York: Harper, 1939); H. S. Dennison, *Organization Engineering* (New York: McGraw-Hill, 1931).

5. Urwick, *The Elements of Administration, op. cit.*, p. 47.

6. See Gaus, *op. cit.* Studies of the problem of morale are instances of the same orientation, having received considerable impetus in recent years from the work of the Harvard Business School group.

7. The creation of informal structures within various types of organizations has received explicit recognition in recent years. See F. J. Roethlisberger and W. J. Dickson, *Management and the Worker* (Cambridge: Harvard University Press, 1941), p. 524; also Barnard, *op. cit.*, c. ix; and Wilbert E. Moore, *Industrial Relations and the Social Order* (New York: Macmillan, 1946), chap. xv.

8. For an analysis of the latter in these terms, see Philip Selznick, "An Approach to a Theory of Bureaucracy," *American Sociological Review* 8 (February 1943).

9. Robert Michels, "Authority," *Encyclopedia of the Social Sciences* (New York: Macmillan, 1931), pp. 319ff.; also Barnard, *op. cit.*, c. xii.

10. For a presentation of this approach having a more general reference than the study of formal organizations, see Talcott Parsons, "The Present Position and Prospects of Systematic Theory in Sociology," in Georges Gurvitch and Wilbert E. Moore (ed.), *Twentieth Century Sociology* (New York: The Philosophical Library, 1945).

11. "Structure" refers to both the relationships within the system (formal plus informal patterns in organization) and the set of needs and modes of satisfaction which characterize the given type of empirical system. As the utilization of this type of analysis proceeds, the concept of "need" will require further clarification. In particular, the imputation of a "stable set of needs" to organizational systems must not function as a new instinct theory. At the same time, we cannot avoid using these inductions as to generic needs, for they help us to stake out our area of inquiry. The author is indebted to Robert K. Merton who has, in correspondence, raised some important objections to the use of the term "need" in this context.

12. For "derived imperative" see Bronislaw Malinowski, *The Dynamics of Culture Change* (New Haven: Yale University Press, 1945), pp. 44ff. For the use of "need" in place of "motive" see the same author's *A Scientific Theory of Culture* (Chapel Hill: University of North Carolina Press, 1944), pp. 89–90.

13. They may also *destroy* those relationships, as noted above, but the need remains, generating one of the persistent dilemmas of leadership.

14. See. R. M. MacIver's discussion of the "dynamic assessment" which "brings the external world selectively into the subjective realm, conferring on it subjective significance for the ends of action." *Social Causation* (Boston: Ginn, 1942), chaps. 11, 12. The analysis of this assessment within the context of organized action yields the implicit knowledge which guides the choice among alternatives. See also Robert K. Merton, "The Unanticipated Consequences of Purposive Social Action," *American Sociological Review* 1 (December, 1936).

15. This is not meant to deprecate the study of organizations as *economies* or formal systems. The latter represent an independent level, abstracted from organizational structures as cooperative or adaptive systems ("organisms").

16. Barnard, *op. cit.*, pp. 158–9.

17. It is perhaps useful to restrict the concept of cooptation to formal organizations, but in fact it probably reflects a process characteristic of all group leaderships. This has received some recognition in the analysis of class structure, wherein the ruling class is interpreted as protecting its own stability by absorbing new elements. Thus Michels made the point that "an aristocracy cannot maintain an enduring stability by sealing itself off hermetically." See Robert Michels, *Umschichtungen in den herrschenden Klassen nach dem Kriege* (Stuttgart: Kohlhammer, 1934), p. 39; also Gaetano Mosca, *The Ruling Class* (New York: McGraw-Hill, 1939), p. 413ff. The alliance or amalgamation of classes in the face of a common threat may be reflected in formal and informal cooptative responses among formal organizations sensitive to class pressures. In a forthcoming volume, *TVA and the Grass Roots*, the author has made extensive use of the concept of cooptation in analyzing some aspects of the organizational behavior of a government agency.

12
Suggestions for a Sociological Approach to the Theory of Organizations

Talcott Parsons

For the purposes of this article the term "organization" will be used to refer to a broad type of collectivity which has assumed a particularly important place in modern industrial societies—the type to which the term "bureaucracy" is most often applied. Familiar examples are the governmental bureau or department, the business firm (especially above a certain size), the university, and the hospital. It is by now almost a commonplace that there are features common to all these types of organization which cut across the ordinary distinctions between the social science disciplines. Something is lost if study of the firm is left only to economists, of governmental organizations to political scientists, and of schools and universities to "educationists."[1]

The study of organization in the present sense is thus only part of the study of social structure as that term is generally used by sociologists (or of "social organization" as ordinarily used by social anthropologists). A family is only partly an organization; most other kinship groups are even less so. The same is certainly true of local communities, regional subsocieties, and of a society as a whole conceived, for example, as a nation. On other levels, informal work groups, cliques of friends, and so on, are not in this technical sense organizations.

THE CONCEPT OF ORGANIZATION

As a formal analytical point of reference, *primacy of orientation to the attainment of a specific goal* is used as the defining characteristic of an organization which distinguishes it from other types of social systems. This criterion has implications for both the external relations and the internal structure of the system referred to here as an organization.

The attainment of a goal is defined as a *relation* between a system (in this case a social system) and the relevant parts of the external situation in which it acts or operates. This relation can be conceived as the maximization, relative to the relevant conditions such as costs and obstacles, of some category of *output* of the system to objects or systems in the external situation. These considerations yield a further important criterion of an organization. An organization is a system which, as the attainment of its goal, "produces" an identifiable something which can be utilized in some way by another system; that is, the output of the organization is, for some other system, an input. In the case of an organization with economic primacy, this output may be a class of goods or services which are either consumable or serve as instruments for a further phase of the

Source: Talcott Parsons, "Suggestions for a Sociological Approach to the Theory of Organizations," *Administrative Science Quarterly* 1 (June 1956): 63–85. Reprinted by permission of *The Administrative Science Quarterly.* Copyright © 1956 *The Administrative Science Quarterly.*

production process by other organizations. In the case of a government agency the output may be a class of regulatory decisions; in that of an educational organization it may be a certain type of "trained capacity" on the part of the students who have been subjected to its influence. In any of these cases there must be a set of consequences of the processes which go on within the organization, which make a difference to the functioning of some other subsystem of the society; that is, without the production of certain goods the consuming unit must behave differently, i.e., suffer a "deprivation."

The availability, to the unit succeeding the organization in the series, of the organization's output must be subject to some sort of terms, the settlement of which is analyzable in the general framework of the ideas of contract or exchange. Thus in the familiar case the economic producer "sells" his product for a money price which in turn serves as a medium for procuring the factors of production, most directly labor services, necessary for further stages of the productive process. It is thus assumed that in the case of all organizations there is something analogous to a "market" for the output which constitutes the attainment of its goal (what Chester I. Barnard calls "organization purpose"); and that directly, and perhaps also indirectly, there is some kind of exchange of this for entities which (as inputs into it) are important means for the organization to carry out its function in the larger system. The exchange of output for input at the boundary defined by the attainment of the goal of an organization need not be the only important boundary-exchange of the organization as a system. It is, however, the one most directly involved in defining the primary characteristics of the organization. Others will be discussed later.

The existence of organizations as the concept is here set forth is a consequence of the division of labor in society. Where both the "production" of specialized outputs and their consumption or ultimate utilization occur within the same structural unit, there is no need for the differentiation of specialized organizations. Primitive societies in so far as their units are "self-sufficient" in both economic and other senses generally do not have clear-cut differentiated organizations in the present sense.

In its internal reference, the primacy of goal-attainment among the functions of a social system gives priority to those processes most directly involved with the success or failure of goal-oriented endeavors. This means essentially the decision-making process, which controls the utilization of the resources of the system as a whole in the interest of the goal, and the processes by which those responsible for such decisions can count on the mobilization of these resources in the interest of a goal. These mechanisms of mobilization constitute what we ordinarily think of as the development of power in a political sense.

What from the point of view of the organization in question is its specified goal is, from the point of view of the larger system of which it is a differentiated part or subsystem, a specialized or differentiated function. This relationship is the primary link between an organization and the larger system of which it is a part, and provides a basis for the classification of types of organization. However, it cannot be the only important link.

This article will attempt to analyze both this link and the other principal ones, using as a point of departure the treatment of the organization as a social system. First, it will be treated as a system which is characterized by all the properties which are essential to any social system. Secondly, it will be treated as a functionally differentiated subsystem of a larger social system. Hence it will be the other subsystems of the larger one which constitute the situation or environment in which the organization operates. An organization, then, will have to be analyzed as the special type of social system organized about the primacy of interest in the attainment of a particular type of system goal. Certain of its special features will derive from goal-primacy in general and others from the primacy of the particular type of goal. Finally, the characteristics of the organization will be defined by the kind of situation in which it has to operate, which will consist of the relations obtaining between it and the other specialized subsystem of the larger system of which it is a part. The latter can for most purposes be assumed to be a society.

THE STRUCTURE OF ORGANIZATIONS

Like any social system, an organization is conceived as having a describable structure. This can be described and analyzed from two points of view, both of which are essential to completeness. The first is the "cultural-institutional" point of view which uses the values of the system and their institutionalization in different functional contexts as its point of departure; the second is the "group" or "role" point of view which takes suborganizations and the roles of individuals participating in the functioning of the organization as its point of departure. Both of these will be discussed, as will their broad relations to each other, but primary attention will be given to the former.

On what has just been called the cultural-institutional level, a minimal description of an organization will have to include an outline of the system of values which defines its functions and of the main institutional patterns which spell out these values in the more concrete functional contexts of goal-attainment itself, adaptation to the situation, and integration of the system. There are other aspects, such as technical lore, ideology, and ritual symbolization, which cannot, for reasons of space, be taken up here.

The main point of reference for analyzing the structure of any social system is its value pattern. This defines the basic orientation of the system (in the present case, the organization) to the situation in which it operates; hence it guides the activities of participant individuals.

In the case of an organization as defined above, this value system must by definition be a subvalue system of a higher-order one, since the organization is always defined as a subsystem of a more comprehensive social system. Two conclusions follow: First, the value system of the organization must imply basic acceptance of the more generalized values of the superordinate system—unless it is a deviant organization not integrated into the superordinate system. Secondly, on the requisite level of generality, the most essential feature of the value system of an organization is the evaluative *legitimation* of its place or "role" in the superordinate system.

Since it has been assumed that an organization is defined by the primacy of a type of goal, the focus of its value system must be the legitimation of this goal in terms of the functional significance of its attainment for the superordinate system, and secondly the legitimation of the primacy of this goal over other possible interests and values of the organization and its members. Thus the value system of a business firm in our society is a version of "economic rationality" which legitimizes the goal of economic production (specified to the requisite level of concreteness in terms of particular goods and services). Devotion of the organization (and hence the resources it controls) to production is legitimized as is the maintenance of the primacy of this goal over other functional interests which may arise within the organization. This is Barnard's "organization purpose."[2] For the business firm, money return is a primary measure and symbol of success and is thus *part* of the goal-structure of the organization. But it cannot be the primary organization goal because profit making is not by itself a function on behalf of the society as a system.

In the most general sense the values of the organization legitimize its existence as a system. But more specifically they legitimize the main functional patterns of operation which are necessary to implement the values, in this case the system goal, under typical conditions of the concrete situation. Hence, besides legitimation of the goal-type and its primacy over other interests, there will be legitimation of various categories of relatively specific subgoals and the operative procedures necessary for their attainment. There will further be normative rules governing the adaptive processes of the organization, the general principles on which facilities can be procured and handled, and there will be rules or principles governing the integration of the organization, particularly in defining the obligations of loyalty of participants to the organization as compared with the loyalties they bear in other roles.

A more familiar approach to the structure of an organization is through its constituent personnel and the roles they play in its functioning. Thus we ordinarily think of an organization as having some kind of "management" or "administration"—a group of people carrying some kind of special responsibility for the organization's affairs, usually formulated as "policy formation" or "decision making." Then under the control of this top group we would conceive of various operative groups arranged in "line" formation down to the lowest in the line of authority. In a somewhat different relation we would also think of various groups performing "staff" functions, usually some kinds of experts who stand in an advisory capacity to the decision-makers at the various levels, but who do not themselves exercise "line" authority.

It seems advantageous for present purposes to carry through mainly with the analysis of the institutional structure of the organization. Using the value system as the main point of reference, the discussion of this structure can be divided into three main headings. The primary adaptive exigencies of an organization concern the procurement of the resources necessary for it to attain its goal or carry out its function; hence one major field of institutionalization concerns the modes of procurement of these resources. Secondly, the organization will itself have to have institutionalized procedures by which these resources are brought to bear in the concrete processes of goal-attainment; and, finally, there will have to be institutional patterns defining and regulating the limits of commitments to this organization as compared with others in which the same persons and other resource-controllers are involved, patterns which can be generalized on a basis tolerable to the society as a whole.

THE MOBILIZATION OF FLUID RESOURCES

The resources which an organization must utilize are, given the social structure of the situation in which it functions, the factors of production as these concepts are used in economic theory.

They are land, labor, capital, and "organization" in a somewhat different sense from that used mainly in this paper.[3]

The factor of land stands on a somewhat different level from the other three. If we treat an organization, for purposes of analysis, as an already established and going concern, then, like any other social system, we can think of it as being in control of certain facilities for access to which it is not dependent on the maintenance of short-run economic sanctions. It has full ownership of certain physical facilities such as physical land and relatively nondepreciating or nonobsolescing buildings. It may have certain traditions, particularly involving technical know-how factors which are not directly involved in the market nexus. The more fully the market nexus is developed, however, the less can it be said that an organization has very important assets which are withdrawn from the market. Even sites of long operation can be sold and new locations found and even the most deeply committed personnel may resign to take other positions or retire, and in either case have to be replaced through the labor market. The core of this aspect of the "land" complex is thus a set of commitments of resources on value grounds.

The two most fluid factors, however, are labor and capital in the economic sense. The overwhelming bulk of personal service takes place in occupational roles. This means that it is *contracted for* on some sector of the labor market. It is not based on ascription of status, through kinship or otherwise, but depends on the specific terms settled between the management of the organization and the incumbent. There are, of course, many types of contract of employment. Some variations concern the agents involved in the settlement of terms; for example, collective bargaining is very different from individual bargaining. Others concern the duration of commitments, varying all the way from a casual relation terminable at will, to a tenure appointment.

But most important, only in a limiting case are the specific ad hoc terms—balancing specifically defined services against specific monetary remuneration—anything like exhaustive of the empirically important factors involved in the contract of employment. The labor market cannot, in the economic sense, closely approach being a "perfect market." It has different degrees and types of imperfection according to whether the employer is one or another type of organization and according to what type of human service is involved. A few of these differences will be noted in later illustrations. Here the essential point is that, with the differentiation of functionally specified organizations from the matrix of diffuse social groupings, such organizations become increasingly dependent on explicit contracts of employment for their human services.

Attention may be called to one particular important differentiation among types of relations existing between the performer of services and the recipients of the ultimate "product." In the typical case of manufacturing industry the typical worker works within the organization. The end result is a physical commodity which is then sold to consumers. The worker has no personal contact with the customer of the firm; indeed no representative of the firm need have such contact except to arrange the settlement of the terms of sale. Where, however, the "product" is a personal service, the situation is quite different; the worker must have personal contact with the consumer during the actual performance of the service.

One way in which service can be organized is the case where neither performer nor "customer" belongs to an organization. Private professional practice is a type case, and doctor and patient, for example, come to constitute a small-scale solidary collectivity of their own. This is the main basis of the sliding scale as a pattern of remuneration. A second mode of organization is the one which assimilates the provision of service to the normal pattern involved in the production of physical commodities; the recipient is a "customer" who pays on a value-of-service basis, with prices determined by commercial competition. This pattern is approached in the case of such services as barbering.

But particularly in the case of professional services there is another very important pattern, where the recipient of the service becomes an operative member of the service-providing organization. The school, university, and hospital are type cases illustrating this pattern. The phrase "member of the university" definitely includes students. The faculty are in a sense dually employed, on the one hand by their students, on the other by the university administration. The transition is particularly clear in the case of the hospital. In private practice the patient is unequivocally the "employer." But in hospital practice the hospital organization employs a professional staff on behalf of the patients, as it were. This taking of the customer *into* the organization has important implications for the nature of the organization.

In a society like ours the requirements of an organization for fluid resources are in one sense and one level overwhelmingly met through financing, i.e., through the provision of money funds at the disposal of the organization.[4] This applies both to physical facilities, equipment, materials, buildings, and to the employment of human services—indeed also to cultural resources in that the rights to use patented processes may be bought.

Hence the availability of adequate financing is always a vital problem for every organization operating in a monetary economy no matter what its goal-type may be; it is as vital for churches, symphony orchestras, and universities as it is for business firms.

The mechanisms through which financial resources are made available differ enormously, however, with different types of organization. All except the "purest" charitable organizations depend to some extent on the returns they receive for purveying some kind of product, be it a commodity, or a service like education or music. But even within this range there is an enormous variation in the adequacy of this return for fully meeting financial needs. The business firm is at one pole in this respect. Its normal expectation is that in the long run it will be able to finance itself adequately from the proceeds of sales. But even here this is true only in the long run; investment of capital in anticipation of future proceeds is of course one of the most important mechanisms in our society.

Two other important mechanisms are taxation and voluntary contributions. In a "free enterprise" economy the general principle governing financing by taxation is that organizations will be supported out of taxation (1) if the goal is regarded as important enough but organizations devoted to it cannot be made to "pay" as private enterprises by providing the service on a commercial basis, *e.g.*, the care of large numbers of persons from the lower income groups who (by current standards) need to be hospitalized for mental illnesses, or (2) if the *ways* in which the services would be provided by private enterprise might jeopardize the public interest, *e.g.*, the provision of military force for the national defense might conceivably be contracted out, but placing control of force to this degree in private hands would constitute too serious a threat to the political stability of the society. Others in these categories are left to the "voluntary" principle, if they are publicly sanctioned, generally in the form of "nonprofit" organizations.

It is important to note that financing of organizations is in general "affected with a public interest" and is in some degree to be regarded as an exercise of political power. This consideration derives from the character of an organization as a goal-directed social system. Every subgoal within the society must to some degree be integrated with the goal-structure of the society as a whole, and it is with this societal goal-structure that political institutions are above all concerned.[5]

The last of the four factors of production is what certain economists, notably Alfred Marshall, have called "organization" in the technical sense referred to above. This refers to the function of *combining* the factors of production in such ways as to facilitate the effective attainment of the organization's goal (in our general sense, in its "economic" or factor-consuming aspects). Its input into the organization stands on a level different from that of labor services and financing since it does not concern the direct facilities for carrying out defined functions in a relatively routine manner, but instead concerns readjustment in the patterns of organization itself. It is therefore, primarily significant in the longer run perspective, and it is involved in processes of structural change in the organization. In its business reference it is what J. A. Schumpeter referred to as "entrepreneurship."[6] Organization in this economic sense is, however, an essential factor in *all* organizational functioning. It necessarily plays a central part in the "founding" stages of any organization. From time to time it is important in later stages, since the kinds of adjustments to changing situations which are possible through the routine mechanisms of recruitment of labor services, and through the various devices for securing adequate financial resources, prove to be inadequate; hence a more fundamental structural change in the organization becomes necessary or desirable. This change would, in the present frame of reference, require a special input of the factor of organization in this technical sense.

The more generalized equivalent of the land factor is treated, except for the longest-run and most profound social changes, as the most constant reference point of all; its essential reference base is the stability of the value system in terms of which the goal of the organization is defined and the commitments involved in it are legitimized. It is from this reference base that the norms defining the broadly expected types of mechanism in the other respects will be derived, particularly those most actively involved in short-run operations, namely the recruitment of human services through the labor market and the financing of the organization.

THE MECHANISMS OF IMPLEMENTATION

The problem of mobilizing fluid resources concerns one major aspect of the external relations of the organization to the situation in which it operates. Once possessing control of the necessary resources, then, it must have a set of mechanisms by which these resources can be brought to bear on the actual process of goal-implementation in a changing situation. From one point of view, there are two aspects of this process. First is the set of relations to the external situation centering around the problem of "disposal" of the "product" of the organization's activities. This involves the basis on which the scale of operations is estimated and on which the settlement of terms with the recipients of this product is arrived at. In the economic context it is the problem of "marketing," but for present purposes it is necessary to generalize this concept to include all products of organization functioning whether they are "sold" or not; for example, the products of a military organization may be said to be disposed of immediately to the executive and legislative branches of the government and through them to the public, but of course in no direct sense are they sold. The second aspect of the process is concerned with the internal mechanisms of the mobilization of resources for the implementation of the goal. For purposes of the present analysis, however, it will not be necessary to treat these internal and external references separately. Both, as distinguished from the mobilization of resources, can be treated together as governed by the "operative code" of the organization.

This code will have to have an essential basis in the value system which governs the organization. In the case of mobilization of resources, this basis concerns the problem of the "claims" of the organization to the resources it needs and hence the settlement of the terms on which they would be available to it. In the operative case it concerns the manner of their utilization within the organization and the relation to its beneficiaries. We may speak of the relevant value-implementation as centering about the question of "authorization" of the measures involved in carrying through the processes of utilization of resources.

There is an important sense in which the focus of all these functions is the process ordinarily called "decision making." We have assumed that goal-attainment has clear primacy in the functioning of the organization. The paramount set of decisions then will be, within the

framework of legitimation previously referred to, the set of decisions as to how, on the more generalized level, to take steps to attain the goal. This is what is generally thought of as the area of *policy* decisions. A second set of decisions concerns implementation in the sense of decisions about the utilization of resources available to the organization. These are the *allocative* decisions and concern two main subject matters: the allocation of responsibilities among personnel, *i.e.*, suborganizations and individuals, and the allocation of fluid resources, *i.e.*, manpower and monetary and physical facilities in accord with these responsibilities. Finally, a third set of decisions concerns maintaining the *integration* of the organization, through facilitating cooperation and dealing with the motivational problems which arise within the organization in relation to the maintenance of cooperation. The first two sets of decisions fall within the area which Barnard calls the problem of "effectiveness"; the third is the locus of the problem of "efficiency" in his sense.[7] Let us consider each of these decision areas in more detail.

Policy Decisions

By policy decisions are meant decisions which relatively directly commit the organization as a whole and which stand in relatively direct connection to its primary functions. They are decisions touching such matters as determination of the nature and quality standards of "product," changes in the scale of operations, problems of the approach of the recipients of the product or service, and organization-wide problems of modes of internal operation.

Policy decisions as thus conceived may be taken at different levels of generality with respect to the functions of the organization. The very highest level concerns decisions to set up a given organization or, conversely, to liquidate it.

Near that level is a decision to merge with one or more other organizations. Then the scale descends through such levels as major changes in type of product or in scale of operations, to the day-to-day decisions about current operation. Broadly, this level of generality scale coincides with a scale of time span of the relevance of decisions; the ones touching the longer-run problems of the organization tend to be the ones on a higher level of generality, involving a wider range of considerations and leading to more serious commitments. An important task for the theory of organization is a systematic classification of these levels of generality of decisions.

As has been noted, the critical feature of policy decisions is the fact that they commit the organization as a whole to carrying out their implications. This area of decisions is the focus of the problem of responsibility. One but only one major aspect of responsibility in turn lies in the fact that all operations of organization to some extent involve risks, and the decision maker on the one hand is to some extent given "credit" for success, and on the other hand is legitimately held responsible for unfavorable consequences. One of the major features of roles of responsibility is the handling of these consequences; this becomes particularly complicated psychologically because it is often impossible to assess accurately the extent to which success or failure in fact stem from particular decisions or result from factors outside the control or predictive powers of the decision-maker. On high levels of responsibility conflicts of moral value may also operate.[8]

Because of the commitment of the organization as a whole, and through this of the interests of everyone participating in the organization to a greater or lesser degree, authorization becomes particularly important at the policy-decision level. This clearly connects with the value system and hence with the problem of legitimacy. It concerns not simply the content of particular decisions, but the right to make them.

Different organizations, according to scale and qualitative type, of course, have different concrete ways of organizing the policymaking process. Often the highest level of policy is placed mainly in the hands of some kind of a board; whereas "management" has responsibility for the next highest levels, with the still lower levels delegated to operative echelons.

Allocative Decisions

Higher policy decisions will concern the general type and quantity of resources brought into the organization and the more general policies toward personnel recruitment and financing. But the operative utilization of these facilities cannot be completely controlled from the center. There must be some allocative organization by which resources are distributed within the organization, and responsibility for their utilization in the various necessary operative tasks is assigned. This means that specialization in the functions of administration or management precludes the incumbents of these functions from also carrying out the main technical procedures involved in the organization-goal, and hence making the main operating decisions at the "work" level. Thus, a commanding general cannot actually man a particular aircraft or command a particular battery of artillery; a university president cannot actively teach all the subjects of instruction for which the university is responsible.

From one point of view, these mechanisms of internal allocation may be treated as "delegations of authority," though this formula will have to be qualified in connection with various cross-cutting considerations of types of competence and so forth. Thus a general, who by training and experience has been an artilleryman, when he is in command does not simply "delegate" authority to the air element under his command; he must in some way recognize the special technical competence of the air people in a field where he cannot have such competence. Similarly a university president who by academic training has been a professor of English does not merely delegate authority to the physicists on his faculty. Both must recognize an independent technical basis for "lower" echelons performing their functions in the ways in which their own technical judgment makes advisable. The technical man can reasonably be held responsible for the *results* of his operations; he cannot, however, be "dictated to" with respect to the technical procedures by which he achieves these results.

Seen in this light, there are two main aspects of the allocative decision process. One concerns mainly personnel (organized in suborganizations, for example, "departments"), the other financial and, at the requisite level, physical facilities. In the case of personnel the fundamental consideration is the allocation of responsibility. Using decisions as the reference point, the primary focus of the responsibility problem is allocation of the responsibility to decide, *i.e.*, the "decision who should decide," as Barnard puts it. Technical operations as such may then be treated as controlled by the allocation of responsibility for decisions.

The second main aspect of the allocation process is the budget. Though generally formalized only in rather large and highly differentiated organizations, analytically the budget is a central conception. It means the allocation of fluid financial resources which in turn can be committed to particular "uses," namely, acquisition of physical facilities and employment of personnel. Allocation of responsibility is definition of the *functions* of humanly organized subsystems of personnel. Budget allocation is giving these suborganizations access to the necessary means of carrying out their assignment. There is a certain important crisscrossing of the two lines in that at the higher level the decision tends to be one of budget, leaving the employment of the relevant personnel to the subsystem to which funds are allocated. The people responsible at the level in question in turn divide the resource stream, devoting part of it to personnel the employment of whom is, subject to general policies, under their control, another part to subbudget allocation of funds to the uses of personnel they employ. This step-down series continues until the personnel in question are given only various types and levels of control or use of physical facilities, and not control of funds.

Coordination Decisions

Two types of operative decisions have so far been discussed, namely policy decisions and allocative decisions. There is a third category which may be called "decisions of coordination," involving what Barnard has called the problems of "efficiency." These decisions are the operative decisions concerned with the integration of the organization as a system. Our two types of fundamental resources have a sharply asymmetrical relation to these decisions as they do to the allocative decisions. Funds (considered apart from their lenders or other suppliers) and physical resources do not have to be motivated to cooperate in organizational tasks, but human agents do. Decisions of policy and decisions of the allocation of responsibility still leave open the question of motivation to adequate performance.

This becomes an integrative problem because the special types of performance required to achieve the many complex contributions to an organization goal cannot be presumed to be motivated by the mere "nature" of the participants independently of the sanctions operating in the organizational situation. What is coordination from the point of view of the operation of the organization is "cooperation" from the point of view of the personnel. The limiting case of non-cooperation is declining to continue employment in the organization, a case of by no means negligible importance where a free labor market exists. But short of this, relative to the goals of the organization, it is reasonable to postulate an inherent centrifugal tendency of subunits of the organization, a tendency reflecting pulls deriving from the personalities of the participants, from the special adaptive exigencies of their particular job situations, and possibly from other sources.

In this situation the management of the organization must, to some degree, take or be ready to take measures to counteract the centrifugal pull, to keep employment turnover at least down to tolerable levels, and internally to bring the performances of subunits and individuals more closely into line with the requirements of the organization than would otherwise be the case. These measures can take any one or a combination of three fundamental forms: (1) coercion—in that penalties for noncooperation are set, (2) inducement—in that rewards for valued performance are instituted, and (3) "therapy"—in that by a complex and judicious combination of measures the motivational obstacles to satisfactory cooperation are dealt with on a level which "goes behind" the overt ostensible reasons given for the difficulty by the persons involved.[9]

INSTITUTIONAL FACTORS IN THE STRUCTURE OF ORGANIZATIONS

So far two problems have been dealt with, that of the adaptation of an organization to the situation in which it must operate, and that of its operative goal-attainment mechanisms. These prove to be capable of formulation in terms of the mechanisms of mobilization of fluid resources and of the central decision-making processes, respectively. There is, however, another central problem area which is not covered by these considerations, namely that of the mechanisms by which the organization is integrated with[10] other organizations and other types of collectivity in the total social system. This is not a matter of the organization in question treating its *social* situation or environment instrumentally, as a source for the procurement of resources or as the functionally defined field in which it produces its goal-attainment output and makes it available on agreed (or somehow settled) terms to other units of the social structure.

The problem concerns rather the *compatibility* of the institutional patterns under which the organization operates with those of other organizations and social units, as related to the integrative exigencies of the society as a whole (or of subsystems wider than the organization in question). It is hence in one aspect a question of the generalizability of the patterns of procedure adopted in the particular organization and hence of their permissibility from a wider social point of view. For example, if a given firm hires and fires on certain bases, will other firms in the same industry be allowed to follow this precedent? Or if the security officers in the Department of Defense follow a given procedure in dealing with alleged security risks, can the same procedure be tolerated in the State Department? If the two sets of procedures are in conflict, can the two organizations continue to differ or must they be subjected to a common set of principles?

It has already been noted that the integrative problem within an organization most directly concerns the human agents. This point can be generalized to interorganizational integration. The central problem concerns the institutionalized norms which can effectively bind the actions of individuals in their commitments to organizations. An important feature of all complex societies is that the normal individual is involved in a multiplicity of roles. From one point of view these roles constitute memberships in or commitments to collectivities, of which in turn organizations are one principal type. The focus of the integrative problem on a transorganizational level, then, is the problem of the determination of the loyalties of participant persons: on the one hand, the level of loyalty he bears to a particular organization (in which, for example, he is employed) and the bases of this loyalty; on the other hand, the way in which this loyalty fits into the larger system of loyalties in which his obligations to a plurality of roles are balanced (for example, to his job, family, and country). Clearly this allocation of loyalties, not within the organization but within the society between collectivities, is intimately connected with values. It cannot be only the values of the organization which govern, it must also be a higher-level value system, since the individual cannot determine his loyalties to the organization only on the basis of the values of that particular organization unless in some special sense it claims, and enforces the claim, to absolute loyalty. This is a limiting case, most nearly exemplified in our time by the totalitarian state.

There are three primary complexes of these integrative patterns which have the same order of hierarchical relation to each other that has been sketched for the case of decision-types. Particularly in a society where ascriptive elements of status are relatively minimized, the focal integrative institution is, from one point of view, that of contract. As applied to organizations, this is primarily relevant to the contract of employment. It is the contract of employment—including not only explicitly agreed terms, but "implicit" understandings and also including what Emile Durkheim called the "noncontractual" elements, *i.e.*, the norms governing the making and implementation of contracts which the parties are not at liberty to alter at will—which defines the individual's obligations to the organization. When for any reason the performance of these obligations is brought into question, the problem of loyalty is raised. Limitations on claims of loyalty made by the organization will arise from one or both of two sources, either the personality of the role-incumbent, in that doing what is asked may conflict with his personal values or may otherwise be motivationally distasteful to him, or from other role-obligations, for example, certain requests for overtime work may conflict with obligations to his family. The institution of contract regulates these possible conflicts through patterns which can apply to the organization in question but which at the same time can be motivationally acceptable to most people as "reasonable" and take into account the interests of the other role-complexes in which the same people are involved. Quite clearly the decisions about what particular personnel to hire may be a prerogative exclusively of the organization; the definitions of the institution of contract can in the nature of the case never be the prerogative of one organization, but, with variations, they must regulate the functioning of every organization in the society.

The contract of employment brings out the central significance of contractual relations most vividly. But essentially the same considerations are involved in contracts where property rights rather than human services are the objects of agreement. Where what is transferred is complete ownership, as in the sale of consumer goods or land or capital goods, problems of loyalty are residual. But contracts of investment and the various types of leases involve such considerations directly, since the holder of property claims against an organization is in a position to influence the operations of the organization, sometimes profoundly, through asserting his "rights." Clearly on the interorganization level these contractual patterns cannot be left to the discretion of the particular organization but must be institutionalized on a wider basis.

Both with respect to human services and with respect to property, elements of compulsion may enter to limit "freedom of contract." The case where the role-incumbent is given no choice may be treated as the limiting one. For each category there are two primary types of such limiting cases. With respect to human service one type is that of ascriptive status—for example, on the medieval manor—where the obligation to work a particular plot of land was based on hereditary serfdom to the lord of the manor. On the other hand, certain organizations in the society may exercise powers of compulsion over certain categories of the population in certain contingencies; conscription of military service is a conspicuous example. In the case of property, there may be ascriptive rights and obligations as exemplified by hereditary ownership of land which was inalienable, or there may be powers which make possible the compulsory relinquishment of property, for example, the taxing power.

The ascriptive case is not of great interest in the present context because it is seldom a feature of organizations in our technical sense. Compulsory contract is, however, of great interest. Essentially it consists of the exercise of authority by an organization of higher-order jurisdiction. It is thus a special combination of the institution of contract, as the definition of the rules under which resources can be made available to organizations, and of the institution of authority, which is the second of the three basic integrative institutions.

The institutionalization of authority may be treated on the interorganizational level as cognate with decision making as a function of the organization itself. Authority is the way in which the binding character of decisions is defined. It is an institutionalized feature of a reciprocal role relationship; there is hence always a double question. First, in what respects and how far is alter bound by ego's decisions and, second, how far and in what respects is ego bound by alter's decisions? We tend to speak of authority only when the relation is relatively one-sided, but the essential elements are present independently of this one-sidedness.

The institutionalization of authority defines, on a basis broader than that of the rules and practices of the organization itself, the ways and their limits in which any given actor, individual or collective, can in a given status in the organization bind others by his decisions and, conversely, the ways and limits in which his action can be bound by the decision of others. Where status in the organization is on a "free" contractual basis, the right to quit is a limiting protection against exposure to authority, and conversely the exerciser of authority is limited in its use by the danger of losing the personnel whose action he seeks to control. Where, as in the military case, the right to quit is severely restricted or altogether eliminated, authority can, of course, go much further.

Although both contract and authority, as institutionalized patterns of the wider society they prescribe, are rules transcending any particular organization, they define obligations which, once entered into, are particularistic. By accepting employment in an organization, an individual accepts a loyalty to that particular organization which, of course, has important limits but which at the same time must be respected within these limits. Authority is also limited, but once in the organization one undertakes responsibilities (*i.e.*, exercises authority) and undertakes to accept the authority of others within the limits of the legitimate range in this organization. These two institutions define the obligations specific to the role in the particular organization which come into force only so far as the incumbent accepts a relation to the organization.

In the conduct of an organization, however, there is a third class of rules or norms which govern conduct independently of any particular organization membership. They are universalistically defined for the society as a whole or for transorganizational sectors of the society's structure. A particularly basic one in our society is the complex having to do with personal freedoms; to take its extreme application, slavery is prohibited not only in that no one may coerce an individual into giving up his personal freedom, but even he himself may not, however voluntary a contractual arrangement, "sell himself" into slavery. The general rules against the use of force in human relations except under carefully regulated circumstances, against the use of outright fraud in almost any case (not, of course, including the withholding of information to which alter is not "entitled") and a variety of other cases fall here. The essential point is that the conduct of the affairs of an organization must in general conform with the norms of "good conduct" as recognized and institutionalized in the society. The most general principle is that no one may legitimately contract to violate these norms, nor may authority be used to coerce people into their violation.

Thus from another point of view the three complexes of institutionalized rules stand in a reverse relation to hierarchical priority. The most universalistic complex just discussed sets the limits in the treatment of human beings and non-human resources within which the conduct of organizations must remain. The institutionalization of authority then defines more specifically how, within these limits, resources may be used within the structure of the organization, while the institution of contract defines the terms on which the resources can be made available at all.

NOTES

1. There is already a considerable literature on organization which cuts across disciplinary lines. It is not the intention of this paper to attempt to review it. Three writers have been particularly important in stimulating the author's thinking in the field: Max Weber, Chester I. Barnard, and Herbert Simon. See particularly, Weber, *Theory of Social and Economic Organization* (New York, 1947), ch. iii; Barnard, *The Functions of the Executive* (Cambridge, Mass., 1938); Simon, *Administrative Behavior: A Study of Decision Making Processes in Administrative Organization* (New York, 1951).

2. Barnard, *op. cit.*, pt. II, ch. vii.

3. This possibly confusing terminological duplication is retained here because organization as a factor is commonly referred to in economic theory.

4. Weber, *op. cit.*, ch. iii.

5. This general thesis of the relation between financing and political power and the public interest has been developed by Parsons and Smelser, *Economy and Society* (London, 1956), especially in chapters ii and iii.

6. J. A. Schumpeter, *The Theory of Economic Development* (Cambridge, Mass.), 1934.

7. Barnard, *op. cit.*, pt. I, ch. v.

8. *Ibid.*, ch. xvii.

9. The famous phenomenon of restriction of production in the informal group as reported by

F. J. Roethlisberger and W. J. Dickson (*Management and the Worker* [Cambridge, Mass., 1939], pt. IV) is a case of relative failure of integration and hence, from one point of view, of failure of management in the function of coordination. It could be handled, from the present point of view, neither by policy decisions (*e.g.*, not to hire "uncooperative workers") nor by allocative decisions (*e.g.*, to hold the shop boss strictly responsible for meeting high production quotas), but only by decisions of coordination, presumably including "therapeutic" measures.

10. Not "adapted to." Adaptation has been considered under the headings already treated.

13
Theories of Bureaucracy
James G. March & Herbert A. Simon

Modern studies of "bureaucracies" date from Weber as to both time and acknowledged intellectual debt.[1] But, in a sense, Weber belongs more to the preceding chapter than he does to the present one. His major interests in the study of organizations appear to have been four: (1) to identify the characteristics of an entity he labelled "bureaucracy"; (2) to describe its growth and the reasons for its growth; (3) to isolate the concomitant social changes; (4) to discover the consequences of bureaucratic organization for the achievement of bureaucratic goals (primarily the goals of a political authority). It is in the last-named interest that Weber most clearly differentiates himself from the other writers who will be considered here. Weber wishes to show to what extent bureaucratic organization is a rational solution to the complexities of modern problems. More specifically, he wishes to show in what ways bureaucratic organization overcomes the decision-making or "computational" limits of individuals or alternative forms of organization (*i.e.*, through specialization, division of labor, etc.).

Consequently, Weber appears to have more in common with Urwick, Gulick, and others than he does with those who regard themselves as his successors. To be sure, Weber goes beyond the "machine" model in significant ways. In particular, he analyzes in some detail the relation between an official and his office. But, in general, Weber perceives bureaucracy as an adaptive device for using specialized skills, and he is not exceptionally attentive to the character of the human organism.

When we turn from Weber to the more recent students of bureaucracy, however, we find them paying increasing attention to the "unanticipated" responses of the organization members.[2] Without denying Weber's essential proposition that bureaucracies are more efficient (with respect to the goals of the formal hierarchy) than are alternative forms of organization, the research and analyses of Merton,[3] Selznick,[4] and Gouldner[5] have suggested important dysfunctional consequences of bureaucratic organization. In addition—explicitly in the case of Gouldner and implicitly in the other two authors—they have hypothesized

Source: From James G. March and Herbert A. Simon, *Organizations*, 36–47. Copyright © 1958 John Wiley & Sons, Inc. Reprinted by permission of John Wiley & Sons, Inc. Footnotes renumbered.

that the unintended consequences of treating individuals as machines actually encourage a continued use of the "machine" model.

The general structure of the theoretical systems of all three writers is remarkably similar. They use as the basic independent variable some form of organization or organizational procedure designed to control the activities of the organization members. These procedures are based primarily on what we have called the machine model of human behavior. They are shown to have the consequences anticipated by the organizational leaders, but also to have other, unanticipated, consequences. In turn, these consequences reinforce the tendency to use the control device. Thus, the systems may be depicted as in Figure 1.

The several systems examined here posit different sets of variables and theoretical relations. However, their structures are sufficiently similar to suggest that these studies in "bureaucracy" belong to a single class of theories.

THE MERTON MODEL

Merton[6] is concerned with dysfunctional organizational learning: organization members generalize a response from situations where the response is appropriate to similar situations where it results in consequences unanticipated and undesired by the organization. Merton asserts that changes in the personality of individual members of the organization stem from factors in the organizational structure. Here personality refers to any fairly reliable connection between certain stimuli and the characteristic responses to them. The label "personality" is attached to such a response pattern when the pattern does not change easily or rapidly.

Merton's system of propositions begins with a *demand for control* (3.1) made on the organization by the top hierarchy. This demand takes the form of an increased *emphasis on the reliability of behavior* (3.2) within the organization [3.2:3.1].[7] From the point of view of the top hierarchy, this represents a need for accountability and predictability of behavior. The techniques used to secure reliability draw upon what has been called here the "machine" model of human behavior. Standard operating procedures are instituted, and control consists largely in checking to ensure that these procedures are, in fact, followed.

Three consequences follow from this emphasis on reliability in behavior and the techniques used to install it:

1. There is a reduction in the *amount of personalized relationships* (3.3) [3.3:3.2]. The bureaucracy is a set of relationships between offices, or roles. The official reacts to other members of the organization not as more or less unique individuals but as representatives of positions that have specified rights and

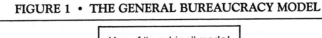

FIGURE 1 • THE GENERAL BUREAUCRACY MODEL

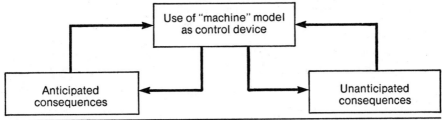

duties. Competition within the organization occurs within closely defined limits; evaluation and promotion are relatively independent of individual achievement (*e.g.*, promotion by seniority).

2. *Internalization of the rules of the organization* (3.4) by the participants is increased [3.4:3.2]. Rules originally devised to achieve organizational goals assume a positive value that is independent of the organizational goals. However, it is important to distinguish two phenomena, both of which have been called the "displacement of goals." In one case, a given stimulus evokes an activity perceived as leading to a preferred state of affairs. In a series of such situations, the repeated choice of the acceptable alternative causes a gradual transfer of the preference from the final state of affairs to the instrumental activity. In the other case, the choice of a desired alternative reveals additional desirable consequences not originally anticipated. The instrumental activity has, therefore, positively valued consequences even when it does not have the originally anticipated outcomes. It is this latter phenomenon (secondary reinforcement) that is operating in the present situation: the organizational setting brings about new personal or subunit consequences through participation in organizationally motivated actions.

3. There is increased *use of categorization as a decision-making technique* (3.5) [3.5:3.2]. To be sure, categorizing is a basic part of thinking in any situation. The special feature involved here is a tendency to restrict the categories used to a relatively small number and to enforce the first formally applicable category rather than search for the possible categories that might be applied and choose among them. An increase in the use of categorization for decision making decreases the *amount of search for alternatives* (3.6) [3.6:3.5].

The reduction in personalized relationships, the increased internalization of rules, and the decreased search for alternatives combine to make the behavior of members of the organization highly predictable; *i.e.*, they result in an increase in the *rigidity of behavior* (3.7) of participants [3.7:3.3, 3.4, 3.6]. At the same time, the reduction in personalized relationships (particularly with respect to internal competition) facilitates the development of an *esprit de corps*, i.e., increases the *extent to which goals are perceived as shared among members of the group* (3.8) [3.8:3.3]. Such a sense of commonness of purpose, interests, and character increases the *propensity of organization members to defend each other against outside pressures* (3.9) [3.9:3.8]. This, in turn, solidifies the tendency toward rigid behavior [3.7:3.9].

The rigidity of behavior has three major consequences. First, it substantially satisfies the original demands for reliability [3.2:3.7]. Thus, it meets an important maintenance need of the system. Further needs of this sort are met by strengthening in-group identification, as previously mentioned [3.2:3.8]. Second, it increases the *defensibility of individual action* (3.10) [3.10:3.7]. Simple categories rigorously applied to individual cases without regard for personal features can only be challenged at a higher level of the hierarchy. Third, the rigidity of behavior increases the *amount of difficulty with clients* (3.11) of the organization [3.11:3.7] and complicates the achievement of client satisfaction—a near-universal organizational goal. Difficulty with clients is further increased by an increase in the *extent of use of trappings of authority* (3.12) by subordinates in the organization [3.11:3.12], a procedure that is encouraged by the in-group's defensiveness [3.12:3.9].

The maintenance of part of the system by the techniques previously outlined produces a continuing pressure to maintain these techniques, as would be anticipated. It is somewhat more difficult to explain why the organization would continue to apply the same techniques in the face of client dissatisfaction. Why do organizational members fail to behave in each case in a manner appropriate to the situation? For the answer one must extend Merton's explicit statements by providing at least one, and perhaps two, additional feedback loops in the system. (It is not enough to say that such behavior becomes a part of the "personality." One must offer some explanation of why this apparently maladaptive learning takes place.)

The second major consequence of rigidity in behavior mentioned above (increased defensibility of individual action) is a deterrent to discrimination that reinforces the emphasis on reliability of behavior [3.2:3.10]. In addition, client dissatisfaction may in itself reinforce rigidity. On the one hand, client pressure at lower levels in the hierarchy tends to increase the *felt need for the defensibility of individual action* (3.13) [3.13:3.11]. On the other hand, remedial action demanded by clients from higher officials in the hierarchy may be misdirected. To the extent to which clients perceive themselves as being victims of discrimination (a perception that is facilitated in American culture by the importance attached to "equal treatment"), the proposals of clients or of the officials to whom they complain will probably strengthen the emphasis on reliability of behavior. This conflict between "service" and "impartiality" as goals for public organizations seems to lie behind a good deal of the literature on public bureaucracies.

We see that Merton's model is a rather complex set of relations among a relatively large number of variables. A simplified version of the model designed to illustrate its major features, is provided in Figure 2.

THE SELZNICK MODEL

Where Merton emphasizes rules as a response to the demand for control, Selznick emphasizes the delegation of authority.[8] Like Merton, however, Selznick wishes to show how the use of a control technique (*i.e.*, delegation) brings about a series of unanticipated consequences. Also, like Merton, Selznick shows how these consequences stem from the problems of maintaining highly interrelated systems of interpersonal relations.

Selznick's model starts with the demand for control made by the top hierarchy. As a result of this demand, an increased *delegation of authority* (3.14) is instituted [3.14:3.1].

Delegation, however, has several immediate consequences. As intended, it increases the *amount of training in specialized competences* (3.15) [3.15:3.14]. Restriction of attention to a relatively small number of problems increases experience within these limited areas and improves the employee's ability to deal with these problems. Operating through this mechanism, delegation tends to decrease the *difference between organizational goals and achievement* (3.16) [3.16:3.15], and thus to stimulate more delegation [3.14:3.16]. At the same time, however, delegation results in departmentalization and an increase in the *bifurcation of interests* (3.17) among the subunits in the organization [3.17:3.14]. The maintenance needs of the subunits dictate a commitment to the subunit goals over and above their contribution to the total organizational program. Many individual needs depend on the continued success and even expansion

FIGURE 2 • THE SIMPLIFIED MERTON MODEL

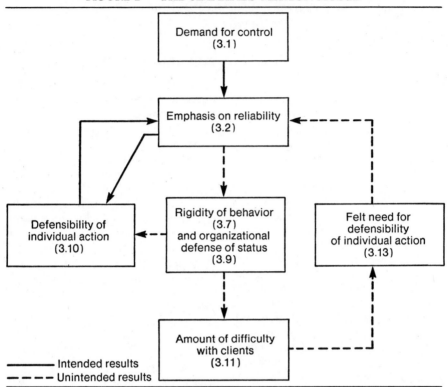

of the subunit. As in the previous example, the activities originally evaluated in terms of the organization goals are seen to have additional important ramifications for the subunits.

Bifurcation of interests is also stimulated by the specialized training that delegation (intendedly) produces. Training results in increased competence and, therefore, in increased *costs of changing personnel* (3.18) [3.18:3.15] and this results, in turn, in further differentiation of subunit goals [3.17:3.18].

The bifurcation within the organization leads to increased *conflict among organizational subunits* (3.19) [3.19:3.17]. As a consequence, the *content of decisions* (3.20) made within the organization depends increasingly upon considerations of internal strategy, particularly

if there is little *internalization of organizational goals by participants* (3.21) [3.20:3.19, 3.21]. As a result there is an increase in the difference between organizational goals and achievement [3.16:3.20] and this results in an increase in delegation [3.14:3.16]. . . .

This effect on daily decisions is accentuated by two other mechanisms in Selznick's system. The struggle for internal control not only affects directly the content of decisions, but also causes greater *elaboration of subunit ideologies* (3.22) [3.22:3.19]. Each subunit seeks success by fitting its policy into the official doctrine of the large organization to legitimize its demands. Such a tactic increases the *internalization of subgoals by participants* (3.23) within subunits [3.23:3.22].

At the same time, the internalization of subgoals is reinforced by a feedback from the daily decisions it influences. The necessity for making daily decisions creates a system of precedents. Decisions depend primarily on the operational criteria provided by the organization, and, among these criteria, subunit goals are of considerable importance [3.20:3.23]. Precedents tend to become habitual responses to the situations for which they are defined as relevant and thus to reinforce the internalization of subunit goals [3.23:3.20]. Obviously, internalization of subgoals is partially dependent on the *operationality of organizational goals* (3.24). By operationality of goals, we mean the extent to which it is possible to observe and test how well goals are being achieved. Variations in the operationality of organizational goals affect the content of daily decisions [3.20:3.24] and thus the extent of subunit goal internalization.

From this it is clear that delegation has both functional and dysfunctional consequences for the achievement of organizational goals. It contributes both to their realization and to their deflection. Surprisingly, the theory postulates that both increases and decreases in goal achievement cause an increase in delegation. Why does not normal learning occur here? The answer seems to be that when goals are not achieved, delegation is—within the framework of the "machine" model—the correct response, and the model does not consider alternatives to simple delegation. On the other hand, the model offers explicitly at least two "dampers" that limit the operation of the dysfunctional mechanisms. As is indicated in Figure 3 where the skeleton of the Selznick model is outlined, there are two (not entirely independent) variables treated as independent but potentially amenable to organizational control, each of which restrains the runaway features of daily decision-making. By suitable changes in the extent to which organi-

zational goals are operational or in the internalization of organizational goals by participants, some of the dysfunctional effects of delegation can be reduced. (To be sure, this ignores the possible effect of such procedures on the maintenance problems of the subunits and the consequent results for the larger organizations, but these are problems we are not prepared to attack at the moment.)

THE GOULDNER MODEL

In terms of number of variables and relations, Gouldner's model[9] is the simplest of the three presented here; but it exhibits the major features of the two previous systems. Like Merton, Gouldner is concerned with the consequences of bureaucratic rules for the maintenance of organization structure. Like both Merton and Selznick, he attempts to show how a control technique designed to maintain the equilibrium of a subsystem disturbs the equilibrium of a larger system, with a subsequent feedback on the subsystem.

In Gouldner's system, the *use of general and impersonal rules* (3.25) regulating the work procedures is part of the response to the demand for control from the top hierarchy [3.25:3.1]. One consequence of such rules is to decrease the *visibility of power relations* (3.26) within the group [3.26:3.25]. The visibility of authority differences within the work group interacts with the *extent to which equality norms are held* (3.27) to affect the *legitimacy of the supervisory role* (3.28) [3.28:3.26, 3.27]. This, in turn, affects the *level of interpersonal tension* (3.29) in the work group [3.29:3.28]. In the American culture of egalitarian norms, decreases in power visibility increase the legitimacy of the supervisory position and therefore decrease tension within the group.

Gouldner argues that these anticipated consequences of rule-making do occur, that the survival of the work group

FIGURE 3 • THE SIMPLIFIED SELZNICK MODEL

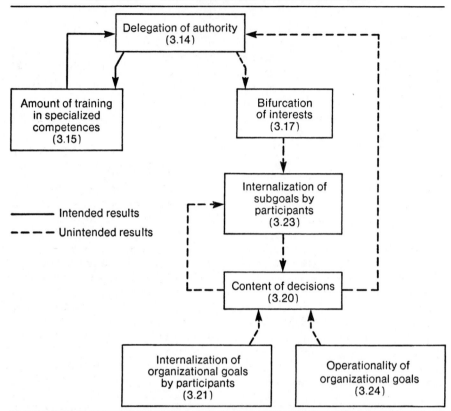

as an operating unit is substantially furthered by the creation of general rules, and that consequently the use of such rules is reinforced [3.25:3.29].

At the same time, however, work rules provide cues for organizational members beyond those intended by the authority figures in the organization. Specifically, by defining unacceptable behavior, they increase *knowledge about minimum acceptable behavior* (3.30) [3.30:3.25]. In conjunction with a low level of internalization of organizational goals, specifying a minimum level of permissible behavior increases the disparity between organization goals and achievement by depressing behavior to the minimum level [3.16:3.21, 3.30].

Performance at the minimum level is perceived by hierarchical superiors as a failure. In short, the internal stabilizing effects of the rules are matched by the unbalance they produce in the larger organization. The response to the unbalance is an increase in the *closeness of supervision* (3.31) over the work group [3.31:3.16]. This response is based on the "machine" model of human behavior: low performance indicates a need for more detailed inspection and control over the operation of the "machine."

In turn, however, close supervision increases the visibility of power relations within the organization [3.26:3.31], raises the tension level in the work group, and thereby upsets the equilibrium originally based on the institution of rules. The broad outline of the model is shown in Figure 4.

Gouldner's model leaves some puzzles unexplained. In particular, why is increased supervision the supervisory response to low performance? It seems reasonable that the tendency to make such a response is affected both by role perceptions and by a third equilibrating process in the system—the individual needs of the supervisors. Thus, the intensity of supervision is a function of the *authoritarianism of supervisors* (3.32) and a function of the *punitivity of supervisory role perception*(3.33) [3.31:3.32, 3.33].

As in the Selznick model, the existence of "dampers" on the system poses the question of their treatment as external variables. Appropriate manipu-lation of equality norms, perceived commonality of interest, and the needs of supervisors will restrict the operation of the dysfunctional features of the system. The failure of top management to use such techniques of control suggests that the system may be incompletely defined.

PROBLEMS OF VERIFICATION

We have sketched three major "models" of bureaucratic behavior. To what extent are the hypotheses empirically verified? Both Selznick and Gouldner base their propositions on extended observations of single organizations in the field. The data on which Merton relies are somewhat less specific but appear to be distilled from a set of generally accepted characterizations of organizational behavior.

FIGURE 4 · THE SIMPLIFIED GOULDNER MODEL

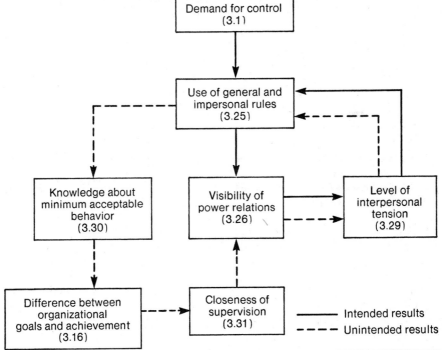

Such evidence raises two major problems. First, what is the role of field research in verifying hypotheses about organizational behavior? The field situation fails to meet many of the major assumptions underlying standard techniques of statistical inference. The second problem is distinctly related to the first. What is the standing of the single case as evidence? For example, one of the knottier complications in this area is deciding what the sample size really is.

At least some of the propositions advanced by these three writers will be reexamined below in different contexts. Some hypotheses relating the closeness of supervision to employee satisfaction are considered later in the present chapter, and some hypotheses concerning organizational conflict can be found in Chapter 5. As we will suggest in those passages, there is evidence for some of the propositions over and above the single field studies discussed here. The evidence is scarcely conclusive and far from complete, but on the whole tends to be consistent with the general models used by Merton, Selznick, and Gouldner. What little we can say beyond that is indicated below.

IMPLICATIONS OF THE BUREAUCRACY MODELS

Other quite comparable models can be added to those examined here. Bendix has discussed limits on technical rationality within an organization and pointed out the intriguing complications involved in the use of spy systems as systems of control.[10] Dubin has presented a model quite similar to that of Merton.[11] Blau has examined the changes in operating procedures that occur at a relatively low level in the hierarchy under the pressure of work group needs.[12]

In the sample of three cases from the "bureaucracy" literature we have

presented (as well as in the others mentioned), complications arise in each of the three ways predicted from the influence model outlined previously. The elaboration of evoking connections, the presence of unintended cues, and organizationally dysfunctional learning appear to account for most of the unanticipated consequences with which these theories deal.

Many of the central problems for the analysis of human behavior in large-scale organizations stem from the operation of subsystems within the total organizational structure. The sociological studies of the work group analyzed here have focussed on the ways in which the needs of individuals, the primary work group, and the large organization interact to affect each other. We now turn to the study of morale and productivity, where we also find that the study of the psychology of work has focussed on the same interactions, with perhaps a greater emphasis on the relations between the needs of individual personalities and the needs of the organization.

NOTES

1. M. Weber, *From Max Weber: Essays in Sociology,* trans, Gerth and Mills (Oxford, 1946). M. Weber, *The Theory of Social and Economic Organization,* trans. Henderson and Parsons (Oxford, 1947).

2. R. K. Merton, "The Unanticipated Consequences of Purposive Social Action," *American Sociological Review* 1 (1936): 894–904. A. W. Gouldner, "Theoretical Requirements of the Applied Social Sciences," *American Sociological Review* 22 (1957): 91–102.

3. R. K. Merton, "Bureaucratic Structure and Personality," *Social Forces* 18 (1940): 560–68.

4. P. Selznick, *TVA and the Grass Roots* (Berkeley, Calif., 1949).

5. A. W. Gouldner, *Patterns of Industrial Bureaucracy* (Glencoe, Ill., 1954).

6. Merton, *Bureaucratic Structure, op. cit.*

7. See pp. 8–9 of this book for an explanation of the numbering system used for the propositions.

8. Selznick, *op. cit.*

9. Gouldner, *Patterns, op. cit.*

10. R. Bendix, "Bureaucracy: The Problem and Its Setting," *American Sociological Review* 12 (1947): 493–507.

11. R. Dubin, "Decision-Making by Management Relations," *Administrative Science Quarterly* 2 (1957): 60–81.

12. P. M. Blau, *The Dynamics of Bureaucracy* (Chicago, 1955).

14
A Behavioral Theory of Organizational Objectives
Richard M. Cyert & James G. March

Organizations make decisions. They make decisions in the same sense in which individuals make decisions: The organization as a whole behaves as though there existed a central coordination and control system capable of directing the behavior of the members of the organization sufficiently to allow the meaningful imputation of purpose to the total system. Because the central nervous system of most organizations appears to be somewhat different from that of the individual system, we are understandably cautious about viewing organization decision-making in quite the same terms as those applied to individual choice. Nevertheless, organizational choice is a legitimate and important focus of research attention.

As in theories of individual choice, theories of organizational decision-making fall into two broad classes. Normative theorists—particularly economic theorists of the firm—have been dedicated to the improvement of the rationality of organizational choice. Recent developments in the application of mathematics to the solution of economic decision-problems are fully and effectively in such a tradition (Cooper, Hitch, Baumol, Shubik, Schelling, Valavanis, and Ellsberg, 1958). The empirical theory of organizational decision-making has a much more checkered tradition and is considerably less well-developed (March and Simon, 1958).

The present efforts to develop a behavioral theory of organizational decision-making represent attempts to overcome the disparity between the importance of decision-making in organizations and our understanding of how, in fact, such decisions are made. The research as a whole, as well as that part of it discussed below, is based on three initial commitments. The first of these is to develop an explicitly empirical theory rather than a normative one. Our interest is in understanding how complex organizations make decisions, not how they ought to do so. Without denying the importance of normative theory, we are convinced that the major current needs are for empirical knowledge.

Source: Mason Haire, ed. *Modern Organization Theory* (New York: John Wiley & Sons, 1959), 76–90.

The second commitment is to focus on the classic problems long explored in economic theory—pricing, resource allocation, and capital investment. This commitment is intended to overcome some difficulties with existing organization theory. By introducing organizational propositions into models of rather complex systems, we are driven to increase the precision of the propositions considerably. At present, anyone taking existing organization theory as a base for predicting behavior within organizations finds that he can make a number of rather important predictions of the general form: If x varies, y will vary. Only rarely will he find either the parameters of the functions or more elaborate predictions for situations in which the *ceteris paribus* assumptions are not met.

The third commitment is to approximate in the theory the process by which decisions are made by organizations. This commitment to a process-oriented theory is not new. It has typified many organization theorists in the past (Marshall, 1919; Weber, 1947). The sentiment that one should substitute observation for assumption whenever possible seems, a priori, reasonable. Traditionally, the major dilemma in organization theory has been between putting into the theory all the features of organizations we think are relevant and thereby making the theory unmanageable, or pruning the model down to a simple system, thereby making it unrealistic. So long as we had to deal primarily with classical mathematics, there was, in fact, little we could do. With the advent of the computer and the use of simulation, we have a methodology that will permit us to expand considerably the emphasis on actual process without losing the predictive precision essential to testing (Cyert and March, in press, 1959).

In models currently being developed there are four major subsystems. Since they operate more or less independently, it is possible to conceive them as the four basic subtheories required for a behavioral theory of organizational decision making: first, the theory of organizational objectives; second, the theory of organizational expectations; third, the theory of organizational choice; fourth, the theory of organizational implementation. In this paper we discuss the first of these only, the theory of organizational objectives.

The Organization as a Coalition

Let us conceive the organization as a coalition. It is a coalition of individuals, some of them organized into subcoalitions. In the business organization, one immediately thinks of such coalition members as managers, workers, stockholders, suppliers, customers, lawyers, tax collectors, etc. In the governmental organization, one thinks of such members as administrators, workers, appointive officials, elective officials, legislators, judges, clientele, etc. In the voluntary charitable organization, one thinks of paid functionaries, volunteers, donors, donees, etc.

This view of an organization as a coalition suggests, of course, several different recent treatments of organization theory in which a similar basic position is adopted. In particular, inducements-contributions theory (Barnard, 1938; Simon, 1947), theory of games (von Neumann and Morgenstern, 1947), and theory of teams (Marschak, in this volume). Each of these theories is substantially equivalent on this score. Each specifies:

1. That organizations include individual participants with (at least potentially) widely varying preference orderings.
2. That through bargaining and side payments the participants in the organization enter into a coalition agreement

for purposes of the game. This agreement specifies a joint preference-ordering (or organizational objective) for the coalition.

3. That thereafter the coalition can be treated as a single strategist, entrepreneur, or what have you.

Such a formulation permits us to move immediately to modern decision theory, which has been an important part of recent developments in normative organization theory. In our view, however, a joint preference ordering is not a particularly good description of actual organization goals. Studies of organizational objectives suggest that to the extent to which there is agreement on objectives, it is agreement on highly ambiguous goals (Truman, 1951; Kaplan, Dirlam, and Lanzillotti, 1958). Such agreement is undoubtedly important to choice within the organization, but it is a far cry from a clear preference ordering. The studies suggest further that behind this agreement on rather vague objectives there is considerable disagreement and uncertainty about subgoals; that organizations appear to be pursuing one goal at one time and another (partially inconsistent) goal at another; and that different parts of the organization appear to be pursuing different goals at the same time (Kaplan, Dirlam, and Lanzillotti, 1958; Selznick, 1949). Finally, the studies suggest that most organization objectives take the form of an aspiration level rather than an imperative to "maximize" or "minimize," and that the aspiration level changes in response to experience (Blau, 1955; Alt, 1949).

In the theory to be outlined here, we consider three major ways in which the objectives of a coalition are determined. The first of these is the bargaining process by which the composition and general terms of the coalition are fixed. The second is the internal organizational process of control by which objectives are stabilized and elaborated. The third is the process of adjustment to experience, by which coalition agreements are altered in response to environmental changes. Each of these processes is considered, in turn, in the next three sections of the paper.

Formation of Coalition Objectives through Bargaining

A basic problem in developing a theory of coalition formation is the problem of handling side payments. No matter how we try we simply cannot imagine that the side payments by which organizational coalitions are formed even remotely satisfy the requirements of unrestricted transferability of utility. Side payments are made in many forms: money, personal treatment, authority, organization policy, etc. A winning coalition does not have a fixed booty which it then divides among its members. Quite to the contrary, the total value of side payments available for division among coalition members is a function of the composition of the coalition; and the total utility of the actual side payments depends on the distribution made within the coalition. There is no conservation of utility.

For example, if we can imagine a situation in which any dyad is a viable coalition (e.g., a partnership to exploit the proposition that two can live more cheaply in coalition than separately), we would predict a greater total utility for those dyads in which needs were complementary than for those in which they were competitive. Generally speaking, therefore, the partitioning of the adult population into male-female dyads is probably more efficient from the point of view of total utility accruing to the coalition than is a partition into sexually homogeneous pairs.

Such a situation makes game theory as it currently exists virtually irrelevant for a treatment of organizational side payments (Luce and Raiffa, 1957). But the problem is in part even deeper than that. The second requirement of such theories as game theory, theory of teams, and inducements-contributions theory, is that after the side payments are made, a joint preference ordering is defined. All conflict is settled by the side-payment bargaining. The employment-contract form of these theories, for example, assumes that the entrepreneur has an objective. He then purchases whatever services he needs to achieve the objective. In return for such payments, employees contract to perform whatever is required of them—at least within the range of permissible requirements. For a price, the employee adopts the "organization" goal.

One strange feature of such a conception is that it describes a coalition asymmetrically. To what extent is it arbitrary that we call wage payments "costs" and dividend payments "profits"—rather than the other way around? Why is it that in our quasi-genetic moments we are inclined to say that in the beginning there was a manager and he recruited workers and capital? For the development of our own theory we make two major arguments. First, the emphasis on the asymmetry has seriously confused our understanding of organizational goals. The confusion arises because ultimately it makes only slightly more sense to say that the goal of a business organization is to maximize profit than it does to say that its goal is to maximize the salary of Sam Smith, Assistant to the Janitor.

Second, despite this there are important reasons for viewing some coalition members as quite different from others. For example, it is clear that employees and management make somewhat different demands on the organization. Ir their

bargaining, side payments appear traditionally to have performed the classical function of specifying a joint preference ordering. In addition, some coalition members (e.g., many stockholders) devote substantially less time to the particular coalition under consideration than do others. It is this characteristic that has usually been used to draw organizational boundaries between "external" and "internal" members of the coalition. Thus, there are important classes of coalition members who are passive most of the time. A condition of such passivity must be that the payment demands they make are of such a character that most of the time they can be met rather easily.

Although we thereby reduce substantially the size and complexity of the coalition relevant for most goal-setting, we are still left with something more complicated than an individual entrepreneur. It is primarily through bargaining within this active group that what we call organizational objectives arise. Side payments, far from being incidental distribution of a fixed, transferable booty, represent the central process of goal specification. That is, a significant number of these payments are in the form of policy commitments.

The distinction between demands for monetary side payments and demands for policy commitments seems to underlie management-oriented treatments of organizations. It is clear that in many organizations this distinction has important ideological and therefore affective connotations. Indeed, the breakdown of the distinction in our generation has been quite consistently violent. Political party-machines in this country have changed drastically the ratio of direct monetary side payments (e.g., patronage, charity) to policy commitments (e.g., economic legislation). Labor unions are conspicuously entering into what has been viewed traditionally as the management prerogatives of policy-making, and demanding payments in that area. Military forces have long since given up the substance—if not entirely the pretense—of being simply hired agents of the regime. The phenomenon is especially obvious in public (Dahl and Lindblom, 1953; Simon, Smithburg, and Thompson, 1950) and voluntary (Sills, 1957; Messinger, 1955) organizations; but all organizations use policy side payments. The marginal cost to other coalition members is typically quite small.

This trend toward policy side payments is particularly observable in contemporary organizations, but the important point is that we have never come close to maintenance of a sharp distinction in the kinds of payments made and demanded. Policy commitments have (one is tempted to say always) been an important part of the method by which coalitions are formed. In fact, an organization that does not use such devices can exist in only a rather special environment.

To illustrate coalition formation under conditions where the problem is not scarce resources for side payments, but varying complementarities of policy demands, imagine a nine-man committee appointed to commission a painting for the village hall. The nine members make individually the following demands:

Committeeman A: The painting must be an abstract monotone.

Committeeman B: The painting must be an impressionistic oil.

Committeeman C: The painting must be small and oval in shape.

Committeeman D: The painting must be small and in oil.

Committeeman E: The painting must be square in shape and multicolored.

Committeeman F: The painting must be an impressionistic square.

Committeeman G: The painting must be a monotone and in oil.

Committeeman H: The painting must be multicolored and impressionistic.

Committeeman I: The painting must be small and oval.

In this case, each potential coalition member makes two simple demands. Assuming that five members are all that are required to make the decision, there are three feasible coalitions. A, C, D, G, and I can form a coalition and commission a small, oval, monotone, oil abstract. B, C, D, H, and I can form a coalition and commission a small, oval, multicolored, impressionistic oil. B, D, E, F, and H can form a coalition and commission a small, square, multicolored, impressionistic oil.

Committeeman D, it will be noted, is in the admirable position of being included in every possible coalition. The reason is clear; his demands are completely consistent with the demands of everyone else.

Obviously at some level of generality the distinction between money and policy payments disappears because any side payment can be viewed as a policy constraint. When we agree to pay someone $35,000 a year, we are constrained to that set of policy decisions that will allow such a payment. Any allocation of scarce resources (such as money) limits the alternatives for the organization. But the scarcity of resources is not the only kind of problem. Some policy demands are strictly inconsistent with other demands. Others are completely complementary. If I demand of the organization that John Jones be shot and you demand that he be sainted, it will be difficult for us both to stay in the organization. This is not because either bullets or haloes are in short supply or because we don't have enough money for both.

To be sure, the problems of policy consistency are *in principle* amenable to explicit optimizing behavior. But they add to the computational difficulties facing the coalition members and make it even more obvious why the bargaining leading to side payment and policy agreements is only slightly related to the bargaining anticipated in a theory of omniscient rationality. The tests of short-run feasibility that they represent lead to the familiar complications of conflict, disagreement, and rebargaining.

In the process of bargaining over side payments many of the organizational objectives are defined. Because of the form the bargaining takes, the objectives tend to have several important attributes. First, they are imperfectly rationalized. Depending on the skill of the leaders involved, the sequence of demands leading to the new bargaining, the aggressiveness of various parts of the organization, and the scarcity of resources, the new demands will be tested for consistency with existing policy. But this testing is normally far from complete. Second, some objectives are stated in the form of aspiration-level constraints. Objectives arise in this form when demands which are consistent with the coalition are stated in this form. For example, the demand, "We must allocate ten percent of our total budget to research." Third, some objectives are stated in a nonoperational form. In our formulation such objectives arise when potential coalition members have demands which are nonoperational or demands which can be made nonoperational. The prevalence of objectives in this form can be explained by the fact that nonoperational objectives are consistent with virtually any set of objectives.

Stabilization and Elaboration of Objectives

The bargaining process goes on more or less continuously, turning out a long series of commitments. But a description of goal formation simply in such terms is not adequate. Organizational objectives are, first of all, much more stable than would be suggested by such a model, and secondly, such a model does not handle very well the elaboration and clarification of goals through day-to-day bargaining.

Central to an understanding of these phenomena is again an appreciation for the limitations of human capacities and time to devote to any particular aspect of the organizational system. Let us return to our conception of a coalition having monetary and policy side payments. These side-payment agreements are incomplete. They do not anticipate effectively all possible future situations, and they do not identify all considerations that might be viewed as important by the coalition members at some future time. Nevertheless, the coalition members are motivated to operate under the agreements and to develop some mutual control-systems for enforcing them.

One such mutual control-system in many organizations is the budget. A budget is a highly explicit elaboration of previous commitments. Although it is usually viewed as an asymmetric control-device (i.e., a means for superiors to control subordinates), it is clear that it represents a form of mutual control. Just as there are usually severe costs to the department in exceeding the budget, so also are there severe costs to other members of the coalition if the budget is not paid in full. As a result, budgets in every organization tend to be self-confirming.

A second major, mutual control-system is the allocation of functions. Division of labor and specialization are commonly treated in management textbooks simply as techniques of rational organization. If, however, we consider the allocation of functions in much the way we would normally view the allocation of resources during budgeting, a somewhat different picture emerges. When we define the limits of discretion, we constrain the individual or subgroup from acting outside those limits. But at the same time, we constrain any other members of the coalition from prohibiting action within those limits. Like the allocation of resources in a budget, the allocation of discretion in an organization chart is largely self-confirming.

The secondary bargaining involved in such mutual control-systems serves to elaborate and revise the coalition agreements made on entry (Thompson and McEwen, 1958). In the early life of an organization, or after some exceptionally drastic organizational upheaval, this elaboration occurs in a context where very little is taken as given. Relatively deliberate action must be taken on everything from pricing policy to paperclip policy. Reports from individuals who have lived through such early stages emphasize the lack of structure that typifies settings for day-to-day decisions (Simon, 1953).

In most organizations most of the time, however, the elaboration of objectives occurs within much tighter constraints. Much of the situation is taken as given. This is true primarily because organizations have memories in the form of precedents, and individuals in the coalition are strongly motivated to accept the precedents as binding. Whether precedents are formalized in the shape of an official standard-operating-procedure or are less formally stored, they remove from conscious consideration many agreements, decisions, and commitments that might well be subject to renegotiation in an organization without a memory

(Cyert and March, to be published, 1960). Past bargains become precedents for present situations. A budget becomes a precedent for future budgets. An allocation of functions becomes a precedent for future allocations. Through all the well-known mechanisms, the coalition agreements of today are institutionalized into semipermanent arrangements. A number of administrative aphorisms come to mind: an unfilled position disappears; see an empty office and fill it up; there is nothing temporary under the sun. As a result of organizational precedents, objectives exhibit much greater stability than would typify a pure bargaining situation. The "accidents" of organizational genealogy tend to be perpetuated.

Changes in Objectives through Experience

Although considerably stabilized by memory and institutionalization-phenomena, the demands made on the coalition by individual members do change with experience. Both the nature of the demands and their quantitative level vary over time.

Since many of the requirements specified by individual participants are in the form of attainable goals rather than general maximizing constraints, objectives are subject to the usual phenomena associated with aspiration levels. As an approximation to the aspiration-level model, we can take the following set of propositions:

1. In the steady state, aspiration level exceeds achievement by a small amount.
2. Where achievement increases at an increasing rate, aspiration level will exhibit short-run lags behind achievement.
3. Where achievement decreases, aspiration level will be substantially above achievement.

These propositions derive from simpler assumptions requiring that current aspiration be an optimistic extrapolation of past achievement and past aspiration. Although such assumptions are sometimes inappropriate, the model seems to be consistent with a wide range of human goal-setting behavior (Lewin, Dembo, Festinger, and Sears, 1944). Two kinds of achievement are, of course, important. The first is the achievement of the participant himself. The second is the achievement of others in his reference group (Festinger, 1954).

Because of these phenomena, our theory of organizational objectives must allow for drift in the demands of members of the organization. No one doubts that aspirations with respect to monetary compensation vary substantially as a function of payments received. So also do aspirations regarding advertising budget, quality of product, volume of sales, product mix, and capital investment. Obviously, until we know a great deal more than we do about the parameters of the relation between achievement and aspiration we can make only relatively weak predictions. But some of these predictions are quite useful, particularly in conjunction with search theory (Cyert, Dill, and March, 1958).

For example, two situations are particularly intriguing. What happens when the rate of improvement in the environment is great enough so that it outruns the upward adjustment of aspiration? Second, what happens when the environment becomes less favorable? The general answer to both of these questions involves the concept of organizational slack (Cyert and March, 1956). When the environment outruns aspiration-level adjustment, the organization secures, or at least has the potentiality of securing, resources in excess of its demands. Some of these resources are simply not obtained—although they are available. Others are used to meet the revised demands of those members of the coalition whose demands adjust most rapidly—usually those most deeply involved in the organization. The excess resources would not be subject to very general bargaining because they do not involve allocation in the face of scarcity. Coincidentally perhaps, the absorption of excess resources also serves to delay aspiration-level adjustment by passive members of the coalition.

When the environment becomes less favorable, organizational slack represents a cushion. Resource scarcity brings on renewed bargaining and tends to cut heavily into the excess payments introduced during plusher times. It does not necessarily mean that precisely those demands that grew abnormally during better days are pruned abnormally during poorer ones; but in general we would expect this to be approximately the case.

Some attempts have been made to use these very simple propositions to generate some meaningful empirical predictions. Thus, we predict that, discounting for the economies of scale, relatively successful firms will have higher unit-costs than relatively unsuccessful ones. We predict that advertising expenditures will be a function of sales in the previous time period at least as much as the reverse will be true.

The nature of the demands also changes with experience in another way. We do not conceive that individual members of the coalition will have a simple listing of demands, with only the quantitative values changing over time. Instead we imagine each member as having a rather disorganized file case full of demands. At any point in time, the member attends to only a rather small subset of his demands, the number and variety depending again on the extent of his involvement in the organization and on the demands of his other commitments on his attention.

Since not all demands are attended to at the same time, one important part of the theory of organizational objectives is to predict when particular units in the organization will attend to particular goals. Consider the safety goal in a large corporation. For the safety engineers, this is a very important goal most of the time. Other parts of the organization rarely even consider it. If, however, the organization has some drastic experience (e.g., a multiple fatality), attention to a safety goal is much more widespread and safety action quite probable.

Whatever the experience, it shifts the attention-focus. In some (as in the safety example), adverse experience suggests a problem area to be attacked. In others, solutions to problems stimulate attention to a particular goal. An organization with an active personnel-research department will devote substantial attention to personnel goals not because it is necessarily a particularly pressing problem but because the subunit keeps generating solutions that remind other members of the organization of a particular set of objectives they profess.

The notion of attention-focus suggests one reason why organizations are successful in surviving with a large set of unrationalized goals. They rarely see the conflicting objectives simultaneously. For example, let us reconsider the case of the pair of demands that John Jones be either (a) shot or (b) sainted. Quite naturally, these were described as inconsistent demands. Jones cannot be simultaneously shot and sainted. But the emphasis should be on *simultaneously*. It is quite feasible for him to be first shot and then sainted, or vice versa. It is logically feasible because a halo can be attached as firmly to a dead man as to a live one and a saint is as susceptible to bullets as a sinner. It

is organizationally feasible because the probability is low that both of these demands will be attended to simultaneously.

The sequential attention to goals is a simple mechanism. A consequence of the mechanism is that organizations ignore many conditions that outside observers see as direct contradictions. They are contradictions only if we imagine a well-established, joint preference ordering or omniscient bargaining. Neither condition exists in an organization. If we assume that attention to goals is limited, we can explain the absence of any strong pressure to resolve apparent internal inconsistencies. This is not to argue that all conflicts involving objectives can be resolved in this way, but it is one important mechanism that deserves much more intensive study.

Constructing a Predictive Theory

Before the general considerations outlined above can be transformed into a useful predictive theory, a considerable amount of precision must be added. The introduction of precision depends, in turn, on the future success of research into the process of coalition formation. Nevertheless, some steps can be taken now to develop the theory. In particular, we can specify a general framework for a theory and indicate its needs for further development.

We assume a set of coalition members, actual or potential. Whether these members are individuals or groups of individuals is unimportant. Some of the possible subsets drawn from this set are viable coalitions. That is, we will identify a class of combinations of members such that any of these combinations meet the minimal standards imposed by the external environment on the organization. Patently, therefore, the composition of the viable set of coalitions will depend on environmental conditions.

For each of the potential coalition members we require a set of demands. Each such individual set is partitioned into an active part currently attended to and an inactive part currently ignored. Each demand can be characterized by two factors; first, its marginal resource requirements, given the demands of all possible other combinations of demands from potential coalition members; second, its marginal consistency with all possible combinations of demands from potential coalition members.

For each potential coalition member we also require a set of problems, partitioned similarly into an active and an inactive part.

This provides us with the framework of the theory. In addition, we need five basic mechanisms. First, we need a mechanism that changes the quantitative value of the demands over time. In our formulation, this becomes a version of the basic aspiration-level and mutual control theory outlined earlier.

Second, we need an attention-focus mechanism that transfers demands among the three possible states: active set, inactive set, not-considered set. We have said that some organizational participants will attend to more demands than other participants and that for all participants some demands will be considered at one time and others at other times. But we know rather little about the actual mechanisms that control this attention factor.

Third, we need a similar attention-focus mechanism for problems. As we have noted, there is a major interaction between what problems are attended to

and what demands are attended to, but research is also badly needed in this area.

Fourth, we need a demand-evaluation procedure that is consistent with the limited capacities of human beings. Such a procedure must specify how demands are checked for consistency and for their resource demands. Presumably, such a mechanism will depend heavily on a rule that much of the problem is taken as given and only incremental changes are considered.

Fifth, we need a mechanism for choosing among the potentially viable coalitions. In our judgment, this mechanism will probably look much like the recent suggestions of game theorists that only small changes are evaluated at a time (Luce and Raiffa, 1957).

Given these five mechanisms and some way of expressing environmental resources, we can describe a process for the determination of objectives in an organization that will exhibit the important attributes of organizational goal-determination. At the moment, we can approximate some of the required functions. For example, it has been possible to introduce into a complete model a substantial part of the first mechanism, and some elements of the second, third, and fourth (Cyert, Feigenbaum, and March, 1959). Before the theory can develop further, however, and particularly before it can focus intensively on the formation of objectives through bargaining and coalition formation (rather than on the revision of such objectives and the selective attention to them), we require greater empirical clarification of the phenomena involved.

BIBLIOGRAPHIC REFERENCES

Alt, R. M. (1949). The internal organization of the firm and price formation: An illustrative case. *Quarterly J. of Econ.*, 63, 92–110.

Barnard, C. I. (1938). *The functions of the executive.* Cambridge: Harvard University Press.

Blau, P. M. (1955). *The dynamics of bureaucracy.* Chicago: University of Chicago Press.

Cooper, W. W., Hitch, C., Baumol, W. J., Shubik, M., Schelling, T. C., Valavanis, S., & Ellsberg, D. (1958). Economics and operations research: A symposium. *The Rev. of Econ. and Stat.*, 40, 195–229.

Cyert, R. M., & March, J. G. (1956). Organizational factors in the theory of oligopoly. *Quarterly J. of Econ.*, 70, 44–64.

Cyert, R. M., Dill, W. R., & March, J. G. (1958). The role of expectations in business decision making. *Adm. Sci. Quarterly*, 3, 307–340.

Cyert, R. M., & March, J. G. (1959). Research on a behavioral theory of the firm. *Management Rev.*

Cyert, R. M., Feigenbaum, E. A., & March, J. G. (1959). Models in a behavioral theory of the firm. *Behavioral Sci.*, 4, 81–95.

Cyert, R. M., & March, J. G. (1960). Business operating procedures. In B. von H. Gilmer (Ed.), *Industrial psychology.* New York: McGraw-Hill.

Dahl, R. A., & Lindblom, C. E. (1953). *Politics, economics, and welfare.* New York: Harper.

Festinger, L. (1954). A theory of social comparison processes. *Human Relations, 7,*117–140.

Kaplan, A. D. H., Dirlam, J. B., & Lanzillotti, R. F. (1958). *Pricing in big business.* Washington: Brookings Institution.

Lewin, L., Dembo, T., Festinger, L., & Sears, P. (1944). Level of aspiration. In J. M. Hunt (Ed.), *Personality and the behavior disorders.* (Vol I). New York: Ronald Press.

Luce, R. D., & Raiffa, H. (1957). *Games and decisions.* New York: John Wiley & Sons.

March, J. G., & Simon, H. A. (1958). *Organizations.* New York: John Wiley & Sons.

Marschak, J. Efficient and viable organization forms. In this volume.

Marshall A. (1919). *Industry and trade.* London: Macmillan.

Messinger, S. L. (1955). Organizational transformation: A case study of a declining social movement. *Amer. sociol. Rev.*, 20, 3–10.

Selznick, P. (1949). *TVA and the grass roots.* Berkeley: University of California Press.

Sills, D. L. (1957). *The volunteers.* Glencoe, IL: Free Press.

Simon, H. A. (1947). *Administrative behavior.* New York: Macmillan.

Simon, H. A., Smithburg, D. W., & Thompson, V. A. (1950). *Public administration.* New York: Alfred A. Knopf.

Simon, H. A. (1953). Birth of an organization: The economic cooperation administration. *Public Adm. Rev.*, 13, 227–236.

Thompson, J. D., & McEwen, W. J. (1958). Organizational goals and environment: Goal setting as an interaction process. *Amer. sociol. Rev.*, 23, 23–31.

Truman, D. B. (1951). *The governmental process.* New York: Alfred A. Knopf.

von Neumann, J., & Morgenstern, O. (1947). *Theory of games and economic behavior.* (2nd ed.) Princeton, NJ: Princeton University Press.

Weber, M. (1947). *The theory of social and economic organization* (A. M. Henderson & T. Parsons, Trans.). New York: Oxford University Press.

CHAPTER III

"Modern" Structural Organization Theory

Usually when someone refers to the structure of an organization, that person is talking about the relatively stable relationships among the positions and groups of positions (units) that comprise the organization. Structural organization theory is concerned with vertical differentiations—hierarchical levels of organizational authority and coordination, and horizontal differentiations between organizational units—for example, between product or service lines, geographical areas, or skills. The organization chart is the ever-present "tool" of a structural organization theorist.

Why do we use the label "modern" to modify structural organization theory? Most organizational theorists from the classical school were structuralists. They focused their attention on the structure—or design—of organizations and their production processes. Some examples that are reprinted in Chapter I include those by Adam Smith, Henri Fayol, Charles Babbage, Daniel McCallum, Frederick Winslow Taylor, and Max Weber. Thus we use the word "modern" (always in quotation marks) merely to differentiate between the structural organization theorists of the 1960s and 1970s and the pre–World War II classical school structuralists.

The "modern" structuralists are concerned with many of the same issues as were the classical structuralists, but their theories have been influenced by and have benefited greatly from advancements in organization theory since World War II. Their roots are in the thinking of Fayol, Taylor, Gulick, and Weber, and their underlying tenets are quite similar: Organizational efficiency is the essence of organizational rationality; the goal of rationality is to increase the production of wealth in terms of real goods and services. However, "modern" structural theories also have been influenced substantially by the neoclassical school, the human relations-oriented theorists, and the systems school.

Bolman and Deal (1984) identify the basic assumptions of the "modern" structural school:

1. Organizations are rational institutions whose primary purpose is to accomplish established objectives; rational organizational behavior is achieved best through systems of defined rules and formal authority. Organizational control and coordination are key for maintaining organizational rationality.

166

2. There is a "best" structure for any organization—or at least a most appropriate structure—in light of its given objectives, the environmental conditions surrounding it (for example, its markets, the competition, and the extent of government regulation), the nature of its products and/or services (the "best" structure for a management consulting firm probably is substantially different from that for a certified public accounting firm), and the technology of the production processes (a coal mining company has a different "best structure" than the "high tech" manufacturer of computer microcomponents).
3. Specialization and the division of labor increase the quality and quantity of production—particularly in highly skilled operations and professions.
4. Most problems in an organization result from structural flaws and can be solved by changing the structure.

What sorts of practical issues are best addressed by "modern" structural organization theory? Is it useful? The most immediate issue in the design of any organization is the question of structure. What should it look like? How should it work? How will it deal with the most common structural questions of specialization, departmentalization, span of control, and the coordination and control of specialized units?

Tom Burns and G. M. Stalker of the Tavistock Institute in London—which is widely acknowledged as the birthplace of the "socio-technical approach" to organizations—developed their widely cited theory of "mechanistic and organic systems" of organization while examining rapid technological change in the British and Scottish electronics industry in the post–World War II years. Their account of "Mechanistic and Organic Systems" from their 1961 book, *The Management of Innovation,* is reprinted here.

Burns and Stalker found that stable conditions may suggest the use of a mechanistic form of organization, where a traditional pattern of hierarchy, reliance on formal rules and regulations, vertical communications, and structured decision making is possible. However, more dynamic conditions—situations in which the environment changes rapidly—require the use of an organic form of organization where there is less rigidity, more participation, and more reliance on workers to define and redefine their positions and relationships. For example, technological creativity, an essential ingredient in an organic system, requires an organizational climate and management systems that are supportive of innovation. The impacts of these two organizational forms on individuals are substantially different. Supervisors and managers find that the mechanistic form provides them with a greater sense of security in dealing with their environment than the organic form, which introduces much greater uncertainty. Burns and Stalker conclude that either form of organization may be appropriate in particular situations.

One of the basic tenets of the "modern" structural school is that rational organizational behavior is achieved best through systems of defined rules and formal authority. Authority is central to "modern" structural organization theory because control and coordination are essential for maintaining organizational rationality. Amitai Etzioni's analysis of "Compliance, Goals, and Effectiveness," which is reprinted here, examines the appropriateness of different types of systems of organizational rules and authority. He examines the "goodness of fit" between different combinations of organizational compliance structures and goal structures. Etzioni's analysis is premised on two propositions: "organizations that have similar compliance structures tend to have similar goals, and organizations that have similar goals tend to have similar compliance structures." Thus organizational effectiveness is necessarily affected by the compatibility between goal structures and compliance structures.

Etzioni uses a three-by-three analytical matrix of organizational goals (order/control goals, economic/financial goals, and cultural/symbolic goals) and compliance structures (coercive compliance, utilitarian compliance, and normative compliance). Etzioni concludes that "organizations that have order goals tend to have a coercive compliance structure; those that have economic goals tend to have a utilitarian compliance structure; and those that serve culture goals tend to have a normative compliance structure." For example, neither a coercive nor a utilitarian compliance structure will yield organizational effectiveness in a religious institution; an effective for-profit business organization with economic/financial goals will tend to use a utilitarian compliance structure rather than a coercive or normative compliance structure. Etzioni's 1961 book, *A Comparative Analysis of Complex Organizations*, was revised, expanded, and republished in 1975. The chapter that is reprinted here, "Compliance, Goals, and Effectiveness," remains unchanged in the 1975 edition.

In "The Concept of Formal Organization," a chapter from their 1962 book, *Formal Organizations: A Comparative Approach*, Peter M. Blau and W. Richard Scott assert that all organizations include both a formal and informal element. The informal organization by its nature is rooted in the formal structure and supports its formal organization by establishing norms for the operation of the organization—which cannot always be spelled out by rules and policies. For these reasons, Blau and Scott maintain that it is impossible to know and understand the true structure of a formal organization without a similar understanding of its parallel informal organization. Clearly, Blau and Scott were influenced by the "classical philosopher" Chester Barnard's 1938 book *The Functions of the Executive*, in which he held that:

> informal organization, although comprising the processes of society which are unconscious as contrasted with those of formal organizations which are conscious, has two important classes of effects: (*a*) it establishes certain attitudes, understandings, customs, habits, institutions, and (*b*) it creates the condition under which formal organization may arise.

Arthur H. Walker and Jay W. Lorsch, in their 1968 *Harvard Business Review* article, "Organizational Choice: Product vs. Function," grapple with one of the perennial questions facing those who would design organizations: should an organization be structured according to product or function? "Should all specialists in a given function be grouped under a common boss, regardless of differences in products they are involved in, or should the various functional specialists working on a single product be grouped together under the same superior?" Walker and Lorsch tackle this problem by examining two firms in the same industry—one organized by product and the other by function. They conclude that either structural arrangement can be appropriate, depending upon the organization's environment and the nature of the organization itself.

In 1776, Adam Smith advocated the division of labor to increase the effectiveness of the factory system of production. In 1922, Max Weber described two strong and opposing forces that have an impact on all organizations: the need for division of labor and specialization, and the need for centralizing authority. Division of labor is an inevitable consequence of specialization by skills, products, or processes. Most "modern" structuralists now use the word *differentiation*—which means essentially the same thing as specialization but also reflects increased appreciation of the myriad and rapidly changing external environmental forces with which organizations interact (for example, different markets, sociopolitical cultures, regulatory environments, technologies, competition, and the economy). Thus, complex differentiation is essential for organizational effectiveness as well as efficiency. However, differentiation *means* diverse forces that "pull organizations apart." Differentiation increases the need for organizational coordination and control that, in the language of "modern" structuralists, is labeled "integration."

Paul R. Lawrence and Jay W. Lorsch have received wide acclaim for their chapter "The Organization-Environment Interface," from their 1969 book, *Developing Organizations: Diagnosis and Action*, which asserts that the single most important problem all organizations must solve is achieving a balance between the conflicting needs for and demands of differentiation and integration. Lawrence and Lorsch advocate a contingency approach to organization theory—an approach that utilizes different organization theories that may be appropriate under different circumstances and conditions. (See Chapter IV for a discussion of contingency theories.)

Matrix organization structures originated with the United States's aerospace program of the 1960s and the aerospace companies' extraordinary and conflicting needs for freedom (for innovation) and order (for regulation and control). Thus, matrix organization theory addresses the same inherent, organizational design need that was described by Max Weber (division of labor versus centralized authority) and Paul Lawrence and Jay Lorsch (differentiation versus integration). However, the enormity, complexity, importance, and temporary nature of the aerospace projects rendered traditional structural solutions to organizational problems inadequate for the task. Thus, great interest developed in matrix structures.

In their book *Matrix* (1977), Stanley Davis and Paul Lawrence define a "matrix as any organization that employs a *multiple command system* that includes not only a multiple command structure but also related support mechanisms and an associated organizational culture and behavior pattern." In their Chapter 2, "The Matrix Organization—Who Needs It?," Davis and Lawrence warn against unquestioning implementation of a matrix. Is a matrix a useful form of organizational structure? According to Davis and Lawrence, only if all necessary conditions exist. A matrix structure is only one element of a matrix organization: matrix systems, culture, and behavior also are needed. Additionally, a matrix organization is not desirable unless: (1) the organization must cope regularly with two or more "critical sectors" (critical sectors include functions, products, services, markets, and/or areas), (2) organizational tasks are uncertain, complex, and highly interdependent, and (3) there are economies of scale.

Henry Mintzberg has emerged as one of the most widely respected management and organizational theorists of the 1970s and 1980s. Since the 1960s, Mintzberg has been compiling a theory of management policy—a field of management and organization theory that has lacked attention. An adaptation of his early conceptual model of management policy is in Figure 1. The model demonstrates why Mintzberg is so influential: He is synthesizing many schools of organization and management theory—and doing so with coherence. His 1979 book, *The Structuring of Organizations,* addresses the first component of the model. (His 1983 book, *Power in and Around Organizations,* addresses the second component of the model. A chapter from it is reprinted in our Chapter V.) In his chapter, "Five Basic Parts of the Organization," which is reprinted here, Mintzberg uses James D. Thompson's (1967) concepts of "pooled, sequential, and reciprocal organizational coupling" to create a model of organizations with five interdependent parts: the strategic apex, the middle line, the operating core, the technostructure, and the support staff. His model is a creative and useful departure from traditional views of formal organization structure.

In the late 1960s and early 1970s, several writers renewed and expanded the historical attacks against the bureaucratic form of organization. Space limitations

FIGURE 1 • MINTZBERG'S BASIC MODEL OF MANAGEMENT POLICY

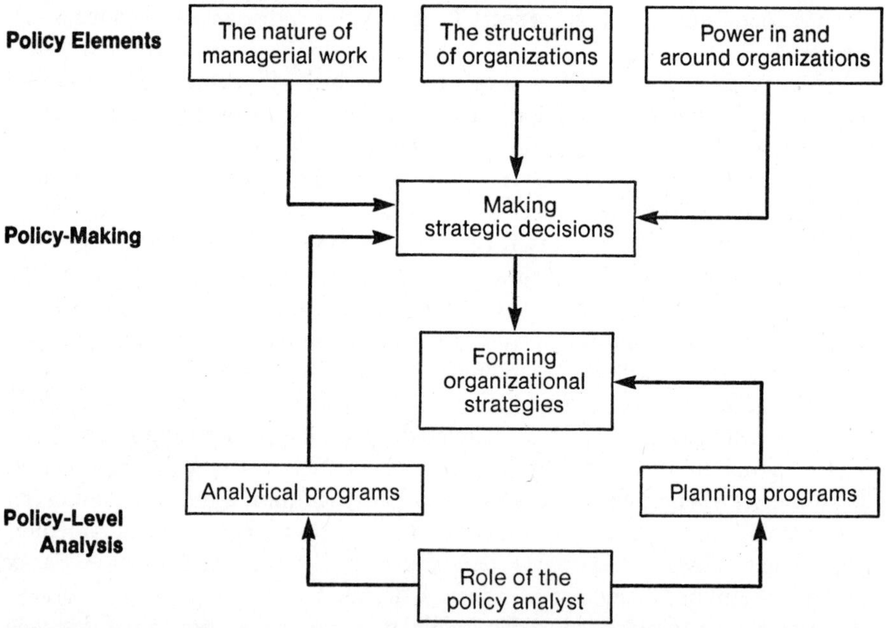

Adapted from Mintzberg, H. (1979). *The structuring of organizations* (p. iv). Englewood Cliffs, NJ: Prentice-Hall.

prohibit including pieces from this important aspect of the "modern" structural school of organization theory, but it is important to be aware of their existence. For example, in *Changing Organizations* (1966), Warren Bennis predicted that bureaucratic organizations as we know them will disappear within this century because they are unable to adapt to rapidly changing environments. Alvin Toffler's chapter in *Future Shock* (1970), titled "Organization: The Coming Ad-hocracy" reflects Bennis's thinking. Bennis and Philip Slater's *The Temporary Society* (1968) extended Bennis's (1966) theme to predict a rise in democracy—within organizations as well as in general society.

Is the bureaucratic form of organization on an inevitable road to extinction? Is it being replaced by systems of temporary democratic networks? If so, it isn't apparent yet. The "modern" structuralists continue to identify new approaches for making bureaucracies more adaptable and effective. In fact, bureaucracies appear to be holding their own quite well, within the field of organization theory as well as in practice. The discipline of Public Administration is even beginning to develop a defensive literature on bureaucracy that increasingly defends and justifies bureaucratic forms of organization because of their efficiency, equity, and representativeness (Kaufman, 1977; Krislov and Rosenbloom, 1981; Goodsell, 1983).

BIBLIOGRAPHIC REFERENCES

Barnard, C. I. (1938). *The functions of the executive*. Cambridge, MA: Harvard University Press.

Bennis, W. G. (1966). *Changing organizations*. New York: McGraw-Hill.

Bennis, W. G., & Slater, P. E. (1968). *The temporary society*. New York: Harper & Row.

Blau, P. M., & Scott, W. R. (1962). *Formal organizations: A comparative approach*. San Francisco: Chandler Publishing.

Bolman, L. G., & Deal, T. E. (1984). *Modern approaches to understanding and managing organizations*. San Francisco: Jossey-Bass.

Burns, T., & Stalker, G. M. (1961). *The management of innovation*. London: Tavistock Publications.

Crozier, M. (1964). *The bureaucratic phenomenon*. Chicago: University of Chicago Press.

Davis, S. M., & Lawrence, P. R. (1977). *Matrix*. Reading, MA: Addison-Wesley Publishing.

Etzioni, A. (1961). *A comparative analysis of complex organizations*. Englewood Cliffs, NJ: Prentice-Hall.

Goodsell, C. T. (1983). *The case for bureaucracy: A public administration polemic*. Chatham, NJ: Chatham House.

Kaufman, H. (1977). *Red tape*. Washington, DC: Brookings Institution.

Krislov, S., & Rosenbloom, D. H. (1981). *Representative bureaucracy and the American political system*. New York: Praeger Publishers.

Lawrence, P. R., & Lorsch, J. W. (1969). *Developing organizations*. Reading, MA: Addison-Wesley Publishing.

Mintzberg, H. (1979). *The structuring of organizations*. Englewood Cliffs, NJ: Prentice-Hall.

Mintzberg, H. (1983). *Power in and around organizations*. Englewood Cliffs, NJ: Prentice-Hall.

Thompson, J. D. (1967). *Organizations in action*. New York: McGraw-Hill.

Thompson, V. A. (1961). *Modern organization*. New York: Alfred A. Knopf.

Toffler, A. (1970). *Future Shock*. New York: Random House.

Walker, A. H., & Lorsch, J. W. (1968, November–December). Organizational choice: Product vs. function. *Harvard Business Review*, 46, 129–138.

15
Mechanistic and Organic Systems
Tom Burns & G. M. Stalker

We are now at the point at which we may set down the outline of the two management systems which represent for us . . . the two polar extremities of the forms which such systems can take when they are adapted to a specific rate of technical and commercial change. The cases we have tried to establish from the literature, as from our research experience exhibited in the last chapter, is that the different forms assumed by a working organization do exist objectively and are not merely interpretations offered by observers of different schools.

Both types represent a "rational" form of organization, in that they may both, in our experience, be explicitly and deliberately created and maintained to exploit the human resources of a concern in the most efficient manner feasible in the circumstances of the concern. Not surprisingly, however, each exhibits characteristics which have been hitherto associated with different kinds of interpretation. For it is our contention that empirical findings have usually been classified according to sociological ideology rather than according to the functional specificity of the working organization to its task and the conditions confronting it.

We have tried to argue that these are two formally contrasted forms of management system. These we shall call the mechanistic and organic forms.

A *mechanistic* management system is appropriate to stable conditions. It is characterized by:

(a) the specialized differentiation of functional tasks into which the problems and tasks facing the concern as a whole are broken down;

(b) the abstract nature of each individual task, which is pursued with techniques and purposes more or less distinct from those of the concern as a whole; *i.e.*, the functionaries tend to pursue the technical improvement of means, rather than the accomplishment of the ends of the concern;

(c) the reconciliation, for each level in the hierarchy, of these distinct performances by the immediate superiors, who are also, in turn, responsible for seeing that each is relevant in his own special part of the main task.

(d) the precise definition of rights and obligations and technical methods attached to each functional role;

(e) the translation of rights and obligations and methods into the responsibilities of a functional position;

(f) hierarchic structure of control, authority, and communication;

Source: From Tom Burns and G. M. Stalker, *The Management of Innovation* (London: Tavistock Publications, 1961), 119–125. Reprinted by permission. References omitted; footnotes retained.

(g) a reinforcement of the hierarchic structure by the location of knowledge of actualities exclusively at the top of the hierarchy, where the final reconciliation of distinct tasks and assessment of relevance is made.[1]

(h) a tendency for interaction between members of the concern to be vertical, *i.e.*, between superior and subordinate;

(i) a tendency for operations and working behavior to be governed by the instructions and decisions issued by superiors;

(j) insistence on loyalty to the concern and obedience to superiors as a condition of membership;

(k) a greater importance and prestige attaching to internal (local) than to general (cosmopolitan) knowledge, experience, and skill.

The *organic* form is appropriate to changing conditions, which give rise constantly to fresh problems and unforeseen requirements for action which cannot be broken down or distributed automatically arising from the functional roles defined within a hierarchic structure. It is characterized by:

(a) the contributive nature of special knowledge and experience to the common task of the concern;

(b) the "realistic" nature of the individual task, which is seen as set by the total situation of the concern;

(c) the adjustment and continual redefinition of individual tasks through interaction with others;

(d) the shedding of "responsibility" as a limited field of rights, obligations and methods. (Problems may not be posted upwards, downwards or sideways as being someone else's responsibility);

(e) the spread of commitment to the concern beyond any technical definition;

(f) a network structure of control, authority, and communication. The sanctions which apply to the individual's conduct in his working role derive more from presumed community of interest with the rest of the working organization in the survival and growth of the firm, and less

from a contractual relationship between himself and a nonpersonal corporation, represented for him by an immediate superior;

(g) omniscience no longer imputed to the head of the concern; knowledge about the technical or commercial nature of the here and now task may be located anywhere in the network; this location becoming the ad hoc centre of control authority and communication;

(h) a lateral rather than a vertical direction of communication through the organization, communication between people of different rank, also, resembling consultation rather than command;

(i) a content of communication which consists of information and advice rather than instructions and decisions;

(j) commitment to the concern's task and to the "technological ethos" of material progress and expansion is more highly valued than loyalty and obedience;

(k) importance and prestige attach to affiliations and expertise valid in the industrial and technical and commercial milieux external to the firm.

One important corollary to be attached to this account is that while organic systems are not hierarchic in the same sense as are mechanistic, they remain stratified. Positions are differentiated according to seniority—*i.e.*, greater expertise. The lead in joint decisions is frequently taken by seniors, but it is an essential presumption of the organic system that the lead, *i.e.*, "authority," is taken by whoever shows himself most informed and capable, *i.e.*, the "best authority." The location of authority is settled by consensus.

A second observation is that the area of commitment to the concern—the extent to which the individual yields himself as a resource to be used by the working organization—is far more extensive in organic than in mechanistic systems. Commitment, in fact, is expected to approach that of the professional scientist to his work, and frequently does. One further consequence of this is that it becomes far less feasible to distinguish "informal" from "formal" organization.

Thirdly, the emptying out of significance from the hierarchic command system, by which co-operation is ensured and which serves to monitor the working organization under a mechanistic system, is countered by the development of shared beliefs about the values and goals of the concern. The growth and accretion of institutionalized values, beliefs, and conduct, in the form of commitments, ideology, and manners, around an image of the concern in its industrial and commercial setting make good the loss of formal structure.

Finally, the two forms of systems represent a polarity, not a dichotomy; there are, as we have tried to show, intermediate stages between the extremities empirically known to us. Also, the relation of one form to the other is elastic, so that a concern oscillating between relative stability and relative change may also oscillate between the two forms. A concern may (and frequently does) operate with a management system which includes both types.

The organic form, by departing from the familiar clarity and fixity of the hierarchic structure, is often experienced by the individual manager as an uneasy, embarrassed, or chronically anxious quest for knowledge about what he should be doing, or what is expected of him, and similar apprehensiveness about what others are doing. Indeed, as we shall see later, this kind of response is necessary if the organic form of organization is to work effectively. Understandably, such anxiety finds expression in resentment when the apparent confusion besetting him is not explained. In these situations, all managers some of the time, and many managers all the time, yearn for more definition and structure.

On the other hand, some managers recognize a rationale of nondefinition, a reasoned basis for the practice of those successful firms in which designation of status, function, and line of responsibility and authority has been vague or even avoided.

The desire for more definition is often in effect a wish to have the limits of one's task more neatly defined—to know what and when one doesn't have to bother about as much as to know what one does have to. It follows that the more definition is given, the more omniscient the management must be, so that no functions are left whole or partly undischarged, no person is overburdened with undelegated responsibility, or left without the authority to do his job properly. To do this, to have all the separate functions attached to individual roles fitting together and comprehensively, to have communication between persons constantly maintained on a level adequate to the needs of each functional role, requires rules or traditions of behavior proved over a long time and an equally fixed, stable task. The omniscience which may then be credited to the head of the concern is expressed throughout its body through the lines of command, extending in a clear, explicitly titled hierarchy of officers and subordinates.

The whole mechanistic form is instinct with this twofold principle of definition and dependence which acts as the frame within which action is conceived and carried out. It works, unconsciously, almost in the smallest minutiae of daily activity. "How late is late?" The answer to this question is not to be found in the rule book, but in the superior. Late is when the boss thinks it is late. Is he the kind of man who thinks 8.00 is the time, and 8.01 is late? Does he think that 8.15 is all right occasionally if it is not a regular thing? Does he think that everyone should be allowed a 5-minute grace after 8.00 but after that they are late?

Settling questions about how a person's job is to be done in this way is nevertheless simple, direct, and economical of effort. We shall, in a later chapter, examine more fully the nature of the protection and freedom (in other respects than his job) which this affords the individual.

One other feature of mechanistic organization needs emphasis. It is a necessary condition of its operation that the individual "works on his own," functionally isolated; he "knows his job," he is "responsible for seeing it's done." He works at a job which is in a sense artificially abstracted from the realities of the situation the concern is dealing with, the accountant "dealing with the costs side," the works manager "pushing production," and so on. As this works out in practice, the rest of the organization becomes part of the problem situation the individual has to deal with in order to perform successfully; *i.e.*, difficulties and problems arising from work or information which has been handed over the "responsibility barrier" between two jobs or departments are regarded as "really" the responsibility of the person from whom they were received. As a design engineer put in,

> When you get designers handing over designs completely to production, it's "their responsibility" now. And you get tennis games played with the responsibility for anything that goes wrong. What happens is that you're constantly getting unsuspected faults arising from characteristics which you didn't think important in the design. If you get to hear of these through a sales person, or a production person, or somebody to whom the design was handed over to in the dim past, then, instead of being a design problem, it's an annoyance caused by that particular person, who can't do his own job—because

you'd thought you were finished with that one, and you're on to something else now.

When the assumptions of the form of organization make for preoccupation with specialized tasks, the chances of career success, or of greater influence, depend rather on the relative importance which may be attached to each special function by the superior whose task it is to reconcile and control a number of them. And, indeed, to press the claims of one's job or department for a bigger share of the firm's resources is in many cases regarded as a mark of initiative, of effectiveness, and even of "loyalty to the firm's interests." The state of affairs thus engendered squares with the role of the superior, the man who can see the wood instead of just the trees, and gives it the reinforcement of the aloof detachment belonging to a court of appeal. The ordinary relationship prevailing between individual managers "in charge of" different functions is one of rivalry, a rivalry which may be rendered innocuous to the persons involved by personal friendship or the norms of sociability, but which turns discussion about the situations which constitute the real problems of the concern—how to make the products more cheaply, how to sell more, how to allocate resources, whether to curtail activity in one sector, whether to risk expansion in another, and so on—into an arena of conflicting interests.

The distinctive feature of the second, organic system is the pervasiveness of the working organization as an institution. In concrete terms, this makes itself felt in a preparedness to combine with others in serving the general aims of the concern. Proportionately to the rate and extent of change, the less can the omniscience appropriate to command organizations be ascribed to the head of the organization; for executives, and even operatives, in a changing firm it is always theirs to reason why. Furthermore, the less definition can be given to status, roles, and modes of communication, the more do the activities of each member of the organization become determined by the real tasks of the firm as he sees them than by instruction and routine. The individual's job ceases to be self-contained; the only way in which "his" job can be done is by his participating continually with others in the solution of problems which are real to the firm, and put in a language of requirements and activities meaningful to them all. Such methods of working put much heavier demands on the individual. The ways in which these demands are met, or countered, will be enumerated and discussed in Part Three.

We have endeavoured to stress the appropriateness of each system to its own specific set of conditions. Equally, we desire to avoid the suggestion that either system is superior under all circumstances to the other. In particular, nothing in our experience justifies the assumption that mechanistic systems should be superseded by organic in conditions of stability.[2] The beginning of administrative wisdom is the awareness that there is no one optimum type of management system.

NOTES

1. This functional attribute to the head of a concern often takes on a clearly expressive aspect. It is common enough for concerns to instruct all people with whom they deal to address correspondence to the firm (*i.e.*, to its formal head) and for all outgoing letters and orders to be signed by the head of the concern. Similarly, the printed letter heading used by Government departments carries instructions for the replies to be addressed to the Secretary, etc. These instructions are not always taken seriously, either by members of the organization or their correspondents, but in one company this practice was insisted upon and was taken to somewhat unusual lengths; *all* correspondence was delivered to the managing director, who would thereafter distribute excerpts to members of the staff, synthesizing their replies into the letter of reply which he eventually sent. Telephone communication was also controlled by limiting the number of extensions, and by monitoring incoming and outgoing calls.

2. A recent instance of this assumption is contained in H. A. Shepard's paper addressed to the Symposium on the Direction of Research Establishments, 1956. "There is much evidence to suggest that the optimal use of human resources in industrial organizations requires a different set of conditions, assumptions, and skills from those traditionally present in industry. Over the past twenty-five years, some new orientations have emerged from organizational experiments, observations, and inventions. The new orientations depart radically from doctrines associated with 'Scientific Management' and traditional bureaucratic patterns.

   The central emphases in this development are as follows:
   1. Wide participation in decision-making, rather than centralized decision-making.
   2. The face-to-face group, rather than the individual, as the basic unit of organization.
   3. Mutual confidence, rather than authority, the integrative force in organization.
   4. The supervisor as the agent for maintaining intragroup and intergroup communication, rather than as the agent of higher authority.
   5. Growth of members of the organization to greater responsibility, rather than external control of the member's performance or their tasks."

16
Compliance, Goals, and Effectiveness
Amitai Etzioni

COMPLIANCE AND ORGANIZATIONAL GOALS

What is the relationship between organizational goals and compliance? We would expect that organizations serving order goals will tend to have a coercive compliance structure; organizations serving economic goals will tend to have a utilitarian compliance structure; and organizations serving culture goals will tend to have a normative compliance structure.

A TYPOLOGY OF GOALS AND COMPLIANCE

	Order	Economic	Culture
Coercive	1	2	3
Utilitarian	4	5	6
Normative	7	8	9

That is, of the nine possible combinations of goals and compliance shown in the accompanying table, we would expect most organizations to reveal one of three combinations (Nos. 1, 5, 9); there are, however, cases in the other six categories. For example, some deviants are segregated and controlled (but not "cured") by the use of normative compliance in rehabilitation centers ("open" prisons). This would be a case in cell No. 7. In the same cell are homes for the aged which house those senile persons who earlier were committed (and to some degree still are) to closed mental hospitals. (Colb, 1956; Drake, 1960, pp. 309–11). Their goal is order since they control actors who otherwise cannot or will not conform to social norms and folkways (Tec and Granick, 1960; Granick and Nahemow, 1960). These persons are controlled by normative means and a minimum of coercion because of their general physical and mental state and, in particular, because of their emotional dependence on the home (Granick, unpublished; Herz and Zelditch, 1952). Camps for conscientious objectors established during World War II in the United States also segregated deviants by predominantly normative means (Dahlke, 1945). Some production is conducted in most coercive organizations, especially in camps of forced labor (No. 2), and in some religious orders (No. 8). Some learning is carried out in strictly utilitarian organizations, such as typing schools and some institutes for the study of foreign languages, where instructors have little if any normative power over students and the student's orientation is calculative (No. 6).

Source: Amitai Etzioni, *A Comparative Analysis of Complex Organizations* (New York: Free Press, 1961), 74–77, 79–86. Reprinted with permission of The Free Press, a division of Macmillan, Inc. from *A Comparative Analysis of Complex Organizations* by Amitai Etzioni. Copyright © 1961 by The Free Press.

Thus there are some cases in cells other than the three cardinal ones (Nos. 1, 5, 9), but these appear to be few and limited in significance. The large majority of organizations reveal one of the three central combinations. Prisons and custodial mental hospitals fall in the first cell; blue- and white-collar industries fall in the fifth cell; religious organizations, universities and colleges, general hospitals, voluntary associations, schools, therapeutic mental hospitals, and professional organizations fall in the ninth cell.

Many organizations serve more than one goal. Sometimes these goals fall in the same general category, as in the case of universities which conduct both teaching and research, two culture goals. Sometimes the same organization serves goals of two different categories, as do forced-labor camps, which are both order- and economic-oriented. Usually, however, there is one predominant goal. The main point for us is that in organizations that serve dual or multiple goals, we would expect to find a parallel "combination" in the compliance structure. For example, the more production-oriented a prison or a forced-labor camp becomes, the more utilitarian (hence, closer to the coercive-utilitarian dual type) we would expect its compliance structure to be.[1] Thus the association between compliance and goals is maintained.

POLITICAL GOALS AND COMPLIANCE

Political goals at first glance seem impossible to place in our typology. It is often suggested that political goals, in particular those of parties, are to attain and maintain power. This is not an order, economic, or culture goal, but in a sense comprehends all three. Nevertheless, if we are to pursue our original objectives we must ask: Granted that all political organizations are power-oriented, how do they differ?

Descriptions of political organizations as oriented to power alone result in part from not observing carefully the distinction between elite goals and organizational goals. The leadership of political organizations may, as Michels suggests, have one predominant interest, to gain and retain power (1959, p. 205). Power is a universal key to all three ends; it may be pursued in order to control or change the allocation of coercion, to affect the allotment of material resources, or to change a normative pattern, as well as to serve various combinations of these goals. However, realization of the power goal requires that it be related to organizational goals which are more acceptable to the rank and file and more legitimate in the eyes of the public (Selznick, 1952, pp. 2–4). Political organizations can be fruitfully classified according to the direction taken by this transformation of power goals into organizational goals.

Some political organizations, such as business unions, "tariff" parties, and the "Greenback" party, and much political activity on the municipal level, are predominantly concerned with allocation or reallocation of material resources and services. These organizations can be seen as oriented to economic goals.

Other political organizations are predominantly concerned with gaining control of command positions over legitimate means of coercion, such as the armed forces and the police. This seems to be the central goal of revolutionary organizations, whatever their ideological orientation, especially shortly before and during the revolutionary episode itself (Brinton, 1938, pp. 405–6), and of groups such as the Latin-American juntas (Christensen, 1951). These organizations can be seen as pursuing an order goal.

Finally, some social movements and radical parties focus on the dissemination of a new ideology. These are often revolutionary parties which are relatively unsuccessful in recruiting members and gaining power, which operate in societies where the existing political structure is well established. Typical examples are Communist parties in Sweden, Norway, and Israel in the fifties (Lipset, 1960, pp. 124 ff.), "long-run" small parties which realize that gaining control of the state or influencing significantly the national allocation of resources is beyond them, and hence devote their limited means to indoctrination of their rank and file, hoping that a change in the situation will open the power structure to them. These political organizations, at this stage, can be perceived as pursuing a culture goal: that of creating and reinforcing commitments to specific ideologies.

In short, the organizational goals of political organizations may be economic, order, or culture goals—or, quite frequently, some combination of these. Thus political goals do not fall in one cell of our classification; instead, we find some type of political goals in all of them. The main point is that *differences in political goals*, as we have defined them, *are associated with differences in the compliance structures* of the organizations serving them.

Political organizations whose goal is the allocation of material resources tend to emphasize, as the means of maintaining the commitment of their members and supporters, continuous allocation of products and services, referred to as "sharing the spoils," "pork-barreling," patronage, and the like. Some such practices are found in most political organizations, but this type tends to use allocation as its central control mechanism (Steffens, 1957; Cook and Cleason, 1959).

Political organizations whose goal is control over the legitimate means of violence are more likely than other political organizations to apply coercion in the control of their members. Revolutionary parties in the revolutionary stage are a well-known illustration (Brinton, 1938, pp. 105 ff.), as are the groups that initiate various coups in Latin America and the Caribbean.

Finally, political organizations with a culture goal, such as indoctrination, tend to emphasize normative compliance and to minimize both the use of coercion and remunerative allocation for internal control purposes (Duverger, 1954, pp. 154 ff.; Lenin, 1952). The major American parties are often contrasted with their European counterparts as being less ideological in their goals and more oriented to the allocation of resources. Similar differences, we would expect, would be found if the involvement of members were compared. For example, one would on the average expect commitment to parties in Western Europe to be higher than in the United States, as reflected, for example, in the proportion of members changing their party affiliation. Thus, if the goals of political organizations are specified, the general proposition concerning relationships between the nature of the goal and the nature of the compliance structure seems to hold.

ORGANIZATIONAL EFFECTIVENESS

The preceding discussion raises the problem of accounting for the fact that certain types of goals and certain types of compliance structures tend to be associated. Are they functional requirements for each other? Could we go so far as to say that one *cannot* rehabilitate in a traditional prison, produce in a religious order, segregate deviants by normative means? The answer seems to be, in one sentence: It is feasible but not effective. The three congruent types of goals and compliance are more effective than the other six combinations, although all nine types are "possible."

Compliance, Goals, and Effectiveness

Let us assume that a wide range of empirical studies has supported our hypothesis about the association between compliance and goals, and has demonstrated that in fact organizations that serve order goals do tend to have a coercive compliance structure; that those serving economic goals tend to have a utilitarian compliance structure; and that those serving culture goals tend to have a normative compliance structure. We have then to explain this association. The first step has been taken above, when we suggested that these three associations are more effective than the other possible six. In other words, effectiveness is our central explanatory intervening variable. In the following paragraphs we attempt to show in some detail why each of the three congruent relationships is more effective than the other two combinations that might be associated with the same goal. In other words, additional intervening variables are introduced. Since these variables account for one relationship at a time, they are naturally on a less abstract and general level than the central intervening variable, that of effectiveness.

Economic Goals and Effective Compliance. There are several reasons why organizations that have economic goals function more effectively when they employ remuneration than when they employ coercion or normative power as their predominant means of control. Production is a rational activity, which requires systematic division of labor, power, and communication, as well as a high level of coordination. It therefore requires also a highly systematic and precise control of performance. This can be attained only when sanctions and rewards can be readily measured and allocated in close relation to performance. Remunerative sanctions and rewards are the only ones that can be so applied, because money differentials are far more precisely measurable than force, prestige, or any other power differentials.

Much production requires some initiative, interest, "care," responsibility, and similar attributes of the lower participants. Engineers and personnel people frequently describe the great damage caused when workers carry out orders to the letter but ignore the spirit of the directive, in order to "get even" with a supervisor. Effective performance requires some degree of voluntary cooperation, which is almost unattainable under coercion. Only the limited types of work that can be effectively controlled through close supervision (e.g., carrying stones to build a pyramid, rowing in the galleys) can be controlled by coercion without great loss of effectiveness. We would therefore expect production in coercive organizations to be of this kind, or to be ineffective. The following statement by work supervisors in a prison may therefore reflect not the inmates' "inherent" inability to work, but their alienation from work under coercion:

> The total result of the prevalence of these attitudes has been to reduce "imprisonment at hard labor" to a euphemism existing chiefly in the rhetoric of sentencing judges and in the minds of the uninformed public. The inmate social system not only has succeeded in neutralizing the laboriousness of prison labor in fact, but also has more or less succeeded in convincing prison authorities of the futility of expecting any improvement in output . . . the prevalent attitudes of work supervisors toward convict labor: "Convicts are inherently unindustrious, unintelligent, unresourceful, and uninterested in honest work." (McCorkle and Korn, 1954, p. 92)

We would also expect either that forced-labor camps will be predominantly punitive, and productivity—that is, *effectiveness*—low; or, that chiefly manual work, of the type described above, will be carried out.

Forced labor in Soviet countries during the Stalin period seems to have been mainly of the highly punitive, relatively ineffective type (Parvilahti, 1960). Moreover, work in these camps consisted typically of building barracks, felling trees, excavation, or performing duties of an orderly in the camp (Rosada and Gwozdz, 1952, p. 26). These jobs, to the degree that their description allows us to judge, are of the routine, simple, easily supervised type, as specified above. The Japanese relocation camps in the United States during World War II were not highly coercive but at the same time did not develop a utilitarian system. Workers were paid 50 cents a day. The consequence was that some work was conducted, but the level of productivity was very low (Leighton, 1945, pp. 72, 86–87, 108, 242–43).

Weber pointed out the advantages of remunerative over coercive control of modern work when he showed that slaves cannot serve as the basis of a rational economy (of the bourgeois capitalist type) whereas free wage labor can. He lists eight reasons, most of them resting on differences in mobility between the two groups. But he also notes that "it has in general been impossible to use slave labour in the operation of tools and apparatus, the efficiency of which required a high level of responsibility and of involvement of the operator's self interest." (1947, p. 253) J. N. Blum (1948) compared the productivity of servile agricultural labor with that of wage labor during the first part of the nineteenth century in Austria-Hungary. He found that wage labor was from two to

two and a half times as effective as servile labor (Ibid., pp. 192–202).

The use of normative power in organizations serving economic goals may lead to highly effective performance, but in general only for work of a particularly gratifying nature, such as research and artistic performance, or for limited periods of time, particularly in crises. Thus, for example, the work of transferring the defeated British army home from Dunkirk, under the pressure of the approaching German army, was conducted by a fleet of volunteers under normative command. Similar efforts on the industrial front take place in the early stages of war.

Normative compliance can be used to conduct "services" of a dramatic nature (in the sense that they have a direct relation to ultimate values), such as fighting fires, helping flood victims, searching for lost children, or collecting money for the March of Dimes and similar causes. But production engaged in by lower participants in typical blue-collar or white-collar industries lacks such qualities. Its relation to ultimate goals is indirect; it is slow to come to fruition; the worker is segregated from the fruits; and activities are highly routinized, spread over long periods of time, and evoke little public interest. Hence production as a rule cannot rely on the moral commitments of lower participants and the normative power of organizational representatives; for example, when a relatively "dramatic" service such as searching for lost children requires continued, routinized activity, the number of volunteers and the level of normative compliance tend to decline rapidly.[2] This is one of the reasons such activities are often delegated to permanent utilitarian organizations, such as the fire department and "professional" fund raisers. In summary, effective production of commodities and services is carried out almost exclusively by utilitarian organizations.

Culture Goals and Effective Compliance. Organizations that serve culture goals have to rely on normative powers because the realization of their goals requires positive and intense commitments of lower participants to the organization—at least to its representatives, and such commitments cannot be effectively attained by other powers.

Studies of charisma, persuasion and influence show that commitment (or identification) of followers to their leaders is the major lever by which the followers' commitments to values are created, transmitted, or extended (Parsons and Shils, 1952, p. 17 ff.). Communication studies demonstrate the low effectiveness of formal communication not supported by informal leaders, and the importance of positive affective interpersonal relations between the priest and the parishioner, the teacher and the student, the political leader and his followers, for effective operation of their respective organizations (Karsh, Seidman, Lilienthal, 1953; Härnqvist, 1956, pp. 88–113). In short, the attainment of culture goals such as the creation, application, or transmission of values requires the development of identification with the organizational representatives.

When participants are alienated from the organization they are less likely to identify with its representatives than if they are committed to it. However, even when commitment to the organization is high, identification with its representatives need not occur. But since normative power is the least alienating and the most committing kind of power, it is the most conducive to the development of identification with representatives and hence to effective service of cultural goals. We shall see below that in organizations that serve economic or order goals rather than culture goals,

identification of followers with organizational representatives is indeed a far less common component of the elite-lower participant relationship (see Chapter V).

Coercion makes identification with organizational representatives very unlikely. This is one of the major reasons rehabilitation work is unsuccessful in prisons and also a reason for the strong objections of progressive educational philosophy to the use of corporal punishment.[3]

In order to build up patients' motivation to be cured, doctors have to attain their nonrational commitment—to achieve normative power over them—since patients do not have the knowledge required to accept the doctors' directions on rational grounds. A similar relationship exists between teacher and students, and other professionals and their clients.

Remuneration cannot serve as the major means of control in organizations serving culture goals because the commitments it tends to build are too mild and rational. Manipulation of pay, fines, and bonuses does not lead to internalization of values. At best it produces superficial, expedient, overt commitment.

In summary, organizations that serve culture goals must, for effective service of these goals, rely predominantly on normative compliance and not on other means of control.

Order Goals and Effective Compliance. Effective service of order goals requires that coercive rather than remunerative or normative power be the predominant means of control of the organization serving this goal.

Remunerative powers as means of control can augment but not replace coercion as the central means of control in serving order goals. Fines, for instance, can be used to a limited degree to punish minor violations of the code in prisons. But in general the income of inmates is too small and violations are too frequent and, in the eyes of the prison, too severe, to be controlled by remuneration. Moreover, control of deviance, the order goal of these organizations, requires that a depriving situation be maintained. Coercive control is typically negative, inflicting deprivations but granting few gratifications. Other types of control tend to balance reward and punishment, if not to stress reward.

Normative compliance is ineffective in the service of order goals since it is, to all intents and purposes, impossible to maintain normative compliance in order-oriented organizations for the large majority of inmates. A small minority of inmates, usually rather atypical—such as middle-class executives committed to open prisons in Sweden for driving while intoxicated, or conscientious objectors—might be controlled by normative means. But most inmates do not allow their behavior to be significantly affected by prison representatives. The social and cultural background, reinforced by inmate social groups, and the prison situation, which is inevitably depriving because of its segregative nature, generate high alienation which does not allow the normative power of the prison to develop. The inmates "oppose, negate and even nullify the ideology and symbols used by the officials." (Weinberg, 1942, p. 720) In short, control by the use of normative power in the prison is in general neither effective nor feasible.

Coercion is common even in custodial mental hospitals, where confinement of deviants and not their punishment is the order goal. One reason for the prevalence of coercion seems to lie in the level of effectiveness demanded by society or by the community in which

the organization is situated. These external collectivities tend to ask both of prisons and of custodial mental hospitals one hundred percent effectiveness in controlling escapes and suicides. This requirement leads to the need to apply coercion, and to apply more coercion than would otherwise be necessary. Lindsay (1947, p. 92) has pointed out that mores, which in other circumstances can rest on what we have referred to here as moral commitments and normative powers, require the support of coercion (their transformation into laws) when they are expected to hold for *all* people *all* the time. Even when the large majority of people are willing to comply, there are some people all the time, and most people sometimes, who are not willing to comply. Hence even when in general normative compliance would do, the expectation of "one hundred percent" performance increases the use of coercion, since the deviating minority can rarely be specified with complete assurance. Sykes made this point in his study of a prison:

> One escape from the maximum security prison is sufficient to arouse public opinion to a fever pitch and an organization which stands or falls on a single case moves with understandable caution. The officials, in short, know on which side their bread is buttered. Their continued employment is tied up with the successful performance of custody. . . . In the light of the public uproar which follows close on the heels of an escape from prison, it is not surprising that the prison officials have chosen the course of treating all inmates as if they were equally serious threats to the task of custody. (1958, pp 18 and 20)

Grusky showed that basically the same situation exists in a minimum-security prison (1959, p. 458). The same point is true for custodial mental hospitals as well, and is one of the reasons why "opening" them has proceeded so slowly.

This association between order goals and coercive compliance illustrates a general point: The specification of an effectiveness model—for example, effective compliance-goal pairs—is influenced by sociocultural environmental factors. This is true because the social groups that set organizational goals tend also to set limits on the means that the organization can legitimately use to attain these goals, including the means that can be used for control purposes. For example, to the degree that the public becomes more tolerant of inmates' escapes, in particular those of mental patients who are a nuisance but do not endanger the public safety (e.g., some types of exhibitionists), less coercion can be applied without loss of effectiveness.[4] Thus for each sociocultural state, the concrete combination of compliance and goals which creates the highest degree of effectiveness differs; but the basic relationship between the type of goal and the type of compliance—as specified in our hypothesis—does not differ. In some cultures, for example, the most effective attainment of order goals requires much coercion; in others, less; but in all cultures in which complex organizations operate, we would expect effective attainment of order goals to require more use of coercion than economic or culture goals; economic goals to be most effectively served by utilitarian structures; and culture goals by normative ones.

Dual compliance structures are found in organizations that serve goals differing in their compliance requirements either because they fall in different categories or because effective attainment of one goal requires development of supplementary tasks belonging to different goal categories. A business union, for example, has to maintain calculative involvement of the members in "normal" periods and to build up their moral involvement in prestrike and strike days. A full examination of the relationship between compound goals and compliance structures is deferred to Chapter XI, since in order to handle the issue additional variables, to be examined in the following chapters, have to be drawn into the analysis.

NOTES

1. On regulations aimed at keeping the level of coercion low in Soviet Hungary's forced-labor camps see Fischer, Kalnoky, and LeNard (1952, p. 9).

2. The shift from wartime to peacetime is therefore the period when military organizations have to shift from more normative to more remunerative controls. Large raises in salaries of N.C.O.s and officers, as well as of enlisted men where there is no conscription, usually come some time after the war, especially when chance of "action" seems remote (*New York Times*, May 31, 1960). It is typical that the Womble Committee of the Department of Defense found in 1953, after the Korean War, that the pay of military personnel "had not kept pace with changes in civilian society." (Janowitz, 1960, p. 50)

3. It is often pointed out that traditional European schools were rather coercive but also quite effective. But the comparison implicit in this statement is misleading, since some important differentiating conditions are not controlled; for one, the European schools were highly selective. This fact may partially account not only for the compliance attained, but also for the high effectiveness. Second, these schools were effective, despite an extensive use of coercion, in part because their students came from families, social classes, and a general sociocultural environment in which the "tolerance for coercion" was considerably higher than it is in modern democratic societies. Hence the alienation produced by coercion was less and the negative effect on discipline, smaller. For studies of Prussian schools which support these points see Arnold (1892), F. E. Keller (1873), and Kerschensteiner (1909). For background of students see *Statistik der Preussischen Volksschule*, published every five years since 1901.

The same points hold for English public schools, whose compliance structure is well depicted in Hughes' *Tom Brown's School Days* and in Hilton's *Goody-bye, Mr. Chips.* For a general discussion of continental schools from this viewpoint see Arnold (1868).

4. In Britain almost all mental hospitals are state hospitals. They draw their inmates from adjacent areas with only very limited possibilities of transfer from one hospital to another (like the public schools in most American cities). Hence one can more readily observe the effect of community tolerance. It is therefore of interest to note that the three most "open" mental hospitals in Britain seem to be located in or close to upper-middle-class communities, which properly are more tolerant of mental patients than the neighborhoods in which the other mental hospitals are located (private communication with John Wing, M.D., and Elizabeth Monck). For a study of community attitude to mental patients in the United States see Cumming and Cumming (1957). See also Aberle (1950).

BIBLIOGRAPHIC REFERENCES

Aberle, D. F. (1950). Introducing preventive psychiatry into a community. *Hum. Org.*, 9: 5–9.

Arnold, M. (1868). *Schools and universities on the continent.* London: McMillan.

Arnold, M. (1892). *Higher schools and universities in Germany.* London: McMillan.

Barber, B. (1957). *Social stratification.* New York: Harcourt Brace, Jovanovich.

Barnard, C. I. (1938). *The functions of the executive.* Cambridge: Harvard University Press.

Blum, J. N. (1948). *Landowners and agriculture in Austria, 1815–1848.* Baltimore: The Johns Hopkins Press.

Brinton, C. (1938). *The anatomy of revolution.* New York: Prentice-Hall.

Buckley, W. (1958). Social stratification and the functional theory of social differentiation. *Am. Sociol. Rev.*, 23; 369–375.

Caplow, T. (1953). The criteria of organizational success. *Soc. Forc.*, 32; 1–9.

Christensen, A. N. (1951). *The evolution of Latin American government.* New York: Holt.

Colb, L. (1956). The mental hospitalization of the aged: Is it being overdone? *Am. J. Psych.*, 112; 627–635.

Cook, F. J., & Cleason, G. (Oct. 31, 1959). The shame of New York. *The Nation* (special issue).

Cumming, Elaine, Clancey, I. L. W., & Cumming, J. (1956). Improving patient care through organizational changes in the mental hospital. *Psychiatry*, 19, 249–261.

Dahlke, O. H. (1945). Values and group behavior in two camps for conscientious objectors. *Soc. Forc.*, 51; 22–33.

Davis, K. (1942). A conceptual analysis of stratification. *Am. Sociol. Rev.*, 7; 309–321.

Davis, K., & Moore, W. E. (1945). Some principles of stratification. *Am. Sociol. Rev.*, 10; 242–249.

Drake, J. T. (1958). *The aged in American society.* New York: Ronald Press.

Duverger, M. (1954). *Political parties.* London: Methuen.

Etzioni, A. (1958). Administration and the consumer. *Admin. Sci. Q.*, 3; 251–264.

Etzioni, A. (1960). Interpersonal and structural factors in the study of mental hospitals. *Psychiatry*, 23; 13–22.

Fischer, J., Kalnoky, H., & LeNard, L. (1952). *Forced labor and confinement without trial in Hungary.* Washington, DC: Mid-European Studies Center.

Georgopoulos, B. S., & Tannenbaum, A. S. (1957). A study of organizational effectiveness. *Am. Sociol. Rev.*, 22, 534–540.

Granick, R. The effect of social isolation on learning of norms in a home for the aged. Unpublished doctoral dissertation, Columbia University (in progress).

Granick, R., & Nahemow, L. D. (February 1960). Preadmission isolation as a factor in adjustment to an old age home. Paper presented to American Psychopathological Association, New York.

Grusky, O. (1959). Role conflict in organization: A study of prison camp officials. *Admin. Sci. Q., 3*; 452–472.

Harnquist, K. (1956). *Adjustment, leadership and group relations.* Stockholm: Almqvist & Wiksell.

Herz, K. G., & Zelditch, M. (Eds.). (1952). *Administration of homes for the aged: Selected papers on management and program planning.* New York: Council of Jewish Federation of Welfare Funds.

Janowitz, M. (1960). *The professional soldier.* Glencoe, IL: Free Press.

Kahn, R. L., Mann, F. C., & Seashore, S. (1956). Introduction. *J. Soc. Issues, 12*; 2–4.

Karsh, B. (1958). *Diary of a strike.* Urbana: University of Illinois.

Karsh, B., Seidman, J., & Lilienthal, D. M. (1953). The union organizer and his tactics: A case study. *Amer. J. Soc., 59*; 113–122.

Keller, F. E. (1873). *Geschichte der Preussischen Volksschulenwesens.* Berlin: Oppenheim.

Kerschensteiner, G. (1909). *Grundfragen der Schulorganization.* Leipzig: Teubner.

Lazarsfeld, P. F., & Rosenberg, M. (Eds.). (1955). *The language of social research.* Glencoe, IL.: Free Press.

Leighton, A. H. (1945). *The governing of men: General principles and recommendations based on experience at a Japanese relocation camp.* Princeton, NJ: Princeton University Press.

Lenin, V. I. (1952). *What is to be done?* Moscow: Foreign Languages Publishing House.

Lindsay, A. D. (1947). *The democratic state.* London: Oxford University Press.

Lipset, S. M. (1960). *Political man.* Garden City, NY: Doubleday.

Lucci, Y. (1960). *The campus YMCA: Highlights from a national study.* New York: Bur. Appl. Soc. Res., Columbia University.

McCorkle, L. W., & Korn, R. (1954). Resocialization within walls. *Annals Am. Acad. Poli. Soc. Sci., 293*; 88–98.

March, J. G., & Simon, H. (1958). *Organizations.* New York: John Wiley & Sons.

Merton, R. K. (1957). The role set: Problems in sociological theory. *Br. J. Sociol., 8*; 106–120.

Michels, R. (1959). *Political parties.* New York: Dover.

Myrdal, G. with the assistance of Sterner, R., & Rose, A. (1944). *An American dilemma.* New York: Harper & Row.

Nagel, E. (1957). *Logic without metaphysics.* Glencoe, IL: Free Press.

Parsons, T., Shils, E. A. *et al.* (1952). *Toward a general theory of action.* Cambridge, MA.: Harvard University Press.

Parvilahti, U. (1960). *Beria's gardens: A slave laborer's experience in the Soviet Utopia.* (A. Blair, Trans.). New York: Dutton.

Rosada, S., & Gwozdz, J. (1952). *Forced labor and confinement without trial in Poland.* Washington, DC: Mid-European Studies Center.

Rosenfeld, Eva. (1951). Social stratification in a "classless" society. *Am. Sociol. Rev., 16*; 766–774.

Schwartz, R. D. (1955). Functional alternatives to inequality. *Am. Sociol. Rev., 20*; 424–430.

Selznick, P. (1952). *The organizational weapon.* New York: McGraw-Hill.

Simpson, R. L. (1959). Vertical and horizontal communication in formal organizations. *Admin. Sci. Q., 4*; 188–196.

Steffens, L. (1957). *The shame of the cities.* New York: Sagamore Press.

Steward, D. D. (1950). Local board: A study of the place of volunteer participation in bureaucratic organization. Unpublished doctoral dissertation, Columbia University.

Sykes, G. M. (1958). *The society of captives.* Princeton, NJ: Princeton University Press.

Talmon-Garber, Y. (1952). Social differentiation in cooperative communities. *Br. J. Sociol., 3*; 339–357.

Tec, N., & Granick R. (1959–60). Social isolation and difficulties in social interaction of residents of a home for aged. *Soc. Prob. 7*; 226–232.

Weber, M. (1947). *The theory of social and economic organization.* London: Wm. Hodge.
Weinberg, K. S. (1942). Aspects of the prison's social structure. *Am. J. Soc.*, 47; 717–726.

17
The Concept of Formal Organization
Peter M. Blau & W. Richard Scott

SOCIAL ORGANIZATION AND FORMAL ORGANIZATIONS

Although a wide variety of organizations exists, when we speak of an organization it is generally quite clear what we mean and what we do not mean by this term. We may refer to the American Medical Association as an organization, or to a college fraternity; to the Bureau of Internal Revenue, or to a union; to General Motors, or to a church; to the Daughters of the American Revolution, or to an army. But we would not call a family an organization, nor would we so designate a friendship clique, or a community, or an economic market, or the political institutions of a society. What is the specific and differentiating criterion implicit in our intuitive distinction of organizations from other kinds of social groupings or institutions? It has something to do with how human conduct becomes socially organized, but it is not, as one might first suspect, whether or not social controls order and organize the conduct of individuals, since such social controls operate in both types of circumstances.

Before specifying what is meant by formal organization, let us clarify the general concept of social organization. "Social organization" refers to the ways in which human conduct becomes socially organized, that is, to the observed regularities in the behavior of people that are due to the social conditions in which they find themselves rather than to their physiological or psychological characteristics as individuals. The many social conditions that influence the conduct of people can be divided into two main types, which constitute the two basic aspects of social organizations: (1) the structure of social relations in a group or larger collectivity of people, and (2) the shared beliefs and orientations that unite the members of the collectivity and guide their conduct.

The conception of structure or system implies that the component units stand in some relation to one another and, as the popular expression "The whole is greater than the sum of its parts" suggests, that the relations between units add new elements to the situation.[1] This aphorism, like so many others, is a half-truth. The sum of fifteen apples, for example, is no more than fifteen times one apple. But a block of ice is more than the sum of the atoms of hydrogen and oxygen that compose it. In the case of the apples, there exist no linkages or relations between the units comprising the whole. In the case of the ice, however, specific connections have been formed between H and O atoms and among H_2O molecules that distinguish ice from hydrogen and oxygen, on the one hand, and from water, on the other. Similarly, a busload of passengers does not constitute a group, since no social relations unify individuals into a common structure.[2] But a busload of club members on a Sunday outing is a group, because a network of social relations links the members into a social structure, a structure which is an emergent characteristic of the collectivity that cannot be reduced to the attributes of its individual members. In short, a network of social relations transforms an aggregate of individuals into a group (or an aggregate of groups into a larger social structure), and the group is more than the sum of the individuals composing it since the structure of social relations is an emergent element that influences the conduct of individuals.

To indicate the nature of social relations, we can briefly dissect this concept. Social relations involve, first, patterns of social interaction: the frequency and duration of the contacts between people, the tendency to initiate these contacts, the direction of influence between persons, the degree of cooperation, and so forth. Second, social relations entail people's sentiments to one another, such as feelings of attraction, respect, and hostility. The differential distribution of social relations in a group, finally, defines its status structure. Each member's status in the group depends on his relations with the others—their sentiments toward and interaction with him. As a result, integrated members become differentiated from isolates, those who are widely respected from those who are not highly regarded, and leaders from followers. In addition to these relations between individuals within groups, relations also develop between groups, relations that are a source of still another aspect of social status, since the standing of the group in the larger social system becomes part of the status of any of its members. An obvious example is the significance that membership in an ethnic minority, say, Puerto Rican, has for an individual's social status.

The networks of social relations between individuals and groups, and the status structure defined by them, constitute the core of the social organization of a collectivity, but not the whole of it. The other main dimension of social organization is a system of shared beliefs and orientations, which serve as standards for human conduct. In the course of social interaction common notions arise as to how people should act and interact and what objectives are worthy of attainment. First, common values crystallize, values that govern the goals for which men strive—their ideals and their ideas of what is desirable—such as our belief in democracy or the importance financial success assumes in our thinking. Second, social norms develop—that is, common expectations concerning how people ought to behave—and social sanctions are used to discourage violations of these norms. These socially sanctioned rules of conduct vary in significance from moral principles or mores, as Sumner calls them, to mere customs or folkways. If values define the ends of human conduct, norms distinguish behavior that is a legitimate means for achieving these ends from behavior that is illegitimate. Finally, aside from the norms to which everybody is expected to conform, differential role expectations also emerge, expectations that become associated with various social positions. Only women in our society are expected to wear skirts, for example. Or, the respected leader of a group is expected to make suggestions, and the other members will turn to him in times of difficulties, whereas group members who have not earned the respect of others are expected to refrain from making suggestions and generally to participate little in group discussions.

These two dimensions of social organization—the networks of social relations and the shared orientations—are often referred to as the social structure and the culture, respectively.[3] Every society has a complex social structure and a complex culture, and every community within a society can be characterized by these two dimensions of social organization, and so can every group within a community (except that the specific term "culture" is reserved for the largest social systems). The prevailing cultural standards and the structure of social relations serve to organize human conduct in the collectivity. As people conform more or less closely to the expectations of their fellows, and as the degree of their conformity in turn influences their relations with others and their social status, and as their status in further turn affects their inclinations to adhere to social norms and their chances to achieve valued objectives, their patterns of behavior become socially organized.

In contrast to the social organization that emerges whenever men are living together, there are organizations that have been deliberately established for a certain purpose.[4] If the accomplishment of an objective requires collective effort, men set up an organization designed to coordinate the activities of many persons and to furnish incentives for others to join them for this purpose. For example, business concerns are established in order to produce goods that can be sold for a profit, and workers organize unions in order to increase their bargaining power with employers. In these cases, the goals to be achieved, the rules the members of the organization are expected to follow, and the status structure that defines the relations between them (the organizational chart) have not spontaneously emerged in the course of social interaction but have been had consciously designed a priori to anticipate and guide interaction and activities. Since the distinctive characteristic of these organizations is that they have been formally established for the explicit purpose of achieving certain goals, the term "formal organization" is used to designate them. And this formal establishment for explicit purpose is the criterion that distinguishes our subject matter from the study of social organization in general.

FORMAL ORGANIZATION AND INFORMAL ORGANIZATION

The fact that an organization has been formally established, however, does not mean that all activities and interactions of its members conform strictly to the official blueprint. Regardless of the time and effort devoted by management to designing a rational organization chart and elaborate procedure manuals, this official plan can never completely determine the conduct and social relations of the organization's members. Stephen Vincent Benét illustrates this limitation when he contrasts the military blueprint with military action:

> If you take a flat map
> And move wooden blocks upon it strategically,
> The thing looks well, the blocks behave as they should.
> The science of war is moving live men like blocks.
> And getting the blocks into place at a fixed moment.
> But it takes time to mold your men into blocks
> And flat maps turn into country where creeks and gullies
> Hamper your wooden squares. They stick in the brush,

They are tired and rest, they straggle
after ripe blackberries.
And you cannot lift them up in your
hand and move them.[5]

In every formal organization there
arise informal organizations. The constituent groups of the organization, like
all groups, develop their own practices,
values, norms, and social relations as
their members live and work together.
The roots of these informal systems are
embedded in the formal organization itself and nurtured by the very formality
of its arrangements. Official rules must
be general to have sufficient scope to
cover the multitude of situations that
may arise. But the application of these
general rules to particular cases often
poses problems of judgment, and informal practices tend to emerge that provide solutions for these problems. Decisions not anticipated by official
regulations must frequently be made,
particularly in times of change, and here
again unofficial practices are likely to
furnish guides for decisions long before
the formal rules have been adapted to
the changing circumstances. Moreover,
unofficial norms are apt to develop that
regulate performance and productivity.
Finally, complex networks of social relations and informal status structures
emerge, within groups and between
them, which are influenced by many
factors besides the organizational chart,
for example by the background characteristics of various persons, their abilities, their willingness to help others,
and their conformity to group norms.
But to say that these informal structures
are not completely determined by the
formal institutions is not to say that
they are entirely independent of it. For
informal organizations develop in response to the opportunities created and
the problems posed by their environment, and the formal organization constitutes the immediate environment of
the groups within it.

When we speak of formal organizations in this book, we do not mean to
imply that attention is confined to formally instituted patterns; quite the contrary. It is impossible to understand the
nature of a formal organization without
investigating the networks of informal
relations and the unofficial norms as well
as the formal hierarchy of authority and
the official body of rules, since the formally instituted and the informally
emerging patterns are inextricably intertwined. The distinction between the
formal and the informal aspects of organizational life is only an analytical one
and should not be reified; there is only
one actual organization. Note also that
one does not speak of the informal organization of a family or of a community.
The term "informal organization" does
not refer to all types of emergent patterns of social life but only to those that
evolve within the framework of a formally established organization. Excluded from our purview are social institutions that have evolved without
explicit design; included are the informally emerging as well as the formally
instituted patterns within formally established organizations.

The decision of the members of a
group to formalize their endeavors and
relations by setting up a specific organization, say, a social and athletic club,
is not fortuitous. If a group is small
enough for all members to be in direct
social contact, and if it has no objectives
that require coordination of activities,
there is little need for explicit procedures or a formal division of labor. But
the larger the group and the more complex the task it seeks to accomplish, the
greater are the pressures to become explicitly organized.[6] Once a group of boys
who merely used to hang around a drug-
store decide to participate in the local
baseball league, they must organize a
team. And the complex coordination of

millions of soldiers with thousands of specialized duties in a modern army requires extensive formalized procedures and a clear-cut authority structure.

Since formal organizations are often very large and complex, some authors refer to them as "large-scale" or as "complex" organizations. But we have eschewed these terms as misleading in two respects. First, organizations vary in size and complexity, and using these variables as defining criteria would result in such odd expressions as "a small large-scale organization" or "a very complex complex organization." Second, although formal organizations often become very large and complex, their size and complexity do not rival those of the social organization of a modern society, which includes such organizations and their relations with one another in addition to other nonorganizational patterns. (Perhaps the complexity of formal organizations is so much emphasized because it is man-made whereas the complexity of societal organization has slowly emerged, just as the complexity of modern computers is more impressive than that of the human brain. Complexity by design may be more conspicuous than complexity by growth or evolution.)

The term "bureaucratic organization" which also is often used, calls attention to the fact that organizations generally possess some sort of administrative machinery. In an organization that has been formally established, a specialized administrative staff usually exists that is responsible for maintaining the organization as a going concern and for coordinating the activities of its members. Large and complex organizations require an especially elaborate administrative apparatus. In a large factory, for example, there is not only an industrial work force directly engaged in production but also an administration composed of executive, supervisory, clerical, and other

staff personnel. The case of a government agency is more complicated, because such an agency is part of the administrative arm of the nation. The entire personnel of, say, a law-enforcement agency is engaged in administration, but administration of different kinds; whereas operating officials administer the law and thereby help maintain social order in the society, their superiors and the auxiliary staff administer agency procedures and help maintain the organization itself.

One aspect of bureaucratization that has received much attention is the elaboration of detailed rules and regulations that the members of the organization are expected to faithfully follow. Rigid enforcement of the minutiae of extensive official procedures often impedes effective operations. Colloquially, the term "bureaucracy" connotes such rule-encumbered inefficiency. In sociology, however, the term is used neutrally to refer to the administrative aspects of organizations. If bureaucratization is defined as the amount of effort devoted to maintaining the organization rather than to directly achieving its objectives, all formal organizations have at least a minimum of bureaucracy—even if this bureaucracy involves no more than a secretary-treasurer who collects dues. But wide variations have been found in the degree of bureaucratization in organizations, as indicated by the amount of effort devoted to administrative problems, the proportion of administrative personnel, the hierarchical character of the organization, or the strict enforcement of administrative procedures and rigid compliance with them.

NOTES

1. For a discussion of some of the issues raised by this assertion, see Ernest Nagel, "On the

Statement 'The Whole is More Than the Sum of Its Parts'," Paul F. Lazarsfeld and Morris Rosenberg (eds.), *The Language of Social Research* (Glencoe, Ill.: Free Press, 1955), pp. 519–527.

2. A purist may, concededly, point out that all individuals share the role of passenger and so are subject to certain generalized norms, courtesy for example.

3. See the recent discussion of these concepts by Kroeber and Parsons, who conclude by defining culture as "transmitted and created content and patterns of values, ideas, and other symbolic-meaningful systems" and social structure or system as "the specifically relational system of interaction among individuals and collectivities."

A. L. Kroeber and Talcott Parsons, "The Concepts of Culture and of Social System," *American Sociological Review,* 23 (1958), p. 583.

4. Sumner makes this distinction between, in his terms, *crescive* and *enacted* social institutions. William Graham Sumner, *Folkways* (Boston: Ginn, 1907), p. 54.

5. From *John Brown's Body.* Holt, Rinehart & Winston, Inc. Copyright, 1927, 1928, by Stephen Vincent Benét. Copyright renewed, 1955, 1956, by Rosemary Carr Benét.

6. For a discussion of size and its varied effects on the characteristics of social organization, see Theodore Caplow, "Organizational Size," *Administrative Science Quarterly,* 1 (1957), pp. 484–505.

18
Organizational Choice: Product versus Function

Arthur H. Walker & Jay W. Lorsch

Of all the issues facing a manager as he thinks about the form of his organization, one of the thorniest is the question of whether to group activities primarily by product or by function. Should all specialists in a given function be grouped under a common boss, regardless of differences in products they are involved in, or should the various functional specialists working on a single product be grouped together under the same superior?

In talks with managers we have repeatedly heard them anguishing over this choice. For example, recently a divisional vice president of a major U.S. corporation was contemplating a major organizational change. After long study,

he made this revealing observation to his subordinate managers:

We still don't know which choice will be the best one. Should the research, engineering, marketing, and production people be grouped separately in departments for each function? Or would it be better to have them grouped together in product departments, each department dealing with a particular product group?

We were organized by product up until a few years ago. Then we consolidated our organization into specialized functional departments, each dealing with all of our products. Now I'm wondering if we wouldn't be better off to divide our operations again into product units. Either way I can see advantages and disadvantages, trade-offs. What criteria should I

Source: Reprinted by permission of the Harvard Business Review. Arthur H. Walker and Jay W. Lorsch, "Organizational Choice: Product versus Function," *Harvard Business Review* (November–December 1968). Copyright © 1968 by the President and Fellows of Harvard College; all rights reserved. Two figures renumbered as tables.

use? How can we predict what the outcomes will be if we change?

Companies that have made a choice often feel confident that they have resolved this dilemma. Consider the case of a large advertising agency that consolidated its copy, art, and television personnel into a "total creative department." Previously they had reported to group heads in their areas of specialization. In a memo to employees the company explained the move:

> Formation of the "total creative" department completely tears down the walls between art, copy, and television people. Behind this move is the realization that for best results all creative people, regardless of their particular specialty, must work together under the most intimate relationship as total advertising people, trying to solve creative problems together from start to finish.
>
> The new department will be broken into five groups reporting to the senior vice president and creative director, each under the direction of an associate creative director. Each group will be responsible for art, television, and copy in their accounts.

But our experience is that such reorganizations often are only temporary. The issues involved are so complex that many managements oscillate between these two choices or try to effect some compromise between them.

In this article we shall explore—from the viewpoint of the behavioral scientist—some of the criteria that have been used in the past to make these choices, and present ideas from recent studies that suggest more relevant criteria for making the decision. We hope to provide a way of thinking about these problems that will lead to the most sensible decisions for the accomplishment of organizational goals.

The dilemma of products versus function is by no means new; managers have been facing the same basic question for decades. As large corporations like Du Pont and General Motors grew, they found it necessary to divide their activities among product divisions.[1] Following World War II, as companies expanded their sales of existing products and added new products and businesses, many of them implemented a transition from functional organizations handling a number of different products to independently managed product divisions. These changes raised problems concerning divisionalization, decentralization, corporate staff activities, and the like.

As the product divisions grew and prospered, many companies extended the idea of product organization further down in their organizations under such labels as "the unit management concept." Today most of the attention is still being directed to these changes and innovations *within* product or market areas below the divisional level.

We are focusing therefore on these organizational issues at the middle and lower echelons of management, particularly on the crucial questions being faced by managers today within product divisions. The reader should note, however, that a discussion of these issues is immensely complicated by the fact that a choice at one level of the corporate structure affects the choices and criteria for choice at other levels. Nonetheless, the ideas we suggest in this article are directly relevant to organizational choice at any level.

ELEMENTS TO CONSIDER

To understand more fully the factors that make these issues so difficult, it is useful to review the criteria often relied on in making this decision. Typically, managers have used technical and economic criteria. They ask themselves, for instance, "Which choice will minimize payroll costs?" Or, "Which will best utilize equipment and specialists?" This approach not only makes real sense in the traditional logic of management, but it has strong support from the classical school of organization theorists. Luther Gulick, for example, used it in arguing for organization by function:

> It guarantees the maximum utilization of up-to-date technical skill and . . . makes it possible in each case to make use of the most effective divisions of work and specialization. . . . [It] makes possible also the economies of the maximum use of labor-saving machinery and mass production. . . . [It] encourages coordination in all of the technical and skilled work of the enterprise. . . . [It] furnishes an excellent approach to the development of central coordination and control.[2]

In pointing to the advantages of the product basis of organization, two other classical theorists used the same approach:

> Product or product line is an important basis for departmentalizing, because it permits the maximum use of personal skills and specialized knowledge, facilitates the employment of specialized capital and makes easier a certain type of coordination.[3]

In sum, these writers on organization suggested that the manager should make the choice based on three criteria:

1. Which approach permits the maximum use of special technical knowledge?
2. Which provides the most efficient utilization of machinery and equipment?
3. Which provides the best hope of obtaining the required control and coordination?

There is nothing fundamentally wrong with these criteria as far as they go, and, of course, managers have been using them. But they fail to recognize the complex set of trade-offs involved in these decisions. As a consequence,

managers make changes that produce unanticipated results and may even reduce the effectiveness of their organization. For example:

> A major manufacturer of corrugated containers a few years ago shifted from a product basis to a functional basis. The rationale for the decision was that it would lead to improved control of production costs and efficiencies in production and marketing. While the organization did accomplish these aims, it found itself less able to obtain coordination among its local sales and production units. The functional specialists now reported to the top officers in charge of production and sales, and there was no mechanism for one person to coordinate their work below the level of division management. As a result, the company encountered numerous problems and unresolved conflicts among functions and later returned to the product form.

This example pinpoints the major trade-off that the traditional criteria omit. Developing highly specialized functional units makes it difficult to achieve coordination or integration among these units. On the other hand, having product units as the basis for organization promotes collaboration between specialists, but the functional specialists feel less identification with functional goals.

BEHAVIORISTS' FINDINGS

We now turn to some new behavioral science approaches to designing organization structure. Recent studies[4] have highlighted three other important factors about specialization and coordination:

- As we have suggested, the classical theorists saw specialization in terms of grouping similar activities, skills, or even equipment. They did not look at its psychological and social consequences. Recently, behavioral scientists (including the authors) have found that there is an important relationship between a unit's or individual's assigned activities and the unit members' patterns of thought and behavior. Functional specialists tend to develop patterns of behavior and thought that are in tune with the demands of their jobs and their prior training, and as a result these specialists (*e.g.*, industrial engineers and production supervisors) have different ideas and orientation about what is important in getting the job done. This is called *differentiation*, which simply means the differences in behavior and thought patterns that develop among different specialists in relation to their respective tasks. Differentiation is necessary for functional specialists to perform their jobs effectively.

• Differentiation is closely related to achievement of coordination, or what behavioral scientists call *integration*. This means collaboration between specialized units or individuals. Recent studies have demonstrated that there is an inverse relationship between differentiation and integration: the more two functional specialists (or their units) differ in their patterns of behavior and thought, the more difficult it is to bring about integration between them. Nevertheless, this research has indicated, achievement of both differentiation and integration is essential if organizations are to perform effectively.

• While achievement of both differentiation and integration is possible, it can occur only when well-developed means of communication among specialists exist in the organization and when the specialists are effective in resolving the inevitable cross-functional conflicts.

These recent studies, then, point to certain related questions that managers must consider when they choose between a product or functional basis of organization.

1. How will the choice affect differentiation among specialists? Will it allow the necessary differences in viewpoint to develop so that specialized tasks can be performed effectively?

2. How does the decision affect the prospects of accomplishing integration? Will it lead, for instance, to greater differentiation, which will increase the problems of achieving integration?
3. How will the decision affect the ability of organization members to communicate with each other, resolve conflicts, and reach the necessary joint decisions?

There appears to be a connection between the appropriate extent of differentiation and integration and the organization's effectiveness in accomplishing its economic goals. What the appropriate pattern is depends on the nature of external factors—markets, technology, and so on—facing the organization, as well as the goals themselves. The question of how the organizational pattern will affect individual members is equally complex. Management must consider how much stress will be associated with a certain pattern and whether such stress should be a serious concern.

To explore in more detail the significance of modern approaches to organizational structuring, we shall describe one recent study conducted in two manufacturing plants—one organized by *product*, the other on a *functional* basis.[5]

PLANT F AND PLANT P

The two plants where this study was conducted were selected because they were closely matched in several ways. They were making the same product; their markets, technology, and even raw materials were identical. The parent companies were also similar: both were large, national corporations that developed, manufactured, and marketed many consumer products. In each case divisional and corporate headquarters were located more than 100 miles from the facilities studied. The plants were separated from other structures at the same site, where other company products were made.

Both plants had very similar management styles. They stressed their desire to foster employees' initiative and autonomy and placed great reliance on selection of well-qualified department heads. They also identified explicitly the same two objectives. The first was to formulate, package, and ship the products in minimum time at specified levels of quality and at minimum costs—that is, within existing capabilities. The second was to improve the capabilities of the plant.

In each plant there were identical functional specialists involved with the manufacturing units and packing unit, as well as quality control, planning and scheduling, warehousing, industrial engineering, and plant engineering. In Plant F (with the *functional* basis of organization), only the manufacturing departments and the planning and scheduling function reported to the plant manager responsible for the product (see Figure 1). All other functional specialists reported to the staff of the divisional manufacturing manager, who was also responsible for plants manufacturing other products. At Plant P (with the *product* basis of organization), all functional specialists with the exception of plant engineering reported to the plant manager (see Figure 2).

State of Differentiation

In studying differentiation, it is useful to focus on the functional specialists' differences in outlook in terms of: orientation toward goals, orientation toward time, and perception of the formality of organization.

Goal Orientation. The bases of organization in the two plants had a marked effect on the specialists' differentiated goal orientations. In Plant F they focused sharply on their specialized goals and objectives. For example, quality control specialists were concerned almost exclusively with meeting quality standards, industrial engineers with methods improvements and cost reduction, and scheduling specialists with how to meet schedule requirements. An industrial engineer in Plant F indicated this intensive interest in his own activity:

> We have 150 projects worth close to a million dollars in annual savings. I guess I've completed some that save as much as $90,000 a year. Right now I'm working on cutting departmental costs. You need a hard shell in this work. No one likes to have his costs cut, but that is my job.

That these intense concerns with specialized objectives were expected is illustrated by the apologetic tone of a comment on production goals by an engineering supervisor at Plant F:

> At times we become too much involved in production. It causes a change in heart. We are interested in production, but not at the expense of our own standards of performance. If we get too much involved, then we may become compromised.

A final illustration is when production employees stood watching while members of the maintenance department worked to start a new production line, and a production supervisor remarked:

> I hope that they get that line going soon. Right now, however, my hands are tied. Maintenance has the job. I can only wait. My people have to wait, too.

This intense concern with one set of goals is analogous to a rifle shot; in a manner of speaking, each specialist took aim at one set of goals and fired at it. Moreover, the specialists identified closely with their counterparts in other plants and at divisional headquarters. As one engineer put it:

FIGURE 1 • ORGANIZATIONAL CHART AT PLANT F

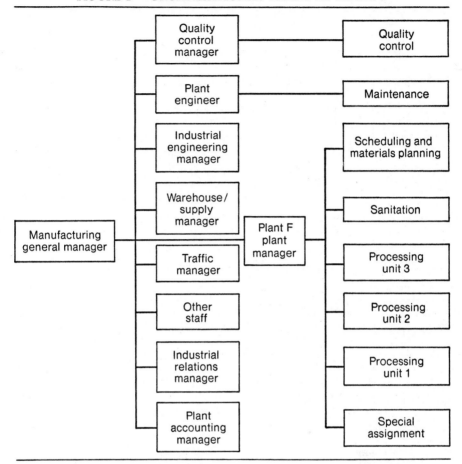

We carry the ball for them (the central office). We carry a project through and get it working right.

At Plant P the functional specialists' goals were more diffuse—like buckshot. Each specialist was concerned not only with his own goals, but also with the operation of the entire plant. For example, in contrast to the Plant F production supervisor's attitude about maintenance, a Plant P maintenance manager said, under similar circumstances:

> We're all interested in the same thing. If I can help, I'm willing. If I have a mechanical problem, there is no member of the operating department who wouldn't go out of his way to solve it.

Additional evidence of this more diffuse orientation toward goals is provided by comments such as these which came from Plant P engineers and managers:

> We are here for a reason—to run this place the best way we know how. There is no reluctance to be open and frank despite various backgrounds and ages.
>
> The changeovers tell the story. Everyone shows willingness to dig in. The whole plant turns out to do cleaning up.

Because the functional specialists at Plant F focused on their individual goals,

FIGURE 2 · ORGANIZATIONAL CHART AT PLANT P

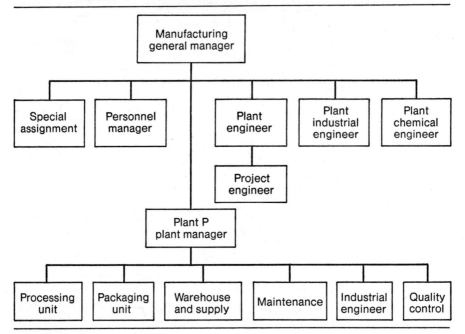

they had relatively wide differences in goals and objectives. Plant P's structure, on the other hand, seemed to make functional specialists more aware of common product goals and reduced differences in goal orientation. Yet, as we shall see, this lesser differentiation did not hamper their performance.

Time Orientation. The two organizational bases had the opposite effect, however, on the time orientation of functional managers. At Plant F, the specialists shared a concern with short-term issues (mostly daily problems). The time orientation of specialists at Plant P was more differentiated. For example, its production managers concentrated on routine matters, while planning and industrial engineering focused on issues that needed solution within a week, and quality control specialists worried about even longer-term problems.

The reason is not difficult to find. Since Plant P's organization led its managers to identify with product goals, those who could contribute to the solution of longer-term problems became involved in these activities. In Plant F, where each unit focused on its own goals, there was more of a tendency to worry about getting daily progress. On the average, employees of Plant P reported devoting 30 percent of their time to daily problems, while at Plant F this figure was 49 percent. We shall have more to say shortly about how these factors influenced the results achieved in the two plants.

Organizational Formality. In the study, the formality of organizational structure in each functional activity was measured by three criteria: clarity of definition of job responsibilities, clarity of dividing lines between jobs, and importance of rules and procedures.

It was found that at Plant F there were fewer differences among functional activities in the formality of organization structure than at Plant P. Plant F employees reported that a uniform degree of structure existed across functional specialties; job responsibilities were well defined, and the distinctions between jobs were clear. Similarly, rules and procedures were extensively relied on. At Plant P, on the other hand, substantial differences in the formality of organization existed. Plant engineers and industrial engineers, for example, were rather vague about their responsibilities and about the dividing line between their jobs and other jobs. Similarly, they reported relatively low reliance on rules and procedures. Production managers, on the other hand, noted that their jobs were well defined and that rules and procedures were more important to them.

The effects of these two bases of organization on differentiation along these three dimensions are summarized in Figure 3. Overall, differentiation was greater between functional specialists at Plant P than at Plant F.

Integration Achieved

While the study found that both plants experienced some problems in accomplishing integration, these difficulties were more noticeable at Plant F. Collaboration between maintenance and production personnel and between production and scheduling was a problem there. In Plant P the only relationship where integration was unsatisfactory was that between production and quality control specialists. Thus Plant P seemed to be getting slightly better integration in spite of the greater differentiation among specialists in that organization. Since differentiation and integration are basically antagonistic, the only way managers at Plant P could get both was by being effective at communication and conflict resolution. They were better at this than were managers at Plant F.

Communication Patterns. In Plant P, communication among employees was more frequent, less formal, and more often of a face-to-face nature than was the case with Plant F personnel. One Plant P employee volunteered:

> Communications are no problem around here. You can say it. You can get an answer.

Members of Plant F did not reflect such positive feelings. They were heard to say:

> Why didn't they tell me this was going to happen? Now they've shut down the line.

FIGURE 3 · DIFFERENTIATION IN PLANTS F AND P

Dimensions of Differentiation	Plant F	Plant P
Goal orientation	More differentiated and focused	Less differentiated and more diffuse
Time orientation	Less differentiated and shorter term	More differentiated and longer term
Formality of structure	Less differentiated, with more formality	More differentiated, with less formality

When we get the information, it is usually too late to do any real planning. We just do our best.

The formal boundaries outlining positions that were more prevalent at Plant F appeared to act as a damper on communication. The encounters observed were often a succession of two-man conversations, even though more than two may have been involved in a problem. The telephone and written memoranda were more often employed than at Plant P, where spontaneous meetings involving several persons were frequent, usually in the cafeteria.

Dealing with Conflict. In both plants, *confrontation* of conflict was reported to be more typical than either the use of power to *force* one's own position or an attempt to *smooth* conflict by "agreeing to disagree." There was strong evidence, nevertheless, that in Plant P managers were coming to grips with conflicts more directly than in Plant F. Managers at Plant F reported that more conflicts were being smoothed over. They worried that issues were often not getting settled. As they put it:

We have too many nice guys here.

If you can't resolve an issue, you go to the plant manager. But we don't like to bother him often with small matters. We should be able to settle them ourselves. The trouble is we don't. So it dies.

Thus, by ignoring conflict in the hope it would go away, or by passing it to a higher level, managers at Plant F often tried to smooth over their differences. While use of the management hierarchy is one acceptable way to resolve conflict, so many disagreements at Plant F were pushed upstairs that the hierarchy became overloaded and could not handle all the problems facing it. So it responded by dealing with only the more immediate and pressing ones.

At Plant P the managers uniformly reported that they resolved conflicts themselves. There was no evidence that conflicts were being avoided or smoothed over. As one manager said:

We don't let problems wait very long. There's no sense to it. And besides, we get together frequently and have plenty of chances to discuss differences over a cup of coffee.

As this remark suggests, the quicker resolution of conflict was closely related to the open and informal communication pattern prevailing at Plant P. In spite of greater differentiation in time orientation and structure, then, Plant P managers were able to achieve more satisfactory integration because they could communicate and resolve conflict effectively.

Performance and Attitudes

Before drawing some conclusions from the study of these two plants, it is important to make two more relevant comparisons between them—their effectiveness in terms of the goals set for them and the attitudes of employees.

Plant Performance. As we noted before, the managements of the two plants were aiming at the same two objectives: maximizing current output within existing capabilities and improving the capabilities of the plant. Of the two facilities, Plant F met the first objective more effectively; it was achieving a higher production rate with greater efficiency and at less cost than was Plant P. In terms of the second objective, however, Plant P was clearly superior to Plant F; the former's productivity had increased by 23 percent from 1963 to 1966 compared with the latter's increment of only 3 percent. One key manager at Plant F commented:

There has been a three- or four-year effort to improve our capability. Our expectations have simply not been achieved. The improvement in performance is just not there. We are still where we were three years ago. But our targets for improvements are realistic.

By contrast, a key manager at Plant P observed:

Our crews have held steady, yet our volume is up. Our quality is consistently better, too.

Another said:

We are continuing to look for and find ways to improve and consolidate jobs.

Employee Attitudes. Here, too, the two organizations offer a contrast, but the contrast presents a paradoxical situation. Key personnel at Plant P appeared to be more deeply involved in their work than did managers at Plant F, and they admitted more often to feeling stress and pressure than did their opposite numbers at Plant F. But Plant F managers expressed more satisfaction with their work than did those at Plant P; they liked the company and their jobs more than did managers at Plant P.

Why Plant P managers felt more involved and had a higher level of stress, but were less satisfied than Plant F managers, can best be explained by linking these findings with the others we have reported.

Study Summary

The characteristics of these two organizations are summarized in Figure 4. The nature of the organization at Plant F seemed to suit its stable but high rate of efficiency. Its specialists concentrated on their own goals and performed well, on the whole. The jobs were well defined and managers worked within procedures and rules. The managers were concerned primarily with short-term matters. They were not particularly effective in communicating with each other and in resolving conflict. But this was not very important to achieve steady, good performance, since the coordination necessary to meet this objective could be achieved through plans and procedures and through the manufacturing technology itself.

As long as top management did not exert much pressure to improve performance dramatically, the plant's managerial hierarchy was able to resolve the few conflicts arising from daily operations. And as long as the organization avoided extensive problem solving, a great deal of personal contact was not very important. It is not surprising therefore that the managers were satisfied and felt relatively little pressure. They attended strictly to their own duties, remained uninvolved, and got the job done. For them, this combination was satisfying. And higher management was pleased with the facility's production efficiency.

The atmosphere at Plant P, in contrast, was well suited to the goal of improving plant capabilities, which it did very well. There was less differentiation between goals, since the functional specialists to a degree shared the product goals. Obviously, one danger in this form of organization is the potential attraction of specialist managers to total goals to the extent that they lose sight of their particular goals and become less effective in their jobs. But this was not a serious problem at Plant P.

Moreover, there was considerable differentiation in time orientation and structure; some specialists worked at the routine and programmed tasks in operating the plant, while others concentrated on longer-term problems to improve manufacturing capability. The latter group was less constrained by formal procedures and job definitions, and

FIGURE 4 • OBSERVED CHARACTERISTICS OF THE TWO ORGANIZATIONS

Characteristics	Plant F	Plant P
Differentiation	Less differentiation except in goal orientation	Greater differentiation in structure and time orientation
Integration	Somewhat less effective	More effective
Conflict management	Confrontation, but also "smoothing over" and avoidance; rather restricted communication pattern	Confrontation of conflict; open, face-to-face communication
Effectiveness	Efficient, stable production; but less successful in improving plant capabilities	Successful in improving plant capabilities, but less effective in stable production
Employee attitudes	Prevalent feeling of satisfaction, but less feeling of stress and involvement	Prevalent feeling of stress and involvement, but less satisfaction

this atmosphere was conducive to problem solving. The longer time orientation of some specialists, however, appeared to divert their attention from maintaining schedules and productivity. This was a contributing factor to Plant P's less effective current performance.

In spite of the higher degree of differentiation in these dimensions, Plant P managers were able to achieve the integration necessary to solve problems that hindered plant capability. Their shared goals and a common boss encouraged them to deal directly with each other and confront their conflicts. Given this pattern, it is not surprising that they felt very involved in their jobs. Also they were under stress because of their great involvement in their jobs. This stress could lead to dissatisfaction with their situation. Satisfaction for its own sake, however, may not be very important; there was no evidence of higher turnover of managers at Plant P.

Obviously, in comparing the performance of these two plants operating with similar technologies and in the same

market, we might predict that, because of its greater ability to improve plant capabilities, Plant P eventually will reach a performance level at least as high as Plant F's. While this might occur in time, it should not obscure one important point: the functional organization seems to lead to better results in a situation where stable performance of a routine task is desired, while the product organization leads to better results in situations where the task is less predictable and requires innovative problem solving.

CLUES FOR MANAGERS

How can the manager concerned with the function versus product decision use these ideas to guide him in making the appropriate choice? The essential step is identifying the demands of the task confronting the organization.

Is it a routine, repetitive task? Is it one where integration can be achieved by plan and conflict managed through the hierarchy? This was the way the task was implicitly defined at Plant F. If this is the nature of the task, or, to put it another way, if management is satisfied with this definition of the task, then the functional organization is quite appropriate. While it allows less differentiation in time orientation and structure, it does encourage differentiation in goal orientation. This combination is important for specialists to work effectively in their jobs.

Perhaps even more important, the functional structure also seems to permit a degree of integration sufficient to get the organization's work done. Much of this can be accomplished through paper systems and through the hardware of the production line itself. Conflict that comes up can more safely be dealt with through the management hierarchy, since the difficulties of resolving conflict are less acute. This is so because the tasks provide less opportunity for conflict and because the specialists have less differentiated viewpoints to overcome. This form of organization is less psychologically demanding for the individuals involved.

On the other hand, if the task is of a problem-solving nature, or if management defines it this way, the product organization seems to be more appropriate. This is especially true where there is a need for tight integration among specialists. As illustrated at Plant P, the product organization form allows the greater differentiation in time orientation and structure that specialists need to attack problems. While encouraging identification with superordinate goals, this organizational form does allow enough differentiation in goals for specialists to make their contributions.

Even more important, to identify with product ends and have a common boss encourages employees to deal constructively with conflict, communicate directly and openly with each other, and

confront their differences, so they can collaborate effectively. Greater stress and less satisfaction for the individual may be unavoidable, but it is a small price to pay for the involvement that accompanies it.

The manager's problem in choosing between product and functional forms is complicated by the fact that in each organization there are routine tasks and tasks requiring problem solving, jobs requiring little interdependence among specialists and jobs requiring a great deal. Faced with these mixtures, many companies have adopted various compromises between product and functional bases. They include (in ascending order of structural complexity):

1. *The use of cross-functional teams to facilitate integration.* These teams provide some opportunity for communication and conflict resolution and also a degree of the common identification with product goals that characterizes the product organization. At the same time, they retain the differentiation provided by the functional organization.

2. *The appointment of full-time integrators or coordinators around a product.* These product managers or project managers encourage the functional specialists to become committed to product goals and help resolve conflicts between them. The specialists still retain their primary identification with their functions.[6]

3. *The "matrix" or grid organization, which combines the product and functional forms by overlaying them.* Some managers wear functional hats and are involved in the day-to-day, more routine activities. Naturally, they identify with functional goals. Others, wearing product or project hats, identify with total product goals and are more involved in the problem-solving activity required to cope with long-range issues and to achieve cross-functional coordination.

These compromises are becoming popular because they enable companies to deal with multiple tasks simultaneously. But we do not propose them as a panacea, because they make sense only for those situations where the differentiation and integration required by the sum of all the tasks make a middle approach necessary. Further, the complexity of interpersonal plus organizational relationships in these forms and the ambiguity associated with them make them difficult to administer effectively and psychologically demanding on the persons involved.

In our view, the only solution to the product versus function dilemma lies in analysis of the multiple tasks that must be performed, the differences between specialists, the integration that must be achieved, and the mechanisms and behavior required to resolve conflict and arrive at these states of differentiation and integration. This analysis provides the best hope of making a correct product or function choice or of arriving at some appropriate compromise solution.

NOTES

1. For a historical study of the organizational structure of U.S. corporations, see Alfred D. Chandler, Jr., *Strategy and Structure* (Cambridge: The M.I.T. Press, 1962).

2. Luther Gulick, "Notes on the Theory of Organization," in *Papers on the Science of Administration*, edited by Luther Gulick and Lyndall F. Urwick (New York Institute of Public Administration, 1917), pp. 23–24.

3. Harold D. Koontz, and C. J. O'Donnell, *Principles of Management* (New York, McGraw-Hill, 2nd ed. 1959), p. 111.

4. See Paul R. Lawrence and Jay W. Lorsch, *Organization and Environment* (Boston, Division of Research, Harvard Business School, 1967); and Eric J. Miller and A. K. Rice, *Systems of Organization* (London, Tavistock Publications, 1967).

5. Arthur H. Walker, *Behavioral Consequences of Contrasting Patterns of Organization* (Boston, Harvard Business School, unpublished doctoral dissertation, 1967).

6. See Paul R. Lawrence and Jay W. Lorsch, "New Management Job: The Integrator," HBR November-December 1967, p. 142.

19
Organization-Environment Interface
Paul R. Lawrence & Jay W. Lorsch

It is no mystery that organizations must carry on transactions with their environment simply to survive, and, even more importantly, to grow. In the first chapter, we identified the quality of these transactions as posing one of the fundamental developmental problems of any organization. Other analysts of organizational affairs have consistently mentioned transactions with the environment as a crucial if not the most crucial

issue. It is an issue that has been dealt with extensively by economists and by specialists in business policy and strategy. They have dealt primarily with the content of these relationships—the actual kind and amount of goods, services, and funds that are part of these transactions. But the issue has not been extensively studied by specialists in the application of behavioral sciences, and attention has not been focused on such

Source: From Paul R. Lawrence and Jay W. Lorsch, *Developing Organizations: Diagnosis and Action* (Reading, Mass.: Addison-Wesley Publishing, 1969), 23–30. Reprinted with permission. Footnotes omitted.

human aspects affecting the quality of these transactions as: What is the quality of the information exchanged across the organizational boundaries? What are the major determinants of the quality? What are its consequences? Such questions have been asked many times of the relations between individuals and groups within the organization, but the boundary-spanning relations have simply not been subjected to comparable scrutiny. It is not surprising therefore, that systematic efforts to diagnose and improve the quality of these organization-environment relations have also lagged behind the effort applied to improving internal relations. It is worth speculating about the reasons for this lack of attention.

Perhaps the focus has been placed on internal transactions because both parties to a faulty relation, being within the institution, tend to bring their troubles to a single source—their shared superior up the chain of command. This focuses attention on the costs of unsatisfactory work relations and triggers corrective action. There is less likelihood that this will happen in connection with boundary transactions. It is, moreover, not so easy to collect information about the status of the boundary-spanning relation since the outside participants may feel no obligation to cooperate. The relative neglect may also be due to the traditional division of labor between academic disciplines. It may be automatically assumed that economists are the experts on boundary transactions while the psychologist and the sociologist are expected to confine their efforts to internal relations. Even within business schools, it is traditional for the functional specialities, such as marketing and finance, to have exclusive concern with the quality of salesman-customer and treasurer-banker relationships. Only recently have such specialists drawn on

behavioral disciplines to aid them in the study of these matters.

The authors themselves became involved in the study and improvement of relations at this interface by approaching the topic through the back door. We had been concerned for some years with the quality of intergroup relations in organizations. This interest led us to the observation that major groups in industry displayed some distinctive characteristics that persisted in spite of efforts from top management toward consistency. We came to the conclusion that this persistence could be accounted for if these groups needed these characteristics to conduct favorable transactions with the segment of the firm's environment with which they were especially involved. So, in order to account for some important sources of intergroup conflict, we began to study each group's relations with its special segment of the environment. Our research findings tended strongly to confirm our theory. This, in turn, led us into a new interest not only in understanding these transactions from a behavioral standpoint, but also in helping organizations and their managers diagnose the quality of these relations and improve them.

THE CERTAINTY-UNCERTAINTY CONTINUUM

Our research findings with specific relevance to this interface can be quickly summarized since they were generally reviewed in Chapter 2. We started our inquiry with the simple notion that the characteristics of an organizational unit would in some way need to match up with those of its segment of the environment if healthy transactional relations were to prevail. We were particularly interested in information flows across these boundaries. It seemed to us that if the sector of the environment involved was in a fairly steady, unchanging state, the amount and complexity of the information needed would be much less than if the opposite were true— namely, if there existed a high degree of uncertainty and change in the relevant part of the environment. As the environment varies along this certainty-uncertainty continuum, we expected to find matching differences in the organizational unit concerned if the transactions were to be sound. We identified four measurable features of groups that we thought might vary with the certainty-uncertainty of their parts of the environment. These were:

1. the degree of reliance on formalized rules and formal communication channels within the unit;
2. the time horizon of managers and professionals in the groups;
3. their orientation toward goals, either diffuse or concentrated; and
4. their interpersonal style, either relationship- or task-oriented.

Using measures of these four characteristics, we made a study of high- and low-performance companies in three different industries, and arrived at the specific conclusion that there was a closer fit in the high-performing organizations than in the low performers between the attributes of each unit and the demands of its relevant part of the environment.

One way to visualize the meaning of these findings is to think again in terms of information flows. In order to relate effectively to its environment, any organization must have reasonably accurate and timely information about the environment and especially about environmental changes. This is clearly an easier job if the environment is relatively stable. The job can be specified in a predetermined set of operating rules. The necessary messages can be handled through the traditional superior-subordinate channels, which may be few and

constricted but are probably less subject to error and relatively inexpensive. Fairly short time horizons are usually adequate to take account of the reactions of such an environment to the firm's actions. This makes it sensible to use a straightforward, task-oriented approach in managerial style.

On the other hand, life in an organizational unit must become more complex in order to deal adequately with an uncertain and rapidly changing sector of the environment. To have more points of contact with the environment, a flatter organization is employed. Formal rules cannot be formulated that will be suitable for any appreciable time period, so it seems better not to rely heavily on them. More of an all-to-all communications pattern is indicated, which can keep environmental clues moving throughout the unit for interpretation at all points instead of just through superior-subordinate channels. A longer time orientation is usually needed. The growth of this necessarily more complex and sophisticated (as well as more costly) communication network is fostered by an interpersonal style that emphasizes building strong relationships rather than just accomplishing the task, per se.

STABILITY VERSUS CHANGE IN THE ENVIRONMENT

Securing and processing relevant information from the environment, while highly critical, is not the only requirement for high-quality transactions at the organization-environment interface. In addition to exchanging information, people at these interfaces must frequently negotiate the terms of exchange of tangible goods and less tangible services of many kinds. These bargaining and/or problem-solving kinds of relationships can also be analyzed in terms of the findings of research. Fouraker has used his findings from experimental research to develop the idea that organizational units with different internal features are more or less effective depending upon whether their environment is characterized by harsh competition for scarce resources or by more beneficent circumstances. In a relatively unchanging environment, it is likely that time has brought more competitors into the struggle and that therefore resources are scarce. In this circumstance, he argues that the organizations which can conduct more favorable transactions will operate with tighter internal controls, more rules, and simpler channels of communication. In short, they will have closed ranks and geared up for a competitive fight. Again, it is a matching process.

At the other extreme is an organization unit dealing with a rapidly changing environment. The resources are plentiful and diverse, but the organization must be capable of creative and flexible problem-solving to discover potential opportunities for conducting more favorable transactions. Here again that unit will thrive which relies not on rules but on a more complex and flatter communication network which serves to stimulate new ideas. Such a unit would be oriented to a longer time perspective. It would thus be matched with the features of its environment as it works at solving the problem of defining and continually redefining the terms of its environmental transactions.

These, then, are the highlights of current research on the matching of organizational units with their respective sectors of the environment. Good matching seems to foster sound transactions at this organization-environment interface. In our research we studied this interface only for the important functions of sales, research, and production; but [Figure 1] indicates how many additional interfaces of this type are relevant to most business organizations. Similar lists could be drawn for other types of organizations.

One of the ways of evolving an overall strategy for any organization is to develop within the organization the capacity to carry on fully adequate transactions at each of these important interfaces, with some special advantages in regard to one or two of them where a favorable exchange is possible. These are areas of "distinctive competence," to use Selznick's term. An organization in which each of its boundary-spanning units is well matched with its corresponding environmental sector is in a desirable position to detect opportunities for new kinds of favorable transactions with the environment and to anticipate newly developing hazards in the environment. This matching process is a highly flexible way to maintain the kind of continuous search that is recommended by a pioneering study recently conducted by Aguilar on how business firms scan their relevant environments.

As the relevant environment changes, however, organizations not only need suitable matched units, but on occasion also need to establish new units to address emerging environmental facts and to regroup old units. For instance, the emergence of the computer as a new environmental fact has led many firms to create a new unit such as management-information services; and the development of newly relevant mathematical techniques has led to the emergence of operations-research groups and long-range planning groups. Such new groups not only draw together people with different technical skills, but also they often need different orientations, structures, and styles to transact their business successfully.

FIGURE 1

Organizational Unit	Relevant Environmental Sector
Sales	Customers and competitors
Research	Science and technology
Production and engineering	Technology and equipment suppliers
Purchasing	Suppliers
Finance	Financial institutions
Personnel	Labor and professional markets
Public relations	The press and legislative bodies
Legal	Governmental regulatory agencies

In addition, as firms grow in terms of product variety and geographical coverage, a need frequently arises to switch the first big structural division of work in the company from the traditional functional basis, implicit in our discussion so far, to some other basis. Valid arguments can be mustered for various choices of first-level structural division, but the soundest arguments will be based on environmental facts. For instance, if different geographical areas require quite different ways of marketing, while the products of a firm are quite similar technically, a first-level split by geography is usually indicated, and vice versa. If, on the other hand, the products and the geographical conditions are relatively homogeneous, an initial division by function is probably the soundest basis.

This analysis of differences and similarities needs to be complemented by an analysis of the intensity of the interdependencies between various units to find the best possible trade-off. Once the primary basis for structurally dividing work is selected, secondary means can be provided not only at lower levels but also by staff groups. In some instances where two factors, such as functions and products, are both highly different and critical, some firms, as in the aerospace industry, are turning to a matrix organization. In such an organization two

bases are used simultaneously as a first-level division of labor.

We have seen that whether we view the environmental transaction primarily as a problem of information exchange or as one of bargaining and problem-solving, we are pointed toward a matching of organizational traits and orientations with environmental features. We are now in a position to explain how we use this method of analysis as a practical tool in helping specific organizations improve the quality of their environmental transactions. We will do this by examining several specific cases.

The first set of cases involves situations where mismatches could be directly addressed by making adjustments in the internal arrangements of the unit concerned. A second set of cases will also be examined where other types of adjustments were needed to improve the matching process:

1. by releasing counterpressures in the organization for consistency among all units;
2. by adjusting units to accommodate shifts in the environment;
3. by creating new units to meet newly important environmental conditions; and
4. by realigning units to cope with the increased scope of the business.

In reviewing these cases emphasis will be given to the variety of variables in the organizational systems that were selected as the initial means of implementing planned change.

Before turning to the cases, however, we need to get a feel for the way problems at this interface are likely to first present themselves to managers and in turn to behaviorally-oriented consultants. Problems at the environment-organization interface are likely to manifest themselves eventually through economic results. For example, at the sales-customer interface, it is in a loss of sales volume; in research and development, it is in a drop in the flow of new products, etc. However, these indicators of interface trouble are fairly slow to show up, and managers learn to be sensitive to earlier clues of difficulty. These often take the form of complaints from the outside—letters from customers, a private word dropped at lunch by a banker,

an important move by a competitor that caught everyone flatfooted. The customer may be saying that your organization is unresponsive, that you cannot seem to tailor your products to his needs, that he is getting tired of fighting his way through your red tape. In other cases, the concern will develop because a competitor seems too frequently to be first with a new-product introduction, or a new marketing technique. Perhaps in the production area it is a failure to realize economies through process innovation or falling behind in the race with rising wages and salaries. Another clue might be that the best specialists are not staying in the company—there is a worrisome amount of turnover among the more promising professionals in the physical or managerial sciences. These are the clues that might well be traced back to human problems at the environment-organization interface.

20
The Matrix Organization—Who Needs It?
Stanley M. Davis & Paul R. Lawrence

At this point we need to remind ourselves that every organization, based on matrix or not, is set up as a way of inducing the desired work behavior on the part of its members. This chapter will address the question of what actual organizational behavior one is trying to induce by using the matrix model as against the more conventional types. Even more importantly we will address the "why" question—under what environmental conditions would one want to induce these "matrix" behaviors? When is the matrix a sensible and practical way to bridge between the specific requirements for healthy survival that are thrust upon an organization and the actual work activities of organizational members? When does such a model serve to channel people's energies into needed tasks.

Source: Stanley M. Davis and Paul R. Lawrence, *Matrix,* © 1977, Addison Wesley Publishing Company, Reading, Massachusetts: pp. 11–24. Reprinted with permission.

Our study of these questions has led us to the conclusion that the matrix is the preferred structural choice when three basic conditions exist simultaneously. This chapter examines these three conditions and their connection to matrix structures, systems, and behavior.

CONDITION 1: OUTSIDE PRESSURE FOR DUAL FOCUS

One of the principal reasons people form organizations is to focus attention and energy on a selected goal. Organizations serve as a lens that catches the sun's rays and bends them into a spot of focused energy. This is the source of the power of organizations and their leaders. It is why organizations can undertake tasks that are "too big" for a single individual or a simple small group. The initial way organizations focus human energy is to group people physically into different organizational units each with a defined boundary and a common boss. These groups are formed around a theme or symbol that identifies their purpose to the rest of the organization. Group members develop their own distinctive way of thinking, working, and relating to each other. They share a common task to be performed as their contribution to the work of the entire organization.

At a simple level, tasks can be "too big" for an individual for two basic reasons. The first is simply because an individual cannot be in two places at the same time. The second is because our mental capacity is finite—one individual cannot be expert and skilled in everything. (If this book had been written a century ago we would have had to add a third basic reason—that human physical strength is finite. But the spread of powered machinery has for all practical purposes removed this constraint.)

When organizations initially form to get around the first constraint, they very naturally tend to set up their organizational units in terms of different physical locations. This tendency is especially apparent in transport and communication companies such as railroads, postal services, telegraph, and telephone. The same principle is at work when we assign a group to look after a defined set of customers. We expect to have the resulting organizational units bear names that identify both the location or set of customers and the service or product provided. We are familiar with the Milwaukee Airport, the New England Telephone Company, Saks Fifth Avenue, etc. This type of organizational grouping tends to focus attention and energy on performing the entire task or service for a given area or set of customers.

When organizations form to get around the second constraint (mental limits) they tend to group people initially around technical specialties so that the group members can enrich and reinforce one another's technical proficiencies. In conventional language this is known as a functional organization that identifies its primary groups with words such as manufacturing, sales, engineering, purchasing, finance, personnel, etc. These labels serve to orient each group to one technical specialty and focus energy accordingly.

Each of these ways of establishing a division of labor is widely used and each division has performed successfully over many years. But which is best, organizing around functions, areas, products, or services? It quite clearly depends on which constraint is more critical. If the geographical coverage is absolutely essential to the existence of an organization such as the telephone service, then it is wise to organize first of all into geographic units that focus on providing a complete service responsive to the special needs of customers in its area, even at the expense of the potential depth of expertise that could be achieved by grouping by technologies. Likewise, when technical expertise is critical to an organization's existence, then initially using functional (technology) groupings is sensible and perhaps essential. In such an arrangement, organizational power will center in these functional groups and the state of technical proficiency can be expected to advance, even at the expense of providing services and products tailored to the special needs of a particular locality or set of customers.

So each mode of organizing has its special strength and its corresponding weakness. But what if both types of constraints are truly critical and equally compelling? What if focusing attention on both is essential to survival? This is, we suggest, the first of the three basic conditions that call out for some form of a matrix design.

It is no accident that matrix first came into widespread use in the aerospace industry. To survive and prosper in the aerospace industry, any firm needs to focus intensive attention *both* on complex technical issues and on the unique project requirements of the customer. These companies can not afford to give a second-level status to either the functional groupings around technical specialties or to the project groupings around unique customer needs. They need to create a balance of power between project-oriented managers and the managers of the engineering and scientific specialists. Neither can be allowed to, arbitrarily, overrule the other. Both orientations need to be brought to bear in a simultaneous fashion on a host of tradeoff decisions involving schedules, costs, and product quality. The needed behavior is epitomized by a picture of two middle managers with equal power, but very

different orientations and goals, sitting down to debate and argue over each and every point in their search for the answers that would optimize decisions for both technical excellence and unique customer requirements. The dual command structure of a matrix serves to induce this kind of simultaneous decision-making behavior. It was to induce this kind of behavior that matrix was developed. The case study of Printer that appears at the end of this chapter presents an example of these outside pressures for maintaining a simultaneous dual focus in an organization that is only beginning to move into a matrix.

CONDITION 2: PRESSURES FOR HIGH INFORMATION-PROCESSING CAPACITY

The second condition that generates pressure to adopt a matrix is the requirement for high information-processing capacity among organizational members. Once any organization is formed to do work "too big" for individuals, it must pay the basic price of organizing—it must establish and maintain a network of communication channels among members. When only one person is doing a job, a single nervous system is used to keep the right and left hands coordinated. When many people are involved in a task, the extra "overhead" cost of coordinating the messages sent back and forth between people must be borne. Since communication uses resources, organization planners try to arrange clusters of people and channels between them to minimize the cost of required communications. The hierarchical pyramid of a conventional organization, depicted with its boxes and lines, represents an attempt to conserve resources by channeling communications through selected managers. Such a communication hierarchy can be supplemented

by rules, job descriptions, standard procedures, schedules and budgets which,
in addition to personal instructions from
the boss, indicate to members what behavior they are expected to engage in
that will fit in a coordinated way with
the work of others. These coordination
arrangements work fine, if they do not
get overloaded with information. But
under certain conditions they do get very
overloaded.

The symptoms of such overloading
are familiar to managers. The issues ur-
gently awaiting managerial action pile
up. The queue to see the boss gets long.
Schedules and budgets start slipping but
nothing gets done about it. Bureaucracy
sets in. There are too many rules, it is
felt, but more probably it is that the
channels are not organized properly. The
communications process bogs down. In
effect, the right hand loses track of what
the left hand is doing.

Why do smart, hardworking, well-
intentioned managers sometimes get
themselves into this situation? Sometimes, better schedules, better budgets,
bigger computers, better rules, and
clearer job descriptions can cure the
problem. As often as not, however, they
are an inadequate cure. There are still
too many real issues that have to get
resolved and not enough hours in the
day to resolve them. Under such conditions only a fundamental redesign of
the organization can relieve the information overload. What conditions tend
to generate an overwhelming need for
information processing and complex
problem solving? Only a special combination of circumstances can lead to a
very high information-processing requirement.

First, the kinds of demands placed
on the organization have to be changing and relatively unpredictable. If the
demands are stable, and therefore reasonably predictable, there is not much

important new information for the organization to cope with. Plans can be
made in advance and the assumptions
about future events that the plans were
made for will prove valid. There will
seldom be a need for quick replanning.
Things can go according to schedule.
But the future frequently holds major
surprises such as sudden changes in
market demand, competitive moves,
technological advances, ecological restrictions and other governmental regulations, currency and stock-market
fluctuations, and the appearance of protest groups. When these surprises occur, plans do not hold up, and large
amounts of new information must be
assimilated and responded to in a coherent way. *Uncertainty* in the external
environment calls for an enriched
information-processing capacity within
the organization.

Second, even these uncertainties
would not be unmanageable if one's organization was doing a simple job such
as making and marketing a single product in a single area, or providing a single
service to a single customer. It should
be remembered that, before the matrix,
the last major change in organization
design occurred in the 1920s and 1930s
when businesses diversified their activities in both product and market terms,
leading to the shift from centralized
functionally departmentalized organizations to decentralized ones based on a
product division design. While the increased complexity of tasks led to a major adaptation in terms of management
and organization, both the centralized
and the decentralized models maintained the traditional singular chain of
command. Information and communication were organized either along functional lines, or by product category or
market unit. Simultaneous diversification of both products/services and markets, however, increased the *complexity*

of an organization's tasks severalfold. When this complexity is "added" to environmental uncertainty, the result is a major multiplication of information processing requirements.

Finally, the question arises concerning how many individuals and groups must be involved in order to make a reasoned response to new events. The more *interdependence* there is among people on any one issue, the greater the information-processing load. If people can accomplish their tasks, no matter how complex and uncertain, by themselves, then they will not have to share information with others and the information-processing load will not be great. If, on the other hand, their tasks are highly interrelated, the opposite is bound to be the case.

So all three generators of the information load—uncertainty, complexity, and interdependence—have to be examined. If all three are high, conventional ways of handling the load tend to break down. If such a compound piling up of information-processing requirements were a rare, once-in-a-hundred occurrence, we could afford to ignore it. But it appears that this set of circumstances is to be the fate of more and more organizations, even in industries that we could label as stable and mature in the recent past. When organizations have to come to terms with heavy information-processing loads, they have to open up and legitimate a more complex communication and decision network.

If the problem were only one of keeping more people informed of events, the response could be handled through increasing the flow of reports, briefings, and informal communications. But, of course, the tough part is weighing the significance of the new information and making decisions that commit the organization to a response that will prove to be wise over time. To accomplish this,

more people simply must be in a position to think and act as general managers—more people who seek out and pull together the relevant information and opinion, who weigh alternatives, who make commitments in the best interest of the whole and who stand ready to be judged by the eventual results. This is the kind of behavior that is called for when managers handle large amounts of complex information for the organization. This behavior on the part of more people is the ultimate cure for information overload.

The matrix design, properly applied, tends to develop more people who think and act in a general management mode. By inducing this kind of action, the matrix increases an organization's information-processing capacity.

The case study at the end of this chapter provides an example of overload and the case studies in the next several chapters describe the information-processing capacity of matrix at work.

CONDITION 3: PRESSURES FOR SHARED RESOURCES

The third and final condition we see as an indication to adopt a matrix is so obvious that its importance is easy to ignore. It is the condition of the organization's being under considerable pressure to achieve economies of scale in human terms and high performance in terms of both costs and benefits by fully utilizing scarce human resources and by meeting high-quality standards.

While all organizations probably feel some degree of pressure for high performance, the amount of such pressure varies a good deal. If an organization has a truly dominant position in a given market, it may not feel much pressure to avoid redundancies in the use of human resources or to attain high-quality outputs. It may feel comfortable increasing its costs by hiring extra specialists to fill out the needs of multiple product divisions, even though these specialists wind up spending much of their time unproductively. On the other hand, it could hire one jack-of-all-trades to perform the jobs of several specialists with a corresponding loss of quality. But when performance pressures are real and strong, the need arises to fully utilize expensive and highly specialized talents. The size of an organization may enable it to acquire skilled human resources in large numbers, but nevertheless there is bound to be an upper limit. Whatever that limit is, when it is reached, pressures will develop to share existing human resources. These internal pressures will be greater when there are external forces pressing to achieve economies of scale. These resources will need to be redeployed in a flexible manner so that people can work on more than one task at a time or at least be readily available for assignment from one task to the next.

A similar argument holds for the sharing of expensive capital resources and physical facilities. For example, several product divisions may need access to a fleet of different test aircraft (helicopters, propeller-driven and jet aircraft) to evaluate their products, but no divisions can afford to maintain them full time. High performance will result from high utilization of such facilities through effective sharing and redeployment of them among specialist groups.

Organizations with conventional designs tend to develop resistances to the rapid redeployment of specialists across organizational lines. Structures are traditionally thought of as stolid and static. They do not change very often, and when they do it is in a discrete quantum jump to another static state. Since environmental and strategic changes tend to evolve in a continual process, the organization is often catching up with already changed circumstances. And each change is experienced by its members as a wrenching of established patterns of behavior and the need to learn new ones. Also, the more rapidly the environment and the firm's strategy change, the shorter will be the duration for which a given structure is appropriate. In such circumstances, it is helpful to think of optimal structural change as being frequent and in small doses, rather than infrequent major shake-ups. Structure, then, becomes flexible, if not fluid; and people can become accustomed to a structure that is always changing but that rarely erupts and causes severe dislocations. The matrix design helps induce the kind of behavior that views rapid redeployment and the shared use of scarce human resources as basic.

REVIEW: THE THREE NECESSARY AND SUFFICIENT CONDITIONS

Based on our observations of why managers adopt a matrix, we initially stated that all three conditions discussed above need to be present simultaneously before a matrix is indicated. Why is not the presence of one or two of these conditions an adequate reason? Our analysis runs as follows: learning how to use a matrix is not easy. A matrix organization is not simply a matter of understanding and creating a formal design. For us:

$$\frac{\text{Matrix}}{\text{Organization}} = \frac{\text{Matrix}}{\text{Structure}} + \frac{\text{Matrix}}{\text{Systems}} + \frac{\text{Matrix}}{\text{Culture}} + \frac{\text{Matrix}}{\text{Behavior}}.$$

The structure involves the dual chains of command that we have spoken about. The system must also operate along two dimensions simultaneously: planning, controlling, appraising and rewarding, etc., along both functional and product lines at the same time. Moreover, every organization has a culture of its own and, as we shall discuss more fully in Chapter 3, for the matrix to succeed the ethos or spirit of the organization must be consonant with the new form. Finally, people's behavior, especially those with two bosses and those who share subordinates, must reflect an understanding, and an ability to work within such overlapping boundaries.

The change to a matrix cannot be accomplished by issuing a new organization chart. People are brought up, by and large, to think in terms of "one person, one boss" and such habits of mind are not easily changed. People must learn to work comfortably and effectively in a different way of managing and organizing. Our experience suggests that successful passage through the early evolution of a matrix, until it is firmly established in its mature form, is a process that will likely take two or three years. That is not a long time in the evolution and life span of an organization, but to those involved in the change, the period of transition can be quite difficult. Furthermore, the limited evidence suggests that going to a matrix will initially add to managerial overhead. So one is ill-advised to view the matrix as one of many exciting new managerial tools and techniques; something that can be tried and discarded if it doesn't seem to be succeeding. The move to a matrix should be a serious decision, made by the top level of management, signalling a major commitment, and thoroughly implemented through many layers of the organization. It is too difficult to undertake superficially, too costly in human terms to attempt haphazardly, and too encompassing to experiment with unnecessarily.

The presence of only two of the three necessary conditions is not sufficient for us to recommend a matrix approach.

There are simpler, partial methods for coping with the additional needs. Taking each partial set of conditions separately:

- It is clear that without performance pressures, the problems generated by conditions 1 and/or 2, the pressure for dual focus and for high information-processing requirements, could be handled without a matrix simply by accepting a lower performance level. One could either take whatever time was needed in a conventional organization design to process all the information up to the top level where a dual focus would be brought into play—at the cost of very slow performance—or one could split the organization into decentralized autonomous parts thereby increasing the information-processing capacity, but at the expense of high costs or low quality.
- The presence of only conditions 1 and/or 3, pressures from two critical sectors and pressures to achieve human economies of scale and performance, could reasonably be handled by creating a small top-management team that represented the dual focus and that given the limited informational requirements could then generate high quality and timely decisions.
- Finally, if only conditions 2 and/or 3 were present—to perform uncertain, complex, and interdependent tasks with scarce human resources—the problem could be solved by placing the most critical focus on the chain of command or line roles while using subordinate or staff positions to represent the less critical focus.

As summarized in Figure 1 there are three environmental conditions, each of which calls for organizational response, and all of which must be present simultaneously for an organization to appropriately adopt and adapt the matrix.

In summarizing the three conditions which call for a matrix, we must point out a very real hazard. It is easy for managers from all kinds of organizations to read over the three conditions and readily nod their heads in a quick agreement

FIGURE 1 • NECESSARY AND SUFFICIENT CONDITIONS

	Environmental Pressure	Behavioral Linkage
Condition 1	Two or more critical sectors; functions, products, services, markets, areas	Balance of power, dual command, simultaneous decision making
Condition 2	Performance of uncertain, complex and interdependent tasks	Enriched information-processing capacity
Condition 3	Economies of scale	Shared and flexible use of scarce human resources

that all three conditions are present in their situation. Such an initial reaction is understandable. After all, most managers feel pressured from multiple sides and swamped with information. If they felt otherwise, they would have trouble justifying their salaries. But a facile reaction is dangerous. Organizations do, in fact, vary in the extent to which they experience these pressures. Until these three conditions are overwhelmingly present, in a literal sense, the matrix will almost certainly be an unnecessary complexity. Caution should be exercised in judging the presence or absence of these conditions and one is well advised to err on the conservative side. Clearly, only a limited, even if growing, number of organizations really need a fully evolved matrix.

While the logic of the three conditions is clear, it may not be clear just exactly how the matrix tends to induce the complex behavior that can simultaneously meet all three pressures. Much of the remainder of the book addresses this question, but at least a partial answer is called for now.

The threefold behavior we are trying to induce with the matrix is (1) the focusing of undivided human effort on two (or more) essential organizational tasks simultaneously, (2) the human processing of a great deal of information and the commitment of the organization to

a balanced reasoned response (a general management response), and (3) the rapid redeployment of human resources to various projects, products, services, clients, or markets. Figure 2 can help in clarifying how the matrix induces these behaviors.

We see here a diamond-shaped organization rather than the conventional pyramid. The top of the diamond represents the same top management symbolized by the top of the pyramid. The two arms of the diamond symbolize the dual chain of command. In the typical case the left arm would array the functional specialist groups or what could be thought of as the resource or input side of the organization. The right arm arrays the various products, projects, markets, clients, services, or areas the organization is set up to provide. This is the output or transaction side of the matrix. Depending on how many people holding a specialist orientation, either resource or output, the organization needs, these groupings can develop several echelons in response to the practical limits of the span of control of any line manager. At the foot of the matrix is the 2-boss manager. This manager is responsible for the performance of a defined package of work. The manager is given agreed-upon financial resources and performance targets by superiors on the output side, and negotiated human and equipment

FIGURE 2 • EXAMPLE OF A MATRIX DESIGN

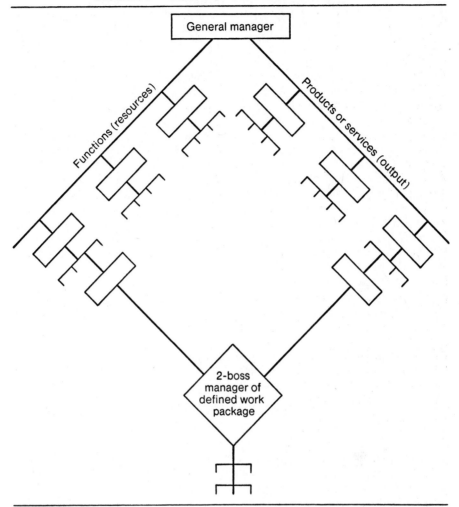

resources from the resource manager. The two streams, taken together, constitute the work package. The manager is responsible for managing these resources to meet performance targets. To perform, the manager must handle high volumes of information, weigh alternatives, make commitments on behalf of the organization as a whole, and be prepared to be judged by the results. This form of organization induces the manager to think and behave like a general manager.

This 2-boss manager is subject to dual demands of both the resource hierarchy and the transaction hierarchy, but can also draw upon their specialized help. The manager who cannot reconcile the dual demands is expected to convene a meeting with the two bosses and present the problem for the two of them to solve. In the resulting debate neither boss can, according to the authority structure, overrule the other. They must search for mutually agreeable and timely solutions.

While they can, if needed, have recourse to their respective two bosses, they cannot refer too many such disputes upward without reflecting on their own managerial capacity. The matrix induces many peer debates on key trade-off decisions. It tends to ensure that each of these decisions are made on their respective merits and not on the basis of any arbitrary form.

When the mix of tasks undertaken by the output or transaction side of the matrix shifts over time, the resources of the other side need to be redeployed. While it is never completely simple to move people from one task to another, the matrix can help this process along. The resource specialists can be engaged in a time-limited way to help any matrix product manager who needs their type of talent. This can be done over and over again without shifting the individual specialist from his or her "home base" resource group. People who are subject to redeployment in conventional organizations almost always develop a very understandable resistance to being uprooted and forced to join up with a set of strangers time after time. They cannot build a reputation for performance that carries them past the occasional mistake. They must work to create relations of trust and mutual respect again and again. While these problems are not totally avoided in a matrix, they can be greatly mitigated. Human resources can be redeployed with a minimum amount of the kind of associated human costs that also usually wind up as economic costs.

Finally, we must point out that even in a fully developed matrix organization, only a relatively small proportion of the total number of people in the organization will be directly in the matrix. Whereas a middle-level manager may have two bosses, those people reporting

beneath that manager are likely to have only one boss. In an organization with 50,000 employees only 500–1,500 may be in the matrix; and in one with 500 people, only 50 may be in the matrix. To keep in perspective the proportion of people that will be affected directly, it may be helpful to envision the diamond of the matrix perched on top of the traditional design of the pyramid. Drawn to scale, proportionate to the numbers of people involved in the matrix, the total organization chart might look like this:

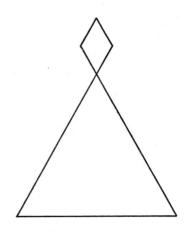

The Printer case study which follows provides a concrete example of an organization that is experiencing the need for a matrix. The case study indicates how the matrix can make a major contribution to inducing the kinds of behavior described above. The matrix that is evolving at Printer can serve as the organizational link between the pressures of the environment and the three kinds of complex behaviors needed to respond to these pressures.

21
The Five Basic Parts of the Organization
Henry Mintzberg

In Chapter 1 organizations were described in terms of their use of the coordinating mechanisms. We noted that, in theory, the simplest organization can rely on mutual adjustment to coordinate its basic work of producing a product or service. Its *operators*—those who do this basic work—are largely self-sufficient.

As the organization grows, however, and adopts a more complex division of labor among its operators, the need is increasingly felt for direct supervision. Another brain—that of a *manager*—is needed to help coordinate the work of the operators. So, whereas the division of labor up to this point has been between the operators themselves, the introduction of a manager introduces a first *administrative* division of labor in the structure—between those who do the work and those who supervise it. And as the organization further elaborates itself, more managers are added—not only managers of operators but also managers of managers. An administrative *hierarchy* of authority is built.

As the process of elaboration continues, the organization turns increasingly to standardization as a means of coordinating the work of its operators. The responsibility for much of this standardization falls on a third group, composed of *analysts*. Some, such as work study analysts and industrial engineers, concern themselves with the standardization of work processes; others, such as quality control engineers, accountants, planners, and production schedulers, focus on the standardization of outputs; while a few, such as personnel trainers, are charged with the standardization of skills (although most of this standardization takes place outside the organization, before the operators are hired). The introduction of these analysts brings a second kind of administrative division of labor to the organization, between those who do and who supervise the work, and those who standardize it. Whereas in the first case managers assumed responsibility from the operators for some of the coordination of their work by substituting direct supervision for mutual adjustment, the analysts assume responsibility from the managers (and the operators) by substituting standardization for direct supervision (and mutual adjustment). Earlier, some of the control over the work was removed from the operator; now it begins to be removed from the manager as well, as the systems designed by the analysts take increasing responsibility for coordination. The analyst "institutionalizes" the manager's job.

We end up with an organization that consists of a core of operators, who do the basic work of producing the products

Source: Henry Mintzberg, *The Structuring of Organizations,* © 1979, pp. 18–34. Reprinted by permission of Prentice-Hall, Englewood Cliffs, New Jersey.

and services, and an *administrative* component of managers and analysts, who take some of the responsibility for coordinating their work. This leads us to the conceptual description of the organization shown in Figure 1. This figure will be used repeatedly throughout the book, sometimes overlaid to show flows, sometimes distorted to illustrate special structures. It emerges, in effect, as the "logo," or symbol, of the book.

At the base of the logo is the *operating core*, wherein the operators carry out the basic work of the organization—the input, processing, output, and direct support tasks associated with producing the products or services. Above them sits the administrative component, which is shown in three parts. First, are the managers, divided into two groups. Those at the very top of the hierarchy, together with their own personal staff, form the *strategic apex*. And those below, who join the strategic apex to the operating core through the chain of command (such as it exists), make up the *middle line*. To their left stands the *technostructure*, wherein the analysts carry out their work of standardizing the work of others, in addition to applying their analytical techniques to help the organization adapt to its environment. Finally, we add a fifth group, the *support staff*, shown to the right of the middle line. This staff supports the functioning of the operating core indirectly, that is, outside the basic flow of operating work. The support staff goes largely unrecognized in the literature of organizational structuring, yet a quick glance at the chart of virtually any large

FIGURE 1 • THE FIVE BASIC PARTS OF ORGANIZATIONS

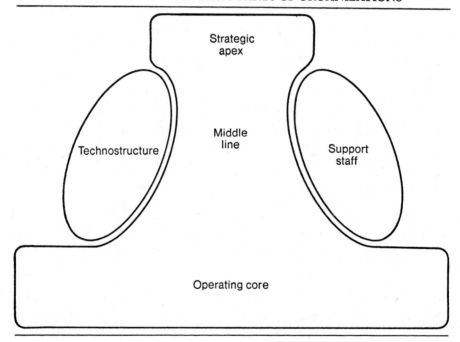

organization indicates that it is a major segment, one that should not be confused with the other four. Examples of support groups in a typical manufacturing firm are research and development, cafeteria, legal council, payroll, public relations, and mailroom.

Figure 1 shows a small strategic apex connected by a flaring middle line to a large, flat operating core. These three parts of the organization are shown in one uninterrupted sequence to indicate that they are typically connected through a single line of formal authority. The technostructure and the support staff are shown off to either side to indicate that they are separate from this main line of authority, and influence the operating core only indirectly.

It might be useful at this point to relate this scheme to some terms commonly used in organizations. The term "middle management," although seldom carefully defined, generally seems to include all members of the organization not at the strategic apex or in the operating core. In our scheme, therefore, "middle management" would comprise three distinct groups—the middle-line managers, the analysts, and the support staff. To avoid confusion, however, the term *middle level* will be used here to describe these three groups together, the term "management" being reserved for the managers of the strategic apex and the middle line.

The word "staff" should also be put into this context. In the early literature, the term was used in contrast to "line": in theory, line positions had formal authority to make decisions, while staff positions did not; they merely advised those who did. (This has sometimes been referred to as "functional" authority, in contrast to the line's formal or "hierarchical" authority.) Allen (1955), for example, delineates the staff's major activities as (1) providing advice, counsel, suggestions, and guidance on planning objectives, policies, and procedures to govern the operations of the line departments on how best to put decisions into practice; and (2) performing specific service activities for the line, for example, installing budgeting systems and recruiting line personnel, "which may include making decisions that the line has asked it to make" (p. 348). As we shall see later, this distinction between line and staff holds up in some kinds of structures and breaks down in others. Nevertheless, the distinction between line and staff is of some use to us, and we shall retain the terms here though in somewhat modified form. *Staff* will be used to refer to the technostructure *and* the support staff, those groups shown on either side in Figure 1. *Line* will refer to the central part of Figure 1, those managers in the flow of formal authority from the strategic apex to the operating core. Note that this definition does not mention the power to decide or advise. As we shall see, the support staff does not primarily advise; it has distinct functions to perform and decisions to make, although these relate only indirectly to the functions of the operating core. The chef in the plant cafeteria may be engaged in a production process, but it has nothing to do with the basic manufacturing process. Similarly, the technostructure's power to advise sometimes amounts to the power to decide, but that is outside the flow of formal authority that oversees the operating core.[1]

Some Conceptual Ideas of James D. Thompson. Before proceeding with a more detailed description of each of the five basic parts of the organization, it will be helpful to introduce at this point some of the important conceptual ideas of James D. Thompson (1967). To

Thompson, "Uncertainty appears as the fundamental problem for complex organizations, and coping with uncertainty, as the essence of the administrative process" (p. 159). Thompson describes the organization in terms of a "technical core," equivalent to our operating core, and a group of "boundary spanning units." In his terms, the organization reduces uncertainty by sealing off this core from the environment so that the operating activities can be protected. The boundary spanning units face the environment directly and deal with its uncertainties. For example, the research department interprets the confusing scientific environment for the organization, while the public relations department placates a hostile social environment.

Thompson and others who have built on his work describe various methods that organizations use to protect their operating cores. Standardization of work processes is, of course, a prime one. Others involve various forms of anticipation—planning, stockpiling, doing preventive maintenance, leveling production, conducting intelligence activities, and so on. Organizations also seek to dominate their environments, and so reduce uncertainty, by fixing prices, creating cartels, and integrating themselves vertically (i.e., becoming their own suppliers and customers).

Thompson also introduces a conceptual scheme to explain the *interdependencies* among organizational members. He distinguishes three ways in which the work can be coupled, shown in Figure 2. First is *pooled coupling*, where members share common resources but are otherwise independent. Figure 2(a) could represent teachers in a school who share common facilities and budgets but work alone with their pupils. In *sequential coupling*, members work in series, as in a relay race where the baton passes from runner to runner. Figure 2(b) could represent a mass production factory, where raw materials enter at one end, are sequentially fabricated and machined, then fed into an assembly line at various points, and finally emerge at the other end as finished products. In *reciprocal coupling*, the members feed their work back and forth among themselves; in effect each receives inputs from and provides outputs to the others. "This is illustrated by the airline which contains both operations and maintenance units. The production of the maintenance unit is an input for operations, in the form of a serviceable aircraft; and the product (or by-product) of operations is an input for maintenance, in the form of an aircraft needing maintenance" (Thompson, 1967, p. 55). Figure 2(c) could be taken to represent this example, or one in a hospital in which the nurse "preps" the patient, the surgeon operates, and the nurse then takes care of the postoperative care.

Clearly, pooled coupling involves the least amount of interdependence among members. Anyone can be plucked out; and, as long as there is no great change in the resources available, the others can continue to work uninterrupted. Pulling out a member of a sequentially coupled organization, however, is like breaking a link in a chain—the whole activity must cease to function. Reciprocal coupling is, of course, more interdependent still, since a change in one task affects not only those farther along but also those behind.

Now let us take a look at each of the five parts of the organization.

THE OPERATING CORE

The operating core of the organization encompasses those members—the operators—who perform the basic work related directly to the production of products and services. The operators perform

FIGURE 2 • POOLED, SEQUENTIAL, AND RECIPROCAL COUPLING
OF WORK

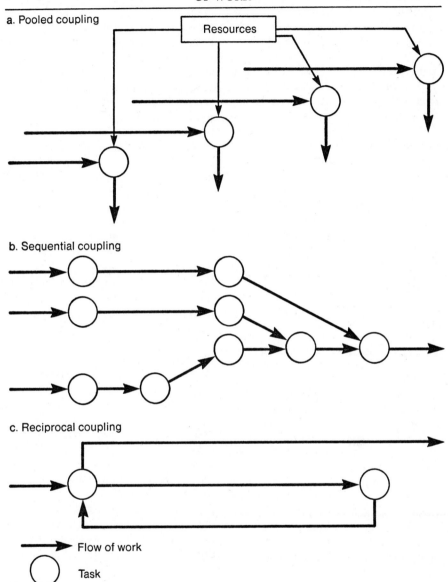

a. Pooled coupling

Resources

b. Sequential coupling

c. Reciprocal coupling

Flow of work

Task

four prime functions: (1) They *secure the inputs* for production. For example, in a manufacturing firm, the purchasing department buys the raw materials and the receiving department takes it in the door. (2) They *transform the inputs into outputs.* Some organizations transform raw materials, for example, by chopping down trees and converting them to pulp and then paper. Others transform individual parts into complete units, for example, by assembling typewriters, while still others transform information or people, by writing consulting reports, educating students, cutting hair, or curing illness. (3) They *distribute the outputs,* for example, by selling and physically distributing what comes out of the transformation process. (4) They *provide direct support* to the input, transformation, and output functions, for example, by performing maintenance on the operating machines and inventorying the raw materials.

Since it is the operating core that the other parts of the organization seek to protect, standardization is generally carried furthest here. How far, of course, depends on the work being done: assemblers in automobile factories and professors in universities are both operators, although the work of the former is far more standardized than that of the latter.

The operating core is the heart of every organization, the part that produces the essential outputs that keep it alive. But except for the very smallest ones, organizations need to build *administrative* components. The administrative component comprises the strategic apex, middle line, and technostructure.

THE STRATEGIC APEX

At the other end of the organization lies the strategic apex. Here are found those people charged with overall responsibility for the organization—the chief executive officer (whether called president, superintendent, Pope, or whatever), and any other top-level managers whose concerns are global. Included here as well are those who provide direct support to the top managers—their secretaries, assistants, and so on.[2] In some organizations, the strategic apex includes the executive committee (because its mandate is global even if its members represent specific interests); in others, it includes what is known as the chief executive office—two or three individuals who share the job of chief executive.

The strategic apex is charged with ensuring that the organization serve its mission in an effective way, and also that it serve the needs of those people who control or otherwise have power over the organization (such as owners, government agencies, unions of the employees, pressure groups). This entails three sets of duties. One already discussed is that of direct supervision. To the extent that the organization relies on this mechanism of coordination, it is the managers of the strategic apex and middle line who effect it. Among the managerial roles (Mintzberg, 1973a) associated with direct supervision are resource allocator, including the design of the structure itself, the assignment of people and resources to tasks, the issuing of work orders, and the authorization of major decisions made by the employees; disturbance handler, involving the resolution of conflicts, exceptions, and disturbances sent up the hierarchy for resolution; monitor, involving the review of employees' activities; disseminator, involving the transmission of information to employees; and leader, involving the staffing of the organization and the motivating and rewarding of them. In its essence, direct supervision at the strategic apex means ensuring that the whole organization function smoothly as a single integrated unit.

But there is more to managing an organization than direct supervision. That is why even organizations with a minimal need for direct supervision, for example the very smallest that can rely on mutual adjustment, or professional ones that rely on formal training, still need managers. The second set of duties of the strategic apex involves the management of the organization's boundary conditions—its relationships with its environment. The managers of the strategic apex must spend a good deal of their time acting in the roles of spokesman, in informing influencial people in the environment about the organization's activities; liaison, to develop high-level contact for the organization, and monitor, to tap these for information and to serve as the contact point for those who wish to influence the organization's goals; negotiator, when major agreements must be reached with outside parties; and sometimes even figurehead, in carrying out ceremonial duties, such as greeting important customers. (Someone once defined the manager, only half in jest, as that person who sees the visitors so that everyone else can get their work done.)

The third set of duties relates to the development of the organization's strategy. Strategy may be viewed as a mediating force between the organization and its environment. Strategy formulation therefore involves the interpretation of the environment and the development of consistent patterns in streams of organizational decisions ("strategies") to deal with it. Thus, in managing the boundary conditions of the organization, the managers of the strategic apex develop an understanding of its environment; and in carrying out the duties

of direct supervision, they seek to tailor a strategy to its strengths and its needs, trying to maintain a pace of change that is responsive to the environment without being disruptive to the organization. Specifically, in the entrepreneur role, the top managers search for effective ways to carry out the organization's "mission" (i.e., its production of basic products and services), and sometimes even seek to change that mission. In a manufacturing firm, for example, management may decide what technical system is best suited for the operating core, what distribution channels most effectively carry the products to the market, what markets these should be, and ultimately, what products should be produced. Top managers typically spend a great deal of their time on various improvement projects, whereby they seek to impose strategic changes on their organizations. Of course, as we shall see later, the process of strategy formulation is not as cut and dried as all that: for one thing, the other parts of the organization, in certain cases even the operating core, can play an active role in formulating strategy; for another, strategies sometimes form themselves, almost inadvertently, as managers respond to the pressures of the environment, decision by decision. But one point should be stressed—the *strategic* apex, among the five parts of the organization, typically plays the most important role in the formulation of its strategy.[3]

In general, the strategic apex takes the widest, and as a result the most abstract, perspective of the organization. Work at this level is generally characterized by a minimum of repetition and standardization, considerable discretion, and relatively long decision-making cycles. Mutual adjustment is the favored mechanism for coordination among the managers of the strategic apex itself.

THE MIDDLE LINE

The strategic apex is joined to the operating core by the chain of middle-line managers with formal authority. This chain runs from the senior managers just below the strategic apex to the *first-line supervisors* (e.g., the shop foremen), who have direct authority over the operators, and embodies the coordinating mechanism that we have called direct supervision. Figure 3 shows one famous chain of authority, that of the U.S. Army, from four-star general at the strategic apex to sergeant as first-line supervisor. This particular chain of authority is *scalar*, that is, it runs in a single line from top to bottom. But as we shall see later, not all need be: some divide and rejoin; a "subordinate" can have more than one "superior."

What do all these levels of managers do? If the strategic apex provides overall direction and the operating core produces the products or services, why does the organization need this whole chain of middle-line managers? One answer seems evident. To the extent that the organization is large and reliant on direct supervision for coordination, it requires middle-line managers. In theory, one manager—the chief executive at the strategic apex—can supervise all the operators. In practice, however, direct supervision requires close personal contact between manager and operator, with the result that there is some limit to the number of operators any one manager can supervise—his so-called span of control. Small organizations can get along with one manager (at the strategic apex); bigger ones require more (in the middle line). As Moses was told in the desert:

> Thou shalt provide out of all the people able men, such as fear God, men of truth, hating covetousness; and place such over them, to be rulers of thousands, and rulers

of hundreds, rulers of fifties, and rulers of tens: and let them judge the people at all seasons: and it shall be, that every great matter they shall bring unto thee, but every small matter they shall judge: so shall it be easier for thyself, and they shall bear the burden with thee. If thou shalt do this thing, and God command thee so, then thou shalt be able to endure, and all this people shall also go to their place in peace (Exodus 18:21–24).

Thus, an organizational *hierarchy* is built as a first-line supervisor is put in charge of a number of operators to form a basic organizational unit, another manager is put in charge of a number of these units to form a higher level unit, and so on until all the remaining units can come under a single manager at the strategic apex—designated the "chief executive officer"—to form the whole organization.

In this hierarchy, the middle-line manager performs a number of tasks in the flow of direct supervision above and below him. He collects "feedback" information on the performance of his own unit and passes some of this up to the managers above him, often aggregating it in the process. The sales manager of the machinery firm may receive information on every sale, but he reports to the district sales manager only a monthly total. He also intervenes in the flow of decisions. Flowing up are disturbances in the unit, proposals for change, decisions requiring authorization. Some the middle-line manager handles himself, while others he passes on up for action at a higher level in the hierarchy. Flowing down are resources that he must allocate in his unit, rules and plans that he must elaborate and projects that he must implement there. For example, the strategic apex in the Postal Service may decide to implement a project to sell "domestograms." Each regional manager and, in turn, each district manager must

FIGURE 3 • THE SCALAR CHAIN OF COMMAND IN THE U.S. ARMY

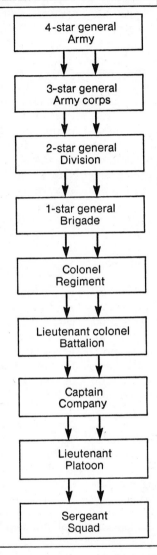

elaborate the plan as it applies to his geographical area.

But like the top manager, the middle manager is required to do more than simply engage in direct supervision. He, too, has boundary conditions to manage, horizontal ones related to the environment of his own unit. That environment may include other units within the larger organization as well as groups outside the organization. The sales manager must coordinate by mutual adjustment with the managers of production and of research, and he must visit some of the organization's customers. The foreman must spend a good deal of time with the industrial engineers who standardize the work processes of the operators and with the supplier installing a new machine in his shop, while the plant manager may spend his time with the production scheduler and the architect designing a new factory. In effect, each middle-line manager maintains liaison contacts with the other managers, analysts, support staffers, and outsiders whose work is interdependent with that of his own unit. Furthermore, the middle-line manager, like the top manager, is concerned with formulating the strategy for his unit, although this strategy is, of course, significantly affected by the strategy of the overall organization.

In general, the middle-line manager performs all the managerial roles of the chief executive, but in the context of managing his own unit (Mintzberg, 1973a). He must serve as a figurehead for his unit and lead its members; develop a network of liaison contacts; monitor the environment and his unit's activities and transmit some of the information he receives into his own unit, up the hierarchy, and outside the chain of command; allocate resources within his unit; negotiate with outsiders; initiate strategic change; and handle exceptions and conflicts.

Managerial jobs do, however, shift in orientation as they descend in the chain of authority. There is clear evidence that the job becomes more detailed and elaborated, less abstract and aggregated, more focused on the work flow itself. Thus, the "real-time" roles of the manager—in particular, negotiation and the handling of disturbances—become especially important at lower levels in the hierarchy (Mintzberg, 1973a, pp. 110–113). Martin (1956) studied the decisions made by four levels of production managers in the chain of authority and concluded that at each successively lower level, the decisions were more frequent, of shorter duration, and less elastic, ambiguous, and abstract; solutions tended to be more pat or predetermined; the significance of

events and interrelationships was more clear; in general, lower-level decision making was more structured.

Figure 4 shows the line manager in the middle of a field of forces. Sometimes these forces become so great—especially those of the analysts to institutionalize his job by the imposition of rules on the unit—that the individual in the job can hardly be called a "manager" at all, in the sense of really being "in charge" of an organizational unit. This is common at the level of first-line supervisor—for example, the foreman in some mass production manufacturing firms and branch managers in some large banking systems.

THE TECHNOSTRUCTURE

In the technostructure we find the analysts (and their supporting clerical staff) who serve the organization by affecting the work of others. These analysts are removed from the operating work flow—they may design it, plan it, change it, or train the people who do it, but they do not do it themselves. Thus, the technostructure is effective only when it can use its analytical techniques to make the work of others more effective.[4]

Who makes up the technostructure? There are the analysts concerned with adaptation, with changing the organization to meet environmental change, and those concerned with control, with stabilizing and standardizing patterns of activity in the organization (Katz and Kahn, 1966). In this book we are concerned largely with the control analysts, those who focus their attention directly on the design and functioning of structure. The control analysts of the technostructure serve to effect standardization in the organization. This is not to say that operators cannot standardize their own work, just as everyone establishes his or her own procedure for getting dressed in the morning, or that

FIGURE 4 · THE LINE MANAGER IN THE MIDDLE

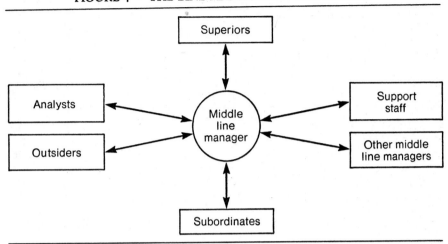

managers cannot do it for them. But in general, the more standardization an organization uses, the more it relies on its technostructure. Such standardization reduces the need for direct supervision, in effect enabling clerks to do what managers once did.

We can distinguish three types of control analysts who correspond to the three forms of standardization: work study analysts (such as industrial engineers), who standardize work processes; planning and control analysts (such as long-range planners, budget analysts, and accountants), who standardize outputs; and personnel analysts (including trainers and recruiters), who standardize skills.

In a fully developed organization, the technostructure may perform at all levels of the hierarchy. At the lowest levels of the manufacturing firm, analysts standardize the operating work flow by scheduling production, carrying out time-and-method studies of the operators' work, and instituting systems of quality control. At middle levels, they seek to standardize the intellectual work of the organization (e.g., by training middle managers) and carry out operations research studies of informational tasks. On behalf of the strategic apex, they design strategic planning systems and develop financial systems to control the goals of major units.

While the analysts exist to standardize the work of others, their own work would appear to be coordinated with others largely through mutual adjustment. (Standardization of skills does play a part in this coordination, however, because analysts are typically highly trained specialists.) Thus, analysts spend a good deal of their time in informal communication. Guetzkow (1965, p. 537), for example, notes that staff people typically have wider communication contacts than line people, and my review of the literature on managerial work (Mintzberg, 1973a, pp. 116–118) showed some evidence that staff managers pay more attention to the information processing roles—monitor, disseminator, spokesman—than do line managers.

SUPPORT STAFF

A glance at the chart of almost any large contemporary organization reveals a great number of units, all specialized, that exist to provide support to the organization outside the operating work flow. Those comprise the *support staff*. For example, in a university, we find the alma mater fund, building and grounds department, museum, university press, bookstore, printing service, payroll department, janitorial service, endowment office, mailroom, real estate office, security department, switchboard, athletics department, student placement office, student residence, faculty club, guidance service, and chaplainery. None is a part of the operating core, that is, none engages in teaching or research, or even supports it directly (as does, say, the computing center or the library), yet each exists to provide indirect support to these basic missions. In the manufacturing firm, these units run the gamut from legal counsel to plant cafeteria.

The surprising thing is that these support units have been all but totally ignored in the literature on organizational structuring. Most often they are lumped together with the technostructure and labeled as the "staff" that provides advice to management. But these support units are most decidedly different from the technostructure—they are not preoccupied with standardization and they cannot be looked upon primarily as advice givers (although they may do some of that, too). Rather, they have distinct functions to perform. The university press publishes books, the faculty club provides a social setting for the professors, the alma mater fund brings in money.

Why do large organizations have so many of these support units? A great many of their services could be purchased from outside suppliers, yet the organization chooses to provide them to itself. Why? Following Thompson's logic, we can argue that the existence of the support staff reflects the organization's attempt to encompass more and more

boundary activities in order to reduce uncertainty, to control its own affairs. By publishing its own books, the university avoids some of the uncertainties associated with the commercial houses; by fighting its own court cases, the manufacturing corporation maintains close control over the lawyers it uses; and by feeding its own employees in the plant cafeteria, it shortens the lunch period and, perhaps, even helps to determine the nutritiousness of their food.

Many support units are self-contained: they are mini-organizations, many with their own equivalent of an operating core, as in the case of the printing service in a university. These units take resources from the larger organization and, in turn, provide specific services to it. But they function independently of the main operating core; that is, they are coupled only in a pooled way. Compare, for example, the maintenance department with the cafeteria in a factory, the first a *direct* service and an integral part of the operating core, coupled reciprocally with it, the second quite separate from it, coupled only in the sharing of space and funds. Other support units, however, do exist in sequential or reciprocal relationships with units above the operating core.

The support units can be found at various levels of the hierarchy, depending on the receivers of their service. In most manufacturing firms, public relations and legal counsel are located near the top, since they tend to serve the strategic apex directly. At middle levels are found the units that support the decisions made there, such as industrial relations, pricing, and research and development. And at the lower levels are found the units with more standardized work, that akin to the work of the operating core—cafeteria, mailroom, reception, payroll. Figure 5 shows all these support groups

FIGURE 5 • SOME MEMBERS AND UNITS OF THE PARTS OF THE MANUFACTURING FIRM

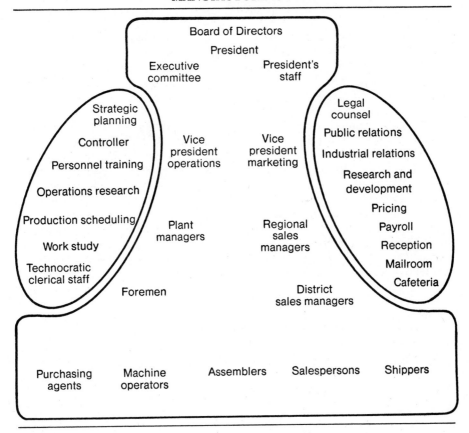

overlaid on our logo, together with typical groups from the other four parts of the organization, again using the manufacturing firm as our example.

Because of the wide variations in the types of support units, we cannot draw a single definitive conclusion about the favored coordinating mechanism for all of them. Each unit relies on whatever mechanism is most appropriate for itself—standardization of skills in the office of legal council, mutual adjustment in the research laboratory, standardization of work processes in the cafeteria. However, because many of the support units are highly specialized and rely on professional staff, standardization of skills may be the single most important coordinating mechanism.

Do the staff groups of the organization—technocratic as well as support—tend to cluster at any special level of the hierarchy? One study of twenty-five organizations (Kaufman and Seidman, 1970) suggested that while the middle lines of organizations tend to form into pyramids, the staff does not. Its form is "extremely irregular"—if anything, inversely pyramidal (p. 446). Hence, while Figure 1 shows the middle line as flaring out toward the bottom, it depicts both the technostructure and the support staff as forming ellipses. Later we shall see that, in fact, the specific shape varies according to the type of structure used by the organization.

The most dramatic growth in organizations in recent decades has been in these staff groups, both the technostructure and the support staff. For example, Litterer (1973, pp. 584–585), in a study of thirty companies, noted the creation of 292 new staff units between 1920 and 1960, nearly ten units per company. More than half these units were in fact created between 1950 and 1960.

Organizations have always had operators and top managers, people to do the basic work and people to hold the whole system together. As they grew, typically they first elaborated their middle-line component, on the assumption in the early literature that coordination had to be effected by direct supervision. But as standardization became an accepted coordinating mechanism, the technostructure began to emerge. The work of Frederick Taylor gave rise to the "scientific management" movement of the 1920s, which saw the hiring of many work study analysts. Just after World War II, the establishment of operations research and the advent of the computer pushed the influence of the technostructure well into the middle levels of the organization, and with the more recent popularity of techniques such as strategic planning and sophisticated financial controls, the technostructure has entrenched itself firmly at the highest levels of the organization as well. And the growth of the support staff has perhaps been even more dramatic, as all kinds of specializations developed during this century—scientific research in a wide number of fields, industrial relations, public relations and many more. Organizations have sought increasingly to bring these as well as the more traditional support functions such as maintenance and cafeteria within their boundaries. Thus, the ellipses to the left and right in the logo have become great bulges in many organizations. Joan Woodward (1965, p. 60) found in her research that firms in the modern process industries (such as oil refining) averaged one staff member for less than three operators, and in some cases the staff people actually outnumbered the operators by wide margins.[5]

NOTES

1. There are other, completely different, uses of the term "staff" that we are avoiding here. The military "chiefs of staff" are really managers of the strategic apex; the hospital "staff" physicians are really operators. Also, the introduction of the line/staff distinction here is not meant to sweep all of its problems under the rug, only to distinguish those involved directly from those involved peripherally with the operating work of organizations. By our definition, the production and sales functions in the typical manufacturing firm are clearly line activities, marketing research and public relations clearly staff. To debate whether engineering is line or staff—does it serve the operating core indirectly or is it an integral part of it?—depends on the importance one imputes to engineering in a particular firm. There is a gray area between line and staff: where it is narrow, for many organizations, we retain the distinction; where it is wide, we shall explicitly discard it.

2. Our subsequent discussion will focus only on the managers of the strategic apex, the work of the latter group being considered an integral part of their own.

3. The preceding discussion on managerial roles is drawn from Mintzberg (1973a); that on strategy formulation, from Mintzberg (1978).

4. This raises an interesting point: that the technostructure has a built-in commitment to change, to perpetual improvement. The modern organization's obsession with change probably derives in part at least from large and ambitious technostructures seeking to ensure their own survival. The perfectly stable organization has no need for a technostructure.

5. Woodward's tables and text here are very confusing, owing in part at least to some line errors in the page makeup. The data cited above are based on Figure 18, page 60, which seems to have the title that belongs to Figure 17 and which seems to relate back to Figure 7 on page 28, not to Figure 8 as Woodward claims.

BIBLIOGRAPHIC REFERENCES

Allen, L. A. (1955, September). The line-staff relationship. *Management Record*, 346–349, 374–376.

Guetzkow, H. (1965). Communications in organizations. In J. G. March (Ed.), *Handbook of organizations* (Chap. 12). Chicago: Rand McNally.

Katz, D., & Kahn, R. L. (1966). *The social psychology of organizations*. New York: John Wiley & Sons.

Kaufman, H., & Seidman, D. (1970). The morphology of organization. *Administrative Science Quarterly*, 439–445.

Litterer, J. A. (1973). *The analysis of organizations* (2nd ed.). New York: John Wiley & Sons. Used with permission.

Martin, N. H. (1956). Differential decisions in the management of an industrial plant. *The Journal of Business*, 249–260.

Mintzberg, H. (1973). *The nature of managerial work*. New York: Harper & Row.

———. (1978). Patterns in strategy formation. *Management Science*, 934–948.

Thompson, J. D. (1967). *Organizations in action*. New York: McGraw-Hill.

Woodward, J. (1965). *Industrial organization: Theory and practice*, New York: Oxford University Press. Used with permission.

CHAPTER IV

Systems and Contingency Theories of Organization

Since World War II, the social sciences have increasingly used systems analysis to examine their assertions about human behavior. The field of management, which to the extent that it deals with human resources can be said to be a social science, has been no exception. Many organization theorists would contend that the systems approach has dominated organization theory since 1966–1967, when two of the most influential modern works in organization theory appeared: Robert Katz and Daniel Kahn's *The Social Psychology of Organizations* (1966), which articulated the concept of organizations as "open systems," and James D. Thompson's coherent statement of the "rational" systems/contingency approach to organizations, in his *Organizations in Action* (1967).

Perhaps the field of organization theory was simply ripe for advancement in the late 1960s. The human relations orientation had lost much of its vigor. The cultural milieu was moving away from the introspective, self-developmental, optimism of the "flower child generation" and the "T-groups" of the early 1960s. We were becoming enamored with computers, statistics, models, information systems, and measurement. Whatever the reasons may be, Katz and Kahn and James D. Thompson provided the intellectual basis for the systems school to emerge as the "mainstream" of organization theory.

The systems school has two major conceptual themes or components: (1) applications of Ludwig von Bertalanffy's (1951) "general systems theory" to organizations, and (2) the use of quantitative tools and techniques to understand complex relationships among organizational variables and, thereby, to optimize decisions. Each will be considered in turn.

The systems school views an organization as a complex set of dynamically intertwined and interconnected elements, including its inputs, processes, outputs, feedback loops, and the environment in which it operates. A change in any element of the system inevitably causes changes in its other elements. The interconnections tend to be complex, dynamic, and often unknown. Thus when management makes decisions involving one organizational element, unanticipated impacts usually occur throughout the organizational system. Systems school organization theorists study

234

interconnections, frequently using organizational decision processes and information and control systems as their focal points for analysis. Whereas classical organization theory tends to be one dimensional and somewhat simplistic, systems theory tends to be multidimensional and complex in its assumptions about organizational cause-and-effect relationships. The classical school viewed organizations as static structures; the systems school sees organizations as dynamic processes of interactions among organizational elements. Organizations are adaptive systems that must adjust to changes in their environment if they are to survive.

Norbert Wiener's classic model of an organization as an adaptive system, from his 1948 book *Cybernetics*, epitomizes these basic theoretical perspectives of the systems school (see Figure 1). *Cybernetics*, a Greek word meaning steersman, was used by Wiener to mean the multidisciplinary study of the structures and functions of control and information processing systems in animals and machines. The basic concept behind cybernetics is self-regulation—biological, social, or technological systems that can identify problems, do something about them, and then receive feedback to adjust themselves automatically. Wiener, a mathematician, developed the concept of cybernetics while working on anti-aircraft systems during World War II. Variations on this simple model of a system have been used extensively by systems school organization theorists for many years—particularly around the development and use of management information systems. We have not been able to locate anyone who used it before Wiener did in 1948.

The systems school's search for order among complex variables has led to an extensive reliance on quantitative analytical methods and models. In these respects, the systems school has close philosophical and methodological ties to the scientific management approach of Frederick Winslow Taylor. Whereas Taylor used quantitative scientific methods to find "the one best way," the systems school uses quantitative scientific methods to find "optimal" solutions. In this realm, the conceptual approaches and purposes between the two schools are strikingly similar. Thus, systems school theory is often called "management science" or "administrative science." But be careful *never* to make the unpardonable error of calling it "scientific management!"

FIGURE 1 • NORBERT WIENER'S MODEL OF AN ORGANIZATION AS
AN ADAPTIVE SYSTEM

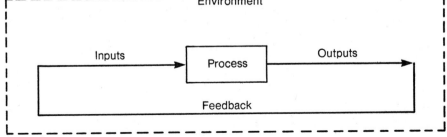

Computers, models, and interdisciplinary teams of analysts are the basic "tools" of the systems school. Studies of organizations done by its members typically use the scientific method and quasi-experimental research techniques, or heuristic computer models. This quantitative orientation reflects the systems school's roots in the years immediately following World War II when the first serious attempts were made to apply mathematical and statistical probability models to organizational processes and decision making. Many of the early efforts started under the label "operations analysis" or "operations research," in defense industry-related "think tanks" like the RAND Corporation of Santa Monica, California. "Operations research" or "operations analysis" refers to the use of mathematical and scientific techniques to develop a quantitative basis for making organizational decisions. See Howard Raiffa's *Decision Analysis* (1968) for an excellent description of the use of mathematical strategies in organizational decision making. During the subsequent decades, defense and aerospace programs provided the development and testing settings for many tools and techniques of operations research, such as PERT, CPM, statistical inference, linear programming, gaming, Monte Carlo methods, and simulation.

Pioneering theories from the neoclassical school provided important conceptual foundations for the systems approach. Herbert Simon and his associates contributed some of the most important of these concepts (see Chapter II). Simon's visionary theories addressed bounded rationality and satisficing in organizational decision making (1957), and programmed and unprogrammed decisions (1960). With James March, Simon also made major contributions in the areas of cognitive limits on rationality, and organizational innovation (1958). Indeed, it was Simon's further work in the areas of management decision making that led to his 1978 Nobel Prize for Economics.

As the systems school ascended to "the center stage" of the field of organization theory during the later half of the 1960s, its focus on computers, information technology, and control systems spawned many heated debates between members of the systems school and human relations-oriented organization theorists over such philosophical issues as computer domination of social structures, increased organizational centralization, and irresolvable conflicts between the individual freedom of organizational members and technology-based organizational confinement. Thus, for example, in 1964, Norbert Wiener, the "father" of cybernetics and a visionary systems-oriented scientist, wrote:

> "Render unto man the things which are man's and unto the computer the things which are the computer's. This would seem the intelligent policy to adopt when we employ men and computers together in common undertakings. It is a policy as far removed from that of the gadget worshipper as it is from the man who sees only blasphemy and the degradation of man in the use of any mechanical adjuvants whatever to thoughts." [An adjuvant is defined as something that serves to help or assist.]

It is important to remember—and easy to forget—that there is a "social systems" side to the systems school, as well as the "management systems" side. The social systems side is rooted in the traditions and philosophies of social psychology, cultural anthropology, and sociology, and in the humanistically oriented classical philosophers of organization theory such as Elton Mayo (1933), Chester Barnard (1938), Roethlisberger and Dickson (1939), and Mary Parker Follett (1940).

If you accept that a system is any organized collection of parts united by prescribed interactions and designed for the accomplishment of specific goals or general purposes, then you can see why modern organization theory is considered to be one aspect of general systems theory. Kenneth E. Boulding's 1956 article "General Systems Theory—The Skeleton of Science," which is reprinted here, is perhaps the best summary and most quoted introduction to the systems concept. Boulding, an economist, builds upon the theories of Ludwig von Bertalanffy (1951), the "father" of general systems theory, *and* integrates Norbert Wiener's (1948, 1950) concept of cybernetics. Boulding's article seeks to provide an orderly framework upon which to "hang the flesh and blood of particular disciplines."

But it remained for Daniel Katz and Robert L. Kahn in their 1966 book, *The Social Psychology of Organizations,* to produce the first major application of existing knowledge of social systems in general to organizations in particular. Open systems theory provided the intellectual basis for merging classical, neoclassical, human relations/behavioral, "modern" structural, and systems perspectives of organizations. Katz and Kahn balance these perspectives through their use of the concept of organizations as "open systems"—systems that must adapt constantly to changing environmental factors. Reprinted here is a chapter from their book, "Organizations and the System Concept." Katz and Kahn conclude that the traditional "closed system" view of organizations has led to a failure to fully appreciate the interdependencies and interactions between organizations and their environments.

Katz and Kahn's concept of open systems has influenced the thinking of many organization theorists. Several articles that are reprinted here and in Chapter IV provide excellent examples. They include James D. Thompson's writing on technology and tasks, Paul Lawrence and Jay Lorsch's chapter on the need to balance between organizational differentiation and integration, and Jay Galbraith's work on information processing models of organizations.

Classical organization theorists saw organizations as rational but closed systems. These systems sought the goal of economic efficiency. As the systems were viewed as "closed" and not subject to influence from the external environment, major attention could be focused on such functions as planning and/or controlling. James D. Thompson, in his influential 1967 book, *Organizations in Action,* classifies most organizations as "open systems." Reprinted here are the first two chapters from his book, in which he suggests that the closed system approach may be realistic at the technical level of organizational operations. Thompson seeks to bridge the gap between "open" and "closed" systems by postulating that organizations "abhor uncertainty" and deal with uncertainty in the environment by creating specific elements designed to cope with the outside world, while other elements are able to focus on the rational nature of technical operations. The dominant technology used by an organization strongly influences its structure, activities, and evaluation/control processes.

In a 1972 *Academy of Management Journal* article, "General Systems Theory: Applications for Organization and Management," Fremont E. Kast and James E.

Rosenzweig examine the "state of the art" of practical applications of systems theory. They attempt to assess the degree of success we have had in utilizing the "key concepts of general systems theory" in the development of "modern organization theory." After discussing some practical problems of applying systems theory to organizations, Kast and Rosenzweig observe that "many managers have used and will continue to use a systems approach and contingency views intuitively and implicitly," thus, systems and contingency views are not new to most managers. They conclude with a call for ways to make systems views more usable by practicing managers.

Kast and Rosenzweig use the phrase "contingency views." Contingency theory is a "close cousin" of systems theory in which the effectiveness of an organizational action (for example, a decision) is viewed as depending upon the relationship between the element in question and all other aspects of the system—at the particular moment. Everything is situational: there are no absolutes or universals. Thus, contingency views of organizations place high importance on rapid, accurate information systems. This linkage between systems theory and the contingency views caused us to place a selection from Jay Galbraith's 1973 book *Designing Complex Organizations* here—rather than in Chapter III on "modern" structural organization theory. Galbraith is in fact a "modern" structuralist who is concerned primarily with organizational design strategies; however, his chapter "Information Processing Model" captures the essence of the systems/contingency perspective on organizations. He constructs theories about the amount of information an organization must process under different levels of (*a*) uncertainty, (*b*) interdependence among organizational elements, *and* (*c*) organizational adaptation mechanisms.

According to Galbraith and other contingency theorists, uncertainty is the gap between the amount of information an organization needs and the amount of information it possesses. Thus, uncertainty limits an organization's ability to plan and to make decisions. The greater the level of uncertainty, the more an organization must use contingency approaches to planning and decision making.

BIBLIOGRAPHIC REFERENCES

Barnard, C. I. (1938). *The functions of the executive.* Cambridge, MA: Harvard University Press.

Bertalanffy, L. von. (1951, December). General systems theory: A new approach to unity of science. *Human Biology, 23,* 303–361.

Bertalanffy, L. von. (1968). *General systems theory: Foundations, development, applications.* New York: George Braziller.

Blumenthal, S. C. (1969). *Management information systems.* Englewood Cliffs, NJ: Prentice-Hall.

Boulding, K. E. (1956, April). General systems theory—The skeleton of science. *Management Science, 2,* 3, 197–208.

Carzo, R., Jr., & Yanouzas, J. N. (1967). *Formal organizations: A systems approach.* Homewood, IL: Richard D. Irwin.

Dearden, J. F., & McFarlan, F. W. (1966). *Management information systems.* Homewood, IL: Richard D. Irwin.

Follett, M. P. (1940). *Dynamic administration: The collected papers of Mary Parker Follett.* E.
    M. Fox & L. Urwick (Eds.). New York: Hippocrene Books.
Galbraith, J. (1973). *Designing complex organizations.* Reading, MA: Addison-Wesley Pub-
    lishing.
Kast, F. E. & Rosenzweig, J. E. (1970). *Organization and management: A systems approach.*
    New York: McGraw-Hill.
Kast, F. E., & Rosenzweig, J. E. (1972, December). General systems theory: Applications
    for organization and management. *Academy of Management Journal,* 447–465.
Katz, D., & Kahn, R. L. (1966). *The social psychology of organizations.* New York: John
    Wiley & Sons.
March, J. G., & Simon, H. A. (1958). *Organizations.* New York: John Wiley & Sons.
Mayo, E. (1933). *The human problems of an industrial civilization.* New York: Viking Press.
Raiffa, H. (1968). *Decision analysis.* Reading, MA: Addison-Wesley Publishing.
Roethlisberger, F. J., & Dickson, W. J. (1939). *Management and the worker.* Cambridge,
    MA: Harvard University Press.
Simon, H. A. (1957). *Administrative behavior* (2nd ed.). New York: Macmillan.
Simon, H. A. (1960). *The new science of management decisions.* New York: Harper & Row.
Thompson, J. D. (1967). *Organizations in action.* New York: McGraw-Hill.
Wiener, N. (1948). *Cybernetics.* Cambridge, MA: MIT Press.
Wiener, N. (1950). *The human use of human beings.* Boston: Houghton Mifflin.
Wiener, N. (1964). *God and golem, inc.* Cambridge, MA: MIT Press.

22
General Systems Theory—The Skeleton of Science

Kenneth E. Boulding

General Systems Theory[1] is a name which has come into use to describe a level of theoretical model-building which lies somewhere between the highly generalized constructions of pure mathematics and the specific theories of the specialized disciplines. Mathematics attempts to organize highly general relationships into a coherent system, a system however which does not have any necessary connections with the "real" world around us. It studies all thinkable relationships abstracted from any concrete situation or body of empirical knowledge. It is not even confined to "quantitative" relationships narrowly defined—indeed, the development of a mathematics of quality and structure is already on the way, even though it is not as far advanced as the "classical" mathematics of quantity and number. Nevertheless because in a sense mathematics contains all theories it contains none; it is the language of theory, but it does not give up the content. At the other extreme we have the separate disciplines and sciences, with their separate bodies of theory. Each discipline

Source: From *Management Science 2* (April 1956): 197–208. Copyright © 1956 The Institute of Management Sciences. Reprinted by permission. Subheads added.

corresponds to a certain segment of the empirical world, and each develops theories which have particular applicability to its own empirical segment. Physics, chemistry, biology, psychology, sociology, economics and so on all carve out for themselves certain elements of the experience of man and develop theories and patterns of activity (research) which yield satisfaction in understanding, and which are appropriate to their special segments.

In recent years increasing need has been felt for a body of systematic theoretical constructs which will discuss the general relationships of the empirical world. This is the quest of General Systems Theory. It does not seek, of course, to establish a single, self-contained "general theory of practically everything" which will replace all the special theories of particular disciplines. Such a theory would be almost without content, for we always pay for generality by sacrificing content, and all we can say about practically everything is almost nothing. Somewhere however between the specific that has no meaning and the general that has no content there must be, for each purpose and at each level of abstraction, an optimum degree of generality. It is the contention of the General Systems Theorists that this optimum degree of generality in theory is not always reached by the particular sciences. The objectives of General Systems Theory then can be set out with varying degrees of ambition and confidence. At a low level of ambition but with a high degree of confidence it aims to point out similarities in the theoretical constructions of different disciplines, where these exist, and to develop theoretical models having applicability to at least two different fields of study. At a higher level of ambition, but with perhaps a lower degree of confidence it

hopes to develop something like a "spectrum" of theories—a system of systems which may perform the function of a "gestalt" in theoretical construction. Such "gestalts" in special fields have been of great value in directing research towards the gaps which they reveal. Thus the periodic table of elements in chemistry directed research for many decades towards the discovery of unknown elements to fill gaps in the table until the table was completely filled. Similarly a "system of systems" might be of value in directing the attention of theorists towards gaps in theoretical models, and might even be of value in pointing towards methods of filling them.

The need for general systems theory is accentuated by the present sociological situation in science. Knowledge is not something which exists and grows in the abstract. It is a function of human organisms and of social organization. Knowledge, that is to say, is always what somebody knows: the most perfect transcript of knowledge in writing is not knowledge if nobody knows it. Knowledge however grows by the receipt of meaningful information—that is, by the intake of messages by a knower which are capable of reorganizing his knowledge. We will quietly duck the question as to what reorganizations constitute "growth" of knowledge by defining "semantic growth" of knowledge as those reorganizations which can profitably be talked about, in writing or speech, by the Right People. Science, that is to say, is what can be talked about profitably by scientists in their role as scientists. The crisis of science today arises because of the increasing difficulty of such profitable talk among scientists as a whole. Specialization has outrun Trade, communication between the disciples becomes increasingly difficult, and the Republic of Learning is breaking up into isolated subcultures with only tenuous lines of communication between them—a situation which threatens intellectual civil war. The reason for this breakup in the body of knowledge is that in the course of specialization the receptors of information themselves become specialized. Hence physicists only talk to physicists, economists to economists—worse still, nuclear physicists only talk to nuclear physicists and econometricians to econometricians. One wonders sometimes if science will not grind to a stop in an assemblage of walled-in hermits, each mumbling to himself words in a private language that only he can understand. In these days the arts may have beaten the sciences to this desert of mutual unintelligibility, but that may be merely because the swift intuitions of art reach the future faster than the plodding leg work of the scientist. The more science breaks into subgroups, and the less communication is possible among the disciplines, however, the greater chance there is that the total growth of knowledge is being slowed down by the loss of relevant communications. The spread of specialized deafness means that someone who ought to know something that someone else knows isn't able to find it out for lack of generalized ears.

It is one of the main objectives of General Systems Theory to develop these generalized ears, and by developing a framework of general theory to enable one specialist to catch relevant communications from others. Thus the economist who realizes the strong formal similarity between utility theory in economics and field theory in physics[2] is probably in a better position to learn from the physicists than one who does not. Similarly a specialist who works with the growth concept—whether the crystallographer, the virologist, the cytologist, the physiologist, the psychologist, the sociologist or the economist—will be more sensitive to the contributions of other fields if he is aware of the many similarities of the growth process in widely different empirical fields.

There is not much doubt about the demand for general systems theory under one brand name or another. It is a little more embarrassing to inquire into the supply. Does any of it exist, and if so where? What is the chance of getting more of it, and if so, how? The situation might be described as promising and in ferment, though it is not wholly clear what is being promised or brewed. Something which might be called an "interdisciplinary movement" has been abroad for some time. The first signs of this are usually the development of hybrid disciplines. Thus physical chemistry emerged in the third quarter of the nineteenth century, social psychology in the second quarter of the twentieth. In the physical and biological sciences the list of hybrid disciplines is now quite long—biophysics, biochemistry, astrophysics are all well established. In the social sciences social anthropology is fairly well established, economic psychology and economic sociology are just beginning. There are signs, even, that Political Economy, which died in infancy some hundred years ago, may have a rebirth.

In recent years there has been an additional development of great interest in the form of "multisexual" interdisciplines. The hybrid disciplines, as their hyphenated names indicate, come from two respectable and honest academic parents. The newer interdisciplines have a much more varied and occasionally even obscure ancestry, and result from the reorganization of material from many different fields of study. Cybernetics, for instance, comes out of electrical engineering, neurophysiology, physics, biology, with even a dash of economics. Information theory, which originated in communications engineering, has important applications in many fields stretching from biology to the social sciences. Organization theory comes out of economics, sociology, engineering, physiology, and Management Science itself is an equally multidisciplinary product.

On the more empirical and practical side the interdisciplinary movement is reflected in the development of interdepartmental institutes of many kinds. Some of these find their basis of unity in the empirical field which they study, such as institutes of industrial relations, of public administration, of international affairs, and so on. Others are organized around the application of a common methodology to many different fields and problems, such as the Survey Research Center and the Group Dynamics Center at the University of Michigan. Even more important than these visible developments, perhaps, though harder to perceive and identify, is a growing dissatisfaction in many departments, especially at the level of graduate study, with the existing traditional theoretical backgrounds for the empirical studies which form the major part of the output of Ph.D. theses. To take but a single example from the field with which I am most familiar. It is traditional for studies of labor relations, money and banking, and foreign investment to come out of departments of economics. Many of the needed theoretical models and frameworks in these fields, however, do not come out of "economic theory" as this is usually taught, but from sociology, social psychology, and cultural anthropology. Students in the department of economics however rarely get a chance to become acquainted with these theoretical models, which may be relevant to their studies, and they become impatient with economic theory, much of which may not be relevant.

It is clear that there is a good deal of interdisciplinary excitement abroad. If this excitement is to be productive, however, it must operate within a certain framework of coherence. It is all too easy for the interdisciplinary to degenerate into the undisciplined. If the interdisciplinary movement, therefore, is not to lose that sense of form and structure which is the "discipline" involved in the various separate disciplines, it should develop a structure of its own. This I conceive to be the great task of general systems theory. For the rest of this paper, therefore, I propose to look at some possible ways in which general systems theory might be structured.

Two possible approaches to the organization of general systems theory suggest themselves, which are to be thought of as complementary rather than competitive, or at least as two roads each of which is worth exploring. The first approach is to look over the empirical universe and to pick out certain general *phenomena* which are found in many different disciplines, and to seek to build up general theoretical models relevant to these phenomena. The second approach is to arrange the empirical fields in a hierarchy of complexity of organization of their basic "individual" or unit of behavior, and to try to develop a level of abstraction appropriate to each.

Some examples of the first approach will serve to clarify it, without pretending to be exhaustive. In almost all disciplines, for instance, we find examples of populations—aggregates of individuals conforming to a common definition, to which individuals are added (born) and subtracted (die) and in which the age of the individual is a relevant and identifiable variable. These populations exhibit dynamic movements of their own, which can frequently be described by fairly simple systems of difference equations. The populations of different species also exhibit dynamic interactions among themselves, as in the theory of Volterra. Models of population change and interaction cut across a great many different fields—ecological systems in biology, capital theory in economics which deals with populations of "goods," social ecology, and even certain problems of statistical mechanics. In all these fields population change, both in absolute numbers and in structure, can be discussed in terms of birth and survival functions relating numbers of births and of deaths in specific age groups to various aspects of the system. In all these fields the interaction of population can be discussed in terms of competitive, complementary, or parasitic relationships among populations of different species, whether the species consist of animals, commodities, social classes or molecules.

Another phenomenon of almost universal significance for all disciplines is that of the interaction of an "individual" of some kind with its environment. Every discipline studies some kind of "individual"—electron, atom, molecule, crystal, virus, cell, plant, animal, man, family, tribe, state, church, firm, corporation, university, and so on. Each of these individuals exhibits "behavior," action, or change, and this behavior is considered to be related in some way to the environment of the individual—that is, with other individuals with which it comes into contact or into some relationship. Each individual is thought of as consisting of a structure or complex of individuals of the order immediately below it—atoms are an arrangement of protons and electrons, molecules of atoms, cells of molecules, plants, animals and men of cells, social organizations of men. The "behavior" of each individual is "explained" by the structure and arrangement of the lower individuals of which it is composed, or by certain principles

of equilibrium or homeostasis according to which certain "states" of the individual are "preferred." Behavior is described in terms of the restoration of these preferred states when they are disturbed by changes in the environment.

Another phenomenon of universal significance is growth. Growth theory is in a sense a subdivision of the theory of individual "behavior," growth being one important aspect of behavior. Nevertheless there are important differences between equilibrium theory and growth theory, which perhaps warrant giving growth theory a special category. There is hardly a science in which the growth phenomenon does not have some importance, and though there is a great difference in complexity between the growth of crystals, embryos, and societies, many of the principles and concepts which are important at the lower levels are also illuminating at higher levels. Some growth phenomena can be dealt with in terms of relatively simple population models, the solution of which yields growth curves of single variables. At the more complex levels structural problems become dominant and the complex interrelationships between growth and form are the focus of interest. All growth phenomena are sufficiently alike however to suggest that a general theory of growth is by no means an impossibility.[3]

Another aspect of the theory of the individual and also of interrelationships among individuals which might be singled out for special treatment is the theory of information and communication. The information concept as developed by Shannon has had interesting applications outside its original field of electrical engineering. It is not adequate, of course, to deal with problems involving the semantic level of communication. At the biological level however the information concept may serve to develop general notions of structuredness and abstract measures of organization which give us, as it were, a third basic dimension beyond mass and energy. Communication and information processes are found in a wide variety of empirical situations, and are unquestionably essential in the development of organization, both in the biological and the social world.

These various approaches to general systems through various aspects of the empirical world may lead ultimately to something like a general field theory of the dynamics of action and interaction. This, however, is a long way ahead.

A second possible approach to general systems theory is through the arrangement of theoretical systems and constructs in a hierarchy of complexity, roughly corresponding to the complexity of the "individuals" of the various empirical fields. This approach is more systematic than the first, leading towards a "system of systems." It may not replace the first entirely, however, as there may always be important theoretical concepts and constructs lying outside the systematic framework. I suggest below a possible arrangement of "levels" of theoretical discourse.

1. FRAMEWORKS LEVEL

The first level is that of the static structure. It might be called the level of *frameworks*. This is the geography and anatomy of the universe—the patterns of electrons around a nucleus, the pattern of atoms in a molecular formula, the arrangement of atoms in a crystal, the anatomy of the gene, the cell, the plant, the animal, the mapping of the earth, the solar system, the astronomical universe. The accurate description of these frameworks is the beginning of organized theoretical knowledge in almost any field, for without accuracy in this description of static relationships no accurate functional or dynamic theory is possible. Thus the Copernican revolution was really the discovery of a new static framework for the solar system which permitted a simpler description of its dynamics.

2. CLOCKWORKS LEVEL

The next level of systematic analysis is that of the simple dynamic system with predetermined, necessary motions. This might be called the level of *clockworks*. The solar system itself is of course the great clock of the universe from man's point of view, and the deliciously exact predictions of the astronomers are a testimony to the excellence of the clock which they study. Simple machines such as the lever and the pulley, even quite complicated machines like steam engines and dynamos fall mostly under this category. The greater part of the theoretical structure of physics, chemistry, and even of economics falls into this category. Two special cases might be noted. Simple equilibrium systems really fall into the dynamic category, as every equilibrium system must be considered as a limiting case of a dynamic system, and its stability cannot be determined except from the properties of its parent dynamic system. Stochastic dynamic systems leading to equilibria, for all their complexity, also fall into this group of systems; such is the modern view of the atom and even of the molecule, each position or part of the system being given with a certain degree of probability, the whole nevertheless exhibiting a determinate structure. Two types of analytical method are important here, which we may call, with the usage of the economists, comparative statics and true dynamics. In comparative statics we compare two equilibrium positions of the system under different values for the basic parameters. These equilibrium positions are usually expressed as the solution of a set of simultaneous equations. The method of comparative statics is to compare the solutions when the parameters of the equations are changed. Most simple mechanical problems are solved in this way. In true dynamics on the other hand we exhibit the system as a set of difference or differential equations, which are then solved in the form of an explicit function of each variable with time. Such a system may reach a position of stationary equilibrium, or it may not—there are plenty of examples of explosive dynamic systems, a very simple one being the growth of a sum at compound interest! Most physical and chemical reactions and most social systems do in fact exhibit a tendency to equilibrium—otherwise the world would have exploded or imploded long ago.

3. THERMOSTAT LEVEL

The next level is that of the control mechanism or cybernetic system, which might be nicknamed the level of the *thermostat*. This differs from the simple stable equilibrium system mainly in the fact that the transmission and interpretation of information is an essential part of the system. As a result of this the equilibrium position is not merely determined by the equations of the system, but the system will move to the maintenance of any *given* equilibrium, within limits. Thus the thermostat will maintain *any* temperature at which it can be set; the equilibrium temperature of the system is not determined solely by its equations. The trick here of course is that the essential variable of

the dynamic system is the *difference* between an "observed" or "recorded" value of the maintained variable and its "ideal" value. If this difference is not zero the system moves so as to diminish it; thus the furnace sends up heat when the temperature as recorded is "too cold" and is turned off when the recorded temperature is "too hot." The homeostasis model, which is of such importance in physiology, is an example of a cybernetic mechanism, and such mechanisms exist through the whole empirical world of the biologist and the social scientist.

4. CELL LEVEL

The fourth level is that of the "open system," or self-maintaining structure. This is the level at which life begins to differentiate itself from not-life: it might be called the level of the *cell*. Something like an open system exists, of course, even in physico-chemical equilibrium systems; atomic structures maintain themselves in the midst of a throughput of electrons, molecular structures maintain themselves in the midst of a throughput of atoms. Flames and rivers likewise are essentially open systems of a very simple kind. As we pass up the scale of complexity of organization towards living systems, however, the property of self-maintenance of structure in the midst of a throughput of material becomes of dominant importance. An atom or a molecule can presumably exist without throughput: the existence of even the simplest living organism is inconceivable without ingestion, excretion, and metabolic exchange. Closely connected with the property of self-maintenance is the property of self-reproduction. It may be, indeed, that self-reproduction is a more primitive or "lower level" system than the open system, and that the gene and the virus, for instance, may be able to reproduce themselves without being open systems. It is not perhaps an important question at what point in the scale of increasing complexity "life" begins. What is clear, however, is that by the time we have got to systems which both reproduce themselves and maintain themselves in the midst of a throughput of material and energy, we have something to which it would be hard to deny the title of "life."

5. PLANT LEVEL

The fifth level might be called the genetic-societal level; it is typified by the *plant,* and it dominates the empirical world of the botanist. The outstanding characteristics of these systems are first, a division of labor among cells to form a cell-society with differentiated and mutually dependent parts (roots, leaves, seeds, etc.), and second, a sharp differentiation between the genotype and the phenotype, associated with the phenomenon of equifinal or "blue-printed" growth. At this level there are no highly specialized sense organs and information receptors are diffuse and incapable of much throughput of information—it is doubtful whether a tree can distinguish much more than light from dark, long days from short days, cold from hot.

6. ANIMAL LEVEL

As we move upward from the plant world towards the animal kingdom we gradually pass over into a new level, the "animal" level, characterized by increased mobility, teleological behavior, and self-awareness. Here we have the development of specialized information-receptors (eyes, ears, etc.) leading to an enormous increase in the intake of information; we have also a great development of nervous systems, leading ultimately to the brain, as an organizer of the information intake into a knowledge structure or "image". Increasingly as we ascend the scale of animal life, behavior is response not to a specific stimulus but to an "image" or knowledge structure or view of the environment as a whole. This image is of course determined ultimately by information received into the organism; the relation between the receipt of information and the building up of an image however is exceedingly complex. It is not a simple piling up or accumulation of information received, although this frequently happens, but a structuring of information into something essentially different from the information itself. After the image structure is well established most information received produces very little change in the image—it goes through the loose structure, as it were, without hitting it, much as a subatomic particle might go through an atom without hitting anything. Sometimes however the information is "captured" by the image and added to it, and sometimes the information hits some kind of a "nucleus" of the image and a reorganization takes place, with far reaching and radical changes in behavior in apparent response to what seems like a very small stimulus. The difficulties in the prediction of the behavior of these systems arises largely because of this intervention of the image between the stimulus and the response.

7. HUMAN LEVEL

The next level is the "human" level, that is of the individual human being considered as a system. In addition to all, or nearly all, of the characteristics of animal systems man possesses self consciousness, which is something different from mere awareness. His image, besides being much more complex than that even of the higher animals, has a self-reflexive quality—he not only knows, but knows that he knows. This property is probably bound up with the phenomenon of language and symbolism. It is the capacity for speech—the ability to produce, absorb, and interpret *symbols*, as opposed to mere signs like the warning cry of an animal—which most clearly marks man off from his humbler brethren. Man is distinguished from the animal also by a much more elaborate image of time and relationship; man is probably the only organization that knows that it dies, that contemplates in its behavior a whole life span, and more than a life span. Man exists not only in time and space but in history, and his behavior is profoundly affected by his view of the time process in which he stands.

8. SOCIAL ORGANIZATIONS LEVEL

Because of the vital importance for the individual man of symbolic images and behavior based on them it is not easy to separate clearly the level of the individual human organism from the next level, that of social organizations. In spite of the occasional stories of feral children raised by animals, man isolated from his fellows is practically unknown. So essential is the symbolic image in human behavior that one suspects that a truly isolated man would not be "human" in the usually accepted sense, though he would be potentially human. Nevertheless it is convenient for some purposes to distinguish the individual human as a system from the social systems which surround him, and in this sense social organizations may be said to constitute another level of organization. The unit of such systems is not perhaps the person—the individual human as such—but the "role"—that part of the person

which is concerned with the organization or situation in question, and it is tempting to define social organizations, or almost any social system, as a set of roles tied together with channels of communication. The interrelations of the role and the person however can never be completely neglected—a square person in a round role may become a little rounder, but he also makes the role squarer, and the perception of a role is affected by the personalities of those who have occupied it in the past. At this level we must concern ourselves with the content and meaning of messages, the nature and dimensions of value systems, the transcription of images into a historical record, the subtle symbolizations of art, music, and poetry, and the complex gamut of human emotion. The empirical universe here is human life and society in all its complexity and richness.

9. TRANSCENDENTAL SYSTEMS LEVEL

To complete the structure of systems we should add a final turret for transcendental systems, even if we may be accused at this point of having built Babel to the clouds. There are however the ultimates and absolutes and the inescapable unknowables, and they also exhibit systematic structure and relationship. It will be a sad day for man when nobody is allowed to ask questions that do not have any answers.

One advantage of exhibiting a hierarchy of systems in this way is that it gives us some idea of the present gaps in both theoretical and empirical knowledge. Adequate theoretical models extend up to about the fourth level, and not much beyond. Empirical knowledge is deficient at practically all levels. Thus at the level of the static structure, fairly descriptive models are available for geography, chemistry, geology, anatomy, and descriptive social science. Even at this simplest level, however, the problem of the adequate description of complex structures is still far from solved. The theory of indexing and cataloging, for instance, is only in its infancy. Librarians are fairly good at cataloging books, chemists have begun to catalog structural formulae, and anthropologists have begun to catalog culture trails. The cataloging of events, ideas, theories, statistics, and empirical data has hardly begun. The very multiplication of records however as time goes on will force us into much more adequate cataloging and reference systems than we now have. This is perhaps the major unsolved theoretical problem at the level of the static structure. In the empirical field there are still great areas where static structures are very imperfectly known, although knowledge is advancing rapidly, thanks to new probing devices such as the electron microscope. The anatomy of that part of empirical world which lies between the large molecule and the cell however, is still obscure at many points. It is precisely this area however—which includes, for instance, the gene and the virus—that holds the secret of life, and until its anatomy is made clear the nature of the functional systems which are involved will inevitably be obscure.

The level of the "clockwork" is the level of "classical" natural science, especially physics and astronomy, and is probably the most completely developed level in the present state of knowledge, especially if we extend the concept to include the field theory and stochastic models of modern physics. Even here however there are important gaps, especially at the higher empirical levels. There is much yet to be known about the sheer mechanics of cells and nervous systems, of brains and of societies.

Beyond the second level adequate theoretical models get scarcer. The last few years have seen great developments at the third and fourth levels. The theory of control mechanisms ("thermostats") has established itself as the new discipline or cybernetics, and the theory of self-maintaining systems or "open systems" likewise has made rapid strides. We could hardly maintain however that much more than a beginning had been made in these fields. We know very little about the cybernetics of genes and genetic systems, for instance, and still less about the control mechanisms involved in the mental and social world. Similarly the processes of self-maintenance remain essentially mysterious at many points, and although the theoretical possibility of constructing a self-maintaining machine which would be a true open system has been suggested, we seem to be a long way from the actual construction of such a mechanical similitude of life.

Beyond the fourth level it may be doubted whether we have as yet even the rudiments of theoretical systems. The intricate machinery of growth by which the genetic complex organizes the matter around it is almost a complete mystery. Up to now, whatever the future may hold, only God can make a tree. In the face of living systems we are almost helpless; we can occasionally cooperate with systems which we do not understand: we cannot even begin to reproduce them. The ambiguous status of medicine, hovering as it does uneasily between magic and science, is a testimony to the state of systematic knowledge in this area. As we move up the scale the absence of the appropriate theoretical systems becomes ever more noticeable. We can hardly conceive ourselves constructing a system which would be in any recognizable sense "aware," much less self-conscious. Nevertheless as we move towards the human and societal level a curious thing happens: the fact that we have, as it were, an inside track, and that we ourselves are the systems which we are studying, enables us to utilize systems which we do not really understand. It is almost inconceivable that we should make a machine that would make a poem: nevertheless, poems *are* made by fools like us by processes which are largely hidden from us. The kind of knowledge and skill that we have at the symbolic level is very different from that which we have at lower levels—it is like, shall we say, the "know how" of the gene as compared with the know how of the biologist. Nevertheless it is a real kind of knowledge and it is the source of the creative achievements of man as artist, writer, architect, and composer.

Perhaps one of the most valuable uses of the above scheme is to prevent us from accepting as final a level of theoretical analysis which is below the level of the empirical world which we are investigating. Because, in a sense, each level incorporates all those below it, much valuable information and insights can be obtained by applying low-level systems to high-level subject matter. Thus most of the theoretical schemes of the social sciences are still at level (2), just rising now to (3), although the subject matter clearly involves level (8). Economics, for instance, is still largely a "mechanics of utility and self interest," in Jevons' masterly phrase. Its theoretical and mathematical base is drawn largely from the level of simple equilibrium theory and dynamic mechanisms. It has hardly begun to use concepts such as information which are appropriate at level (3), and makes no use of higher level systems. Furthermore, with this crude apparatus it has achieved a modicum of success, in the sense that anybody trying to manipulate an economic

system is almost certain to be better off if he knows some economics than if he doesn't. Nevertheless at some point progress in economics is going to depend on its ability to break out of these low-level systems, useful as they are as first approximations, and utilize systems which are more directly appropriate to its universe—when, of course, these systems are discovered. Many other examples could be given—the wholly inappropriate use in psychoanalytic theory, for instance, of the concept of energy, and the long inability of psychology to break loose from a sterile stimulus-response model.

Finally, the above scheme might serve as a mild word of warning even to Management Science. This new discipline represents an important breakaway from overly simple mechanical models in the theory of organization and control. Its emphasis on communication systems and organizational structure, on principles of homeostasis and growth, on decision processes under uncertainty, is carrying us far beyond the simple models of maximizing behavior of even ten years ago. This advance in the level of theoretical analysis is bound to lead to more powerful and fruitful systems. Nevertheless we must never quite forget that even these advances do not carry us much beyond the third and fourth levels, and that in dealing with human personalities and organizations we are dealing with systems in the empirical world far beyond our ability to formulate. We should not be wholly surprised, therefore, if our simpler systems, for all their importance and validity, occasionally let us down.

I chose the subtitle of my paper with some eye to its possible overtones of meaning. General Systems Theory is the skeleton of science in the sense that it aims to provide a framework or structure of systems on which to hang the flesh and blood of particular disciplines and particular subject matters in an orderly and coherent corpus of knowledge. It is also, however, something of a skeleton in a cupboard—the cupboard in this case being the unwillingness of science to admit the very low level of its success in systematization, and its tendency to shut the door on problems and subject matters which do not fit easily into simple mechanical schemes. Science, for all its successes, still has a very long way to go. General Systems Theory may at times be an embarrassment in pointing out how very far we still have to go, and in deflating excessive philosophical claims for overly simple systems. It also may be helpful however in pointing out to some extent *where* we have to go. The skeleton must come out of the cupboard before its dry bones can live.

NOTES

1. The name and many of the ideas are to be credited to L. von Bertalanffy, who is not, however, to be held accountable for the ideas of the present author! For a general discussion of Bertalanffy's ideas see General System Theory: A New Approach to Unity of Science, *Human Biology* (December 1951), Vol. 23, p. 303–361.

2. See A. G. Pikler, Utility Theories in Field Physics and Mathematical Economics, *British Journal for the Philosophy of Science* (1955), Vol. 5, pp. 47 and 303.

3. See "Towards a General Theory of Growth" by K. E. Boulding, *Canadian Journal of Economics and Political Science* (August 19, 1953), 326–340.

23
Organizations and the System Concept
Daniel Katz & Robert L. Kahn

The aims of social science with respect to human organizations are like those of any other science with respect to the events and phenomena of its domain. The social scientist wishes to understand human organizations, to describe what is essential in their form, aspects, and functions. He wishes to explain their cycles of growth and decline, to predict their effects and effectiveness. Perhaps he wishes as well to test and apply such knowledge by introducing purposeful changes into organizations—by making them, for example, more benign, more responsive to human needs.

Such efforts are not solely the prerogative of social science, however; common sense approaches to understanding and altering organizations are ancient and perpetual. They tend, on the whole, to rely heavily on two assumptions: that the location and nature of an organization are given by its name; and that an organization is possessed of built-in goals—because such goals were implanted by its founders, decreed by its present leaders, or because they emerged mysteriously as the purposes of the organizational system itself. These assumptions scarcely provide an adequate

Source: Daniel Katz and Robert L. Kahn, *The Social Psychology of Organizations,* 14–29. Copyright © 1966 John Wiley & Sons, Inc. Reprinted by permission of John Wiley & Sons, Inc. Footnotes renumbered.

basis for the study of organizations and at times can be misleading and even fallacious. We propose, however, to make use of the information to which they point.

The first problem in understanding an organization or a social system is its location and identification. How do we know that we are dealing with an organization? What are its boundaries? What behavior belongs to the organization and what behavior lies outside it? Who are the individuals whose actions are to be studied and what segments of their behavior are to be included?

The fact that popular names exist to label social organizations is both a help and a hindrance. These popular labels represent the socially accepted stereotypes about organizations and do not specify their role structure, their psychological nature, or their boundaries. On the other hand, these names help in locating the area of behavior in which we are interested. Moreover, the fact that people both within and without an organization accept stereotypes about its nature and functioning is one determinant of its character.

The second key characteristic of the common sense approach to understanding an organization is to regard it simply as the epitome of the purposes of its designer, its leaders, or its key members. The teleology of this approach is again both a help and a hindrance. Since human purpose is deliberately built into organizations and is specifically recorded in the social compact, the bylaws, or other formal protocol of the undertaking, it would be inefficient not to utilize these sources of information. In the early development of a group, many processes are generated which have little to do with its rational purpose, but over time there is a cumulative recognition of the devices for ordering group life and a deliberate use of these devices.

Apart from formal protocol, the primary mission of an organization as perceived by its leaders furnishes a highly informative set of clues for the researcher seeking to study organizational functioning. Nevertheless, the stated purposes of an organization as given by its by-laws or in the reports of its leaders can be misleading. Such statements of objectives may idealize, rationalize, distort, omit, or even conceal some essential aspects of the functioning of the organization. Nor is there always agreement about the mission of the organization among its leaders and members. The university president may describe the purpose of his institution as one of turning out national leaders; the academic dean sees it as imparting the cultural heritage of the past, the academic vice-president as enabling students to move toward self-actualization and development, the graduate dean as creating new knowledge, the dean of men as training youngsters in technical and professional skills which will enable them to earn their living, and the editor of the student newspaper as inculcating the conservative values which will preserve the status quo of an outmoded capitalistic society.

The fallacy here is one of equating the purposes or goals of organizations with the purposes and goals of individual members. The organization as a system has an output, a produce or an outcome, but this is not necessarily identical with the individual purposes of group members. Though the founders of the organization and its key members do think in teleological terms about organization objectives, we should not accept such practical thinking, useful as it may be, in place of a theoretical set of constructs for purposes of scientific analysis. Social science, too frequently in the past, has been misled by such short-cuts and has equated popular phenomenology with scientific explanation.

In fact, the classic body of theory and thinking about organizations has assumed a teleology of this sort as the easiest way of identifying organizational structures and their functions. From this point of view an organization is a social device for efficiently accomplishing through group means some stated purpose; it is the equivalent of the blueprint for the design of the machine which is to be created for some practical objective. The essential difficulty with this purposive or design approach is that an organization characteristically includes more and less than is indicated by the design of its founder or the purpose of its leader. Some of the factors assumed in the design may be lacking or so distorted in operational practice as to be meaningless, while unforeseen embellishments dominate the organizational structure. Moreover, it is not always possible to ferret out the designer of the organization or to discover the intricacies of the design which he carried in his head. The attempt by Merton to deal with the latent function of the organization in contrast with its manifest function is one way of dealing with this problem.[1] The study of unanticipated consequences as well as anticipated consequences of organizational functioning is a similar way of handling the matter. Again, however, we are back to the purposes of the creator or leader, dealing with unanticipated consequences on the assumption that we can discover the consequences anticipated by him and can lump all other outcomes together as a kind of error variance.

It would be much better theoretically, however, to start with concepts which do not call for identifying the purposes of the designers and then correcting for them when they do not seem to be fulfilled. The theoretical concepts should begin with the input, output, and functioning of the organization as a system and not with the rational purposes of its leaders. We may want to utilize such purposive notions to lead us to sources of data or as subjects of special study, but not as our basic theoretical constructs for understanding organizations.

Our theoretical model for the understanding of organizations is that of an energic input-output system in which the energic return from the output reactivates the system. Social organizations are flagrantly open systems in that the input of energies and the conversion of output into further energic input consist of transactions between the organization and its environment.

All social systems, including organizations, consist of the patterned activities of a number of individuals. Moreover, these patterned activities are complementary or interdependent with respect to some common output or outcome; they are repeated, relatively enduring, and bounded in space and time. If the activity pattern occurs only once or at unpredictable intervals, we could not speak of an organization. The stability or recurrence of activities can be examined in relation to the *energic input* into the system, the *transformation of energies within the system,* and the *resulting product or energic output.* In a factory the raw materials and the human labor are the energic input, the patterned activities of production the transformation of energy, and the finished product the output. To maintain this patterned activity requires a continued renewal of the inflow of energy. This is guaranteed in social systems by the energic return from the product or outcome. Thus the outcome of the cycle of activities furnishes new energy for the initiation of a renewed cycle. The company which produces automobiles sells them and by doing so obtains the means of securing new raw materials, compensating its labor force, and continuing the activity pattern.

In many organizations outcomes are converted into money and new energy is furnished through this mechanism. Money is a convenient way of handling energy units both on the output and input sides, and buying and selling represent one set of social rules for regulating the exchange of money. Indeed, these rules are so effective and so widespread that there is some danger of mistaking the business of buying and selling for the defining cycles of organization. It is a commonplace executive observation that businesses exist to make money, and the observation is usually allowed to go unchallenged. It is, however, a very limited statement about the purposes of business.

Some human organizations do not depend on the cycle of selling and buying to maintain themselves. Universities and public agencies depend rather on bequests and legislative appropriations, and in so-called voluntary organizations the output reenergizes the activity of organization members in a more direct fashion. Member activities and accomplishments are rewarding in themselves and tend therefore to be continued, without the mediation of the outside environment. A society of bird watchers can wander into the hills and engage in the rewarding activities of identifying birds for their mutual edification and enjoyment. Organizations thus differ on this important dimension of the source of energy renewal, with the great majority utilizing both intrinsic and extrinsic sources in varying degree. Most large-scale organizations are not as self-contained as small voluntary groups and are very dependent upon the social effects of their output for energy renewal.

Our two basic criteria for identifying social systems and determining their functions are (1) tracing the pattern of energy exchange or activity of people as it results in some output and (2) ascertaining how the output is translated into energy which reactivates the pattern. We shall refer to organizational functions or objectives not as the conscious purposes of group leaders or group members but as the outcomes which are the energic source for a maintenance of the same type of output.

This model of an energic input-output system is taken from the open system theory as promulgated by von Bertalanffy.[2] Theorists have pointed out the applicability of the system concepts of the natural sciences to the problems of social science. It is important, therefore, to examine in more detail the constructs of system theory and the characteristics of open systems.

System theory is basically concerned with problems of relationships, of structure, and of interdependence rather than with the constant attributes of objects. In general approach it resembles field theory except that its dynamics deal with temporal as well as spatial patterns. Older formulations of system constructs dealt with the closed systems of the physical sciences, in which relatively self-contained structures could be treated successfully as if they were independent of external forces. But living systems, whether biological organisms or social organizations, are acutely dependent upon their external environment and so must be conceived of as open systems.

Before the advent of open-system thinking, social scientists tended to take one of two approaches in dealing with social structures; they tended either (1) to regard them as closed systems to which the laws of physics applied or (2) to endow them with some vitalistic concept like entelechy. In the former case they ignored the environmental forces affecting the organization and in the latter case they fell back upon some magical purposiveness to account for organizational functioning. Biological theorists, however, have rescued us from this trap by pointing out that the concept of the open system means that we neither have to follow the laws of traditional physics, nor in deserting them do we have to abandon science. The laws of Newtonian physics are correct generalizations but they are limited to closed systems. They do not apply in the same fashion to open systems which maintain themselves through constant commerce with their environment, i.e., a continuous inflow and outflow of energy through permeable boundaries.

One example of the operation of closed versus open systems can be seen in the concept of entropy and the second law of thermodynamics. According to the second law of thermodynamics a system moves toward equilibrium; it tends to run down, that is, its differentiated structures tend to move toward dissolution as the elements composing them become arranged in random disorder. For example, suppose that a bar of iron has been heated by the application of a blowtorch on one side. The arrangement of all the fast (heated) molecules on one side and all the slow molecules on the other is an unstable state, and over time the distribution of molecules becomes in effect random, with the resultant cooling of one side and heating of the other, so that all surfaces of the iron approach the same temperature. A similar process of heat exchange will also be going on between the iron bar and its environment, so that the bar will gradually approach the temperature of the room in which it is located, and in so doing will elevate somewhat the previous temperature of the room. More technically, entropy increases toward a maximum and equilibrium occurs as the physical system attains the state of the most probable distribution of its elements. In social systems, however, structures tend to become more elaborated rather than less differentiated. The rich may grow richer and the poor may grow poorer. The open system does not run down, because it can import energy from the world around it. Thus the operation of entropy is counteracted by the importation of energy and the living system is characterized by negative rather than positive entropy.

COMMON CHARACTERISTICS OF OPEN SYSTEMS

Though the various types of open systems have common characteristics by virtue of being open systems, they differ in other characteristics. If this were not the case, we would be able to obtain all our basic knowledge about social organizations through the study of a single cell.

The following nine characteristics seem to define all open systems.

1. Importation of Energy

Open systems import some form of energy from the external environment. The cell receives oxygen from the blood stream; the body similarly takes in oxygen from the air and food from the external world. The personality is dependent upon the external world for stimulation. Studies of sensory deprivation show that when a person is placed in a darkened soundproof room, where he has a minimal amount of visual and auditory stimulation, he develops hallucinations and other signs of mental stress.[3] Deprivation of social stimulation also can lead to mental disorganization.[4] Köhler's studies of the figural after-effects of continued stimulation show the dependence of perception upon its energic support from the external world.[5] Animals deprived of visual experience from birth for a prolonged period never fully recover their visual capacities.[6] In other words, the functioning personality is heavily dependent upon the continuous inflow of stimulation from the external environment. Similarly, social organizations must also draw renewed supplies of energy from other institutions, or people, or the material environment. No social structure is self-sufficient or self-contained.

2. The Through-Put

Open systems transform the energy available to them. The body converts starch and sugar into heat and action. The personality converts chemical and electrical forms of stimulation into sensory qualities, and information into thought patterns. The organization creates a new product, or processes materials, or trains people, or provides a service. These activities entail some reorganization of input. Some work gets done in the system.

3. The Output

Open systems export some product into the environment, whether it be the invention of an inquiring mind or a bridge constructed by an engineering firm. Even the biological organism exports physiological products such as carbon dioxide from the lungs which helps to maintain plants in the immediate environment.

4. Systems as Cycles of Events

The pattern of activities of the energy exchange has a cyclic character. The product exported into the environment furnishes the sources of energy for the repetition of the cycle of activities. The energy reinforcing the cycle of activities can derive from some exchange of the product in the external world or from the activity itself. In the former instance, the industrial concern utilizes raw materials and human labor to turn out materials and human labor to turn out

a product which is marketed, and the monetary return is used to obtain more raw materials and labor to perpetuate the cycle of activities. In the latter instance, the voluntary organization can provide expressive satisfactions to its members so that the energy renewal comes directly from the organizational activity itself.

The problem of structure, or the relatedness of parts, can be observed directly in some physical arrangement of things where the larger unit is physically bounded and its subparts are also bounded within the larger structure. But how do we deal with social structures, where physical boundaries in this sense do not exist? It was the genius of F. H. Allport which contributed the answer, namely that the structure is to be found in an interrelated set of events which return upon themselves to complete and renew a cycle of activities.[7] It is events rather than things which are structured, so that social structure is a dynamic rather than a static concept. Activities are structured so that they comprise a unity in their completion or closure. A simple linear stimulus-response exchange between two people would not constitute social structure. To create structure, the responses of A would have to elicit B's reactions in such a manner that the responses of the latter would stimulate A to further responses. Of course the chain of events may involve many people, but their behavior can be characterized as showing structure only when there is some closure to the chain by a return to its point of origin with the probability that the chain of events will then be repeated. The repetition of the cycle does not have to involve the same set of phenotypical happenings. It may expand to include more subevents of exactly the same kind or it may involve similar activities directed toward the same outcomes. In the individual organism the eye may move in such a way as to have the point of light fall upon the center of the retina. As the point of light moves, the movements of the eye may also change but to complete the same cycle of activity, i.e., to focus upon the point of light.

A single cycle of events of a self-closing character gives us a simple form of structure. But such single cycles can also combine to give a larger structure of events or an event system. An event system may consist of a circle of smaller cycles or hoops, each one of which makes contact with several others. Cycles may also be tangential to one another from other types of subsystems. The basic method for the identification of social structures is to follow the energic chain of events from the input of energy through its transformation to the point of closure of the cycle.

5. Negative Entropy

To survive, open systems must move to arrest the entropic process; they must acquire negative entropy. The entropic process is a universal law of nature in which all forms of organization move toward disorganization or death. Complex physical systems move toward simple random distribution of their elements and biological organisms also run down and perish. The open system, however, by importing more energy from its environment than it expends, can store energy and can acquire negative entropy. There is then a general trend in an open system to maximize its ratio of imported to expended energy, to survive and even during periods of crisis to live on borrowed time. Prisoners in concentration camps on a starvation diet will carefully conserve any form of energy expenditure to make the limited food intake go as far as possible.[8] Social organizations will seek to improve their

survival position and to acquire in their reserves a comfortable margin of operation.

The entropic process asserts itself in all biological systems as well as in closed physical systems. The energy replenishment of the biological organism is not of a qualitative character which can maintain indefinitely the complex organizational structure of living tissue. Social systems, however, are not anchored in the same physical constancies as biological organisms and so are capable of almost indefinite arresting of the entropic process. Nevertheless the number of organizations which go out of existence every year is large.

6. Information Input, Negative Feedback, and the Coding Process

The inputs into living systems consist not only of energic materials which become transformed or altered in the work that gets done. Inputs are also informative in character and furnish signals to the structure about the environment and about its own functioning in relation to the environment. Just as we recognize the distinction between cues and drives in individual psychology, so must we take account of information and energic inputs for all living systems.

The simplest type of information input found in all systems is negative feedback. Information feedback of a negative kind enables the system to correct its deviations from course. The working parts of the machine feed back information about the effects of their operation to some central mechanism or subsystem which acts on such information to keep the system on target. The thermostat which controls the temperature of the room is a simple example of a regulatory device which operates on the basis of negative feedback. The automated power plant would furnish more complex examples. Miller emphasizes the critical nature of negative feedback in his proposition: *"When a system's negative feedback discontinues, its steady state vanishes, and at the same time its boundary disappears and the system terminates."*[9] If there is no corrective device to get the system back on its course, it will expend too much energy or it will ingest too much energic input and no longer continue as a system.

The reception of inputs into a system is selective. Not all energic inputs are capable of being absorbed into every system. The digestive system of living creatures assimilates only those inputs to which it is adapted. Similarly, systems can react only to those information signals to which they are attuned. The general term for the selective mechanisms of a system by which incoming materials are rejected or accepted and translated for the structure is coding. Through the coding process, the "blooming, buzzing confusion" of the world is simplified into a few meaningful and simplified categories for a given system. The nature of the functions performed by the system determines its coding mechanisms, which in turn perpetuate this type of functioning.

7. The Steady State and Dynamic Homeostasis

The importation of energy to arrest entropy operates to maintain some constancy in energy exchange, so that open systems which survive are characterized by a steady state. A steady state is not motionless or a true equilibrium. There is a continuous inflow of energy from the external environment and a continuous export of the products of the system, but the character of the system, the ratio of the energy exchanges and the relations between parts, remains the same. The catabolic and anabolic processes of tissue breakdown and restoration within the body preserve a steady state so that the organism from time to time is not the identical organism it was but a highly similar organism. The steady state is seen in clear form in the homeostatic processes for the regulation of body temperature; external conditions of humidity and temperature may vary, but the temperature of the body remains the same. The endocrine glands are a regulatory mechanism for preserving an evenness of physiological functioning. The general principle here is that of Le Châtelier who maintains that any internal or external factor making for disruption of the system is countered by forces which restore the system as closely as possible to its previous state.[10] Krech and Crutchfield similarly hold, with respect to psychological organization, that cognitive structures will react to influences in such a way as to absorb them with minimal change to existing cognitive integration.[11]

The homeostatic principle does not apply literally to the functioning of all complex living systems, in that in counteracting entropy they move toward growth and expansion. This apparent contradiction can be resolved, however, if we recognize the complexity of the subsystems and their interaction in anticipating changes necessary for the maintenance of an overall steady state. Stagner has pointed out that the initial disturbance of a given tissue constancy within the biological organism will result in mobilization of energy to restore the balance, but that recurrent upsets will lead to actions to anticipate the disturbance:

> We eat before we experience intense hunger pangs. . . . energy mobilization for forestalling tactics must be explained in terms of a *cortical tension* which reflects the visceral-proprioceptive pattern of the original biological disequilibration. . . . *Dynamic homeostasis* involves the

maintenance of tissue constancies by establishing a constant physical environment—by reducing the variability and disturbing effects of external stimulation. Thus the organism does not simply restore the prior equilibrium. A new, more complex and more comprehensive equilibrium is established.[12]

Though the tendency toward a steady state in its simplest form is homeostatic, as in the preservation of a constant body temperature, the basic principle is *the preservation of the character of the system.* The equilibrium which complex systems approach is often that of a quasi-stationary equilibrium, to use Lewin's concept.[13] An adjustment in one direction is countered by a movement in the opposite direction and both movements are approximate rather than precise in their compensatory nature. Thus a temporal chart of activity will show a series of ups and downs rather than a smooth curve.

In preserving the character of the system, moreover, the structure will tend to import more energy than is required for its output, as we have already noted in discussing negative entropy. To insure survival, systems will operate to acquire some margin of safety beyond the immediate level of existence. The body will store fat, the social organization will build up reserves, the society will increase its technological and cultural base. Miller has formulated the proposition that the rate of growth of a system—within certain ranges—is exponential if it exists in a medium which makes available unrestricted amounts of energy for input.[14]

In adapting to their environment, systems will attempt to cope with external forces by ingesting them or acquiring control over them. The physical boundedness of the single organism means that such attempts at control over the environment affect the behavioral system rather than the biological system of the individual. Social systems will move, however, towards incorporating within their boundaries the external resources essential to survival. Again the result is an expansion of the original system.

Thus, the steady state which at the simple level is one of homeostasis over time, at more complex levels becomes one of preserving the character of the system through growth and expansion. The basic type of system does not change directly as a consequence of expansion. The most common type of growth is a multiplication of the same type of cycles or subsystems—a change in quantity rather than in quality. Animal and plant species grow by multiplication. A social system adds more units of the same essential type as it already has. Haire has studied the ratio between the sizes of different subsystems in growing business organizations.[15] He found that though the number of people increased in both the production subsystem and the subsystem concerned with the external world, the ratio of the two groups remained constant. Qualitative change does occur, however, in two ways. In the first place, quantitative growth calls for supportive subsystems of a specialized character not necessary when the system was smaller. In the second place, there is a point where quantitative changes produce a qualitative difference in the functioning of a system. A small college which triples its size is no longer the same institution in terms of the relation between its administration and faculty, relations among the various academic departments, or the nature of its instruction.

In time, living systems exhibit a growth or expansion dynamic in which they maximize their basic character. They react to change or they anticipate change through growth which assimilates the new energic inputs to the nature of their structure. In terms of Lewin's quasista-tionary equilibrium the ups and downs of the adjustive process do not always result in a return to the old level. Under certain circumstances a solidification or freezing occurs during one of the adjustive cycles. A new base line level is thus established and successive movements fluctuate around this plateau which may be either above or below the previous plateau of operation.

8. Differentiation

Open systems move in the direction of differentiation and elaboration. Diffuse global patterns are replaced by more specialized functions. The sense organs and the nervous system evolved as highly differentiated structures from the primitive nervous tissues. The growth of the personality proceeds from primitive, crude organizations of mental functions to hierarchically structured and well-differentiated systems of beliefs and feelings. Social organizations move toward the multiplication and elaboration of roles with greater specialization of function. In the United States today medical specialists now outnumber the general practitioners.

One type of differentiated growth in systems is what von Bertalanffy terms progressive mechanization. It finds expression in the way in which a system achieves a steady state. The early method is a process which involves an interaction of various dynamic forces, whereas the later development entails the use of a regulatory feedback mechanism. He writes:

> It can be shown that the *primary* regulations in organic systems, that is, those which are most fundamental and primitive in embryonic development as well as in evolution, are of such nature of dynamic interaction. . . . Superimposed are those regulations which we may call *secondary*, and which are controlled by fixed

arrangements, especially of the feedback type. This state of affairs is a consequence of a general principle of organization which may be called progressive mechanization. At first, systems—biological, neurological, psychological or social—are governed by dynamic interaction of their components; later on, fixed arrangements and conditions of constraint are established which render the system and its parts more efficient, but also gradually diminish and eventually abolish its equipotentiality.[16]

9. Equifinality

Open systems are further characterized by the principle of equifinality, a principle suggested by von Bertalanffy in 1940.[17] According to this principle, a system can reach the same final state from differing initial conditions and by a variety of paths. The well-known biological experiments on the sea urchin show that a normal creature of that species can develop from a complete ovum, from each half of a divided ovum, or from the fusion product of two whole ova. As open systems move toward regulatory mechanisms to control their operations, the amount of equifinality may be reduced.

SOME CONSEQUENCES OF VIEWING ORGANIZATIONS AS OPEN SYSTEMS

In the following chapter we shall inquire into the specific implications of considering organizations as open systems and into the ways in which social organizations differ from other types of living systems. At this point, however, we should call attention to some of the misconceptions which arise both in theory and practice when social organizations are regarded as closed rather than open systems.

The major misconception is the failure to recognize fully that the organization is continually dependent upon inputs from the environment and that the inflow of materials and human energy is not a constant. The fact that organizations have built-in protective devices to maintain stability and that they are notoriously difficult to change in the direction of some reformer's desires should not obscure the realities of the dynamic interrelationships of any social structure with its social and natural environment. The very efforts of the organization to maintain a constant external environment produce changes in organizational structure. The reaction to changed inputs to mute their possible revolutionary implications also results in changes.

The typical models in organizational theorizing concentrate upon principles of internal functioning as if these problems were independent of changes in the environment and as if they did not affect the maintenance inputs of motivation and morale. Moves toward tighter integration and coordination are made to insure stability, when flexibility may be the more important requirement. Moreover, coordination and control become ends in themselves rather than means to an end. They are not seen in full perspective as adjusting the system to its environment but as desirable goals within a closed system. In fact, however, every attempt at coordination which is not functionally required may produce a host of new organizational problems.

One error which stems from this kind of misconception is the failure to recognize the equifinality of the open system, namely that there are more ways than one of producing a given outcome. In a closed physical system the same initial conditions must lead to the same final result. In open systems this is not true even at the biological level. It is much less true at the social level. Yet in practice we insist that there is one best way of assembling a gun for all recruits, one best way for the baseball player to hurl the ball in from the outfield and that we standardize and teach these best methods. Now it is true under certain conditions that there is one best way, but these conditions must first be established. The general principle, which characterizes all open systems, is that there does not have to be a single method for achieving an objective.

A second error lies in the notion that irregularities in the functioning of a system due to environmental influences are error variances and should be treated accordingly. According to this conception, they should be controlled out of studies of organizations. From the organization's own operations they should be excluded as irrelevant and should be guarded against. The decisions of officers to omit a consideration of external factors or to guard against such influences in a defensive fashion, as if they would go away if ignored, is an instance of this type of thinking. So is the now outmoded "public be damned" attitude of businessmen toward the clientele upon whose support they depend. Open system theory, on the other hand, would maintain that environmental influences are not sources of error variance but are integrally related to the functioning of a social system, and that we cannot understand a system without a constant study of the forces that impinge upon it.

Thinking of the organization as a closed system, moreover, results in a failure to develop the intelligence or feedback function of obtaining adequate information about the changes in environmental forces. It is remarkable how weak many industrial companies are in their market research departments when they are so dependent upon the market. The prediction can be hazarded that organizations in our society will increasingly move toward the improvements of the facilities for research in assessing environmental forces. The reason is that we are in the process of correcting our misconception of the organization as a closed system.

Emery and Trist have pointed out how current theorizing on organizations still reflects the older closed system conceptions. They write:

> In the realm of social theory, however, there has been something of a tendency to continue thinking in terms of a "closed" system, that is, to regard the enterprise as sufficiently independent to allow most of its problems to be analyzed with reference to its internal structure and without reference to its external environment. . . . In practice the system theorists in social science . . . did "tend to focus on the statics of social structure and to neglect the study of structural change." In an attempt to overcome this bias, Merton suggested that "the concept of dysfunction, which implied the concept of strain, stress and tension on the structural level, provides an analytical approach to the study of dynamics and change." This concept has been widely accepted by system theorists but while it draws attention to sources of imbalance within an organization it does not conceptually reflect the mutual permeation of an organization and its environment that is the cause of such imbalance. It still retains the limiting perspectives of "closed system" theorizing. In the administrative field the same limitations may be seen in the otherwise invaluable contributions of Barnard and related writers.[18]

SUMMARY

The open-system approach to organizations is contrasted with common-sense approaches, which tend to accept popular names and stereotypes as basic organizational properties and to identify the purpose of an organization in terms of the goals of its founders and leaders.

The open-system approach, on the other hand, begins by identifying and mapping the repeated cycles of input, transformation, output, and renewed input which comprise the organizational pattern. This approach to organizations represents the adaptation of work in biology and in the physical sciences by von Bertalanffy and others.

Organizations as a special class of open systems have properties of their own, but they share other properties in common with all open systems. These include the importation of energy from the environment, the through-put or transformation of the imported energy into some product form which is characteristic of the system, the exporting of that product into the environment, and the re-energizing of the system from sources in the environment.

Open systems also share the characteristics of negative entropy, feedback, homeostasis, differentiation, and equifinality. The law of negative entropy states that systems survive and maintain their characteristic internal order only so long as they import from the environment more energy than they expend in the process of transformation and exportation. The feedback principle has to do with information input, which is a special kind of energic importation, a kind of signal to the system about environmental conditions and about the functioning of the system in relation to its environment. The feedback of such information enables the system to correct for its own malfunctioning or for changes in the environment, and thus to maintain a steady state or homeostasis. This is a dynamic rather than a static balance, however. Open systems are not at rest but tend toward differentiation and elaboration, both because of subsystem dynamics and because of the relationship between growth and survival.

Finally, open systems are characterized by the principle of equifinality, which asserts that systems can reach the same final state from different initial conditions and by different paths of development.

Traditional organizational theories have tended to view the human organization as a closed system. This tendency has led to a disregard of differing organizational environments and the nature of organizational dependency on environment. It has led also to an overconcentration on principles of internal organizational functioning, with consequent failure to develop and understand the processes of feedback which are essential to survival.

NOTES

1. Merton, R. K. 1957. *Social theory and social structure*, rev. ed. New York: Free Press.

2. von Bertalanffy, L. 1956. General System theory. *General Systems*. Yearbook of the Society for the Advancement of General System Theory, 1, 1–10.

3. Solomon, P., *et al.* (Eds.) 1961. *Sensory deprivation*. Cambridge, Mass: Harvard University Press.

4. Spitz, R. A. 1945. Hospitalism: an inquiry into the genesis of psychiatric conditions in early childhood. *Psychoanalytic Study of the Child*, 1, 53–74.

5. Kohler, W., and H. Wallach. 1944. Figural after-effects: an investigation of visual processes. *Proceedings of the American Philosophical Society*, 88, 269–357. Also, Kohler, W., and D. Emery. 1947. Figural after-effects in the third dimension of visual space. *American Journal of Psychology*, 60, 159–201.

6. Melzack, R., and W. Thompson. 1956. Effects of early experience on social behavior. *Canadian Journal of Psychology*, 10, 82–90.

7. Allport, F. H. 1962. A structuronomic conception of behavior: individual and collective. I. Structural theory and the master problem of social psychology. *Journal of Abnormal and Social Psychology*, 64, 3–30.

8. Cohen, E. 1954. *Human behavior in the concentration camp*. London: Jonathan Cape.

9. Miller, J. G. 1955. Toward a general theory for the behavioral sciences. *American Psychologist*, 10, 513–531; quote from p. 529.

10. See Bradley, D. F., and M. Calvin. 1956. Behavior: imbalance in a network of chemical transformations. *General Systems*. Yearbook of the Society for the Advancement of General System Theory, 1, 56–65.

11. Krech, D., and R. Crutchfield. 1948. *Theory and problems of social psychology*. New York: McGraw-Hill.

12. Stagner, R. 1951. Homeostasis as a unifying concept in personality theory. *Psychological Review*, 58, 5–17; quote from p. 5.

13. Lewin, K. 1947. Frontiers in group dynamics. *Human Relations*, 1, 5–41.

14. Miller, *op cit*.

15. Haire, M. 1959. Biological models and empirical histories of the growth of organizations. In M. Haire (Ed.), *Modern organization theory*, New York: Wiley, 272–306.

16. von Bertalanffy. 1956, *op cit*, p. 6.

17. von Bertalanffy, L. 1940. Der organismus als physikalisches system betrachtet. *Naturwissenschaften*, 28, 521 ff.

18. Emery, F. E., and E. L. Trist. 1960. Sociotechnical systems. In *Management sciences models and techniques*. Vol. 2, London: Pergamon Press; quote from p. 84.

24
Organizations in Action
James D. Thompson

STRATEGIES FOR STUDYING ORGANIZATIONS

Complex organizations—manufacturing firms, hospitals, schools, armies, community agencies—are ubiquitous in modern societies, but our understanding of them is limited and segmented.

The fact that impressive and sometimes frightening consequences flow from organizations suggests that some individuals have had considerable insight into these social instruments. But insight and private experiences may generate private understandings without producing a public body of knowledge adequate for the preparation of a next generation of administrators, for designing new styles of organizations for new purposes, for controlling organizations, or for appreciation of distinctive aspects of modern societies.

What we know or think we know about complex organizations is housed in a variety of fields or disciplines, and communication among them more nearly resembles a trickle than a torrent.[1] Although each of the several schools has its unique terminology and special heroes, Gouldner was able to discern two fundamental models underlying most of the literature.[2] He labeled these the "rational" and "natural-system" models of organizations, and these labels are indeed descriptive of the results.

To Gouldner's important distinction we wish to add the notion that the rational model results from a *closed-system*

strategy for studying organizations, and that the natural-system model flows from an *open-system strategy.*

Closed-System Strategy

• *The Search for Certainty.* If we wish to predict accurately the state a system will be in presently, it helps immensely to be dealing with a *determinate system.* As Ashby observes, fixing the present circumstances of a determinate system will determine the state it moves to next, and since such a system cannot go to two states at once, the transformation will be unique.[3]

Fixing the present circumstances requires, of course, that the variables and relationships involved by few enough for us to comprehend and that we have control over or can reliably predict all of the variables and relations. In other words, it requires that the system be closed or, if closure is not complete, that the outside forces acting on it be predictable.

Now if we have responsibility for the future states or performance of some system, we are likely to opt for a closed system. Bartlett's research on mental processes, comparing "adventurous thinking" with "thinking in closed systems," suggests that there are strong human tendencies to reduce various forms of knowledge to the closed-system variety, to rid them of all ultimate uncertainty.[4] If such tendencies appear in puzzle-solving as well as in everyday situations, we would especially expect them to be emphasized when responsibility and high stakes are added. Since much of the literature about organizations has been generated as a by-product of the search for improved efficiency or performance, it is not surprising that it employs closed-system assumptions—employs a rational model—about organizations. Whether we consider *scientific management,* [5] *administrative management,* [6] or *bureaucracy,* [7] the ingredients of the organization are deliberately chosen for their necessary contribution to a goal, and the structures established are those deliberately intended to attain highest efficiency.

Three Schools in Caricature. Scientific management, focused primarily on manufacturing or similar production activities, clearly employs economic efficiency as its ultimate criterion, and seeks to maximize efficiency by planning procedures according to a technical logic, setting standards, and exercising controls to ensure conformity with standards and thereby with the technical logic. Scientific management achieves conceptual closure of the organization by assuming that goals are known, tasks are repetitive, output of the production process somehow disappears, and resources in uniform qualities are available.

Administrative-management literature focuses on structural relationships among production, personnel, supply, and other service units of the organization; and again employs as the ultimate criterion economic efficiency. Here efficiency is maximized by specializing tasks and grouping them into departments, fixing responsibility according to such principles as span of control or delegation, and controlling action to plans. Administrative management achieves closure by assuming that ultimately a master plan is known, against which specialization, departmentalization, and controls are determined. (That this master plan is elu-

sive is shown by Simon. [8]) Administrative management also assumes that production tasks are known, that output disappears, and that resources are automatically available to the organization.

Bureaucracy also follows the pattern noted above, focusing on staffing and structure as means of handling clients and disposing of cases. Again the ultimate criterion is efficiency, and this time it is maximized by defining offices according to jurisdiction and place in a hierarchy, appointing experts to offices, establishing rules for categories of activity, categorizing cases or clients, and then motivating proper performance of expert officials by providing salaries and patterns for career advancement. [The extended implications of the assumptions made by bureaucratic theory are brought out by Merton's discussion of "bureaucratic personality."[9]] Bureaucratic theory also employs the closed system of logic. Weber saw three holes through which empirical reality might penetrate the logic, but in outlining his "pure type" he quickly plugged these holes. Policymakers, somewhere above the bureaucracy, could alter the goals, but the implications of this are set aside. Human components—the expert officeholders—might be more complicated than the model describes, but bureaucratic theory handles this by divorcing the individual's private life from his life as an officeholder through the use of rules, salary, and career. Finally, bureaucratic theory takes note of outsiders—clientele—but nullifies their effects by depersonalizing and categorizing clients.

It seems clear that the rational-model approach uses a closed-system strategy. It also seems clear that the developers of the several schools using the rational model have been primarily students of performance or efficiency, and only incidentally students of organizations. Having focused on control of the organization as a target, each employs a closed system of logic and conceptually closes the organization to coincide with that type of logic, for this elimination of uncertainty is the way to achieve determinateness. The rational model of an organization results in everything being functional—making a positive, indeed an optimum, contribution to the overall result. All resources are appropriate resources, and their allocation fits a master plan. All action is appropriate action, and its outcomes are predictable.

It is no accident that much of the literature on the management or administration of complex organizations centers on the concepts of *planning* or *controlling*. Nor is it any accident that such views are dismissed by those using the open-system strategy.

Open-System Strategy

The Expectation of Uncertainty. If, instead of assuming closure, we assume that a system contains more variables than we can comprehend at one time, or that some of the variables are subject to influences we cannot control or predict, we must resort to a different sort of logic. We can, if we wish, assume that the system is determinate by nature, but that it is our incomplete understanding which forces us to expect surprise or the intrusion of certainty. In this case we can employ a natural-system model.

Approached as a natural system, the complex organization is a set of interdependent parts which together make up a whole because each contributes something and receives something from the whole, which in turn is interdependent with some larger environment. Survival of the system is taken to be the goal, and the parts and their relationships presumably are determined through evolutionary processes. Dysfunctions are conceivable, but it is assumed that an offending part will adjust to produce a net positive contribution or be disengaged, or else the system will degenerate.

Central to the natural-system approach is the concept of homeostasis, or self-stabilization, which spontaneously, or naturally, governs the necessary relationships among parts and activities and thereby keeps the system viable in the face of disturbances stemming from the environment.

Two Examples in Caricature. Study of the *informal organization* constitutes one example of research in complex organizations using the natural-system approach. Here attention is focused on variables which are not included in any of the rational models—sentiments, cliques, social controls via informal norms, status and status striving, and so on. It is clear that students of informal organization regard these variables not as random deviations or error, but as patterned, adaptive responses of human beings in problematic situations.[10] In this view the formal organization is a spontaneous and functional development, indeed a necessity, in complex organizations, permitting the system to adapt and survive.

A second version of the natural-system approach is more global but less crystallized under a label. This school views the organization as a unit in interaction with its environment, and its view was perhaps most forcefully expressed by Chester Barnard[11] and by the empirical studies of Selznick[12] and Clark.[13] This stream of work leads to the conclusion that organizations are not autonomous entities; instead, the best laid plans of managers have unintended consequences and are conditioned or upset by other social units—other complex organizations or publics—on whom the organization is dependent.

Again it is clear that in contrast to the rational-model approach, this research area focuses on variables not subject to complete control by the organization and hence not contained within a closed system of logic. It is also clear that students regard interdependence of organization and environment as inevitable or natural, and as adaptive or functional.

Choice or Compromise?

The literature about organizations, or at least much of it, seems to fall into one of the two categories, each of which at best tends to ignore the other and at worse denies the relevance of the other. The logics associated with each appear to be incompatible, for one avoids uncertainty to achieve determinateness, while the other assumes uncertainty and indeterminateness. Yet the phenomena treated by each approach, as distinct from the explanations of each, cannot be denied.

Viewed in the large, complex organizations are often effective instruments for achievement, and that achievement flows from planned, controlled action. In every sphere—educational, medical, industrial, commercial, or governmental—the quality or costs of goods or services may be challenged and questions may be raised about the equity of distribution within the society of the fruits of complex organizations. Still millions live each day on the assumption that a reasonable degree of purposeful, effective action will be forthcoming from the many complex organizations on which they depend. Planned action, not random behavior, supports our daily lives. Specialized, controlled, patterned action surround us.

There can be no question but that the rational model of organizations directs our attention to important phenomena—to important "truth" in the sense that complex organizations viewed in the large exhibit some of the patterns and results to which the rational model attends, but which the natural-system model tends to ignore. But it is equally evident that phenomena associated with the natural-system approach also exist in complex organizations. There is little

room to doubt the universal emergence of the informal organization. The daily news about labor-management negotiations, interagency jurisdictional squabbles, collusive agreements, favoritism, breeches of contract, and so on, are impressive evidence that complex organizations are influenced in significant ways by elements of their environments, a phenomenon addressed by the natural-system approach but avoided by the rational. Yet most versions of the natural-system approach treat organizational purposes and achievements as peripheral matters.

It appears that each approach leads to some truth, but neither alone affords an adequate understanding of complex organizations. Gouldner calls for a synthesis of the two models, but does not provide the synthetic model.

Meanwhile, a serious and sustained elaboration of Barnard's work[14] has produced a newer tradition which evades the closed- versus open-system dilemma.

A Newer Tradition

What emerges from the Simon-March-Cyert stream of study is the organization as a problem-facing and problem-solving phenomenon. The focus is on organizational processes related to choice of courses of action in an environment which does not fully disclose the alternatives available or the consequences of those alternatives. In this view, the organization has limited capacity to gather and process information or to predict consequences of alternatives. To deal with situations of such great complexity, the organization must develop processes for *searching* and *learning,* as well as for *deciding.* The complexity, if fully faced, would overwhelm the organization, hence it must set limits to its definitions of situations; it must make decisions in *bounded rationality.*[15] This requirement involved replacing the maximum-efficiency criterion with one of satisfactory accomplishment, decision making now involving *satisficing* rather than *maximizing*. [16]

These are highly significant notions, and it will become apparent that this book seeks to extend this "newer tradition." The assumptions it makes are consistent with the open-system strategy, for it holds that the processes going on within the organization are significantly affected by the complexity of the organization's environment. But this tradition also touches on matters important in the closed-system strategy: performance and deliberate decisions.

But despite what seem to be obvious advantages, the Simon-March-Cyert stream of work has not entirely replaced the more extreme strategies, and we need to ask why so many intelligent men and women in a position to make the same observations we have been making should continue to espouse patently incomplete views of complex organizations.

The Cutting Edge of Uncertainty. Part of the answer to that question undoubtedly lies in the fact that supporters of each strategy have had different purposes in mind, with open-system strategists attempting to understand organizations per se, and closed-system strategists interested in organizations mainly as vehicles for rational achievements. Yet this answer does not seem completely satisfactory, for these students could not have been entirely unaware of the challenges to their assumptions and beliefs.

We can suggest now that rather than reflecting weakness in those who use them, the two strategies reflect something fundamental about the cultures surrounding complex organizations—the fact that our culture does not contain concepts for simultaneously thinking about rationality and indeterminateness. These appear to be incompatible concepts, and we have no ready way of thinking about something as half-closed, half-rational. One alternative, then, is

the closed-system approach of ignoring uncertainty to see rationality; another is to ignore rational action in order to see spontaneous processes. The newer tradition with its focus on organizational coping with uncertainty is indeed a major advance. It is notable that a recent treatment by Crozier starts from the bureaucratic position but focuses on coping with uncertainty as its major topic. [17]

Yet in directing our attention to processes for meeting uncertainty, Simon, March, and Cyert may lead us to overlook the useful knowledge amassed by the older approaches. If the phenomena of rational models are indeed observable, we may want to incorporate some elements of those models; and if natural-system phenomena occur, we should also benefit from the relevant theories. For purposes of this volume, then, *we will conceive of complex organizations as open systems, hence indeterminate and faced with uncertainty, but at the same time as subject to criteria of rationality and hence needing determinateness and certainty.*

The Location of Problems

As a starting point, we will suggest that the phenomena associated with open- and closed-system strategies are not randomly distributed through complex organizations, but instead tend to be specialized by location. To introduce this notion we will start with Parsons' suggestion that organizations exhibit three distinct levels of responsibility and control—*technical, managerial,* and *institutional.* [18]

In this view, every formal organization contains a suborganization whose "problems" are focused around effective performance of the technical function—the conduct of classes by teachers, the processing of income tax returns and the handling of recalcitrants by the bureau, the processing of material and supervision of these operations in the case of physical production. The primary exigencies to which the technical suborganization is oriented are those imposed by the nature of the technical task, such as the materials, which must be processed and the kinds of cooperation of different people required to get the job done effectively.

The second level, the managerial, *services* the technical suborganization by (1) mediating between the technical suborganization and those who use its products—the customers, pupils, and so on—and (2) procuring the resources necessary for carrying out the technical functions. The managerial level *controls*, or administers, the technical suborganization (although Parsons notes that its control is not unilateral) by deciding such matters as the broad technical task which is to be performed, the scale of operations, employment and purchasing policy, and so on.

Finally, in the Parsons formulation, the organization which consists of both technical and managerial suborganizations is also part of a wider social system which is the source of the "meaning," or higher-level support which makes the implementation of the organization's goals possible. In terms of "formal" controls, an organization may be relatively independent; but in terms of the meaning of the functions performed by the organization and hence of its "rights" to command resources and to subject its customers to discipline, it is never wholly independent. This overall articulation of the organization and the institutional structure and agencies of the community is the function of the third, or institutional, level of the organization.

Parsons' distinction of the three levels becomes more significant when he points out that at each of the two points of articulation between them there is a *qualitative* break in the simple continuity of "line" authority because the functions at each level are qualitatively different.

Those at the second level are not simply lower-order spellings-out of the top-level functions. Moreover, the articulation of levels and of functions rests on a two-way interaction, with each side, by withholding its important contribution, in a position to interfere with the functioning of the other and of the larger organization.

If we now reintroduce the conception of the complex organization as an open system subject to criteria of rationality, we are in a position to speculate about some dynamic properties of organizations. As we suggested, the logical model for achieving complete technical rationality uses a closed system of logic—closed by the elimination of uncertainty. In practice, it would seem, the more variables involved, the greater the likelihood of uncertainty, and it would therefore be advantageous for an organization subject to criteria of rationality to remove as much uncertainty as possible from its *technical core* by reducing the number of variables operating on it. Hence if both resource-acquisition and output-disposal problems—which are in part controlled by environmental elements and hence to a degree uncertain or problematic—can be removed from the technical core, the logic can be brought closer to closure, and the rationality, increased.

Uncertainty would appear to be greatest, at least potentially, at the other extreme, the institutional level. Here the organization deals largely with elements of the environment over which it has no formal authority or control. Instead, it is subjected to generalized norms, ranging from formally codified law to informal standards of good practice, to public authority, or to elements expressing the public interest.

At this extreme the closed system of logic is clearly inappropriate. The organization is open to influence by the environment (and vice versa) which can change independently of the actions of the organization. Here an open system of logic, permitting the intrusion of variables penetrating the organization from outside, and facing up to uncertainty, seems indispensable.

If the closed-system aspects of organizations are seen most clearly at the technical level, and the open-system qualities appear most vividly at the institutional level, it would suggest that a significant function of the managerial level is to mediate between the two extremes and the emphases they exhibit. If the organization must approach certainty at the technical level to satisfy its rationality criteria, but must remain flexible and adaptive to satisfy environmental requirements, we might expect the managerial level to mediate between them, ironing out some irregularities stemming from external sources, but also pressing the technical core for modifications as conditions alter. One exploration of this notion was offered in Thompson.[19]

Possible Sources of Variation. Following Parsons' reasoning leads to the expectation that differences in technical functions, or *technologies*, cause significant differences among organizations, and since the three levels are interdependent, differences in technical functions should also make for differences at managerial and institutional levels of the organization. Similarly, differences of the institutional structures in which organizations are imbedded should make for significant variations among organizations at all three levels.

Relating this back to the Simon-March-Cyert focus on organizational processes of searching, learning, and deciding, we can also suggest that while these adaptive processes may be generic, the ways in which they proceed may well vary with differences in technologies or in environments.

Recapitulation

Most of our beliefs about complex organizations follow from one or the other of two distinct strategies. The closed-system strategy seeks certainty by incorporating only those variables positively associated with goal achievement and subjecting them to a monolithic control network. The open-system strategy shifts attention from goal achievement to survival, and incorporates uncertainty by recognizing organizational interdependence with environment. A newer tradition enables us to conceive of the organization as an open system, indeterminate and faced with uncertainty, but subject to criteria of rationality and hence needing certainty.

With this conception the central problem for complex organizations is one of coping with uncertainty. As a point of departure, we suggest that organizations cope with uncertainty by creating certain parts specifically to deal with it, specializing other parts in operating under conditions of certainty or near certainty. In this case, articulation of these specialized parts becomes significant.

We also suggest that technologies and environments are major sources of uncertainty for organizations, and that differences in those dimensions will result in differences in organizations. To proceed, we now turn to a closer examination of the meaning of "rationality," in the context of complex organizations.

RATIONALITY IN ORGANIZATIONS

Instrumental action is rooted on the one hand in *desired outcomes* and on the other hand in *beliefs about cause/effect relationships.* Given a desire, the state of man's knowledge at any point in time dictates the kinds of variables required and the manner of their manipulation to bring that desire to fruition. To the extent that the activities thus dictated by man's beliefs are judged to produce the desired outcomes, we can speak of technology, or *technical rationality.*

Technical rationality can be evaluated by two criteria: instrumental and economic. The essence of the instrumental question is whether the specified actions do in fact produce the desired outcome, and the instrumentally perfect technology is one which inevitably achieves such results. The economic question in essence is whether the results are obtained with the least necessary expenditure of resources, and for this there is no absolute standard. Two different routes to the same desired outcome may be compared in terms of cost, or both may be compared with some abstract ideal, but in practical terms the evaluation of economy is relative to the state of man's knowledge at the time of evaluation.

We will give further consideration to the assessment of organizational action in a later chapter, but it is necessary to distinguish at this point between the instrumental and economic questions because present literature and organization gives considerable attention to the economic dimension of technology but hides the importance of the instrumental question, which in fact takes priority. The cost of doing something can be considered only after we know that the something can be done.

Complex organizations are built to operate technologies which are found to be impossible or impractical for individuals to operate. This does not mean, however, that technologies operated by complex organizations are instrumentally perfect. The instrumentally perfect technology would produce the desired outcome inevitably, and this perfection is approached in the case of continuous processing of chemicals or in mass manufacturing—for example, of automobiles. A less perfect technology will produce the desired outcome only part of the time; nevertheless, it may be incorporated into complex organizations, such as the mental hospital, because desire for the possible outcome is intense enough to settle for possible rather than highly probable success. Sometimes the intensity of desire for certain kinds of outcomes, such as world peace, leads to the creation of complex organizations, such as the United Nations to operate patently imperfect technologies.

Variations in Technologies

Clearly, technology is an important variable in understanding the actions of complex organizations. In modern societies the variety of desired outcomes for which specific technologies are available seems infinite. A complete but simple typology of technologies which has found order in this variety would be quite helpful. Typologies are available for industrial production[20] and for mental therapy[21] but are not general enough to deal with the range of technologies found in complex organizations. Lacking such a typology, we will simply identify three varieties which are (1) widespread in modern society and (2) sufficiently different to illustrate the propositions we wish to develop.

The Long-Linked Technology.[22] A long-linked technology involves serial interdependence in the sense that act Z can be performed only after successful completion of act Y, which in turn rests on act X, and so on. The original symbol of technical rationality, the mass production assembly line, is of this long-linked nature. It approaches instrumental perfection when it produces a single kind of standard product, repetitively and at a constant rate. Production of only one kind of product means that a single technology is required, and this in turn permits the use of clear-cut criteria for the selection of machines and tools, construction of work-flow arrangements, acquisition of raw materials, and selection of human operators. Repetition of the productive process provides experience as a means of eliminating imperfections in the technology; experience can lead to the modification of machines and provide the basis for scheduled preventive maintenance. Repetition means that human motions can also be examined, and through training and practice, energy losses and errors minimized. It is in this setting that the scientific-management movement has perhaps made its greatest contribution.

The constant rate of production means that, once adjusted, the proportion of resources involved can be standardized to the point where each contributes to its capacity; none need to be underemployed. This of course makes important contributions to the economic aspect of the technology.

The Mediating Technology. Various organizations have, as a primary function, the linking of clients or customers who are or wish to be interdependent. The commercial bank links depositors and borrowers. The insurance firm links those who would pool common risks. The telephone utility links those who would call and those who would be called. The post office provides a possible linkage of virtually every member of the modern society. The employment agency mediates the supply of labor and the demand for it.

Complexity in the mediating technology comes not from the necessity of having each activity geared to the requirements of the next but rather from the fact that the mediating technology requires operating in *standardized ways*, and *extensively*; e.g., with multiple clients

or customers distributed in time and space.

The commercial bank must find and aggregate deposits from diverse depositors; but however diverse the depositors, the transaction must conform to standard terms and to uniform bookkeeping and accounting procedures. It must also find borrowers; but no matter how varied their needs or desires, loans must be made according to standardized criteria and on terms uniformly applied to the category appropriate to the particular borrower. Poor risks who receive favored treatment jeopardize bank solvency. Standardization permits the insurance organization to define categories of risk and hence to sort its customers or potential customers into appropriate aggregate categories; the insured who is not a qualified risk but is so defined upsets the probabilities on which insurance rests. The telephone company became viable only when the telephone became regarded as a necessity, and this did not occur until equipment was standardized to the point where it could be incorporated into one network. Standardization enables the employment agency to aggregate job applicants into categories which can be matched against standardized requests for employees.

Standardization makes possible the operation of the mediating technology over time and through space by assuring each segment of the organization that other segments are operating in compatible ways. It is in such situations that the bureaucratic techniques of categorization and impersonal application of rules have been most beneficial.[23]

The Intensive Technology. This third variety we label *intensive* to signify that a variety of techniques is drawn upon in order to achieve a change in some specific object; but the selection, combination, and order of application are determined by feedback from the object itself. When the object is human, this intensive technology is regarded as "therapeutic," but the same technical logic is found also in the construction industry[24] and in research where the objects of concern are nonhuman.

The intensive technology is most dramatically illustrated by the general hospital. At any moment an emergency admission may require some combination of dietary, x-ray, laboratory, and housekeeping or hotel services, together with the various medical specialities, pharmaceutical services, occupational therapies, social work services, and spiritual or religious services. Which of these, and when, can be determined only from evidence about the state of the patient.

In the construction industry, the nature of the crafts required and the order in which they can be applied depend on the nature of the object to be constructed and its setting; including, for example, terrain, climate, weather. Organized or team research may draw from a variety of scientific or technical skills, but the particular combination and the order of application depend on the nature of the problem defined.

The development of military combat teams, with a multiplicity of highly skilled capacities to be applied to the requirements of changing circumstances, represents a shift toward the intensive technology in military operations.[25]

The intensive technology is a custom technology. Its successful employment rests in part on the availability of all the capacities potentially needed, but equally on the appropriate custom combination of selected capacities as required by the individual case or project.

Boundaries of Technical Rationality. Technical rationality, as a system of cause/effect relationships which lead to a desired result, is an abstraction. It is instrumentally perfect when it becomes a closed system of logic. The closed system of logic contains all relevant variables, and only relevant variables. All other influences, or *exogenous variables*, are excluded; and the variables contained in the system vary only to the extent that the experimenter, the manager, or the computer determines they should.

When a technology is put to use, however, there must be not only desired outcomes and knowledge of relevant cause/effect relationships, but also power to control the empirical resources which correspond to the variables in the logical system. A closed system of action corresponding to a closed system of logic would result in instrumental perfection in reality.

The mass production assembly operation and the continuous processing of chemicals are more nearly perfect, in application, than the other two varieties discussed above because they achieve a high degree of control over relevant variables and are relatively free from disturbing influences. Once started, most of the action involved in the long-linked technology is dictated by the internal logic of the technology itself. With the mediating technology, customers or clients intrude to make difficult the standardized activities required by the technology. And with the intensive technology, the specific case defines the component activities and their combination from the larger array of components contained in the abstract technology.

Since technical perfection seems more nearly approachable when the organization has control over all the elements involved,

Proposition 2.1: Under norms of rationality, organizations seek to seal off their core technologies from environmental influences.

Organizational Rationality

When organizations seek to translate the abstractions called technologies into action, they immediately face problems for which the core technologies do not provide solutions.

Mass production manufacturing technologies are quite specific, *assuming* that certain inputs are provided and finished products are somehow removed from the premises before the productive process is clogged; but mass production technologies do not include variables which provide solutions to either the input- or output-disposal problems. The present technology of medicine may be rather specific if certain tests indicate an appendectomy is in order, if the condition of the patient meets certain criteria, and if certain medical staff, equipment, and medications are present. But medical technology contains no cause/effect statements about bringing sufferers to the attention of medical practitioners, or about the provision of the specified equipment, skills, and medications. The technology of education rests on abstract systems of belief about relationships among teachers, teaching materials, and pupils; but learning theories assume the presence of these variables and proceed from that point.

One or more technologies constitute the core of all purposive organizations. But this technical core is always an incomplete representation of what the organization must do to accomplish desired results. Technical rationality is a necessary component but never alone sufficient to provide *organizational rationality*, which involves acquiring the inputs which are taken for granted by the technology, and dispensing outputs which again are outside the scope of the core technology.

At a minimum, then, organizational rationality involves three major component activities: (1) input activities, (2) technological activities, and (3) output activities. Since these are interdependent, organizational rationality requires that they be appropriately geared to one another. The inputs acquired must be within the scope of the technology, and it must be within the capacity of the organization to dispose of the technological production.

Not only are these component activities interdependent, but both input and output activities are interdependent with environmental elements. Organizational rationality, therefore, never conforms to closed-system logic but demands the logic of an open system. Moreover, since the technological activities are embedded in and interdependent with activities which are open to the environment, the closed system can never be completely attained for the technological component. Yet we have offered the proposition that organizations subject to rationality norms seek to seal off their core technologies from environmental influences. How do we reconcile these two contentions?

> Proposition 2.2: Under norms of rationality, organizations seek to buffer environmental influences by surrounding their technical cores with input and output components.

To maximize productivity of a manufacturing technology, the technical core must be able to operate as if the market will absorb the single kind of product at a continuous rate, and as if inputs flowed continuously, at a steady rate and with specified quality. Conceivably both sets of conditions could occur; realistically they do not. But organizations reveal a variety of devices for approximating these "as if" assumptions, with input and output components meeting fluctuating environments and converting them into steady conditions for the technological core.

Buffering on the input side is illustrated by the stockpiling of materials and supplies acquired in an irregular market, and their steady insertion into the production process. Preventive maintenance, whereby machines or equipment are repaired on a scheduled basis, thus minimizing surprise, is another example of buffering by the input component. The recruitment of dissimilar personnel and their conversion into reliable performers through training or indoctrination is another; it is most dramatically illustrated by basic training or boot camp in military organizations.[26]

Buffering on the output side of long-linked technologies usually takes the form of maintaining warehouse inventories and items in transit or in distributor inventories, which permits the technical core to produce at a constant rate, but distribution to fluctuate with market conditions.

Buffering on the input side is an appropriate and important device available to all types of organizations. Buffering on the output side is especially important for mass-manufacturing organizations, but is less feasible when the product is perishable or when the object is inextricably involved in the technological process, as in the therapeutic case.

Buffering of an unsteady environment obviously brings considerable advantages to the technical core, but it does so with costs to the organization. A classic problem in connection with buffering is how to maintain inventories, input or output, sufficient to meet all needs without recurring obsolescence as needs change. Operations research recently has made important contributions toward this problem of "run out versus obsolescence," both of which are costly.

Thus while a fully buffered technological core would enjoy the conditions for maximum technical rationality, organizational rationality may call for compromises between conditions for maximum technical efficiency and the energy required for buffering operations. In an unsteady environment, then, the organization under rationality norms must seek other devices for protecting its technical core.

Proposition 2.3: Under norms of rationality, organizations seek to smooth out input and output transactions.

Whereas buffering absorbs environmental fluctuations, smoothing or leveling involves attempts to reduce fluctuations in the environment. Utility firms—electric, gas, water, or telephone—may offer inducements to those who use their services during "trough" periods, or charge premiums to those who contribute to "peaking." Retailing organizations faced with seasonal or other fluctuations in demand, may offer inducements in the form of special promotions or sales during slow periods. Transportation organizations such as airlines may offer special reduced fare rates on light days or during slow seasons.

Organizations pointed toward emergencies, such as fire departments, attempt to level the need for their services by activities designed to prevent emergencies, and by emphasis on early detection so that demand is not allowed to grow to the point that would overtax the capacity of the organization. Hospitals accomplish some smoothing through the scheduling of nonemergency admissions.

Although action by the organization may thus reduce fluctuations in demand, complete smoothing of demand is seldom possible. But a core technology interrupted by constant fluctuation and change must settle for a low degree of technical rationality. What other services do organizations employ to protect core technologies?

Proposition 2.4: Under norms of rationality, organizations seek to anticipate and adapt to environmental changes which cannot be buffered or leveled.

If environmental fluctuations penetrate the organization and require the technical core to alter its activities, then environmental fluctuations are exogenous variables within the logic of technical rationality. To the extent that environmental fluctuations can be anticipated, however, they can be treated as *constraints* on the technical core within which a closed system of logic can be employed.

The manufacturing firm which can correctly forecast demand for a particular time period can thereby plan or schedule operations of its technical core at a steady rate during that period. Any changes in technical operations due to changes in the environment can be made at the end of the period on the basis of forecasts for the next period.

Organizations often learn that some environmental fluctuations are patterned, and in these cases forecasting and adjustment appear almost automatic. The post office knows, for example, that in large commercial centers large volumes of business mail are posted at the end of the business day, when secretaries leave offices. Recently the post office has attempted to buffer that load by promising rapid treatment of mail posted in special locations during morning hours. Its success in buffering is not known at this writing, but meanwhile the post office schedules its technical activities to meet known daily fluctuations. It can also anticipate heavy demand during November and December, thus allowing its input components lead time in acquiring additional resources.

Banks likewise learn that local conditions and customs result in peak loads at predictable times during the day and week, and can schedule their operations to meet these shifts.[27]

In cases such as these, organizations have amassed sufficient experience to know that fluctuations are patterned with a high degree of regularity or probability; but when environmental fluctuations are the result of combinations of more dynamic factors, anticipation may require something more than the simple projection of previous experience. It is in these situations that forecasting emerges as a specialized and elaborate activity, for which some of the emerging management-science or statistical-decision theories seem especially appropriate.

To the extent that environmental fluctuations are unanticipated they interfere with the orderly operation of the core technology and thereby reduce its performance. When such influences are anticipated and considered as constraints for a particular period of time, the technical core can operate as if it enjoyed a closed system.

Buffering, leveling, and adaptation to anticipated fluctuations are widely used devices for reducing the influence of the environment on the technological cores of organizations. Often they are effective, but there are occasions when these devices are not sufficient to ward off environmental penetration.

Proposition 2.5: When buffering, leveling, and forecasting do not protect their technical cores from environmental fluctuations, organizations under norms of rationality resort to rationing.

Rationing is most easily seen in organizations pointed toward emergencies, such as hospitals. Even in nonemergency situations hospitals may ration beds to physicians by establishing priority systems for nonemergency admissions. In emergencies, such as community disasters, hospitals may ration pharmaceutical dosages or nursing services by dilution—by assigning a fixed number of nurses to a larger patient population. Mental hospitals, especially state mental hospitals, may ration technical services by employing primarily organic-treatment procedures—electroshock, drugs, insulin—which can be employed more economically than psychoanalytic or *milieu* therapies.[28] Teachers and caseworkers in social welfare organizations may ration effort by accepting only a portion of those seeking service, or if not empowered to exercise such discretion, may concentrate their energies on the more challenging cases or on those which appear most likely to yield satisfactory outcomes.[29]

But rationing is not a device reserved for therapeutic organizations. The post office may assign priority to first-class mail, attending to lesser classes only when the priority task is completed. Manufacturers of suddenly popular items may ration allotments to wholesalers or dealers, and if inputs are scarce, may assign priorities to alternative uses of those resources. Libraries may ration book loans, acquisitions, and search efforts.[30]

Rationing is an unhappy solution, for its use signifies that the technology is not operating at its maximum. Yet some system of priorities for the allocation of capacity under adverse conditions is essential if a technology is to be instrumentally effective—if action is to be other than random.

The Logic of Organizational Rationality. Core technologies rest on closed systems of logic, but are invariably embedded in a larger organizational rationality which pins the technology to a time and place, and links it with the larger environment through input and output activities. Organizational rationality thus calls for an open-system logic, for when the organization is opened to environ-

mental influences, some of the factors involved in organizational action become *constraints*; for some meaningful period of time they are not variables but fixed conditions to which the organization must adapt. Some of the factors become *contingencies*, which may or may not vary, but are not subject to arbitrary control by the organization.

Organizational rationality therefore is some result of (1) constraints which the organization must face, (2) contingencies which the organization must meet, and (3) variables which the organization can control.

Recapitulation

Perfection in technical rationality requires complete knowledge of cause/effect relations plus control over all of the relevant variables, or closure. Therefore, under norms of rationality (Prop. 2.1), organizations seek to seal off their core technologies from environmental influences. Since complete closure is impossible (Prop. 2.2), they seek to buffer environmental influences by surrounding their technical cores with input and output components.

Because buffering does not handle all variations in an unsteady environment, organizations seek to smooth input and output transactions (Prop. 2.3), and to anticipate and adapt to environmental changes which cannot be buffered or smoothed (Prop. 2.4), and finally, when buffering, leveling, and forecasting do not protect their technical cores from environmental fluctuations (Prop. 2.5), organizations resort to rationing.

These are maneuvering devices which provide the organization with some self-control despite interdependence with the environment. But if we are to gain understanding of such maneuvering, we must consider both the direction toward which maneuvering is designed and the nature of the environment in which maneuvering takes place.

NOTES

1. William R. Dill, "Desegregation or Integration? Comments about Contemporary Research on Organizations," in *New Perspectives in Organization Research*, eds. W. W. Cooper, Harold J. Leavitt, and Maynard W. Shelly II (New York: John Wiley & Sons, Inc., 1964). James G. March, "Introduction," in *Handbook of Organizations*, ed. James G. March (Chicago: Rand McNally, 1965).

2. Alvin W. Gouldner, "Organizational Analysis," in *Sociology Today*, eds. Robert K. Merton, Leonard Broom, and Leonard S. Cottrell, Jr. (New York: Basic Books, 1959).

3. W. Ross Ashby, *An Introduction to Cybernetics* (London: Chapman and Hall, Ltd., 1956).

4. Sir Frederic Bartlett, *Thinking: An Experimental and Social Study* (New York: Basic Books, 1958).

5. Frederick W. Taylor, *Scientific Management* (New York: Harper & Row, 1911).

6. Luther Gulick and L. Urwick, eds., *Papers on the Science of Administration* (New York: Institute of Public Administration, 1937).

7. Max Weber, *The Theory of Social and Economic Organization*, ed. Talcott Parsons, trans. A. M. Henderson and Talcott Parsons (New York: Free Press, 1947).

8. Herbert A. Simon, *Administrative Behavior*, 2nd ed. (New York: Macmillan, 1957).

9. Robert K. Merton, "Bureaucratic Structure and Personality," in *Social Theory and Social Structure*, rev. ed., ed. Robert K. Merton (New York: Free Press, 1957).

10. Fritz J. Roethlisberger and W. J. Dickson, *Management and the Worker* (Cambridge, Mass.: Harvard University Press, 1939).

11. Chester I. Barnard, *The Functions of the Executive* (Cambridge, Mass.: Harvard University Press, 1938).

12. Philip Selznick, *TVA and the Grass Roots* (Berkeley, Calif.: University of California Press, 1949).

13. Burton R. Clark, *Adult Education in Transition* (Berkeley, Calif.: University of California Press, 1956).

14. Simon, *Administrative Behavior*. James G. March and Herbert A. Simon, *Organizations* (New York: John Wiley & Sons, Inc., 1958). Richard M. Cyert and James G. March, *A Behavioral Theory of the Firm* (Englewood Cliffs, N.J.: Prentice-Hall, 1963).

15. Herbert A. Simon, *Models of Man, Social and Rational* (New York: John Wiley & Sons, Inc., 1957).

16. *Ibid.*

17. Michel Crozier, *The Bureaucratic Phenomenon* (Chicago: The University of Chicago Press, 1964).

18. Talcott Parsons, *Structure and Process in Modern Societies* (New York: Free Press, 1960).

19. James D. Thompson, "Decision-making, the Firm, and the Market," in *New Perspectives in Organization Research*, eds., W. W. Cooper et al. (New York: John Wiley & Sons, Inc., 1964).

20. Joan Woodward, *Industrial Organization: Theory and Practice* (London: Oxford University Press, 1965).

21. Robert W. Hawkes, "Physical Psychiatric Rehabilitation Models Compared," (Paper presented at the Ohio Valley Sociological Society, 1962).

22. The notions in this section rest especially on conversations some years ago with Frederick L. Bates. For a different but somewhat parallel analysis of work flows, see Robert Dubin, "Stability of Human Organizations," in *Modern Organization Theory*, ed. Mason Haire (New York: John Wiley & Sons, Inc., 1959).

23. Weber, *Theory of Organization*. Merton, *Social Theory and Structure*.

24. Arthur L. Stinchcombe, "Bureaucratic and Craft Administration of Production: A Comparative Study," *Administrative Science Quarterly* 4 (September 1959): 168–87.

25. Morris Janowitz, "Changing Patterns of Organizational Authority: The Military Establishment," *Administrative Science Quarterly* 3 (March 1959): 473–93.

26. Sanford M. Dornbusch, "The Military Academy as an Assimilating Institution," *Social Forces* 33 (May 1955): 316–21.

27. Chris Argyris, *Organization of a Bank* (New Haven, Conn.: Labor and Management Center, Yale University, 1954).

28. Ivan Belknap, *The Human Problems of a State Mental Hospital* (New York: McGraw Hill, 1956).

29. Peter M. Blau, *The Dynamics of Bureaucracy* (Chicago: The University of Chicago Press, 1955).

30. Richard L. Meier, "Communications Overload," *Administrative Science Quarterly* 7 (March 1963): 521–44.

25

General Systems Theory: Applications for Organization and Management

Fremont E. Kast & James E. Rosenzweig

Biological and social scientists generally have embraced systems concepts. Many organization and management theorists seem anxious to identify with this movement and to contribute to the development of an approach which purports to offer the ultimate—the unification of all science into one grand conceptual model. Who possibly could resist? General systems theory seems to provide a relief from the limitations of more mechanistic approaches and a rationale for rejecting "principles" based on relatively "closed-system" thinking. This theory provides the paradigm for organization and management theorists to "crank into their systems model" all of the diverse knowledge from relevant underlying disciplines. It has become almost mandatory to have the word "system" in the title of recent articles and books (many of us have compromised and placed it only in the subtitle).[1]

But where did it all start? This question takes us back into history and brings to mind the long-standing philosophical arguments between mechanistic and organismic models of the 19th and early 20th centuries. As Deutsch says:

Both mechanistic and organismic models were based substantially on experiences and operations known before 1850. Since then, the experience of almost a century

of scientific and technological progress has so far not been utilized for any significant new model for the study of organization and in particular of human thought [12, p. 389].

General systems theory even revives the specter of the "vitalists" and their views on "life force" and most certainly brings forth renewed questions of teleological or purposeful behavior of both living and nonliving systems. Phillips and others have suggested that the philosophical roots of general systems theory go back even further, at least to the German philosopher Hegel (1770–1831) [29, p. 56]. Thus, we should recognize that in the adoption of the systems approach for the study of organizations we are not dealing with newly discovered ideas—they have a rich genealogy.

Even in the field of organization and management theory, systems views are not new. Chester Barnard used a basic systems framework.

A cooperative system is a complex of physical, biological, personal, and social components which are in a specific systematic relationship by reason of the cooperation of two or more persons for at least one definite end. Such a system is evidently a subordinate unit of larger systems from one point of view; and itself embraces subsidiary systems—physical,

Source: Fremont E. Kast and James E. Rosenzweig, "General Systems Theory: Applications for Organization and Management," *Academy of Management Journal* (December 1972): 447–465.

biological, etc.—from another point of view. One of the systems comprised within a cooperative system, the one which is implicit in the phrase "cooperation of two or more persons," is called an "organization" [3, p. 65].

And Barnard was influenced by the "systems views" of Vilfredo Pareto and Talcott Parsons. Certainly this quote (dressed up a bit to give the term "system" more emphasis) could be the introduction to a 1972 book on organizations.

Miller points out that Alexander Bogdanov, the Russian philosopher, developed a theory of tektology or universal organization science in 1912 which foreshadowed general systems theory and used many of the same concepts as modern systems theorists [26, p. 249–250].

However, in spite of a long history of organismic and holistic thinking, the utilization of the systems approach did not become the accepted model for organization and management writers until relatively recently. It is difficult to specify the turning point exactly. The momentum of systems thinking was identified by Scott in 1961 when he described the relationship between general systems theory and organization theory.

> The distinctive qualities of modern organization theory are its conceptual-analytical base, its reliance on empirical research data, and above all, its integrating nature. These qualities are framed in a philosophy which accepts the premise that the only meaningful way to study organization is to study it as a system . . . Modern organization theory and general system theory are similar in that they look at organization as an integrated whole [33, pp. 15–21].

Scott said explicitly what many in our field had been thinking and/or implying—he helped us put into perspective the important writings of Herbert Simon, James March, Talcott Parsons, George Homans, E. Wight Bakke, Kenneth Boulding, and many others.

But how far have we really advanced over the past decade in applying general systems theory to organizations and their management? Is it still a "skeleton," or have we been able to "put some meat on the bones?" The systems approach has been touted because of its potential usefulness in understanding the complexities of "live" organizations. Has this approach really helped us in this endeavor or has it compounded confusion with chaos? Herbert Simon describes the challenge for the systems approach:

> In both science and engineering, the study of "systems" is an increasingly popular activity. Its popularity is more a response to a pressing need for synthesizing and analyzing complexity than it is to any large development of a body of knowledge and technique for dealing with complexity. If this popularity is to be more than a fad, necessity will have to mother invention and provide substance to go with the name [35, p. 114].

In this article we will explore the issue of whether we are providing substance for the term *systems approach* as it relates to the study of organizations and their management. There are many interesting historical and philosophical questions concerning the relationship between the mechanistic and organistic approaches and their applicability to the various fields of science, as well as other interesting digressions into the evolution of systems approaches. However, we will resist those temptations and plunge directly into a discussion of the key concepts of general systems theory, the way in which these ideas have been used by organization theorists, the limitations in their application, and some suggestions for the future.

KEY CONCEPTS OF GENERAL SYSTEMS THEORY

The key concepts of general systems theory have been set forth by many writers [6, 7, 13, 17, 25, 28, 39] and have been used by many organization and management theorists [10, 14, 18, 19, 22, 23, 24, 32]. It is not our purpose here to elaborate on them in great detail because we anticipate that most readers will have been exposed to them in some depth. Figure 1 provides a very brief review of those characteristics of systems which seem to have wide acceptance. The review is far from complete. It is difficult to identify a "complete" list of characteristics derived from general systems theory; moreover, it is merely a first-order classification. There are many derived second- and third-order characteristics which could be considered. For example, James G. Miller sets forth 165 hypotheses, stemming from open systems theory, which might be applicable to two or more levels of systems [25]. He suggests that they are *general* systems theoretical hypotheses and qualifies them by suggesting that they are propositions applicable to general systems *behavior* theory and would thus exclude nonliving systems. He does not limit these propositions to individual organisms, but considers them appropriate for social systems as well. His hypotheses are related to such issues as structure, process, subsystems, information, growth, and integration. It is obviously impossible to discuss all of these hypotheses; we want only to indicate the extent to which many interesting propositions are being posed which might have relevance to many different types of systems. It will be a very long time (if ever) before most of these hypotheses are validated; however, we are surprised at how many of them can be agreed with intuitively, and we can see their possible verification in studies of social organizations.

We turn now to a closer look at how successful or unsuccessful we have been in utilizing these concepts in the development of "modern organization theory."

A BEGINNING: ENTHUSIASTIC BUT INCOMPLETE

We have embraced general systems theory but, really, how completely? We could review a vast literature in modern organization theory which has explicitly or implicitly adopted systems theory as a frame of reference, and we have investigated in detail a few representative examples of the literature in assessing the "state of the art" [18, 19, 22, 23, 31, 38]. It was found that most of these books professed to utilize general systems theory. Indeed, in the first few chapters, many of them did an excellent job of presenting basic systems concepts and showing their relationship to organizations; however, when they moved further into the discussion of more specific subject matter, they departed substantially from systems theory. The studies appear to use a "partial systems approach" and leave for the reader the problem of integrating the various ideas into a systemic whole. It also appears that many of the authors are unable, because of limitations of knowledge about subsystem relationships, to carry out the task of using general systems theory as a conceptual basis for organization theory.

Furthermore, it is evident that each author had many "good ideas" stemming from the existing body of knowledge or current research on organizations which did not fit neatly into a "systems model." For example, they might discuss leadership from a relatively closed-system

FIGURE 1 • KEY CONCEPTS OF GENERAL SYSTEMS THEORY

Subsystems or Components: A system by definition is composed of interrelated parts or elements. This is true for all systems—mechanical, biological, and social. Every system has at least two elements, and these elements are interconnected.

Holism, Synergism, Organicism, and Gestalt: The whole is not just the sum of the parts; the system itself can be explained only as a totality. Holism is the opposite of elementarism, which views the total as the sum of its individual parts.

Open Systems View: Systems can be considered in two ways: (1) closed or (2) open. Open systems exchange information, energy, or material with their environments. Biological and social systems are inherently open systems; mechanical systems may be open or closed. The concepts of open and closed systems are difficult to defend in the absolute. We prefer to think of open-closed as a dimension; that is, systems are relatively open or relatively closed.

Input-Transformation-Output Model: The open system can be viewed as a transformation model. In a dynamic relationship with its environment, it receives various inputs, transforms these inputs in some way, and exports outputs.

System Boundaries: It follows that systems have boundaries which separate them from their environments. The concept of boundaries helps us understand the distinction between open and closed systems. The relatively closed system has rigid, impenetrable boundaries; whereas the open system has permeable boundaries between itself and a broader suprasystem. Boundaries are relatively easily defined in physical and biological systems, but are very difficult to delineate in social systems, such as organizations.

Negative Entropy: Closed, physical systems are subject to the force of entropy which increases until eventually the entire system fails. The tendency toward maximum entropy is a movement to disorder, complete lack of resource transformation, and death. In a closed system, the change in entropy must always be positive; however, in open biological or social systems, entropy can be arrested and may even be transformed into negative entropy—a process of more complete organization and ability to transform resources—because the system imports resources from its environment.

Steady State, Dynamic Equilibrium, and Homeostasis: The concept of steady state is closely related to that of negative entropy. A closed system eventually must attain an equilibrium state with maximum entropy—death or disorganization. However, an open system may attain a state where the system remains in dynamic equilibrium through the continuous inflow of materials, energy, and information.

Feedback: The concept of feedback is important in understanding how a system maintains a steady state. Information concerning the outputs or the process of the system is fed back as an input into the system, perhaps leading to changes in the transformation process and/or future outputs. Feedback can be both positive and negative, although the field of cybernetics is based on negative feedback. Negative feedback is informational input which indicates that the system is deviating from a prescribed course and should readjust to a new steady state.

Hierarchy: A basic concept in systems thinking is that of hierarchical relationships between systems. A system is composed of subsystems of a lower order and is also part of a suprasystem. Thus, there is a hierarchy of the components of the system.

Internal Elaboration: Closed systems move toward entropy and disorganization. In contrast, open systems appear to move in the direction of greater differentiation, elaboration, and a higher level of organization.

Multiple Goal-Seeking: Biological and social systems appear to have multiple goals or purposes. Social organizations seek multiple goals, if for no other reason than that they are composed of individuals and subunits with different values and objectives.

Equifinality of Open Systems: In mechanistic systems there is a direct cause and effect relationship between the initial conditions and the final state. Biological and social systems operate differently. Equifinality suggests that certain results may be achieved with different initial conditions and in different ways. This view suggests that social organizations can accomplish their objectives with diverse inputs and with varying internal activities (conversion processes).

point of view and not consider it in relation to organizational technology, structure, or other variables. Our review of the literature suggests that much remains to be done in applying general systems theory to organization theory and management practice.

SOME DILEMMAS IN APPLYING GST TO ORGANIZATIONS

Why have writers embracing general systems theory as a basis for studying organizations had so much difficulty in following through? Part of this difficulty may stem from the newness of the paradigm and our inability to operationalize "all we think we know" about this approach. Or it may be because we know too little about the systems under investigation. Both of these possibilities will be covered later, but first we need to look at some of the more specific conceptual problems.

Organizations as Organisms

One of the basic contributions of general systems theory was the rejection of the traditional closed-system or mechanistic view of social organizations. But, did general systems theory free us from this constraint only to impose another, less obvious one? General systems theory grew out of the organismic views of von Bertalanffy and other biologists; thus, many of the characteristics are relevant to the living organism. It is conceptually easy to draw the analogy between living organisms and social organizations. "There is, after all, an intuitive similarity between the organization of the human body and the kinds of organizations men create. And so, undaunted by the failures of the human-social analogy through time, new theorists try afresh in each epoch" [2, p. 660]. General systems theory would have us accept this analogy between organism and social organization. Yet, we have a hard time swallowing it whole. Katz and Kahn warn us of the danger:

> There has been no more pervasive, persistent, and futile fallacy handicapping the social sciences than the use of the physical model for the understanding of social structures. The biological metaphor, with its crude comparisons of the physical parts of the body to the parts of the social system, has been replaced by more subtle but equally misleading analogies between biological and social functioning. This figurative type of thinking ignores the essential difference between the socially contrived nature of social systems and the physical structure of the machine or the human organism. So long as writers are committed to a theoretical framework based upon the physical model, they will miss the essential social-psychological facts of the highly variable, loosely articulated character of social systems [19, p. 31].

In spite of this warning, Katz and Kahn do embrace much of the general systems theory concepts which are based on the biological metaphor. We must be very cautious about trying to make this analogy too literal. We agree with Silverman who says, "It may, therefore, be necessary to drop the analogy between an organization and an organism: organizations may be systems but not necessarily *natural* systems" [34, p. 31].

Distinction between Organization and an Organization

General systems theory emphasizes that systems are organized—they are composed of interdependent components in some relationship. The social organization would then follow logically as just another system. But, we are perhaps being caught in circular thinking. It is true that all systems (physical, biological, and social) are by definition organized, but are all systems organizations?

Rapoport and Horvath distinguish "organization theory" and "the theory of organizations" as follows:

> We see organization theory as dealing with general and abstract organizational principles; it applies to any system exhibiting organized complexity. As such, organization theory is seen as an extension of mathematical physics or, even more generally, of mathematics designed to deal with organized systems. The theory of organizations, on the other hand, purports to be a social science. It puts real human organizations at the center of interest. It may study the social structure of organizations and so can be viewed as a branch of sociology; it can study the behavior of individuals or groups as members of organizations and can be viewed as a part of social psychology; it can study power relations and principles of control in organizations and so fits into political science [30, pp. 74–75].

Why make an issue of this distinction? It seems to us that there is a vital matter involved. All systems may be considered to be organized, and more advanced systems may display differentiation in the activities of component parts—such as the specialization of human organs. However, all systems *do not* have purposeful entities. Can the heart or lungs be considered as purposeful entities in themselves or are they only components of the larger purposeful system, the human body? By contrast, the social organization is composed of two or more purposeful elements. "An organization consists of elements that have and can exercise their own wills" [1, p. 669]. Organisms, the foundation stone of general systems theory, do not contain purposeful elements which exercise their own will. This distinction between the organism and the social organization is of importance. In much of general systems theory, the concern is primarily with the way in which the *organism* responds to environmentally generated inputs.

Feedback concepts and the maintenance of a steady state are based on internal adaptations to environmental forces. (This is particularly true of cybernetic models.) But, what about those changes and adaptations which occur from *within* social organizations? Purposeful elements within the social organization may initiate activities and adaptations which are difficult to subsume under feedback and steady state concepts.

Open and Closed Systems

Another dilemma stemming from general systems theory is the tendency to dichotomize all systems as opened or closed. We have been led to think of physical systems as closed, subject to the laws of entropy, and to think of biological systems as open to their environment and, possibly, becoming negentropic. But applying this strict polarization to social organizations creates many difficulties. In fact, most social organizations and their subsystems are "partially open" and "partially closed." Open and closed are a matter of degree. Unfortunately, there seems to be a widely held view (often more implicit than explicit) that *open-system thinking is good and closed-system thinking is bad.* We have not become sufficiently sophisticated to recognize that both are appropriate under certain conditions. For example, one of the most useful conceptualizations set forth by Thompson is that the social organization *must seek* to use closed-system concepts (particularly at the technical core) to reduce uncertainty and to create more effective performance at this level.

Still Subsystems Thinking

Even though we preach a general systems approach, we often practice subsystems thinking. Each of the academic disciplines and each of us personally have limited perspective of the system we are studying. While proclaiming a broad systems viewpoint, we often dismiss variables outside our interest or competence as being irrelevant, and we only open our system to those inputs which we can handle with our disciplinary bag of tools. We are hampered because each of the academic disciplines has taken a narrow "partial systems view" and find comfort in the relative certainty which this creates. Of course, this is not a problem unique to modern organization theory. Under the more traditional process approach to the study of management, we were able to do an admirable job of delineating and discussing planning, organizing, and controlling as separate activities. We were much less successful in discussing them as integrated and interrelated activities.

How Does Our Knowledge Fit?

One of the major problems in utilizing general systems theory is that we know (or think we know) more about certain relationships than we can fit into a general systems model. For example, we are beginning to understand the two-variable relationship between technology and structure. But, when we introduce another variable, say psychosocial relationships, our models become too complex. Consequently, in order to discuss all the things we know about organizations, we depart from a systems approach. Perhaps it is because we know a great deal more about the elements or subsystems of an organization than we do about the interrelationships and interactions between these subsystems. And, general systems theory forces us to consider those relationships about which we know the least—a true dilemma. So we continue to elaborate on those aspects of the organization which we know best—a partial systems view.

Failure to Delineate a Specific System

When the social sciences embraced general systems theory, the total system became the focus of attention and terminology tended toward vagueness. In the utilization of systems theory, we should be more precise in delineating the specific system under consideration. Failure to do this leads to much confusion. As Murray suggests:

> I am wary of the word "system" because social scientists use it very frequently without specifying which of several possible different denotations they have in mind; but more particularly because, today, "system" is a highly cathected term, loaded with prestige; hence, we are all strongly tempted to employ it even when we have nothing definite in mind and its only service is to indicate that we subscribe to the general premise respecting the interdependence of things—basic to organismic theory, holism, field theory, interactionism, transactionism, etc. . . . . When definitions of the units of a system are lacking, the term stands for no more than an article of faith, and is misleading to boot, insofar as it suggests a condition of affairs that may not actually exist [27, pp. 50–51].

We need to be much more precise in delineating both the boundaries of the system under consideration and the level of our analysis. There is a tendency for current writers in organization theory to accept general systems theory and then to move indiscriminately across systems boundaries and between levels of systems without being very precise (and letting their readers in on what is occurring). James Miller suggests the need for clear delineation of levels in applying systems theory, "It is important to follow one procedural rule in systems theory in order to avoid confusion. Every discussion should begin with an identification of the level of reference, and the discourse should not change to another level without a specific statement that this is occurring" [25, p. 216]. Our field is replete with these confusions about systems levels. For example, when we use the term *organizational behavior* are we talking about the way the organization behaves as a system or are we talking about the behavior of the individual participants? By goals, do we mean the goals of the organization or the goals of the individuals within the organization? In using systems theory we must become more precise in our delineation of systems boundaries and systems levels if we are to prevent confusing conceptual ambiguity.

Recognition That Organizations Are "Contrived Systems"

We have a vague uneasiness that general systems theory truly does not recognize the "contrived" nature of social organizations. With its predominate emphasis on natural organisms, it may understate some characteristics which are vital for the social organization. Social organizations do not occur naturally in nature; they are contrived by man. They have structure; but it is the structure of events rather than of physical components, and it cannot be separated from the processes of the system. The fact that social organizations are contrived by human beings suggests that they can be established for an infinite variety of purposes and do not follow the same life-cycle patterns of birth, growth, maturity, and death as biological systems. As Katz and Kahn say:

> Social structures are essentially contrived systems. They are made of men and are imperfect systems. They can come apart at the seams overnight, but they can also outlast by centuries the biological organisms which originally created them. The

cement which holds them together is essentially psychological rather than biological. Social systems are anchored in the attitudes, perceptions, beliefs, motivations, habits, and expectations of human beings [19, p. 33].

Recognizing that the social organization is contrived again cautions us against making an exact analogy between it and physical or biological systems.

Questions of Systems Effectiveness

General systems theory with its biological orientation would appear to have an evolutionary view of system effectiveness. That living system which best adapts to its environment prospers and survives. The primary measure of effectiveness is perpetuation of the organism's species. Teleological behavior is therefore directed toward survival. But, is survival the only criterion of effectiveness of the social system? It is probably an essential but not all-inclusive measure of effectiveness.

General systems theory emphasizes the organism's survival goal and does not fully relate to the question of the effectiveness of the system in its suprasystem—the environment. Parsonian functional-structural views provide a contrast. "The *raison d'etre* of complex organizations, according to this analysis, is mainly to benefit the society in which they belong, and that society is, therefore, the appropriate frame of reference for the evaluation of organizational effectiveness" [41, p. 896].

But, this view seems to go to the opposite extreme from the survival view of general systems theory—the organization exists to serve the society. It seems to us that the truth lies somewhere between these two viewpoints. And it is likely that a systems viewpoint (modified from the species survival view of general systems theory) will be most appropriate. Yuchtman and Seashore suggest:

> The organization's success over a period of time in this competition for resources—i.e., its bargaining position in a given environment—is regarded as an expression of its overall effectiveness. Since the resources are of various kinds, and the competitive relationships are multiple, and since there is interchangeability among classes of resources, the assessment of organizational effectiveness must be in terms not of any single criterion but of an open-ended multidimensional set of criteria [41, p. 891].

This viewpoint suggests that questions of organizational effectiveness must be concerned with at least three levels of analysis. The level of the environment, the level of the social organization as a system, and the level of the subsystems (human participants) within the organization. Perhaps much of our confusion and ambiguity concerning organizational effectiveness stems from our failure to clearly delineate the level of our analysis and, even more important, our failure really to understand the relationships among these levels.

Our discussion of some of the problems associated with the application of general systems theory to the study of social organizations might suggest that we completely reject the appropriateness of this model. On the contrary, we see the systems approach as the new paradigm for the study of organizations; but, like all new concepts in the sciences, one which has to be applied, modified, and elaborated to make it as useful as possible.

SYSTEMS THEORY PROVIDES THE NEW PARADIGM

We hope the discussion of GST and organizations provides a realistic appraisal. We do not want to promote the value of the systems approach as a matter of faith; however, we do see systems theory as vital to the study of social organizations and as providing the major new paradigm for our field of study.

Thomas Kuhn provides an interesting interpretation of the nature of scientific revolution [20]. He suggests that major changes in all fields of science occur with the development of new conceptual schemes or "paradigms." These new paradigms do not just represent a step-by-step advancement in "normal" science (the science generally accepted and practiced) but, rather, a revolutionary change in the way the scientific field is perceived by the practitioners. Kuhn says:

> The historian of science may be tempted to exclaim that when paradigms change, the world itself changes with them. Led by a new paradigm, scientists adopt new instruments and look in new places. Even more important, during revolutions scientists see new and different things when looking with familiar instruments in places they have looked before. It is rather as if the professional community has been suddenly transported to another planet where familiar objects are seen in a different light and are joined by unfamiliar ones as well. . . . Paradigm changes do cause scientists to see the world of their research-engagement differently. Insofar as their only recourse to that world is through what they see and do, we may want to say that after a revolution scientists are responding to a different world [20, p. 110].

New paradigms frequently are rejected by the scientific community. (At first they may seem crude and limited—offering very little more than older paradigms.) They frequently lack the apparent sophistication of the older paradigms which they ultimately replace. They do not display the clarity and certainty of older paradigms which have been refined through years of research and writing. But, a new paradigm does provide for a "new start" and opens up new directions which were not possible under the old. "We must recognize how very limited in both scope and precision a paradigm can be at the time of its first appearance. Paradigms gain their status because they are more successful than their competitors in solving a few problems that the group of practitioners has come to recognize as acute. To be more successful is not, however, to be either completely successful with a single problem or notably successful with any large number" [20, p. 23].

Systems theory does provide a new paradigm for the study of social organizations and their management. At this stage it is obviously crude and lacking in precision. In some ways it may not be much better than older paradigms which have been accepted and used for a long time (such as the management process approach). As in other fields of scientific endeavor, the new paradigm must be applied, clarified, elaborated, and made more precise. But, it does provide a fundamentally different view of the reality of social organizations and can serve as the basis for major advancements in our field.

We see many exciting examples of the utilization of the new systems paradigm in the field of organization and management. Several of these have been referred to earlier [7, 13, 19, 22, 23, 24, 31, 38], and there have been many others. Burns and Stalker made substantial use of systems views in setting forth their concepts of mechanistic and organic managerial systems [8]. Their studies of the characteristics of these two organization types lack precise definition to the variables and relationships, but their colleagues have used the systems approach to look at the relationship of organizations to their environment and also among the technical, structural, and behavioral characteristics within the organization [24]. Chamberlain used a system view in studying enterprises and their

environment, which is substantially different from traditional microeconomics [9]. The emerging field of "environmental sciences" and "environmental administration" has found the systems paradigm vital.

Thus, the systems theory paradigm is being used extensively in the investigation of relationships between subsystems within organizations and in studying the environmental interfaces. But, it still has not advanced sufficiently to meet the needs. One of the major problems is that the practical need to deal with comprehensive systems of relationships is overrunning our ability to fully understand and predict these relationships. *We vitally need the systems paradigm but we are not sufficiently sophisticated to use it appropriately.* This is the dilemma. Do our current failures to fully utilize the systems paradigm suggest that we reject it and return to the older, more traditional, and time-tested paradigms? Or do we work with systems theory to make it more precise, to understand the relationships among subsystems, and to gather the informational inputs which are necessary to make the systems approach really work? We think the latter course offers the best opportunity.

Thus, we prefer to accept current limitations of systems theory, while working to reduce them and to develop more complete and sophisticated approaches for its application. We agree with Rapoport who says:

> The system approach to the study of man can be appreciated as an effort to restore meaning (in terms of intuitively grasped understanding of wholes) while adhering to the principles of *disciplined* generalizations and rigorous deduction. It is, in short, an attempt to make the study of man both scientific and meaningful [7, p. xxii].

We are sympathetic with the second part of Rapoport's comment, the need to apply the systems approach but to make disciplined generalizations and rigorous deductions. This is a vital necessity and yet a major current limitation. We do have some indication that progress (although very slow) is being made.

WHAT DO WE NEED NOW?

Everything is related to everything else—but how? General systems theory provides us with the macro paradigm for the study of social organizations. As Scott and others have pointed out, most sciences go through a macro-micro-macro cycle or sequence of emphasis [33]. Traditional bureaucratic theory provided the first major macro view of organizations. Administrative management theorists concentrated on the development of macro "principles of management" which were applicable to all organizations. When these macro views seemed incomplete (unable to explain important phenomena), attention turned to the micro level—more detailed analysis of components or parts of the organization, thus the interest in human relations, technology, or structural dimensions.

The systems approach returns us to the macro level with a new paradigm. General systems theory emphasizes a very high level of abstraction. Phillips classifies it as a third-order study [29] that attempts to develop macro concepts appropriate for all types of biological, physical, and social systems.

In our view, we are now ready to move down a level of abstraction to consider second-order systems studies or mid-range concepts. These will be based on general systems theory but will be more concrete and will emphasize more specific characteristics and relationships in social organizations. They will operate within the broad paradigm of systems theory but at a less abstract level.

What should we call this new mid-range level of analysis? Various authors have referred to it as a "contingency view," a study of "patterns of relationships," or a search for "configurations among subsystems." Lorsch and Lawrence reflect this view:

> During the past few years there has been evident a new trend in the study of organizational phenomena. Underlying this new approach is the idea that the internal functioning of organizations must be consistent with the demands of the organization task, technology, or external environment, and the needs of its members if the organization is to be effective. Rather than searching for the panacea of the one best way to organize under all conditions, investigators have more and more tended to examine the functioning of organizations in relation to the needs of their particular members and the external pressures facing them. Basically, this approach seems to be leading to the development of a "contingency" theory of organization with the appropriate internal states and processes of the organization contingent upon external requirements and member needs [21, p. 1].

Numerous others have stressed a similar viewpoint. Thompson suggests that the essence of administration lies in understanding basic configurations which exist between the various subsystems and with the environment. "The basic function of administration appears to be co-alignment, not merely of people (in coalitions) but of institutionalized action—of technology and task environment into a viable domain, and of organizational design and structure appropriate to it [38, p. 157].

Bringing these ideas together we can provide a more precise definition of the contingency view:

> The contingency view of organizations and their management suggests that an organization is a system composed of subsystems and delineated by identifiable boundaries from its environmental suprasystem.

The contingency view seeks to understand the interrelationships within and among subsystems as well as between the organization and its environment and to define patterns of relationships or configurations of variables. It emphasizes the multivariate nature of organizations and attempts to understand how organizations operate under varying conditions and in specific circumstances. Contingency views are ultimately directed toward suggesting organizational designs and managerial systems most appropriate for specific situations.

But, it is not enough to suggest that a "contingency view" based on systems concepts of organizations and their management is more appropriate than the simplistic "principles approach." If organization theory is to advance and make contributions to managerial practice, it must define more explicitly certain patterns of relationships between organizational variables. This is the major challenge facing our field.

Just how do we go about using systems theory to develop these midrange or contingency views. We see no alternative but to engage in intensive comparative investigation of many organizations following the advice of Blau:

> A theory of organization, whatever its specific nature, and regardless of how subtle the organizational processes it takes into account, has as its central aim to establish the constellations of characteristics that develop in organizations of various kinds. Comparative studies of many organizations are necessary, not alone to test the hypotheses implied by such a theory, but also to provide a basis for initial exploration and refinement of the theory by indicating the conditions on which relationships, originally assumed to hold universally are contingent. . . . Systematic research on many organizations that provides the data needed to determine the interrelationships between several organizational features is, however, extremely rare [5, p. 332].

Various conceptual designs for the comparative study of organizations and their subsystems are emerging to help in the development of a contingency view. We do not want to impose our model as to what should be considered in looking for these patterns of relationships. However, the tentative matrix shown in Figure 2 suggests this approach. We have used as a starting point the two polar organization types which have been emphasized in the literature—closed/stable/mechanistic and open/adaptive/organic.

We will consider the environmental suprasystem and organizational subsystems (goals and values, technical, structural, psychosocial, and managerial) plus various dimensions or characteristics of each of these systems. By way of illustration we have indicated several specific subcategories under the Environmental Suprasystem as well as the Goals and Values subsystem. This process would have to be completed and extended to all of the subsystems. The next step would be the development of appropriate descriptive language (based on research and conceptualization) for each relevant characteristic across the continuum of organization types. For example, on the "stability" dimension for Goals and Values we would have High, Medium, and Low at appropriate places on the continuum. If the entire matrix were filled in, it is likely that we would begin to see discernible patterns of relationships among subsystems.

We do not expect this matrix to provide *the* midrange model for every one. It is highly doubtful that we will be able to follow through with the field work investigations necessary to fill in all the squares. Nevertheless, it does illustrate a possible approach for the translation of more abstract general systems theory into an appropriate midrange model which is relevant for organization theory and management practice. Frankly, we see

FIGURE 2 • MATRIX OF PATTERNS OF RELATIONSHIPS BETWEEN ORGANIZATION TYPES AND SYSTEMS VARIABLES

Organizational Supra- and Subsystems	Continuum of Organization Types	
	Closed/Stable/Mechanistic	Open/Adaptive/Organic
Environmental relationships		
General nature	Placid	Turbulent
Predictability	Certain, determinate	Uncertain, Indeterminate
Boundary relationships	Relatively closed; limited to few participants (sales, purchasing, etc.); fixed and well-defined	Relatively open; many participants have external relationships; varied and not clearly defined
Goals and values		
Organizational goals in general	Efficient performance, stability, maintenance	Effective problem-solving, innovation, growth
Goal set	Single, clear-cut	Multiple, determined by necessity to satisfy a set of constraints
Stability	Stable	Unstable
Technical		
Structural		
Psychosocial		
Managerial		

this as a major long-term effort on the part of many researchers, investigating a wide variety of organizations. In spite of the difficulties involved in such research, the endeavor has practical significance. Sophistication in the study of organizations will come when we have a more complete understanding of organizations as total systems (configurations of subsystems) so that we can prescribe more appropriate organizational designs and managerial systems. Ultimately, organization theory should serve as the foundation for more effective management practice.

APPLICATION OF SYSTEMS CONCEPTS TO MANAGEMENT PRACTICE

The study of organizations is an applied science because the resulting knowledge is relevant to problem-solving in on-going institutions. Contributions to organization theory come from many sources. Deductive and inductive research in a variety of disciplines provide a theoretical base of propositions which are useful for understanding organizations and for managing them. Experience gained in management practice is also an important input to organization theory. In short, management is based on the body of knowledge generated by practical experience *and* eclectic scientific research concerning organizations. The body of knowledge developed through theory and research should be translatable into more effective organizational design and managerial practices.

Do systems concepts and contingency views provide a panacea for solving problems in organizations? The answer is an emphatic *no;* this approach does not provide "ten easy steps" to success in management. Such cookbook approaches, while seemingly applicable and easy to grasp, are usually shortsighted, narrow in

perspective, and superficial—in short, unrealistic. Fundamental ideas, such as systems concepts and contingency views, are more difficult to comprehend. However, they facilitate more thorough understanding of complex situations and increase the likelihood of appropriate action.

It is important to recognize that many managers have used and will continue to use a systems approach and contingency views intuitively and implicitly. Without much knowledge of the underlying body of organization theory, they have an intuitive "sense of the situation," are flexible diagnosticians, and adjust their actions and decisions accordingly. Thus, systems concepts and contingency views are not new. However, if this approach to organization theory and management practice can be made more explicit, we can facilitate better management and more effective organizations.

Practicing managers in business firms, hospitals, and government agencies continue to function on a day-to-day basis. Therefore, they must use whatever theory is available, they cannot wait for the *ultimate* body of knowledge (there is none!). Practitioners should be included in the search for new knowledge because they control access to an essential ingredient—organizational data—and they are the ones who ultimately put the theory to the test. Mutual understanding among managers, teachers, and researchers will facilitate the development of a relevant body of knowledge.

Simultaneously with the refinement of the body of knowledge, a concerted effort should be directed toward applying what we do know. We need ways of making systems and contingency views more usable. Without oversimplification, we need some relevant guidelines for practicing managers.

The general tenor of the contingency view is somewhere between simplistic, specific principles and complex, vague notions. It is a midrange concept which recognizes the complexity involved in managing modern organizations but uses patterns of relationships and/or configurations of subsystems in order to facilitate improved practice. The art of management depends on a reasonable success rate for actions in a probabilistic environment. Our hope is that systems concepts and contingency views, while continually being refined by scientists/researchers/theorists, will also be made more applicable.

NOTE

1. An entire article could be devoted to a discussion of ingenious ways in which the term "systems approach" has been used in the literature pertinent to organization theory and management practice.

BIBLIOGRAPHIC REFERENCES

1. Ackoff, Russell L., "Towards a System of Systems Concepts," *Management Science* (July 1971).
2. Back, Kurt W., "Biological Models of Social Change," *American Sociological Review* (August 1971).
3. Barnard, Chester I., *The Functions of the Executive* (Cambridge, Mass.: Harvard University Press, 1938).
4. Berrien, F. Kenneth, *General and Social Systems* (New Brunswick, NJ: Rutgers University Press, 1968).
5. Blau, Peter M., "The Comparative Study of Organizations," *Industrial and Labor Relations Review* (April 1965).
6. Boulding, Kenneth E., "General Systems Theory: The Skeleton of Science," *Management Science* (April 1956).
7. Buckley, Walter, ed., *Modern Systems Research for the Behavioral Scientist* (Chicago: Aldine Publishing, 1968).
8. Burns, Tom and G. M. Stalker, *The Management of Innovation* (London: Tavistock Publications, 1961).
9. Chamberlain, Neil W., *Enterprise and Environment: The Firm in Time and Place* (New York: McGraw-Hill, 1968).
10. Churchman, C. West, *The Systems Approach* (New York: Dell Publishing Company, Inc., 1968).
11. DeGreene, Kenyon, ed., *Systems Psychology* (New York: McGraw-Hill, 1970).
12. Deutsch, Karl W., "Toward a Cybernetic Model of Man and Society," in Walter Buckley, ed., *Modern Systems Research for the Behavioral Scientist* (Chicago: Aldine Publishing, 1968).
13. Easton, David, *A Systems Analysis of Political Life* (New York: John Wiley & Sons, 1965).
14. Emery, F. E. and E. L. Trist, "Socio-technical Systems," in C. West Churchman and Michele Verhulst, eds., *Management Sciences: Models and Techniques* (New York: Pergamon Press, 1960).
15. Emshoff, James R., *Analysis of Behavioral Systems* (New York: Macmillan, 1971).
16. Gross, Bertram M., "The Coming General Systems Models of Social Systems," *Human Relations* (November 1967).
17. Hall, A. D. and R. E. Eagen, "Definition of System," *General Systems, Yearbook for the Society for the Advancement of General Systems Theory*, Vol. 1 (1956).
18. Kast, Fremont E. and James E. Rosenzweig, *Organization and Management Theory: A Systems Approach* (New York: McGraw-Hill, 1970).
19. Katz, Daniel and Robert L. Kahn, *The Social Psychology of Organizations* (New York: John Wiley & Sons, 1966).

20. Kuhn, Thomas S., *The Structure of Scientific Revolutions* (Chicago: University of Chicago Press, 1962).
21. Lorsch, Jay W. and Paul R. Lawrence, *Studies in Organizational Design* (Homewood, IL: Irwin-Dorsey, 1970).
22. Litterer, Joseph A., *Organizations: Structure and Behavior*, Vol. 1 (New York: John Wiley & Sons, 1969).
23. ———, *Organizations: Systems, Control and Adaptation*, Vol. 2 (New York: John Wiley & Sons, 1969).
24. Miller, E. J. and A. K. Rice, *Systems of Organizations* (London: Tavistock Publications, 1967).
25. Miller, James G., "Living Systems: Basic Concepts," *Behavioral Science* (July 1965).
26. Miller, Robert F., "The New Science of Administration in the USSR," *Administrative Science Quarterly* (September 1971).
27. Murray, Henry A., "Preparation for the Scaffold of a Comprehensive System," in Sigmund Koch, ed., *Psychology: A Study of a Science*, Vol. 3 (New York: McGraw-Hill, 1959).
28. Parsons, Talcott, *The Social System* (New York: Free Press, 1951).
29. Phillips, D. C., "Systems Theory—A Discredited Philosophy," in Peter P. Schoderbek, *Management Systems* (New York: John Wiley & Sons, 1971).
30. Rapoport, Anatol and William J. Horvath, "Thoughts on Organization Theory," in Walter Buckley, ed., *Modern Systems Research for the Behavioral Scientist* (Chicago: Aldine Publishing, 1968).
31. Rice, A. K., *The Modern University* (London: Tavistock Publications, 1970).
32. Schein, Edgar, *Organizational Psychology*, rev. ed. (Englewood Cliffs, NJ: Prentice-Hall, 1970).
33. Scott, William G., "Organization Theory: An Overview and an Appraisal," *Academy of Management Journal* (April 1961).
34. Silverman, David, *The Theory of Organizations* (New York: Basic Books, 1971).
35. Simon, Herbert A., "The Architecture of Complexity," in Joseph A. Litterer, *Organizations: Systems, Control and Adaptation*, Vol. 2 (New York: John Wiley & Sons, 1969).
36. Springer, Michael, "Social Indicators, Reports, and Accounts: Toward the Management of Society," *The Annals of the American Academy of Political and Social Science* (March 1970).
37. Terreberry, Shirley, "The Evolution of Organizational Environments," *Administrative Science Quarterly* (March 1968).
38. Thompson, James D., *Organizations in Action* (New York: McGraw-Hill, 1967).
39. von Bertalanffy, Ludwig, *General System Theory* (New York: George Braziller, 1968).
40. ———, The Theory of Open Systems in Physics and Biology," *Science* (January 13, 1950).
41. Yuchtman, Ephraim and Stanley E. Seashore, "A System Resource Approach to Organizational Effectiveness," *American Sociological Review* (December 1967).

<u>26</u>
Information Processing Model
Jay Galbraith

In this chapter the basic model is created and the overall structure of the framework is outlined. Subsequent chapters will expand the major strategies put forth in the framework. Of necessity, the remainder of the chapter is fairly abstract. The purpose is to conceive of organizations as information-processing networks and to explain why and through what mechanisms uncertainty and information relate to structure. In order to accomplish this explanation, the basic bureaucratic mechanical model is created. The value of the model is not that it describes reality but that it creates a basis from which various strategies are formed to adapt the bureaucratic structure for handling greater complexity.

MECHANISTIC MODEL

In order to develop the model and the design strategies, assume that we have a task which requires several thousand employees divided among many subtasks. For example, the task of designing and manufacturing an aircraft or space capsule requires a group to design the capsule, a group to design the manufacturing methods, a group to fabricate parts and components, a group to assemble the parts, and a group to test the completed unit. The result is a division of labor which involves considerable interdependence and therefore coordination among the groups. The workflow is shown schematically in Figure 1.

In order to complete the task at a high level of performance, the activities that take place in the various groups must be coordinated. The behavior of the product design engineer must be consistent with the behavior of the process design engineers, etc. Although the behavior of several thousand people must be coordinated, it is impossible for all of them to communicate with each other. The organization is simply too large to permit face-to-face communication to be the mechanism for coordination. The organization design problem is to create mechanisms by which an integrated pattern of behavior can be obtained across all the interdependent groups. In order to see what these mechanisms are and the conditions under which they are appropriate, let us start with a very predictable task and slowly increase the degree of task uncertainty.

First we have a task, like the one represented in Figure 1 in which there is a high degree of division of labor, a high level of performance, and relatively large size. A good deal of information must be processed to coordinate the interdependent subtasks. As the degree of uncertainty increases, the amount of information processing during task execution increases. Organizations must evolve strategies to process the greater amount of information necessary to maintain the level of performance. Let us follow the history of a fictitious

Source: Jay Galbraith, *Designing Complex Organizations*, © 1973, Addison-Wesley Publishing Company, Reading, Mass., pp. 8–21. Reprinted with permission.

FIGURE 1 • HORIZONTAL WORKFLOW ACROSS A FUNCTIONAL DIVISION OF LABOR

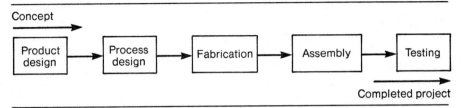

organization performing the task represented in Figure 1 and observe the mechanisms that are created to deal with increasing information loads caused by increasing task uncertainty.

Rules, Programs, Procedures

The simplest method of coordinating interdependent subtasks is to specify the necessary behaviors in advance of their execution in the form of rules or programs.[1] In order to make effective use of programs, the organization's employees are taught the job-related situations with which they will be faced and the behaviors appropriate to those situations. Then as situations arise daily, the employees act out the behaviors appropriate to the situations. If everyone adopts the appropriate behavior, the resultant aggregate response is an integrated or coordinated pattern of behavior.

The primary virtue of rules is that they eliminate the need for further communication among the subunits. If an organization has hundreds of employees, they cannot all communicate with each other in order to guarantee coordinated action. To the extent that the job-related situations can be anticipated in advance and rules derived for them, integrated activity is guaranteed without communication. These rules and programs perform the same functions for organizations that habits perform for individuals. They eliminate the need for treating each

situation as new. The amount of communication and decision making is reduced each time a situation is repeatedly encountered. In addition, rules provide a stability to the organization's operations. As people come and go through an organization, the rules provide a memory for handling routine situations.

The best example of a programmed task is the automobile assembly operation. Each employee learns a specific set of behaviors for each possible situation he will face, e.g., station wagon, convertible, deluxe sedan, standard sedan, etc. For assembly operations the programs and procedures are created by engineers. In other situations individuals simply program themselves. That is, after confronting the same situation many times, individuals coordinate their behavior by following the same approach as in the past. Many standard operating procedures arise in this manner.

The use of rules and programs as coordination devices is limited, however. It is limited to those job-related situations which can be anticipated in advance and to which an appropriate response can be identified. As the organization faces new and different situations, the use of rules must be supplemented by other integrating devices.

Hierarchy

As the organization that depends on rules encounters situations it has not faced before, it has no ready-made response. When a response is developed for the new situation it must take into account all the subtasks that are affected. The information collection and problem solving activities may be substantial. To handle this task new roles are created, called managerial roles, and arranged in a hierarchy as shown in Figure 2.[2] The occupants of these roles handle the information collection and decision-making tasks necessitated by uncertainty.

Then as unanticipated events arise, the problem is referred to the manager who has the information to make a new decision. In addition, the hierarchy is also a hierarchy of authority and reward power, so that the decisions of the role occupants are effective determinants of the behavior of the task performers. In this manner the hierarchy of authority is employed on an exception basis. That is, the new situation, for which there is no preplanned response, is referred upward in the hierarchy to permit the creation of a new response. Since the process we are describing remains rather mechanical, the new situation is referred upward in the hierarchy to that point where a shared superior exists for all subunits affected by the new situation. For example, in Figure 2, if a problem arises during testing which requires

product design work, it is referred to the general manager. If a situation arises affecting assembly and fabrication, it is referred to manager No. 2.

It is important to point out that the hierarchy is employed *in addition to, not instead of,* the use of rules. That is, the rules achieve coordination for the uniform and repetitive situations, whereas the new and unique situations are referred upward. This combination guarantees an integrated coordinated organizational response to the situations which the organization faces.

The weakness of hierarchical communication systems is that each link has a finite capacity for handling information. As the organization's subtasks increase in uncertainty, more exceptions arise which must be referred upward in the hierarchy. As more exceptions are referred upward, the hierarchy becomes overloaded. Serious delays develop between the upward transmission of information about new situations and a response to that information downward. In this situation, the organization must develop new processes to supplement rules and hierarchy.

Targeting or Goal Setting

As task uncertainty increases, the volume of information from the points of action to points of decision making

FIGURE 2 • HIERARCHICAL ORGANIZATION STRUCTURE

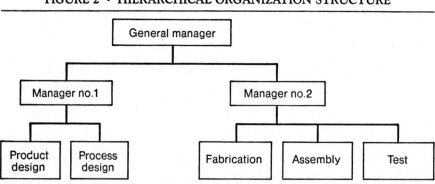

overload the hierarchy. In this situation it becomes more efficient to bring the points of decision down to the points of action where the information originates. This can be accomplished by increasing the amount of discretion exercised by employees at lower levels of the organization. However, as the amount of discretion exercised at lower levels of the organization is increased, the organization faces a potential behavior control problem. That is, how can the organization be sure that the employees will consistently choose the appropriate response to the job-related situations which they will face?

In order to increase the probability that employees will select the appropriate behavior, organizations make two responses to deal with the behavior control problem.[3] The first change involves the substitution of craft or professional training of the work force for the detailed centralized programming of the work processes.[4] This is illustrated by a comparison between manufacturing industries and construction industries. In mass production, the work processes that are planned in advance are:

1. the location at which a particular task will be performed
2. the movement of tools, of materials and of workers to this work place and the most efficient arrangement of these workplace characteristics
3. sometimes the particular movements to be performed in getting the task done
4. the schedules and time allotments for particular operations
5. inspection criteria for particular operations.

In construction all these characteristics of the work process are governed by the worker in accordance with the empirical lore that makes up craft principles.[5] These two descriptions represent a shift from control based on supervision and surveillance to control based on selection of responsible workers. Workers who have the appropriate skills and attitudes are selected.

Professionalization by itself may not be sufficient to shift decision making to lower levels of the organization. The reason is that in the presence of interdependence, an alternative which is based on professional or craft standards may not be best for the whole organization. Thus alternatives which are preferred from a local or departmental perspective may not be preferred from a global perspective. The product design that is technically preferred may not be preferred by the customer, may be costly to produce, or may require a schedule which takes too long to complete. In order to deal with the problem, organizations undertake processes to set goals or targets to cover the primary interdependencies.

An example of the way goals are used can be demonstrated by considering the design group responsible for an aircraft wing structure. The group's interdependence with other design groups is handled by technical specifications elaborating the points of attachment of the wing to the body, forces transmitted at these points, centers of gravity, etc. The group also has a set of targets (not to be exceeded) for weight, design man-hours to be used, and a completion date. They are given minimum stress specifications below which they cannot design. The group then designs the structures and assemblies which combine to form the wing. They need not communicate with any other design group on work related matters if they and the interdependent groups are able to operate within the planned targets.

Thus goal setting helps coordinate interdependent subtasks and still allows discretion at the local subtask level. Instead of specifying specific behaviors through rules and programs, the organization specifies targets to be achieved and allows the employees to select behaviors appropriate to the target.[6]

The ability of the design groups to operate within the planned targets, however, depends partly on the degree of task uncertainty. If the task is one that has been performed before, the estimates of man-hours, weight, due date, etc., will probably be realized. If it is a new design involving new materials, the estimates will probably be wrong. The targets will have to be set and reset throughout the design effort.

The violation of planned targets usually requires additional decision making and hence additional information processing. The additional information processing takes place through the hierarchy in the same way that rule exceptions were handled. Problems are handled on an exception basis. They are raised to higher levels of the hierarchy for resolution. The problem rises to the first level at which a shared superior exists for all affected subunits. A decision is made, and the new targets are communicated to the subunits. In this manner the behavior of the interdependent subunits remains integrated.

However, as the organization performs more uncertain tasks, such as designing and building a 747 jumbo jet, the hierarchical channels become overloaded once again. The organization does not have the information to estimate how many man-hours are needed to design the new titanium wings. How much weight will the wings require? Will it take 9 months, a year, or 18 months to complete the design? The information necessary to make these decisions can only be discovered during the actual design. The decisions must be made and remade each time new information is discovered. The volume of information processing can overwhelm an organization behaving in the mechanical fashion

outlined in this chapter. The organization must adopt a strategy to either reduce the information necessary to coordinate its activities or increase its capacity to process more information. In the next section these strategies are identified and integrated into the framework. Subsequent chapters explain the strategies in detail.

DESIGN STRATEGIES

The ability of an organization to successfully coordinate its activities by goal setting, hierarchy, and rules depends on the combination of the frequency of exceptions and the capacity of the hierarchy to handle them. As task uncertainty increases, the number of exceptions increases until the hierarchy is overloaded. Then the organization must employ new design strategies. Either it can act in two ways to reduce the amount of information that is processed, or it can act in two ways to increase its capacity to handle more information. An organization may choose to develop in both of these ways. The two methods for reducing the need for information and the two methods for increasing processing capacity are shown schematically in Figure 3. The effect of all these actions is to reduce the number of exceptional cases referred upward into the organization through hierarchical channels.

Creation of Slack Resources

An organization can reduce the number of exceptions that occur by simply reducing the required level of performance. In the example of the wing design, the scheduled time, weight allowance, or man-hours could be increased. In each case more resources could be consumed. These additional resources are called slack resources.[7]

FIGURE 3 • ORGANIZATION DESIGN STRATEGIES

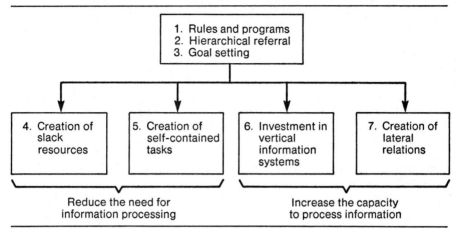

Reduce the need for information processing / Increase the capacity to process information

Slack resources are an additional cost to the organization or the customer. However, the longer the scheduled time available, the lower the likelihood of a target being missed. The fewer the exceptions, the less the overload on the hierarchy. Thus the creation of slack resources, through reduced performance levels, reduces the amount of information that must be processed during task execution and prevents the overloading of hierarchical channels. Whether the organization chooses this strategy depends on the relative costs of the other three strategies for handling the overload.

Creation of Self-Contained Tasks

The second method for reducing the amount of information processed is to change from the functional task design to one in which each group has all the resources it needs to perform its task. In the example of the 747, self-contained units could be created around major sections of the aircraft—wing, cabin, tail, body, etc. Each group would have its own product engineers, process engineers, fabricating and assembly operations, and test facilities. In other situations, groups can be created around product lines, geographical areas, projects, client groups, markets, etc., each of which would contain the input resources necessary for the task.

The strategy of self-containment shifts the basis of the authority structure from one based on input, resource, skill, or occupational categories, to one based on output or geographical categories. The shift reduces the amount of information processing through several mechanisms—two are described here.

First, it reduces the amount of output diversity faced by a single collection of resources. For example, a professional organization with multiple skill specialties that provides service to three different client groups must schedule the use of these specialties across three demands for their services and determine priorities when conflicts occur. But if the organization changes to three groups, one for each client category, each with its own full complement of specialties, the schedule conflicts across client groups disappears, and there is no need to process information to determine priorities.

The second source of information reduction occurs through a reduced division of labor. The functional or re-source specialized structure pools the demand for skills across all output categories. In the example above, each client generates approximately one-third of the demand for each skill. Since the division of labor is determined by the extent of the market, the division of labor must decrease as the demand decreases. In the professional organization, each client group may have generated a need for one-third of a computer programmer. The functional organization would have hired one programmer and shared him across the groups. In the self-contained structure, there is insufficient demand in each group for a programmer, and so the professionals must do their own programming. Specialization is reduced but there is no problem of scheduling the programmer's time across the three possible uses for it.

Thus the first two strategies reduce overloads on the hierarchy by reducing the number of exceptions that occur. The reduction occurs by reducing the level of performance, diversity of output, or division of labor. According to the theory put forth earlier, reducing the level of performance, etc., reduces the amount of information required to co-ordinate resources in creating the organization's services or products. In this way, the amount of information to be acquired and processed during task execution, and as a consequence the amount of task uncertainty, is reduced.

In contrast, the other two strategies take the required level of information as given, and create processes and mechanisms to acquire and process information during task execution.

Investment in Vertical Information Systems

The organization can invest in mechanisms which allow it to process information acquired during task performance without overloading the hierarchical communication channels. The investment occurs according to the following logic. After the organization has created its plan or set of targets for weight, stress, budget, and schedule, unanticipated events occur which generate exceptions requiring adjustments to the original plan. At some point when the number of exceptions becomes substantial, it is preferable to generate a new plan rather than make incremental changes in the old one with each exception. The issue is then how frequently plans should be revised—yearly, quarterly, or monthly? The greater the uncertainty, the greater the frequency of replanning. The greater the frequency of replanning, the greater the resources, such as clerks, computer time, input-output devices, etc., required to process information about relevant factors.

Providing more information more often may simply overload the decision maker. Investment may be required to increase the capacity of the decision maker by employing computers, various man-machine combinations, assistants-to, etc. The cost of this strategy is the cost of information processing resources.

The investment strategy is to collect information at the points of origin and direct it, at appropriate times, to the appropriate places in the hierarchy. The strategy increases the information processing at planning time while reducing the number of exceptions which have overloaded the hierarchy.

Creation of Lateral Relations

The last strategy is to selectively employ lateral decision processes which cut across lines of authority. The strategy moves the level of decision making down to where the information exists rather than bringing it up to the points of decision. It decentralizes decisions but without creating self-contained groups. Several mechanisms are employed. The number and types depend upon the level of uncertainty.

The simplest form of lateral relation is direct contact between two people who share a problem. If a problem arises in testing (see Figure 3), the manager of test may contact the manager of assembly and secure the necessary change. Direct contact avoids the upward referral to another manager and removes overloads from the hierarchy.

In some cases there is a large volume of contact between two subtasks such as process design and assembly. Under these circumstances a new role, a liaison role, may be created to handle the interdepartmental contacts.

As tasks of higher uncertainty are encountered, problems are detected in testing which require the joint efforts of product and process design, assembly, and testing. Rather than refer the problem upwards, managers of these areas form a task force or team to jointly resolve the issue. In this manner interdepartmental group problem solving becomes a mechanism to decentralize decisions and reduce hierarchical overloads.

As more decisions and more decisions of consequence are made at lower levels of the organization through interdepartmental groups, problems of leadership arise. The response is the creation of a new role, an integrating role.[8] The function of the role is to represent the general manager in the interdepartmental decisions for a particular brand, product line, project, country, or geographical unit. These roles are called product managers in commercial firms, project managers in aerospace, and unit managers in hospitals.

After the role is created the issue is, how much and what kind of influence does the role occupant need in order to achieve integration for the project, unit, or product. Mechanisms from supporting information and budget control all the way to dual reporting relations and the matrix design are employed under various circumstances described in later chapters.

In summary, lateral relations permit the moving of decisions to lower levels of the organization and yet guarantee that all information is included in the process. The cost of the strategy is the greater amounts of managerial time that must be spent in group processes and the overhead expense of liaison and integrating roles.

Choice of Strategy

Four strategies have been briefly presented. The organization can choose to follow one or some combination of several if it chooses. It will choose that strategy which is least expensive in its environmental context.

It is important to note that the four strategies are hypothesized to be an exhaustive set of alternatives. That is, if the organization is faced with greater uncertainty, due to technological change, higher performance standards, increased competition, or diversified product line to reduce dependence, the amount of information processing is increased. *The organization must adopt at least one of the four strategies when faced with greater uncertainty.* If it does not consciously choose one of the four, then the first, reduced performance standards, will happen automatically. The task information requirements and the capacity of the organization to process information are always matched. If the organization does not consciously match them, reduced performance through budget overruns or schedule overruns will occur in order to bring about equality. Thus the organization should be planned and designed simultaneously with the planning of the strategy and resource allocations. But if the strategy involves introducing new products, entering new markets etc., then some provision for increased information must be made. Not to decide is to decide, and it is to decide upon slack resources as the only strategy for removing hierarchical overload.

SUMMARY

This chapter has introduced the basic theory upon which the remainder of the book will build. Starting from the observation that uncertainty appears to make a difference in type of organization structure, it was postulated that uncertainty increased the amount of information that must be processed during task execution. Therefore perceived variation in organization form was hypothesized to be variation in the capability of the organization to process information about events that could not be anticipated in advance.

Uncertainty was conceived as the relative difference in the amount of information required and the amount possessed by the organization. The amount required was a function of the output diversity, division of labor, and level of performance. In combination the task uncertainty, division of labor, diversity of output, and level of performance determine the amount of information that must be processed.

Next the basic, mechanistic bureaucratic model was introduced along with explanations of its information processing capabilities. It was shown that hierarchical communication channels can coordinate large numbers of interdependent subtasks but have a limited capacity to remake decisions. In response four strategies were articulated which either reduced the amount of information or increased the capacity of the organization to process more information. The way to decrease information was to reduce the determinants of the amount of information: performance levels, diversity, and division of labor. The strategies to increase capacity were to invest in the formal, hierarchical information process and to introduce lateral decision processes. Each of these strategies has its effects and costs. Subsequent chapters will discuss each strategy in more detail. In addition, case studies will be presented which highlight the various choices.

NOTES

1. James G. March and Herbert A. Simon, *Organizations* (New York: John Wiley, 1958), 142–150.

2. For a more detailed discussion of hierarchical arrangements, see James C. Emery, *Organizational Planning and Control Systems* (New York: Macmillan, 1969), 11–12.

3. There are two aspects to this problem. First, individuals may choose behaviors which are ineffective because they do not have the information or knowledge to make a rational choice. This is the cognitive problem addressed here. The other aspect is that individuals may have goals which are different from organizational goals. Processes for dealing with this problem have been discussed already in this series. See Richard Beckhard, *Organization Development: Strategies and Models* (Reading, Mass.: Addison-Wesley, 1969), 35–40.

4. Arthur Stinchcombe, "Bureaucratic and Craft Administration of Production: A Comparative Study," *Administrative Science Quarterly* (September 1959): 168–187.

5. Ibid., p. 170.

6. Here again there are motivation questions. How difficult should the goals be? Should incentives be attached to them? Should the manager participate in setting them? See John Campbell, Marvin Dunette, Edward Lawler, III, and Karl Weick, Jr., *Managerial Behavior, Performance and*

Effectiveness (New York: McGraw-Hill, 1970), Chapter 15.

7. James G. March and Herbert A. Simon, *Organizations* (New York: John Wiley, 1958); and Richard Cyert and James G. March, *A Behav-* *ioral Theory of the Firm* (Englewood Cliffs, N.J.: Prentice-Hall, 1963).

8. Paul Lawrence and Jay Lorsch, *Organization and Environment* (Boston: Division of Research, Harvard Business School, 1967), Chapter 3.

CHAPTER V

Power and Politics

The neatest thing about power is that we all understand it. We may have first discovered power as children when our mothers said, "Don't do that!" And we learn about power in organizations as soon as we go to school. Most of us have a pretty good intuitive grasp of the basic concepts of organizational power by the time we reach the third grade. So, the newest thing about power in organizations is not our understanding of it, but rather our intellectualizing about it.

Ordinary people—as well as scholars—have hesitated to talk about power. First, for many, power is not a subject for polite conversation. We have often equated power with force, brutality, unethical behavior, manipulation, connivance, and subjugation. Rosabeth Moss Kanter (1979) contends that "power is America's last dirty word. It is easier to talk about money—and much easier to talk about sex—than it is to talk about power." Second, many of the important pieces from the power school are quite recent, and the theoretical grounding of the school is not as advanced as it is in the classical, "modern" structural, and systems schools. For both of the above reasons, fewer people have been exposed to analyses of organizational power. So, it will be useful to start our introduction to the power and politics school by contrasting some of its basic assumptions with those of its immediate predecessors, the "modern" structural and systems schools.

In both the "modern" structural and the systems schools of organization theory, organizations are assumed to be institutions whose primary purpose is to accomplish established goals. Those goals are set by people in positions of formal authority. In these two schools, the primary questions for organization theory involve how best to design and manage organizations to achieve their declared purposes effectively and efficiently. The personal preferences of organizational members are restrained by systems of formal rules, authority, and by norms of rational behavior (see Chapters III and IV for more complete discussions).

The power school rejects these assumptions about organizations as being naive, unrealistic, and therefore of minimal practical value. Instead, organizations are viewed as being complex systems of individuals and coalitions, each having its own interests, beliefs, values, preferences, perspectives, and perceptions. The coalitions compete with each other continuously for scarce organizational resources. Conflict is inevitable. Influence—and the power and political activities through which influence is acquired and maintained—is the primary "weapon" for use in competition and conflicts. Thus, power, politics, and influence are critically important and permanent facts of organizational life.

304

Only rarely are organizational goals established by those in positions of formal authority. Goals result from ongoing maneuvering and bargaining among individuals and coalitions. Coalitions tend to be transitory: They shift with issues and often cross vertical and horizontal organizational boundaries. (For example, they may include people at several levels in the organizational hierarchy and from different product, functional, and/or geographical divisions or departments.) Thus, organizational goals change with shifts in the balance of power among coalitions. J. V. Baldridge (1971) found that organizations had many conflicting goals, and different sets of goals take priority as the balance of power changes among coalitions—as different coalitions gain and use enough power to control them. Why are organizational goals so important in the theory of organizational power and politics? Because they provide the "official" rationale and the legitimacy for resource allocation decisions.

Power relations are permanent features of organizations primarily because specialization and the division of labor result in the creation of many small, interdependent organization units with varying degrees of importance. The units compete with each other for scarce resources—as well as with the transitory coalitions. As James D. Thompson points out in *Organizations in Action* (1967), a lack of balance in the interdependence among units sets the stage for the use of power relations. Jeffery Pfeffer emphasizes this point in his "Preface" to *Power in Organizations* (1981): "Those persons and those units that have the responsibility for performing the more critical tasks in the organization have a natural advantage in developing and exercising power in the organization. . . .power is first and foremost a structural phenomenon, and should be understood as such."

The "modern" structural school of organization theory places high importance on "legitimate authority" (authority that flows down through the organizational hierarchy) and formal rules (promulgated and enforced by those in authority) to ensure that organizational behavior is directed toward the attainment of established organizational goals. Structuralists tend to define power synonymously with authority. In contrast, John Kotter (1985) argues that in today's organizational world, the gap is increasing between the power one needs to get the job done and the power that automatically comes with the job (authority). The power and politics school views authority as only one of the many available sources of organizational power, and power is aimed in *all* directions—not just down through the hierarchy. For example, Robert W. Allen and Lyman W. Porter divide their 1983 book of readings on *Organizational Influence Processes* into three parts. Following the introductory overview, the remaining parts are on downward influence (authority), lateral influence, and upward influence.

Other forms of power and influence often prevail over authority-based power. Several of this chapter's selections identify different sources of power in organizations, so we list only a few here as examples: control over scarce resources (for example, office space, discretionary funds, current and accurate information, and time and skill to work on projects), easy access to others who are perceived as having power (for example, important customers or clients, members of the board of directors, or someone else with formal authority or who controls scarce resources), a central place in a potent coalition, ability to "work the organizational rules" (knowing how to get things done or to prevent others from getting things done), and credibility (for, example, that one's word can be trusted).

By now, you should be wondering just what power, politics, and influence are. Many definitions have been proposed, and Jeffrey Pfeffer explores the advantages and limitations of some of the better ones in his chapter on "Understanding the Role of Power in Decision Making," from his 1981 book, *Power in Organizations*, which is reprinted here. We like the following definition of power, which is a blending of definitions proposed by Gerald Salancik and Jeffrey Pfeffer (1977), and Robert Allen and Lyman Porter (1983): "Power is the ability to get things done the way one wants them done; it is the latent ability to influence people." It offers several advantages for understanding organizations. First, it emphasizes the relativity of power. As Pfeffer points out, "power is context or relationship specific. A person is not 'powerful' or 'powerless' in general, but only with respect to other social actors in a specific social relationship."

Second, the phrase "the way one wants them done" is a potent reminder that conflict and the use of power often are over the choice of methods, means, approaches, and/or "turf." They are not limited to battles about outcomes. This point is important because power is primarily a structural phenomenon—a consequence of the division of labor and specialization. For example, competing organizational coalitions often form around professions: hospital nurses versus paramedics, sociologists versus mathematicians in a college of liberal arts, business school–educated staff specialists versus generalists from the "school of hard knocks" in a production unit, or social workers versus educators in a center for incarcerated youth. Organizational conflicts among people representing different professions, educational backgrounds, sexes, and ages frequently do not involve goals. They center on questions about the "right" of a profession, academic discipline, sex, or age group to exercise its perception of its "professional rights," to control the way things will be done, or to protect its "turf" and status. Why is this point important? Because it reemphasizes that organizational behavior and decisions frequently are not "rational"—as the word is used by the "modern" structural school and the systems school, meaning "directed toward the accomplishment of established organizational goals." Thus, this definition of power highlights a fundamental reason why the power and politics school rejects the basic assumptions of the "modern" structural school and the systems school as being naive and unrealistic, and considers those theories of organization to be of minimal value.

Jeffrey Pfeffer's chapter, "Understanding the Role of Power in Decision Making," provides an excellent synopsis of the power and politics perspective on organizations. We have placed it first among this chapter's selections in order to provide the reader with a macroperspective on the school. His basic theme is that power and politics are fundamental concepts for understanding behavior in organizations. He defines the concepts of power, authority, and organizational politics, and he identifies the "place of power" in the literature of organization theory.

Discussions of power and politics go back to Aristotle and other writers from antiquity. All of political theory is concerned with the exercise of power. Herbert Kaufman (1964) has even thought to apply the ancient field of political theory to the comparatively young concepts of organization theory. Those who would limit themselves to the wisdom of modern writers would seem to be putting intellectual blinders on themselves. Remember, it is frequently said of those who rise to rule the nation's largest organizations that they are "natural politicians."

One of the most influential of all political theorists, is Niccolo Machiavelli (1469–1527), the most famous management and political analyst of the Italian Renaissance. His book of advice to would-be leaders, *The Prince* (1513), is the progenitor of all "how to succeed" books that advocate practical rather than moral actions. In 1967, Antony Jay reintroduced Machiavelli's concepts to a modern audience with his best-selling book, *Management and Machiavelli: An Inquiry into the Politics of Corporate Life*, which took Machiavelli's insights for managing a state and applied them to the problem of power and politics in organizations. In his introductory chapter, reprinted here, Jay draws advice for modern managers from Machiavelli's principles for governing conquered colonies. He shows how Machiavelli's thinking can be applied effectively to the managing of modern organizations; for example, in establishing control over merged and acquired firms, and in deciding between conducting functions in-house or contracting them out. Jay concludes that Machiavelli's principles are as valid now as they were four hundred and fifty years ago, because they are "rooted in human nature."

David Mechanic's influential and pioneering 1962 *Administrative Science Quarterly* article, "Sources of Power of Lower Participants in Complex Organizations," which is reprinted here, examines sources of influence and power that can be aimed at targets who possess more formal authority than the potential "influencer" possesses. As John Kotter (1977) points out, power is related to dependence, and lower-level organizational members have an arsenal of weapons with which to make others dependent upon them. They include expertise, effort and interest, attractiveness (or charisma), location and position in the organization, coalitions, and rules. This is an intellectualization of something we all know instinctively—that some people are treated like prima donnas or "get away with murder" in organizations because they possess some special skill that gives them power in the context of their organization. The most ready examples are "Hawkeye" and "Trapper" from the MASH movie and television series. If they were not badly needed surgeons at the battlefront, they would have been court-martialled years ago.

In her 1979 *Harvard Business Review* article, "Power Failure in Management Circuits," which is reprinted here, Rosabeth Moss Kanter argues that executive and managerial power is a necessary ingredient for moving organizations toward their goals. "Power can mean efficacy and capacity" for organizations. The ability of managers to lead effectively cannot be predicted by studying their styles or traits; it requires knowledge of a leader's real power sources. Kanter identifies three groups of positions within organizations that are particularly susceptible to powerlessness: first line supervisors, staff professionals, and top executives. However, she carefully distinguishes between "power" and "dominance, control, and oppression." Her primary concern is that at higher organizational levels, the power to "punish, to prevent, to sell off, to reduce, to fire, all without appropriate concern for consequences" grows, but the power needed for positive accomplishments does not. Managers who perceive themselves as being powerless and who think their subordinates are discounting them tend to use more dominating or punishing forms of influence. Thus, in large organizations, powerlessness (or perceived powerlessness) can be a more substantive problem than possession of power. By empowering others, leaders actually can acquire more "productive power"—the power needed to accomplish organizational goals. "Power Failure in Management Circuits" also contains an embedded subarticle on the particular problems that power poses for women managers.

Henry Mintzberg describes his 1983 book *Power in and Around Organizations* as a discussion of a theory of organizational power. Organizational behavior is viewed as a power game. The "players" are "influencers" with varying personal needs, who attempt to control organizational decisions and actions. "Thus, to understand the behavior of the organization, it is necessary to understand which influencers are present, what needs each seeks to fulfill in the organization, and how each is able to exercise power to fulfill them." His chapter, "The Power Game and the Players," which is reprinted here, focuses on the "influencers"—who they are and where their power comes from. Eleven groups of possible influencers are listed: five are in the "external coalition" and six in the "internal coalition." The external coalition consists of the owners, "associates" (suppliers, clients, trading partners, and competitors), employee associations (unions and professional associations), the organization's various publics (at large), and the corporate directors (which includes representatives from the other four groups in the external coalition and also some internal influencers). The internal coalition is comprised of six groups of influencers: the chief executive officer, operators (the organization's "producers"), line managers, analysts (staff specialists), and the support staff. The final "actor" in Mintzberg's internal coalition is the ideology of the organization—"the set of beliefs shared by its internal influencers that distinguishes it from other organizations." Factors like organizational ideology actually are more representative of our final school of organization theory, the organizational culture school, which is discussed in the next chapter.

BIBLIOGRAPHIC REFERENCES

Allen, R. W., & Porter, L. W. (1983). *Organizational influence processes.* Glenview, IL: Scott, Foresman.

Baldridge, J. V. (1971). *Power and conflict in the university.* New York: John Wiley & Sons.

Cummings, L. L., & Staw, B. M. (Eds.). (1981). *Research in organizational behavior* (Vol. 3). Greenwich, CT: JAI Press.

Cyert, R. M., & March, J. G. (1963). *A behavioral theory of the firm.* Englewood Cliffs, NJ: Prentice-Hall.

Jay, A. (1967). *Management and Machiavelli.* New York: Holt, Rinehart & Winston.

Kanter, R. M. (1977). *Men and women of the corporation.* New York: Basic Books.

Kanter, R. M. (July-August 1979). Power failure in management circuits. *Harvard Business Review, 57,* 65–75.

Kaufman, H. (March 1964). Organization theory and political theory. *American Political Science Review, 58,* 5–14.

Kotter, J. P. (July-August 1977). Power, dependence, and effective management. *Harvard Business Review, 55,* 125–136.

Kotter, J. P. (1985). *Power and influence: Beyond formal authority.* New York: Free Press.

Mechanic, D. (December 1962). Sources of power of lower participants in complex organizations. *Administrative Science Quarterly, 7,* 3, 349–364.

Mintzberg, H. (1983). *Power in and around organizations.* Englewood Cliffs, NJ: Prentice-Hall.

Pfeffer, J. (1981). *Power in organizations.* Boston: Pitman Publishing.

Porter, L. W., Allen, R. W., & Angle, H. L. (1981). The politics of upward influence in organizations. In L. L. Cummings & B. M. Staw (Eds.), *Research in Organizational Behavior,* Vol. 3 (pp. 408–422). Greenwich, CT: JAI Press.

Salancik, G. R., & Pfeffer, J. (1977). Who gets power—and how they hold on to it: A strategic-contingency model of power. *Organizational Dynamics, 5,* 2–21.

Thompson, J. D. (1967). *Organizations in action.* New York: McGraw-Hill.

Tushman, M. L. (April 1977). A political approach to organizations: A review and rationale. *The Academy of Management Review, 2,* 206–216.

Yates, D., Jr. (1985). *The politics of management.* San Francisco: Jossey-Bass.

27
Understanding the Role of Power in Decision Making
Jeffrey Pfeffer

More than 40 years ago Harold Lasswell (1936) defined politics as the study of who gets what, when, and how. Certainly, who gets what, when, and how, are issues of fundamental importance in understanding formal organizations. Nevertheless, organizational politics and organizational power are both topics which are made conspicuous by their absence in management and organization theory literature (Allen, et al., 1979). Why?

It is certainly not because the terms *power* and *politics* are concepts used infrequently in everyday conversation. Both are often used to explain events in the world around us. Richard Nixon's behavior while in the presidency has been ascribed to a need for power. Budget allocations among various federal programs are described as being the result of politics. Success in obtaining a promotion may be attributed to an individual's ability to play office politics. The fact that certain business functions (such as finance) or occupational specialties (such as law) are frequently important in organizations is taken to reflect the power of those functions or occupations. There are few events that are not ascribed to the effects of power and politics. As Dahl (1957: 201) noted, "The

Source: Jeffrey Pfeffer, *Power in Organizations* (Marshfield, Mass.: Pitman Publishing, 1981), 1–32.

concept of power is as ancient and ubiquitous as any that social theory can boast."

Power and politics are not neglected because they lack relevance in explaining what occurs in organizations. The theme of this book is that these are fundamental concepts for understanding behavior in organizations. For the moment, we can briefly summarize this literature by noting that there is evidence that power affects outcomes ranging from the allocation of budgets to organizational subunits (Pfeffer and Salancik, 1974; Pfeffer, Salancik, and Leblebici, 1976; Salancik and Pfeffer, 1974), to succession to executive and administrative positions (Zald, 1965; Pfeffer and Salancik, 1978: Ch. 9) to the design and redesign of formal organizational structures (Pfeffer, 1978a).

Power has been neglected for several reasons. First, the concept of power is itself problematic in much of the social science literature. In the second place, while power is something, it is not everything. There are other competing perspectives for understanding organizational decision making. These perspectives are frequently persuasive, if for no other reason than that they conform more closely to socially held values of rationality and effectiveness. And third, the concept of power is troublesome to the socialization of managers and the practice of management because of its implications and connotations.

Therefore, we begin at the beginning, with a discussion of these issues as they affect the study and analysis of power and politics in organizations. It is important to understand what power is and what it isn't; what alternative perspectives exist on organizational choice processes; and the place of power in the organization theory literature. With that as background, it will be possible then to proceed to the analysis of organizations using a political perspective.

THE CONCEPT OF POWER

The very pervasiveness of the concept of power, referred to in the earlier quote from Robert Dahl, is itself a cause for concern about the utility of the concept in assisting us to understand behavior in organizations. Bierstedt (1950: 730) noted that the more things a term could be applied to the less precise was its meaning. Dahl (1957: 201) wrote, ". . . a Thing to which people attach many labels with subtly or grossly different meanings in many different cultures and times is probably not a Thing at all but many Things." March (1966) has suggested that in being used to explain almost everything, the concept of power can become almost a tautology, used to explain that which cannot be explained by other ideas, and incapable of being disproved as an explanation for actions and outcomes.

Most definitions of power include an element indicating that power is the capability of one social actor to overcome resistance in achieving a desired objective or result. For instance, Dahl (1957: 202–203) defined power as a relation among social actors in which one social actor, A, can get another social actor B, to do something that B would not otherwise have done. Power becomes defined as force, and more specifically, force sufficient to change the probability of B's behavior from what it would have been in the absence of the application of the force. Emerson's (1962: 32) definition is quite similar: "The power of actor A over actor B is the amount of resistance on the part of B which can be potentially overcome by A." Bierstedt (1950: 738) also wrote of power as having incidence only in cases of social opposition. Power may be tricky to define, but it is not that difficult to recognize: "the ability of those who possess power to bring about the outcomes they desire" (Salancik and Pfeffer, 1977b: 3).

It is generally agreed that power characterizes relationships among social actors. A given social actor, by which we mean an individual, subunit, or organization, has more power with respect to some social actors and less power with respect to others. Thus, power is context or relationship specific. A person is not "powerful" or "powerless" in general, but only with respect to other social actors in a specific social relationship. To say, for example, that the legal department in a specific firm is powerful, implies power with respect to other departments within that firm during a specific period of time. That same legal department may not be at all powerful with respect to its interactions with the firm's outside counsel, various federal and state regulatory agencies, and so forth. And, the power of the department can and probably will change over time.

Although power is relationship or context specific, it is not necessarily specifically related to a limited set of decision issues. Whether or not power is generalizable across decision issues is an empirical question, not a matter of definition. Indeed, one of the interesting aspects in the study of power in organizations is the determination of under what circumstances power is general across decisions, and in what cases the power of a particular social actor is more issue-specific.

Most studies of power in organizations have focused on hierarchical power, the power of supervisors over subordinates, or bosses over employees. The vertical, hierarchical dimension of power is important in understanding social life, but it is not the only dimension of power. As Perrow (1970: 59) wrote, "It is my impression that for all the discussion and research regarding power in organizations, the preoccupation with interpersonal power has led us to neglect one of the most obvious aspects of this subject: in complex organizations, tasks are divided up between a few major departments or subunits, and all of these subunits are not likely to be equally powerful." Implicit in this statement is the recognition that power is, first of all, a structural phenomenon, created by the division of labor and departmentation that characterize the specific organization or set of organizations being investigated. It is this more structural approach to power that constitutes the focus of this book, although at times we will consider what individual characteristics affect the exercise of structurally determined power.

It should be evident why power is somewhat tricky to measure and operationalize. In order to assess power, one must be able to estimate a) what would have happened in the absence of the exercise of power; b) the intentions of the actor attempting to exercise power; and c) the effect of actions taken by that actor on the probability that what was desired would in fact be likely to occur. Because the ability to diagnose power distributions is critical to understanding and acting effectively in organizations, we will consider the diagnosis of power in some detail in the next chapter. For now, it should be recognized that the definition and assessment of power are both controversial and problematic.

THE CONCEPT OF AUTHORITY

It is important to distinguish between power and authority. In any social setting, there are certain beliefs and practices that come to be accepted within that setting. The acceptance of these practices and values, which can include the distribution of influence within the social setting, binds together those within the setting, through their common perspective. Activities which are accepted and expected within a context are then said to be legitimate within that context. The distribution of power within a social setting can also become legitimated over time, so that those within the setting expect and value a certain pattern of influence. When power is so legitimated, it is denoted as authority. Weber (1947) emphasized the critical role of legitimacy in the exercise of power. By transforming power into authority, the exercise of influence is transformed in a subtle but important way. In social situations, the exercise of power typically has costs. Enforcing one's way over others requires the expenditure of resources, the making of commitments, and a level of effort which can be undertaken only when the issues at hand are relatively important. On the other hand, the exercise of authority, power which has become legitimated, is expected and desired in the social context. Thus, the exercise of authority, far from diminishing through use, may actually serve to enhance the amount of authority subsequently possessed.

Dornbusch and Scott (1975), in their book on evaluation in organizations, made a similar point with respect to the evaluation process. They noted that in formal organizations, some people have the right to set criteria, to sample output, and to apply the criteria to the output that is sampled. Persons with such authority or evaluation rights are expected to engage in these authorized activities, and, instead of being punished for doing so, are punished when they fail to do so.

The transformation of power into authority is an important process, for it speaks to the issue of the institutionalization of social control. As such, we will return to this issue when political strategies are considered and when we take up the topic of institutionalized power. For the moment, it is sufficient to note that within formal organizations, norms and expectations develop that make the exercise of influence expected and accepted. Thus, social control of one's behavior by others becomes an expected part of organizational life. Rather than seeing the exercise of influence within organizations as a contest of strength or force, power, once it is transformed through legitimation into authority, is not resisted. At that point, it no longer depends on the resources or determinants that may have produced the power in the first place.

The transformation of power into authority can be seen most clearly in the relationship between supervisors and subordinates in work organizations. As Mechanic (1962) noted, lower level organizational members have, in reality, a great amount of power. If they refused to accept and accede to the instructions provided by higher level managers, those managers would have difficulty carrying out sanctions and operating the organization. Furthermore, the lower level participants have power that comes from specialized knowledge about the work process and access to information that higher level managers may not have. Thus, Mechanic (1962) argued, what is interesting is not that subordinates accept the instructions of managers because of the greater power possessed by the managers. Rather, it is interesting that in spite of the considerable degree of power possessed by lower level employees, these employees seldom attempt to exercise their power or to resist the instructions of their managers.

The point that is being made is important. Although it is true that the manager may have the power to fire employees, to control the amount of money they get paid, and to affect their promotion opportunities in the future, in most organizations such powers are severely limited and, in any event, are seldom exercised. Employees do not consciously compare their power (to withhold labor services, to quit, to withhold information, to do the work poorly) with the power that the manager has (to use and withhold rewards and sanctions), and then decide whether or not to comply depending on the relative power balance. Rather, most of the time in most work settings the authority of the manager to direct the work activities is so legitimated and taken for granted, that issues of relative power and sanctions seldom become consciously considered. Subordinates obey not because the supervisor has the power to compel them to; rather, they follow reasonable instructions related to the control of their work behavior because they expect that such directions will be given and followed. In this way, power becomes transformed into authority, and control can be exercised almost regardless of the balance of power possessed by the interacting groups.

When social understanding and social consensus develops to accept, ratify, and even prefer the distribution of power, then the power becomes legitimated and becomes authority. Authority is maintained not only by the resources or sanctions that produced the power, but also by the social pressures and social norms that sanction the power distribution and which define it as normal and acceptable. Such social acceptance and social approval adds stability to the situation and makes the exercise of power easier and more effective. Legitimation, of course, occurs in a specific social context, and what is legitimate in one setting may be illegitimate in another. The degree and kind of supervisor-subordinate control exercised in U.S. organizations, for instance, may be perceived as illegitimate in the organizations of countries where there is more worker self-management and industrial democracy. Legitimation of power is thus ultimately problematic and far from inevitable. The examination of the conditions under which power and social control become legitimated and transformed into authority is an important undertaking in trying to understand the governance and control of organizations.

DEFINITION OF ORGANIZATIONAL POLITICS

The task of defining the term organizational politics is as difficult as that of defining power. The problem is to distinguish between political activity and organizational or administrative activity in general. As in the case of power, if politics refers to all forms of administrative or managerial action, then the term becomes meaningless because it includes every behavior.

From Lasswell's (1936) definition of politics as who gets what, when, and how, and from Wildavsky's (1979) descriptions of the politics of the budgetary process, the inference is that politics involves how differing preferences are resolved in conflicts over the allocation of scarce resources. Thus, politics involves activities which attempt to influence decisions over critical issues that are not readily resolved through the introduction of new data and in which there are differing points of view. For our purposes, organizational politics will be defined as:

> Organizational politics involves those activities taken within organizations to acquire, develop, and use power and other resources to obtain one's preferred outcomes in a situation in which there is uncertainty or dissensus about choices.

If power is a force, a store of potential influence through which events can be affected, politics involves those activities or behaviors through which power is developed and used in organizational settings. Power is a property of the system at rest; politics is the study of power in action. An individual, subunit, or department may have power within an organizational context at some period of time; politics involves the exercise of power to get something accomplished, as well as those activities which are undertaken to expand the power already possessed or the scope over which it can be exercised. This definition is similar to that provided by Allen, et al. (1979: 77): "Organizational politics involve intentional acts of influence to enhance or protect the self-interest of individuals or groups."

From the definition of power, it is clear that political activity is activity which is undertaken to overcome some resistance or opposition. Without opposition or contest within the organization, there is neither the need nor the expectation that one would observe political activity. And, because political activity is focused around the acquisition and use of power, it can be distinguished from activity involved in making decisions which uses rational or bureaucratic procedures. In both rational and bureaucratic models of choice, there is no place for and no presumed effect of political activity. Decisions are made to best achieve the organization's goals, either by relying on the best information and options that have been uncovered, or by using rules and procedures which have evolved in the organization. Political activity, by contrast, implies the conscious effort to muster and use force to overcome opposition in a choice situation.

It is useful to contrast the definition adopted here with another one found in the literature. Mayes and Allen (1977: 675) defined organizational politics as:

> Organizational politics is the management of influence to obtain ends not sanctioned by the organization or to obtain sanctioned ends through non-sanctioned influence means.

This definition has two problems. First, what is or what is not sanctioned within an organization, in terms of both means and ends, are the results of power and political activity within the organization. To say that an activity is not sanctioned is to say that those undertaking the activity do not have the power in the organization to have their definition of the world generally accepted. Under the definition proposed by Mayes and Allen (1977), the powerful would not engage in political activity (since what they do is likely to be organizationally sanctioned) and the powerless would almost inevitably engage in political activity. The second problem with this definition is that it gives the concept of organizational politics a sense of sinfulness. This may be nice for the sales of books with such a term in the title, but it diverts attention from the inevitability of power and politics in organizations as well as from the functional outcomes that often emerge from political activity.

To assess the consequences of political activity on an a priori basis as implied by Mayes and Allen, is to presume that the system knows in advance what is best for it. Influence means that are not sanctioned, which are used to accomplish nonsanctioned ends, are categorized by Mayes and Allen (1977: 675) as being organizationally dysfunctional political behavior. Such a categorization is less likely to be readily accepted when applied to a larger political context, such as the protests against the war in Vietnam. These protests sometimes used nonsanctioned means to accomplish an end which was clearly not sanctioned by the authorities. The definition put forward by Mayes and Allen is important because it is a reflection of the schizophrenia with which concepts such as power and politics have been treated in the literature. Power and politics are fine for understanding and diagnosing events on a national or governmental level; at the level of formal organizations, however, power and politics are considered to be either pejorative terms or illegitimate as analytical concepts for use in understanding bureaucratic or rational systems of decision making.

It is clearly important to be able to distinguish between political activity and administrative action in general, and to distinguish between outcomes produced by social power and outcomes that occur by chance, because of precedent, or because of the application of rational decision procedures. At the same time, analysis should not be unnecessarily diverted by the interminable definitional and theoretical controversies that fill the literature surrounding these concepts. In a study of eighty-seven managerial personnel, Allen, et al. (1979: 77–78) reported:

> Respondents were asked to describe organizational political tactics and personal characteristics of effective political actors. . . . No definition of organizational politics was given to the respondents, nor did any of them ask what was meant by the term.

Similarly, in an interview study of twenty-nine department heads at the University of Illinois, during which each respondent was asked to rate the power of his and the other departments on the campus, only one department head found it necessary to ask for clarification of what was meant by the term *power*. It seems fair to state that *power* and *politics*

are terms that have some shared meanings in the world of organizational actors. We shall see when we consider the assessment of power in organizations that such shared meanings guide and are anchored in consensually shared judgments concerning the distribution of power in organizational settings.

THE PLACE OF POWER IN ORGANIZATION THEORY LITERATURE

If *power* and *politics* are terms which are used frequently in everyday conversation, understood at least at an intuitive level by practicing managers and administrators, and, as we shall demonstrate later, can help account for careers, budgets, structure, the relative size of personnel components, and their persistence over time, why then is power neglected in the literature of organization theory? One reason has already been suggested—the issues associated with the definition and measurement of these concepts. A second issue, that of competing perspectives for analyzing organizational choice processes, will be considered later in the chapter. For the moment, consider the place of power in the literature of organization theory and the role served by such literature.

Examination of the major textbooks now current in the field will indicate that the subject of power is either not mentioned at all in the subject index or, if it is, it receives short shrift in terms of the number of pages devoted to it. When the subject of power is found in the index, it is frequently associated with a discussion of the individual bases of power (e.g., French and Raven, 1968) or the need for power. Size, technology, and environment all receive much more time and attention, even in those books with a presumably more sociological perspective. And, in specialized books dealing with topics such as organization design or organization development, power typically receives no mention at all, even though it is a particularly critical variable for some of these more specialized concerns.

It is, of course, possible that this book and its treatment of organizations seriously overstates the importance of power and politics as phenomena of concern and as explanations for behavior in organizations. This argument however, not only flies in the face of a small but growing body of empirical research, but also the popular explanations for organizational phenomena which are found in sources such as *Fortune, Business Week,* or the *Wall Street Journal.* If power is unimportant, it is not only this author that has been fooled; I have plenty of company in the business press.

A more likely explanation for the neglect of power in the management and organizational behavior literature is found by considering the role of management writing in the management process, and the position of a topic such as power as implied by the various functions served by management writing. The argument to be developed is relatively straightforward: management writing serves a variety of functions; in virtually all of these functions there is a strong component of ideology and values; topics such as power and politics are basically incompatible with the values and ideology being developed; therefore, it is reasonable, if not theoretically useful, to ignore topics which detract from the functions being served by the writing, and this includes tending to ignore or to downplay the topics of power and politics.

To ask what functions are served by management writing, we can begin by asking who reads management books.

The answer is that there are three important categories of persons who read management books, though the books they read are not necessarily the same: students in undergraduate and graduate programs in management and administration who read the books to acquire knowledge about the profession and practice of management; practicing managers and administrators in public and private sector organizations; and the general public, including those not involved with or in private business organizations. Consider next, what books or writings are needed in each case.

In the case of students, there is little doubt that one of the important functions of business education is socialization. This statement reflects both the more general importance of socialization in the educational process, and the specific prominence of socialization with respect to certain occupations and professions. It is not in just the fields of medicine and law that socialization plays an important part in the educational process. Although less frequently empirically examined, there are important considerations of socialization in the education of young, aspiring managers (e.g. Schein, 1968). Socialization involves the inculcation of norms and values that are central to the profession and that are, not incidentally, useful to the organizations in which the professionals are going to work. There is no norm so central to the existing practice and ideology of management as the norm of rationality. The political purposes served by this norm will be developed in more detail in Chapters 5 and 6, but will be briefly summarized here. Rationality and rational choice models focus attention on the development of technologies to more effectively achieve a goal or set of goals, such as profit or efficiency. Concern is directed toward the development of alternatives, the development of sophisticated techniques for evaluating the alternatives, their possible consequences, and the assembling of information that facilitates the evaluation of performance along these specified dimensions. What is less salient and less central in this process of rational choice is the origin of these objectives or criteria and who benefits and who loses by having decisions made to optimize these particular decision criteria as opposed to others.

It is, we are suggesting, not by accident that in choosing among alternatives given certain specified preferences (March, 1978) the role of preferences has been neglected in theories of choice, relative to the role of technologies. It is around preferences, and the values and beliefs implicit in these preferences, that conflicts of interest emerge. And such conflicts may cause a diversion of effort from goal attainment which is not favored by those whose goals are being served well by the present arrangement. The point is that, by even raising the issue of preferences or criteria as problematic, the institutionalized nature of goals such as profits or efficiency is challenged and is threatened by the mere fact of the challenge. It is in this sense that all normative theories of organization, whether within the domains of economics, organizational design, organizational development, or whatever, are inevitably political; it is also the case that most or perhaps all of the descriptive theories are equally political. These theories are political in the sense that each takes for granted certain assumptions about the world and how it operates, thereby causing the indoctrination of these assumptions. The result is the unconscious, or at best semiconscious, acceptance of the implicit values by a widely varying set of participants.

Some actors may benefit from the application of these values and some may lose. This same point has been nicely developed by Walter Nord (1974) in his critique of modern human resource management theory. It is equally and inevitably applicable to all organization theory.

In the socialization of professional managers, there are some components which are distinctly different from the socialization of other professionals. First, in contrast to doctors, lawyers, and to a lesser extent accountants, the professional manager will not practice in a relatively small organization with the legal structure of a partnership. Rather, he or she will work in a much larger organization which is legally structured as a corporation. The manager, then, can be expected to operate in a setting substantially more bureaucratized and in which there is a lesser likelihood of attaining such a great amount of ownership or control. Thus, the socialization must focus not so strongly on developing values that will serve the professional in solo or small group practice, but rather that will facilitate the manager's integration into large, formalized bureaucracies. Clearly, the acceptance of legitimate authority as implemented through a hierarchical structure is more important in the socialization of managers. Such authority will be more readily accepted to the extent that it *is perceived* to be legitimate. Given the social values stressing universalism and rationality, any organizational authority system and decision-making apparatus that operates according to these values will appear to be more legitimate and will encourage compliance on the part of the managers.

To socialize students into a view of business that emphasizes power and politics would not only make the compliance to organizational authority and the acceptance of decision outcomes and procedures problematic, but also it might cause recruitment problems into the profession. It is certainly much more noble to think of oneself as developing skills toward the more efficient allocation and use of resources—implicitly for the greater good of society as a whole—than to think of oneself as engaged with other organizational participants in a political struggle over values, preferences, and definitions of technology. Technical rationality, as a component of the managerial task, provides legitimation and meaning for one's career, fulfilling a function similar to healing the sick for doctors, or serving the nation's system of laws and justice for attorneys.

For the second group of practicing managers, as well as for the student, the ideology of rationality and efficiency provides an explanation for career progress, or lack thereof, that is much more likely to lead to the acceptance of one's position rather than to an attempt at making a radical change. The theoretical foundations of economics, including human capital and labor market theories, emphasize the universalistic nature of the wage determination process. It is scarcely an exaggeration to note that the inclusion of socioeconomic background in multiple regressions explaining wages or change in wages is what distinguishes a sociological from an economic approach to the issues of stratification and inequality. The theory that efficiency considerations, bureaucratic rationality, or both, drive out power and politics, reassures those in or entering into the corporate world, that their success in rising through the ranks will be more a function of their marginal product than of their ability to diagnose power distributions and play politics. Inequality in outcomes becomes justified by the presumed decision-making processes which produce such outcomes; this process is deemed legitimate and accepted because of its association with valued social ideals. This acceptance of one's place and rewards in the organization clearly can discourage the unionization of the workforce, and can help to provide continuing motivation and purposefulness to work when career blockages or other career problems occur.

In this way, the ideology of efficiency and rationality provides comforting explanations for practicing managers who find the progress of their careers blocked or less than what they might like, or feel a general sense of malaise about their work and their future. The invisible hands of marginal productivity and human capital have put them where they deserve to be. If power is to be considered at all, it is in terms of individually-oriented political strategies (e.g. Korda, 1975), which provide the managers with the illusion that, with a few handy hints, they can improve their lot in the organization. Explanations which focus on structural variables, as most of the explanations for power and politics developed here do, are less popular, as they provide no easy palliatives and imply a need for much more fundamental change in terms of affecting decision outcomes.

For the third set of readers of the management literature, the general public, the emphasis on rationality and efficiency and the deemphasis on power and politics, assures them that the vast power and wealth controlled by organizations is, indeed, being effectively and legitimately employed. In this sense, organization theory and economic theory frequently find themselves fulfilling similar roles in explaining the status quo in terms which both justify and legitimate it. The theory of perfect competition or markets argues that when market processes are allowed to operate unimpeded by the intervention of politicians or monopolists, the best allocation results are obtained. Even those writers who have noted the existence of transaction costs and resulting problems (e.g. Williamson, 1975) have argued from a premise assuming efficiency interests on the part of the various economic actors involved.

In a similar fashion, the literature of organizational behavior has been dominated by a parallel form of functionalism. The strategic contingencies theories of organizational design (Lawrence and Lorsch, 1967; Galbraith, 1973; Woodward, 1965; Pennings, 1975) argued that there existed some optimal organizational design, given the organization's technology, size or environmental uncertainty. The assumption was implicit in much of this work that if such contingencies could be uncovered, the implementation of the rational structures would be straightforward. The search for empirical regularities between context and structure presumes some functional imperative for organizations, as a collectivity, to be roughly in correspondence with the requirements of their technologies or environments. Discussion of the size of the administrative component (Pondy, 1969; Blau and Schoenherr, 1971), the degree of centralization and formalization present in organizations (Burns and Stalker, 1961; Thompson, 1967), and the degree of differentiation (Lawrence and Lorsch, 1967; Thompson, 1967), all proceeded from a premise of functional rationality, though only Thompson took pains to make this assumption explicit.

The ideology of functional rationality—decision making oriented toward the improvement of efficiency or performance—provides a legitimation of formal organizations, for the general public as well as for those working within specific organizations. Bureaucracies are, as Perrow (1972) argued, tremendous stores of resources and energy, both human and financial. Bureaucracies also represent concentrations of energy on a scale seldom seen in the history of the world. The legitimation and justification of these concentrations of power are clearly facilitated by theories arguing that efficiency, productivity, and effectiveness are the dominant dynamics underlying the operation of organizations.

To maintain that organizations are less than totally interested in efficiency, effectiveness or market performance is to suggest that it is legitimate to raise questions concerning the appropriateness of the concentration of power and energy they represent and makes it possible to introduce political concerns into the issues of corporate governance. The introduction of these concerns makes the present control arrangements less certain and permanent and would be resisted by all of those who benefit from the status quo.

The argument, then, is that the very literature of management and organizational behavior (as well, we might add, of much of economics, though that is a topic worthy of separate development) is itself political (Edelman, 1964), and causes support to be generated and opposition to be reduced as various conceptions of organizations are created and maintained in part through their very repetition. In this literature, efficiency-enhancing or profit-increasing behavior are not being taken as hypotheses about motivation and causes for action, but rather as accepted facts. Then, a theory is developed which is both consistent with these assumptions and finds excuses for why so much variation in actual decisions and behaviors is missed. Another way of seeing the very strong ideological basis and bias in organization theory is to contrast explanations of organizations developed in the U.S. with those found in the writings of European organizational scholars (e.g., Karpik, 197‿ ‿ozier, 1964). The European treatment of organizations and of knowledge about organizations takes a much more context-specific, historical view. Organizations are much more clearly related to the broader social issues of power and politics in the society and it is assumed that conceptions of organizations themselves are products of a social construction of reality which also constitutes an ingredient of politics played out on a macro-social level.

Two other sources are also consistent with our position concerning the ideological foundation and political use of organization theory and writings on management. Nehrbass (1979) recently reviewed several streams of research, including the quality of working life studies and the research dealing with participatory decision making, and noted that, in spite of limited empirical research results, certain normatively-valued conceptions remained not only prominent in the literature, but, in fact, the dominant point of view and accepted as established truth. The persistent misinterpretation of the data from the Hawthorne studies (Carey, 1967) is another instance of the willingness of researchers to let values rather than data structure their conclusions. We would add to Nehrbass' list the issue of the premises for decisions made within organizations. Efficiency, effectiveness and profit are normatively valued and legitimate, while conceptions of organizations as political systems are much less consistent with dominant ideology and values. Thus, research demonstrating the non-rationality of decision procedures in organizations or in individuals has been met with relative neglect. The theories of organizations found explicitly or implicitly stated in the principal textbooks and in scholarly research presume bureaucratically rational functional imperatives for management and organizations.

Baritz (1960) has undertaken one of the more systematic examinations of the relationship between research and knowledge on the one hand, and society on the other, in his study of the employment of social scientists in industry, the incorporation of social science, particularly industrial psychology, into management thought, and the consequences of this relationship in the development of critical social theory. Although Baritz focused primarily on the use of the employment relationship to control the direction and development of social science inquiry, it is clear that there are many other forms of influence. These include the part-time relationships afforded by consulting opportunities, business firm contributions to universities, business funding of research, and the employment of graduates trained in the various social science skills and ideologies.

Baritz presented details concerning the perceived increase of the importance of social science by business executives which developed during the twentieth century. He noted:

> American management came to believe in the importance of understanding human behavior because it became convinced that this was one sure way of improving its main weapon in the struggle for power, the profit margin (1960: 191–192).

This awareness on the part of management was encouraged by the claims made by social scientists concerning their utility in the solving of industrial problems.

Baritz argued that the cooperation between industry and social scientists, which was eagerly embraced by both parties, hindered the development of social science knowledge and its effective use in society more generally.

> As part of the bureaucratization of virtually every aspect of American life, most

industrial social scientists labored in industry as technicians, not as scientists . . . they were hemmed in by the very organization charts which they had helped to contrive. And the usual industrial social scientist, because he accepted the norms of the elite dominant in his society, was prevented from functioning critically, was compelled by his own ideology and the power of America's managers to supply the techniques helpful to managerial goals. In what should have been a healthful tension between mind and society, the industrial social scientist in serving the industrial elite had to abandon the wider obligations of the intellectual who is a servant of his own mind (Baritz, 1960: 194).

Research and recommendations were colored by and tailored to the wishes of those who either directly employed the social scientists or who indirectly employed them through the support of research and programs within universities. The response on the part of social scientists was, Baritz argued, to ignore this aspect of their work. As in the case of organization theory generally, issues of preferences, values and politics were submerged and therefore ignored. "From the pioneers in industrial psychology to the sophisticated human-relations experts of the 1950's, almost all industrial social scientists have either backed away from the political and ethical implications of their work or have faced these considerations from the point of view of management" (Baritz, 1960:199). Clearly, this was true for Mayo, one of the founders of the human relations movement, a researcher involved in the Hawthorne experiments, and an individual who has had a lasting impact on the direction taken by organizational research in the U.S. "Mayo throughout his inquiring and productive life ignored labor, power and politics" (Baritz, 1960: 200).

Baritz argued that because of the influence of the management elite on social science, the problems investigated tended to be both trivial and regarded from a point of view which either vindicated the status quo or accepted as starting premises certain goals, objectives, and values established by industry. This point has been echoed by Pugh (1966). Baritz's critique focused primarily on industrial psychology. It could be updated to include the research in organizations conducted since his study, and expanded to include other social sciences, including economics. What is important is not that science has come under these same influences in the same way that one might expect in considering power-dependence relationships. Rather, the critical thing is the extent to which, under the guise of objectivity and data, the ideological bases and premises of much of the study of organizations remain systematically submerged and ignored.

A study of the sociology of organizational science, although an interesting endeavor, is well beyond the scope of this book. Nevertheless, some casual observations about the political and ideological role of organizational behavior literature are in order. Consider a sampling of books randomly selected from the card catalogue of a major U.S. business school library with the terms power or politics in the title. Most of the books are by authors who are either European, political scientists, or sociologists. Few, if any, are in or from U.S. business schools. One could, in general, make the statement that the assumptions and topics covered by organization research are explainable by the political and social context in which researchers are working. This observation has already been made about social psychologists by Cartwright who noted:

It is true, of course, that the substantive content of the knowledge attained in any field of science is ultimately determined by the intrinsic nature of the phenomena under investigation, since empirical research is essentially a process of discovery with an internal logic of its own. But it is equally true that the knowledge attained is the product of a social system and, as such, is basically influenced by the properties of that system and by its cultural, social and political environment (1979: 82).

A study of the politics of knowledge in the organizational behavior area, which traces changes in research issues, conclusions, and expressed values and ideologies, and relates these to changes in funding patterns, consultancy, social values, and political trends in the society in general, and to cultural differences, would be productive in terms of developing data and explanations for the phenomena discussed in this section.

Models of organizations which emphasize power and politics have their own political problems. It is important for those analyzing organizations to be able to figure out the kind of analytical framework that can be most usefully employed to diagnose the particular organization of interest. Kaplan's (1964) parable of the hammer is relevant. Because one has a hammer, one tends to use it on everything and for every task. Similarly, there is a tendency to take a noncontingent approach to the analysis of organizations, and to see them all as rational, bureaucratic, or political. Just as it is difficult to play football with baseball equipment, it is difficult to diagnose or effectively operate in an organization unless its dominant paradigm or mode of operation is understood. Furthermore, in order to evaluate the validity of a political approach to organizational analysis, there must be some alternatives with which to compare the model. For both of these reasons—to place the political model in a broader context of

competing perspectives on organizational decision making and to raise issues relevant to diagnosing the form of system one is dealing with—we will describe the major contending models of organizational decision making.

RATIONAL CHOICE MODELS

The model of rational choice is prominent in the social choice literature. It is not only prescribed as being the best way to make choices in organizations, but frequently claims to be descriptive of actual choice processes as well. The rational model presumes that events are "purposive choices of consistent actors" (Allison, 1971: 11). It is important to recognize, therefore, that the rational model presumes and assumes that "behavior reflects purpose or intention" (Allison, 1971: 13). Behavior is not accidental, random, or rationalized after the fact; rather, purpose is presumed to pre-exist and behavior is guided by that purpose. With respect to understanding organizations or other social collectivities, the rational model further presumes that there is a unified purpose or set of preferences characterizing the entity taking the action. As Allison (1971: 28–29) has noted:

> What rationality adds to the concept of purpose is *consistency*: consistency among goals and objectives relative to a particular action; consistency in the application of principles in order to select the optimal alternative (emphasis in original).

The rational choice model presumes that there are goals and objectives that characterize organizations. As Friedland (1974) has noted, rationality cannot be defined apart from the existence of a set of goals. Thus, all rational choice models start with the assumption of a goal or consistent goal set. In the case of subjective expected utility maximization models (Edwards, 1954), the goals are called utilities for various outcomes, associated with the pleasure or pain producing properties of the outcomes. In the language of economics and management science, the goals are called the objectives or objective function to be maximized. Occasionally, goals are called preferences, referring to the states of the world the social actor prefers. Rational choice models require that these goals be consistent (March, 1976: 70).

Given a consistent set of goals, the next element in theories of rational choice is a set of decision-making alternatives to be chosen. Alternatives are presumed to be differentiable one from the other, so that each is uniquely identified. Such alternatives are produced by a search process. Until Simon (1957) introduced the concept of satisficing, it was generally assumed that search was costless and that large numbers of alternatives would be considered. Simon's contribution was to introduce the concept of bounded rationality, which held that persons had both limited capacities to process information and limited resources to devote to search activities. Thus a search for alternatives would be conducted only until a satisfactory alternative was uncovered. The concept of satisfaction was defined in terms of the social actor's level of aspiration (March and Simon, 1958).

Be they many or few, once a set of alternatives are uncovered, the next step in the rational decision-making process involves the assessment of the likely outcomes or consequences of the various possible courses of action. If there is risk or uncertainty involved, then estimates of the probability of the occurrence of various consequences would be used in making statements about the values of the consequences of different choices. At this stage in the decision process, it is assumed that consequences can be fully and completely anticipated, albeit with some degree of uncertainty. In other words, everything that can possibly occur as a result of the decision is presumably specified, though which of the various possibilities will actually occur may be subject to chance.

Then, a rational choice involves selecting that course of action or that alternative which maximizes the social actor's likelihood of attaining the highest value for achievement of the preferences or goals in the objective function. In rational choice, decisions are related systematically to objectives (March, 1976: 70); that decision is made which shows the most promise of enabling the social actor to maximize the attainment of objectives. "Rationality refers to consistent, value-maximizing choice within specified constraints" (Allison, 1971: 30).

It is clear that in analyzing choice processes in organizations or other social collectivities, the assumption of consistency and unity in the goals, information and decision processes is problematic. However, one of the advantages of the rational model is that it permits prediction of behavior with complete certainty and specificity if one knows (or assumes one knows) the goals of the other organization. Allison (1971: 13), in reviewing foreign policy analysis, has argued that this advantage is one important reason that "most contemporary analysts . . . proceed *predominantly* . . . in terms of this framework when trying to explain international events." The rational choice model facilitates the prediction of what the other social actor will do, assuming various goals; turning the model around, various goals can be inferred (though scarcely unambiguously) from the behavior of the other actor. It is inevitably the case that "an imaginative analyst can construct an account of value-maximizing choice for any action or set of actions performed" (Allison, 1971: 35).

Thus, to preserve the diagnostic and analytic properties of the rational model, goal consistency, and congruity are assumed. In economic theory, the goal of the firm is assumed to be profit maximization. In the theory of finance, the goal is assumed to be the maximization of shareholder wealth. In theories of public bureaucracies, the goals are presumed to be those that are part of the agency's mission and which enable it to fulfill its assigned role in society. As Stava (1976:209) has noted in discussing choice in larger political bodies, "legal-bureaucratic theories mostly argue that resources are allocated . . . according to some universalistic rules applied in a neutral way and in accord with the prima facie needs of the society." For society, one could as easily substitute the word organization. Stava continued by noting that decisions were presumed to be both formally neutral and rational. "They are neutral in the sense that the necessary value premises for the decisions are given or treated as given. . . . The decisions should also be (formally) rational. This means that they are intended to realize goals" (Stava, 1976: 209).

DIAGNOSING THE USE OF RATIONAL DECISION MAKING

How can one tell if the organization one is investigating is, in fact, best described in terms of the rational model? One can certainly not tell by investigating the decision outcomes. Any such outcomes can be consistent with rational choice, if the appropriate goals or preferences are assumed. Rational choice describes a *process* of selecting the best alternative course of action. It seems reasonable, then, to diagnose the presence or absence of rationality in decision making by considering the process by which choices are made.

Chaffee (1980), in reviewing the literature on decision making, has developed a set of seven criteria for defining the requirements of rational choice processes in terms of the collection and use of information:

1. Information is received prior to the decision being made;
2. Information is problem-centered and goal-directed;
3. Information documents the existence of and the need to solve the problem or reach the goal;
4. Information includes consideration of more than one alternative for reaching the goal or solving the problem;
5. Information has logical internal consistency in terms of posited cause-effect relationships.
6. Information is oriented toward maximization, in that it demonstrates the value of the various alternatives considered in reaching the goal;
7. Information identifies the value premises on which it is based.

One final condition could be added, which is that the choice is made to accept that alternative which, on the basis of the information provided, seems to provide the best likelihood of achieving the goals or solving the problem.

It is, of course, the case that given a belief and social norms favoring rationality, such a process might be followed to legitimate a decision made, for instance, on political grounds. Thus, it is reasonable to argue that the fulfillment of a process similar to that outlined above is a necessary but not sufficient condition to provide conclusive evidence for the operation of a rational decision making process.

The process concerns outlined above can be usefully coupled with another type of consideration to provide a better way of assessing whether or not the organization in question is operating according to the rational model. In particular, political models of organizations imply that decisions are made on the basis of the preferences of actors within the organization, without regard to the welfare of the whole organization (e.g., Stagner, 1969). Nagel (1975: 29) has defined power as "an actual or potential causal relation between the preferences of an 'actor' regarding an outcome and the outcome itself." By contrast, rational choice involves the selection of the goal-maximizing alternative regardless of which particular interests within the organization favor that alternative. This suggests that rational organizations can be distinguished from more political organizations by investigating the extent to which the choices made consistently reflect the preferences of certain groups within the organizations, or whether such choices are relatively uncorrelated with the prior preferences and positions of the same groups. The rational model presumes that information and value-maximization dictate choice; the political model presumes that parochial interests and preferences control choice. Then, choice should be relatively uncorrelated with the preferences of the same groups and highly correlated with information and the selection of the best alternative.

BUREAUCRATIC MODELS OF DECISION MAKING

The rational model of choice implies the need for some substantial information processing requirements in organizational decision making. These may be unrealistic or unattainable in some cases, and organizations may operate using standard operating procedures and rules rather than engaging in rational decision making on a continuous basis. The bureaucratic model of organizations substitutes procedural rationality for substantive rationality (Simon, 1979); rather than having choices made to maximize values, choices are made according to rules and processes which have been adaptive and effective in the past.

The best explication of what is meant by bureaucratically-rational decision processes can be found in March and Simon (1958) and Cyert and March (1963). In this framework, goals are viewed as systems of constraints (Simon, 1964) which decisions must satisfy. Because of bounded rationality, search is limited and stops as soon as a satisfactory alternative is found. Uncertainty tends to be avoided in that, rather than making comprehensive assessments of risk and probabilities, decisions are made with relatively short time horizons. Conflict among different alternatives or points of view is never fully resolved, and priorities and objectives are attended to sequentially, first, for instance, worrying about profit, then about market share, then personnel problems, and so forth. Throughout this process, organizations learn and adapt, and their learning and knowledge takes the form of rules of action or standard operating procedures, repertoires of behavior which are activated in certain situations and which provide a program, a set of behaviors for organizational participants, that serve as a guide to action and choice.

Seen from this perspective, decisions are viewed "less as deliberate choices and more as *outputs* of large organizations functioning according to standard patterns of behavior" (Allison, 1971: 67). It is presumed that "most of the behavior is determined by previously established procedures" (Allison, 1971: 79). The model of organizations as bureaucratically rational presumes less conscious foresight and less clearly defined preferences and information. Both rely on habitual ways of doing things and the results of past actions, and constrain how the organization proceeds to operate in the future. Decisions are not made as much as they evolve from the policies, procedures, and rules which constitute the organization and its memory.

Perhaps one of the best examples to consider in understanding the difference between the rational choice model and the bureaucratic model is to examine the effect of precedence on budgeting decisions. The literature on governmental budgeting, for instance (Wildavsky, 1979; Davis, Dempster, and Wildavsky, 1966; Wildavsky and Hammond, 1965), indicates that the best predictor of this year's budget is last year's budget. Analysis of governmental budgeting indicates that precedence, coupled with some very simple rules for handling increased requests, can account for most of the variation in resource allocations. That this process is not perceived as completely rational is evidenced by the fact that great time and attention has been spent on developing alternative resource allocation schemes, such as Planning-Programming-Budgeting Systems (PPBS) and zero-based budgeting. The advocates of these systems argue that what was allocated last year may have little to do with rational, value maximizing goal attainment, and it is necessary to more systematically relate decisions to preferences and new information.

Of course, most of these new decision making processes have had tremendous problems in their implementation. Precedence and other similar simple rules may not be optimal, but they are at least computationally easy and require less heroic assumptions about information processing capacities. Furthermore, one could argue that except in circumstances of sudden and dramatic change in the contingencies confronting the organization, incremental change as might occur through incremental budgeting is sufficient to maintain effective operations through the process of making small adjustments to the organization's operations. Thus, bureaucratic rationality, it is argued, can perhaps effectively substitute for substantive rationality.

DISTINGUISHING BUREAUCRATIC ORGANIZATIONS

It is relatively simple to distinguish between organizations which operate under the bureaucratic model and those which operate under the rational model. Bureaucratic organizations will typically have much less extensive information search and analysis activities, and rely more heavily on rules, precedent, and standard operating procedures. Less time and resources will be spent on decision making, and fewer alternatives will be considered before actions are taken. Indeed, it is the difference in the amount of analysis, search, and focused attention on goal attainment, that constitutes the difference between the bureaucratic and rational models.

Distinguishing between the bureaucratic and political models of organization may be somewhat more difficult. After all, if the distribution of power is stable in the organization, which is a reasonable assumption, particularly over relatively short time periods, and if power and politics determine organizational decisions, then organizational choices will be relatively stable over time. But, this stability is also characteristic of the use of precedent in decision making, which is one of the hallmarks of bureaucratic organizations. One way of distinguishing, then, would involve looking at the correlates of the incremental changes in decisions and allocations made within the organization. While both models might be consistent with the use of precedent for the bulk of the decisions, there are some implicit differences in how incremental resources will be allocated. In bureaucratic organizations, changes in resource allocation patterns should either follow a proportional basis, be based on some standard measure of operations and performance, or reflect an attempt to shift the resources to better achieve the goals and values of the organization. By contrast, political models of organizations would suggest that power would best predict changes and shifts in decisions and allocations.

Research which attempts to explore the use of rules and standard operating procedures in organizations has typically involved the use of computer programs which simulate the operation of such rules (e.g., Cyert and March, 1963; Crecine, 1967; Gerwin, 1969). Unfortunately, the validation of such models is complex because there may be many ways in which an observed outcome can be produced. This means that just because the application of a set of decision rules produces results that mirror what occurs in an organization, it is not necessarily true that these rules are actually guiding the organization's decision making.

DECISION PROCESS MODELS

Although they exist within much the same tradition as the bureaucratic model of organizations, decision process models differ in that they presume even less rationality and more randomness in organizational functioning. As power models depart from bureaucratic rationality by removing the assumption of consistent, overall organizational objectives and shared beliefs about technology, decision process models depart even

further by removing the presumption of predefined, known preferences held by the various social actors. Decision process models posit that there are no overall organizational goals being maximized through choice, and no powerful actors with defined preferences who possess resources through which they seek to obtain those preferences. Stava (1976: 209) described decision process models as follows:

> In *decision process theories* it is presumed that policy is the outcome of a choice made by one or several decision-makers. Which choice is made is determined by the situation in which the decision-maker finds himself. This situation is, in turn, largely caused by the processes preceding the choice. It is impossible, then, to predict policies without knowing the details of the preceding processes.

March (1966: 180) argued that in such decision process models, although one might posit that the various actors have preferences and varying amounts of power, the concept of power does not add much to the prediction of behavior and choice in such systems.

More recently, March (1978) and others (e.g., Weick, 1969) have questioned whether or not the concept of preferences makes sense at any level of analysis, individual or organizational. One of the arguments raised is that instead of preferences guiding choice, choice may determine preferences. In other words, one only knows what one likes after it has been experienced; or, as Weick has argued, one only knows what one has done after he or she has done it, since the meaning of action is retrospective and follows the action rather than preceeds it. In this framework, goals are seen as the products of sense making activities which are carried on after the action has occurred to explain that action or rationalize it. The action itself is presumed to be the result of habit, custom, or the influence of other social actors in the environment.

One example of a decision process model of social choice is the garbage can model (Cohen, March, and Olsen, 1972). The basic idea of the model is that decision points are opportunities into which various problems and solutions are dumped by organizational participants. "In a garbage can situation, a decision is an outcome of an interpretation of several relatively independent 'streams' within an organization" (Cohen, March, and Olsen, 1976: 26). The streams consist of problems, solutions (which are somebody's product), participants, and choice opportunities. The decision process models developed by March and his colleagues emphasize the problematic nature of participation by various social actors in choices. They note that systems are frequently so overloaded with problems, solutions, and decision opportunities that any given social actor will attend to only certain decisions.

Cohen, March, and Olsen (1972) developed a simulation of the garbage can decision process. One of the important conclusions emerging from that simulation is:

> . . . that although the processes within the garbage can are understandable and in some ways predictable, events are not dominated by intention. The processes and the outcomes are likely to appear to have no close relation with the explicit intention of actors. In situations in which load is heavy and the structure is relatively unsegmented, intention is lost in context dependent flow of problems, solutions, people, and choice opportunities (Cohen, March, and Olsen, 1976: 37).

March (1966) had earlier begun to explore the role of chance in organizational choice situations, and the garbage can simulation represents the formal incorporation of chance and randomness in a theory of choice.

The garbage can model emerged largely from a study of universities and university presidents (Cohen and March, 1974). Universities were characterized as organized anarchies, and garbage can decision process models were believed to be particularly appropriate in such contexts, although the assertion is also made that elements of these models are found in most organizations. Weiner (1976) has summarized some of the main features and assumptions of the organized anarchy model of organizations. First, "the existing theory of organized anarchies does not require that decisions be reached or problems solved by a specified time . . . the theory holds that such requirements are neither generated within the organization nor imposed by the organization's environment" (Weiner, 1976: 226). The garbage can model then, presumes and assumes no deadlines. Decisions are worked on until they are made. The theory also suggests that "the stream of problems entering or leaving an organization" is a "flow that is independent of the other streams of choices, solutions and energy. . . . The theory holds further that problems move autonomously among choice opportunities in search for a choice process in which the problem can be resolved" (Weiner, 1976: 243). Decision making is viewed as an activity which absorbs the energy of those available, works on problems, and comes up with solutions which are determined in large measure by a random stream of events.

DISTINGUISHING ORGANIZED ANARCHIES

The key concept used in diagnosing whether or not the organization is an organized anarchy which can best be understood by using decision process organizational models is that of intention. Not only are there presumed to be no overarching organizational goals, but presumably intention is problematic even at the level of subunits and groups within the organization. Action occurs, but it is not primarily motivated by conscious choice and planning. Although not made explicit, there should be relatively little consistency or consensus over behavior in an organized anarchy. Events should unfold in ways predictable only by considering the process, and not through consideration of value maximization, precedent, power, or force.

If that seems like a difficult requirement to fulfill, those who advocate the decision process model of organizations argue that much of the consistency and intentionality observed in organizations is imputed by those doing the observing rather than being a characteristic of the organization being observed. Much as in Allison's (1971) treatment of foreign policy analysis, goals are imputed to organizations by observers rather than being actual properties of the organizations themselves. Similarly, rules and power may also be imputed rather than actually be properties of the system under study.

Although decision process models provide a language for describing the randomness that is sometimes observed, they do not provide a great amount of predictive power. Their theme is that such prediction is largely impossible, except for the use of complex programs of decision routines. Their de-emphasis of intention makes them unpopular with those who view the world in a more proactive, strategic fashion.

POLITICAL MODELS OF ORGANIZATIONS

One criticism that has been leveled against rational choice models is that they fail to take into account the diversity of interests and goals within organizations. March (1962) described business firms as political coalitions. The coalitional view of organizations was developed by Cyert and March (1963) in their description of organizational decision making. In bureaucratic theories of organizations, the presumption is that through control devices such as rewards based on job performance or seniority, rules that ensure fair and standardized treatment for all, and careers within the organization, the operation of self-interest can be virtually eliminated as an influence on organizational decision making. Economic or incentive theories of organizations argue that through the payment of a wage, particularly when compensation is made contingent on performance, individuals hired into the organization come to accept the organization's goals. Political models of organizations assume that these control devices, as well as others such as socialization, are not wholly effective in producing a coherent and unified set of goals or definitions of technology. Rather, as Baldridge (1971: 25) has argued, political models view organizations as pluralistic and divided into various interests, subunits, and subcultures. Conflict is viewed as normal or at least customary in political organizations. Action does not presuppose some overarching intention. Rather, action results "from games among players who perceive quite different faces of an issue and who differ markedly in the actions they prefer" (Allison, 1971: 175). Because action results from bargaining and compromise, the resulting decision seldom perfectly reflects the preferences of any group or subunit within the organization.

Political models of choice further presume that when preferences conflict, the power of the various social actors determines the outcome of the decision process. Power models hypothesize that those interests, subunits, or individuals within the organization who possess the greatest power, will receive the greatest rewards from the interplay of organizational politics. In such models, power "is an intervening variable between an initial condition, defined largely in terms of the individual components of the system, and a terminal state, defined largely in terms of the system as a whole" (March, 1966: 168–169). Power is used to overcome the resistance of others and obtain one's way in the organization.

To understand organizational choices using a political model, it is necessary to understand who participates in decision making, what determines each player's stand on the issues, what determines each actor's relative power, and how the decision process arrives at a decision; in other words, how the various preferences become combined (majority rule; unanimity; ⅔ vote; etc.) (Allison, 1971: 164). A change in any one of these aspects—relative power, the rules of decision making, or preferences—can lead to a change in the predicted organizational decision.

DISTINGUISHING POLITICAL MODELS OF ORGANIZATIONS

March (1966) has argued that it is often difficult to distinguish chance models from power or force models in terms of the predictions that each would make. He argued that evidence for force models would include: whether or not power is stable over time, whether or not power is stable over subject matter, whether or not power is correlated with other attributes, and whether or not power could be experimentally manipulated. These are important criteria to keep in mind when thinking about the evidence for a political model of organizations to be presented in this book.

It is clear that a political or power model of choice need not assume that all issues are equally important and, therefore, equally worthy of effort. Incorporating ideas of activation in force or power models makes their testing even more difficult.

Power models can be distinguished from rational models if it can be demonstrated that either no overarching organizational goal exists or even if such a goal does exist, decisions are made which are inconsistent with maximizing the attainment of the goal. Power can be distinguished from chance or organized anarchy models by demonstrating that actors in organizations have preferences and intentions which are consistent across decision issues and which they attempt to have implemented. Further evidence for political models would come from finding that measures of power in social systems, rather than goals, precedent, or chance, bring about decision outcomes. Indeed, the ability to measure and operationalize power is critical both for diagnosing political systems and for testing political models of organizations.

SUMMARY

One of the points of Allison's (1971) analysis of the Cuban missile crisis is that it is not necessary to choose between analytical frameworks. Each may be partly true in a particular situation, and one can obtain a better understanding of the organization by trying to use all of the models rather than by choosing among them. This point is different than saying that some organizations are characterized more by the political model and others by the rational model. Allison's argument is that insight can be gained from the application of all the frameworks in the same situation. This statement is true, but only within limits. At some point, the various perspectives will begin to make different predictions about what will occur, and will generate different recommendations concerning the strategy and tactics to be followed. At that point, the participant will need to decide where to place his or her bets.

As we have already discussed, discovering which perspective best describes a particular organization is not easy, and the world will do little to make it easier. Some of the perspectives are more accepted and acceptable than others. This means that language will be used to make it seem that the organization is operating according to the more accepted paradigms. It also means that there will be various informational and other types of social influence imposed on the observer to make him construct a particular view of the organization.

In Figure 1, the four decision models described in this chapter are briefly summarized along eight relevant dimensions. The ability to perfectly distinguish between the models, using a single dimension in a particular situation, is likely to be limited. However, by considering the dimensions in combination and by using comparative frames of reference, it becomes feasible to assess the extent to which the organization in question is operating according to one or the other of the models.

It is evident from the title of this book what my view is concerning the relative applicability of the four models of organizational decision making. Circumstances of bureaucratically rational decision making occur only in certain conditions on an infrequent basis. As Thompson and Tuden (1959) have argued, consensus on both goals and technology, or the connections between actions and consequences, are necessary in order for computational forms of decision making to be employed. Where there is disagreement over goals, compromise is used; when there is disagreement over technology, judgment is employed; and when there is disagreement

about both, Thompson and Tuden characterize the decision situation as one requiring inspiration. In the case of judgment, compromise, and inspiration, it is the relative power of the various social actors that provides both the sufficient and necessary way of resolving the decision.

Furthermore, if intention is not always a guiding force in the taking of action and if preferences are not always clear or consistent, then there are at least some participants in organizations who know what they want and have the social power to get it. The randomness implied by the decision process model of organizations is inconsistent with the observation that in organizational decision making, some actors seem to usually get the garbage, while others manage to get the can.

Standard operating procedures, rules, and behavior repertoires clearly exist and are important in organizations. Much organizational decision making involves issues that are neither important nor contested, and in such cases, standard operating procedures are sufficient to get the decisions made in an inexpensive fashion. However, it is necessary to be aware that these various rules, norms, and procedures have in themselves implications for the distribution of power and authority in organizations and for how contested decisions should be resolved. The rules and processes themselves become important focal points for the exercise of power. They are not always neutral and not always substantively rational. Sometimes they are part and parcel of the political contest that occurs within organizations.

One of the reasons why power and politics characterize so many organizations is because of what some of my students have dubbed the Law of Political Entropy: given the opportunity, an organization will tend to seek and maintain a political character. The argument

FIGURE 1 • OVERVIEW OF FOUR ORGANIZATIONAL DECISION-
MAKING MODELS

	Model			
Dimension	Rational	Bureaucratic	Decision Process/ Organized Anarchy	Political Power
Goals, preferences	Consistent within and across social actors	Reasonably consistent	Unclear, ambiguous, may be constructed ex post to rationalize action	Consistent within social actors; inconsistent, pluralistic within the organization
Power and control	Centralized	Less centralized with greater reliance on rules	Very decentralized, anarchic	Shifting coalitions and interest groups
Decision process	Orderly, substantively rational	Procedural rationality embodied in programs and standard operating procedures	Ad hoc	Disorderly, characterized by push and pull of interests
Rules and norms	Norm of optimization	Precedent, tradition	Segmented and episodic participation in decisions	Free play of market forces; conflict is legitimate and expected
Information and computational requirements	Extensive and systematic	Reduced by the use of rules and procedures	Haphazard collection and use of information	Information used and withheld strategically
Beliefs about action-consequence relationships	Known at least to a probability distribution	Consensually shared acceptance of routines	Unclear, ambiguous technology	Disagreements about technology
Decisions	Follow from value-maximizing choice	Follow from programs and routines	Not linked to intention; result of intersection of persons, solutions, problems	Result of bargaining and interplay among interests
Ideology	Efficiency and effectiveness	Stability, fairness, predictability	Playfulness, loose coupling, randomness	Struggle, conflict, winners and losers

is that once politics are introduced into a situation, it is very difficult to restore rationality. Once consensus is lost, once disagreements about preferences, technology, and management philosophy emerge, it is very hard to restore the kind of shared perspective and solidarity which is necessary to operate under the rational model. If rationality is indeed this fragile, and if the Law of Political Entropy is correct, then over time one would expect to see more and more organizations characterized by the political model.

BIBLIOGRAPHIC REFERENCES

Allen, R. W., Madison, D. L., Porter, L. W., Renwick, P. A., & Mayes, B. T. (1979). Organizational politics: Tactics and characteristics of its actors. *California Management Review, 22,* 77–83.

Allison, G. T. (1971). *Essence of decision.* Boston: Little, Brown.

Baldridge, J. V. (1971). *Power and conflict in the university.* New York: John Wiley & Sons.

Baritz, J. H. (1960). *The servants of power.* Middletown, CT: Wesleyan University Press.

Bierstedt, R. (1950). An analysis of social power. *American Sociological Review, 15,* 730–738.

Blau, P. M. (1964). *Exchange and power in social life.* New York: John Wiley & Sons.

————, and Schoenherr, R. A. (1971). *The structure of organizations.* New York: Basic Books.

Burns, T., & Stalker, G. M. (1961). *The management of innovation.* London: Tavistock.

Carey, A. (1967). The Hawthorne studies: A radical criticism. *American Sociological Review, 32,* 403–416.

Cartwright, D. (1979). Contemporary social psychology in historical perspective. *Social Psychology Quarterly, 42,* 82–93.

Crozier, M. (1964). *The bureaucratic phenomenon.* Chicago: University of Chicago Press.

Cyert, R. M., and March, J. G. (1963). *A behavioral theory of the firm.* Englewood Cliffs, NJ: Prentice-Hall.

Dahl, R. A. (1957). The concept of power. *Behavioral Science, 2,* 201–215.

Dornbusch, S. M., & Scott, W. R. (1975). *Evaluation and the exercise of authority: A theory of control applied to diverse organizations.* San Francisco, CA: Jossey-Bass.

Edelman, M. (1964). *The symbolic uses of politics.* Urbana, IL: University of Illinois Press.

Emerson, R. M. (1(1962). Power-dependence relations. *American Sociological Review, 27,* 31–41.

French, J. R. P., Jr., & Raven, B. (1968). The bases of social power. In D. Cartwright & A. Zander (Eds.), *Group dynamics* (3rd ed.). (pp. 259–269). New York: Harper & Row.

Galbraith, J. R. (1973). *Designing complex organizations.* Reading, MA: Addison-Wesley Publishing.

Kaplan, A. (1964). *The conduct of inquiry.* Scranton, PA: Chandler Publishing Co.

Karpik, L. (1978). Organizations, institutions and history. In Lucien Karpik (Ed.), *Organization and environment: Theory, issues and reality* (pp. 15–68). Beverly Hills, CA: Sage.

Korda, M. (1975). *Power.* New York: Ballantine Books.

Lasswell, H. D. (1936). *Politics: Who gets what, when, how.* New York: McGraw-Hill.

Lawrence, P. R., & Lorsch, J. W. (1967). *Organization and environment.* Boston: Graduate School of Business Administration, Harvard University.

March, J. G. (1962). The business firm as a political coalition. *Journal of Politics, 24,* 662–678.

————. (1966). The power of power. In D. Easton (Ed.). *Varieties of political theory* (pp. 39–70). Englewood Cliffs, NJ: Prentice-Hall.

————. (1978). Bounded rationality, ambiguity, and the engineering of choice. *Bell Journal of Economics, 9,* 587–608.

Mayes, B. T., & Allen, R. W. (1977). Toward a definition of organizational politics. *Academy of Management Review, 2,* 672–678.

Mechanic, D. (1962). Sources of power of lower participants in complex organizations. *Administrative Science Quarterly, 7,* 349–364.

Nehrbass, R. G. (1979). Ideology and the decline of management theory. *Academy of Management Review, 4,* 427–431.

Nord, W. R. (1974). The failure of current applied behavioral science: A Marxian perspective. *Journal of Applied Behavioral Science, 10,* 557–578.

Pennings, J. M. (1975). The relevance of the structural-contingency model for organizational effectiveness. *Administrative Science Quarterly, 20,* 393–410.

Perrow, C. (1961). The analysis of goals in complex organizations. *American Sociological Review, 26,* 859–866.

————. (1970). Departmental power and perspectives in industrial firms. In M. N. Zald (Ed.), *Power in organizations* (pp. 59–89). Nashville: Vanderbilt University Press.

————. (1972). *Complex organizations: A critical essay.* Glenview, IL: Scott, Foresman.

Pfeffer, J. (1978a). The micropolitics of organizations. In M. W. Meyer and Assoc., (Eds.), *Environments and organizations* (pp. 29–50). San Francisco: CA: Jossey-Bass.

Pfeffer, J., & Salancik, G. R. (1974). Organizational decision making as a political process: The case of a university budget. *Administrative Science Quarterly, 19,* 135–151.

————. (1978). *The external control of organizations: A resource dependence perspective.* New York: Harper & Row.

————, & Leblebici, H. (1976). The effect of uncertainty on the use of social influence in organizational decision making. *Administrative Science Quarterly, 21,* 227–245.

Pondy, L. R. (1969). Effects of size, complexity, and ownership on administrative intensity. *Administrative Science Quarterly, 14,* 47–60.

Pugh, D. S. (1966). Modern organization theory. *Psychological Bulletin, 66,* 235–251.

Salancik, G. R., & Pfeffer, J. (1974). The bases and use of power in organizational decision making: The case of a university. *Administrative Science Quarterly, 19,* 453–473.

————. (1977b). Who gets power—and how they hold on to it: A strategic-contingency model of power. *Organizational Dynamics, 5,* 3–21.

Schein, E. H. (1968). Organizational socialization and the profession of management. *Industrial Management Review, 9,* 1–16.

Thompson, J. D. (1967). *Organizations in action.* New York: McGraw-Hill.

Weber, M. (1947). *The theory of social and economic organization.* New York: Free Press.

Wildavsky, A. (1979). *The politics of the budgeting process* (3rd ed.). Boston: Little, Brown.

Williamson, O. E. (1975). *Markets and hierarchies: Analysis and antitrust implications.* New York: Free Press.

Woodward, J. (1965). *Industrial organization: Theory and practice.* London: Oxford University Press.

Zald, M. N. (1965). Who shall rule? A political analysis of succession in a large welfare organization. *Pacific Sociological Review, 8,* 52–60.

28
Sources of Power of Lower Participants in Complex Organizations

David Mechanic

This paper explores various factors that account for the power of secretaries, hospital attendants, prison inmates, and other lower participants within organizations. Power is seen as resulting from access to and control over persons, information, and instrumentalities. Among the variables discussed affecting power are normative definitions, perception of legitimacy, exchange, and coalitions. Personal attributes related to power include commitment, effort, interest, willingness to use power, skills, and attractiveness. Finally, various attributes of social structure are discussed which also help to account for the power of lower participants: time spent in the organization, centrality of position, duality of power structures, and replaceability of persons.[1]

It is not unusual for lower participants[2] in complex organizations to assume and wield considerable power and influence not associated with their formally defined positions within these organizations. In sociological terms they have considerable personal power but no authority. Such personal power is often attained, for example, by executive secretaries and accountants in business firms, by attendants in mental hospitals, and even by inmates in prisons. The personal power achieved by these lower participants does not necessarily result from unique personal characteristics, although these may be relevant, but results rather from particular aspects of their location within their organizations.

INFORMAL VERSUS FORMAL POWER

Within organizations the distribution of authority (institutionalized power) is closely if not perfectly correlated with the prestige of positions. Those who have argued for the independence of these variables[3] have taken their examples from diverse organizations and do not deal with situations where power is clearly comparable.[4] Thus when Bierstedt argues that Einstein had prestige but no power, and the policeman power but no prestige, it is apparent that he is comparing categories that are not comparable. Generally persons occupying high-ranking positions within organizations have more authority than those holding low-ranking positions.

One might ask what characterizes high-ranking positions within organizations. What is most evident, perhaps, is that lower participants recognize the right of higher-ranking participants to exercise power, and yield without difficulty to demands they regard as legitimate. Moreover, persons in high-ranking positions tend to have considerable

Source: David Mechanic, "Sources of Power of Lower Participants in Complex Organizations," in *Administrative Science Quarterly* 7 (December 1962): 349–364; reprinted by permission of *The Administrative Science Quarterly.* Copyright © 1962 *The Administrative Science Quarterly.*

access and control over information and persons both within and outside the organization, and to instrumentalities or resources. Although higher supervisory personnel may be isolated from the task activities of lower participants, they maintain access to them through formally established intermediary positions and exercise control through intermediary participants. There appears, therefore, to be a clear correlation between the prestige of positions within organizations and the extent to which they offer access to information, persons, and instrumentalities.

Since formal organizations tend to structure lines of access and communication, access should be a clue to institutional prestige. Yet access depends on variables other than those controlled by the formal structure of an organization, and this often makes the informal power structure that develops within organizations somewhat incongruent with the formally intended plan. It is these variables that allow work groups to limit production through norms that contravene the goals of the larger organization, that allow hospital attendants to thwart changes in the structure of a hospital, and that allow prison inmates to exercise some control over prison guards. Organizations, in a sense, are continuously at the mercy of their lower participants, and it is this fact that makes organizational power structure especially interesting to the sociologist and social psychologist.

Clarification of Definitions

The purpose of this paper is to present some hypotheses explaining why lower participants in organizations can often assume and wield considerable power which is not associated with their positions as formally defined within these organizations. For the purposes of this analysis the concepts "influence," "power,"

and "control" will be used synonymously. Moreover, we shall not be concerned with type of power, that is, whether the power is based on reward, punishment, identification, power to veto, or whatever.[5] Power will be defined as *any force that results in behavior that would not have occurred if the force had not been present*. We have defined power as a force rather than a relationship because it appears that much of what we mean by power is encompassed by the normative framework of an organization, and thus any analysis of power must take into consideration the power of norms as well as persons.

I shall also argue, following Thibaut and Kelley,[6] that power is closely related to dependence. To the extent that a person is dependent on another, he is potentially subject to the other person's power. Within organizations one makes others dependent upon him by controlling access to information, persons, and instrumentalities, which I shall define as follow:

a. *Information* includes knowledge of the organization, knowledge about persons, knowledge of the norms, procedures, techniques, and so forth.

b. *Persons* include anyone within the organization or anyone outside the organization upon whom the organization is in some way dependent.

c. *Instrumentalities* include any aspect of the physical plant of the organization or its resources (equipment, machines, money, and so on).

Power is a function not only of the extent to which a person controls information, persons, and instrumentalities, but also of the importance of the various attributes he controls.[7]

Finally, following Dahl,[8] we shall agree that comparisons of power among persons should, as far as possible, utilize comparable units. Thus we shall strive for clarification by attempting to oversimplify organizational processes; the goal is to set up a number of hypothetical statements of the relationship between variables taken two at a time, "all other factors being assumed to remain constant."

A Classic Example

Like many other aspects of organizational theory, one can find a classic statement of our problem in Weber's discussion of the political bureaucracy. Weber indicated the extent to which bureaucrats may have considerable power over political incumbents, as a result, in part, of their permanence within the political bureaucracy, as contrasted to public officials, who are replaced rather frequently.[9] Weber noted how the low-ranking bureaucrat becomes familiar with the organization—its rules and operations, the work flow, and so on, which gives him considerable power over the new political incumbent, who might have higher rank but is not as familiar with the organization. While Weber does not directly state the point, his analysis suggests that bureaucratic permanence has some relationship to increased access to persons, information, and instrumentalities. To state the hypothesis suggested somewhat more formally:

H1　Other factors remaining constant, organizational power is related to access to persons, information, and instrumentalities.

H2　Other factors remaining constant, as a participant's length of time in an organization increases, he has increased access to persons, information, and instrumentalities.

While these hypotheses are obvious, they do suggest that a careful scrutiny of the organizational literature, especially that dealing with the power or counter-power of lower participants, might lead to further formalized statements, some

considerably less obvious than the ones stated. This kind of hypothesis formation is treated later in the paper, but at this point I would like to place the discussion of power within a larger theoretical context and discuss the relevance of role theory to the study of power processes.

IMPLICATIONS OF ROLE THEORY FOR THE STUDY OF POWER

There are many points of departure for the study of power processes within organizations. An investigator might view influence in terms of its sources and strategies; he might undertake a study of the flow of influence; he might concentrate on the structure of organizations, seeing to what extent regularities in behavior might be explained through the study of norms, roles, and traditions; and, finally, more psychologically oriented investigators might concentrate on the recipients of influence and the factors affecting susceptibility to influence attempts. Each of these points of departure leads to different theoretical emphases. For our purposes the most important emphasis is that presented by role theorists.

Role theorists approach the question of influence and power in terms of the behavioral regularities which result from established identities within specific social contexts like families, hospitals, and business firms. The underlying premise of most role theorists is that a large proportion of all behavior is brought about through socialization within specific organizations, and much behavior is routine and established through learning the traditional modes of adaptation in dealing with specific tasks. Thus the positions persons occupy in an organization account for much of their behavior. Norms and roles serve as mediating forces in influence processes.

While role theorists have argued much about vocabulary, the basic premises underlying their thought have been rather consistent. The argument is essentially that knowledge of one's identity or social position is a powerful index of the expectations such a person is likely to face in various social situations. Since behavior tends to be highly correlated with expectations, prediction of behavior is therefore possible. The approach of role theorists to the study of behavior within organizations is of particular merit in that it provides a consistent set of concepts which is useful analytically in describing recruitment, socialization, interaction, and personality, as well as the formal structure of organizations. Thus the concept of role is one of the few concepts clearly linking social structure, social process, and social character.

Many problems pertaining to role theory have been raised. At times it is not clear whether role is regarded as a real entity, a theoretical construct, or both. Moreover, Gross has raised the issue of role consensus, that is, the extent to which the expectations impinging upon a position are held in common by persons occupying reciprocal positions to the one in question.[10] Merton has attempted to deal with inevitable inconsistencies in expectations of role occupants by introducing the concept of role-set which treats differences in expectations as resulting, in part, from the fact that any position is differently related to a number of reciprocal positions.[11] Furthermore, Goffman has criticized role theory for its failure to deal adequately with commitment to roles[12]— a factor which Etzioni has found to be related intimately to the kind of power exercised in organizations.[13] Perhaps these various criticisms directed at role theory reflect its importance as well as

its deficiencies, and despite the difficulties involved in role analysis, the concept of role may prove useful in various ways.

Role theory is useful in emphasizing the extent to which influence and power can be exercised without conflict. This occurs when power is integrated with a legitimate order, when sentiments are held in common, and when there are adequate mechanisms for introducing persons into the system and training them to recognize, accept, and value the legitimacy of control within the organization. By providing the conditions whereby participants within an organization may internalize the norms, these generalized rules, values, and sentiments serve as substitutes for interpersonal influence and make the workings of the organization more agreeable and pleasant for all.

It should be clear that lower participants will be more likely to circumvent higher authority, other factors remaining constant, when the mandates of those in power, if not the authority itself, are regarded as illegitimate. Thus as Etzioni points out, when lower participants become alienated from the organization, coercive power is likely to be required if its formal mandates are to be fulfilled.[14]

Moreover, all organizations must maintain control over lower participants. To the extent that lower participants fail to recognize the legitimacy of power, or believe that sanctions cannot or will not be exercised when violations occur, the organization loses, to some extent, its ability to control their behavior. Moreover, in-so-far as higher participants can create the impression that they can or will exert sanctions above their actual willingness to use such sanctions, control over lower participants will increase. It is usually to the advantage of an organization to externalize and impersonalize controls, however, and if possible to develop positive sentiments toward its rules.

In other words, an effective organization can control its participants in such a way as to make it hardly perceivable that it exercises the control that it does. It seeks commitment from lower participants, and when commitment is obtained, surveillance can be relaxed. On the other hand, when the power of lower participants in organizations is considered, it often appears to be clearly divorced from the traditions, norms, and goals and sentiments of the organization as a whole. Lower participants do not usually achieve control by using the role structure of the organization, but rather by circumventing, sabotaging, and manipulating it.

SOURCES OF POWER OF LOWER PARTICIPANTS

The most effective way for lower participants to achieve power is to obtain, maintain, and control access to persons, information, and instrumentalities. To the extent that this can be accomplished, lower participants make higher-ranking participants dependent upon them. Thus dependence together with the manipulation of the dependency relationship is the key to the power of lower participants.

A number of examples can be cited which illustrate the preceding point. Scheff, for example, reports on the failure of a state mental hospital to bring about intended reform because of the opposition of hospital attendants.[15] He noted that the power of hospital attendants was largely a result of the dependence of ward physicians on attendants. This dependence resulted from the physician's short tenure, his lack of interest

in administration, and the large amount of administrative responsibility he had to assume. An implicit trading agreement developed between physicians and attendants, whereby attendants would take on some of the responsibilities and obligations of the ward physician in return for increased power in decision-making processes concerning patients. Failure of the ward physician to honor his part of the agreement resulted in information being withheld, disobedience, lack of cooperation, and unwillingness of the attendants to serve as a barrier between the physician and a ward full of patients demanding attention and recognition. When the attendant withheld cooperation, the physician had difficulty in making a graceful entrance and departure from the ward, in handling necessary paper work (officially his responsibility), and in obtaining information needed to deal adequately with daily treatment and behavior problems. When attendants opposed change, they could wield influence by refusing to assume responsibilities officially assigned to the physician.

Similarly, Sykes describes the dependence of prison guards on inmates and the power obtained by inmates over guards.[16] He suggests that although guards could report inmates for disobedience, frequent reports would give prison officials the impression that the guard was unable to command obedience. The guard, therefore, had some stake in ensuring the good behavior of prisoners without use of formal sanctions against them. The result was a trading agreement whereby the guard allowed violations of certain rules in return for co-operative behavior. A similar situation is found in respect to officers in the Armed Services or foremen in industry. To the extent that they require formal sanctions to bring about co-operation, they are usually perceived by their superiors as less valuable to the organization. For a good leader is expected to command obedience, at least, if not commitment.

FACTORS AFFECTING POWER

Expertise

Increasing specialization and organizational growth has made the expert or staff person important. The expert maintains power because high-ranking persons in the organization are dependent upon him for his special skills and access to certain kinds of information. One possible reason for lawyers obtaining many high governmental offices is that they are likely to have access to rather specialized but highly important means to organizational goals.[17]

We can state these ideas in hypotheses, as follows:

> H3   Other factors remaining constant, to the extent that a low-ranking participant has important expert knowledge not available to high-ranking participants, he is likely to have power over them.

Power stemming from expertise, however, is likely to be limited unless it is difficult to replace the expert. This leads to two further hypotheses:

> H4   Other factors remaining constant, a person difficult to replace will have greater power than a person easily replaceable.
>
> H5   Other factors remaining constant, experts will be more difficult to replace than nonexperts.

While persons having expertise are likely to be fairly high-ranking participants in an organization, the same hypotheses that explain the power of lower participants are relevant in explaining the comparative power positions of intermediate- and high-ranking persons.

The application of our hypothesis about expertise is clearly relevant if we look at certain organizational issues. For example, the merits of medical versus lay hospital administrators are often debated. It should be clear, however, that all other factors remaining unchanged, the medical administrator has clear advantage over the lay administrator. Where lay administrators receive preference, there is an implicit assumption that the lay person is better at administrative duties. This may be empirically valid but is not necessarily so. The special expert knowledge of the medical administrator stems from his ability legitimately to oppose a physician who contests an administrative decision on the basis of medical necessity. Usually hospitals are viewed primarily as universalistic in orientation both by the general public and most of their participants. Thus medical necessity usually takes precedence over management policies, a factor contributing to the poor financial position of most hospitals. The lay administrator is not in a position to contest such claims independently, since he usually lacks the basis for evaluation of the medical problems involved and also lacks official recognition of his competence to make such decisions. If the lay administrator is to evaluate these claims adequately on the basis of professional necessity, he must have a group of medical consultants or a committee of medical men to serve as a buffer between medical staff and the lay administration.

As a result of growing specialization, expertise is increasingly important in organizations. As the complexity of organizational tasks increases, and as organizations grow in size, there is a limit to responsibility that can be efficiently exercised by one person. Delegation of responsibility occurs, experts and specialists are brought in to provide information and research, and the higher participants become dependent upon them. Experts have tremendous potentialities for power by withholding information, providing incorrect information, and so on, and to the extent that experts are dissatisfied, the probability of organizational sabotage increases.

Effort and Interest

The extent to which lower participants may exercise power depends in part on their willingness to exert effort in areas where higher-ranking participants are often reluctant to participate. Effort exerted is directly related to the degree of interest one has in an area.

> H6 Other factors remaining constant, there is a direct relationship between the amount of effort a person is willing to exert in an area and the power he can command.

For example, secretarial staffs in universities often have power to make decisions about the purchase and allocation of supplies, the allocation of their services, the scheduling of classes, and, at times, the disposition of student complaints. Such control may in some instances lead to sanctions against a professor by polite reluctance to furnish supplies, ignoring his preferences for the scheduling of classes, and giving others preference in the allocation of services. While the power to make such decisions may easily be removed from the jurisdiction of the lower participant, it can only be accomplished at a cost—the willingness to allocate time and effort to the decisions dealing with these matters. To the extent that responsibilities are delegated to lower participants, a certain degree of power is likely to accompany the responsibility. Also, should the lower participant see his perceived rights

in jeopardy, he may sabotage the system in various ways.

Let us visualize a hypothetical situation where a department concludes that secretarial services are being allocated on a prejudicial basis as a result of complaints to the chairman of the department by several of the younger faculty. Let us also assume that, when the complaint is investigated, it is found to be substantially correct; that is, some of the younger faculty have difficulty obtaining secretarial services because of preferences among the secretarial staff. If in attempting to eliminate discretion by the secretarial staff, the chairman establishes a rule ordering the allocation of services on the basis of the order in which work appears, the rule can easily be made ineffective by complete conformity to it. Deadlines for papers, examinations, and the like will occur, and flexibility in the allocation of services is required if these deadlines are to be met. Thus the need for flexibility can be made to conflict with the rule by a staff usually not untalented in such operations.

When an organization gives discretion to lower participants, it is usually trading the power of discretion for needed flexibility. The cost of constant surveillance is too high, and the effort required too great; it is very often much easier for all concerned to allow the secretary discretion in return for co-operation and not too great an abuse of power.

> H7 Other factors remaining constant, the less effort and interest higher-ranking participants are willing to devote to a task, the more likely are lower participants to obtain power relevant to this task.

Attractiveness

Another personal attribute associated with the power of low-ranking persons in an organization is attractiveness or what some call "personality." People who are viewed as attractive are more likely to obtain access to persons, and, once such access is gained, they may be more likely to succeed in promoting a cause. But once again dependence is the key to the power of attractiveness, for whether a person is dependent upon another for a service he provides, or for approval or affection, what is most relevant is the relational bond which is highly valued.

> H8 Other factors remaining constant, the more attractive a person, the more likely he is to obtain access to persons and control over these persons.

Location and Position

In any organization the person's location in physical space and position in social space are important factors influencing access to persons, information, and instrumentalities.[18] Propinquity affects the opportunities for interaction, as well as one's position within a communication network. Although these are somewhat separate factors, we shall refer to their combined effect as centrality[19] within the organization.

> H9 Other factors remaining constant, the more central a person is in an organization, the greater is his access to persons, information, and instrumentalities.

Some low participants may have great centrality within an organization. An executive's or university president's secretary not only has access, but often controls access in making appointments and scheduling events. Although she may have no great formal authority, she may have considerable power.

Coalitions

It should be clear that the variables we are considering are at different levels of analysis; some of them define attributes of persons, while others define attributes of communication and organization. Power processes within organizations are particularly interesting in that there are many channels of power and ways of achieving it.

In complex organizations different occupational groups attend to different functions, each group often maintaining its own power structure within the organization. Thus hospitals have administrators, medical personnel, nursing personnel, attendants, maintenance personnel, laboratory personnel, and so on. Universities, similarly, have teaching personnel, research personnel, administrative personnel, maintenance personnel, and so on. Each of these functional tasks within organizations often becomes the sphere of a particular group that controls activities relating to the task. While these tasks usually are co-ordinated at the highest levels of the organization, they often are not co-ordinated at intermediate and lower levels. It is not unusual, however, for coalitions to form among lower participants in these multiple structures. A secretary may know the man who manages the supply of stores, or the person assigning parking stickers. Such acquaintances may give her the ability to handle informally certain needs that would be more time-consuming and difficult to handle formally. Her ability to provide services informally makes higher-ranking participants in some degree dependent upon her, thereby giving her power, which increases her ability to bargain on issues important to her.

Rules

In organizations with complex power structures lower participants can use their knowledge of the norms of the organization to thwart attempted change. In discussing the various functions of bureaucratic rules, Gouldner maintains that such rules serve as excellent substitutes for surveillance, since surveillance in addition to being expensive in time and effort arouses considerable hostility and antagonism.[20] Moreover, he argues, rules are a functional equivalent for direct, personally given orders, since they specify the obligations of workers to do things in specific ways. Standardized rules, in addition, allow simple screening of violations, facilitate remote control, and to some extent legitimize punishment when the rule is violated. The worker who violates a bureaucratic rule has little recourse to the excuse that he did not know what was expected, as he might claim for a direct order. Finally, Gouldner argues that rules are "the 'chips' to which the company staked the supervisors and which they could use to play the game";[21] that is, rules established a punishment which could be withheld, and this facilitated the supervisors' bargaining power with lower participants.

. While Gouldner emphasizes the functional characteristics of rules within an organization, it should be clear that full compliance to all the rules at all times will probably be dysfunctional for the organization. Complete and apathetic compliance may do everything but facilitate achievement of organizational goals. Lower participants who are familiar with an organization and its rules can often find rules to support their contention that they not do what they have been asked to do, and rules are also often a rationalization for inaction on their part. The following of rules becomes especially complex when associations and unions become involved, for there are then two sets of rules to which the participant can appeal.

What is suggested is that rules may be chips for everyone concerned in the game. Rules become the "chips" through which the bargaining process is maintained. Scheff, as noted earlier, observed that attendants in mental hospitals often took on responsibilities assigned legally to the ward physician, and when attendants refused to share these responsibilities the physician's position became extremely difficult.[22]

The ward physician is legally responsible for the care and treatment of each ward patient. This responsibility requires attention to a host of details. Medicine, seclusion, sedation and transfer orders, for example, require the doctor's signature. Tranquilizers are particularly troublesome in this regard since they require frequent adjustment of dosage in order to get the desired effects. The physician's order is required to each change in dosage. With 150 patients under his care on tranquilizers, and several changes of dosages a week desirable, the physician could spend a major portion of his ward time in dealing with this single detail.

Given the time-consuming formal chores of the physician, and his many other duties, he usually worked out an arrangement with the ward personnel, particularly the charge (supervisory attendant), to handle these duties. On several wards, the charge called specific problems to the doctor's attention, and the two of them, in effect, would have a consultation. The charge actually made most of the decisions concerning dosage change in the back wards. Since the doctor delegated portions of his formal responsibilities to the charge, he was dependent on her good will toward him. If she withheld her cooperation, the physician had absolutely no recourse but to do all the work himself.[23]

In a sense such delegation of responsibility involves a consideration of reward and cost, whereby the decision to be made involves a question of what is more valuable—to retain control over an area, or to delegate one's work to lower participants.

There are occasions, of course, when rules are regarded as illegitimate by lower participants, and they may disregard them. Gouldner observed that, in the mine, men felt they could resist authority in a situation involving danger to themselves.[24] They did not feel that they could legitimately be ordered to do anything that would endanger their lives. It is probably significant that in extremely dangerous situations organizations are more likely to rely on commitment to work than on authority. Even within nonvoluntary groups dangerous tasks are regarded usually as requiring task commitment, and it is likely that commitment is a much more powerful organizational force than coercive authority.

SUMMARY

The preceding remarks are general ones, and they are assumed to be in part true of all types of organizations. But power relationships in organizations are likely to be molded by the type of organization being considered, the nature of organizational goals, the ideology of organizational decision making, the kind of commitment participants have to the organization, the formal structure of the organization, and so on. In short, we have attempted to discuss power processes within organizations in a manner somewhat divorced from other major organizational processes. We have emphasized variables affecting control of access to persons, information, and facilities within organizations. Normative definitions, perception of legitimacy, exchange, and coalitions have all been viewed in relation to power processes. Moreover, we have dealt with some attributes of persons related to power: commitment, effort, interest, willingness to use power, skills, attractiveness, and so on. And we have discussed some

other variables: time, centrality, complexity of power structure, and replaceability of persons. It appears that these variables help to account in part for power exercised by lower participants in organizations.

NOTES

1. Paper presented at the Ford Foundation Seminar in the Social Science of Organizations, University of Pittsburgh, June 10–22, 1962.

2. The term "lower participants" comes from Amitai Etzioni, *A Comparative Analysis of Complex Organizations* (New York, 1961) and is used by him to designate persons in positions of lower rank: employees, rank-and-file, members, clients, customers, and inmates. We shall use the term in this paper in a relative sense denoting position vis-à-vis a higher-ranking participant.

3. Robert Bierstedt, An Analysis of Social Power, *American Sociological Review*, 15 (1950), 730–738.

4. Robert A. Dahl, The Concept of Power, *Behavioral Science*, 2 (1957), 201–215.

5. One might observe, for example, that the power of lower participants is based primarily on the ability to "veto" or punish. For a discussion of bases of power, see John R. P. French, Jr., and Bertram Raven, "The Bases of Social Power," in D. Cartwright and A. Zander, eds., *Group Dynamics* (Evanston, Ill., 1960), pp. 607–623.

6. John Thibaut and Harold H. Kelley, *The Social Psychology of Groups* (New York, 1959). For a similar emphasis on dependence, see Richard M. Emerson, Power-Dependence Relationships, *American Sociological Review*, 27(1962), 31–41.

7. Although this paper will not attempt to explain how access may be measured, the author feels confident that the hypotheses concerned with access are clearly testable.

8. *Op. cit.*

9. Max Weber, "The Essentials of Bureaucratic Organization: An Ideal-Type Construction," in Robert Merton *et al.*, *Reader in Bureaucracy* (Glencoe, Ill., 1952), pp. 18–27.

10. Neal Gross, Ward S. Mason, and Alexander W. McEachern, *Explorations in Role Analysis* (New York, 1958).

11. Robert Merton, The Role-Set: Problems in Sociological Theory, *British Journal of Sociology*, 8 (1957), 106–120.

12. Erving Goffman, *Encounters* (Indianapolis, Ind., 1961), pp. 85–152.

13. Etzioni, *op. cit.*

14. *Ibid.*

15. Thomas J. Scheff, Control over Policy by Attendants in a Mental Hospital, *Journal of Health and Human Behavior*, 2 (1961), 93–105.

16. Gresham M. Sykes, "The Corruption of Authority and Rehabilitation," in A. Etzioni, ed., *Complex Organizations* (New York, 1961), pp. 191–197.

17. As an example, it appears that 6 members of the cabinet, 30 important subcabinet officials, 63 senators, and 230 congressmen are lawyers (*New Yorker*, April 14, 1962, p. 62). Although one can cite many reasons for lawyers holding political posts, an important one appears to be their legal expertise.

18. There is considerable data showing the powerful effect of propinquity on communication. For summary, see Thibaut and Kelley, *op. cit.*, pp. 39–42.

19. The concept of centrality is generally used in a more technical sense in the work of Bavelas, Shaw, Gilchrist, and others. For example, Bavelas defines the central region of a structure as the class of all cells with the smallest distance between one cell and any other cell in the structure, with distance measured in link units. Thus the most central position in a pattern is the position closest to all others. Cf. Harold Leavitt, "Some Effects of Certain Communication Patterns on Group Performance," in E. Maccoby, T. N. Newcomb, and E. L. Hartley, eds., *Readings in Social Psychology* (New York, 1958), p. 559.

20. Alvin W. Gouldner, *Patterns of Industrial Bureaucracy* (Glencoe, Ill., 1954).

21. *Ibid.*, p. 173.

22. Scheff, *op. cit.*

23. *Ibid.*, p. 97.

24. Gouldner, *op. cit.*

29
Management and Machiavelli
Antony Jay

The new science of management is in fact only a continuation of the old art of government, and when you study management theory side by side with political theory, and management case histories side by side with political history, you realize that you are only studying two very similar branches of the same subject. Each illuminates the other, but since history has been studied to excess, and management hardly at all, it is not surprising that it is management situations which are illuminated more often.

It was Machiavelli who brought this truth home to me. Machiavelli is not at the moment required reading in business colleges or on management training courses. In his introduction to the Everyman edition, Herbert Butterfield, Regius Professor of Modern History at Cambridge, claims no modern relevance for his writings: "The chief significance of his work today," he says, "lies in the fact that it marks a stage in the development of the scientific method, whether in statecraft, or in general political analysis, or in the broader fields of history."

Source: Antony Jay, *Management and Machiavelli: An Inquiry into the Politics of Corporate Life* (New York: Holt, Rinehart & Winston, 1967), 3–10. Copyright © 1967 by Antony Jay. Reprinted by permission of Curtis Brown, Ltd..

And yet in fact Machiavelli, however marginal his relevance to academic historians, is bursting with urgent advice and acute observations for top management of the great private and public corporations all over the world.

Although the connection became clear to me in a sudden flash, a moment of what Arthur Koestler calls "bisociation," I can see that I had been working toward it for some time. I was one of the middle management of a large and growing corporation of some 20,000 people with a gross revenue around $100 million a year. I was fascinated, perhaps (in view of my lowly position) precociously fascinated, with the problems of management and leadership and organization, not just of that particular corporation but of any modern corporation that faces the problems of great size and continued growth. It seemed to me then that this scale of operation was still, for most industrial nations, such a new one that we were all probing, pioneering, and guessing, with few helpful precedents and little accumulated wisdom to guide us; each firm was working by trial and error, and all too often repeating the errors of others rather than learning from them.

I was discussing this at lunch with a friend who is chairman of an industrial engineering group. I asked if he and his fellow managers had formulated any laws or amassed a body of folk wisdom about the right way to treat a firm when you have taken it over. He had made some extremely interesting observations from his own experience: One of them was that a staff of four hundred represents the critical number in a firm taken over. It is the number which separates the personal boss from the high-level manager. A man may run a firm of four hundred or fewer people extremely well, but that is the maximum he can run personally, knowing all their names, without too

much delegated authority. If you expand that firm to, say, 1,100, you may destroy him: Instead of all being people he knows by name, they become pegs on a board; instead of just doing and deciding he has to do a lot of explaining and educating; instead of checking up on everything himself, he has to institute a system and establish procedures. All this demands skills quite different from those he built his success on, and ones which he may well lack.

This however was only an isolated observation. There did not seem to be any generally accepted body of opinion, any guiding principles, for the taking over of firms, even though it was (and is) one of the chief problems facing thousands of top managements all over the Western world. Many managers had made their own observations, but they were not collated, and when takeovers happened every firm had to work out how to do it on its own, and from scratch.

The next day, while this conversation was very much in my mind, I was reading Machiavelli's *The Prince*. I thought I was browsing agreeably among the remote political problems of Renaissance Italian states, when suddenly I encountered a sentence which was so utterly relevant to the previous day's discussion that in a few seconds it transformed my attitude to the book, to Machiavelli, to management, and to political history. It seemed like a direct answer to the question of how you make a taken-over firm into a part of your own organization, capable of operating to the same standards and worthy to carry a part of your reputation. The passage (Chapter III) reads:

> The other and better course is to send colonies to one or two places, which may be as keys to that state, for it is necessary either to do this or else to keep there a great number of cavalry and infantry. A prince does not spend much on colonies,

for with little or no expense he can send them out and keep them there, and he offends a minority only of the citizens from whom he takes lands and houses to give them to the new inhabitants; and those whom he offends, remaining poor and scattered, are never able to injure him; whilst the rest being uninjured are easily kept quiet, and at the same time are anxious not to err for fear it should happen to them as it has to those who have been despoiled. In conclusion, I say that these colonies are not costly, they are more faithful, they injure less, and the injured, as has been said, being poor and scattered, cannot hurt. Upon this, one has to remark that men ought either to be well treated or crushed, because they can avenge themselves of lighter injuries, of more serious ones they cannot; therefore the injury that is to be done to a man ought to be of such a kind that one does not stand in fear of revenge.

In other words: "Put small management teams of your own into one or two key factories, because otherwise you'll use up half your staff in giving orders and issuing requests, and then checking that they've been properly fulfilled. By comparison a management team does not cost much, and the only people who will be upset are the former managers whose jobs they have taken over. And since they are no longer in the firm they cannot cause any trouble, while the rest of the staff will not protest as long as they still have their old jobs, particularly while they have the example of the fired managers to keep them on their toes. The guiding principle is that senior men in taken-over firms should either be warmly welcomed and encouraged, or sacked; because if they are sacked they are powerless, whereas if they are simply downgraded they will remain united and resentful and determined to get their own back." This, though Machiavelli does not mention it in this context, is the principle on which the Romans founded their

empire (which was one of the most spectacular examples of successful large-scale management); generosity (full Roman citizenship) or brutality (executions and enslavement, full military garrisons) but not the sort of half-hearted severity that left the defeated enemy resentful and still in being. Since reading that passage I have tried out Machiavelli's principle on several managers who have had to cope with takeovers; they are with him to a man.

Of course this might simply have been a happy coincidence. Many writers have taken elegant analogies from history—the British Broadcasting Corporation has been most persuasively compared with the democratic centralism of the Kremlin—to decorate or illuminate their observations on management. But this seemed altogether too close to be an accident; and the next chapter, when looked at in this new light, also became extremely relevant and up to date:

> The principalities of which one has record are found to be governed in two different ways: either by a prince, with a body of servants, who assist him to govern the kingdom as ministers by his favour and permission; or by a prince and barons, who hold that dignity by antiquity of blood and not by grace of the prince. Such barons have states and their own subjects, who recognize them as lords and hold them in natural affection. The examples of these two governments in our time are the Turk and the King of France. The entire monarchy of the Turk is governed by one lord, the others are his servants; and, dividing his kingdom into sanjaks, he sends there different administrators, and shifts and changes them as he chooses. But the King of France is placed in the midst of an ancient body of lords, acknowledged by their own subjects, and beloved by them; they have their own prerogatives, nor can the king take these away except at his peril.

Anyone who has worked in large organizations must instantly recognize these two basic methods of management. The British civil service is well known to be Turkish in outlook, rotating managers (especially at the lower levels) at a hectic speed. The Foreign Office is particularly religious in its observance, making sure that none of its embassy staffs stay for more than a few years in one place. This, according to Machiavelli, ensures that the goodwill and hopes of benefit of the foreign governments are directed toward the central government in London, and not to the person of its representative. It is the sort of organization which often develops under a very tough and strong top man. According to Machiavelli, it is very hard to force or intrigue your way to the top of such an organization, but comparatively easy to run it once you are there.

At the other pole, the Frankish organization, it is much easier to take over the top position but much harder to achieve anything when you reach it. When a strong and active leader is succeeded by a weak or lazy one, the organization will tend to revert from Turkish to Frankish—the barons are strong when the king is weak. Oxford and Cambridge universities are notorious examples of the Frankish system—it is entirely suitable that the body appointed to inquire into the running of Oxford University should have been known as the Franks Commission. The feudal baronies are the colleges, and the heads of colleges rule them from appointment until retirement with as much freedom from interference as they can arrange. And they arrange it very well; the central government of the university comes under the chancellor, a figurehead, and the vice-chancellor, who is the head of one of the colleges appointed for one year only in strict rotation—an excellent way to ensure that the power of the colleges is never reduced. It is autonomy of the colleges and the impotence of the

university which have always defeated university reform.

The BBC television service, when I belonged to it, was another excellent instance of Frankish government. All the programs of any consequence were produced by four great departments—drama, talks, light entertainment, and outside broadcasts. They were four powerful baronies, and the barons of the last three had all succeeded to the title after being heir apparent (assistant head). And they had been baron or heir apparent for ten, nine, and seventeen years respectively. The fourth was new, but his predecessor had been baron for nine years, and heir apparent for one year before that. In that time there had been all sorts of convulsions in the central government: First there was a controller with an assistant controller, then a second controller with no assistant, then a third controller with a new assistant, then the same controller with two chiefs of programs, and then shortly after I left a fourth controller with two chiefs of programs. It was the continuity of the barons that smoothed out these convulsions; but, according to Machiavelli, it must have meant that the new rulers found it difficult to exercise much control over the actual domains of the barons—the content and quality of the programs they produced.

A few pages later there is another parallel, of particular significance to the manufacturing industries. To translate it into modern terms, Machiavelli discusses whether you should, ideally, manufacture and assemble your product entirely in your own works, or whether you should contract it out to associated companies, or to independent contractors. He argues that associated companies are liable to their own industrial disputes and production and delivery crises which are beyond your control and of a higher priority to them than your order; that independent contractors will delay or scamp your work if a much more lucrative urgent contract crops up; that if you succeed with a product which another firm is making for you, then you place yourself at their mercy; and that you should therefore make everything you possibly can in your own shop. Few production managers would question this conclusion. In fact he expresses it in terms of whether you should defend your state with an army formed by your own citizens, or with auxiliaries, or with mercenaries; he points out that allies may withdraw (or withhold) their troops if they are attacked themselves; or, if they fight and win, that they will then start dictating to you; that mercenaries are always liable to desert to another prince, or even to your enemy, if he pays better; and that an army of your own citizens is the only one you can really trust. The differences are differences of application; the principle, being rooted in human nature, is the same in both cases, and is just as valid now as it was 450 years ago.

The root of the matter is that the great modern corporations are so similar to independent or semi-independent states of the past that they can only be fully understood in terms of political and constitutional history, and management can only be properly studied as a branch of government.

30
Power Failure in Management Circuits
Rosabeth Moss Kanter

Power is America's last dirty word. It is easier to talk about money—and much easier to talk about sex—than it is to talk about power. People who have it deny it; people who want it do not want to appear to hunger for it; and people who engage in its machinations do so secretly.

Yet, because it turns out to be a critical element in effective managerial behavior, power should come out from undercover. Having searched for years for those styles or skills that would identify capable organization leaders, many analysts, like myself, are rejecting individual traits or situational appropriateness as key and finding the sources of a leader's real power.

Access to resources and information and the ability to act quickly make it possible to accomplish more and to pass on more resources and information to subordinates. For this reason, people tend to prefer bosses with "clout." When employees perceive their manager as influential upward and outward, their status is enhanced by association and they generally have high morale and feel less critical or resistant to their boss.[1] More powerful leaders are also more likely to delegate (they are too busy to do it all themselves), to reward talent, and to build a team that places subordinates in significant positions.

Powerlessness, in contrast, tends to breed bossiness rather than true leadership. In large organizations, at least, it is powerlessness that often creates ineffective, desultory management and petty, dictatorial, rules-minded managerial styles. Accountability without power—responsibility for results without the resources to get them—creates frustration and failure. People who see themselves as weak and powerless and find their subordinates resisting or discounting them tend to use more punishing forms of influence. If organizational power can "ennoble," then, recent research shows, organizational powerlessness can (with apologies to Lord Acton) "corrupt."[2]

So perhaps power, in the organization at least, does not deserve such a bad reputation. Rather than connoting only dominance, control, and oppression, *power* can mean efficacy and capacity—something managers and executives need to move the organization toward its goals. Power in organizations is analogous in simple terms to physical power: it is the ability to mobilize resources (human and material) to get things done. The true sign of power, then, is accomplishment—not fear, terror, or tyranny. Where the power is "on," the system can be productive; where the power is "off," the system bogs down.

But saying that people need power to be effective in organizations does not tell us where it comes from or why some people, in some jobs, systematically seem to have more of it than others. In this article I want to show that to discover the sources of productive power, we have to look not at the *person*—as conventional classifications of effective managers and employees do—but at the *position* the person occupies in the organization.

WHERE DOES POWER COME FROM?

The effectiveness that power brings evolves from two kinds of capacities: first, access to the resources, information, and support necessary to carry out a task; and, second, ability to get cooperation in doing what is necessary. (Figure 1 identifies some symbols of an individual manager's power.)

Both capacities derive not so much from a leader's style and skill as from his or her location in the formal and informal systems of the organization—in both job definition and connection to other important people in the company. Even the ability to get cooperation from subordinates is strongly defined by the manager's clout outward. People are more responsive to bosses who look as if they can get more for them from the organization.

We can regard the uniquely organizational sources of power as consisting of three "lines":

1. *Lines of Supply.* Influence outward, over the environment, means that managers have the capacity to bring in the things that their own organizational domain needs—materials, money, resources to distribute as rewards, and perhaps even prestige.

2. *Lines of Information.* To be effective, managers need to be "in the know" in both the formal and the informal sense.

3. *Lines of Support.* In a formal framework, a manager's job parameters need to allow for nonordinary action, for a show of discretion or exercise of judgment. Thus managers need to know that they can assume innovative, risk-taking activities without having to go through the stifling multi-layered approval process. And, informally, managers need the backing of other important figures in the organization whose

FIGURE 1 • SOME COMMON SYMBOLS OF A MANAGER'S
ORGANIZATIONAL POWER (INFLUENCE UPWARD AND OUTWARD)

To What Extent a Manager Can—

Intercede favorably on behalf of someone in trouble with the organization.

Get a desirable placement for a talented subordinate.

Get approval for expenditures beyond the budget.

Get above-average salary increases for subordinates.

Get items on the agenda at policy meetings.

Get fast access to top decision makers.

Get regular, frequent access to top decision makers.

Get early information about decisions and policy shifts.

tacit approval becomes another resource they bring to their own work unit as well as a sign of the manager's being "in."

Note that productive power has to do with *connections* with other parts of a system. Such systemic aspects of power derive from two sources—job activities and political alliances:

1. Power is most easily accumulated when one has a job that is designed and located to allow *discretion* (nonroutinized action permitting flexible, adaptive, and creative contributions), *recognition* (visibility and notice), and *relevance* (being central to pressing organizational problems).

2. Power also comes when one has relatively close contact with *sponsors* (higher-level people who confer approval, prestige, or backing), *peer networks* (circles of acquaintanceship that provide reputation and information, the grapevine often being faster than formal communication channels), and *subordinates* (who can be developed to relieve managers of some of their burdens and to represent the manager's point of view).

When managers are in powerful situations, it is easier for them to accomplish more. Because the tools are there, they are likely to be highly motivated and, in turn, to be able to motivate subordinates. Their activities are more likely to be on target and to net them successes. They can flexibly interpret or shape policy to meet the needs of particular areas, emergent situations, or sudden environmental shifts. They gain the respect and cooperation that attributed power brings. Subordinates' talents are resources rather than threats. And, because powerful managers have so many lines of connection and thus are oriented outward, they tend to let go of control downward, developing more independently functioning lieutenants.

The powerless live in a different world. Lacking the supplies, information, or support to make things happen easily, they may turn instead to the ultimate weapon of those who lack productive power—oppressive power: holding others back and punishing with whatever threats they can muster.

Figure 2 summarizes some of the major ways in which variables in the organization and in job design contribute to either power or powerlessness.

POSITIONS OF POWERLESSNESS

Understanding what it takes to have power and recognizing the classic behavior of the powerless can immediately

FIGURE 2 • WAYS ORGANIZATIONAL FACTORS CONTRIBUTE TO
POWER OR POWERLESSNESS

Factors	Generates Power when Factor Is	Generates Powerlessness when Factor Is
Rules inherent in the job	few	many
Predecessors in the job	few	many
Established routines	few	many
Task variety	high	low
Rewards for reliability/predictability	few	many
Rewards for unusual performance/innovation	many	few
Flexibility around use of people	high	low
Approvals needed for nonroutine decisions	few	many
Physical location	central	distant
Publicity about job activities	high	low
Relation of tasks to current problem areas	central	peripheral
Focus of tasks	outside work unit	inside work unit
Interpersonal contact in the job	high	low
Contact with senior officials	high	low
Participation in programs, conferences, meetings	high	low
Participation in problem-solving task forces	high	low
Advancement prospects of subordinates	high	low

help managers make sense out of a number of familiar organizational problems that are usually attributed to inadequate people:

> The ineffectiveness of first-line supervisors.
> The petty interest protection and conservatism of staff professionals.
> The crises of leadership at the top.

Instead of blaming the individuals involved in organizational problems, let us look at the positions people occupy. Of course, power or powerlessness in a position may not be all of the problem. Sometimes incapable people *are* at fault and need to be retrained or replaced. (See the ruled insert on pages 354–356 for a discussion of another special case, women.) But where patterns emerge, where the troubles associated with some

units persist, organizational power failures could be the reason. Then, as Volvo President Pehr Gyllenhammar concludes, we should treat the powerless not as "villains" causing headaches for everyone else but as "victims."[3]

First-Line Supervisors

Because an employee's most important work relationship is with his or her supervisor, when many of them talk about "the company," they mean their immediate boss. Thus a supervisor's behavior is an important determinant of the average employee's relationship to work and is in itself a critical link in the production chain.

Yet I know of no U.S. corporate management entirely satisfied with the performance of its supervisors. Most see them as supervising too closely and not training their people. In one manufacturing company where direct laborers were asked on a survey how they learned their job, on a list of seven possibilities "from my supervisor" ranked next to last. (Only company training programs ranked worse.) Also, it is said that supervisors do not translate company policies into practice—for instance, that they do not carry out the right of every employee to frequent performance reviews or to career counseling.

In court cases charging race or sex discrimination, first-line supervisors are frequently cited as the "discriminating official."[4] And, in studies of innovative work redesign and quality of work life projects, they often appear as the implied villains; they are the ones who are said to undermine the program or interfere with its effectiveness. In short, they are often seen as "not sufficiently managerial."

The problem affects white-collar as well as blue-collar supervisors. In one large government agency, supervisors in field offices were seen as the source of problems concerning morale and the flow of information to and from headquarters. "Their attitudes are negative," said a senior official. "They turn people against the agency; they put down senior management. They build themselves up by always complaining about headquarters, but prevent their staff from getting any information directly. We can't afford to have such attitudes communicated to field staff."

Is the problem that supervisors need more management training programs or that incompetent people are invariably attracted to the job? Neither explanation suffices. A large part of the problem lies in the position itself—one that almost universally creates powerlessness.

First-line supervisors are "people in the middle," and that has been seen as the source of many of their problems.[5]

But by recognizing that first-line supervisors are caught between higher management and workers, we only begin to skim the surface of the problem. There is practically no other organizational category as subject to powerlessness.

First, these supervisors may be at a virtual dead end in their careers. Even in companies where the job used to be a stepping stone to higher-level management jobs, it is now common practice to bring in MBAs from the outside for those positions. Thus moving from the ranks of direct labor into supervision may mean, essentially, getting "stuck" rather than moving upward. Because employees do not perceive supervisors as eventually joining the leadership circles of the organization, they may see them as lacking the high-level contacts needed to have clout. Indeed, sometimes turnover among supervisors is so high that workers feel they can outwait—and outwit—any boss.

Second, although they lack clout, with little in the way of support from above, supervisors are forced to administer programs or explain policies that they have no hand in shaping. In one company, as part of a new personnel program supervisors were required to conduct counseling interviews with employees. But supervisors were not trained to do this and were given no incentives to get involved. Counseling was just another obligation. Then managers suddenly encouraged the workers to bypass their supervisors or to put pressure on them. The personnel staff brought them together and told them to demand such interviews as a basic right. If supervisors had not felt powerless before, they did after that squeeze from below, engineered from above.

The people they supervise can also make life hard for them in numerous ways. This often happens when a supervisor has himself or herself risen up from the ranks. Peers that have not made it are resentful or derisive of their former colleague, whom they now see as trying to lord it over them. Often it is easy for workers to break rules and let a lot of things slip.

Yet first-line supervisors are frequently judged according to rules and regulations while being limited by other regulations in what disciplinary actions they can take. They often lack the resources to influence or reward people; after all, workers are guaranteed their pay and benefits by someone other than their supervisors. Supervisors cannot easily control events; rather, they must react to them.

In one factory, for instance, supervisors complained that performance of their job was out of their control: they could fill production quotas only if they had the supplies, but they had no way to influence the people controlling supplies.

The lack of support for many first-line managers, particularly in large organizations, was made dramatically clear in another company. When asked if contact with executives higher in the organization who had the potential for offering support, information, and alliances

diminished their own feelings of career vulnerability and the number of headaches they experienced on the job, supervisors in five out of seven work units responded positively. For them *contact* was indeed related to a greater feeling of acceptance at work and membership in the organization.

But in the two other work units where there was greater contact, people perceived more, not less, career vulnerability. Further investigation showed that supervisors in these business units got attention only when they were in trouble. Otherwise, no one bothered to talk to them. To these particular supervisors, hearing from a higher-level manager was a sign not of recognition or potential support but of danger.

It is not surprising, then, that supervisors frequently manifest symptoms of powerlessness: overly close supervision, rules-mindedness, and a tendency to do the job themselves rather than to train their people (since job skills may be one of the few remaining things they feel good about). Perhaps this is why they sometimes stand as roadblocks between their subordinates and the higher reaches of the company.

Women Managers Experience Special Power Failures

The traditional problems of women in management are illustrative of how formal and informal practices can combine to engender powerlessness. Historically, women in management have found their opportunities in more routine, low-profile jobs. In staff positions, where they serve in support capacities to line managers but have no line responsibilities of their own, or in supervisory jobs managing "stuck" subordinates, they are not in a position either to take the kinds of risks that build credibility or to develop their own team by pushing bright subordinates.

Such jobs, which have few favors to trade, tend to keep women out of the mainstream of the organization. This lack of clout, coupled with the greater difficulty anyone who is "different" has in getting into the information and support networks, has meant that merely by organizational situation women in management have been more likely than men to be rendered structurally powerless. This is one reason those women who have achieved power have often had family connections that put them in the mainstream of the organization's social circles.

A *disproportionate number of women managers are found among first-line supervisors or staff professionals; and they, like men in those circumstances, are likely to be organizationally powerless. But the behavior of other managers can contribute to the powerlessness of women in management in a number of less obvious ways.*

One way other managers can make a woman powerless is by patronizingly overprotecting her: putting her in "a safe job," not giving her enough to do to prove herself, and not suggesting her for high-risk, visible assignments. This protectiveness is sometimes born of "good" intentions to give her every chance to succeed (why stack the deck against her?). Out of managerial concerns, out of awareness that a woman may be up against situations that men simply do not have to face, some very well-meaning managers protect their female managers ("It's a jungle, so why send her into it?").

Overprotectiveness can also mask a manager's fear of association with a woman should she fail. One senior bank official at a level below vice president told me about his concerns with respect to a high-performing, financially experienced woman reporting to him. Despite his overwhelmingly positive work experiences with her, he was still afraid to recommend her for other assignments because he felt it was a personal risk. "What if other managers are not as accepting of women as I am?" he asked. "I know I'd be sticking my neck out; they would take her more because of my endorsement than her qualifications. And what if she doesn't make it? My judgment will be on the line."

Overprotection is relatively benign compared with rendering a person powerless by providing obvious signs of lack of managerial support. For example, allowing someone supposedly in authority to be bypassed easily means that no one else has to take him or her seriously. If a woman's immediate supervisor or other managers listen willingly to criticism of her and show they are concerned every time a negative comment comes up and that they assume she must be at fault, then they are helping to undercut her. If managers let other people know that they have concerns about this person or that they are testing her to see how she does, then they are inviting other people to look for signs of inadequacy or failure.

Furthermore, people assume they can afford to bypass women because they "must be uninformed" or "don't know the ropes." Even though women may be respected for their competence or expertise, they are not necessarily seen as being informed beyond the technical requirements of the job. There may be a grain of historical truth in this. Many women come to senior management positions as "outsiders" rather than up through the usual channels.

Also, because until very recently men have not felt comfortable seeing women as businesspeople (business clubs have traditionally excluded women), they have tended to seek each other out for informal socializing. Anyone, male or female, seen as organizationally naive and lacking sources of "inside dope" will find his or her own lines of information limited.

Finally, even when women are able to achieve some power on their own, they have not necessarily been able to translate such personal credibility into an organizational power base. To create a network of supporters out of individual clout requires that a person pass on and share power, that subordinates and peers be empowered by virtue of their connection with that person. Traditionally, neither men nor women have seen women as capable of sponsoring others, even though they may be capable of achieving and succeeding on their own. Women have been viewed as the recipients of sponsorship rather than as the sponsors themselves.

(As more women prove themselves in organizations and think more self-consciously about bringing along young people, this situation may change. However, I still hear many more questions from women managers about how they can benefit from mentors, sponsors, or peer networks than about how they themselves can start to pass on favors and make use of their own resources to benefit others.)

Viewing managers in terms of power and powerlessness helps explain two familiar stereotypes about women and leadership in organizations: that no one wants a woman boss (although studies show that anyone who has ever had a woman boss is likely to have had a positive experience), and that the reason no one wants a woman boss is that women are "too controlling, rules-minded, and petty."

The first stereotype simply makes clear that power is important to leadership. Underneath the preference for men is the assumption that, given the current distribution of people in organizational leadership positions, men are more likely than women to be in positions to achieve power and, therefore, to share their power with others. Similarly, the "bossy woman boss" stereotype is a perfect picture of powerlessness. All of those traits are just as characteristic of men who are powerless, but women are slightly more likely, because of circumstances I have mentioned, to find themselves powerless than are men. Women with power in the organization are just as effective—and preferred—as men.

Recent interviews conducted with about 600 bank managers show that, when a woman exhibits the petty traits of powerlessness, people assume that she does so "because she is a woman." A striking difference is that, when a man engages in the same behavior, people assume the behavior is a matter of his own individual style and characteristics and do not conclude that it reflects on the suitability of men for management.

Staff Professionals

Also working under conditions that can lead to organizational powerlessness are the staff specialists. As advisers behind the scenes, staff people must sell their programs and bargain for resources, but unless they get themselves entrenched in organizational power networks, they have little in the way of favors to exchange. They are seen as useful adjuncts to the primary tasks of the organization but inessential in a day-to-day operating sense. This disenfranchisement occurs particularly when staff jobs consist of easily routinized administrative functions which are out of the mainstream of the currently relevant areas and involve little innovative decision making.

Furthermore, in some organizations, unless they have had previous line experience, staff people tend to be limited in the number of jobs into which they can move. Specialists' ladders are often very short, and professionals are just as likely to get "stuck" in such jobs as people are in less prestigious clerical or factory positions.

Staff people, unlike those who are being groomed for important line positions, may be hired because of a special expertise or particular background. But management rarely pays any attention to developing them into more general organizational resources. Lacking growth prospects themselves and working alone or in very small teams, they are not in a position to develop others or pass on power to them. They miss out on an important way that power can be accumulated.

Sometimes staff specialists, such as house counsel or organization development people, find their work being farmed out to consultants. Management considers them fine for the routine work, but the minute the activities involve risk or something problematic, they bring in outside experts. This treatment says something not only about their expertise but also about the status of their function. Since the company can always hire talent on a temporary basis, it is unclear that the management really needs to have or considers important its own staff for these functions.

And, because staff professionals are often seen as adjuncts to primary tasks, their effectiveness and therefore their contribution to the organization are often hard to measure. Thus visibility and recognition, as well as risk taking and relevance, may be denied to people in staff jobs.

Staff people tend to act out their powerlessness by becoming turf-minded. They create islands within the organization. They set themselves up as the only ones who can control professional standards and judge their own work. They create sometimes false distinctions between themselves as experts (no one else could possibly do what they do) and lay people, and this continues to keep them out of the mainstream.

One form such distinctions take is a combination of disdain when line managers attempt to act in areas the professionals think are their preserve and of subtle refusal to support the managers' efforts. Or staff groups battle with each other for control of new "problem areas," with the result that no one really handles the issue at all. To cope with their essential powerlessness, staff groups may try to elevate their own status and draw

boundaries between themselves and others.

When staff jobs are treated as final resting places for people who have reached their level of competence in the organization—a good shelf on which to dump managers who are too old to go anywhere but too young to retire—then staff groups can also become pockets of conservatism, resistant to change. Their own exclusion from the risk-taking action may make them resist *anyone's* innovative proposals. In the past, personnel departments, for example, have sometimes been the last in their organization to know about innovations in human resource development or to be interested in applying them.

Top Executives

Despite the great resources and responsibilities concentrated at the top of an organization, leaders can be powerless for reasons that are not very different from those that affect staff and supervisors: lack of supplies, information, and support.

We have faith in leaders because of their ability to make things happen in the larger world, to create possibilities for everyone else, and to attract resources to the organization. These are their supplies. But influence outward—the source of much credibility downward—can diminish as environments change, setting terms and conditions out of the control of the leaders. Regardless of top management's grand plans for the organization, the environment presses. At the very least, things going on outside the organization can deflect a leader's attention and drain energy. And, more detrimental, decisions made elsewhere can have severe consequences for the organization and affect top management's sense of power and thus its operating style inside.

In the go-go years of the mid-1960s, for example, nearly every corporation officer or university president could look—and therefore feel—successful. Visible success gave leaders a great deal of credibility inside the organization, which in turn gave them the power to put new things in motion.

In the past few years, the environment has been strikingly different and the capacity of many organization leaders to do anything about it has been severely limited. New "players" have flexed their power muscles: the Arab oil bloc, government regulators, and congressional investigating committees. And managing economic decline is quite different from managing growth. It is no accident that when top leaders personally feel out of control, the control function in corporations grow.

As powerlessness in lower levels of organizations can manifest itself in overly routinized jobs where performance measures are oriented to rules and absence of change, so it can at upper levels as well. Routine work often drives out nonroutine work. Accomplishment becomes a question of nailing down details. Short-term results provide immediate gratifications and satisfy stockholders or other constituencies with limited interests.

It takes a powerful leader to be willing to risk short-term deprivations in order to bring about desired long-term outcomes. Much as first-line supervisors are tempted to focus on daily adherence to rules, leaders are tempted to focus on short-term fluctuations and lose sight of long-term objectives. The dynamics of such a situation are self-reinforcing. The more the long-term goals go unattended, the more a leader feels powerless and the greater the scramble to prove that he or she is in control of daily events at least. The more he is involved in the organization as a short-term Mr. Fix-it, the more out of control of long-term objectives he is, and the more ultimately powerless he is likely to be.

Credibility for the top executives often comes from doing the extraordinary: exercising discretion, creating, inventing, planning, and acting in nonroutine ways. But since routine problems look easier and more manageable, require less change and consent on the part of anyone else, and lend themselves to instant solutions that can make any leader look good temporarily, leaders may avoid the risky by taking over what their subordinates should be doing. Ultimately, a leader may succeed in getting all the trivial problems dumped on his or her desk. This can establish expectations even for leaders attempting more challenging tasks. When Warren Bennis was president of the University of Cincinnati, a professor called him when the heat was down in a classroom. In writing about this incident, Bennis commented, "I suppose he expected me to grab a wrench and fix it."[6]

People at the top need to insulate themselves from the routine operations of the organization in order to develop and exercise power. But this very insulation can lead to another source of powerlessness—lack of information. In one multinational corporation, top executives who are sealed off in a large, distant office, flattered and virtually babied by aides, are frustrated by their distance from the real action.[7]

At the top, the concern for secrecy and privacy is mixed with real loneliness. In one bank, organization members were so accustomed to never seeing the top leaders that when a new senior vice president went to the branch offices to look around, they had suspicion, even fear, about his intentions.

Thus leaders who are cut out of an organization's information networks understand neither what is really going on at lower levels nor that their own isolation may be having negative effects. All too often top executives design "beneficial" new employee programs or declare a new humanitarian policy (e.g., "Participatory management is now our style") only to find the policy ignored or mistrusted because it is perceived as coming from uncaring bosses.

The information gap has more serious consequences when executives are so insulated from the rest of the organization or from other decision makers that, as Nixon so dramatically did, they fail to see their own impending downfall. Such insulation is partly a matter of organizational position and, in some cases, of executive style.

For example, leaders may create closed inner circles consisting of "doppelgängers," people just like themselves, who are their principal sources of organizational information and tell them only what they want to know. The reasons for the distortions are varied: key aides want to relieve the leader of burdens, they think just like the leader, they want to protect their own positions of power, or the familiar "kill the messenger" syndrome makes people close to top executives reluctant to the bearers of bad news.

Finally, just as supervisors and lower-level managers need their supporters in order to be and feel powerful, so do top executives. But for them sponsorship may not be so much a matter of individual endorsement as an issue of support by larger sources of legitimacy in the society. For top executives the problem is not to fit in among peers; rather, the question is whether the public at large and other organization members perceive a common interest which they see the executives as promoting.

If, however, public sources of support are withdrawn and leaders are open to public attack or if inside constituencies fragment and employees see their interests better aligned with pressure groups than with organizational leadership, then powerlessness begins to set in.

When common purpose is lost, the system's own politics may reduce the capacity of those at the top to act. Just as managing decline seems to create a much more passive and reactive stance than managing growth, so does mediating among conflicting interests. When what is happening outside and inside their organizations is out of control, many people at the top turn into decline managers and dispute mediators. Neither is a particularly empowering role.

Thus when top executives lose their own lines of supply, lines of information, and lines of suport, they too suffer from a kind of powerlessness. The temptation for them then is to pull in every shred of power they can and to decrease the power available to other people to act. Innovation loses out in favor of control. Limits rather than targets are set. Financial goals are met by reducing "overhead" (people) rather than by giving people the tools and discretion to increase their own productive capacity. Dictatorial statements come down from the top, spreading the mentality of powerlessness farther until the whole organization becomes sluggish and people concentrate on protecting what they have rather than on producing what they can.

When everyone is playing "king of the mountain," guarding his or her turf jealously, then king of the mountain becomes the only game in town.

TO EXPAND POWER, SHARE IT

In no case am I saying that people in the three hierarchical levels described are always powerless, but they are susceptible to common conditions that can contribute to powerlessness. Figure 3

FIGURE 3 • COMMON SYMPTOMS AND SOURCES OF
POWERLESSNESS FOR THREE KEY ORGANIZATIONAL POSITIONS

Position	Symptoms	Sources
First-line supervisors	Close, rules-minded supervision	Routine, rules-minded jobs with little control over lines of supply
	Tendency to do things oneself, blocking of subordinates' development and information	Limited lines of information
	Resistant, underproducing subordinates	Limited advancement or involvement prospects for oneself/subordinates
Staff professionals	Turf protection, information control	Routine tasks seen as peripheral to "real tasks" of line organization
	Retreat into professionalism	Blocked careers
	Conservative resistance to change	Easy replacement by outside experts
Top executives	Focus on internal cutting, short-term results, "punishing"	Uncontrollable lines of supply because of environmental changes
	Dictatorial top-down communications	Limited or blocked lines of information about lower levels of organization
	Retreat to comfort of like-minded lieutenants	Diminished lines of support because of challenges to legitimacy (e.g., from the public or special interest groups)

summarizes the most common symptoms of powerlessness for each level and some typical sources of that behavior.

I am also distinguishing the tremendous concentration of economic and political power in large corporations themselves from the powerlessness that can beset individuals even in the highest positions in such organizations. What grows with organizational position in hierarchical levels is not necessarily the power to accomplish—productive power—but the power to punish, to prevent, to sell off, to reduce, to fire, all without appropriate concern for consequences. It is that kind of power—oppressive power—that we often say corrupts.

The absence of ways to prevent individual and social harm causes the polity to feel it must surround people in power with constraints, regulations, and laws that limit the arbitrary use of their authority. But if oppressive power corrupts, then so does the absence of productive power. In large organizations, powerlessness can be a bigger problem than power.

David C. McClelland makes a similar distinction between oppressive and productive power:

The negative . . . face of power is characterized by the dominance-submission mode: if I win, you lose. . . . It leads to simple and direct means of feeling powerful [such as being aggressive]. It does not often lead to effective social leadership for the reason that such a person tends to treat other people as pawns. People who feel they are pawns tend to be passive and useless to the leader who gets his satisfaction from dominating them. Slaves are the most inefficient form of labor ever devised by man. If a leader wants to have far-reaching influence, he must make his followers feel powerful and able to accomplish things on their own. . . . Even the most dictatorial leader does not succeed if he has not instilled in at least some of his followers a sense of power and the strength to pursue the goals he has set.[8]

Organizational power can grow, in part, by being shared. We do not yet know enough about new organizational forms to say whether productive power is infinitely expandable or where we reach the point of diminishing returns. But we do know that sharing power is different from giving or throwing it away. Delegation does not mean abdication.

Some basic lessons could be translated from the field of economics to the realm of organizations and management. Capital investment in plants and equipment is not the only key to productivity. The productive capacity of nations, like organizations, grows if the skill base is upgraded. People with the tools, information, and support to make more informed decisions and act more quickly can often accomplish more. By empowering others, a leader does not decrease his power; instead he may increase it—especially if the whole organization performs better.

This analysis leads to some counterintuitive conclusions. In a certain tautological sense, the principal problem of the powerless is that they lack power. Powerless people are usually the last ones to whom anyone wants to entrust more power, for fear of its dissipation or abuse. But those people are precisely the ones who might benefit most from an injection of power and whose behavior is likely to change as new options open up to them.

Also, if the powerless bosses could be encouraged to share some of the power they do have, their power would grow. Yet, of course, only those leaders who feel secure about their own power outward—their lines of supply, information, and support—can see empowering subordinates as a gain rather than a loss. The two sides of power (getting it and giving it) are closely connected.

There are important lessons here for both subordinates and those who want to change organizations, whether executives or change agents. Instead of resisting or criticizing a powerless boss, which only increases the boss's feeling of powerlessness and need to control, subordinates instead might concentrate on helping the boss become more powerful. Managers might make pockets of ineffectiveness in the organization more productive not by training or replacing individuals but by structural solutions such as opening supply and support lines.

Similarly, organizational change agents who make a new program or policy to succeed should make sure that the change itself does not render any other level of the organization powerless. In making changes, it is wise to make sure that the key people in the level or two directly above and in neighboring functions are sufficiently involved, informed, and taken into account, so that the program can be used to build their own sense of power also. If such involvement is impossible, then it is better to move these people out of the territory altogether than to leave behind a group from whom some power has been removed and who might resist and undercut the program.

In part, of course, spreading power means educating people to this new definition of it. But words alone will not make the difference; managers will need the real experience of a new way of managing.

Here is how the associate director of a large corporate professional department phrased the lessons that he learned in the transition to a team-oriented, participatory, power-sharing management process:

"Get in the habit of involving your own managers in decision making and approvals. But don't abdicate! Tell them what you want and where you're coming from. Don't go for a one-boss grass roots 'democracy.' Make the mangement hierarchy work for you in participation. . . .

"Hang in there, baby, and don't give up. Try not to 'revert' just because everything seems to go sour on a particular day. Open up—talk to people and tell them how you feel. They'll want to get you back on track and will do things to make that happen—because they don't really want to go back to the way it was. . . . Subordinates will push you to 'act more like a boss,' but their interest is usually more in seeing someone else brought to heel than getting bossed themselves."

Naturally, people need to have power before they can learn to share it. Exhorting managers to change their leadership styles is rarely useful by itself. In one large plant of a major electronics company, first-line production supervisors were the source of numerous complaints from managers who saw them as major roadblocks to overall plant productivity and as insufficiently skilled supervisors. So the plant personnel staff undertook two pilot programs to increase the supervisors' effectiveness. The first program was based on a traditional competency and training model aimed at teaching the specific skills of successful supervisors. The second program, in contrast, was designed to empower the supervisors by directly affecting their flexibility, access to resources, connections with higher-level officials, and control over working conditions.

After an initial gathering of data from supervisors and their subordinates, the personnel staff held meetings where all the supervisors were given tools for developing action plans for sharing the data with their people and collaborating on solutions to perceived problems. But then, in a departure from common practice in this organization, task forces of supervisors were formed to develop new systems for handling job and career issues common to them and their people. These task forces were given budgets, consultants, representation on a plant-wide project steering committee alongside managers at much higher levels, and wide latitude in defining the nature and scope of the changes they wished to make. In short, lines of supply, information, and support were opened to them.

As the task forces progressed in their activities, it became clear to the plant management that the hoped-for changes in supervisory effectiveness were taking place much more rapidly through these structural changes in power than through conventional management training; so the conventional training was dropped. Not only did the pilot groups design useful new procedures for the plant, astonishing senior management in several cases with their knowledge and capabilities, but also, significantly, they learned to manage their own people better.

Several groups decided to involve shop-floor workers in their task forces; they could now see from their own experience the benefits of involving subordinates in solving job-related problems. Other supervisors began to experiment with ways to implement "participatory management" by giving subordinates more control and influence without relinquishing their own authority.

Soon the "problem supervisors" in the "most troubled plant in the company" were getting the highest possible performance ratings and were considered models for direct production management. The sharing of organizational power from the top made possible the productive use of power below.

One might wonder why more organizations do not adopt such empowering strategies. There are standard answers: that giving up control is threatening to people who have fought for every shred of it; that people do not want to share power with those they look down on; that managers fear losing their own place and special privileges in the system; that "predictability" often rates higher than "flexibility" as an organizational value; and so forth.

But I would also put skepticism about employee abilities high on the list. Many modern bureaucratic systems are designed to minimize dependence on individual intelligence by making routine as many decisions as possible. So it often comes as a genuine surprise to top executives that people doing the more routine jobs could, indeed, make sophisticated decisions or use resources entrusted to them in intelligent ways.

In the same electronics company just mentioned, at the end of a quarter the pilot supervisory task forces were asked to report results and plans to senior management in order to have their new budget requests approved. The task forces made sure they were well prepared, and the high-level executives were duly impressed. In fact, they were *so* impressed that they kept interrupting the presen-

tations with compliments, remarking that the supervisors could easily be doing sophisticated personnel work.

At first the supervisors were flattered. Such praise from upper management could only be taken well. But when the first glow wore off, several of them became very angry. They saw the excessive praise as patronizing and insulting. "Didn't they think we could think? Didn't they imagine we were capable of doing this kind of work?" one asked. "They must have seen us as just a bunch of animals. No wonder they gave us such limited jobs."

As far as these supervisors were concerned, their abilities had always been there, in latent form perhaps, but still there. They as individuals had not changed—just their organizational power.

NOTES

1. Donald C. Pelz, "Influence: A Key to Effective Leadership in the First-Line Supervisor," *Personnel*, November 1952, p. 209.

2. See my book, *Men and Women of the Corporation* (New York: Basic Books, 1977), pp. 164–205; and David Kipnis, *The Powerholders* (Chicago: University of Chicago Press, 1976).

3. Pehr G Gyllenhammar, *People at Work* (Reading, Mass.: Addison-Wesley, 1977), p. 133.

4. William E. Fulmer, "Supervisory Selection: The Acid Test of Affirmative Action," *Personnel*, November-December 1976, p. 40.

5. See my chapter (coauthor, Barry A. Stein), "Life in the Middle: Getting In, Getting Up, and Getting Along," in *Life in Organizations*, eds. Rosabeth M. Kanter and Barry A. Stein (New York: Basic Books, 1979).

6. Warren Bennis, *The Unconscious Conspiracy: Why Leaders Can't Lead* (New York: AMACOM, 1976).

7. See my chapter, "How the Top is Different," in *Life in Organizations*.

8. David C. McClelland, *Power: The Inner Experience* (New York: Irvington Publishers, 1975), p. 263. Quoted by permission.

31
The Power Game and the Players
Henry Mintzberg

The core of this book is devoted to the discussion of a theory of organizational power. It is built on the premise that organizational behavior is a power game in which various players, called *influencers*, seek to control the organization's decisions and actions. The organization first comes into being when an initial group of influencers join together to pursue a common mission. Other influencers are subsequently attracted to the organization as a vehicle for satisfying some of their needs. Since the needs of influencers vary, each tries to use his or her own levers of power—*means or systems of influence*—to control decisions and actions. How they succeed determines what configuration of organizational power emerges. Thus, to understand the behavior of the organization, it is necessary to understand which influencers are present, what needs each seeks to fulfill in the organization, and how each is able to exercise power to fulfill them.

Of course, much more than power determines what an organization does. But our perspective in this book is that power is what matters, and that, if you like, everyone exhibits a lust for power (an assumption, by the way, that I do not personally favor, but that proves useful for the purposes of this book). When our conclusions here are coupled with those of the first book in this series, *The Structuring of Organizations* (Mintzberg 1979a, which will subsequently be referred to as the *Structuring* book), a more complete picture of the behavior of organizations emerges.

THE EXERCISE OF POWER

Hirschman (1970) notes in a small but provocative book entitled *Exit, Voice, and Loyalty,* that the participant in any system has three basic options:

> To stay and contribute as expected, which Hirschman calls *loyalty* (in the vernacular, "Shut up and deal")
>
> To leave, which Hirschman calls *exit* ("Take my marbles and go")
>
> To stay and try to change the system, which Hirschman refers to as *voice* ("I'd rather fight than switch")

Should he or she choose voice, the participant becomes what we call an influencer.[1] Those who exit—such as the client who stops buying or the employee who seeks work elsewhere—cease to be influencers, while those who choose loyalty over voice—the client who buys without question at the going rate, the employees who do whatever they are told quietly—choose not to participate as active influencers (other than to support implicitly the existing power structure).

Source: Henry Mintzberg, *Power in and around Organizations,* © 1983, pp. 22–30. Reprinted by permission of Prentice-Hall, Englewood Cliffs, New Jersey.

To resort to voice, rather than exit, is for the customer or member to make an attempt at changing the practices, policies, and outputs of the firm from which one buys or of the organization to which one belongs. Voice is here defined as any attempt at all to change, rather than to escape from, an objectionable state of affairs . . . (Hirschman 1970, p. 30)[2]

For those who stay and fight, what gives power to their voice? Essentially the influencer requires (1) some source or basis of power, coupled with (2) the expenditure of energy in a (3) politically skillful way when necessary. These are the three basic conditions for the exercise of power. In Allison's concise words, "Power . . . is an elusive blend of . . . bargaining advantages, skill and will in using bargaining advantages . . ." (1971, p. 168).

The General Bases of Power

In the most basic sense, the power of the individual in or over the organization reflects some *dependency* that it has—some gap in its own power as a system, in Crozier's view, an "uncertainty" that the organization faces (Crozier 1964; also Crozier and Friedberg 1977). This is especially true of three of the five bases of power we describe here.[3] Three prime bases of power are control of (1) a resource, (2) a technical skill, or (3) a body of knowledge, any one critical to the organization. For example, a monopolist may control the raw material supply to an organization, while an expert may control the repair of important and highly complex machinery. To serve as a basis of power, a resource, skill or body of knowledge must first of all be *essential* to the functioning of the organization. Second, it must be *concentrated*, in short supply or else in the hands of one person or a small number of people who cooperate to some extent. And third it must be *nonsubstitutable*, in

other words irreplaceable. These three characteristics create the dependency—the organization needs something, and it can get it only from the few people who have it.

A fourth general basis of power stems from legal prerogatives—exclusive rights or privileges to impose choices. Society, through its governments and judicial system, creates a whole set of legal prerogatives which grant power—*formal power*—to various influencers. In the first place, governments reserve for themselves the power to authorize the creation of the organization and thereafter impose regulations of various sorts on it. They also vest owners and/or the directors of the organization with certain powers, usually including the right to hire and fire the top executives. And these executives, in turn, usually have the power to hire and perhaps fire the rest of the employees, and to issue orders to them, tempered by other legal prerogatives which grant power to employees and their associations.

The fifth general basis of power derives simply from access to those who can rely on the other four. That access may be personal. For example, the spouses and friends of government regulators and of chief executives have power by virtue of having the ear of those who exercise legal prerogatives. The control of an important constituency which itself has influence—the customers who buy or the accountants who control costs—can also be an important basis for power. Likewise power flows to those who can sway other influencers through the mass media—newspaper editors, TV commentators, and the like.

Sometimes access stems from favors traded: Friends and partners grant each other influence over their respective activities. In this case, power stems not from dependency but from *reciprocity*, the gaining of power in one sphere by the giving up of power in another. As we shall see in many examples in this book, the organizational power game is characterized as much by reciprocal as by dependency—one-sided, or "asymmetrical"—relationships.[4]

Will and Skill

But having a basis for power is not enough. The individual must act in order to become an influencer, he or she must expend energy, use the basis for power. When the basis is formal, little effort would seem to be required to use it. But many a government has passed legislation that has never been respected, in many cases because it did not bother to establish an agency strong enough to enforce it. Likewise managers often find that their power to give orders means little when not backed up by the effort to ensure that these are in fact carried out. On the other hand, when the basis of power is informal, much effort would seem to be required to use it. If orders cannot be given, battles will have to be won. Yet here too, sometimes the reverse is true. In universities, for example, power often flows to those who take the trouble to serve on the committees. As two researchers noted in one study: "Since few people were involved and those who were involved wandered in and out, someone who was willing to spend time being present could often become influential" (March and Romelaer 1976, p. 272). In the game of power, it is often the squeaky wheel that gets the grease.

In effect, the requirement that energy be expended to achieve outcomes, and the fact that those with the important bases of power have only so much personal energy to expend, means that power gets distributed more widely than our discussion of the bases of power would suggest. Thus, one article shows how the attendants in a mental hospital, at the bottom of the formal hierarchy, could block policy initiatives from the top because collectively they were willing and able to exert far more effort than could the administrators and doctors (Scheff 1961, discussed at greater length in Chapter 13). What this means is that influencers pick and choose their issues, concentrating their efforts on the ones most important to them, and, of course, those they think they can win. Thus Patchen (1974) finds that each influencer stakes out those areas that affect him or her most, deferring elsewhere to other influencers.

Finally, the influencer must not only have some basis for power and expend some energy, but often he or she must also do it in a clever manner, with political skill. Much informal and even formal power backed by great effort has come to naught because of political ineptness. Managers, by exploiting those over whom they have formal power, have often provoked resistance and even mutiny; experts regularly lose reasonable issues in meetings because they fail to marshall adequate support. Political skill means the ability to use the bases of power effectively—to convince those to whom one has access, to use one's resources, information, and technical skills to their fullest in bargaining, to exercise formal power with a sensitivity to the feelings of others, to know where to concentrate one's energies, to sense what is possible, to organize the necessary alliances.

Related to political skill is a set of intrinsic leadership characteristics—charm, physical strength, attractiveness, what Kipnis calls "personal resources" (1974, p. 88). *Charisma* is the label for that mystical quality that attracts followers to an individual. Some people become powerful simply because others support them; the followers pledge loyalty to a single voice.

Thus power derives from some basis for it coupled with the efforts and the abilities to use the basis. We shall assume this in the rest of the book, and look more concretely at the channels through which power is exercised, what we call the *means* and *the systems of influence*—the specific instruments influencers are able to use to effect outcomes.

THE CAST OF PLAYERS IN ORDER OF APPEARANCE

Who are these influencers to whom we have referred? We can first distinguish *internal* from *external* influencers. The internal influencers are the full-time employees who use voice, those people charged with making the decision and taking the actions on a permanent, regular basis; it is they who determine the outcomes, which express the goals pursued by the organization. The external influencers are nonemployees who use their bases of influence to try to affect the behavior of the employees.[5] The first two sections of our theory, on the elements of power, describe respectively the *External Coalition*, formed by the external influencers, and the *Internal Coalition*, formed by the internal influencers.

(As the word *coalition* was retained in this book only after a good deal of consideration, it is worth explaining here why it was chosen. In general, an attempt was made to avoid jargon whenever it was felt to be possible—for example, employing "chief executive officer" instead of "peak coordinator." "Coalition" proved to be a necessary exception. Because there are no common labels—popular or otherwise—to distinguish the power in from that around the organization, one had to be selected. But why *coalition?* Because it seems to fit best, even though it may be misleading to the reader at first. The word *coalition* is normally used for a group of people who band together to win some issue. As the Hickson research team at the University of Bradford notes, it has the connotation of "engineered agreements and alliances" (Astley et al. 1980, p. 21). Ostensibly, we are not using the word in this sense, at least not at first. We use it more in the sense that Cyert and March (1963) introduced it, as a set of people who bargain among themselves to determine a certain distribution of organizational power. But as we proceed in our discussion, the reader will find the two meanings growing increasingly similar. For one thing, in the External or Internal Coalition, the various influencers band together around or within the same organization to satisfy their needs. They do form some sort of "coalition." As Hickson et al. note in an earlier publication, "it is their coalition of interests that sustains (or destroys) [the] organization" (1976, p. 9).[6] More importantly, we shall see that the external and internal influencers each typically form rather stable systems of power, usually focussed in nature. These become semipermanent means to distribute benefits, and so resemble coalitions in the usual meaning of the term.)

Our power play includes ten groups of possible influencers, listed below in order of appearance. The first four are found in the External Coalition:

- First are the *owners*, who hold legal title to the organization. Some of them perhaps conceived the idea of founding the organization in the first place and served as brokers to bring the initial influencers together.
- Second are the *associates*, the suppliers of the organization's input resources, the clients for its output products and services, as well as its trading partners and competitors. It should be noted that only those associates who resort to voice—for example, who engage in contacts of other than a purely economic nature—are

counted as influencers in the External Coalition.
- Third are the *employee associations*, that
is, unions and professional associations.
Again these are included as influencers to
the extent that they seek to influence the
organization in other than purely economic ways, that is, to use voice to affect
decisions and actions directly. Such employee associations see themselves as representatives of more than simple suppliers
of labor resources. Note that employee
associations are themselves considered *external* influencers, even though they represent people who can be internal influencers. Acting collectively, through their
representatives, the employees choose to
exert their influence on the organization
from outside of its regular decision-making
and action-taking channels, much as do
owners and clients. (Singly, or even collectively but in different ways, the employees can of course bring their influence
to bear directly on these processes, as internal influencers. Later we shall in fact
see that it is typically their impotence in
the Internal Coalition that causes them
to act collectively in the External Coalition.)
- A fourth category comprises the organization's various *publics*, groups representing special or general interests of the public at large. We can divide these into three:
(1) such general groups as families, opinion leaders, and the like; (2) special interest groups such as conservation movements or local community institutions; and
(3) government in all of its forms—national, regional, local, departments and
ministries, regulatory agencies, and so on.
- Another group of influencers, which is
really made up of representatives from
among the other four, as well as from the
internal influencers, are the *directors* of the
organization. These constitute a kind of
"formal coalition." This group stands at
the interface of the External and Internal
Coalitions, but because it meets only in-
termittently, and for other reasons we shall
discuss in Chapter 6, it is treated as part
of the External Coalition.

The Internal Coalition comprises six
groups of influencers:

- First is the top or general management of
the organization, Papandreou's peak coordinator. We shall refer to this by the
single individual at the top of the hierarchy of authority, in standard American
terminology, the *chief executive officer*, or
CEO.[7]
- Second are the *operators*, those workers
who actually produce the products and
services, or who provide the direct support
to them, such as the machine operators
in the manufacturing plant or the doctors
and nurses in the hospital.
- Third are the managers who stand in the
hierarchy of line authority from the CEO
down to the first-line supervisors to whom
the operators formally report. We shall
refer to these simply as the *line managers*.
- Fourth are the *analysts of the technostructure*, those staff specialists who concern
themselves with the design and operation
of the systems for planning and for formal
control, people such as work study analysts, cost accountants, and long-range
planners.
- Fifth is the *support staff*, comprising those
staff specialists who provide indirect support to the operators and the rest of the
organization, in a business firm, for example, the mailroom staff, the chef in the
cafeteria, the researchers, the public relation officers, and the legal counsel.[8]
- Finally, there is an eleventh actor in the
organizational power system, one that is
technically inanimate but in fact shows
every indication of having a life of its own,
namely the *ideology* of the organization—
the set of beliefs shared by its internal
influencers that distinguishes it from other
organizations.

Figure 1 shows the position of each
of these eleven groups schematically. The
Internal Coalition is shown in the center, with the Chief Executive Officer at
the top, followed, according to the formal hierarchy of authority, by the line
managers and then the operators. (In
some parts of the discussion, we shall
accept these notions of formal authority,
in others, we shall not. For now, we
retain them.) Shown at either side to

FIGURE 1 • THE CAST OF PLAYERS

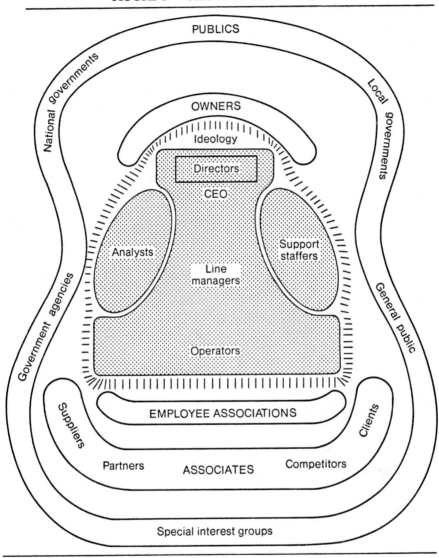

represent their roles as staff members are the analysts and the support staff. Above the CEO is shown the board of directors to which the CEO formally reports. And emanating from the organization is a kind of aura to represent its ideology. Surrounding all this are the various groups of the External Coalition. The owners are shown closest to the top of the hierarchy, and to the board of directors, where they are often inclined to exert their influence. The associates are shown surrounding the operating core where the operators work, the suppliers on the left (input) side and the clients on the right (output) side, with the partners and competitors in between. The employee associations are shown closest to the operators, whom they represent, while the various publics are shown to form a ring around the entire power system, in effect influencing every part of it. Thus the organization of Figure 1 can be seen to exist in a complex field of influencer forces.

Each of these eleven groups of players in the organizational power game will be discussed in turn, together with the means of influence they have at their disposal. We assume in this discussion that each is driven by the needs inherent in the roles they play. For example, owners will be described as owners, not as fathers, or Episcopalians, or power-hungry devils. People are of course driven by a variety of needs—by intrinsic values such as the need for control or autonomy, or in Maslow's (1954) needs hierarchy theory, by physiological, safety, love, esteem, and self-actualization needs; by the values instilled in them as children or developed later through socialization and various identifications; by the need to exploit fully whatever skills and abilities they happen to have; by their desire to avoid repetition of painful experiences or to repeat successful ones; by opportunism, the drive to exploit whatever opportunities happen to present themselves. All of these needs contribute to the makeup of each influencer and lead to an infinite variety of behaviors. All are, therefore, important to understand. But they are beyond the scope of this book. Here we focus on those behaviors that are dictated strictly by role. We assume throughout that each group discussed above is driven to gain power in or over the organization—in other words, is an influencer; our discussion then focusses on what ends each seeks to attain, what means or systems of influence each has at its disposal, and how much power each tends to end

up with by virtue of the role it plays in the power coalition to which it happens to belong. This is the point of departure for the discussion of our theory.

NOTES

1. Some writers call the influencer a "stakeholder" since he or she maintains a stake in the organization the way a shareholder maintains shares. Others use the term "claimant," in that he or she has a claim on the organization's benefits. Both these terms, however, would include those who express loyalty as well as voice.

2. There are some interesting linkages among these three options, as Hirschman points out. Exit is sometimes a last resort for frustrated voice, or in the case of a strike (temporary exit), a means to supplement voice. The effect of exit can be "galvanizing" when voice is the norm, or vice versa, as in the case of Ralph Nader who showed consumers how to use voice instead of exit against the automobile companies (p. 125). Of course, an inability to exit forces the disgruntled individual to turn to voice, Hirschman also makes the intriguing point that exit belongs to the study of economics, voice to that of political science. In economic theory, the customer or employee dissatisfied with one firm is supposed to shift to another: ". . . one either exits or one does not; it is impersonal" (p. 15). In contrast, voice is "a far more 'messy' concept because it can be graduated, all the way from faint grumbling to violent protest . . . voice is political action par excellence" (p. 16). But students of political science also have a "blind spot": ". . . exit has often been branded as *criminal*, for it has been labelled desertion, defection, and treason" (p. 17).

3. Related discussions of bases of power can be found in Allison (1971), Crozier and Friedberg (1977), Jacobs (1974), Kipnis (1974), Mechanic (1962), and Pfeffer and Salancik (1978).

4. French and Raven's (1959) five categories of power, as perhaps the most widely quoted typology of power, should be related to these five bases of power. Their "reward" and "coercive" power are used formally by those with legal prerogatives and may be used informally by those who control critical resources, skills, or knowledge (for example, to coerce by holding these back). Their "legitimate" power corresponds most closely to our legal prerogatives and their

"expert" power to our critical skills and knowledge. Their fifth category, "referent" power, is discussed below in our section on political skill.

5. As we shall soon see, there are some circumstances in which external influencers can impose decisions directly on the organization, and other in which full-time employees acting in concert through their associations behave as external influencers by trying to affect the behavior of the senior managers. As Pfeffer and Salancik (1978, p. 30) point out, actors can be part of the organization as well as its environment. Nevertheless, the distinction between full-time employees—those individuals with an intensive and regular commitment to the organization—and others will prove to be a useful and important one in all that follows.

6. It might be noted that the Hickson group in the 1980 publication cited earlier (as Astley et al.) decided to replace the word *coalition* by *constellation*. That was tried in this book, but dropped as not having quite the right ring to it.

7. An alternate term which appears frequently in the more recent literature is *dominant coalition*. But we have no wish to prejudice the discussion of the power of one of our groups of influencers by the choice of its title.

8. For a more elaborate description of each of these five groups as well as clarification of the differences between technocratic and support staff and of line and staff in general, see Chapter 2 of the *Structuring* book.

BIBLIOGRAPHIC REFERENCES

Allison, G. T. (1971). *Essence of decision: Explaining the Cuban missile crisis*. Boston: Little, Brown. Copyright © 1971 by Graham T. Allison. Reprinted by permission of the publisher.

Astley, W. G., Axelsson, R., Butler, R. J., Hickson, D. J., & Wilson, D. C. (1980). Decision making: Theory III. Working Paper, University of Bradford Management Centre. Used with permission.

Crozier, M. (1964). *The bureaucratic phenomenon*. Chicago: University of Chicago Press. Used with permission.

——. (1974). Why is France blocked? In H. J. Leavitt, L. Pinfield, & E. J. Webb (Eds.). *Organizations of the future: Interaction with the external environment*. New York: Praeger. Used with permission.

——, & Friedberg, E. (1977). *L'acteur et le système*. Paris: Editions du Seuil.

Cyert, R. M., & March, J. G. (1963). *A behavioral theory of the firm*. Englewood Cliffs, NJ: Prentice-Hall.

French, J. R. P., Jr., & Raven, B. (1959). The bases of social power. In D. Cartwright (Ed.). *Studies in social power* (pp. 150–67). Ann Arbor: Institute for Social Research, University of Michigan.

Hickson, D. J., Butler, R. J., Axelsson, R., & Wilson, D. (1976). Decisive coalitions. Paper presented to International Conference on Coordination and Control of Group and Organizational Performance, Munich, West Germany.

Hirschman, A. O. (1970). *Exit, voice, and loyalty: Responses to decline in firms, organizations, and states*. Cambridge, MA: Harvard University Press.

Jacobs, D. (1974). Dependency and vulnerability: An exchange approach to the control of organizations. *Administrative Science Quarterly*, 45–59.

Kipnis, D. (1974). The powerholder. In J. T. Tedeschi (Ed.), *Perspectives on social power* (pp. 82–122). Chicago: Aldine.

March, J. G., & Romelaer, P. J. (1976). Position and presence in the drift of decisions. In J. G. March & J. P. Olsen (Eds.), *Ambiguity and choice in organizations*. Bergen, Norway: Universitetsforlaget.

Maslow, A. H. (1954). *Motivation and personality*. New York: Harper & Row.

Mechanic, D. (1962). Sources of power of lower participants in complex organizations. *Administrative Science Quarterly*, 349–64.

Mintzberg, H. (1979a). *The structuring of organizations: A synthesis of the research*. Englewood Cliffs, NJ: Prentice-Hall.

Patchen, M. (1974). The locus and basis of influence on organizational decisions. *Organizational Behavior and Human Performance*, 195–221.

Pfeffer, N., and Salamcik, G. R. (1978). *The external control of organizations: A resource dependence perspective*. New York: Harper & Row.

Scheff, T. J. (1961). Control over policy by attendants in a mental hospital. *Journal of Health and Human Behavior*, 93–105.

CHAPTER VI

The Organizational Culture School

The newest and most controversial of the schools of organization theory is the organizational culture school. Its theories are based upon assumptions about organizations and people that depart radically from those of the "mainline" schools of organization theory. Secondly, the organizational culture school does not believe that quantitative, experimental-type, "scientific" research is especially useful for studying organizations. In these respects, it shares similarities with the power and politics school.

What is organizational culture? First of all, it is the culture that exists in an organization, something akin to a societal culture. It is comprised of many intangible things such as values, beliefs, assumptions, perceptions, behavioral norms, artifacts, and patterns of behavior. It is the unseen and unobservable force that is always behind organizational activities that can be seen and observed. According to Kilmann and others (1985), organizational culture is a social energy that moves people to act. "Culture is to the organization what personality is to the individual—a hidden, yet unifying theme that provides meaning, direction, and mobilization."

Secondly, organizational culture is a recent, emerging school of organization theory—another way of viewing, thinking about, studying, and trying to understand organizations. Like the power and politics school, the organizational culture perspective represents a "counterculture" within organization theory. Its assumptions, theories, and approaches are very different from those of the dominant "modern" structural and systems schools. The organizational culture school challenges the basic views of the "modern" structural and systems schools about, for example, how organizations make decisions, and how and why people in organizations behave as they do.

In both the "modern" structural and the systems schools of organization theory, organizations are assumed to be institutions whose primary purpose is to accomplish established goals. Those goals are set by people in positions of formal authority. In these two schools, the primary questions for organization theory involve how best to design and manage organizations to achieve their declared purposes effectively and efficiently. The personal preferences of organizational members are restrained by systems of formal rules, authority, and by norms of rational

373

behavior. In a 1982 *Phi Delta Kappan* article, Karl Weick argues that four organizational conditions must exist in order for basic assumptions of the structuralists and systemists to be valid:

1. A self-correcting system of interdependent people.
2. Consensus on objectives and methods.
3. Coordination achieved through sharing information.
4. Predictable organizational problems and solutions.

But, unfortunately, Weick is forced to conclude that these conditions seldom exist in modern organizations.

Consequently, the organizational culture school rejects the assumptions of the "modern" structural and systems schools. Instead, it assumes that many organizational behaviors and decisions are almost "predetermined" by the patterns of basic assumptions existing in the organization. Those patterns of assumptions continue to exist and to influence behaviors, because they repeatedly lead people to make decisions that usually "worked" for the organization. With repeated use, the assumptions slowly drop out of peoples' consciousness, but continue to influence organizational decisions and behaviors—even when the organization's environment changes. They become the underlying, unquestioned—but virtually forgotten—reasons for "the way we do things here"—even when the ways are no longer appropriate. They are so basic, so pervasive, and so totally accepted as "the truth" that no one thinks about or remembers them. Thus a strong organizational culture controls organizational behavior; for example, it can block an organization from making changes needed to adapt to a changing environment.

From the organizational culture perspective, the personal preferences of organizational members are not restrained by systems of formal rules, authority, and by norms of rational behavior. Instead, they are controlled by cultural norms, values, beliefs, and assumptions. Thus, in order to understand or predict how an organization will behave under different circumstances, one must know what its patterns of basic assumptions are—its organizational culture.

Every organizational culture is different, for several reasons. First, what has "worked" repeatedly for one organization does not for another, so the basic assumptions differ. Second, an organization's culture is partially shaped by many factors including, for example, the societal culture in which it resides, its technologies, markets, competition, and the personality of its founder(s) or dominant leaders. Some organizational cultures are more distinctive than others; some organizations have strong, unified, pervasive cultures, whereas others have weaker cultures; some organizational cultures are quite pervasive, whereas others have many "subcultures" existing in different functional or geographical areas.

Knowledge of an organization's structure, information systems, strategic planning processes, markets, technology, goals, and so forth, will give clues about an organization's culture, but not accurately or reliably. As a consequence, an organization's behavior can not be understood or predicted by studying its structural or systems elements; its organizational culture must be studied. And, the quantitative quasi-experimental research methods used by the "modern" structural and systems schools *can not* identify or measure unconscious, virtually forgotten basic assumptions. Van Maanen, Dabbs, and Faulkner, in their 1982 book, *Varieties of Qualitative Research*, describe a growing wave of disenchantment with the use of quantitative quasi-experimental research methods for studying organizations, mainly because they have produced very little useful knowledge about organizations over the last twenty years. Yet, quantitative research using quasi-experimental designs, control groups, computers, multivariate analyses, heuristic models, and the like are the essential "tools" of the systems and "modern" structural schools. More and more, the organizational culture school (and the power and politics school) are turning to qualitative research methods like ethnography and participant observation.

Earlier, we said that the organizational culture school represents a "counterculture" within the field of organization theory. The reasons should be becoming evident. The organizational culture school believes that the "modern" structural and systems schools of organization theory are using the wrong "tools" (or "lenses") to look at the wrong organizational elements in their attempts to understand and predict organizational behavior. In other words, they are wasting their time.

It takes courage to challenge the basic views of a "mainstream" school in any profession or academic discipline. Yet this is just what the organizational culture and the power and politics perspectives are doing when they advocate such radically different ways of looking at and working with organizations. For example, from the organizational culture perspective, AT&T's basic problems since deregulation and court-ordered splintering of the Bell System are not in its structure, information systems, or people. Rather, they rest in an organizational culture that no longer is appropriate for AT&T's deregulated world. The long-standing AT&T culture has been centered on assumptions about (1) the value of technical superiority, (2) AT&T's possession of technical superiority, and thus (3) AT&T's rightful dominance in the telephone and telecommunications market. Therefore, working to improve things like AT&T's goals, structure, differentiation and integration processes, strategic plans, and information systems will not solve AT&T's monumental problems. The solution requires changing an ingrained organizational culture: changing basic *unconscious* assumptions about what makes for success in a competitive telephone and communications market.

Lee Iacocca faced a similar problem (but different in its content) when he took over leadership of the Chrysler Corporation. Chrysler was a "loser"—in just about every way—in the eyes of employees, potential employees, investors, car dealers, financers, suppliers, and car buyers. It was simply *assumed* that Chrysler could not compete head-on. Iacocca had to change not only an organizational culture, but also *everybody's perception* of that culture. Chrysler needed and got in Iacocca what Warren Bennis (1984) and Tichy and Ulrich (1984) have called a "transformational leader," one who could totally transform an imbedded organizational culture by creating a new vision of and for the organization, and successfully selling that vision—by rallying commitment and loyalty to make the vision become a reality.

In Chapter V, we said that much of the important writing from the power school is quite recent, and the theoretical grounding of the school is not as well developed as, for example, it is in the classical, "modern" structural, and systems schools. Comparatively, the organizational culture school is still in its infancy. Thus, the organizational culture school suffers from the problems and limitations of youthfulness. Although phrases like "organizational culture" and "culture of a factory" can be found in a few books on management written as early as the 1950s (for example, Elliott Jaques's 1951 book *The Changing Culture of a Factory,* and William H. Whyte, Jr.'s, 1956 book about conformity in businesses, *The Organization Man*), few students of management or organizations paid much attention to the nature and content of organizational culture until the late 1970s.

During the 1960s and early 1970s, several books on organizational and professional socialization processes received wide attention. As useful as these earlier works were, they *assumed* the presence of organizational or professional cultures, and proceeded to examine issues involving the match between individuals and cultures. Some of the more widely read of these were the 1961 book, *Boys in White,* by Becker, Geer, Hughes, and Strauss, which chronicled the processes used to socialize medical students into the medical profession; Herbert Kaufman's 1960 study of how the United States Forest Service developed the "will and capacity to conform" among its remotely stationed rangers in *The Forest Ranger;* Ritti and Funkhouser's 1977 humorous-but-serious look at *The Ropes to Skip and the Ropes to Know*"; John Van Maanen's articles on "Police Socialization" (1975) and "Breaking in: Socialization to Work" (1976). During this period, Edgar H. Schein contributed significantly to the knowledge about both organizational and professional socialization processes in numerous writings including, for example, "How to Break in the College Graduate" (1964), "Organizational Socialization and the Profession of Management" (1968), and *Career Dynamics: Matching Individual and Organizational Needs* (1978). Once again, however, these earlier writings did not address important questions such as how cultures are formed or changed, how cultures affect leadership, or the relationship between culture and strategic planning (establishing organizational directions); rather, they focused on the process of socializing employees into existing organizational cultures and the impacts of existing cultures on organizational members.

An entirely different orientation to culture and organizational culture started to appear in the organization theory literature in the late 1970s. This orientation is known as the "symbolic frame," "symbolic management," or "organizational symbolism." Lee Bolman and Terrence Deal (1984) identify the basic tenets of the "symbolic frame" as

1. The meaning or the interpretation of what is happening in organizations is more important than what actually is happening.
2. Ambiguity and uncertainty, which are prevalent in most organizations, preclude rational problem solving and decision-making processes.
3. People use symbols to reduce ambiguity and to gain a sense of direction when they are faced with uncertainty.

Symbols are things like flags, logos, and creeds that carry a wider (or different) meaning than their intrinsic content. For example, the United States flag is a symbol because it embodies values, traditions, and emotions. Symbols also can be things such as words, phrases, organizational structures, management information systems, an office next to the president's, wood as opposed to steel office furniture, romanticized stories about organizational heroes, and ritualistic ceremonies—if they carry meanings that go beyond their intrinsic content. Thus, the focus of organizational symbolism is on the creation and management of the meaning of symbols.

The manipulation of symbols and the dramaturgy of symbolic acts are essential elements of managing people in organizations. While such manipulations may be conscious or unconscious on the part of management, they are invariably there. Frequently, symbolic acts are easily identifiable because of their obvious *beau geste* quality. They form an integral part of everyday manners and courtesies. When an organization's chief executive accidently meets a lower-echelon employee in a crowded elevator and says, "How's your job coming along?" the executive is not using words to ask a question; the words are used simply to communicate sociability—a symbolic ritual. It would be quite out of place and both annoying and surprising to the executive if the employee actually answered the question instead of replying with a simple, "Fine, thank you." In cases like these, language ceases to be an instrument of communication and becomes a symbol—a thing that carries a different meaning than its intrinsic content. Similar symbolic machinations are important devices for both control and motivation in any social system.

In their 1967 book, *The Social Construction of Reality*, Peter Berger and Thomas Luckmann define meanings as "socially constructed realities." In other words, things are not real in and of themselves; the perceptions of them are, in fact, reality. As W. I. Thomas said (1923), "If people believe things are real, they are real in their consequences." According to the organizational culture school, meanings (realities) are established by and among the people in organizations—*by the organizational culture.* Experimenters have shown that there is a strong relation between culturally determined values and the perception of symbols. People will distort their perceptions of symbols according to the need for that which is symbolized (Davis, 1963). Thus, organizational symbolism is an integral part of the organizational culture perspective.

Symbolic management attracted only limited attention during the 1970s. The turning point for the organizational culture (and symbolism) perspective did not arrive until 1981 or 1982. Then, almost overnight, organizational culture became a very hot topic in books, journals, and periodicals aimed at both management practitioners and academicians. Only a few are listed here: Thomas Peters and Robert Waterman, Jr.'s, 1982 best-seller, *In Search of Excellence*; Terrence Deal and Allan Kennedy's 1982 book, *Corporate Cultures*; Stanley Davis's 1984 book, *Managing Corporate Culture; Fortune* Magazine's 1983 story on "The Corporate Culture Vultures"; and *Business Week's* May 14, 1984, cover story, "Changing a Corporate Culture." Certainly, both William Ouchi's 1981 best-seller, *Theory Z*, and Richard Pascale and Anthony Athos's *The Art of Japanese Management* (1981) belong to the organizational culture school.

Despite this wave of "popular" literature on organizational culture in the early 1980s, the first good comprehensive, theoretically based, integrative writing on organizational culture did not appear until 1984 or 1985. Today, there are only three or four such books. Edgar Schein's (1985) *Organizational Culture and Leadership* is the most notable. Sathe's (1985) *Culture and Related Corporate Realities* is a theoretically sound textbook with readings and cases. Sergiovanni and Corbally's (1984) *Leadership and Organizational Culture* is a stimulating collection of theoretical papers mostly concerned with education administration. Kilmann, Saxton, Serpa, and Associates' (1985) *Gaining Control of the Corporate Culture* contains many excellent articles by most of the better-known writers from the organizational culture school.

The youthfulness of the organizational culture school continues to cause problems for it and places limitations on its usefulness. Because of its youth, minimal consensus exists about much of anything concerned with organizational culture. The disagreements start with what an organizational culture is. As one would expect, they are even more pronounced and heated about its nature, components, usefulness, and methods for studying and applying it. There are only a few organizational culture issues upon which there is wide consensus. They include:

1. Organizational cultures exist.
2. Each organizational culture is relatively unique.
3. Organizational culture is a socially constructed concept.
4. Organizational culture provides organizational members with a way of understanding and making sense of events and symbols.
5. Organizational culture is a powerful lever for guiding organizational behavior. It functions as "organizational control mechanisms, informally approving or prohibiting some patterns of behavior" (Martin & Siehl, 1983).

Beyond these five basic points, agreement about organizational culture is very limited. Note that these basic points say nothing about what organizational culture is. Agreement is essentially limited to its existence, its relative uniqueness, and a few functions it performs. The lack of agreement about such basic issues creates problems for those who are inclined to use the organizational culture perspective; and even casts doubt on the very legitimacy of the perspective.

A few theorists' views on changing organizational culture provide a good example of the lack of agreement within the school. Should a manager even try to change an organizational culture? If so, what change strategy should be used? Allen and Kraft (1982) advocate changing organizational cultures by modifying behavioral norms. Stanley Davis (1984) disagrees, arguing for chief executive officer-imposed, top-to-bottom, organization-wide change processes. Vijay Sathe (1985), and Martin and Siehl (1983) predict failure for any single-strategy cultural change program. Edgar Schein (1985) cautions that attempts to change organizational cultures may be harmful and should be tried only if the conditions are right.

The first selection reprinted here is Edgar H. Schein's chapter from his 1985 book, *Organizational Culture and Leadership*, titled "Defining Organizational Culture." Schein proposes a "formal definition" of organizational culture that appears to be gaining acceptance from other writers, and he presents a model of "levels of culture," which is helpful for sorting through some of the conflicting viewpoints about organizational culture that are discussed above.

In "The Making of an Organizational Saga," from his widely cited 1970 book, *The Distinctive College: Antioch, Reed & Swarthmore*, Burton R. Clark examines how sagas and stories help to provide stability and continuity through symbolism during and between the times of risks and tensions that inevitably accompany the stages in the development of organizational distinctiveness. Clark's study represents an excellent example of the use of qualitative research methods to *explain* rather than simply to *understand* organizational phenomena.

Thomas J. Peter's 1978 *Organizational Dynamics* article, "Symbols, Patterns, and Settings: An Optimistic Case for Getting Things Done," explores the manipulation of symbols and settings for accomplishing organizational change. He proposes a "simple" classification of change tools and techniques for use under different circumstances. He concludes that managers have a multitude of symbolic change tools available to them, and thus there is reason for cautious optimism about their ability to create change.

Meryl Reis Louis' article, "Organizations as Culture-Bearing Milieux," from L. Pondy, P. Frost, G. Morgan, and T. Dandridge's 1983 book, *Organizational Symbolism*, provides a cogent overview of the cultural perspective. She describes "meaning" as "emergent"—as a socially constructed reality influenced by shared interpretations of symbols and social ideals, which help organizational members interpret experience and, thus, guide behavior. She explores culture from the psychological and sociological contexts, and argues for the use of qualitative research methods for expanding existing knowledge of organizations.

Our final article, "The Role of Symbolic Management: How Can Managers Effectively Transmit Organizational Culture," by Caren Siehl and Joanne Martin, is reprinted from the 1984 book *Leaders and Managers*, edited by James G. Hunt, D. M. Hosking, C. A. Schriesheim, and R. Stewart. Siehl and Martin describe an empirical research study they conducted that identified some of the ways in which the managers of a business created, transmitted, and maintained a system of shared values. They argue that organizational culture is a "powerful phenomenon" that should not be left to chance. Managers need to learn how to recognize, control, and change organizational culture.

BIBLIOGRAPHIC REFERENCES

Allen, R. F., & Kraft, C. (1982). *The organizational unconscious.* Englewood Cliffs, NJ: Prentice-Hall.

Becker, H. S., Geer, B., Hughes E. C., & Strauss, A. L. (1961). *The boys in white: Student culture in medical school.* Chicago: University of Chicago Press.

Bennis, W. G. (1984). Transformative power and leadership. In T. J. Sergiovanni & J. E. Corbally (Eds.), *Leadership and organizational culture* (pp. 64–71). Urbana, IL: University of Illinois Press.

Berger, P. L., & Luckmann, T. (1967). *The social construction of reality.* Garden City, NY: Doubleday Anchor.

Business Week. (May 14, 1984). Changing a corporate culture: Can J&J move from band-aids to high tech?, pp. 130–138.

Clark, B. R. (1970). *The distinctive college: Antioch, Reed & Swarthmore.* Chicago: Aldine Publishing.

Davis, J. C. (1963). *Human nature in politics: The dynamics of political behavior.* New York: John Wiley & Sons.

Davis, S. M. (1984). *Managing corporate culture.* Cambridge, MA: Ballinger.

Fortune. (October 17, 1983). The corporate culture vultures, pp. 66–71.

Hunt, J. G., Hosking, D. M., Schriesheim, C. A., & Stewart, R. (Eds.). *Leaders and managers.* New York: Pergamon Press.

Jaques, E. (1951). *The changing culture of a factory.* London: Tavistock Institute.

Kaufman, H. (1960). *The forest ranger.* Baltimore, MD: The Johns Hopkins Press.

Kilmann, R. H., Saxton, M. J., Serpa, R., & Associates (Eds.). (1985). *Gaining control of the corporate culture.* San Francisco: Jossey-Bass.

Louis, M. R. (1983). Organizations as culture-bearing milieux. In L. R. Pondy, P. J. Frost, G. Morgan, & T. C. Dandridge (Eds.). *Organizational symbolism* (pp. 39–54). Greenwich, CT: JAI Press.

Martin, J., & Siehl, C. (Autumn 1983). Organizational culture and counterculture: An uneasy symbiosis. *Organizational Dynamics,* 52–64.

Ouchi, W. G. (1981). *Theory Z.* Reading, MA: Addison-Wesley Publishing.

Pascale, R. T., & Athos, A. G. (1981). *The art of Japanese management.* New York: Simon & Schuster.

Peters, T. J. (Autumn 1978). Symbols, patterns, and settings: An optimistic case for getting things done. *Organizational Dynamics,* 3–23.

Pondy, L. R., Frost, P. J., Morgan, G., & Dandridge, T. C. (Eds.). *Organizational symbolism.* Greenwich, CT: JAI Press.

Ritti, R. R., & Funkhouser, G. R. (1977). *The ropes to skip and the ropes to know.* New York: John Wiley & Sons.

Sathe, V. (1985). *Culture and related corporate realities.* Homewood, IL: Richard D. Irwin.

Schein, E. H. (1964). How to break in the college graduate. *Harvard Business Review, 42,* 68–76.

Schein, E. H. (1968). Organizational socialization and the profession of management. *Industrial Management Review, 9,* 1–15.

Schein, E. H. (1978). *Career dynamics: Matching individual and organizational needs.* Reading, MA: Addison-Wesley Publishing.

Schein, E. H. (1985). *Organizational culture and leadership.* San Francisco: Jossey-Bass.

Sergiovanni, T. J., & Corbally, J. E. (Eds.). (1984). *Leadership and organizational culture.* Urbana, IL: University of Illinois Press.

Siehl, C., & Martin, J. (1984). The role of symbolic management: How can managers effectively transmit organizational culture? In J. G. Hunt, D. M. Hosking, C. A. Schriesheim, & R. Stewart (Eds.), *Leaders and Managers* (pp. 227–239). New York: Pergamon Press.

Thomas, W. I. (1923). *The unadjusted girl.* New York: Harper Torchbooks, 1967.

Tichy, N. M., & Ulrich, D. O. (Fall 1984). The leadership challenge—A call for the transformational leader. *Sloan Management Review, 26(1),* 59–68.

Van Maanen, J. (1975). Police socialization. *Administrative Science Quarterly, 20,* 207–228.

Van Maanen, J. (1976). Breaking in: Socialization to work. In R. Dubin (Ed.), *Handbook of work, organization and society* (pp. 67–130). Chicago: Rand McNally.

Van Maanen, J. (Ed.). (1979, 1983). *Qualitative methodology.* Beverly Hills, CA: Sage Publications.

Van Maanen, J., Dabbs, J. M., Jr., & Faulkner, R. R. (Eds.). (1982). *Varieties of qualitative research.* Beverly Hills, CA: Sage Publications.

Weick, K. E. (June 1982). Administering education in loosely coupled schools. *Phi Delta Kappan,* 673–676.

Whyte, W. H., Jr. (1956). *The organization man.* New York: Simon & Schuster.

32
Defining Organizational Culture
Edgar H. Schein

Most of us—whether students, employees, managers, researchers, or consultants—live in organizations and have to deal with them. Yet we continue to find it amazingly difficult to understand and justify much of what we observe and experience in our organizational life. Too much seems to be "bureaucratic," or "political," or just plain "irrational." People in positions of authority, especially our immediate bosses, often frustrate us or act incomprehensibly, and those we consider the "leaders" of our organizations often disappoint us and fail to meet our aspirations. The fields of organizational psychology and sociology have developed a variety of useful concepts for understanding individual behavior in organizations and the ways in which organizations structure themselves. But the dynamic of why and how they grow, change, sometimes fail, and—perhaps most important of all—do things that don't seem to make any sense continues to elude us.

The concept of organizational culture holds promise for illuminating this difficult area. I will try to show that a deeper understanding of cultural issues in organizations is necessary not only to decipher what goes on in them but, even more important, to identify what may be the priority issues for leaders and leadership. Organizational cultures are created by leaders, and one of the most decisive functions of leadership may well be the creation, the management, and—if and when that may become necessary—the destruction of culture. Culture and leadership, when one examines them closely, are two sides of the same coin, and neither can really be understood by itself. In fact, there is a possibility—underemphasized in leadership research—that the *only thing of real importance that leaders do is to create and manage culture* and that the unique talent of leaders is their ability to work with culture. If the concept of leadership as distinguished from management and administration is to have any value, we must recognize the centrality of this culture management function in the leadership concept.

But before we examine closely the tie to leadership, we must fully understand the concept of organizational culture. I would like to begin with two examples from my own consulting experience. In the first case (Company A), I was called in to help a management group improve its communication, interpersonal relationships, and decision making. After sitting in on a number of meetings, I observed, among other things, high levels of interrupting, confrontation, and debate; excessive emotionality about proposed courses of action; great frustration over the difficulty of getting a point of view across; and a sense that

Source: Edgar H. Schein, *Organizational Culture and Leadership* (San Francisco, Calif.: Jossey-Bass, 1985), 1–22.

every member of the group wanted to win all the time. Over a period of several months, I made many suggestions about better listening, less interrupting, more orderly processing of the agenda, the potential negative effects of high emotionality and conflict, and the need to reduce the frustration level. The group members said that the suggestions were helpful, and they modified certain aspects of their procedure, such as lengthening some of their meetings. However, the basic pattern did not change, no matter what kind of intervention I attempted. I could not understand why my efforts to improve the group's problem-solving process were not more successful.

In the second case (Company B), I was asked, as part of a broader consultation project, to help create a climate for innovation in an organization that felt a need to become more flexible in order to respond to its increasingly dynamic business environment. The organization consisted of many different business units, functional groups, and geographical groups. As I got to know more about these units and their problems, I observed that some very innovative things were going on in many places in the company. I wrote several memos describing these innovations, added other ideas from my own experience, and gave the memos to my contact person in the company, hoping that he would distribute them to other managers who might benefit from the ideas. I also gave the memos to those managers with whom I had direct contact. After some months I discovered that whoever got my memo thought it was helpful and on target, but rarely, if ever, did the memo get past the person to whom I gave it. I suggested meetings of managers from different units to stimulate lateral communication, but found no support at all for such meetings. No matter what

I did, I could not seem to get information flowing, especially laterally across divisional, functional, or geographical boundaries. Yet everyone agreed in principle that innovation would be stimulated by more lateral communication and encouraged me to keep on helping.

I did not really understand what happened in either of these cases until I began to examine my own assumptions about how things should work in these organizations and began to test whether my assumptions fitted those operating in my client systems. This step of examining the shared assumptions in the client system takes one into "cultural" analysis and will be the focus from here on. Such analysis is, of course, common when we think of ethnic or national cultures, but not sufficient attention has been paid to the possibility that groups and organizations within a society also develop cultures that affect in a major way how the members think, feel, and act. Unless we learn to analyze such organizational cultures accurately, we cannot really understand why organizations do some of the things they do and why leaders have some of the difficulties that they have. The concept of organizational culture is especially relevant to gaining an understanding of the mysterious and seemingly irrational things that go on in human systems. And culture *must* be understood if one is to get along at all, as tourists in foreign lands and new employees in organizations often discover to their dismay.

But a concept is not helpful if we misuse it or fail to understand it. My primary purpose in undertaking this book, therefore, is to explain the concept of organizational culture, show how it can best be applied, and relate it to leadership. To put it more precisely, I hope to accomplish the following things in this book:

1. Provide a clear, workable definition of organizational culture that takes into account the accumulated insights of anthropologists, sociologists, and psychologists. Much attention also will be given to what culture *is not*, because there has been a tendency in the last few years to link culture with virtually everything.

2. Develop a conceptual "model" of how culture works—that is, how it begins, what functions it serves, what problems it solves, why it survives, why and how it changes, and whether it can be managed and, if so, how. We need a dynamic evolutionary model of organizational culture, a model that tells us what culture *does*, not only what it is. In our rush to create more effective organizations in the last few years, we may well have latched on to culture as the new panacea, the cure for all our industrial ailments. How valid is this notion, and, if it is valid, how can we use culture constructively?

3. Show how culture, as a conceptual tool, can illuminate individual psychological behavior; what goes on in small groups and in geographically or occupationally based communities; how large organizations work; and how societal, multinational issues can be better understood through increased cultural insight. A dynamic model of culture will be especially useful in improving our understanding of how human systems evolve over time.

4. Show how culture and leadership are really two sides of the same coin. One cannot understand one without the other.

Underlying these several purposes is a chronic fear I have that both students of culture and those consultants and managers who deal with culture in a more pragmatic way continue to misunderstand its real nature and significance. In both the popular and the academic literature, I continue to see simplistic, cavalier statements about culture, which not only confuse matters but positively mislead the reader and promise things that probably cannot be delivered. For example, all the recent writings about improving organizational effectiveness through creating "strong" and "appropriate" cultures continue to proliferate the possibly quite *incorrect* assumption that culture can be changed to suit our purposes. Suppose we find that culture can only "evolve" and that groups with "inappropriate" or "weak" cultures simply will not survive. The desire to change culture may become tantamount to destroying the group and creating a new one, which will build or evolve a new culture. Leaders do at times have to do this, but under what conditions is it possible or practical? Are we aware that we may be suggesting something very drastic when we say "Let's change the culture"?

So throughout this book I will be hammering away at the idea that culture is a *deep* phenomenon, that culture is *complex* and difficult to understand, but that the effort to understand it is worthwhile because much of the mysterious and the irrational in organizations suddenly becomes clear when we do understand it.

A Formal Definition of Organizational Culture

The word "culture" has many meanings and connotations. When we combine it with another commonly used word, "organization," we are almost certain to have conceptual and semantic confusion. In talking about organizational culture with colleagues and members of organizations, I often find that we agree "it" exists and is important in its effects but that we have completely different ideas of what the "it" is. I have also had colleagues tell me pointedly that they do *not* use the concept of culture in their work, but when I ask them what it is they do *not* use, they cannot define "it" clearly. Therefore, before launching into the reasons for studying "it," I must give a clear definition of what I will mean by "it."

Some common meanings are the following:

1. *Observed behavioral regularities* when people interact, such as the language used and the rituals around deference and demeanor (Goffman, 1959, 1967; Van Maanen, 1979b).

2. The *norms* that evolve in working groups, such as the particular norm of "a fair day's work for a fair day's pay" that evolved in the Bank Wiring Room in the Hawthorne studies (Homans, 1950).

3. The *dominant values espoused* by an organization, such as "product quality" or "price leadership" (Deal and Kennedy, 1982).

4. The *philosophy* that guides an organization's policy toward employees and/or customers (Ouchi, 1981; Pascale and Athos, 1981).

5. The *rules* of the game for getting along in the organization, "the ropes" that a newcomer must learn in order to become an accepted member (Schein, 1968, 1978; Van Maanen, 1976, 1979b; Ritti and Funkhouser, 1982).

6. The *feeling* or *climate* that is conveyed in an organization by the physical layout and the way in which members of the organization interact with customers or other outsiders (Tagiuri and Litwin, 1968).

All these meanings, and many others, do, in my view, *reflect* the organization's culture, but none of them *is* the essence of culture. I will argue that the term "culture" should be reserved for the deeper level of *basic assumptions* and *beliefs* that are shared by members of an organization, that operate unconsciously, and that define in a basic "taken-for-granted" fashion an organization's view of itself and its environment. These

assumptions and beliefs are *learned* responses to a group's problems of *survival* in its external environment and its problems of *internal integration*. They come to be taken for granted because they solve those problems repeatedly and reliably. This deeper level of assumptions is to be distinguished from the "artifacts" and "values" that are manifestations or surface levels of the culture but not the essence of the culture (Schein, 1981a, .1983, 1984; Dyer, 1982).

But this definition immediately brings us to a problem. What do we mean by the word "group" or "organization," which, by implication, is the locale of a given culture (Louis, 1983)? Organizations are not easy to define in time and space. They are themselves open systems in constant interaction with their many environments, and they consist of many subgroups, occupational units, hierarchical layers, and geographically dispersed segments. If we are to locate a given organization's culture, where do we look, and how general a concept are we looking for?

Culture should be viewed as a property of an independently defined stable social unit. That is, if one can demonstrate that a given set of people have shared a significant number of important experiences in the process of solving external and internal problems, one can assume that such common experiences have led them, over time, to a shared view of the world around them and their place in it. There has to have been enough shared experience to have led to a shared view, and this shared view has to have worked for long enough to have come to be taken for granted and to have dropped out of awareness. Culture, in this sense, is a *learned product of group experience* and is, therefore, to be found only where there is a definable group with a significant history.

Whether or not a given company has a single culture in addition to various subcultures then becomes an empirical question to be answered by locating stable groups within that company and determining what their shared experience has been, as well as determining the shared experiences of the members of the total organization. One may well find that there are several cultures operating within the larger social unit called the company or the organization: a managerial culture, various occupationally based cultures in functional units, group cultures based on geographical proximity, worker cultures based on shared hierarchical experiences, and so on. The organization as a whole may be found to have an overall culture if that whole organization has a significant shared history, but we cannot assume the existence of such a culture ahead of time.

This concept of culture is rooted more in theories of group dynamics and group growth than in anthropological theories of how large cultures evolve. When we study organizations, we do not have to decipher a completely strange language or set of customs and mores. Rather, our problem is to distinguish—within a broader host culture—the unique features of a particular social unit in which we are interested. This social unit often will have a history that can be deciphered, and the key actors in the formation of that culture can often be studied, so that we are not limited, as the anthropologist is often limited, by the lack of historical data.

Because we are looking at evolving social units within a larger host culture, we also can take advantage of learning theories and develop a dynamic concept of organizational culture. Culture is learned, evolves with new experiences, and can be changed if one understands the dynamics of the learning process. If one is concerned about managing or changing culture, one must look to what we know about the learning and unlearning of complex beliefs and assumptions that underlie social behavior.

The word "culture" can be applied to any size of social unit that has had the opportunity to learn and stabilize its view of itself and the environment around it—its basic assumptions. At the broadest level, we have *civilizations* and refer to Western or Eastern cultures; at the next level down, we have *countries* with sufficient ethnic commonality that we speak of American culture or Mexican culture. But we recognize immediately that within a country we also have various *ethnic groups* to which we attribute different cultures. Even more specific is the level of *occupation, profession,* or *occupational community*. If such groups can be defined as stable units with a shared history of experience, they will have developed their own cultures. Finally, we get to the level of analysis that is the focus of this book—*organizations*. Within organizations we will find subunits that can be referred to as *groups*, and such groups may develop group cultures.

To summarize, at any of these structural levels, I will mean by "culture": *a pattern of basic assumptions—invented, discovered, or developed by a given group as it learns to cope with its problems of external adaptation and internal integration—that has worked well enough to be considered valid and, therefore, to be taught to new members as the correct way to perceive, think, and feel in relation to those problems.*

Because such assumptions have worked repeatedly, they are likely to be taken for granted and to have dropped out of awareness. Note that the definition does not include overt behavior patterns. I believe that overt behavior is always determined both by the cultural predisposition (the assumptions, perceptions, thoughts, and feelings that are patterned) and by the situational contingencies that arise from the external environment. Behavioral regularities could thus be as much a reflection of the environment as of the culture and should, therefore, not be a prime basis for *defining* the culture. Or, to put it another way, when we observe behavior regularities, we do not know whether we are dealing with a cultural artifact or not. Only after we have discovered the deeper layers that I am defining as the culture can we specify what is and what is not an artifact that reflects the culture.

Two Case Examples

To illustrate the problem of definition, I will briefly review the two company examples mentioned earlier. In Company A, hereafter referred to as Action Company, one encounters at the visible level an organization with open office landscape architecture; extreme informality of dress and manners; an absence of status symbols (so that it is hard to decipher who has what status in the organization); a very dynamic environment in the sense of rapid pace, enthusiasm, intensity, energy, and impatience; and, finally, a high level of interpersonal confrontation, argumentativeness, and conflict. One also discovers that people are constantly busy going to meetings of various sorts and expressing considerable ambivalence about committees and meetings. Committees are considered frustrating but necessary, and the level of debate and argument within meetings is intense.

If one goes beyond these surface phenomena and talks to people about what they do and why, one discovers some of their *values:* high regard for individual creativity, an absolute belief in individual accountability, but, at the same time, a strong commitment to obtaining consensus on important matters before moving ahead to a decision. Individuals at all levels in the organization are expected to think for themselves and take what they consider to be the correct course of action, even if it means going against a previous decision. Insubordination is positively valued if the action leads to a better outcome. The language one hears in the company reflects these values in that it glorifies "arguing back," "doing the right thing," and so on.

Inquiries about what the "boss" wants are typically considered irrelevant, giving one the impression that authority is not much respected in the organization. In fact, there are frequent complaints that decisions made at higher levels do not get implemented, that people at lower levels feel they can reverse a decision if their insight tells them to do something different, and that insubordination is rarely if ever punished. When people in higher authority positions are asked why they are not more decisive, why they let groups work things out, they state that they are "not smart enough" to make the decision by themselves. Consequently, they stimulate group debate and argument and create the kind of group atmosphere that I described above.

To understand this behavior, one must seek the *underlying assumptions* and premises on which this organization is based. The founding group comes from an engineering background, is intensely practical and pragmatic in its orientation, has built a strong and loyal "family" spirit that makes it possible to confront and have conflict without risk of loss of membership, and clearly believes that "truth" lies not in revealed wisdom or authority but in "what works," both technologically and in the marketplace. The assumption that the individual is the source of ideas but that no one individual is smart enough to evaluate his or her own ideas is at the root of the organization's problem-solving/decision-making model. Thus, creativity is always strongly encouraged, but new ideas have to be sold to all potentially affected parties before they will be blessed by higher authority.

Without understanding these assumptions, one cannot decipher most of the behavior observed, particularly the seeming incongruity between intense individualism and intense commitment to group work and consensus. Similarly, one cannot understand why there is simultaneously intense conflict with authority figures and intense loyalty to the organization without also understanding the assumption "We are one family who will take care of each other." Finally, without these assumptions one cannot decipher why a group would want a consultant to help it become more effective, yet ignore most of the suggestions on how to be more effective.

I now realize that what the group members meant by "effective" was, within their cultural assumptions, to be better at sorting out the truth. The group was merely a means to an end; the real process going on in the group was a basic, deep search for solutions that one could have confidence in because they stood up. Once I shifted my focus to improving the *decision* process instead of the *group* process, my interventions were more quickly acted on. For example, I began to help more with agenda setting, time management, clarifying some of the debate, summarizing, consensus testing once debate was running dry, and in other ways focusing on the "task process" rather than the "interpersonal process." But the basic confrontive, interruptive style continued because the culture of the group legitimized operating that way, based on the assumption that truth is determined through confrontive debate.

Company B, hereafter referred to as the Multi Company, offers a sharp contrast. Multi is headquartered in Europe, and most of its managers are European. At the level of what is visible, it is more formal—the formality symbolized by large buildings and offices with closed doors; a hushed atmosphere in the corridors; obvious deference rituals among people who meet each other in the hall; many status symbols, such as private dining rooms for senior managers (in contrast to Action's open cafeteria); the frequent use of academic and other titles, such as Dr. so-and-so; a slower, more deliberate pace; and much more emphasis on planning, schedules, punctuality, and formal preparation of documents for meetings.

Multi managers come across as much more serious, more thoughtful, less impulsive, more formal, and more concerned about protocol. Whereas Action ties rank and salary fairly strictly to the actual job being performed by the individual, Multi has a system of managerial ranks based on length of service, overall performance, and the personal background of the individual rather than on the actual job being performed at a given time.

In meetings I observed much less direct confrontation and much more respect for individual opinion. Recommendations made by managers in their specific area of accountability are generally respected and implemented. Insubordination tends *not* to be tolerated. Rank and status thus clearly have a higher value in Multi than in Action, whereas personal negotiating skill and the ability to get things done in an ambiguous social environment have a higher value in Action than in Multi.

I could not understand the culture of Multi, however, until I attempted to circulate memos to the various branches of the Multi organization. Although I was supposed to "stimulate innovation," the ideas never got to certain managers unless I presented them personally. When I asked one of my colleagues in the organization *why* the information did not circulate freely, he indicated that unsolicited ideas might not be well received. Only if information was asked for was it acceptable to offer ideas, unless they came down the hierarchy as an official position. To provide unsolicited information or ideas could be seen as a challenge to the information base the manager was using, and that might be regarded as an insult, implying that the person challenged had not thought deeply enough about his own problem or was not really on top of his job.

To understand this and related behavior, it was necessary to consider the underlying assumptions that this company had evolved. It had grown and achieved much of its success through fundamental discoveries made by a number of basic researchers in the company's central research laboratories. Whereas in Action truth is discovered through conflict and debate, in Multi truth has come more from the wisdom of the scientist/researcher. Both companies believe in the individual, but the differing assumptions about the nature of truth led to completely different attitudes toward authority and the role of conflict.

In Multi authority is much more respected, and conflict tends to be avoided. The individual is given areas of freedom by the boss and then is totally respected in those areas. If the role occupant is not well enough educated or skilled enough to make decisions, he is expected to train himself. If he performs poorly in the meantime, that will be tolerated. In both companies there is a "tenure" assumption that once someone

has been accepted he is likely to remain unless he fails in a major way.

In Action conflict is valued, and the individual is expected to take initiative and fight for ideas in every arena. In Multi conflict is suppressed once a decision has been made. In Action it is assumed that, if a job is not challenging or is not a good match between what the organization needs and what the individual can give, the individual should be moved to a new assignment or would quit anyway. In Multi the person would be expected to be a good soldier and do the job. Both companies are successful, yet in certain respects their cultures are almost totally different.

Recognition of these assumptions has led me to change my role as a consultant at Multi. I found that if I gave information directly, even if it was unsolicited, it was accepted because I was an "expert." If I wanted information to circulate, I sent it out to the relevant parties on my own initiative. But I have not yet found reliable mechanisms for stimulating lateral communication as a means of achieving the basic goal of increasing innovativeness.

Levels of Culture

Throughout the previous discussion, I have referred to various cultural "elements," such as the physical layout of an organization's offices, rules of interaction that are taught to newcomers, basic values that come to be seen as the organization's ideology or philosophy, and the underlying conceptual categories and assumptions that enable people to communicate and to interpret everyday occurrences. As Figure 1 shows, I distinguish among these elements by treating basic assumptions as the essence—what culture really is—and by treating values and behaviors as observed manifestations of the cultural es-

FIGURE 1 • LEVELS OF CULTURE AND THEIR INTERACTION

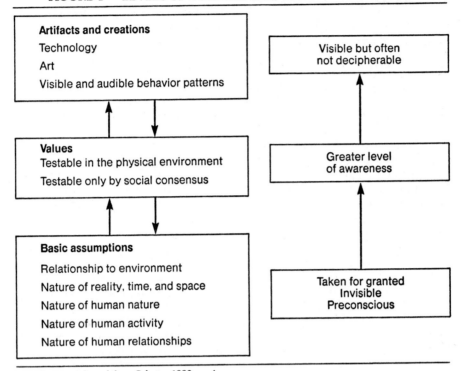

Source: Adapted from Schein, 1980, p. 4.

sence. In a sense these are "levels" of the culture, and they need to be carefully distinguished to avoid conceptual confusion.

Level 1: Artifacts. The most visible level of the culture is its artifacts and creations—its constructed physical and social environment. At this level one can look at physical space, the technological output of the group, its written and spoken language, artistic productions, and the overt behavior of its members. Since the insiders of the culture are not necessarily aware of their own artifacts, one cannot always ask about them, but one can always observe them for oneself.

Every facet of a group's life produces artifacts, creating the problem of clas-

sification. In reading cultural descriptions, one often notes that different observers choose to report on different sorts of artifacts, leading to noncomparable descriptions. Anthropologists have developed classification systems, but these tend to be so vast and detailed that cultural essence becomes difficult to discern.

Moreover, whereas it is easy to observe artifacts—even subtle ones, such as the way in which status is demonstrated by members—the difficult part is figuring out what the artifacts mean, how they interrelate, what deeper patterns, if any, they reflect. What has been called the "semiotic" approach to cultural analysis (Spradley, 1979; Frake, 1964; Barley, 1983; Manning, 1979; Van

Maanen, 1977) deals with this problem by collecting enough data on how people communicate to enable one to understand, from the point of view of the insider, what meanings are to be attached to the visible behavior. If the anthropologist lives in the cultural environment long enough, the meanings gradually become clear.

If one wants to achieve this level of understanding more quickly, one can attempt to analyze the central values that provide the day-to-day operating principles by which the members of the culture guide their behavior.

Level 2: Values. In a sense all cultural learning ultimately reflects someone's original values, their sense of what "ought" to be, as distinct from what is. When a group faces a new task, issue, or problem, the first solution proposed to deal with it can only have the status of a value because there is not as yet a shared basis for determining what is factual and real. Someone in the group, usually the founder, has convictions about the nature of reality and how to deal with it, and will propose a solution based on those convictions. That individual may regard the proposed solution as a belief or principle based on facts, but the group cannot feel that same degree of conviction until it has collectively shared in successful problem solution. For example, in a young business if sales begin to decline, the leader may say "We must increase advertising" because of his* belief that "advertising always increases sales." The group, never having experienced this situation before, will hear that assertion as a statement of the leader's *values:* "He thinks that one should always advertise more when one is in trouble." What the leader

*The author uses *his* and *he* for reasons of convenience and acknowledges the inequity of the traditional use of masculine pronouns.

initially proposes, therefore, cannot have any status other than a value to be questioned, debated, and challenged.

If the solution works, and the group has a shared perception of that success, the value gradually starts a process of *cognitive transformation* into a belief and, ultimately, an assumption. If this transformation process occurs—and it will occur only if the proposed solution continues to work, thus implying that it is in some larger sense "correct" and must reflect an accurate picture of reality—group members will tend to forget that originally they were not sure and that the values were therefore debated and confronted. As the values begin to be taken for granted, they gradually become beliefs and assumptions and drop out of consciousness, just as habits become unconscious and automatic. Thus, if increased advertising consistently results in increased sales, the group begins to believe that the leader is "right" and has an understanding of how the world really works.

Not all values undergo such transformation. First of all, the solution based on a given value may not work reliably. Only those values that are susceptible of physical or social validation, and that continue to work reliably in solving the group's problems, will become transformed into assumptions. Second, certain value domains, those dealing with the less controllable elements of the environment or with aesthetic matters, may not be testable at all. In such cases consensus through social validation is still possible, but it is not automatic. By social validation I mean that values about how people should relate to each other, exercise power, define what is beautiful, and so on, can be validated by the experience that they reduce uncertainty and anxiety. A group can learn that the holding of certain beliefs and assumptions is necessary as a basis for maintaining the group.

Many values remain conscious and are explicitly articulated because they serve the normative or moral function of guiding members of the group in how to deal with certain key situations. For example, if a company states explicitly in its charter and other public documents that it strongly values people, it may be doing so because it wants everyone to operate by that value, even without any historical experience that such a value actually improves its performance in its environment. A set of values that become embodied in an ideology or organizational philosophy thus can serve as a guide and as a way of dealing with the uncertainty of intrinsically uncontrollable or difficult events. Such values will predict much of the behavior that can be observed at the artifactual level. But if those values are not based on prior cultural learning, they may also come to be seen only as what Argyris and Schön (1978) have called "espoused values," which predict well enough what people will *say* in a variety of situations but which may be out of line with what they will actually *do* in situations where those values should be operating. Thus, the company may *say* that it values people, but its record in that regard may contradict what it says.

If the espoused values are reasonably congruent with the underlying assumptions, then the articulation of those values into a philosophy of operating can be helpful in bringing the group together, serving as a source of identity and core mission (Ouchi, 1981; Pascale and Athos, 1981; Peters and Waterman, 1982). But in analyzing values one must discriminate carefully between those that are congruent with underlying assumptions and those that are, in effect, either rationalizations or aspirations for the future.

If we can spell out the major espoused values of an organization, have we then described and understood its culture? And how do we know whether we have

really understood it? The answer often lies in our own feelings as observers and analysts. Even after we have listed and articulated the major values of an organization, we still may feel that we are dealing only with a list that does not quite hang together. Often such lists of values are not patterned, sometimes they are even mutually contradictory, sometimes they are incongruent with observed behavior. Large areas of behavior are often left unexplained, leaving us with a feeling that we understood a piece of the culture but still do not have the culture as such in hand. To get at that deeper level of understanding, to decipher the pattern, to predict future behavior correctly, we have to understand more fully the category of "basic assumptions."

Level 3: Basic Underlying Assumptions. When a solution to a problem works repeatedly, it comes to be taken for granted. What was once a hypothesis, supported by only a hunch or a value, comes gradually to be treated as a reality. We come to believe that nature really works this way. Basic assumptions, in this sense, are different from what some anthropologists call "dominant value orientations" (Kluckhohn and Strodtbeck, 1961) in that such dominant orientations reflect the *preferred* solution among several basic alternatives, but all the alternatives are still visible in the culture, and any given member of the culture could, from time to time, behave according to variant as well as dominant orientations. Basic assumptions, in the sense in which I want to define that concept, have become so taken for granted that one finds little variation within a cultural unit. In fact, if a basic assumption is strongly held in a group, members would find behavior based on any other premise inconceivable. For example, in a group whose basic assumption is that the individual's rights supersede those of the group, members would find it inconceivable that they should commit suicide or in some other way sacrifice themselves to the group even if they had dishonored the group. In a company in a capitalist country, it is inconceivable that one might sell products at a financial loss or that it does not matter whether a product works.

What I am calling basic assumptions are congruent with what Argyris has identified as "theories-in-use," the implicit assumptions that actually guide behavior, that tell group members how to perceive, think about, and feel about things (Argyris, 1976; Argyris and Schön, 1974). Basic assumptions, like theories-in-use, tend to be nonconfrontable and nondebatable. To relearn in the area of "theories-in-use," to resurrect, reexamine, and possibly change basic assumptions—a process that Argyris and others have called "double-loop learning"—is intrinsically difficult because assumptions are, by definition, not confrontable or debatable.

Clearly, such unconscious assumptions can distort data. If we assume, on the basis of past experience or education, that other people will take advantage of us whenever they have an opportunity (essentially what McGregor, 1960, meant by his "Theory X"), we expect to be taken advantage of and then interpret the behavior of others in a way that coincides with those expectations. We observe people sitting idly at their desk and perceive them as loafing rather than thinking out an important problem; we perceive absence from work as shirking rather than doing work at home. In contrast, if we assume—as the previously mentioned Action Company does—that everyone is highly motivated and competent (McGregor's "Theory Y"), we will act in accordance with that assumption. Thus, if someone at Action Company is absent or seems to be idle,

the managers ask themselves what has happened to their job assignment process, not what is wrong with the individual. The person is still seen as motivated, but the environment is perceived as somehow turning him or her off. Managerial energy then goes into redesigning the work or the environment to enable the person to become productive once again.

Unconscious assumptions sometimes lead to "Catch 22" situations, as illustrated by a common problem experienced by American supervisors in some other cultures. A manager who comes from an American pragmatic tradition assumes and takes it for granted that solving a problem always has the highest priority. When that manager encounters a subordinate who comes from a different cultural tradition, in which good relationships and protecting the superior's "face" are assumed to have top priority, the following scenario can easily result.

The manager proposes a solution to a given problem. The subordinate knows that the solution will not work, but his unconscious assumption requires that he remain silent because to tell the boss that the proposed solution is wrong is a threat to the boss's face. It would not even occur to the subordinate to do anything other than remain silent or even reassure the boss that they should go ahead and take the action.

The action is taken, the results are negative, and the boss, somewhat surprised and puzzled, asks the subordinate what he would have done. When the subordinate reports that he would have done something different, the boss quite legitimately asks why the subordinate did not speak up sooner. This question puts the subordinate into an impossible bind because the answer itself is a threat to the boss's face. He cannot possibly explain his behavior without committing the very sin he is trying to avoid in the first place—namely, embarrassing the boss. He might even lie at this point and argue that what the boss did was right and only bad luck or uncontrollable circumstances prevented it from succeeding.

From the point of view of the subordinate, the boss's behavior is incomprehensible because it shows lack of self-pride, possibly causing the subordinate to lose respect for that boss. To the boss the subordinate's behavior is equally incomprehensible. He cannot develop any sensible explanation of his subordinate's behavior that is not cynically colored by the assumption that the subordinate at some level just does not care about effective performance and therefore must be gotten rid of. It never occurs to the boss that another assumption—such as "One never embarrasses a superior"—is operating and that, to the subordinate, that assumption is even more powerful than "One gets the job done."

In this instance probably only a third party or some cross-cultural education could help to find common ground whereby both parties could bring their implicit assumptions to the surface. And even after they have surfaced, such assumptions would still operate, forcing the boss and the subordinate to invent a new communication mechanism that would permit each to remain congruent with his culture—for example, agreeing that, before any decision is made and before the boss has stuck his neck out, the subordinate will be asked for suggestions and for factual data that would not be face threatening.

I have dwelled on this long example to illustrate the potency of implicit, unconscious assumptions and to show that such assumptions often deal with fundamental aspects of the culture. But such assumptions are hard to locate. If we examine carefully an organization's artifacts and values, we can try to infer the underlying assumptions that tie things together. Such assumptions can usually be brought to the surface in interviews if both the interviewer and the interviewee are committed to trying to piece together the cultural pattern. But this requires detective work and commitment, not because people are reluctant to surface their assumptions but because they are so taken for granted. Yet when we do surface them, the cultural pattern suddenly clarifies and we begin to feel we really understand what is going on and why.

Ethnographic versus Clinical Perspective

In reviewing my own "data base," the sources of my own knowledge about organizational culture, I have found it necessary to distinguish the perspective of the *ethnographer* from that of the *clinician*. The ethnographer obtains concrete data in order to understand the culture he is interested in, presumably for intellectual and scientific reasons. Though the ethnographer must be faithful to the observed and experienced data, he brings to the situation a set of concepts or models that motivated the research in the first place. The group members studied are often willing to participate but usually have no particular stake in the intellectual issues that may have motivated the study.

In contrast, a "clinical perspective" is one where the group members are clients who have their own interests as the prime motivator for the involvement of the "outsider," often labeled "consultant" or "therapist" in this context. In the typical ethnographic situation, the researcher must obtain the cooperation of the subjects; in the clinical situation, the client must get the cooperation of the helper/consultant. The psychological contract between client and helper is completely different from that between researcher and subject, leading to a different kind of relationship between them, the revelation of different kinds of data, and the use of different criteria for when enough has been "understood" to terminate the inquiry.

Clients call in helpers when they are frustrated, anxious, unhappy, threatened, or thwarted; when their rational, logical approaches to things do not work. Inevitably, then, the clinical view brings one to the topic of the "irrational" in organizations. I have found and hope to show in this book that one of the simplest ways of understanding the seemingly irrational is to relate such phenomena to culture, because culture often explains things that otherwise seem mysterious, silly, or "irrational."

Consultants also bring with them their models and concepts for obtaining and analyzing information, but the function of those models is to provide insight into how the client can be *helped*. In order to provide help, the consultant must "understand" at some level. Some theories, in fact, argue that only by attempting to change a system (that is, giving help) does one demonstrate any real level of understanding (Lewin, 1952; Schein, 1980). For me this criterion has always been the relevant one for "validating" my understanding, even though that understanding often is incomplete,

since the clinical relationship does not automatically license the helper to inquire into areas the client may not wish to pursue or considers irrelevant. On the other hand, the level of understanding is likely to be deeper and more dynamic.

The point of spelling all this out now is to let the reader know that my data base is a clinical one, not an ethnographic one. I have not been a participant-observer in organizations other than the ones I had membership in, but in being a consultant I have spent long periods of time in client organizations. I believe that this clinical perspective provides a useful counterpoint to the pure ethnographic perspective, because the clinician learns things that are different from what an ethnographer learns. Clients are motivated to reveal certain things when they are paying for help that may not come out if they are only "willing" to be studied.

So this kind of inquiry leads, I believe, to a "deeper" analysis of culture as a phenomenon—deeper in the sense of its impact on individual members of the organization. This perspective also leads inevitably to a more dynamic view of how things work, how culture begins, evolves, changes, and sometimes disintegrates. And, as we will see, this perspective throws into high relief what leaders and other change agents can or cannot do to change culture deliberately.

BIBLIOGRAPHIC REFERENCES

Argyris, C. (1976). *Increasing leadership effectiveness.* New York: Wiley-Interscience.

Argyris, C., & Schön, D. A. (1974). *Theory in practice: Increasing professional effectiveness.* San Francisco: Jossey-Bass.

Argyris, C., & Schön, D. A. (1978). *Organizational learning.* Reading, MA: Addison-Wesley Publishing.

Barley, S. R. (1983). Semiotics and the study of occupational and organizational cultures. *Administrative Science Quarterly, 28,* 393–413.

Deal, T. E., & Kennedy, A. A. (1982). *Corporate cultures.* Reading, MA: Addison-Wesley Publishing.

Dyer, W. G., Jr. (1982). Culture in organizations. A case study and analysis. Unpublished paper, Sloan School of Management, MIT.

Frake, C. O. (1964). Notes on queries in ethnography. *American Anthropologist*, 66, 132–145.

Goffman, E. (1959). *The presentation of self in everyday life*. New York: Doubleday.

Homans, G. (1950). *The human group*. New York: Harcourt Brace Jovanovich.

Kluckhohn, F. R., & Strodtbeck, F. L. (1961). *Variations in value orientations*. New York: Harper & Row.

Lewin, K. (1952). Group decision and social change. In G. E. Swanson, T. N. Newcomb, & E. L. Hartley (Eds.), *Readings in Social Psychology* (rev. ed.). New York: Holt, Rinehart & Winston.

Louis, M. R. (1983). Organizations as culture bearing milieux. In L. R. Pondy & others (Eds.), *Organizational symbolism*. Greenwich, CT: JAI Press.

McGregor, D. M. (1960). *The human side of enterprise*. New York: McGraw-Hill.

Manning, P. (1979). Metaphors of the field: Varieties of organizational discourse. *Administrative Science Quarterly*, 24, 660–671.

Ouchi, W. G. (1981). *Theory Z*. Reading, MA: Addison-Wesley Publishing.

Pascale, R. T., & Athos, A. G. (1981). *The art of Japanese management*. New York: Simon & Schuster.

Peters, T. J., & Waterman, R. H., Jr. (1982). *In search of excellence*. New York: Harper & Row.

Ritti, R. R., & Funkhouser, G. R. (1982). *The ropes to skip and the ropes to know*. Columbus, OH: Grid.

Schein, E. H. (1968). Organizational socialization and the profession of management. *Industrial Management Review*, 9, 1–15.

Schein, E. H. (1978). *Career dynamics: Matching individual and organizational needs*. Reading, MA: Addison-Wesley Publishing.

Schein, E. H. (1980). *Organizational psychology* (3rd ed.). Englewood Cliffs, NJ: Prentice-Hall. (First published 1965, 2nd ed. 1970.)

Schein, E. H. (1981a). Does Japanese management style have a message for American managers? *Sloan Management Review*, 23, 55–68.

Schein, E. H. (Summer 1983). The role of the founder in creating organizational culture. *Organizational Dynamics*, pp. 13–28.

Schein, E. H. (1984). Coming to a new awareness of organizational culture. *Sloan Management Review*, 25, 3–16.

Spradley, J. P. (1979). *The ethnographic interview*. New York: Holt, Rinehart & Winston.

Tagiuri, R., & Litwin, G. H. (Eds.). (1968). *Organizational climate: Exploration of a concept*. Boston: Division of Research, Harvard Graduate School of Business.

Van Maanen, J. (1976). Breaking in: Socialization to work. In R. Dubin (Ed.), *Handbook of work, organization and society*. Chicago: Rand McNally.

Van Maanen, J. (1977). Experiencing organizations. In J. Van Maanen (Ed.), *Organizational careers: Some new perspectives*. New York: John Wiley & Sons.

Van Maanen, J. (1979b). The self, the situation, and the rules of interpersonal relations. In W. Bennis & others, *Essays in interpersonal dynamics*. Homewood, IL: Dorsey Press.

33
The Making of an Organizational Saga
Burton R. Clark

THE LEADER, THE GROUP, AND THE COMMUNITY

The three case studies and the foregoing discussion suggest how distinctiveness is achieved in an American college. It is initiated by a single individual, or a small band, in a setting conducive in normative and structural openness. It is sustained by a much larger number of people, on and off campus, through many interlocking components of durable organization.

When we look for how distinctive emphasis gets under way, we find typically a single individual, usually the president, or a very small group. The innovator formulates a new idea, a mission; he has, with varying degrees of deliberateness, found his way to a particular college that is in a particular stage of development and that is structurally open, and he starts to design appropriate means of embodying his idea in the organization and to enhance the conduciveness of the setting. Although this is the function of the strong president, it can likely be performed also by a unified junta.

When we look for the way distinctive emphasis is maintained in a college, we find it typically firmly expressed in interlocking stable structures. The key structure is usually a tenured faculty armed with power. The senior faculty members are personally committed to the emphasis, are collectively the center of power or are so powerful that they can veto attempts at change, and are replaced over time in such a way as to continue the embodiment of the historic purpose in faculty values.

The question of who is most important in the making of a distinctive college, one raised often in educational circles, becomes then not a useful question. It leads toward simple answers and polarized arguments that obscure more than they reveal. For example, if we ask: "Is not Antioch the lengthened shadow of Morgan, a creature of his ideals and introduced practices?" the answer "yes" is a partial truth that overlooks the essential work of full development and institutionalization that took place under Henderson in the thirties; the essential, permanent commitment of the senior faculty; and the essential expression of an Antioch legend in student subculture, public image, and social base. If we answer the same question with a flat "no," we underestimate the great impact of one man in designing a change and getting it under way. The question requires an answer informed by an awareness of the stages of development in a college; the differing roles of the leader and the group in initiating and sustaining a distinctive style; and the complicated, ongoing interaction of purpose, leadership, environment, and the means of organization. The question of how

Source: Burton R. Clark, The Distinctive College: Antioch, Reed and Swarthmore (Chicago: Aldine Publishing, 1970), 255–262.

distinctiveness is achieved must at least be broken into the two parts of how it was initiated and how it is sustained. That the question can be further specified and fruitfully posed in other ways has been demonstrated in earlier discussion.

We may note particularly that distinctiveness in a college involves and encourages those characteristics of group life commonly referred to as community. It offers an educationally relevant definition of the difference of the group from all others. And salient elements in the distinctiveness become foci of personal awareness and of a sense of things held in common with others currently on the scene, those who have been there before, and those yet to arrive. Distinctiveness captures loyalty, inducing men to enlist and to stay against the lures of careerism. And it arrests the most transient members, the students, extending their devotion for years to come.

In turn, the conditions most favorable to the existence of a community assist in the development and maintenance of distinctive character. One such condition in a formal organization is singularity of purpose. Group integration is promoted when all are headed in the same direction. A second condition is smallness of size, which allows informal as well as formal links across the specializations and internal divisions inherent in formal organization. An aggregate of strangers brought together to pursue a common purpose within a small organization is more likely to develop a community than is an aggregation set to multiple purposes in a large enterprise. These conditions favor frequent and intense interaction across the system and encourage convergent rather than divergent personal experiences leading toward a sense of oneness. They then obviously can be put to the service of distinctiveness.

However, other conditions can sometimes compensate. Multipurpose universities of the size of ten thousand can still have a relatively strong sense of community and a distinctive character, e.g., Harvard and Yale. Here, long tradition, slow growth, high status, and units promoting intensive interaction combine to combat the structural and subjective fragmentation inherent in largeness and multiplicity of purpose. Tradition contributes an aura. Slow growth helps preserve a sense of unity, by granting time for the assimilation of newcomers into established staff and of new thought into traditional conceptions. High status encourages close identification with the institution: Harvard professor and Yale man are terms usually seized rather than resisted by those entitled to them. Structures promoting interaction—the Harvard residential houses, the Yale residential colleges—help students cope psychologically and socially with the potential stress of individual detachment among thousands of strangers. But these conditions are in short supply in American colleges and universities. The common situation is one of little tradition, rapid growth, modest status, and weak structures for promoting interaction. With these conditions, large size and multiple purpose sharply diminish the possibilities for a sense of community and for distinctive character in the whole.

We may also reflect on the achievement of distinctiveness by asking about its failure to occur. The explanatory scheme here suggests three main sources of nonoccurrence. One is lack of will, or essentially no man with a mission. The second is the absence of structurally conducive conditions for the introduction and early working-out of the mission. The third is weakness or breakdown in the structures of institutionalization, the major components of the organization highlighted earlier, whose embodiment of the mission to an important degree turns it into a saga. Thus we have the denial of distinctiveness when the mission-oriented leader cannot be found or induced to come to the organization; or having arrived, cannot loosen the organization from its web of traditional expectations and commitments; or having broken tradition and established the mission, the mission does not endure because one or more major structural supports develop weakly or give way. The latter problems include weakness in the social base, as nonbelievers stiffen their resistance and withhold support; attenuation of belief in the faculty, as nonselective recruitment introduces nonbelievers; fragmentation of the student subculture, as a growing student body becomes more heterogeneous and draws from the youth of a new age; and loss of unity and distinctiveness in curricular practices, as adaptations are made to placate external and internal interests. Above all, as emphasized, vulnerability lies in weak power of the believing group, for then agents of change can divert the organization to a new course.

THE RISKS AND TENSIONS OF DISTINCTIVENESS

Distinctive colleges, because they attempt to be special and not all things to all men, are likely to have one or more distinctive strains, exhibiting in higher degree tensions found elsewhere. In emphasizing one value, they underplay, oppose, or ignore others. In securing the loyalty of one segment of society, they may secure the hostility of others. In committing the organization strongly to one path of action, they find it difficult at a later time to take another route or otherwise to adapt as new demands are made upon them.

Among the three colleges of this study, we have seen a number of tensions and risks: the strain between adult responsibility and the freedom of students; the struggle between specialization and general education; the split between teaching and research; the risk of being a cult in a hostile countryside; the danger of getting cut off from ordinary funding sources. At Antioch, as we have seen, the freedom of students was a persisting source of institutional strain, presenting problems with which only a true believer would willingly live. The salient commitment to general education also produced a severe problem when the more specialized interests of modern academic men demanded to be served. And for decades the general liberality, nonconformity, and political action have produced local disdain and hostility, complicating severely the task of raising necessary funds. To become distinctive the college lived through two decades of being heavily in debt. After the retirement of the debt, the college continued to find its fund-raising efforts heavily mortgaged by its reputation. Antioch has had only a few quiet years since 1920, and it has had very few financially easy years.

Reed has shared with Antioch a deep institutional strain over student freedom. The internal anxiety and the external antipathy have been an enduring part of institutional affairs. One president after another has found student behavior his cross to bear, and trustees could hardly help resting uneasy, no matter how strong their pride in accomplishments. The college proved better oriented than Antioch for an age of specialization in that its posture was not rooted in an equally broad version of general education; but its dogged commitment to teaching meant stubborn resistance to the interest in research growing everywhere in the academic world.

And no other college of similar national standing has had such a problem of fund-raising. In its business affairs, it was a shoestring operation, with all that that entails in administrative anxiety, lack of physical plant, and underpayment of faculty. The strain and the risk have been high, again only tolerable to determined men who are sure they are right.

Of the three colleges, Swarthmore has been least subject to strain because of distinctiveness. To effect a major change it did not undergo the uncertainties of new organization or the difficulties of crisis. The change was more evolution-ary and considerably better funded than was the case in the other two colleges. But Swarthmore could have lived an eas-ier life if it had stayed more in the nor-mal mold. The many changes of the twenties and thirties had to be fought out; alumni resistance made the whole effort a precarious one for several years and a matter of some stress for a longer period. Although the college was well oriented (for its size) for the growing interests in specialization and research, it, too, had to struggle to attract and hold an appropriate faculty against the lures of the universities. Even more than Antioch and Reed, the college could not make do with faculty members whose job alternatives were in average small colleges. Student brightness alone would make this foolhardy, and the self-con-cept and national leadership role of the college made it highly inappropriate. As a result, the college pitted itself against Ivy League universities in recruitment, not a soft road for any small college to travel. And then, too, the college found student freedom and nonconformity a steady source of strain within its mem-bership and especially with the sur-rounding community.

The ultimate risk of distinctive char-acter is that of success in one era breed-ing rigidity and stagnation in a later one.

Commitments are precise rather than diffuse, sharply made rather than dully connected, articulated rather than un-spoken; in short, they constitute a for-mula for later trouble. But in such mat-ters, involving stages of organizational development and degrees of openness to later change, we know little about com-pelling restraints and open options. Surely the organization that turns a mis-sion into a saga, a good idea into a fruit-ful legend, moves, in the full flush of success, toward the possibility of its dis-tinctiveness becoming an antiquated mode, one from which it cannot unhook itself until torn by trouble. But surely, just as ordinary routinized colleges can vary in degree of openness to change, distinctively fixed colleges can also vary. Among the three colleges, for example, one can speculate that Reed is the least open to change. The Reed capacity, one may say the Reed necessity, to endure through sheer stubbornness gives it a sharp problem of adaptability. Swarth-more appears in a middle ground, con-servative in habit but with possible flex-ibility within its open Quaker ethos and its general institutional health. Antioch appears the most open to change, even to diffusion of hard-won character. Its central educational values leave the cur-riculum exposed: To believe that the young learn from work in jobs off campus and from campus experiences outside the classroom is to unbutton things, for then why not this and why not that, why not course credit for making pottery or for living and working three months with a farm family in France? The ideals of so-cial reform, strongest at Antioch, also spill over into a sense that one's own campus can stand improvement. The values institutionalized at Antioch have, in general, left the college somewhat ex-perimental-minded, with a passion for self-study and for leadership in experi-mental-college circles.

In the face of the common institutional danger that distinctiveness may lead in time to rigidity and stagnation, we may note several features that are favorable to change and that are likely to be present in all distinctively excellent colleges. One feature is the challenge of bright students. To have a bright student body is to have a steady infiltration of critical minds. The faculty and administration then come under heavy pressure to remain alert, first in the performance of traditional practice, and second to the possibilities of altering practices to meet the changing needs and demands of the students. In the best colleges, the students tend to become brighter than the faculty. Many faculty members must then struggle to maintain their credibility as teachers, reading widely and critically, staying abreast of the latest perspectives and findings of the discipline so that they at least know more than the students even if their mental gears do not go around so fast. On affairs that engage the whole campus, the bright students offer rational arguments that are qualitatively different from those of students at average small colleges. At an Antioch or Reed or Swarthmore, time and again one can observe students getting the best of an administrator in an argument, driving him back against the wall as he tries to give a rational explanation for traditional controls over student behavior. In such settings, effective administrators not only must be intelligent and quick but also must be capable of adapting to the changing nature of sophisticated youth.

A second feature favorable to change is the expression of new views that occurs when the authority structure is relatively democratic and when discussion is relatively open. The students, faculty, and administrators who flow in from the outside, not as well socialized to what the college has been, as are the old-timers, are often the source of new thought. In time, on the average, they become socialized or they go away. The chance for them to express themselves in influential ways while they are young in the organization becomes an important factor in change. Forms of organization at Antioch, for example, have allowed young faculty members to have influence. The young ones do not sit in hushed silence, in awe or fear of their elders, as young men do in many small colleges. With the faculty meeting allowing a reasonable chance for men to be equal, Young Turks cannot be ignored. Community government, in addition, has allowed the voices of students to be heard. As a result, the oligarchs are not completely in control. There is always a group with a new plan that must be considered and in some cases adopted. Other leading colleges, in somewhat lesser degree, usually possess this source of adaptation.

Finally, sources of openness to change are found in the tensions and risks, described earlier in the section, that inhere in distinctive character. The tensions force small crises in organizational viability; the risks generate anticipation that present character may not be able to cope with future pressures. The small crises and worries about the future are commonly generated by problems of finance and retention of faculty. The frequent annual deficit shocks everyone when, in the current year, it jumps to a new high. The normal loss of faculty members to other places becomes abnormal and threatening when four associate professors leave in a single year. Such events can be taken as signs of a gathering storm, for if repeated because the college has become out of joint with the times, then the institution, beloved character and all, will decline in health and quality.

THE REWARDS OF A SAGA

When we hold educational ideals in mind, the making of a college is much more than raising money, erecting buildings, recruiting professors, organizing courses, and enrolling students. Past minimal competence lies the problem of whether the operations of the college will reflect to a significant degree certain educational and social values. To build effectively is to incorporate purpose effectively, and not any purpose but purpose congruent with the general ideals of a class of organizations and of a large social institution; e.g., the ideals of the liberated arts college and the ideals of excellence in higher learning. The reflected purpose can be a specific imitation of what the leading colleges of a given period are doing; and that is hard to do, requiring as it does supportive settings that are in short supply and organizational means that must be obtained in a competitive market. Even more difficult is to find the specific formula that allows the college to reflect general values in a new, highly productive, and esteemed form. The vision that drives the best educational leaders is to approach a general ideal of man by developing new organizational devices and practices.

Antioch, Reed, and Swarthmore are among the handful of colleges that, through ingenuity and persistence in the four decades of 1920 to 1960, came to reflect most fully distinctive excellence in liberal education on the American scene. Their stories tell us how they did it and suggest what is essential and what may be accidental to doing as well in other efforts. Optimistically, we see elements of organizational development that could be widely replicated. The common elements discussed here can at least inform the images of the future held by college administrators and faculties.

Pessimistically, however, we see conditions, men, and events that have rarely conspired. No one should suggest that it is easy to get purpose and men together under conditions that permit effective expression of cherished educational ideals.

Either way, we find at root in these successful cases a willingness to risk much, personally and organizationally, to try a different route. The personal commitment required of many actors in the situation can be set in motion by the charisma of a single man. It can be fully invested and steadily carried over the years, however, only by a fusing of an idea and the organization. Careerist motives are not enough; an embodied idea is the institutional chariot to which individual motive becomes chained. When the idea is in command, men are indifferent to personal cost. They often are not even aware of how much they have risked and how much they sometimes have sacrificed. As ideologues, as believers, they do not care. They are proud of what they have been through, what they have done, and what they stand for. They feel highly involved in a worthwhile collective effort and wish to remain with it. For the organization the richly embellished institutional definition that we call a saga can then be invaluable in maintaining viability in a competitive market. It is also invaluable as a foundation for trust within the institutional group, easing communication and cooperation.

The individual and group returns are thus considerable. In offering so much thrill and pleasure, a saga maximizes for the individual the esthetic rewards of administration and group membership. The organizational means become beautiful ends in themselves. In turn, in binding and motivating the individual, even in fusing personal and organizational identities, the legend becomes a precious resource for those who fashion the enterprise, a resource created out of the social components of organization. In such efforts, the task—and the reward—of the institutional leader is to create and initiate an activating mission. The task—and the reward—of the institutional group is to have purpose and organization become a saga.

34

Symbols, Patterns, and Settings: An Optimistic Case for Getting Things Done

Thomas J. Peters

The most important decisions are often the least apparent.
                                    Karl Weick

What tools come to mind when you think about changing an organization? If you came up through the ranks in the 1950s and 1960s, the answer is quite likely to be divisionalizing and developing a strategic planning system. Shifting the organizational structure and inventing new processes are still options for change. But increasingly thorny and overlapping international, competitive, and regulatory problems call for increasingly complex responses—and such responses are getting increasingly difficult to devise and problematical in their application.

It is reasonable to propose, however, that an effective set of change tools is actually embedded in senior management's daily message sending and receiving activities, and that these tools can be managed in such a way as to energize and redirect massive, lumbering business and government institutions.

The tools will be characterized as symbols (the raw material), patterns (the systematic use of the raw material), and settings (the showcase for the systematic use).

It is not suggested that these tools merely be added to the traditional arsenal of formal change instruments—primarily structure and process. Rather, it will be argued that historically effective prescriptions are losing some of their impact, and their formal replacements—such as the matrix structure—have comparatively little leverage. Moreover, the typical top management is seldom around for much more than five or six years—too little time in which to leave a distinctive and productive stamp on a large, history-bound institution solely by means of the available formal change alternatives. Hence effective change may increasingly depend on systematic use of

Note: The author wholeheartedly acknowledges the help of Anne Hartman Peters in the preparation of this article, along with the thoughtful comments of Anthony G. Athos, Harold J. Leavitt, and Eugene J. Webb.

Source: Thomas J. Peters, "Symbols, Patterns, and Settings: An Optimistic Case for Getting Things Done," *Organizational Dynamics*, (Autumn 1978). Reprinted, by permission of the publisher, from *Organizational Dynamics*, Autumn 1978.

the informal change mechanisms, derived from coherent daily actions.

PESSIMISM: FROM RATIONAL MEN TO GARBAGE CANS

Many leading organizational researchers seem to imply "You'll never get much done." James March describes organizations as "garbage cans," in which problems, participants, and choices circle aimlessly around, connecting—with resultant decisions—only occasionally. Other colorful metaphors or contrived terms have sought to convey similar images of confusion: for example, "organizational seesaws" (William Starbuck), "organized chaos" (Igor Ansoff), "loosely coupled systems" (Karl Weick). The theory of resource dependency developed by Jeffery Pfeffer and Gerald Salancik depicts the typical executive as having but a single course for inducing stable outcomes: Diversify to cope with uncertainty by reducing dependence on any one source of supply or market segment. The common message seems to be one of nearly unrelieved pessimism: It is a confusing, messy world.

It would be hard to quarrel with the researchers' descriptions of the complexity and ambiguity of real life in organizations. The trouble is that most of them fail to address in any but the most general terms the question of whether (and how) one can operate in such a world.

In the face of such pessimism, I argue that actually senior management has an array of underutilized tools at hand to help it come to grips with organizational complexity. In the words of British researcher Rosemary Stewart, ". . . managers tend to exaggerate the amount of choice that they have while failing to appreciate the nature of some of the choices that are available to them."

It may be well to begin by briefly examining the origin of the pessimistic views. Herbert Simon, the most noted analyst of organizational complexity, coined the term *satisficing* in 1957 to suggest that organizations seek satisfactory rather than optimal solutions to problems.

Simon and his successors were reacting to decades of management and organization theorizing in search of reliable management prescriptions. The quest for certainties in management began at least as early as Frederick Taylor's time and motion studies and soon expanded to a search for highly rational principles of management—for example, optimal spans of control and rules of delegation. After the Hawthorne experiments, a competing form of prescriptive certainty, based on an opposite set of assumptions about human nature, emerged. Enhancing participation in decision making became a substitute panacea.

When Simon and his successors revolted against the quest for certainty, their line of attack (based on descriptions of ambiguity in managerial settings) was not surprisingly marked by a refusal to develop prescriptions for the management of change. Their complex models in general provide little comfort for the struggling executive. It is in fact commonplace in organizational behavior articles to dismiss most practical advice as "not contingent enough." The contingency theorists correctly assert that different organizational solutions work in different settings. In practice, this frequently seems to imply that every solution is unique, hence the search for generally useful principles is essentially futile.

Carefully reading the work of the leading architects of complexity, one can, however, unearth the rudiments of some practical prescriptions for beleaguered managers. Almost as an aside, for example, Michael Cohen and James March in *Leadership and Ambiguity*, a study of university presidents, offer "eight basic tactical rules for those who seek to influence the course of decisions." The sorts of rules that Cohen and March propose (see Figure 1) have a particularly startling property: Although, as the authors demonstrate, some such tools as these may be the most effective change vehicles available in today's environment, they are too "trivial" to be at the forefront of most managers' minds—one

reason, perhaps, why they have not been explored.

The author's research has focused on what many audiences have called the "theory of the small win." Patterns of consistent, moderate size, clear-cut outcomes—patterns of small wins—are a special subclass of managerial activity patterns influencing future change. The effectiveness of these patterns was first validated in laboratory experiments with M.B.A. graduates. In addition, patterns of small wins were repeatedly noted in the literature of business and politics.

FIGURE 1 • RULES FOR MANAGING CHANGE

Rule	Interpretation
1. Spend time	Spending time exerts, in itself, a "claim" on the decision-making system.
2. Persist	Having more patience than other people often results in adoption of a chosen course of action.
3. Exchange status for substance	One of the most effective ways to gather support for programs is to reward allies with visible tokens of recognition.
4. Facilitate opposition participation	Often those outside the formal decision centers overestimate the feasibility of change; encouraged to participate, they will often become more realistic.
5. Overload the system	Bureaucracies chew up most projects, but on the other hand, some sneak through; merely launching more projects is likely to result in more successes.
6. Provide garbage cans	Organizations endlessly argue issues; to induce desired outcomes, put "throw-away" issues at the top of agendas (to absorb debate) saving substantive issues for later.
7. Manage unobtrusively	Certain actions can influence the organization pervasively but almost imperceptibly; moreover, the resulting changes will persist with little further attention.
8. Interpret history	By articulating a particular version of events, the leader can alter people's perception of what has been happening; whoever writes the minutes influences the outcome.

Successful executives in both the private and public sectors apparently often attend to manageable situations where the value of their own persistence and ability to control intermediate events maximizes their influence on subsequent outcomes. Strings of these controlled successes are used over time to shape and manage attention and perceptions, thereby affecting the course of interactions and outcomes.

During the past year, several colleagues and I have been testing similar change techniques in a handful of large American and European corporations. The results so far obtained by sensitive application of these "mundane tools"—as practical alternatives to ponderous weapons such as structural overhauls—have been impressive enough to give grounds for cautious optimism. Based on these experiences, I will propose in the following pages a simple set of change instruments whose practical value seems to warrant trial and application on a broader scale.

A FRAMEWORK FOR THINKING ABOUT CHANGE

In the minds of senior managers, what does it mean to induce effective change? Surely speed of effect and control over outcomes would be near the top of any list of criteria. Consider the typology derived from these two dimensions:

Category 1: High control, low speed.
Category 2: High control, high speed.
Category 3: Low control, high speed.
Category 4: Low control, low speed.

Our revised view of organizational change may be considered in the framework of this categorization. First, some historical change tools will be assigned to each category; next, the apparently decreasing effectiveness of several tools will be discussed; last,

some alternative change levers will be suggested.

Historically, the most regularly considered tools for change have been formal processes, structure, and human resource development programs. The first two of these levers have been at the forefront of organization change in the past; the third has never attained its purported full potential.

The modern planning system is the most typical formal process. Its roots go back decades. Planning, as managers generally think of it today, received its major impetus during World War II. Strategic planning systems burgeoned in the 1960s; General Electric and Texas Instruments, among others, have attributed much of their continuing success to the planning revolution. Planning tends to affect organizational outcomes over a period of years, as experience and skill accumulate at many levels within the organization. Historically, then, planning systems are perhaps the most important and typical change tool in Category 1 (high control, low speed).

Structural solutions, especially decentralization and divisionalization, have commonly been employed for strategically realigning increasingly complex organizations into manageable, typical product-line-oriented chunks. Having reached its highwater mark in the United States in the years after World War II, decentralization spread to Europe in the 1960s in response to the U.S. multinational invasion. The vast majority of major business enterprises today are organized on the divisional principle—or some variation thereof, for example, GE's recent sectoral reorganization. Working out the problems of divisionalization took years in many cases, but noticeable change more often than not came quickly and was generally in the hoped-for direction. Thus it seems fair to consider this historical solution as the leading candidate for Category 2 (high control, high speed) change tools.

An obvious candidate for Category 4 (low control, low speed) change appears to be human resource development, particularly typified by bottom-up team building. Numerous organizations, under a wide range of circumstances, have noted the benefits of team building. By and large, however, organizational development, no matter what its form, seems not to have had the hoped-for impact. Chief executives are frequently unaware of ongoing experiments in their own organizations. Few corporations with stable, energetic cultures attribute much of their success to formal application of behavioral science techniques.

TRADITIONAL TOOLS: WHAT'S HAPPENED

Meanwhile, something rather disturbing has been happening to the traditional, controlled-change tools. In effect, they have largely been migrating to the low-speed, low-control category. Left with no obvious set of replacement tools, the senior manager may well adopt the pessimistic view noted earlier.

Over time, government and competitive pressures requiring recentralization along various dimensions have nibbled away at the decentralization principle until most organizations today are a hodgepodge of centralized and decentralized activities. The matrix structure, which has arisen in response to these conflicting demands, has as often as not multiplied rather than resolved coordination problems. Even the foremost advocates of the matrix, for example Paul Lawrence and Jay Galbraith, point to imposing lists of pathologies leading to failures—or at least significant delay in implementation.

Similarly, strategic planning systems are no longer viewed as a panacea by many executives. Their greatest value often came soon after they were put in place: They provided novel perspectives on the business. Now, in many large organizations, the strategic planning system has become a rather routine and highly politicized part of the bureaucracy. It is seldom the font of new directions or the spearhead of rapid adaptation to changing economic or political conditions.

SOME SPECULATIONS

My thesis in this article is that there are a variety of practical controlled change tools appropriate to today's complex and ambiguous organization settings. Most have been around a long time and need only to be consciously packaged and managed. Some are rather new. Few have been thought of as major instruments for achieving organizational redirection. Almost all are associated with the informal organization.

Figure 2 arrays some of these change tools along the previously noted dimensions of controllability and speed of change, and Figure 3 presents some mundane change tools. By briefly assessing the reasons for the failure or obsolescence of the conventional tools and their successors (shown here as having drifted to the low-control, low-speed category), a very general rationale for the nature of the new change-tool candidates can be developed. Then each new category of tools can be assessed in turn.

There are at least two reasons why the conventional solutions have failed to achieve their full promise or have declined in effectiveness. One is that none of them takes time explicitly into account. In the case of structural solutions, management typically miscalculates in two different ways. On the one

FIGURE 2 • SPECULATION ABOUT CURRENT CHANGE TOOLS

		Speed of Short-Term Change	
		Low	**High**

Control over Direction of Change	**High**	Manipulation of symbols—*a*
		Patterns of activity—*b*
		Settings for interaction—*c*
		
		1
			Single element structural thrust
			  focusers
			Total systems of top managers'
			  interaction
			Dominating value
			2

	Low	4 Overdetermined approaches: • Complex planning systems • Multiple project teams • Matrix structures Underdetermined approaches: • Bottom-up team building	3 Change for change sake: • Structure • Senior managers

FIGURE 3 • MUNDANE TOOLS

a—Symbols:	Calendars Reports Agenda Physical settings Public statements Staff organization
b—Patterns:	Positive reinforcement Frequency and consistency of behavior Implementation/solution bias Experimenting mode
c—Settings:	Role of modeling Location Agenda control Presentation format Questioning approaches Deadline management Use of minutes

hand, it grossly underestimates the growing time lag between changed structure and changed behavior. On the other hand, it overestimates their durability under growing environmental pressures and consequently tends to leave them in place long after they have outlived their effectiveness.

The second reason for the weakness of conventional solutions is over- or underdetermination. Several solutions seem to rest on an overestimation of managers' ability to determine the best way to accomplish great purposes—overdetermination. For example, complex planning systems, multiple project teams, and the matrix structure proceed from the implicit assumption that effective organizing flows from figuring out the correct wiring diagram—an assumption increasingly at odds with today's organizational tasks. Koppers' chief executive officer, Fletcher Byrom, recently remarked, "Of all the things that I have observed about corporations, the most disturbing has been a tendency toward over-organization, producing a rigidity that is intolerable in an era of rapidly accelerating change."

At the other end of the spectrum—underdetermination—bottom-up team building has been based on the opposite presumption: Overall organizational purposes can be largely ignored; seeding effective new behavior patterns at the bottom of the organization or in the ranks of middle management will somehow eventuate in desirable organizational performance levels.

The proposed "new" change tools partially address both issues. First, they explicitly take time into account, recognizing both that change typically comes slowly as the result of the application of many tools and that the organizational focus of prime importance today is temporary and will almost certainly have changed substantially four or

five years hence. Second, they are tools of the experimenter: That is, they neither assume an ability to fix organizational arrangements with much precision—the failing of overdetermination—nor do they ignore purposiveness—the failing of underdetermination.

OBSESSION WITH THE MUNDANE

Cell 1 of Figure 2 (high control, low speed change), the realm of what my colleagues and I have come to call "mundane tools," reflects the notion that the management of change—small or large—is inextricably bound up with the mundane occurrences that fill an executive's calendar.

By definition, managing the daily stream of activities might be said to consist of the manipulation of symbols, the creation of patterns of activity, and the staging of occasions for interaction. The mundane tools are proposed as direct alternatives to structural manipulation and other grand solutions to strategic organization needs. Conscious experimentation with these tools can provide a sound basis for controlled, purposive change.

Manipulation of Symbols

Because they have so often been applied by the media to the performances of politicians intent on reshaping or repairing an image, the terms *symbolic behavior* and *symbol manipulation* have lately acquired something of a perjorative connotation: symbol versus substance. In a much more basic sense, however, symbols are the very stuff of management behavior. Executives, after all, do not synthesize chemicals or operate lift trucks; they deal in symbols. And their overt verbal communications are only part of the story. Consciously or unconsciously, the senior executive is constantly acting out the vision and goals he is trying to realize in an organization that is typically far too vast and complex for him to control directly.

What mundane tools might best aid the executive interested in effecting change through symbol manipulation? To signal watchers, which includes nearly everyone in his organization, there is no truer test of what he really thinks is important than the way he spends his time. As Eli Ginsberg and Ewing W. Reilley have noted:

> Those a few echelons from the top are always alert to the chief executive. Although they attach importance to what he says, they will be truly impressed only by what he does.

Is he serious about making a major acquisition? The gossip surrounding his calendar—Has he seen the investment banker?—provides clues for senior and junior management alike.

As reported in *Fortune*, Roy Ash's early activities after assuming the reins at Addressograph-Multigraph suggest mastery of the calendar and other mundane tools:

> Instead of immediately starting to revamp the company, Ash spent his first several months visiting its widely scattered operations and politely asking a lot of searching questions. . . . His predecessors had always summoned subordinates to the headquarters building, which had long lived up to its official name, the Tower. Rather than announcing his ideas, Ash demonstrated them. He left his office door open, placing his own intercom calls to arrange meetings, and always questioned people in person, not in writing. Then he removed some of the company's copying machines "to stop breeding paperwork." Spotting a well-written complaint from an important customer in Minneapolis, Ash quickly flew off to visit him. As he now explains, "I wanted the word to get around our organization that I'm aware of what's going on." Ash's next dramatic step to reshape company attitudes will be moving its headquarters to Los Angeles . . . he justifies the move primarily on psychological grounds. "We must place ourselves in a setting where—partly through osmosis—we get a different idea of our future." For much the same reason, he wants to change the corporation's name, too.

Calendar behavior includes review of reports and the use of agenda and minutes to shape expectations. What kinds of questions is the executive asking? Does he seem to focus on control of operating costs, quality, market share? How is his memory about what was "assumed" last month? Last quarter? What kinds of feedback is he giving? What sorts of issues get onto his agenda?

Other symbolic actions include the use of physical settings and public statements. By attending operating meetings in the field, the top man can provide vital evidence of his concerns and the directions he wants to pursue. By touching or ignoring a particular theme, a public statement—boilerplate to a skeptical outsider—can lead to a rash of activity. In a talk to investment bankers, a president devoted a paragraph to new departures in an R&D area that had previously been underfunded. Almost overnight, a wealth of new proposals began bubbling up from a previously disenchanted segment of the labs.

Last, his use of his personal staff—its size, their perquisites, how much probing he allows them to do—will indicate, not only the chief executive's style of doing business, but the direction of his substantive concerns as well.

The executive's ability to manage the use of symbols is at the heart of the case for optimism. Laterally at his fingertips, he has powerful tools—his day-timer and phone—for testing the possibilities of change and, over time, substantially shifting the focus of the organization.

Patterns of Activity

Success or failure in exploiting these simple tools is seen in the pattern of their use. Richard E. Neustadt in *Presidential Power* maintained:

> The professional reputation of a President in Washington is made or altered by the man himself. No one can guard it for him; no one saves him from himself. . . . His general reputation will be shaped by signs of pattern in the things he says and does. These are the words and actions he has chosen, day by day.

In short, the mundane tools that involve the creation and manipulation of symbols over time have impact to the extent that they reshape beliefs and expectations. Frequent, consistent, positive reinforcement is an unparalleled shaper of expectations—and, therefore, inducer of change.

Patterns of positive reinforcement can be applied in at least two ways: (1) use of praise and design of positive reinforcement schemes for individuals (or groups), and (2) allowing the bad to be displaced by the good, instead of trying to legislate it out of existence.

The White House, for example, has historically made meticulous use of the tools of praise. Selecting the attendees for major events and controlling the use of various classes of presidential letters of praise is a key activity controlled by very senior staff and the President himself.

Along the same lines, a research vice-president, responsible for about 2,000 scientists, has his executive assistant provide him with a sample of about 50 reports produced each month. He sends personal notes to the authors, often junior, of the best half-dozen or so.

Without touching on the complex ramifications of reinforcement theory, these instances merely support the point

that senior managers are signal transmitters, and signals take on meaning as they are reiterated. Moreover, there is ample evidence that giving prominence to positive efforts and exposing them to the light of day induces constructive change far more effectively than trying to discourage undesired activities through negative reinforcement. As an associate of mine succinctly observed, "It's a hell of a lot easier to add a new solution than attack an old problem." An example illustrates the point in a broader context:

> The information system unit of a multibillion-dollar conglomerate had a disastrously bad reputation. Rather than "clean house" or develop better procedures, the vice-president/systems installed, with some fanfare, "Six Programs of Excellence." Six reasonably sizable projects—out of an agenda of over 100—were singled out for intensive management attention. The effort was designed to build, from the inside out, a reputation for excellence that would gradually increase user confidence and group motivation alike.

Frequency and consistency are two other primary attributes of effective pattern shaping. A pattern of frequent and consistent small successes is such a powerful shaper of expectations that its creation may be worth the deferral of ambitious short-term goals:

> In one large company, the top team wished to establish a climate in which new product development would be viewed more favorably by all divisional managers. Rather than seeking an optimal product slate the first year—with the attendant likelihood of a high failure rate—the top team instead consistently supported small new product thrusts that gradually "made believers out of the operators."

Since consistency becomes a driving force in inducing major change over time, the executive committed to change ought to be constantly on the lookout for opportunities to reinforce activities, even trivial activities, that are congruent with his eventual purpose. He scours his in-basket for solutions—bits of completed action—to be singled out as exemplars of some larger theme. Support of completed actions typically generates further actions consistent with the rewarded behavior. The executive who keeps on testing tools to produce this result will find that by varying his patterns of reinforcement he can substantially influence people's behavior over time, often several levels down in the organization. (Figure 4 offers advice to pattern shapers based on my research.)

Settings for Interaction

The third class of mundane tools is settings. Senior management's development of a symbolic pattern of activities occurs somewhere. These are some of the setting variables that can directly reinforce or attenuate the impact of the symbolic message:

Presence or Absence of Top Managers. Psychologists now agree on the high impact of modeling behavior—the most significant finding of the last decade, according to many. The senior executive's presence and his minor actions can bring to life and rather precisely shape an institutional point of view—about investment, competitive response, the importance of tight controls. The careers of top executives abundantly reflect their intuitive awareness of this point.

Location of Groups and Meetings. Moving a meeting or a staff unit or a new activity is often a dramatic signal that something new is afoot. At one company, the previously isolated top team began holding meetings in the field, thus signaling a sincere intent to make decentralization work after three previous failures.

Agenda Control. Since agenda directly symbolize priorities, agenda management can be a potent change tool.

A division's top team changed its basic approach to management by suddenly devoting more than half its meeting time to issues of project implementation, previously a relatively minor item on its agenda. To cope with the new questions they were getting from the top, managers throughout the organization were soon following suit.

Attendance. Who attends which meetings, and who presents material, can signal new approaches to management and new substantive directions. When one company president decided to force his vice presidents, instead of junior staff, to present reviews and proposals, the atmosphere of his meetings perceptibly changed. All at once, heated battles between analytic guns-for-hire over numerical nuances were replaced by sober discussion of the issues.

Presentation/Decision Memorandum Formats. Format control can shift managers' focus to new issues and fundamentally reshape the process of organizational learning. One management team vastly improved its approach to problem solving by meticulously starting every decision presentation with an historical review of "the five key assumptions." At a second major corporation, the chief executive brought to life his major theme—focus on the competition—by requiring all decision documents to include much greater depth of competitive analysis.

Questioning Approaches. Among the clearest indicators of the direction or redirection of interest are the sorts of questions the top team consistently asks. Accounts of the working methods of Roy Ash, Harold Geneen, and others stress their unique questioning style and its pervasive effect on the issues the organization worries about. For instance, *Forbes* describes how A. W. Clausen of the Bank of America shifted concern from revenue to profit: "Ask an officer,

FIGURE 4 • GUIDING ASSERTIONS FOR THE PATTERN SHAPER

- The world is a stream of problems that can be activated, bound in new ways, or by-passed.
- His associates are pattern watchers and are acutely aware of his and their impact, over time, on each other.
- Above all, timing is important.
- An early step in analyzing a situation is careful assessment of the levers he does or does not control.
- Most change occurs incrementally, and major change typically emerges over a long period of time.
- Much of the change induced in subordinates results from consciously acting as a model himself.
- Frequent rewards—directed at small, completed actions—effectively shape behavior over time.
- Good questioning, focusing on the short term, helps him and his subordinates learn about system responses to small nudges one way or another.
- Creating change in organizations is facilitated by unusual juxtaposition of traditional elements with small problem-making subunits that seed changes.
- Long-term goals are of secondary importance since control of change follows from learning about multiple, small, real-time adjustments.
- Consistency in delivering small, positive outcomes is an efficient and effective way to manipulate others' perceptions when attempting to induce change.
- Patience, persistence, self-control, and attention to the mundane are often keys to achieving small, consistent outcomes.
- Surprise should usually be avoided in an attempt to present stable expectations to peers, subordinates, and bosses.
- It is possible approximately to calculate the opportunity value of others' and one's own time, thus substantially increasing the ability to pick change opportunities.
- Adding new solutions is often better than tackling old problems; that is, as much or more change and learning can ensue from the effective implementation of new solutions as from time-consuming efforts to overcome typically deep-seated resistance to old problems.

'How's business,' and you'd immediately hear how many loans he's made. I tried to leave my stamp by making everyone aware of profit."

Approaches to Follow-Up. Effective use of minutes, ticklers, and history can become the core of top management's real control system. Genuine accountability was introduced into a lax management organization by introducing a "blue blazer" system that made follow-up a way of life. In tracking issues, whenever operating executives' proposals had been modified by staff, the impact of the changes was explicitly noted. This put the staff and its contribution on stage. Accountability was further substantially sharpened by revamping a previous forecast-tracking procedure to highlight assumptions and outcomes.

Professor Serge Muscovici has asserted that:

Social status, leadership, majority pressure . . . are not decisive factors in social influence. A minority can modify the opinions and norms of a majority, irrespective of their relative power or social status, as long as, all other things being equal, the organization of its actions and the expression of its opinions and objectives obey the conditions . . . of consistency, autonomy, investment, and fairness.

Fairness takes on added meaning on the context of mundane management tools, intended as they are to shape expectations, over time, through minor shifts of emphasis. To be effective, the management of expectations must be unfailingly honest, realistic, and consistent. Violation of this property, especially if perceived as intentional, automatically destroys the effectiveness of patterned symbolic manipulation.

Richard Neustadt captures the essence of the use of mundane tools:

> [Franklin D. Roosevelt] had a strong feeling for a cardinal fact in government: That Presidents don't act on policies, program, or personnel in the abstract; they act in the concrete as they meet deadlines set by due dates, act on documents awaiting signatures, vacant posts waiting appointees, officials seeking interviews, newsmen seeking answers, audiences awaiting for a speech.

Note that the tools he mentions are all at hand. Though rarely disruptive or threatening, they have the potential to revolutionize an organization's ways of thinking and doing over time—particularly if, instead of being used intuitively and implicitly, they are consciously packaged and managed.

MAJOR CHANGE VIA TEMPORARY FOCUS

Big bureaucracies are run largely on inertia. Salesmen make their calls, products roll off the line, and checks get processed without any intervention by senior management. The task of today's slate of top managers, then, might well be viewed as time-bound: "How do we make a distinctive, productive difference over the next four years?" Or, "How do we leave our mark?"

It has been suggested above that certain prescriptions—undertaking structural shakeups or introducing new formal processes—are less effective than they once were in altering corporate perspectives. Constructing temporary systems to redirect the organization's attention and energies may be a better way to coax along institutional change. The high-impact devices proposed for this purpose are a natural extension of the mundane tools just discussed, in that in and of themselves they act as strong signals (or accumulations of symbols) of attention to new corporate directions.

Major—but limited—shifts in emphasis have been accomplished by public and private bureaucracies through three kinds of temporary focusing mechanisms: single-element focusers, systems of interaction, and dominating values. Each of these focusing mechanisms is discussed below.

Single-Element Focusers

To begin with, single-element focusers have been used time and again as a strategic signaling and implementing device. Consider how General Motors, a massive bureaucracy by any definition, recently adapted more swiftly than any other major automobile maker to the need to downsize its entire product line:

> The project center [says *Fortune*] was probably GM's single most important managerial tool in carrying out that bold decision. . . . It has eliminated a great deal of redundant effort, and has speeded numerous new technologies into production. Its success . . . rests on the same delicate

balance between the powers of persuasion and coercion that underlines GM's basic system of coordinated decentralization.

Some other business examples of single-element focusers similarly wrested the attention of major organizations—temporarily—to something new:

Harris Corporation created an interdivisional technology manager to oversee transfer of technology—Harris's "main strategic thrust"—between previously isolated groups.

Product family managers—three to five senior men with small staffs—were introduced as a means of wrenching the attention of two huge functional bureaucracies toward the marketplace; the creation of these high-visibility positions was thought to be a clearer, more efficient signal of strategic redirection than a major structural shift. Similarly, the establishment of just one job, executive vice-president for marketing, at White Consolidated is credited with sprucing up the long-stagnant sales of White's newly acquired Westinghouse appliance group.

ITT's product group managers are a free-wheeling band of central staff problem solvers and questioners who have brought a common market-based orientation to a highly diversified conglomerate.

An oil company's central technology staff (a roving group of top-ranking geologists and engineers) has markedly upgraded exploration and production quality.

In surveying these and other instances of success, some common threads can be identified (see Figure 5). Most important of these is singleness of focus. That is, the single-element focuser should not be confused with multiple-team project management. Its effectiveness rests on achieving a limited, temporary focus on one, or at most two, major new items. Note, also, that the structural manifestations tend to be about half staff, half line. On one hand, the focusing element

often has the look of a traditional staff unit, but its manager, as the unmistakable agent of the top team's highest priority, visibly intrudes on operating managers' territory.

Kenneth Arrow, the Nobel laureate economist, describes an analogous approach to galvanizing massive government institutions into acting on new agenda: "Franklin D. Roosevelt . . . saw the need of assigning new tasks to new bureaus even though according to some logic [such a task] belonged in the sphere of an existing department." Congressional Budget Office Deputy Director Robert Levine summarizes the thesis this way:

Since it seems impossible . . . to change overall public bureaucratic systems substantially either by changing their direction at the top by devices like program budgeting, or by changing their culture à la organization development, it may be useful to look for a third class of solutions . . . specifically, trying to treat bureaucratic units as if they were competing business units. . . . Even if it worked very well, this would be less well than program budgeting or organization development if they worked well. But the contention here is that in the real world this alternative concept is substantially more likely to work.

System of Interaction

Attention-directing organization elements are only the first of the three high-impact focusing mechanisms to be considered here. The second is the construction of a coherent system of senior management interaction, again with the purpose of shifting management attention either to some new direction or to some new method of reaching overall consensus. Under some circumstances, this second mechanism might even be preferred to the first. On the one hand, a system of forums has perhaps less symbolic impact than a single high-visibility element. On the other hand, however,

FIGURE 5 • ATTRIBUTES OF SINGLE-ELEMENT FOCUSING DEVICES

Success Characteristic	Related Failure Mode
Focus: limited number of "devices," no more than two and preferably one.	Use usually simultaneously—of many devices (e.g., teams, meetings) dilutes attention and can become just a bureaucratic encumbrance.
Focus within focus: The limited device must, moreover, have a limited agenda and not take on everything at once.	Limited devices charged with turning the world around in 12 months are likely to fail (i.e., a failure of expectation).
Incumbent: Manned with a very senior contender(s) for the top.	Selection of good men, but not those recognized as members of "the top ten" or sure-fire top ten contenders.
Startup: Either a pilot element (e.g., one product family manager of an eventual set of five) or a "pilot decision," (e.g., a visible output—perhaps a decision—by the new event/process) will affect acceptance.	Groups/processes invented, but no clear sign of early progress or shift of emphasis.
Need: A clear-cut, agreed-upon business need for the element exists.	The new element's agenda is not clear and/or is not viewed as urgent.
CEO role: CEO is reinforcer of project *and* lets it make its mark.	CEO nonsupporter or a supporter but preempts the new role by continuing to play the game by the old rules.
Conscience: Systems—formal or informal—to "watch" the top team and ensure that actions are being taken consistent with the purpose of the shift.	Element "implemented," but top team regularly takes decisions inconsistent with purpose.
Implementation duration: Even though single device, implementation should be expected to take a couple of years at least.	Since it is only a simple new element, put it in place and let it go.

such a system does directly manipulate the agenda of senior managers.

Systems of forums designed to turn top management's eyes to new horizons range from one company's five "management forums"—a formal system of interaction designed to force regular discussion of strategic issues—to a president's regular informal breakfast meetings where senior executives, free of their staffs and the attendant bureaucratic insulation, engage in untrammeled discussion of key issues.

One particularly striking class of forums is special operating or strategic review sessions. Texas Instruments, ITT, and Emerson Electric, among others, focus top-management direction setting in regular sessions where—as everyone in the organization knows—"things get done" or "the buck stops." Another notable example is cited by *Fortune*:

> One of the enduring questions of management, a subject of constant concern and endless analysis, is how a large corporation can best monitor and direct operations spread over many industries and throughout many parts of the world. A number of companies have sought the answer in ponderous and elaborate management mechanisms. . . . But there is at least one large

company whose top management continues to rely on plain, old-fashioned, face-to-face contact. Richard B. Loynd, the president and chief operating officer of Eltra Corp. . . . visits each of Eltra's thirteen divisions as many as eight times a year, and puts managers through formal grillings that last several hours at a time. The people at Eltra call this the "hands-on" management technique. Loynd says: "I think I spend more time with our operating people than the president of any other major company."

Invariably, like the single-element focusers, these systems are temporary in nature. Since most of them tend to become rigid and lose their unique value in the course of time, they need to be modified at intervals. One executive reports:

> The monthly breakfast meeting finally got the chairman and his operating presidents away from staff. For two years these sessions, preliminary to the regular monthly review, became the real decision-making/ enervating forum. But then the staffs caught on. One by one, *they* began coming to breakfast.

Dominating Value

The discussion of change mechanisms has had a consistent undercurrent. The three classes of mundane tools have been presented as apparently trivial signaling devices for redirecting organizational attention and energy over time toward a theme, while the first two major change tools have been characterized as just larger-scale or agglomerated devices for the same purpose.

One final tool, which may be labeled the *dominating value*, addresses the role and utilization of the theme itself. It is, on the one hand, more delicate than the other tools, in that its use demands consummate political commitment-building skills and a shrewd sense of timing. In another sense it is more robust than

the others, in that, if handled effectively, it can generate substantial, sustained energy in large institutions. For the senior manager, therefore, thinking about and acting on the value management process is, although imprecise, extremely practical.

Business researchers have coined various terms for an effective, predominant institutional belief. Richard Normann calls it a business idea or growth idea. He devotes an entire book, *Management and Statesmanship*, to documenting a case for the power of an effective, simply articulated business idea and describing the unique role and leverage of top management in indirectly guiding the process of belief establishment and change. He argues that "the interpretation of ongoing and historical events and the associated adjustment and regulation of the dominating idea is probably the most crucial of the processes occurring in the company."

Some other recent scholarly work, well-grounded in the leading edge of social science findings, provides a corroborating point of view. Andrew Pettigrew's anthropological study of the creation of organization culture is representative:

> One way of approaching the study of the entrepreneur's relationship with his organization is to consider the entrepreneur as a symbol creator, an ideologue, a formulator of organizational vocabularies, and a maker of ritual and myth. Stylistic components of a vision, which may be crucial, might include the presence of a dramatically significant series of events, rooting the vision back into history, and thus indicating the vision was more than a fad. Visions with simple, yet ambiguous content expressed in symbolic language are not only likely to be potent consciousness raisers, but also flexible enough to sustain the ravages of time and therefore the certitude of events. Visions contain new and old terminology perhaps organized into metaphors with which it is hoped to create

new meanings. Words can move people from a state of familiarity to a state of awareness. Some people have the capacity to make words walk. I suspect this is one of the unexplored characteristics of successful entrepreneurs.

Louis Pondy, in "Leadership is a Language Game," quite similarly equates leadership effectiveness with the capacity to achieve what he calls "language renewal."

Roy Ash puts the same notion in more concrete terms:

At a sufficiently high level of abstraction, he says, "all businesses are the same." Ash's plans for testing that theory are summed up in the notes that he continually pencils on yellow legal pads. One of the most revealing of these notes says: "Develop a much greater attachment of everybody to the bottom line—more agony and ecstasy." As he sees it, the really important change in a company is a process of psychological transformation.

If one combs the literature for the lessons extracted by business leaders, the crucial role of a central belief emerges. The biographies of Cordiner at GE, Vail at AT&T, Greenewalt at Du Pont, and Watson at IBM all stress the quest to give operational force and meaning to a dominant, though imprecise, idea. Such accounts may be dismissed as self-serving, but it would seem a bit more cynical than even these times call for to write off the extraordinary consistency of so many closing statements.

Among active business leaders, the pattern of evidence is repeated. Richard Pascale, for example, has described the management style of several particularly effective chief executive officers. He notes the recurrence of a simple, overarching theme captured in a few words: for example, Harold Geneen's ceaseless "search for the unshakable facts," reflected in all kinds of organizational arrangements from structural contrivances—his controllers reporting to the

chief executive and his intrusive product group managers—through interaction mechanisms—the famed ITT monthly review sessions. Further examples dot the business press:

A. W. Clausen at Bank of America: "Stay around Tom Clausen for about 15 minutes and he'll talk about laying pipe," says *Forbes.* "That's his shorthand for anticipating events and readying a response. Subordinates lay pipe to Clausen when they tell him about potential problems; he lays the pipe the other way when he sketches his expectations. The expression isn't especially catchy, the process isn't particularly glamorous. But it does help to explain why Bank of America isn't facing huge loan losses— and this big, slow-moving tortoise seems perfectly able to keep up with the flashier, more dynamic hares."

John DeButts at AT&T incessantly uses the term *the system is the solution.* The concept, professed by DeButts in every setting from management meetings to television commercials, is aimed at starting the process of shifting the massive million-person Bell System's focus to the market place.

Tom Jones at Northrup, Fortune notes, has been particularly successful at gaining more than a fair share of defense contracts—largely, he believes, by bringing to life the theme "Everybody at Northrup is in marketing."

Walter Spencer at Sherwin Williams, according to *Forbes,* spent his five years as CEO working to introduce a "marketing orientation" into a previously manufacturing-dominated institution. Says Spencer: "When you take a 100-year old company and change the culture of the organization, and try to do that in Cleveland's traditional business setting—well, it takes time; you just have to keep hammering away at everybody. . . . The changeover to marketing is probably irreversible now. It's not complete, but we've brought along a lot of young managers with that philosophy, and once you've taken a company this far, you can't go back.

When the scholarly research and the anecdotal evidence are drawn together, some characteristic attributes of an effective dominating value can be discussed:

It is both loose and tight. That is, it connotes a clear directional emphasis—focus on the competition, stand for quality, become low-cost producer—but ample latitude for supporting initiatives.

It must, almost always, emerge rather than be imposed. Though it may be crystallized in a succinct phrase, it usually represents the end product of time-consuming consensus-building processes that may have gone on for a year or more.

Just as it cannot be imposed by fiat, it cannot be changed at will. Typically, a major shift in the dominant belief can be brought about only when an important change is perceived to be at hand. The process of gaining commitment requires so much emotional commitment and institutional energy that it can be repeated only infrequently.

It has a reasonably predictable life cycle. Beginning with a great deal of latitude, it becomes progressively less flexible over time—though never approaching the rigidity of a quantified goal.

It may be a definition or characterization of the past, meant primarily to mark the end of a period and provide the energy to start a search for new modes of organizational behavior. For example, one might choose to label the past five years as "the era of tight control" in order to suggest that something now coming to an end should be replaced with something new, as yet unspecified.

It imposes choices. Despite the general nature of most effective beliefs, they do require management to face up to the limits of the organization's capacities. Of course, any huge enterprise does a bit of everything, but, for example, a choice to stress controls, if effectively implemented, is likely also a choice not to push harder for new products.

It can be anything from a general management principle to a reasonably specific major business decision. At the management-principles end, it can become a commitment to something like "fact-based analysis." At the business-decision end, it can be a commitment to a revised position for a key product line. In the middle are hybrids such as "enhanced focus on competition."

It suggests movement (e.g., toward becoming the industry quality leader or dominating a particular market niche), thus implying some sort of tension or imbalance. Few leaders have been noted for achieving balance. Most have been known for going from somewhere to somewhere else.

Figure 6 gives a graphic portrayal of the essentials of the process I have been discussing. It depicts a five- to nine-year cycle of strategic transition marked by the tightening, executing, loosening, and redirecting search for an operational dominating value.

CHANGE FOR CHANGE'S SAKE

At least one significant tool remains to be considered: namely, change for its own sake.

This is the device assigned, in Figure 2, to Cell 3 (low-control, high-speed change). Sometimes things are such a muddle that significant change for its own sake is a good bet to produce, on balance, a more desirable outcome than any directionally managed program.

In *The Economist*, Norman McRae recently observed:

. . . the most successful companies have been those restless enough to be unsure what their management styles should be.

FIGURE 6 • FIVE- TO NINE-YEAR CYCLE OF STRATEGIC
TRANSITION

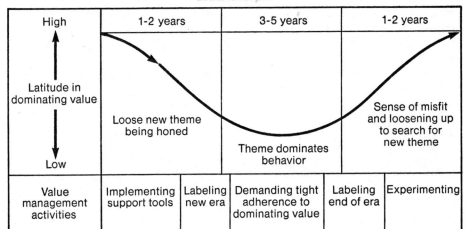

Successful big American corporations today will often centralize their policy making, and get a significant initial gain in effectiveness; but then, as time passes, will find that this does not work because the central planners do not know what is really going on out in the field. So these corporations will then decentralize, and get a significant initial gain in effectiveness. This constant reorganization is in fact very sensible, and is a main reason why I judge that big American corporations are still the most efficient day-to-day business operators in the world.

A somewhat less radical dose of the same medicine is the rather arbitrary reshuffling of top team member responsibilities, even when it results in a seemingly less rational match of skills to tasks. A fresh juxtaposition of perspectives, per se, is often of value.

At least one word of warning about high-early impact, low-control prescriptions is in order. The secret of their success is novelty. Routine reorganizing or all-too-regular shakeups of top team assignments all too readily evoke the sense of déjà vu. "Nobody on the top team has been in the same job for more than 15 months," remarks an executive of a high-technology company. "Of course, all they do is trade bureaucratic barbs. That's all they've got. No one sees the results of his own initiatives."

Although it certainly merits much more discussion, the analysis of this last class of tools must necessarily be cut short at this point.

IN CONCLUSION: LIMITS AND OPTIMISM

The purpose of this essay has been twofold: first, to provide a simple classification of change tools and some speculative hypotheses in support of the case for pessimism about the old favorites among them; second, to suggest that for the alert senior manager, today's organizational garbage cans are still full of powerful change tools—tools that he uses intuitively, and therefore not systematically, but which nevertheless are numerous and potentially powerful enough to justify a measure of optimism.

A limited measure, to be sure. Even with a mastery of all the change tools reviewed here, today's senior manager is unlikely to be able to develop real consensus, commitment, and change in more than a single new direction. Richard Neustadt's metaphor captures the essence of his role:

> Presidential power is the power to persuade. Underneath our images of Presidents-in-boots, astride decisions, are the half-observed realities of President-in-sneakers, stirrups in hand, trying to induce particular department heads . . . to climb abroad.

As he tries to coax his senior colleagues aboard, the senior executive has at his command a variety of settings—settings in which he can experiment, implement, and build patterns to provide a general conception of what's possible. He can, with luck and to a limited extent, grasp control of the signaling system to point a general direction and mark out limited areas of expected new institutional excellence. By adroitly managing agenda, he can nudge the day-to-day decision-making system, thus simultaneously imparting new preferences and testing new initiatives.

And some day, in retrospect, he may be able to see himself as an experimenter who attempted to build consensus on a practical (and flexible) vision of what was possible over a five-year time horizon, and through incessant attention to the implementation of small, adaptive steps, eventually made that vision a reality.

If so, he should be well content.

BIBLIOGRAPHIC REFERENCES

Richard Pascale in "Three Chief Executives: The Effect of Style on Implementation" (Research Paper 357, Stanford Graduate School of Business) developed with the subjects' cooperation, detailed case studies of Harold Geneen, Roy Ash, and Ed Carlson. He meticulously describes the links between their everyday behavior patterns, supporting organizational systems, and effectiveness.

John Kotter and Paul Lawrence in *Mayors in Action* (John Wiley & Sons, 1974) discuss in a series of case studies the relationship, for example, between mayoral agenda setting and implementation success.

Four studies of bureaucratic politics offer particularly detailed analyses of the mundane attributes of influence accumulation and exercise: Graham Allison's *Essence of Decision* (Little, Brown, 1971); Edward Banfield's *Political Influence* (Free Press, 1961); Robert Caro's *The Power Broker* (Alfred A. Knopf, 1974); and Richard Neustadt's *Presidential Power* (John Wiley & Sons, 1960).

Henry Mintzberg's unique observational study of senior executives, *The Nature of Managerial Work* (Harper & Row, 1973), vividly portrays the fragmented nature of real senior-management activity. If one finds his analysis credible, then presumably the kinds of change levers discussed in this article are of particular importance.

H. Edward Wrapp's "Good Managers Don't Make Policy Decisions" (*Harvard Business Review*, September-October 1967) and James Quinn's "Strategic Goals: Process and Politics" (*Sloan Management Review*, Fall 1977) provide good examples of effective muddling-about processes that typically attend development of what is called a dominating value in this paper.

The notion of organizations as temporary systems discussed in the paper is treated at length by E. J. Miller and A. K. Rice in *Systems of Organization* (Tavistock, 1967).

Last, James March and Johan Olsen's *Ambiguity and Choice* (Universitelforlaget: Norway, 1976) proposes and supports a novel, complex model of organizational choice. The decision-making environment they describe clearly calls for radically different management prescriptions. The tools offered in this paper seem, to the author, to be reasonably consistent with their view of the world.

35
Organizations as Culture-Bearing Milieux
Meryl Reis Louis

Any social group, to the extent that it is a distinctive unit, will have to some degree a culture differing from that of other groups, a somewhat different set of common understandings around which action is organized, and these differences will find expression in a language whose nuances are peculiar to that group. Members of churches speak differently from members of tavern groups; more importantly, members of any particular church or tavern group have cultures, and languages in which they are expressed, which differ somewhat from those of other groups of the same general type (Becker & Geer, 1970, p. 134).

My aim in this paper is to present a view of organizations as culture-bearing milieux, that is, as distinctive social units possessed of a set of common understandings for organizing action (e.g., what we're doing together in this particular group, appropriate ways of doing in and among members of the group) and languages and other symbolic vehicles for expressing common understandings. The timeliness of such a view is indicated in several trends in the organizational sciences. First, there has been a growing dissatisfaction with traditional research efforts, especially those grounded in essentially positivistic views of organizations. Many have become disillusioned with fundamental inadequacies in traditional methods and the meager grasp and leverage on organizational

phenonema they have provided (Silverman, 1970; Burrell & Morgan, 1979; Pondy & Mitroff, 1979; Van Maanen, 1979b; Evered & Louis, 1981).

Simultaneously, there has been a groundswell of interest in things cultural in organizations. Organizational researchers have undertaken studies of symbols, myths, legends and metaphors, of language systems and other artifacts of organizational cultures (Clarke, 1970; Mitroff & Kilmann, 1976; Wilkins & Martin, 1979; Dandridge, Mitroff & Joyce, 1980; Evered, in this volume, pp. 125–143). Additionally, there has been an increasing concern with cognitive processes of individuals in organizations, with issues of how individuals make meaningful their interactions and encounters in daily organization life (Van Maanen, 1979a; Weick, 1979; Louis, 1980b).

A final impetus for developing a cultural view of organizations stems from a practical problem faced by increasing numbers of organizational participants. With the rising rate of voluntary turnover at all organizational levels has come a greater appreciation for cultural aspects of organizations by participants. Specifically, recognition of the need to become acculturated, to "learn the ropes," when entering an unfamiliar organizational setting suggests that some cultural stratum is present in any organization, and that its mastery is critical

Source: L. R. Pondy and others, eds., *Organizational Symbolism* (Greenwich, Conn.: JAI Press, 1983), 39–54.

for the well-functioning of new organizational members (Schutz, 1964; Van Maanen, 1977; Louis, 1980a, 1980b).

The concept of culture is not new. It has long been used by anthropologists, among others, in studying ethnic and/or national groups through ethnographic and cross-cultural research. For example, Beres & Portwood (1979, p. 141) have proposed a comprehensive model of the influence of ethnic/national culture in the development of an individual's frame of reference and, in particular, orientations to work. They define culture as a "cognitive frame of reference and a pattern of behavior transmitted to members of a group from previous generations of the group," emphasize the role of socialization in the transmission of culture, suggest the need to consider psychological, social and historical dimensions, review deficiencies in cross-cultural research, and provide results of a test of one segment of the model. Although organizational (versus ethnic) culture is not considered per se, their paper offers a recent perspective on cross-cultural research and a conceptualization of cultural influence processes (or, more appropriately, factors in the process) directly relevant to work on organizational culture.

What is new and what is my particular aim here is to map dimensions of culture relevant in organizations and to suggest that researchers incorporate a cultural view of organizations into the repertoire of perspectives on organizations. The discussion will focus on several questions: What constitutes a cultural perspective? What are psychological and sociological processes and contexts of cultural phenomena in organizations? And in what ways are organizations culture-bearing milieux? While this effort is necessarily exploratory (we are just beginning to map the territory and this will be a brief essay), the purpose is

to broadly consider what a cultural view of organizations might entail. [1]

A CULTURAL PERSPECTIVE

The idea of culture rests on the premise that the full meaning of things is not given a priori in the things themselves. Instead, meaning results from interpretation. Consider, for instance, a hiker encountering a fallen tree. The significance to the hiker of a tree laying across the trail depends on whether he is idly strolling through the morning woods, scouting ahead for hazards for other hikers on a pack train, making a getaway from a minimum security prison, or surveying drought damage in the forest. Whether the hiker views the fallen tree as the result of drought or of prison guards and, more basically, whether causes of the tree falling are relevant, depend on the larger historical and situational contexts of the hiker. The meaning as the significance of some event, utterance, etc. may derive from any of several aspects of the situation in which meaning is to be assigned. Meaning may involve definition, consequence, antecedents, and/or intention (Black, 1962, p. 193), as the example of the hiker demonstrates.

In a cultural view, meaning is produced through an *in situ* interpretive process. The process encompasses universal, cultural and individual levels of interpretation. The universal level refers to the broad set of objective or physically feasible meanings or relevances of each thing. For instance, universally speaking, dogs can be eaten, worshipped, or befriended, but not flown. These basic physical constraints are what Weick (1979) referred to as "grains of truth."

The cultural level refers to the set of potential meanings or relevances indigenous to the local social group. In one sense, this local code is a subset of the universal set of feasible relevances. In another sense, the local code is an elaboration of the universal set. Each of the objective or physically feasible meanings may be exploded into a whole range of meanings. For instance, consider the myriad social meanings of dog in our society—companion, family member, guide dog for the blind, shepherd, guard dog, drug detective. This array of meanings derives less from objective features or universal meanings of the creature dog and more from the creative differentiation from universal meanings into contextually relevant cultural meanings. The cultural code describes the repertoire of meanings that may appropriately be assigned to a thing by members of the particular social system. That, strictly speaking, dogs are befriended, but not eaten or worshiped in 1980 America reflects the code of relevances for dog in our Western culture.

The final level in interpretation is the individual one. Here the person's idiosyncratic adaptation of cultural codes leads to a set of personal codes of relevance. In turn, personal codes are applied in the moment of encountering a thing and meaning is produced. Whether you greet or run from the dog in front of you at this moment depends on your history with dogs and your recognition of this one as your neighbor's friendly puppy.

So, from the universe of feasible relevances of any thing, a cultural set of possible meanings appropriate through time and space for the social group is carved out, and based on this cultural code, social system members derive their own codes of relevance. As I have indicated in Figure 1, the universal can be thought of as an objective realm. Only at the universal level is meaning given a priori. The cultural stratum can be thought of as an intersubjective realm, studied through clinical means.

With few exceptions researchers in the organizational sciences have proceeded as if study of the universal stratum *alone* were sufficient to produce understandings of organizational behavior; organizational phenomena have been studied implicitly as universal matters devoid of any cultural component.[2] It is time to begin studying cultural phenomena as distinct aspects of organizational life. It is increasingly clear that much of what matters in organizational life takes place at the cultural level. From the "informal organization" first recognized in the Hawthorne studies to the "organizational politics" currently in vogue among researchers, cultural phenomena pervade organizational life. Yet, by and large, cultural phenomena seem to elude, be overlooked by, and/or remain on the fringe of mainstream organizational science. I suspect this is due in part to the lack of a coherent integral image conveyed in symbols and language sufficient to distinguish it from other images (e.g., culture versus machine). And so, in the following pages, I will begin to flesh out and give language to such an image. (The paradox is that traditional images, ideals and language of organizational science [i.e., our culture] tend to blind us to supplementary images of organization phenomena.)

The next two sections will consider aspects of culture relevant to a view of organizations as culture-bearing milieux. For purposes of discussion, a distinction is made between what goes on inside any one individual vis-à-vis cultural processes and what goes on outside the person; that is, between persons or, more generally, within the social system. The former is termed the psychological context and the latter the sociological context of culture.

CULTURE IN ORGANIZATIONS: THE SOCIOLOGICAL CONTEXT

In a brief but classic statement, Kroeber and Parsons (1958) define culture as the

FIGURE 1 • LEVELS OF INTERPRETATION IN PRODUCING
MEANING

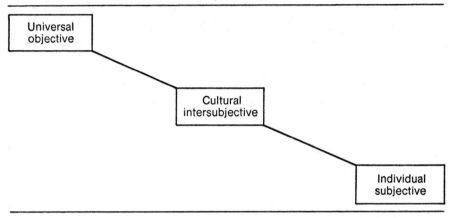

". . . transmitted and created content and patterns of values, ideas, and other symbolic-meaningful systems as factors in the shaping of human behavior . . ." as distinct from social system, or ". . . the specifically relational system of interaction among individuals and collectivities" (pp. 86–87). As discussed above, the codes of meaning or relevance indigenous to a social system serve as behavior-shaping social ideals (i.e., "thou shalt," "thou shalt not"). Social ideals constitute a system of values and relevances by which individuals and institutions set goals and aspirations, sanction behavior, and judge performances. A set of social ideals is represented in a kind of hierarchy or prioritization of meanings, a coherent meaning system. A cultural view then encompasses the system of social ideals and the set of symbolic devices (i.e., myths, rituals, signs, metaphors, special languages) that embody and are used to convey the ideals. While these symbolic devices are used to convey the local culture, they are simultaneously the artifacts of that culture.

Culture provides for social system continuity, control, identity and integration of members. The stability (through time) of shared ideals across generations of social system members provides continuity and serves a homeostatic function.[3] The stability (through space) of the standards or goals conveyed in the commonly-held set of ideals serves the control function of deviance detection and reduction.[4] Ouchi's (1979) work on control by clan illustrates this function. Further, ideals shared among members provide for the integration of individuals into the social group, a kind of individual-to-institution linking. Etzioni's (1961) work on moral involvement of organization members illustrates the integrating function of culture.[5]

More diffusely, culture embodies the identity of the social group. What we, as members, stand for and how we deal with one another and with outsiders is carried in and through our culture. Discussions of corporate personality are concerned at least implicitly, with the identity aspect of organizational culture (O'Toole, 1979).

CULTURE IN ORGANIZATIONS: THE PSYCHOLOGICAL CONTEXT

At the individual level, ". . . human beings act toward things on the basis of the meanings that the things have for them . . ." (Blumer, 1969, p. 2). And those meanings, or significances, are the products of an in situ interpretive process. Meaning is essentially and endlessly negotiated by social system members. In one sense of negotiated, meaning production represents navigation of an experiential landscape by which one controls one's course or position. In the other sense of negotiated, it represents bargaining among alternative meanings differentially preferred by the various parties to an interaction.

At the micro-interactional level, the navigational aspect of cultural processes produces the individual's definition of the situation.[6] Features as landmarks are identified and interpreted in light of present sociological position and destination. In an interaction, the person's individualized version of the local set of social ideals (i.e., personal code of meanings or frame of reference) guides perception, interpretation, and action. Through a series of steps, it allows the individual to assess whether, for instance, a particular performance constitutes a job well done. First, one's culturally derived meaning system facilitates the identification of a performance from a continuous stream of experience, or parsing as Weick (1969) refers to it. What is noticed is, to a great extent, given in our cultural set. Second, it directs attention to certain features of the performance considered worth assessing. Third, it provides the yardstick for assessing those features of the performance. Fourth, assessment or interpretation guides action; or, as W. I. Thomas (1928, p. 584) has phrased it, "If men define situations as real, they are real in their consequences." Responses are made in terms of features assessed and assessments of those features.

The psychological context of cultural processes has been discussed at length by Schutz (1964, 1970b) who has shown how the individual's interpretive scheme or meaning system is embedded and operational in a particular culture. As a result of this communal embeddedness of members' meaning systems, meaning produced in situ is extensively intersubjective. Discussions of specific subprocesses in which individuals make meaning in social interaction based on an intersubjective perspective are found in McHugh (1968) and Louis (1980b).

Figure 2 reviews the aspects of a cultural perspective outlined so far.

CULTURE IN ORGANIZATIONAL SETTINGS

Ways in which organizations can be viewed as culture-bearing milieux and critical issues encountered in doing so are explored in this section. In addition, we will consider defining characteristics of cultural participation (e.g., physical versus psychological connection, self-perception, competence) and issues of boundary and perspective in studying culture in organizations.

Organizations provide regularly-convening settings in which cultures may develop; thus, an organizational setting is analogous to a petri dish. Whether or not, or, more precisely, the extent to which, a particular organizational setting fosters the development of a local culture depends on a great many factors, only a few of which seem apparent at this stage of study. Some organizational settings may "bear" (in the sense of supporting the development of) elaborate cultures, while, in others, no appreciable culture may develop. In the latter

FIGURE 2 • ASPECTS OF CULTURAL PERSPECTIVE

Sociological Context		Psychological Context
Shared Ideals	Symbolic Devices	Interpretive Scheme
Cultural system of relevances Through the functions of culture, social systems achieve: Continuity—transtemporal stability Control—contemporaneous stability Integration of individual members Identity of social group		Personal system of relevances Within a culture: Meaning is emergent and intersubjective Individuals negotiate meaning Negotiation as: Navigation Bargaining The *in situ* interpretive process: Perception → Negotiation → Meaning ⇒ Definition of situation → Behavior

case, the settings may be characterized by more purely instrumental involvement of members and individually-oriented behaviors. This is analogous at the organizational level to what Hall (1976) has referred to at the societal level as a "low-context" setting. Further, multiple nested and/or overlapping cultures may be borne by any given organization in correspondence to the potential multitude of physical/sociological/cognitive settings convened within the bounds of organizational activities. For example, somewhat distinct local cultures may form in each of several departments within a division of an organization, and at the level of the division as an organizational setting. In this view, then, the organization provides the setting or milieu in and through which cultures may develop; thus, the phrase, "organizations as culture-bearing milieux".

Several features of organizational settings are hypothesized to contribute to the development of local cultures, regardless of the organizational level at which culture is investigated (e.g., whether we consider organization-wide culture or the work-group culture). For

instance, more extensive cultures are expected to be associated with: stability of membership; the extent to which key members "consistently point to (a set of) general ideas or frameworks (Wilkins, in this volume, pp. 81–92); "members' perceptions of the relative youth and smallness of the organization; identification of human qualities of key people (i.e., idiosyncracies, personal values, interpersonal style); impermeability of organizational boundaries (e.g., for purposes of product secrecy in an R&D lab or societal privacy in a nudist colony); membership restrictions (essential acquired or innate attributes, e.g., education or experience, sex or race). There are undoubtedly other features of organizational settings that contribute to the development of local cultures which remain to be identified through further study.

I believe we will discover in future studies that patterns of features, the relative importance of some over others, will differ depending on the organizational level (e.g., organization-wide versus work-group) at which we are investigating cultures in organizations. Additionally, I believe we will discover different cultural processes and culture-shaping processes in operation depending on the developmental stage of the organizational unit qua setting under study. For instance, in entrepreneurships (organizations in early stages of development), culture-creating processes are expected to be in evidence. Stories and the values they convey are being shaped from the actions of key people. In contrast, cultural revitalization in mature or stagnating organizations (mid and late stages) may be fostered through the development and dissemination of new images and accompanying rationales for breaking with the past. The literal bringing in of "young blood" in the form of new leadership is often used to symbolically represent a new "life for the organization."

Changes in organizational settings can alternatively disrupt or support local cultures. For instance, the imposition of new technology may disrupt the local culture. Witness the example documented by Trist and Bamforth (1951) in their coal-mining studies. Previous to the change, task planning, coordination and control, interpersonal bonds and interfamily relationships were facilitated and mediated by the work group culture. The new technology imposed a different set of interpersonal relationships and externalized planning and control. The basic features of the work-group setting were altered; the structural arrangements in and of the work-group were dismantled and reassembled. Like a spider's web between garden tools resting against the walls of a shed, the web of the work-group culture was torn when the tools were rearranged.

Changes in organizational settings can also foster new cultural developments. For instance, establishing an identified task team creates a setting in and through which a local culture may develop. Creation of project teams, new geographically distinct divisions, and even matrix structures all represent the convening of potentially culture-bearing milieux. Each "new" unit created in an organizational change effort (e.g., adding project teams) may be new "in name only;" that is, it may be made up of people who have been members of the organization doing tasks done before in buildings and at desks long familiar. But, what matters is the "name." Organizational settings refer essentially to sociologically and cognitively identifiable spaces, not merely or even necessarily to physical aspects of setting; identifiability is facilitated by shared namings of space and/or by physical bounding of space. So, in a number of ways, organizational settings represent milieux which may foster, enhance, hinder, and/or disrupt the development of local cultures, depending on specific features of the setting.

In terms of membership in a particular organizational culture, an individual may be a member of a social system and its culture by virtue of regular ongoing physical presence and participation in face-to-face interactions with other members. One may also be a member of a culture by virtue of affiliation without necessarily being physically present in a face-to-face interaction system. For instance, being a member of the Academy of Management constitutes membership in a social system which convenes in the strict physical sense only once a year. Yet the culture of the Academy of Management seems clearly distinguishable from the culture of the Association for Humanistic Psychology or other professional groups. Further, membership by affiliation may be purely informal, as in the case of "regulars" at the culture-rich Monterey Jazz Festival, which convenes 3 days per year and has done so for more than 25 years. Thus, in two distinct ways, as opportunities for affiliation and as physically convening social systems, organizations can be seen as culture-bearing milieux.

An individual may be a member of a social system and participate superficially or deeply in the local culture. What determines the level of cultural membership is the individual's self-perception. This is particularly true when we consider cultures in work organizations as opposed to national and ethnic group cultures. In contrast to participation in a culture of birth, participation in an organizational culture is more temporary or transitory and more a matter of voluntary choice (though not necessarily the product of a conscious rational decision process). Ultimately, one is a participant in a particular culture to the extent that one considers him or herself to be a member.

In addition to self-perception as a factor in cultural participation, the competence of the participation must be considered. Competence is more at issue in organizational culture than societal culture in part because of the relative frequency with which individuals change organizations and therefore have an opportunity and an attendant need to master a new culture. Has the person sufficiently internalized core ideals and values, and appreciated key symbols? Adequate grasp of the local intersubjective or social reality is necessary in order for the individual to function within the culture.

In an organizational setting, the definition of a situation by an individual may be guided by several nested and/or overlapping cultural systems. These may be differentially dominant depending on the individual, his or her tenure in the social system, the congruence among cultural systems, the situation to be defined, etc. For instance, incongruence between overlapping cultures may result for individuals who have both professional and organizational affiliations (e.g., an attorney or CPA working at GM corporate headquarters). Similarly, nested cultures can exert incompatible pulls on individuals. This is illustrated in the case of the division manager torn between loyalty to his division and loyalty to the company, particularly when performance is assessed at divisional profit centers. Such situations have been studied in terms of role conflict and organizational commitment without adequate attention to relevant cultural elements.

The prevalence of nested and overlapping cultures (by affiliation and/or physical colocation) and the self-perceptual nature of cultural membership indicate the need to clarify issues of boundary and perspective in conducting organizational research. In studying culture, especially when organizations are studied at a distance, from the outside (Evered & Louis, 1981), one can't tell whether a particular boundary—e.g., the IBM culture as a whole—is a meaningful level of analysis, a substantially rich culture in comparison with other nested or overlapping cultures—e.g., the culture of IBM systems engineers in which individuals are simultaneously members. As well, different members of IBM may consider different boundaries relevant; they may consider their dominant affiliation at the organization-wide, or subunit or functional specialty level. The challenge, then, is to identify which culture(s) is being studied and from whose points of view.

In addition to the organizational phenomena previously identified (e.g., control systems, nature of involvement, role conflict, organizational/professional commitment), a number of other phenomena (e.g., organizational climate, goal setting/performance feedback) imply that cultural processes are present in organizations and suggest vehicles for studying culture in organizations. Organizational climate has dealt at least conceptually almost directly with culture in organizations. Goal setting and performance feedback, which serve to guide and assess actions of organizational members, can be seen through a cultural view as the formalization and individualization of shared social ideals.

CONCLUSION

In this essay I have proposed that organizations be viewed as culture-bearing milieux. Essential ingredients of a cultural perspective were outlined and a number of organizational phenomena implicated in a cultural perspective were identified. A key premise of a cultural view is that meaning is emergent and intersubjectively negotiated. It was proposed that shared social ideals, frames of reference and symbols for conveying them are indigenous to social systems in organizations, as elsewhere; and that these aid members in interpreting experience and that they facilitate expression and guide behavior.

Conceptual development is needed to flesh out a cultural perspective. For instance, it may be useful to develop what seem to be natural categories of cultural facets. Prescriptive, descriptive, and expressive facets correspond on first glance to the cultural manifestations of, respectively, shared ideals, present images of local life, and symbol sets. And, by viewing culture as the context of individual action, the temporal/real-time, self-referencing, context-embedded, and actionable qualities of culture could be studied in much the same way that discourse is studied distinctly from language (Ricoeur, 1971).

Traditional analytic, etic-oriented research strategies (e.g., survey research) must be supplemented with more synthetic emic-oriented strategies in order to tap contextual aspects of phenomena and the perspectives of system members. Ethnography, participant observation, and intensive case study techniques may be appropriate. Certain types of interaction analysis may also be appropriate in that they reveal communicative codes (e.g., sociolinguistics), native knowledge (especially as in Frake's work [1964] on elicitation frames), and information management schemes (e.g., Mehan, 1978) constituting the underlying structures by which people organize each other and build environments for one another. (See McDermott & Roth [1978] for a review of interactional approaches and Cicourel [1978] for a comparative illustration of three models of discourse analysis.) Whatever specific methods are used, appropriate study of cultural phenomena requires that researchers avoid objectifying intersubjective phenomena and consider critical issues of boundary and perspective.

Culture in organizations needs to be studied both as a primary focus (i.e., cultural processes in organizations) and as an additional level of analysis (i.e., cultural aspects of organizational phenomena). There are abundant opportunities to study culture as a primary focus. For instance, at the sociological level, evolution of culture could be examined by studying the initial convening and early history of a social system, its shared ideals, metaphors, and symbol systems. Pittigrew's (1979) work in tracing the development of a newly established organization illustrates this type of study. The start of a project team, the commissioning and initial staffing of a new ship in the Navy, and the beginning of classes each semester are all situations in which the evolution of culture in organizations can be studied. And what happens during a corporate takeover, the shifts in priorities, images, and even languages reflect sometimes massive and sudden alterations of culture.

I close this essay by suggesting a final rationale for adding a view of organizations as culture-bearing milieux to our repertoire of perspectives on organizations. Historically, organizational scientists have adopted a reductionistic approach in studying organizational phenomena. Parts and pieces have been studied; 2 to 5 variable causal models have predominated (e.g., in studies of leadership, technology, structure). Results and conclusions about organizational functioning drawn from such research have been weak and necessarily tentative. Perhaps progress in the organizational sciences has suffered due to a pattern of pursuing the whole by exclusively examining the parts, without a balanced recognition that the whole, especially in the case of organizations, is greater than the sum of the parts. In contrast to the traditional reductionistic approach, considerations of culture require, support, and themselves imply a more holistic and integrative approach to studying organizational phenomena. The themes and images characterizing particular cultures are lost when examined piecemeal. When considered as a whole, the character of a culture is rather readily detected, for instance, through its imprint on social system members. In sum then, a cultural perspective might help us to move from a fairly exclusive reliance on a reductionistic approach to more diverse and, in particular, more holistic approaches to organizational inquiry.

NOTES

1. This paper was completed in 1980. Since then, organizational scientists have written much on this subject; my thinking has evolved; I have become concerned that our pursuit of culture may not prove fruitful (Louis, 1983). My notions of culture in organizational settings have been influenced by writings in cultural anthropology, sociology, linguistics, and philosophy. The works of Schutz (1964, 1970a, 1970b), Berger and Luckmann (1966), Geertz (1973), Thomas (1951) and Ball (1972) have been particularly influential. Basic material on anthropological approaches to meaning and culture, can be found in Hammel and Simmons (1970), Spradley (1972), Gamst and Norbeck (1976). Nida (1964) provides a helpful and detailed discussion of linguistic, referential and emotive meanings.

2. A detailed critique of deficiencies arising from the exclusive use of universalistic approaches in organizational research is found in Louis (1981). Discussions in Ritzer (1975), Burrell and Morgan (1979), and Pondy and Mitroff (1979) provide other characterizations of limitations of traditional perspectives on organizations.

3. See Buckley (1967, p. 206) for a discussion of systemic origins of this function.

4. McHugh's (1968) temporal and spatial themes are analogous at the individual psychological level to what is suggested here at the social systems level.

5. This emphasis on stabilizing functions of culture is not meant to suggest that cultural systems are static. On the contrary, they are more appropriately viewed as in-process, evolving and emergent. For example, the changing attitudes toward career/family trade-offs that are being reflected in changes in work cultures in America illustrate the evolving character of culture.

6. "The definition of the situation" is used here to refer to the meanings given by the individual to particular experiences in an immediate sense, that is, in the moment of experience; the interpretive scheme refers to the meaning set that the setting and social system typically has for the individual, across particular situations.

BIBLIOGRAPHIC REFERENCES

Ball, D. W. (1972). The definition of situation: Some theoretical and methodological consequences of taking W. I. Thomas seriously. *Journal for the Theory of Social Behaviour*, 2, 61–82.

Becker, H. S., & Geer, B. (1970). Participant observation and interviewing: A comparison. In W. J. Filstead (Ed.), *Qualitative methodology*. Chicago: Rand McNally.

Beer, M. (1980). *Organization change and development: A systems view*. Santa Monica, CA: Goodyear.

Beres, M. E., & Portwood, J. D. (1979). Explaining cultural differences in the perceived role of work: An intranational cross-cultural study. In G. N. England, A. Negandhi, & B. Wilpert (Eds.), *Organizational functioning in a cross-cultural perspective*. Kent, OH.: Kent State University Press.

Berger, P., & Luckmann, T. (1966). *The social construction of reality: A treatise in the sociology of knowledge*. New York: Anchor Books.

Black, M. (1962). Meaning. In D. D. Runes (Ed.). *Dictionary of philosophy*. Patterson, NJ: Littlefield, Adams & Co.

Blumer, H. (1969). *Symbolic interactionism: Perspective and method*. Englewood Cliffs, NJ: Prentice-Hall.

Buckley, W. (1967). *Sociology and modern systems theory*. Englewood Cliffs, NJ: Prentice-Hall.

Burrell, G., & Morgan, G. (1979). *Sociological paradigms and organisational analysis*. London: Heinemann.

Cicourel, A. V. (1978). *Three models of discourse analysis: The role of social structure*. Unpublished paper, Department of Sociology, University of California, San Diego.

Clarke, B. (1970). *The distinctive college: Antioch, Reed and Swarthmore*. Chicago: Aldine Publishing.

Dandridge, T. C., Mitroff, I. I., & Joyce, W. F. (1980). Organizational symbolism: A topic to expand organizational analysis. *Academy of Management Review*, 5, 77–82.

Etzioni, A. (1961). *A comparative analysis of complex organizations*. New York: Free Press.

Evered, R., & Louis, M. R. (191981). Alternative perspectives in the organizational sciences: 'Inquiry from the inside' and 'Inquiry from the outside.' Under review with the *Academy of Management Review*, 6, 385–395.

Frake, C. O. (1964). Notes on queries in ethnography. *American Anthropologist*, 66, 1323–1145.

Gamst, F. C., & Norbeck, E. (1976). *Ideas of culture: Sources and uses*. New York: Holt, Rinehart & Winston.

Geertz, C. (1973). *The interpretation of cultures*. New York: Basic Books.

Hall, E. T. (1976). *Beyond culture*. New York: Anchor Press.

Hammel, E. A., & Simmons, W. S. (1970). *Man makes sense: A reader in modern cultural anthropology*. Boston: Little, Brown.

Harrison, R. (1972). Understanding your organization's character. *Harvard Business Review*, 5(3), 119–128.

Kroeber, A. L., & Parsons, T. (1958). The concepts of culture and of social systems. *American Sociological Review*, 23, 582–583.

Louis, M. R. (1980). Career transitions: Varieties and commonalities. *Academy of Management Review*, 5, 329–340. (a)

Louis, M. R. (1980). Surprise and sense making: What newcomers experience in entering unfamiliar organizational settings. *Administrative Science Quarterly*, 25, 226–251. (b)

Louis, M. R. (1981). Culture in organizations: The need for and consequences of viewing organizations as culture-bearing milieux. *Human Systems Management*, 2, 246–258.

Louis, M. R. Prerequisites for fruitful research on organizational culture. Unpublished paper.

McDermott, R. P., & Roth, D. R. (1978). The social organization of behavior: Interactional approaches. *Annual Review of Anthropology*, 7, 321–345.

McHugh, P. (1968). *Defining the situation: The organization of meaning in social interaction*. New York: Bobbs-Merrill.

Mehan, H. (1978). Structuring school structure. *Harvard Educational Review*, 48, 32–64.

Mitroff, I. I., & Kilmann, R. (1976). On organizational stories: An approach to the design and analysis of organizations through myths and stories. In R. H. Kilmann, L. R. Pondy & D. P. Slevin (Eds.), *The management of organization design: Strategies and implementation*. New York: Elsevier.

Nida, E. A. (1964). *Toward a science of translating*. Leiden: E. J. Brill.

O'Toole, J. J. (1979). Corporate and managerial cultures. In C. L. Cooper (Ed.), *Behavioral problems in organizations*. Englewood Cliffs, NJ: Prentice-Hall.

Ouchi, W. G. (1979). A conceptual framework for the design of organizational control mechanisms. *Management Science, 25*, 833–848.

Pettigrew, A. M. (1979). On studying organizational cultures. *Administrative Science Quarterly, 24*, 570–581.

Pike, K. L. (1954). *Language in relation to a unified theory of the structure of human behavior.* Glendale, CA: Summer Institute of Linguistics.

Pondy, L. R., & Mitroff, I. I. (1979). Beyond open system models of organization. In B. M. Staw (Ed.), *Research in organizational behavior* (Vol. 1). Greenwich CT: JAI Press.

Ricoeur, P. (1979). The model of the text: Meaningful action considered as a text. In P. Rabinow & W. M. Sullivan (Eds.), *Interpretive social science: A reader.* Berkeley: University of California Press. (Reprinted from *Social Research*, 1971, *38.*)

Ritzer, G. (1975). *Sociology: A multiple paradigm science.* Boston: Allyn & Bacon.

Schutz, A. (1964). *Collected papers II: Studies in social theory.* (Arvid Brodersen, Ed.) The Hague: Martinus Nijhoff.

Schutz, A. (1970). *On phenomenology and social relations.* (Helmut R. Wagner, Ed.) Chicago: The University of Chicago Press. (a)

Schutz, A. (1970). *Reflections on the problem of relevance.* (Richard M. Zaner, Ed.) New Haven, CT: Yale University Press. (b)

Silverman, D. (1970). *The theory of organizations.* New York: Basic Books.

Spradley, J. P. (1972). *Culture and cognition: Rules, maps, and plans.* San Francisco: Chandler.

Thomas, W. I. (1951). *Social behavior and personality: Contribution of W. I. Thomas to theory and social research.* (Edmund H. Volkart, Ed.) New York: Social Science Research Council.

Trist, E. L., & Bamforth, K. W. (1951). Some social and psychological consequences of the Longwall method of coal-getting. *Human Relations, 4*, 1–38.

Van Maanen, J. (1977). Experiencing organization: Notes on the meaning of careers and socialization. In J. Van Maanen (Ed.), *Organizational careers: Some new perspectives.* New York: John Wiley & Sons.

Van Maanen, J. (1979). On the understanding of interpersonal relations. In W. Bennis, J. Van Maanen, E. H. Schein, & F. I. Steele (Eds.), *Essays in interpersonal dynamics.* Homewood, IL: Dorsey Press. (a)

Van Maanen, J. (1979). Reclaiming qualitative methods for organizational research: A preface. *Administrative Science Quarterly, 24*, 520–526. (b)

Weick, K. E. (1969). *The social psychology of organizing.* Reading, MA: Addison-Wesley Publishing.

Weick, K. E. (1979). Cognitive processes in organizations. In B. M. Staw (Ed.), *Research in organizational behavior* (Vol. 1). Greenwich, CT: JAI Press.

Wilkins, A., & Martin, J. (1979). *Organizational legends.* Unpublished paper, Stanford University.

36

The Role of Symbolic Management: How Can Managers Effectively Transmit Organizational Culture?

Caren Siehl & Joanne Martin

The success of an organizational leader is contingent upon the development of shared meaning through a coherent system of beliefs and guiding values (Peters, 1981). Selznick (1957) clearly argued that:

> The formation of an institution is marked by the making of value commitments, that is, choices which fix the assumptions of policy makers as to the nature of the enterprise, its distinctive aims, methods and roles. The institutional leader is primarily an expert in the promotion and protection of values. Leadership fails when it concentrates on sheer survival. Institutional survival, properly understood, is a matter of maintaining values and distinctive identity. (pp. 152 & 153)

While chairman of the board of IBM, Thomas J. Watson, Jr. (1963) posited a similar argument when he said that, "The basic philosophy, spirit, and drive of an organization have far more to do with its relative achievements than do technological or economic resources, organizational structure, innovation, and timing. All these things weigh heavily on success, but they are transcended by how the people in the organization believe in its basic precepts and how faithfully they carry them out." (p. 13)

Previous research and theory, as the preceding paragraph indicates, suggest that one of the critical tasks of management involves the construction and maintenance of a system of shared values. Such values are one component of the phenomenon known as organizational culture.

Although definitions of culture are available, their primary shared attribute is vagueness. An amalgamation of some of the more interesting definitions would result in the following: organizational culture can be thought of as the glue that holds an organization together through a sharing of patterns of meaning. The culture focuses on the values, beliefs, and expectations that members come to share (i.e., Baker, 1980; Gamst & Norbeck, 1976; Pfeffer, 1981a; Van Maanen & Schein, 1979).

It is important to reduce the vagueness of such definitions if culture is to be developed and managed by organizational leaders. A more concrete and complete definition of organizational culture would suggest that a culture consists of three components: content, forms, and strategies.

The first component, the content of an organizational culture, can be viewed as the core values of the organization. These values define the basic philosophy or mission of the company. Sometimes

Source: James G. Hunt and others, eds., *Leaders and Managers: International Perspectives on Managerial Behavior and Leadership* (New York: Pergamon Press, 1984), 227–239.

the core values concern technical issues such as one which Ken Olson, the founder and president of Digital Equipment Corporation expresses as: "Our job is to make a good product. Growth is not our primary goal. After making good products, growth is the natural occurrence" (*Fortune*, Apr. 23, 1979). Or they can be financial in nature, as is reflected in an underlying value of Data General: "We're in this business to make money. It just so happens that the computer business is the best way to do that. But if we could make more money selling rye bread, we should consider doing that" (Herb Richman in *Fortune*, Apr. 23, 1979). Oftentimes the core values are humanistic and emphasize the importance of the people and customers of the organization. Values of this type include Dana Corporation's "Productivity through people" and IBM's "IBM means service" and "Respect for the individual." DuPont's "Better things for better living through chemistry," and GE's "Progress is our most important product" are other examples of underlying beliefs that shape the way people interact and process information about the organization.

It is suggested that the content of the culture can be communicated through the second component of culture, cultural forms. Such forms are oftentimes indirect, implicit, and subtle means of value transmission. Organizational researchers have studied a number of potential cultural forms including: special language or jargon (e.g., Edelman, 1977; Hirsch, 1980; Pondy, 1978); organizational stories and scripts (e.g., Clark, 1970; Martin, 1982; Wilkins, 1978); rituals and ceremonies (e.g., Gephart, 1978; Moch & Huff, 1980; Smircich, In press, 1983); and physical arrangements, such as dress and decor (e.g., Edelman, 1971; Pfeffer, 1981a).

The third component of culture, not dealt with in previous culture research, consists of strategies that managers can use as a means of reinforcing the content or underlying values of the culture. Strategies teach, support, and demonstrate behavior and attitudes that are appropriate for a particular cultural context. Potential strategies include recruitment policies, training programs, compensation, promotion practices, and other management systems. For example, if a culture values a people-oriented management style, successful users of this style should receive more promotions than other managers.

The development of strong organizational culture is important because cultures serve four, perhaps five, useful functions. First, cultures offer a shared interpretation of organizational events, so that members know how they are expected to behave (e.g., Bougon, Weick, & Binkhorst, 1977; Lodahl & Gordon, 1972; Martin, Harrod, & Siehl, 1980; Martin, 1982). Second, in addition to these cognitive functions, strong cultures have emotional impact, lending an aura of excitement, if not inspiration, to employees' work lives. For example, cultures can generate commitment to a set of corporate values or management philosophy, so that employees feel they are working for something they can believe in (e.g., Clark, 1970; Edelman, 1977; Martin & Powers, in press; Ouchi, 1980; Selznick, 1957; Sproull, 1979; Wilkins, 1978). Organizational cultures also generate commitment by giving members a sense of community. Values shared among employees provide for the integration of individuals into the work setting, a kind of individual-to-organization linking (Louis, 1980a). Such a sharing of values can bind members to the organization (Ouchi, 1981; Wilkins, 1978). Third, culture creates and maintains boundaries. In- versus out-groups arise that help to define who is and who is not behaving appropriately within the organizational context. Fourth, cultures also serve as organizational control mechanisms, formally labeling some patterns of behavior as prohibited (e.g., Ouchi & Price, 1978; Salancik, 1977; Wilkins, in press). Finally, the presence of a strong humanistic culture has been tied by implication, if not firm empirical evidence, to increased productivity or profitability (Ouchi, 1981; Pascale & Athos, 1981).

Although earlier research provides support for the important functions served by culture, questions remain as to how a manager can create, maintain, and transmit a shared culture in order to reap the benefits of increased commitment, cognitive sense making, and control. The study that is the subject of this chapter addresses two issues that are central to furthering the understanding of the process by which managers can transmit and reinforce the content of culture, or the underlying value system.

First, how can managers transmit the content of culture, the core values, in a believable, credible manner? One way that managers could communicate the values would be to use explicit forms of communication. Examples of explicit forms include quantitative figures, broad policy statements, and rules and procedures. Managers might prefer to use explicit, unambiguous means of communication so that misunderstandings and differences in interpretation will not occur.

It is predicted, however, that managers will do just the opposite and use implicit forms of communication to transmit values. Previous research, as described earlier, suggests that the values may be transmitted through one or more of the following implicit forms: jargon, organizational stories, and rituals. Other forms that have been relatively unexplored in previous research include humor and the role modeling of appropriate behavior.

Managers may use implicit forms because the core values, especially those of a humanistic nature, tend to be abstract and hypothetical. Research has shown that people have a difficult time remembering or believing information when it is communicated directly in an abstract manner (Martin, Harrod, & Siehl, 1980; Martin, Patterson, & Price, 1979). If managers use explicit language and quantitative figures to express values, their remarks may be forgotten or considered less than credible, particularly if those values have a humanistic tone and are hard to justify in purely financial terms. Without the use of implicit, cultural forms, it is likely that values would be dismissed by employees as propaganda or superficial platitudes. Cultural forms are concrete, yet they communicate values indirectly. For example, the value-relevant message of an organizational story is usually implicit while the events, characters, and action line of the story are specific, detailed, and concrete.

Second, can managers use a strategy, such as a formal training program, to reinforce the core values? Earlier research findings suggest that structured training programs, because they remove new employees from the work setting, do not increase cultural understanding (Louis, 1980b).

Contrary to previous research, however, it is predicted that the use of a formal training program by management can be more effective in reinforcing the core values than continued on-the-job interaction. A training program is predicted to be a powerful management strategy because new employees are isolated from the daily demands of learning a new job. The training manager can indirectly and subtly focus attention on core values. Values can be consistently and redundantly reinforced in the controlled environment of a training program.

In summary, the present study addresses several basic issues left unresolved by previous research on the development and management of a shared value system. First, how can managers transmit the cultural content or value system? It is predicted that managers will communicate the values implicitly using such forms as: rituals or ceremonies, humor, and role modeling. Second, can the strategy of a structured training program be used by management to reinforce the value system? It is predicted that a formal training program is more effective than continued on-the-job interaction.

METHOD

This study was conducted in a field setting at a large, high-technology corporation, referred to below as XYZ. This organization was selected because it has consciously attempted to create and maintain a distinctive organizational culture in the face of changes caused by sustained organizational growth.

Design: Stage One

The study had a two-stage design. The first stage utilized qualitative methods to determine the content and form of this particular organizational culture. The first author conducted open-ended, indepth interviews with managers at various levels of the corporate hierarchy. In addition, she attended as an observer a one-week recognition event for top-level and rising middle-level managers. Activities included observation of formal group sessions on such topics as the company's unique culture and philosophy of management, informal socializing, and

participation in organizational rituals, such as award ceremonies. By the end of this stage of the research process, the researchers were familiar with and understood the shared interpretation of many elements of XYZ's organizational culture. A brief description of the results of the qualitative stage of the study is included in a later section of this chapter.

Design: Stage Two

The second stage of the study had a two-group quasi-experimental design. The subjects were newly hired sales trainees. Within two days of beginning work, all subjects were asked to complete a questionnaire. A cover letter with the questionnaire requested the voluntary assistance of the trainees. The trainees were assured that the confidentiality of their responses would be maintained and that no one at XYZ would have access to their individual responses. The response rate was 87 percent.

During the first six weeks of an eight-week period, all subjects studied written orientation material, which included cultural information, and participated in a one-day orientation session. During the last two weeks of this eight-week period, half of the subjects (group 1) participated in a ten-day structured training program, while the training of the other half of the subjects (group 2) was deferred for scheduling reasons until after the study was completed. Although the subjects could not be randomly assigned by the researchers to the two groups, the subjects whose training was deferred did not differ in any apparent way from the trained subjects. Subsequent analyses, as described below, confirmed this. The training program was led by a first-line manager and guest speakers included the regional manager, district manager, and other first-line managers. Those subjects (group 2) who did not attend the formal training class continued to study product and market information at their home offices. Their activities during the last two-week period did not differ from those of the preceding six weeks. The first author attended the orientation session and eight of the ten days of the training class, including several after-hours social events.

At the end of the eight-week period, all subjects completed a second version of the questionnaire. At this time only half of the subjects had participated in the training program and consequently had been exposed to the management strategy. Figure 1 summarizes the two-group design and the timing of this second stage of the study.

Questionnaire Design

Qualitative data collected during the first stage of the study were used to design questionnaires for use in the second stage of the study. All versions of the questionnaire (items were counterbalanced across two time periods) had four sections: special language/jargon; organizational stories; questions about company goals; and an indirect measure of ideological commitment. The content of the items in each of these sections was tailored to reflect the culture of XYZ. Although these items were closed-ended quantitative measures, they represent an attempt to provide subtle and sensitive measures of cultural knowledge and commitment. For this reason, the items are described in some detail below.

Special Language/Jargon. This section of the questionnaire consisted of a vocabulary test of 20 words or phrases of particular relevance to XYZ employees. The jargon was obtained during interviews with managers of XYZ. Subjects were asked to define each word or phrase. Twelve of the words or phrases had technical meanings, such as MOF (Master Order Form), while eight were used by managers to transmit underlying values of the culture, for example, "working the issue" (confronting disagreement and continuing the discussion until genuine consensus is reached). Definitions were coded as totally correct, partially correct (a synonym or more abstract form of the word), or incorrect. Intercoder reliability was perfect, with coders reaching 100 percent agreement after a brief training session.

Organizational Stories. Four stories, frequently told during the in-depth interviews, were summarized. Subjects were first asked how much of the story they had heard. (Subjects responded to these and other items on 11-point scales, with higher scores indicating greater cultural knowledge and more commitment.) Three morals to the story were

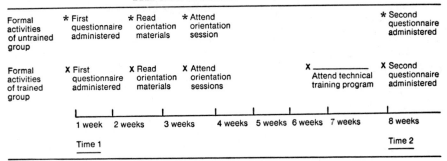

FIGURE 1 • DESIGN OF SECOND STAGE OF STUDY: TIMING OF
THE MANAGEMENT STRATEGY

then offered and subjects were asked to decide the extent to which each represented the appropriate interpretation of the story. Although all three morals for each story were logically plausible, data from the first stage of the study indicated that one moral was generally considered to be the "correct" interpretation by management, one moral was obviously "incorrect," and one was ambiguous. The "correct" moral reflected a shared value of XYZ. To the extent that a subject's judgment followed management's pattern, the subject would be demonstrating knowledge of a shared interpretation of meaning particular to this organizational setting. For example, one study concerned a lower-level employee:

> Susan Sanders, a secretary of a sales unit in Northern California, had been working for XYZ for about two years. She was well respected by everyone—her manager, the sales people, and other secretaries. She was extremely skillful and her performance had been rated as excellent. Owing to her efforts, Susan's manager did not need to direct his attention to proofreading or correction tasks. Susan also had a pleasant personality. In fact, she was one of those people who was generally cheerful, even on bad days. During her second year with XYZ, Susan's husband, who worked for another company, was promoted to a new job in Arizona. Although he would be losing a valued employee, Susan's manager approved her request for a transfer to an XYZ office in Arizona. This office was not hiring at the time but gladly accepted her transfer, knowing that her skills would be helpful in some capacity in the future.

The three morals offered for this story were:

1. "We believe that people are clearly our most important asset and we take pride in treating our employees well." ("Correct.")
2. "Employees are one part of the financial structure of XYZ and are as im-

portant as their contribution to the bottom-line." ("Incorrect.")
3. "Because good employees are hard to find, we feel it is to XYZ's advantage to try to meet the needs of such people." ("Ambiguous." Logically plausible, pragmatic rather than humanistic, an interpretation or moral not offered by XYZ management.)

Company Goal Identification. In stage one of this study, the top managers had identified a number of XYZ's corporate goals that embody the underlying values of the company, for example, meeting social and environmental commitments to communities surrounding corporate facilities. Subjects were asked to rate the importance of each of five such goals to XYZ and to themselves personally. This provided a measure of the accuracy with which subjects perceived the company's values and a measure of the subjects' personal ideological commitment to those values.

Indirect Measure of Ideological Commitment. Direct measures of subjects' commitment to the corporate ideology are subject to social desirability effects, even given anonymity, and thus, have unavoidable demand characteristics. To overcome this problem, commitment was also assessed using an indirect measure of error-choice. These measures consisted of statements taken from published material about XYZ company. A key numerical fact in each statement was left blank. Subjects were instructed to fill in the blank with one of two predesignated choices. Subjects were not aware that both alternatives were actually incorrect. One of the choices was biased in a direction designed to make the company look better than in fact it was; the other choice was biased in a negative, anticompany direction. For example, one item estimated sales-force turnover at either 12 or 16 percent, when the actual turnover rate was 14 percent. Ideological commitment to the company should be reflected in a disproportionate preference for the positive bias, procompany alternatives. The plus or minus difference is not meaningful in itself. It is the change in the cumulative bias from Time 1 to Time 2, irrespective of the bias at Time 1, that will indicate an increase or decrease in commitment.

RESULTS AND DISCUSSION

The qualitative data are presented first, so that the richness and the texture of XYZ's organizational culture are familiar. These data are used primarily to address the first question raised in the introduction to this chapter. The quantitative data are then presented and discussed in the context of both questions.

Qualitative Results

During the course of the in-depth interviews, the observation of the managerial recognition event, and the training class, four core values were emphasized by management: (1) The family of an employee is an integral concern of the company; (2) XYZ doesn't undercut the future by considering only the short-term consequences of decisions; (3) XYZ believes that people are clearly the most important asset of the company; and (4) XYZ is different: we build a unique product and our people are unique also.

The qualitative data answer the question of how managers can transmit values in a believable, credible manner. The four shared values were transmitted in several different forms. One form was the organizational story. For example, the following story, or a slight variation of it, was told repeatedly: A prospective employee was qualified for a sales position with XYZ but had specific family constraints on his ability to relocate. XYZ offered the salesman a job in his desired location even though his experience made him better suited to sell to a different market. This story clearly articulates the first shared value, as stated above, of commitment to be supportive and understanding of employees' families.

The observation of the orientation day suggested that managers can also transmit the underlying values or content of the culture in the form of organizational rituals. Rituals are repeated behavior patterns that are stylized or formalized (Smircich, in press). XYZ's orientation session was designed by management to be highly ritualistic. The setting, the sequence of events, and the controlling characters did not vary from one session to the next. The ritual had the specific purpose of introducing aspects of XYZ culture and, in general, of demonstrating the third central value of XYZ: the company cares about people. As the orientation manager told us, "Most new employees go through buyer's remorse. They aren't totally confident that they made the right job decision. All we want to do today is let them know that XYZ really is happy to have them on board. We want them to share our ideal of giving 100 percent to each other and to XYZ."

In addition, within the ritual of the orientation session, other aspects of XYZ's culture were communicated by the leader of the organization (the company president and founder) through the use of a special videotape. The videotape portrayed the president giving a tour of the historic company headquarters. He related the pivotal values of the philosophy of management and the culture in the form of organizational stories, drawing on incidents from the company's history to make his points. For example, one story concerned the leader's commitment to the second central value: avoid the folly of considering only the short-term consequences of decisions.

Organizational values were also transmitted in the form of special language. By definition, this language should be unique to XYZ and best understood by XYZ employees. Interestingly, the content of the language also emphasized the fourth of the central values as discussed, the value that stressed the uniqueness of the company, its people, and its products. Managers used the jargon to express the underlying values and to help emphasize organizational boundaries.

Humor was also used by management to convey the content of XYZ culture. For example, in the beginning of the training program, laughter was scarce. Most jokes were understandable to an outsider. They contained little jargon and the causes of laughter were fairly universal objects such as foolish mistakes, sexual innuendo, and general tension. By the end of the training program, laughter was more frequent. This could be due to increased cohesion and openness among the participants. Understanding of these jokes, however, required more knowledge of the unique culture as well, as the jokes contained considerable XYZ jargon. In addition the targets of the jokes were usually outgroups, such as competitive companies. Thus, humor tended to define the ingroup, out-group boundary, with the new employees gradually, through their laughter, coming to act like in-group members. In accord with the fourth core value of XYZ, the new employees were coming to define the in-group, their company, as unique and distinct from other groups.

The observation of the training class also provided support for the hypothesis that cultural information may be transmitted by managers through the role modeling of appropriate behavior. The training managers modeled behavior as a means of teaching the new employees what would be expected in this particular corporate environment. The employees observed a specific instance of behavior and developed a minitheory concerning situations in which this behavior pattern would be appropriate. For example, one role-modeling incident concerned the third of the central values of XYZ, that the company's employees are its most important asset. A minitheory illustrating the application of this value was built around the belief that the company should not give up on low-performing employees.

A powerful enactment of this minitheory was observed during the second day of the training program. The trainees had been made aware of the need to be prepared for a test to be given during the afternoon of the second day. Just before breaking for lunch, the manager held an "impromptu" review session. She asked several sample exam questions of each individual, beginning with the last person in the last row and moving sequentially through the class. One trainee appeared to be completely unprepared and failed to answer a single question correctly. Rather than reprimanding this employee publicly or privately, the manager was encouraging and offered additional study help during lunch. Later that afternoon, the manager summarized the relevant minitheory, saying, "We believe that if an employee is failing to perform, we owe that person assistance."

Discussion of Qualitative Results

The purpose of gathering the qualitative data was twofold. The first objective was to address, to the extent possible, the two issues raised in the introduction to this chapter. The first issue concerned the transmission of values by managers. The qualitative data provided evidence that managers can transmit underlying values using at least five forms: organizational stories, special language, rituals, humor, and the role modeling of appropriate behavior. The first three of these forms have been suggested by previous culture research. The latter two forms represent an understudied means by which managers can transmit cultural information and values, particularly new information that has not yet been institutionalized in the company's history, language, or ritualized ceremonies.

The qualitative data cannot provide a test of the second issue to be addressed: whether a structured training program can be an effective management strategy for reinforcing underlying values. The qualitative data do provide a basis for the subsequent quantitative investigation of this issue. Observation of the training program indicated that subjects were learning the company jargon and organizational stories. Whether they were gaining an equivalent or better understanding of the values than those subjects not involved in the training class can be tested using quantitative methods. Comparisons of the two groups would yield information about the efficacy with which one cultural strategy, a structured training program, transmitted values.

The second objective of collecting the qualitative data was to gain a sense of the content of the culture of this particular organization. The highlights of the qualitative data, summarized above, indicate that the content of XYZ's culture primarily concerned four values central to the company's philosophy of management. Some aspects of this information about the content of XYZ's culture were used to develop the quantitative measures discussed in the next section of this chapter.

To summarize, the qualitative data answered the question of how a manager can transmit values. In addition,

the data provided a picture of the richness and complexity of the content and forms of the corporate culture. The quantitative data, discussed below, build on this qualitative information to address the question of whether managers can use the strategy of a training program to reinforce values.

Quantitative Results

To ensure that any difference at Time 2 between the trained and untrained groups was due to the presence or absence of the structured training class, the Time 1 results for the two groups (prior to any training) were compared. As expected, at Time 1 both groups' responses to the questionnaire items were generally not significantly different more often than would be expected by chance. There was, therefore, no reason to suspect that the two groups differed initially in any substantive way.

Changes in knowledge of the value system and commitment to the values that occurred between Time 1 and Time 2 were then examined. First, the results for the trained group (those employees exposed to the management strategy) will be described. (More detailed presentation of these data and analyses are available in Siehl & Martin, 1982.) By Time 2, after the formal training program, the trained group of new employees had come to interpret the values transmitted by the organizational stories in a fashion similar to that of the managers interviewed in stage one of the study. Averaging across the stories, at Time 2 the "correct" morals to the stories were rated as highly appropriate interpretations of the stories, the "neutral" morals were rated near the midpoint of the scale, as they had been at Time 1, and the "incorrect" morals to the stories received lower ratings. For the "correct" and "incorrect" morals, these differences between Time 1 and

Time 2 were strongly significant for each of the stories. These results clearly support the conclusion that by Time 2 the subjects exposed to the training program had come to adopt the shared interpretation of the meaning of the values transmitted by these organizational stories.

At Time 2, the trained group showed high levels of ideological commitment to the values and goals underlying the XYZ corporate culture. Averaging across the five corporate goals articulated by top management, at Time 2 the trained subjects felt that these goals were highly important to the company and to themselves personally. Although these ratings of the importance of the goals to the company at Time 2 represented an increase over the Time 1 ratings for the trained group, two of these differences were not significant, two were marginally significant, and one was significant. A similar pattern of effects was found in the analysis of the ratings of the personal importance of these corporate goals. Although at Time 2 ratings were higher, or for one goal equal, the differences between Time 1 and Time 2 for the personal importance ratings were significant for only two of the five goals. For each of these measures of ideological commitment, the patterns of results are similar and the same explanation for that pattern can be offered: ideological commitment was at a high enough level at Time 1 that a ceiling effect prevented some of the Time 2 differences from being significantly higher. Nevertheless, as expected, commitment increased over time for these trained subjects.

The second type of ideological commitment measure minimized demand characteristics. The indirect error-choice test showed that the trained subjects had a strong tendency to make errors that were favorable to the company. For the trained subject, this bias, indicating ideological commitment, was significantly stronger at Time 2 than at Time 1. To summarize the commitment results for the trained group, the high levels of ideological commitment found at Time 1 increased following participation in the management strategy of a structured training program, and, for measures where ceiling effects were not present, these increases in commitment were significant.

Turning now to the untrained group (employees not exposed to the management strategy), a quite different pattern of results was found. By Time 2, there was no significant improvement in the untrained subjects' abilities to identify the "correct" or "incorrect" morals to the stories. Unlike the trained group, the untrained subjects showed no significant change in their willingness to endorse the shared values expressed by the organizational stories. The various measures of ideological commitment also showed relatively little change for the untrained group. The untrained subjects showed only slight increases in commitment, smaller increases than were shown by the trained group. None was significant.

An additional set of analyses were done comparing the trained and untrained groups at Time 2. The results confirm those reported above, with the trained group showing greater overall understanding of the value system and higher levels of commitment to the values of the company than the untrained group.

Discussion of Quantitative Results

The quantitative data addressed both questions raised in the introduction. The first of these questions concerned the cultural forms used to transmit knowledge about the corporation's values. The quantitative measures used two such forms: jargon and stories. Over time the subjects came to understand the meaning of words and phrases unique to this organizational setting, became more familiar with the organization's stories, and came to endorse the same interpretation of those stories as management. Both of these forms, then, were successfully used by management to communicate the content of the organization's culture, that is, the underlying value system.

The second question concerned the use by managers of a cultural strategy, a formal training program, to reinforce the underlying value system of the company. Over time the trained subjects showed a significant increase in their familiarity with the shared values transmitted by the organizational stories. A similar change in ideological commitment levels was also found for the trained subjects. In contrast to the trained subjects, the untrained subjects showed no significant increases in cultural knowledge or commitment. These results suggest that a formal training program is a powerful strategy that managers can use to reinforce underlying values.

CONCLUSION

As was proposed earlier, one of the critical tasks of the manager and leader is the creation and maintenance of a system of shared values. The present study makes the contribution of addressing several issues that are basic to furthering the understanding of how a manager can create such a value system. First, managers can use implicit, cultural forms, such as organizational stories, rituals, and role modeling, effectively to express and communicate core values. Second, the use by management of a strategy, such as a formal training program, can be a powerful means of reinforcing the value system and generating employee commitment.

The present study also suggests several questions that are worthy of future research. It was learned that managers can communicate values through a variety of cultural forms. This gives rise to such questions as the following: Under what circumstances are the different forms used by managers? When are they more or less effective?

In addition, it is acknowledged that culture is a powerful phenomenon that plays important functions in organizational life. Do managers want to allow such a phenomenon with far-reaching effects to develop and change in an uncontrolled manner? One would think not. What other specific strategies can be employed to promote the development of a widely shared value system? How can new strategies be designed?

It would be useful if managers could know how to recognize culture, how to control culture, and ultimately, how to change culture. Continued research efforts that attempt to extend present theory would be of value to both practicing managers and social scientists.

BIBLIOGRAPHIC REFERENCES

Baker, E. (Autumn 1980). Managing organizational culture. *The McKinsey Quarterly*, 51–61.

Bougon, M., Weick, K., & Binkhorst, D. (1977). Cognition in organizations: An analysis of the Utrecht Jazz Orchestra. *Administrative Science Quarterly, 22*, 606–639.

Clark, B. (1970). *The distinctive college: Antioch, Reed and Swarthmore*. Chicago: Aldine Publishing.

Edelman, M. (1971). *Politics as symbolic action.* Chicago: Markham.

Edelman, M. (1977). *Political language.* New York: Academic Press.

Gamst, F. C., & Norbeck, E. (Eds.). (1976). *Ideas of culture: Sources and uses.* New York: Holt, Rinehart &Winston.

Gephart, R. P. (1978). Status degradation and organizational succession: An ethnomethodological approach. *Administrative Science Quarterly, 23,* 553–581.

Hirsch, P. (August 1980). *Ambushes, shootouts, and knights of the roundtable: The language of corporate takeovers.* Paper presented at the meeting of the Academy of Management, Detroit.

Lodahl, J., & Gordon, G. (1972). The structure of scientific fields and the functioning of university graduate departments. *American Sociological Review, 34,* 57–72.

Louis, M. R. (August 1980a). *Learning the ropes: What helps new employees become acculturated.* Paper presented at the meeting of the Academy of Management, Detroit.

Louis, M. R. (1980b). Surprise and sense making: What newcomers experience in entering unfamiliar organizational settings. *Administrative Science Quarterly, 25,* 226–251.

Martin, J. (1982). Stories and scripts in organizational settings. In A. Hastorf & A. Isen (Eds.), *Cognitive social psychology.* New York: Elsevier.

Martin, J., Harrod, W., & Siehl, C. (September 1980). *The development of knowledge structures.* Paper presented at the meetings of the American Psychological Association, Montreal.

Martin, J., Patterson, K., & Price, R. (June 1979). *The effects of level of abstraction of a script on accuracy of recall, predictions and beliefs* (Research paper No. 520). Stanford, CA: Stanford University, Graduate School of Business.

Martin, J., & Powers, M. (in press). Truth or corporate propaganda: The value of a good war story. In L. Pondy, P. Frost, G. Morgan, & T. Dandridge (Eds.), *Organizational symbolism.* Greenwich, CT: JAI Press.

Moch, M., & Huff, A. S. (August 1980). *Chewing out ass: The enactment of power relationships through language and ritual.* Paper presented to the meetings of the Academy of Management, Detroit.

Ouchi, W. G. (1980). Markets, clans, and hierarchies. *Administrative Science Quarterly, 25,* 129–141.

Ouchi, W. G. (1981). *How American business can meet the Japanese challenge.* Reading, MA: Addison-Wesley Publishing.

Ouchi, W. G., & Price, R. (1978). Hierarchies, clans and Theory Z: A new perspective on organizational development. *Organization Dynamics, 7,* 25–44.

Pascale, R. T., & Athos, A. G. (1981). *The art of Japanese management.* New York: Simon & Schuster.

Peters, T. J. (1981). *Putting excellence into management.* Unpublished manuscript, Stanford University, Stanford, CA.

Pfeffer, J. (1981a). Management as symbolic action: The creation and maintenance of organizational paradigms. In L. L. Cummings & B. M. Staw (Eds.), *Research in organizational behavior* (Vol. 3). Greenwich, CT: JAI Press.

Pondy, L. R. (1978). Leadership is a language game. In M. McCall & M. Lombardo (Eds.), *Leadership: Where else can we go?* Durham, NC: Duke University Press.

Salancik, G. R. (1977). Commitment and the control of organizational behavior and belief. In B. Staw & G. R. Salancik (Eds.), *New directions in organizational behavior.* Chicago: St. Clair Press.

Selznick, P. (1957). *Leadership and administration.* Evanston, IL: Row, Peterson.

Siehl, C., & Martin, J. (1982). *Learning organizational culture.* Unpublished manuscript, Stanford University.

Smircich, L. (in press). Organizations as shared meaning. In L. Pondy, P. Frost, G. Morgan, & T. Dandridge (Eds.), *Organizational symbolism.* Greenwich, CT: JAI Press.

Sproull, L. S. (1981). Beliefs in organizations. In P. C. Nystrom & W. H. Starbuck (Eds.), *Handbook of organizational design*. London: Oxford University Press.

Van Maanen, J., & Schein, E. (1979). Toward a theory of organizational socialization. In L. Cummings & B. Staw (Eds.), *Research in organizational behavior* (Vol. 1). Greenwich, CT: JAI Press.

Watson, T. (1963). *A business and its beliefs: The ideas that helped build IBM*. New York: McGraw-Hill.

Wilkins, A. (1978). *Organizational stories as an expression of management philosophy: Implications for social control in organizations*. Unpublished doctoral dissertation, Stanford University.

Wilkins, A. (in press). Organizational control. In L. Pondy, P. Frost, G. Morgan, & T. Dandridge (Eds.), *Organizational symbolism*. Greenwich, CT: JAI Press.

ABOUT THE AUTHORS

Jay M. Shafritz is a professor in the Graduate School of Public and International Affairs at the University of Pittsburgh. Previously he has taught at the University of Colorado in Denver, the University of Houston in Clear Lake City, the State University of New York in Albany, and Rensselaer Polytechnic Institute. He is the author, coauthor, and editor of more than two dozen books on public, private and nonprofit management, including *The Facts on File Dictionary of Public Administration, The Facts on File Dictionary of Personnel Management and Labor Relations,* and *The MBA's Dictionary* (with Daniel Oran). Dr. Shafritz received his master's degree from the Baruch College of the City University of New York and his Ph.D. from Temple University.

J. Steven Ott teaches organization and management courses at the University of Maine. Previously he was Executive Vice President of Applied Management Corporation, a Denver-based management consulting firm. He has applied organization theory to the management of public, private, and nonprofit organizations for more than twenty years. He is a frequent speaker at management seminars and conferences, provides intra- and inter-organizational process leadership, and instructs graduate-level courses in management and organization theory at the University of Colorado in Denver. Dr. Ott has written several books and various articles, most recently *The Facts on File Dictionary of Nonprofit Organization Management* (with Jay M. Shafritz). Dr. Ott earned his bachelor's degree from the Pennsylvania State University, his master's degree from the Sloan School of Management at the Massachusetts Institute of Technology, and his doctorate from the University of Colorado in Denver.

A NOTE ON THE TYPE

Goudy Old Style is one of American Frederick W. Goudy's earlier type designs and the printing industry has made use of it in both books and advertising since the late teens of this century. Like many of Mr. Goudy's types, his Old Style is a classic typeface and the capitals were modeled on renaissance lettering. The text of this book was adapted from Goudy's original design for the Penta 202 System.

Composed by Carlisle Graphics, Dubuque, Iowa.

Printed and bound by Kingsport Press, Kingsport, Tennessee.